THE PRIVATE LIVES OF NOËL AND GERTIE

SHERIDAN MORLEY

THE PRIVATE LIVES OF NOËL AND GERTIE

TWO CLASSIC BIOGRAPHIES IN ONE VOLUME

A TALENT TO AMUSE

A BRIGHT PARTICULAR STAR

OBERON BOOKS

LONDON

The individual dedications in these books, to my first wife and our three now adult children, of course remain as first written; but I would like to dedicate this joint edition to my darling Ruth Leon, whose love for, and understanding of, an always difficult husband has made these past ten years of my life so much happier than they would have been in any other company

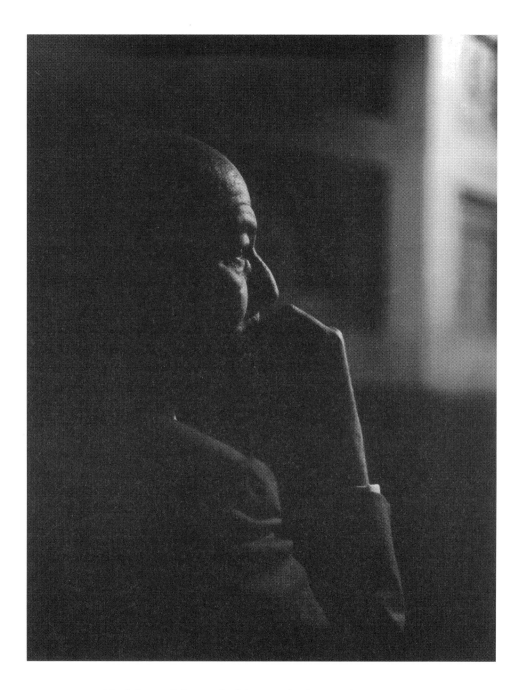

Noel Coward directs *Sail Away* at the Savoy Theatre, 1962

Contents

A BRIGHT PARTICULAR STAR, 331

Illustrations

Frontispiece: Noël Coward directing *Sail Away* at the Savoy Theatre in 1962 (photo: John Timbers)

The following pictures were all supplied courtesy of the Raymond Mander and Joe Mitchenson Theatre Collection.
Photographs copyright © the copyright holders.

A Talent to Amuse

Noël Coward at two; at five; at seven. (photo: Robert Turnbull)
The programme for Coward's first appearance.
In *The Great Name,* 1911.
In *I'll Leave it to You,* 1920.
In *Polly with a Past,* 1921.
In *The Vortex,* 1924. (photo: Sasha)
Noël Coward, mid-Twenties.
In *The Constant Nymph,* 1926.
In *This Year of Grace,* New York, 1928.
Noël Coward, drawn by Max Beerbohm, 1929.
With Gertrude Lawrence, Laurence Olivier and Adrianne Allen in *Private Lives,* 1930. (photos: Sasha)
Noël Coward, London, late-Twenties. (photo: Dorothy Wilding)
Cavalcade, 1931.
In *Design for Living,* 1933.
In *Conversation Piece,* 1934. (photo: Sasha)
With Gertrude Lawrence in *Tonight at Eight-Thirty.* (photos: Sasha)
A scene from *In Which We Serve,* 1942.
With troops in Malta, 1943.
With Norman Hackforth, the Arakan, 1944.
At Blue Harbour, Jamaica. (photo: Amador Packer)
At the Desert Inn, Las Vegas, 1955. (photo: William Claxton)
With Mary Martin in *Together with Music,* 1955. (photo: CBS Television Network)
Noël Coward in three roles, *Suite in Three Keys,* 1966. (photos: Angus McBean)
Receiving his Hon. Doctor of Letters, 1972.

A Bright Particular Star

Gertie Lawrence at ten; at twelve.

As Leader of the Frolics at Murray's Club, 1920.

Gertie and Noël Coward in *London Calling!*, 1923.

As 'Parisian Pierrot' and 'Poor Little Rich Girl' from *London Calling!*

Fallen Babies: Gertie and Bea Lillie.

Cast and audience after the première of Charlot's *Revue* of 1925.

With P. G. Wodehouse during *Oh, Kay!*

Gertie and Douglas Fairbanks.

With Leslie Howard in *Candlelight* in 1929.

Gertie and Noël Coward in 'Family Album' from *Tonight at Eight-Thirty*, 1936.

As Lisa, the *Lady in the Dark*, Broadway, 1941. (photo: Vandamm)

Gertie as a driver for the American Red Cross. (photo: Pamela Chatworthy)

With Raymond Massey in *Pygmalion*, 1946. (photo: Vandamm)

In Daphne du Maurier's *September Tide*, 1949. (photo: Angus McBean)

With Yul Brynner in *The King and I*, 1951. (photo: Vandamm)

Introduction

These two biographies, only now for the first time published together, date from 1969 (*A Talent to Amuse*) and 1981 (*A Bright Particular Star*), and their original prefaces will tell you individually how they came into existence.

But they have a connection which I have never before explained, and it is this. When I was asked, or rather commanded by Noël to write his first (and indeed my first) biography, I kept my distance from him: we had agreed from the outset that it should be a critical biography rather than a fan book, and Noël had characteristically himself given me his 'enemies list', with all their phone numbers. 'Start with them, dear boy,' he said briskly, 'and you'll have a much more interesting story to tell; the friends can come later.'

He also agreed, amazingly, that he didn't really want to see the book (despite all the help and access and papers he had given me) until it was at least in proof, whereupon he sent the telegram I still have framed on this desk: 'Darling, boy, I am simply wild about me. Love Noël'.

It was then that we really became friends; in 1969 I helped to organise one of the very first gala charity concerts ever held in this country, at midnight on the eve of his seventieth birthday, and that too we called *A Talent to Amuse*. I then had the huge delight of covering live for BBC television the 70th birthday dinner given at the Savoy Hotel the following evening in his honour by his old friend Lord Mountbatten.

The following day there was to be a Foyles Literary Lunch to launch my book, but Noël, now somewhat frail, was unable to appear; instead, as he said in another cable I cherish to this day, 'I am sending my understudy, a promising little comedian called Sir Charles Chaplin'.

It was indeed Chaplin who chaired that lunch, and in my own copy of *A Talent to Amuse* I have his drawing of the Little Tramp. But by now, I knew I really wanted Noël as a friend rather than just the subject of my first book; we were immensely lucky with both reviews and sales here and in America, and Noël was always warmed by success, especially when he had made it available to someone else as well, in this case me.

As I have said elsewhere, he had already agreed to be godfather to my son Hugo, born while I was writing *A Talent to Amuse*; to this day, it is widely assumed that it is I rather than my son who is the godson, but in fact I never met Noël until 1964 when, just down from Oxford and a newscaster at ITN, I went for the first time to interview him for *The Times* and found that wonderful blithe spirit leaping around the river suite of the Savoy and starting on a new movie, *Bunny Lake is Missing*, for Otto Preminger.

One morning while I was interviewing Noël the star of the picture, the American actor Keir Dullea, popped his head around the door to introduce himself: 'I'm Keir Dullea,' he said winningly; Noël looked up briefly: 'Keir Dullea,' he said, 'Gone Tomorrow.'

Although my grandmother Gladys Cooper had known Noël since the early 1920s, and indeed gave him his first major postwar success with *Relative Values* in 1951, they were not what might have been called close. Noël, a stickler for accuracy and insistent that all lines be learnt before the first rehearsal, came head to head against Gladys's staunch determination never to learn lines at all unless absolutely necessary, For almost two years, nightly at the Savoy, she would turn the exit line 'I am going into the study' into the vastly more intriguing 'I am going into the understudy.'

And although my father Robert was of course also an actor, he was not exactly typecast for Noël's slim, elegant, dressing-gowned heroes, so it wasn't until that Gala night in 1969 that I had the joy of introducing them together on stage, though my mother Joan had known him rather longer. On one occasion he had phoned her, searching as usual for her mother Gladys, the morning after Ma had given birth to my brother in her own bed at home. She now answered the phone to an amazed Coward, who so far from congratulating her on the recent birth said 'It's disgusting, having children in your own bed and then answering the telephone; just like those African women who have babies behind trees whenever you are not looking in their direction.'

Ma of course forgave him, as one always forgave Coward; and now another generation, my son and my first wife and I, began seeing Noël whenever we could; on one occasion, I think my son's third birthday, a vast Rolls Royce drew up outside our terraced house in Dulwich, thereby blocking at least two other driveways on either side. It was occupied by a uniformed chauffeur and, alone on the back seat, a vast teddy bear sporting a label around its neck reading simply 'love Noël.'

He was to live for another three years, but they were to be of increasingly ill health, so now we would usually travel out to Switzerland to see him; the last time we met was on one of those Swiss weekends just before he went out to New York and then on to Jamaica, where he died suddenly in March 1973.

Late one night, at his amazingly English house just above Lake Geneva (a friend once complained that unlike chalets further up towards Gstaad, Chalet Coward has no real alpine views; 'this house,' retorted Noël, 'has the best view of a tax advantage I have ever seen') he and I were talking by the piano in his living room about Gertie, who had now been dead for all of twenty years.

You know [said Noël] there's one thing wrong with *A Talent to Amuse*. You seem to think of me in the book as a rather isolated and lonely figure, and now to some extent perhaps I am, though with darling Graham [Payn] and Coley [Cole Lesley, his lifelong secretary and servant], I can never really complain. But you see I always thought of myself as half of a double-act, Noël and Gertie, and I thought we would go on forever, whatever happened, doing play after play and musical after musical even into our eighties, like Sybil Thorndike and Lewis Casson or Jessica Tandy and Hume Cronyn in New York.

It didn't, as you will discover from these two biographies, work out like that; and it is I believe at least arguable that, after Gertie's sudden and unexpected death, Noël never again wrote a truly great play or song. So much of his best work had always been written for her, and it is even I think possible that the reason in *Blithe Spirit* for Elvira being a ghost is that Gertie, for whom the role was clearly intended, had already by 1941 settled into a new American marriage. Noël and Gertie were now separated by that marriage, by the war and by the Atlantic, and they were never really to get together again, except for a few brief performances in *Tonight at Eight-Thirty* after the war when Noël stood in for an ailing Graham Payn on tour in California.

It was Noël, that last night in Switzerland, who asked me to write the book about Gertie, precisely because he felt she had left so little behind to remember her by; in London she had only ever made one post-war appearance, and that in a shortlived drama by Daphne du Maurier called *September Tide*. 'Do you,' I asked Noël idiotically, 'still think a lot about her?' There was a long pause: 'Every night when I close my eyes,' he eventually said to me, 'and every morning when I wake up, I see her in that white Molyneux dress on that *Private Lives* terrace of the hotel in France, and she never goes away.'

No doubt, as they say in the second most famous balcony scene (after *Romeo and Juliet*) in all stage history, no doubt anywhere.

That is, in the end, why these two books belong together as much as Noël and Gertie themselves did, and why I am so grateful to James Hogan at Oberon for bringing them together for the first time; I feel, in this year of Noël's centenary, that a circle has at last been completed.

Sheridan Morley
London 1999

A TALENT TO AMUSE

For Margaret and for Hugo
and now
for Alexis and Juliet as well

Prologue

Like a first child, a first book is the one you worry about the most: others may turn out better or brighter in the end, but the first is the one whose conception and gestation and arrival you never forget. It is now getting on for thirty years since *A Talent to Amuse* first appeared in print, and although since then I've published more than a dozen other titles, this is the one that still matters most to me. I remember the room in Paddington where I started typing it; the house in Dulwich where l finished it; the smell of the proofs; the morning the reviews appeared (in those far-off days that was still the morning of publication, which gave the event an immediate theatricality I much enjoyed and much miss in today's world of delayed and staggered press reaction) and the sudden, marvellous, magical realisation that a book which in preparation nobody else seemed terribly excited about was in fact going to be the one that everybody wanted for Christmas.

This biography was written over a three-year period from 1966, and it happily coincided with the last great change in Noël's professional and private fortunes: when I began writing, he was still widely, if wrongly, regarded as an exiled relic from some pre-war world of lost glamour. A couple of months after the book came out, at the time of his seventieth birthday, he was given (by a Labour government) the knighthood that established him as the grand old man of the British theatre. The renaissance had come, and unlike most he had lived to see it himself.

Because I come from a family of actors, and because my son Hugo, who was born during the writing of this book, became the last of Noël's many godchildren, there has developed a curious but unchangeable theory that I too must have known Coward from childhood. In fact we first met in 1964 when I was twenty-three and working as a newscaster and scriptwriter for ITN. This being by definition an evening job, I used to spend some of my mornings writing arts-page profiles for *The Times*.

The Arts Editor of *The Times* in those days was a marvellously avuncular figure called John Lawrence, of whom it was always said that once, left in charge of the Obituaries during a holiday period, he had run by mistake one for the then Duke of Norfolk who subsequently telephoned in understandable indignation to correct the error. 'But, Your Grace, replied Lawrence, ever a careful man, 'may I first of all establish precisely from where you are now telephoning?'

He always knew precisely from where I was telephoning: the flat in Paddington, to ask if there was anybody in town he would like interviewed. One morning the news was that Noël Coward had come to London to start auditioning for a National Theatre revival of *Hay Fever* which he was himself to direct: 'He's getting on a bit now,' said Lawrence, 'and hasn't had a success in a long time, but he's just the sort of chap for our readers and I think you might like him.'

I had never met Coward before, and was almost totally unprepared for what I found. At that time, popular legend had it that he was more or less finished – a sixty-four-year-old writer of old-fashioned drawing room comedies, hopelessly out of touch artistically with the post-Osborne theatre, and equally out of touch socially with the country he had abandoned for financial reasons a decade earlier. I think I expected to meet a rather embittered old gentleman somewhere halfway from Somerset Maugham to the Duke of Windsor, living on his memories and surrounded by albums of photographs by Cecil Beaton. What I actually found, in the opulent surroundings of the river suite at the Savoy, was a blithe and sprightly spirit leaping around in his shirt sleeves organising not only the *Hay Fever* casting, but also rehearsals for a musical called *High Spirits* which was to open in the same season, and a forthcoming film appearance in an Otto Preminger thriller. Yet he remained courteous enough and relaxed enough to give an inexperienced and uneasy journalist an interview of such elegance, charm and wit that almost every one of the hundreds, if not thousands, I have done since has inevitably seemed something of an anti-climax.

The result of that first meeting was, as I recall it, an appallingly patronising profile for *The Times* in which I suggested that the old master still had a spark or two of life in him, and remarked mildly that one or two of his plays perhaps deserved a better fate than to be held up as examples of everything that Kenneth Tynan and the Royal Court had been erected to destroy. It was not, at the time, a distinctly popular view, but the more I began to think about and read Coward, the more convinced I became that the history of British entertainment in the first half of this century was essentially the history of his own career – from child actor through revues and musical comedies to patriotic epics like *Cavalcade* and such classic comedies as *Private Lives* and *Blithe Spirit* – and that is before you even start to think about the cabaret songs or the movies like *Brief Encounter* or the poems or the novel or the short stories or the paintings or the productions he staged.

I rapidly became obsessed with Coward, but it was a curiously unfashionable obsession for the mid-Sixties: indeed I was solemnly told by one magazine editor that my future as a drama critic looked decidedly shaky unless I stopped talking about Noël and started talking about Wesker pretty damn quick. Yet the tide was already on the turn: the decision by Olivier to make Coward the first living British dramatist to have a production at the National might have been regarded by many as just the repayment of an old debt (since Olivier had been given one of his first great West End successes in *Private Lives*) but it undoubtedly started a slow process of canonisation.

By the time *Hay Fever* had opened, I had already started to think it was curious that there had only ever been one attempt at a Coward biography (a slim and wildly inaccurate volume published in 1933) and that his own autobiographies gave no account at all of the years 1931–39 or 1945 to the present. So I wrote to him suggesting that it was about time somebody wrote his life, and that on balance he might do worse than me. In my innocence of publishing customs, I also suggested that as it was his life we were talking about, he would of course be entitled to a cut of the proceeds – if there were ever to be any – which at that time did not appear altogether inevitable.

Noël replied at once: yes, he agreed that it was about time for a biography and that my 'curious fascination' with his work probably qualified me to write it. As, however, I had never written a book, he suggested that perhaps I would like to send him a couple of trial chapters about his childhood: if he approved of them, he would open up his files and give me his friends telephone numbers. I went away and wrote about the first quarter of the book, sent it to him and was duly summoned to another meeting at the Savoy at which he gave me his approval to go ahead, as well as access to a vast number of scrapbooks that his mother had kept since his earliest appearances in school plays.

I told him I was hoping to write a critical theatrical biography, rather than a fan book or a cuttings job, and that I wanted to talk to his enemies as well as his friends. He seemed to approve of that, and made only one reservation: there was to be no mention in the book of his homosexuality. His private life had, he said, always been just that: it had never been allowed to affect his work, and his reason for not wanting it made public in his lifetime was purely pragmatic. Noël was still living on his royalties, and in difficult times these tended to come from records and anthologies of short stories as well as from theatres. His audience was not, he reckoned, exclusively made up of a post-war generation prepared to allow the artist absolute sexual freedom: his followers still included large numbers of old ladies and gentlemen who would have been deeply shocked by homosexual revelations, and at a time when he still needed all the friends he could get, he saw no reason to alienate a whole section of his constituency. It needs to be recalled that the laws on homosexuality had not then been reformed, and that at least one distinguished leading actor, a contemporary friend of Coward's, was still living in the shadow of a notorious court case of the early 1950s.

This book took me two more years to research and write, and although along the way I came to agree with Coward that his private life had indeed played remarkably little part in an existence almost wholly given over to work, I still felt that there needed to be some reference to it somewhere.

At last I thought I'd found a way of changing Coward's mind: in about 1966 the drama and television critic T. C. Worsley, a figure of impeccable Establishment credentials and some literary distinction, published a memoir entitled *Flannelled Fools* in which he revealed lifelong homosexuality. Empires did not totter, membership of the Garrick was not withdrawn, and at last it seemed that the prejudice was fading. Armed with the book and its very favourable critical reaction in the serious press, I went to stay with Noël in Switzerland and suggested that where Worsley had beaten down the barricades, he too could slip through without too great a scandal. Noël disagreed: 'There is', he said memorably, 'one essential difference between me and Cuthbert Worsley. The British public at large would not care if Cuthbert Worsley had slept with mice.'

And that was more or less that, though Noël was always the first to make it clear that his demand for sexual privacy only applied in his own lifetime, and that after he was dead I was at liberty to rewrite this entire book if I so chose. In fact, I haven't: with the exception of this prologue and an epilogue, I have not altered or added anything for the simple reason that to have changed any of it would have meant changing all of it and there really isn't the need. As his own diaries (which Graham Payn and I edited for publication in 1982) indicate, his was not a life which lends itself to 'amazing revelations' of any kind.

This was, then, always intended to be a career book and it remains just that. Since its first publication have come many other biographies, including Cole Lesley's *Life of Noël Coward* (in America *Remembered Laughter*) which will give you a better idea of what Noël was like to live with on a day-to-day basis, and I would suggest that the two books need to be considered together as mirror images of the professional and the domestic man.

Three decades on, there are of course stylistic as well as tense changes I would make were I starting this book again: but the only and brief section I would actually want to rewrite from the point of view of content rather than style would be in Chapter 29, where I deal with Coward's last full-length play *A Song at Twilight.* Here I believe, for the first and only time, Noël did allow his private life to surface seriously in his work: though he always maintained that if the play was about anybody it was about either Max Beerbohm or Somerset Maugham rather than himself. In its discussion of the public's intolerance of homosexuality, it has always seemed to me a lot closer to home than any of the light comedies. As a play it was however not his best, and as autobiography it flew in the face of one of the many maxims which Coward made his own – never complain, never explain.

This book is by way of being an explanation: when I began it there was curiously little critical or public interest in the craftsmanship of Coward's plays and songs, in his professional longevity and resilience, or in the way that his work so perfectly reflected the changing social attitudes of the Twenties and Thirties. It was in the hope of arousing that interest that I started to write, and the intention was to chronicle the way in which Coward had kept himself constantly, professionally and uniquely in high definition across half a century.

Because I had Coward's approval for the project, I also had access to the hundred and fifty people I've thanked in the acknowledgments, many of them alas no longer with us. This book is about their memories as well as my research, and without them it would never have been possible.

But I believe
That since my life began,
The most I've had is just
A talent to amuse...

Bitter-Sweet, 1929.

1

1899–1910

I was born in Teddington, Middlesex, an ordinary middle-class boy. I was not gutter,
I didn't gnaw kippers' heads in the gutter as Gertrude Lawrence quite untruthfully
always insisted that she did. Nor was my first memory the crunch of carriage wheels
in the drive. Because we hadn't got a drive.

So from the very beginning the legend of Noël Coward is destroyed by the
facts. One had imagined him born into a rich London family, Mayfair
possibly or at worst Belgravia, and one had hoped to find him at a tender age
photographed on a bearskin rug murmuring witticisms through a few clenched
baby teeth and perhaps a tiny cigarette holder. But no such luck – indeed, no
such photographs; though there is one of him aged about two, looking
alarmingly coy and another at the age of five in what could well have been an
all-midget revival of *HMS Pinafore.*

Faced with starting the book in Teddington, Middlesex, one almost envies
any biographer of Mr Coward's life-long friend and frequent partner, Gertrude
Lawrence. She at least had the foresight to start life in romantic, impoverished,
if (as Coward claims) fictional surroundings. There she was, dancing to barrel
organs in the street and putting pennies into fortune-telling machines, one of
which was obliging enough to turn out a card reading 'A star danced, and
under it you were born.' All splendid material for a theatrical life story but
not, alas, for that of Mr Coward.

He was born, in ample time for Christmas and the new century, on the
morning of December 16th 1899; the Boer War was supplying the headlines,
Queen Victoria was eighty, and in Paris Oscar Wilde was living out the last few
months of his life in exile. Noël's mother, who at that time was thirty-six, had
been the last of six children of one Captain and Mrs Veitch. The Captain was
an archetypal, side-whiskered naval figure with twin passions for the sea and
painting both of which were later to be inherited by his grandson; as an artist
the Captain was splendid at landscapes but rather less good at depicting people,
a problem he overcame by cutting figures out of magazines and sticking them
on to his backgrounds. His family consisted of three girls and two boys as well
as a faintly dotty relation called Borby who had fallen out of a porthole on to
her head early in life and had never been quite the same since.

By 1883 the Captain's two sons had died, and two of his daughters had
married; the rest of the family (Noël's grandmother, his mother, Aunt Vida
and of course Borby) all moved in that year to Teddington in Middlesex,

which was then a small, unsuburban Thames-side village where some of the French royal family were still living in exile. There was now not much money left in Mrs Veitch's household, and by this time no man was left alive to support it, though for a while they scraped together just about enough to keep up the all-important appearances of the time. Their life in Teddington at the end of the last century centred around St Alban's church opposite Peg Woffington's cottage in the High Street, and it was there in about 1890 that Violet Agnes Veitch met Arthur Sabin Coward.

St Alban's was, and still is, a huge old church modelled on Rheims Cathedral. At the time of Noël's birth it had been in Teddington for about half a century and seemed to be almost totally supported, in the choir at least, by members of his father's family which was large and deeply musical. Noël's paternal grandfather had been the organist at the Crystal Palace and his Uncle Jim, in the years before he took almost exclusively to the bottle, was the organist at St Alban's except for the month of August when every year he used to travel to Paris and deputize for Guilmant at the organ of Notre Dame. Noël's father worked as a salesman for Metzler's during the week (Sir Henry Wood, founder of the Promenade concerts, remembered 'very enjoyable times in Metzler's going through the marvellous Mustel organs that they used to sell, and no one ever displayed them with such a wonderful technique as did Arthur Coward') and every Sunday he was to be found in the St Alban's church choir together with his brothers Randolph, Walter and Percy and his sisters Hilda, Myrrha, Ida and Nellie. Later in life Aunt Hilda, who had sung most of the solos, moved about half a dozen miles north-west and became known locally as the Twickenham Nightingale.

Noël's parents had actually met during choir practice in the church where they both sang loudly and frequently, and a prolonged courtship was carried out under the raised eyebrows of the local vicar, the Reverend F. Leith Boyd, who used to preach hell-fire sermons at the surprised old ladies of his congregation until he mellowed enough to become vicar of St Paul's in Knightsbridge. At about this time, shortly before their marriage, Noël's mother and father were also to be seen together in a number of amateur theatricals, though these were apparently restricted to the town hall in Teddington.

In 1892, soon after their marriage at St Alban's, the Cowards had a son whom they christened Russell. He lived only until he was six, when he died of spinal meningitis. Mrs Coward remained convinced however throughout her long life that Russell had died because as a baby she had had him inoculated; this conviction made her determined never to allow herself or any of her family to be vaccinated against anything ever again, a determination that remained unshakeable even when her third son, Eric, became a tea planter in Ceylon and laid himself open to every tropical disease imaginable, one of which eventually killed him.

A year and a half after Russell's death, while the Cowards were still living at Waldegrave Road in Teddington, they had a second son; born within ten days of Christmas, he was christened Noël and, much to his subsequent fury, given the middle name of Peirce after an old school-friend of his mother's who had been called Miss Peirce.

One of the family's neighbours in Teddington at that time was R. D. Blackmore, the author of *Lorna Doone;* asked by Mrs Coward to be one of Noël's godfathers, he declined on the grounds that Russell had been his godson and that therefore his godparenthood might be unlucky.

Coward's early memories seem inextricably bound up with the church in Teddington where his parents met, and where he was christened on February 10th 1900. He is reputed to have behaved impeccably at the font, though there was a nasty ecclesiastical scene about two years later when the young Master had to be forcibly restrained from dancing in one of the aisles.

At the time of Noël's birth Sir Henry Irving, then beyond doubt the head of the acting profession, was on tour in America. In his absence, Frank Benson was at the Lyceum doing a Shakespeare season with a company that included Henry Ainley and Harcourt Williams. It was still the high summer of the actor-managers: Beerbohm Tree was at Her Majesty's, playing Bottom in *A Midsummer Night's Dream* with Julia Neilson as Oberon; Charles Wyndham had just opened a theatre bearing his own name in the Charing Cross Road, and George Alexander was giving his *Rupert of Hentzau* at the St James's. Melodramas were at the beginning of a slow decline, though Drury Lane still had one called *The Price of Peace,* which offered its spectacle-crazed audiences scenes in Battersea Park, an ice-skating rink, and, amazingly, the terrace at the House of Commons.

In general revivals were preferred to new plays, by actors and audiences alike; W. S. Gilbert called the English dramatists of his time 'steady and stolidly', and the critic J. T. Grein noted that 'so long as Shakespeare draws the crowd… we need not bewail the poverty of our contemporary drama', though in fact both Bernard Shaw and, in Ireland, W. B. Yeats were writing prolifically by 1900.

Noël Coward spent the first five years of his life in Teddington, during which time electric trams appeared in the High Street, the village grew enormously, and his own family there diminished considerably: most of the uncles and aunts followed Hilda's example and moved away, some rather further than Twickenham. Uncle Percy actually moved as far as Australia, having married a professional pianist whom he abandoned on arrival there. In 1905 what was left of the Coward family in Teddington – Noël himself, his parents and a devoted maid called Emma who was inclined to hum the works of Gilbert and Sullivan through her teeth - found they could no longer afford to live there; reluctantly, having rejected the idea of emigrating to join Uncle Percy in Australia because they couldn't raise the fares, they moved a few miles away to a small villa half-way down Lenham Road in Sutton; but many years later Noël recaptured at least some of his memories of Teddington in a nostalgic poem called *Personal Reminiscence*:

I cannot remember
I cannot remember
The house where I was born
But I know it was in Waldegrave Road
Teddington, Middlesex
Not far from the border of Surrey
An unpretentious abode
Which, I believe,
Economy forced us to leave
In rather a hurry.
But I *can* remember my grandmother's Indian shawl
Which, although exotic to behold,
Felt cold.
Then there was a framed photograph in the hall
Of my father wearing a Norfolk jacket,
Holding a bicycle and a tennis racquet
And leaning against a wall
Looking tenacious and distinctly grim
As though he feared they'd be whisked away from him.
I can also remember with repulsive clarity
Appearing at a concert in aid of charity
At which I sang, not the 'Green Hill Far Away', that you know
But the one by Gounod.
I remember a paper-weight, made of quartz
And a sombre Gustave Doré engraving
Illustrating the 'Book of Revelations'
Which, I am told, upset my vibrations.
I remember too a most peculiar craving
For 'Liquorice All-Sorts'.
Then there was a song, 'Oh that we two were Maying'
And my uncle, who later took to the bottle, playing
And playing very well
An organ called the 'Mustel'
In the Autumn quietness of suburban roads
And seeing the winter river flooding
And swirling over the tow-path by the lock.
I remember my cousin Doris in a party frock

With 'broderie anglaise' at the neck and sleeves
And being allowed to stir the Christmas pudding
On long ago, enchanted Christmas Eves.

By the time the family moved across the Surrey border to Sutton, where their villa had a coloured glass front door and little else to recommend it, Noël's father (who had begun his career as a 'corresponding clerk' and been so described on Noël's baptism register) had stopped selling pianos for Metzler's and was now working for Payne's, a newer but less successful piano firm, as a travelling salesman. On one occasion his travels took him as far as Naples, which to some extent made up for an otherwise monotonous round of calls. Soon after the family had settled themselves in Surrey, Noël's brother Eric was born; Noël remembered him at that early age as bright red and singularly unattractive. Other outstanding moments of his early life in Sutton include a nasty encounter with Miss Willington, the headmistress of the local school, whom Noël bit, and an even nastier one with a neighbouring bull-terrier, who bit Noël. His first term at a day school did, however, lead to Coward's appearance at an end of term concert at the Public Hall in Sutton on July 23rd 1907, when he gave the assembled parents a rendering of 'Coo' from Lionel Monckton's musical *A Country Girl*. He came fifteenth on the bill, and followed it with a sickly number about birds and trees and smiling fields called 'Time Flies'.

The school concert was a qualified success, and a few months later Coward was to be found giving his all in public once again, this time by the sea at Bognor where during the family's summer holiday he won first prize and a rather nasty box of chocolates for singing 'Come along with me to the Zoo, Dear' in a competition organized on the beach by Uncle George's Concert Party, even though this particular Uncle was no relation.

In 1908 the Cowards moved again, this time to Number 70, Prince of Wales Mansions, overlooking Battersea Park, where they stayed until the spring of 1913. In these years the family's money troubles got considerably worse and they lived with what Ruth Gordon has called 'the dark brown taste of poverty' in their mouths. Noël's father's income from the piano firm was very small indeed, so once installed in Battersea his mother decided to follow the example of Aunt Ida who had by now set up a boarding house near Victoria Station in Ebury Street. Thus the Battersea household was soon joined by two paying guests, a Mr Baker and a Mr Denston, who dressed for dinner and were fond of musical soirées afterwards. 'The circumstances of my early life', wrote Noël later, 'were liable to degenerate into refined gentility unless carefully watched.'

But in spite of the genteel poverty surrounding it, Noël's childhood was cast in the classic theatrical mould; the precocious son of a doting mother, by the time he was eight he was already in proud possession of a toy theatre and looking forward to annual visits to the real theatres that were no longer so very far from his home. He used to save his pocket money and go once a week to see Gertie Millar in *The Quaker Girl* at the Adelphi; she possessed a magic that Noël was never to forget. For hours he would wait outside the stage door in the hope of seeing her, and once she even gave him some flowers from a bouquet which he kept for years reverently pressed in a bound volume of *Chums*.

In public, he was the kind of child who would suddenly burst into unexplained howls of fury, leaving passers-by with the distinct impression that his doting mother was ill-treating him. But left to himself, he was not too precocious to make a few friends around the neighbourhood, some of whom initiated him in the basic doorbell game. In Noël's case, however, it was played with a difference; instead of ringing the bell and then running away, he would ring it and then stand there, smiling seraphically but saying nothing, while a distraught housewife tried to find out what he wanted.

One of the joys of living at the top of a large number of flats was that the people who lived below used to leave prams on the landings outside their front doors. These could then be tied by Noël to their door-knockers, so that when the unfortunate lady of the house opened her front door from the inside, her pram came at her. Living in the next door flat to Noël at this time was an infant James Cameron who remembered that his family's enthusiasm for the 'gifted boy' across the landing waned somewhat after Noël tried to tip a pram with Cameron in it down the landing stairs.

In the meantime, Uncle Walter had gone on to become organist at the Chapel Royal in St James's; and soon after his brother's family moved to Battersea it was decided that his nephew should go to the Chapel Royal School then run in Clapham by Mr Claud Selfe who had a passion for making his boys swing Indian clubs and pursue other manly sports. The idea was that Noël should try for a place in the choir when he was old enough, but this did not entirely appeal to Coward himself who didn't much like the look of the other choirboys; even at the age of nine he was alert enough to realize that he might find more exciting things to do with his early life than spend it singing sacred music. But he joined the school, and when the day came for his first audition, he did his best; dressed in an Eton suit he gave a comprehensive if overacted version of Gounod's 'There is a Green Hill Far Away'. Dr Alcock, the choirmaster, was not impressed. He told Mrs Coward that her boy was far too young, that though she insisted Noël's voice had once moved the ex-Queen of Portugal to tears it really wasn't quite good enough for the Chapel Royal, and that he hadn't got a vacancy in any case. Mrs Coward, with the superb loyalty and dauntless pride of all theatrical mothers in time of crisis, rapidly overcame her disappointment and decided that Noël's failure had in fact been a blessing in disguise. Dr Alcock, she said, was obviously silly and didn't know a good voice when he heard one; moreover, she added that in her opinion, the whole choir looked exceedingly common, including Uncle Walter.

During the first decade of this century, the years when Coward was growing up in suburban London, the theatre was going through a quiet revolution. No longer were the actors in charge; Irving's influence was on the decline (he died a few hours after a performance of *Becket* at Bradford, on October 13th 1905) and instead these were the years of the writers – of such men as Bernard Shaw, J. M. Barrie, John Galsworthy, Arthur Wing Pinero, Henry Arthur Jones and, in Ireland, J. M. Synge. The theatre of ideas, which had begun with translations of Ibsen in the 1890s, was carried forward by the playwrights of the 1900s, though on the other side of the footlights Beerbohm Tree, George Alexander, Charles Wyndham and Seymour Hicks preserved the status quo of what J. C. Trewin has called the 'Theatre Theatrical' of the time. Tree had by now succeeded to the mantle of Irving in spite of the fact that his *Hamlet* was described by W. S. Gilbert as 'funny, without being vulgar.'

In these years, for the first time, the theatre in this country acquired a sort of social respectability as well as a social conscience. In 1895 Queen Victoria had given Irving the first theatrical knighthood ever, but it was her son Edward VII who finally set a seal of official (or at least royal) approval on the stage; between his accession in 1902 and his death in 1910 he went to a hundred and forty London productions, and organized almost thirty command performances at Sandringham or Windsor Castle. During his brief reign London saw six new plays by Pinero, ten by Henry Arthur Jones and almost twenty by Bernard Shaw, who in 1900 had sworn 'never again will I cross the threshold of a theatre – that subject is exhausted and so am I.'

When Noël Coward was one, Sarah Bernhardt was fifty-six and playing in *L'Aiglon* at Her Majesty's; when he was three, the Abbey Theatre in Dublin was founded and Granville Barker published his plans for a National Theatre; when he was four, the Vedrenne-Barker seasons started at the Royal Court, Synge wrote *Riders to the Sea,* Beerbohm Tree founded the Royal Academy of Dramatic Art and Barrie wrote *Peter Pan;* when he was five, London's first permanent cinema was opened, Henry Irving died, Shaw wrote *Man and Superman,* Ellen Terry's son, Gordon Craig, published his *Art of the Theatre* and Pinero wrote *His House in Order;* when he was six, the modern theatre's first attack on social injustice was made by Galsworthy in *The Silver Box,* Henrik Ibsen died, and Gerald du Maurier played 'Raffles'; when he was seven, *The Merry Widow* opened at Daly's, Miss Horniman opened the first repertory theatre in Manchester and

W. S. Gilbert was knighted; when he was eight, there were four plays by Somerset Maugham running in the West End, a record that Coward himself was to equal with three plays and a revue in 1925.

Soon after his defeat at the Chapel Royal choir audition, Coward got his first taste of life in the country. His mother, bored with Battersea and depressed by the kind of genteel poverty in which the family were living, decided to let the flat for six months; the lodgers went to lodge elsewhere and Noël and Eric were sent to stay with their grandmother and aunts Vida and Borby in Southsea, while their parents looked around Hampshire for a cottage. Coward's memories here are of the grey warships that lay at anchor off Spithead, the dawning of his lifelong devotion to the navy, and of a sort of desolation that even at the age of nine he seems to have sensed around Southsea. In the meantime Mrs Coward found a cottage at Meon, near Tichfield in Hampshire, and it was there that the family spent the next six months while an operatic lady called Mrs Davis rented the flat at Battersea.

Bay Tree Cottage in Meon was very small indeed, possessed of a thatched roof and an outside lavatory at the end of the garden which a local goat had to be discouraged from using. While the Cowards were coping with country life for the first time, the German Emperor paid a State Visit to Britain, in celebration of which all the battleships in the nearby Solent were lit up and Noël's family had a moonlight picnic with fireworks on the cliffs. The rest of their stay in Hampshire was uneventful, except for one occasion when Noël and his mother were nearly caught by their landlord while stealing his plums, and another when Noël wrote a brief drama which unwisely he decided to have acted by three little girls, sisters, who were holidaying nearby. They failed to share his enthusiasm for the piece, and during the performance (staged in a bell tent with evergreens for scenery) were prone to drying up and then giggling inanely. Afterwards the indignant playwright hit one of them over the head with a wooden spade and the whole thing deteriorated into a row between the parents concerned. One of the three girls, Joan Spurgin, never forgot the drama; Noël made her and her two sisters Joyce and Nancy, forego their combined pocket money – all of sixpence – with which he then bicycled two miles into Tichfield to buy ribbon for their various disguises. When they weren't actually rehearsing (and before the row which put an abrupt end to their friendship), the girls took Noël on endless picnics at which he taught them to make and, indeed, to consume nasturtium leaf sandwiches followed by stinging nettle tea. Joan remembered 'a friendly and likeable boy who always wanted things done his way, but whose charm made one want to please him.'

When the six months were up, the operatic lady decided she would like a little longer in Battersea, so the Cowards returned to Southsea for Christmas with Noël's grandmother. Immediately afterwards he was sent back to London to be there in ample time for the first day of the new term at the Chapel Royal School: the plan was that the rest of the family should return a week later and reinstall themselves in Battersea. Noël spent the week staying with his Uncle Randolph in St George's Square, and for the first time in his life was deeply unhappy. At the best of times he was not fond of school anyway, and during this one week early in 1909 he became obsessed with the idea that he would never see his mother again:

> The dramatic scenes I visualized were terrifying; first the fatal telegram arriving at the house, and my aunt and uncle calling me into the drawing-room on the first floor to break the news, then a tear-sodden journey in the train, and Auntie Vida meeting me at Fratton Junction, very small and morose, in black. Then, as a fitting climax, I imagined the front bedroom enshrouded in a funereal twilight with the blinds down and Mother lying still and dead under a sheet like a waxwork.

So far from being still and dead, his mother returned from the country in splendid health and Noël returned happily to their flat in Battersea; it was perhaps the first time that he became aware of his deep devotion to the woman who remained the most powerful figure in Noël's life until she died almost fifty years later at the age of ninety-one.

In the next year Noël started to sing a good deal, sometimes in church, but more often at concerts which he preferred because there the audience applauded. After his performance at one of these, given in a private house, the hostess was heard to murmur 'how sweetly pretty' – though whether she was referring to Noël's voice or his general deportment is not clear. His mother, having discovered with a good deal of pride but not much surprise that her boy had talent, soon decided that the time had come to train it.

So for six weeks early in 1910 every Thursday and Friday afternoon, Noël set off across the city to a dancing academy run in Hanover Square by Miss Janet Thomas. He enjoyed the lessons only slightly less than the journey through London, on which, travelling alone, he was able to accost old ladies in trains with gruesome stories of a sordid but entirely mythical home life. On successful afternoons they would take pity on this angelic child sobbing about his drunken father and diseased tubercular sisters, and Noël would be treated to a large tea in Fuller's; on one less successful afternoon he was pinched on the knee by a clergyman and decided there and then to abandon the whole practice. During these weeks, apart from perfecting a theatrical ability to tell lies convincingly, Noël also acquired a penchant for travelling alone which stayed with him until his sixties. Though not an anti-social man, he travelled like all writers in search of material and found this easier to pick up on those occasions when he was alone. It is true that in this way he laid himself open to the endless stories of innumerable bores in countless hotel bars, but that would appear, as Maugham also discovered, to be the price paid.

Just before the end of the dancing lessons an advertisement in the *Daily Mirror* announced that Miss Lila Field was in search of 'talented boy with attractive appearance' to play in her all-children production of *The Goldfish,* a piece she had written herself. Mrs Coward replied to the advertisement at once, and soon afterwards Noël clambered back into his Eton suit and went off to an audition room near Baker Street. There he sang 'Liza Ann' unaccompanied, an achievement he followed with a brisk dance while his mother, in the absence of a pianist, sang. Miss Field, unlike Dr Alcock at Chapel Royal, was impressed. She told Mrs Coward that she would like to engage her boy for the part of Prince Mussel in the play, and that the fee would be one and a half guineas a week. There was a terrible pause, at the end of which Mrs Coward murmured that she would not, alas, be able to afford it. Miss Field laughed politely, explained that it was she who would be paying, and Noël Coward had his first job.

It was 1910 and to celebrate his triumph, the boy actor and his mother went to Selfridge's for ice-cream sodas.

2

1910–1913

I can remember. I can remember.
The months of November and December
Were filled for me with peculiar joys,
So different from those of other boys.

For other boys would be counting the days
Until end of term and holiday times
But I was acting in Christmas plays
While they were taken to pantomimes.

I didn't envy their Eton suits,
Their children's dances and Christmas trees.
My life had wonderful substitutes
For such conventional treats as these.

I didn't envy their country larks,
Their organized games in panelled halls:
While they made snowmen in stately parks,
I was counting the curtain calls.

Rehearsals for *The Goldfish* were held twice a week for many months; this was partly because there seemed to be some difficulty in finding a theatre, and mainly because the cast kept changing as various mothers grew impatient and withdrew their children. Some however did last the course, among them a girl called June, who later married Lord Inverclyde, and a ten year old boy called Alfred Willmore who later translated his name back to its original Irish and became known as Micheál MacLiammóir. For him as for Noël it was the first professional engagement:

> I went into this room in Hanover Square – it was a big studio with a polished floor on which I nearly fell over. And I was ten and I presume Noël was too and I remember this beautiful autumn day in 1910; there were a lot of children there, a crowd of children, and among them was one who looked strangely grown up, more poised than all the others. The voice was very mature and the eyes were already observant, not cynical but shrewd and humorous and ambiguous – in a way they seemed to tell you nothing. I was very miserable on that day, and Noël after a few preliminary boyish grins, was the first person who spoke to me. I think he asked how much work I'd done; I do know that during the course of that

conversation I asked him what he wanted to be when he grew up. He electrified me by saying: 'An actor of course, otherwise I wouldn't be here. What do you want to be?' And then I said miserably that I didn't really know – I was sure it wasn't an actor by that time because I was hopelessly at sea with all the other children. But Noël evidently knew even then exactly what he wanted to do with his life; he was a lively, brilliant, settled, quarrelsome, vivid boy. He was also extraordinarily urbane for his age, already enjoying phrases, and I remember that I had enough sense of words myself to notice how he enjoyed saying brisk and beautifully balanced things like 'Mother nearly had a fit in Oxford Street today'. And I thought how typically perfect – she didn't have colly-wobbles in Hampstead, she had a fit in Oxford Street.

Noël was Jack in the play and I was Charlie in the first act and the Goldfish in the second. I forget any of the lines I said – they were quite colourless and meant nothing to me. But Noël's first was, 'Crumbs, how exciting', and then I remember him saying 'boo' behind a little girl's ear – her name was Dolly – and then she said, 'Oh Jack, you brute! To frighten me like that!' And he said, 'Oh really, Dolly, good gracious! If you start like that when anybody comes up behind you at your age, you'll have electric wires sticking out all over you when you grow up.' Noël had then exactly the same cadence that we all know so well now. I don't think I've ever known a man in my life who has changed less.

MacLiammóir was getting £2 a week for his first engagement, *9/6d.* more than Noël was being paid for wearing a small black hat and executing a dance later described by the *Daily Mirror* as 'spirited'. *The Goldfish* was a fairy story in three acts, with music by Lila Field herself and lyrics by Ayre O'Naut. Originally it had been a one-act play performed by a cast entirely consisting of girls, but the 1911 production which opened on January 27th for a week of matinées at the Little Theatre with Noël as 'Prince Mussel', June Tripp as 'Princess Sole' and Micheál MacLiammóir as 'King Goldfish' was an entirely reorganized undertaking. Miss Field herself, a daunting character who also wrote a fashion column and found time to be a lady aviator, took complete charge. After the production she was engaged in a rather bitter correspondence with Noël's mother, who claimed only to have received one week's salary for her boy, but by the time she and Noël next met some forty years later all that was forgotten, and he was persuaded to add an introduction to *The Goldfish* which Miss Field was hoping to publish. In fact it never appeared in print, but this in part is what Noël wrote:

Rehearsals, sometimes sporadic, sometimes daily, had taken place in basements, gymnasiums, dance-halls, and even private houses of members of the cast with furniture pushed back and tea served afterwards with little cakes, drop scones, and, on one occasion, watercress sandwiches.

During the week immediately before production when there was no longer any doubt that the play was at last going to open, the excitement rose to fever pitch – anxious mothers, clutching their offsprings shoes, shawls and 'Dorothy' bags, lined the walls of rehearsal rooms whispering sibilantly and now and then swaying slightly as the winds of rumour eddied around them – 'Miss Field has said this – Miss Field has said that'.

Everything, Life and Death and the stars in their courses depended on what Miss Field had said.

Occasionally, there was an outburst of hysteria – faces were slapped, tears were shed; mothers bowed icily to each other and sat tight-lipped, watching with disdain the cavortings of their rivals' progeny, who, serenely unaware of those primaeval undertones, were enjoying themselves tip-top.

Finally, the great day dawned. The curtain rose, I think, at 2 pm. but it may have been 2.30; however, it did definitely rise disclosing a pretty garden scene crowded with bright and eager children all hell bent on future stardom, and all under fourteen years of age with the exception of one who shall be forever nameless, for we suspected then and I still suspect that she was nineteen if she was a day. The opening chorus was led by a radiant fair little girl and a plumpish, very assured little boy in a white knicker-bocker suit. The girl was described in the programme as 'Little June Tripp' and the boy was Master Noël Coward. They sang with extreme abandon 'School, School, Goodbye to School'. Fifteen years later, on that same stage, Master Noël Coward, grown to man's estate, was portraying with equal abandon a drug addict in his own play *The Vortex*.

I remember clearly, so very clearly, Master Alfred Willmore as King Goldfish singing 'I lived within my bowl of glass – Heigho – a prisoner I' – Master Burford Hampden as the ruthless King Starfish: 'I am a really first class King, O'er the sea my praises ring' – and of course, my own song as Prince Mussel the Court Jester:

Fairest Queen you'll never guess
How I praise your loveliness,
I've a heart that loves you so…
But alas you must not know.

I remember hearing for the first time in my life an audience in a theatre laughing and applauding. I remember for the first time the drying size on canvas, the pungency of hot gelatine in the limelights and footlights, the unforgettable indescribable dressing-room smell, greasepaint, face-powder, new clothes and cold cream. I remember, I remember the house where I was born: that, actually, I cannot remember at all; but I certainly remember the theatre where I was born and the play in which I was born and that play is *The Goldfish*, which retains for one rapidly ageing little boy a magic that will never die.

In the six months that followed Coward's first appearance at the Little Theatre, *The Goldfish* was revived twice; first at the Crystal Palace for two performances, during one of which a rat ate Noël's powder-puff in the dressing-room, and then at the Court Theatre in Sloane Square where they played for a week in another condensed version. This last engagement brought a number of notices in the press: *The Stage* found Noël 'resourceful' in his singing, the *Daily Telegraph* considered that his 'robust appearance gave excellent point to his woebegone song of love for the Queen of the Coral Islands' and the *American Register* announced rather surprisingly that 'all Mayfair flocked to the performance.' These reviews must have made up for the disappointment of Noël's first notice, in the *Daily Telegraph* of January 28th 1911. This, referring to the earlier production of *The Goldfish,* had read simply 'Among other tiny artists who deserve a congratulatory pat on the back are Miss Noël Coward, Miss Nellie Terriss and Miss Peggie Bryant.'

The girls in the production included a very young Ninette de Valois, though it was June who retained the most vivid impressions of the young Coward. She remembered 'a boy with elfin ears and a foul temper', and recorded that when he hit her over the head with a ballet slipper it was MacLiammóir who came to her rescue. June's sole line in the play was apparently, 'Let us run away to little Sunny Cove', and at one performance she failed even to get that out:

> Everything seemed set for fair as the curtain parted; but somewhere along the line, between supervising the sketchy scenery and making certain that none of the actors got locked in the lavatory, Miss Field had slipped up. Instead of the little painted blocks of wood, representing cakes, which we had used at rehearsals, there were real pastries on the table. And, when my cue came, I was completely immobilized by a chocolate éclair. Ninette chirped her line, 'What shall we do?', and after a short but deathly silence I heard a slightly cracked voice say 'Let us run away to little Sunny Cove.' Turning indignantly I beheld Noël Coward closing his lips in a triumphant smirk. I could have throttled him.

Later, at home Mrs Howard-Tripp did not exactly endear herself to her daughter June by retelling the story of Noël's step taken into the breach: 'What a brilliant boy!' she enthused. 'What superb presence of mind! Mark my words, he'll go a long way'. Without warning, June was quietly sick over the table-cloth.

Noël has said that *The Goldfish* was the play in which he was born: but it was not really the play in which he got his theatrical education. For that he had to wait until later in 1911 when, at the end of the summer, he was sent by Bellew and Stock, Theatrical Agents, to see a gentleman called E. M. Tarver. By this time Noël's official schooling had become a bit sparse, as even when he wasn't actually rehearsing or playing in a show he was inclined to wander off to Waterloo Station to watch the trains, or else potter up and down the embankment wearing an alarming red beard made from crêpe hair bought from the local chemist for a penny. He skipped school yet again to keep his appointment with Tarver, then the stage manager for Charles Hawtrey's company at the Prince of Wales, who was looking for a boy to play the page in the last act of a new comedy called *The Great Name* which was due to open in a few days time. Tarver decided that Coward would do, and engaged him for two pounds a week (of which Messrs Bellew and Stock took four shillings in commission). Noël only had one line, addressed to Hawtrey himself who as a composer was discovered in one scene playing a piano in the artists room at the Queen's Hall. Noël had to enter as the page-boy and demand, 'Stop that noise at once, please. In there they're playing *The Meistersingers*. Making such a horrible noise. We're used to good music here.' As they were within three days of the first night by the time Noël joined the company, he and his mother carefully rehearsed and re-rehearsed the line at home, with Mrs Coward trying out her skills as a director and the dining-room table pushed back to make more room.

Fully rehearsed and thoroughly aware of all the possible emotions that could be worked into his one line as Cannard the page-boy, Noël presented himself at the Prince of Wales, performed it at the top of his voice, and made an exit that would not have disgraced a chorus girl in the Ziegfeld Follies. Hawtrey swivelled round on the piano stool and watched the small boy's departing back with a look of glazed horror. Then, interrupting the rehearsal and sending for his stage manager, Hawtrey murmured, 'Tarver, never let me see that boy again'. Later, however, he relented, and Noël was allowed to play the part on condition he be re-rehearsed by Tarver and make rather less of a meal out of what was meant to be an insignificant walk-on.

The Great Name, which opened on September 7th 1911, was not a marked success; nevertheless, Hawtrey's play remained at the Prince of Wales until the last week in October and in that time Noël learnt a great deal about the theatre from him. Charles Hawtrey was, before Gerald du Maurier, the first of the new 'naturalistic' actors of the time. Coming directly after a period of great declamation in the theatre, Hawtrey in contrast appeared to act on the stage very much as he would in real life. In fact his casual, soft-spoken, throwaway style hid as much care, as much projection and as much technique as the more obvious theatricality of Irving or Beerbohm Tree.

But Hawtrey did not appear to be 'acting' in the way that his predecessors did, and Coward, astute eleven-year-old child that he was, realized that here was a man from whom he could learn – by what he taught and, more important, by the way he acted on stage.

During the six weeks of *The Great Name,* Hawtrey was haunted by a small, adoring child who followed him around like a sheep, seizing every opportunity to chatter at him, get his autograph (seventeen times, in a book covered with sweet peas) or just stare at him. The effect on Hawtrey was convulsive; not only did he once miss an entrance because Coward was talking to him but he also began to believe that the child was really haunting him, and that wherever he turned in his life there Coward would be. On one occasion, Hawtrey was coming down the main staircase at Buckingham Palace after an official reception, and there at the bottom of the stairs. Looking up at him, was a small child dressed as a page-boy. He swore it was Coward, who to this day can hear Hawtrey's quiet voice edged with exasperation murmuring, 'Go away, boy, for God's sake, leave me alone.'

But however unsettling the effect on Hawtrey, the effect on Noël was precisely what he had intended; he learnt. He learnt about the theatre, about being an actor and above all he learnt about comedy; Coward credited Hawtrey with everything he was to learn about getting laughs in the theatre, and the main lesson seems to have been that before you can hope to get your laughs you have got to help the other actor get his. What Coward thought of Hawtrey, and how much he owes to him, we know, but what Hawtrey thought of Coward is not on record although it may be of interest to note that in the three hundred pages of his autobiography (edited by Somerset Maugham and published in 1924) the only mention of Noël is as one of a list of actors who were in the original company of *Where the Rainbow Ends* and who subsequently made good in the theatre.

By now, like it or not and Noël patently did, he was a child actor; one of that small, select band along with Master Robert Andrews, Master Philip Tonge, Master Reggie Sheffield, Master Harold French, Master Alfred Willmore and the others who earned up to five pounds a week for their eager mothers by appearing on the stage at the earliest possible moment. London in those days must have been a socially tight-knit city, and certainly the acting world was of such proportions that everybody knew everybody. Each Christmas there was the massive scramble by boy and girl actors alike to get into one of the seasonal plays or pantomimes, followed by the resultant fury of their mothers if they failed. In fact the children, left to themselves, generally got on very well indeed with one another; but among the parents, and notably among the mothers who used to meet at Lyons Corner House in Coventry Street to discuss the careers of their young, there was – on their children's behalf – all the massive jealousy and temperament that one normally associates with opera stars.

Mrs Coward, to her everlasting credit, had some reservations about making her elder surviving son into a child actor; on the other hand the money was undoubtedly needed, and Noël was evidently happy in what he was doing. One evening at about this stage in Noël's childhood, Mrs Coward went with her sister-in-law Ida to see Anna Eva Fay who was doing her celebrated mind-reading act on the stage of the London Coliseum. She invited questions from the audience and Mrs Coward, sitting up in the gallery worrying about Noël's theatrical life, sent down a question not explaining what Noël did, but simply saying that it made him very tired and asking whether she should keep him at it. After a good deal of mind-searching and clutching at her forehead Miss Fay announced from the stage that whatever Mrs Coward's son was doing she should keep him at it, since one day he would be a very great success indeed. Relieved and delighted Mrs Coward hurried home to tell Noël, who had never for one moment doubted it anyway. Ida, who had hoped that Miss Fay would provide an answer to where she had mislaid a roll of barbed wire, was less enthusiastic.

Before *The Great Name* folded, Coward was again in rehearsal for Hawtrey and again playing a page-boy, though this time the theatre was the Savoy, the part was a better one, and the play was *Where the Rainbow Ends*. This, like all Noël's appearances on the professional stage until he was fourteen, necessitated a visit to the Bow Street Magistrates Court. There he and his mother, together with the business manager of whatever was the production concerned, would apply for a licence. Usually these were given as a matter of course to child actors, and on the few occasions when a magistrate was brave enough to stand up to Mrs Coward and ask if acting was in her boy's best interests, he was treated to a lengthy speech in which Mrs Coward explained that if the boy was not allowed to act he would doubtless go into a decline and have to be sent to a sanatorium. Not surprisingly the licence was then granted and Noël returned happily to his work in the theatre.

It was on December 21st that Hawtrey first presented *Where the Rainbow Ends* at the Savoy Theatre, and in the opening production of the play that was to become a children's classic second only to *Peter Pan* Noël played William, a good part though one that disappears after the first act. That year Reginald Owen who, under the pseudonym of John Ramsey was the co-author, played St George of England and the Savoy Hotel was advertising dinner for 5 shillings after the show.

The company seems to have been a happy one except for minor squabbles over the mother of the leading boy, Philip Tonge, who used to wash out her gloves in the dressing-room until some of the other boys, Noël among them, complained to the management which effectively discouraged her. Master Tonge's leading lady was a child actress called Esmé Wynne; she played Rosamund and became later the first real friend of his own age that Noël had ever had. Hawtrey's management, concerned by the generally low status of child actors and kept under the strict surveillance of the London County Council, fell over themselves to make the cast feel at home. Thus the life of a child actor with Hawtrey wasn't at all a bad one, and he noted with pride that many of them looked a good deal better and healthier after the run of *The Rainbow* than when they first came to rehearsals.

The first night of *The Rainbow* brought with it a cable to Coward from Hawtrey that read 'Best of luck and I hope a good hard smack. Charles Hawtrey', referring presumably to some long-forgotten business in the first act. It also brought some good notices: the *Referee* considered that 'Master Noël Coward... also deserves praise', *The Era* felt that 'the role of William the spiteful page-boy was smartly acted by Master Noël Coward' and *The Birmingham Daily Post* thought he played a 'thankless part with much skill and effect.'

Most of the children in *The Rainbow* came from that source of almost all English stage children, Italia Conti. But Coward, contrary to popular belief, was never a Conti child and though Miss Conti once tried to persuade him that as his part in the play was over by the end of the first act, he might like to join the rest of her team playing hyenas and frogs in the other acts, Mrs Coward decided that her boy's prestige as one of the principals would definitely suffer if he were to be seen crawling about in a hot hyena skin.

The run also gave Coward his first taste of direction; once the play had opened, the children ('all we clever little tots', in Noël's phrase) were encouraged by Hawtrey to stage special matinées of their own devising for families and loyal friends. On February 2nd, the sole performance of a one-act piece called *The Daisy Chain* by Dot Temple, who played Betty Blunders in *The Rainbow* was directed by a twelve-year-old Noël Coward. Later on in the run, when Philip Tonge produced a play called *The Prince's Bride* by Esmé Wynne, Noël was billed as the stage manager; it was at this moment, according to Esmé Wynne writing in 1962, that 'Noël decided to become a playwright and a Man of the Theatre'.

The beginning of 1912 found Noël out of work once *The Rainbow* ended its Christmas season, but after a few depressing months trailing round agents' offices and having sixpenny lunches at Lyons he was back at the Savoy, this time appearing as 'The Mushroom' in *An Autumn Idyll,* an artistic ballet arranged and produced by a lady called Ruby Ginner. The ballet was set to music by Chopin, and told of a day in the life of an Autumn Leaf, played by Miss Ginner herself with Mr Alan Trotter as The Wind and members of Miss Ginner's dancing school as Winter Mists. Noël was intended to supply some of the more lighthearted moments in his role as a carefree mushroom, and he was partnered by Joan Carrol, dressed as a toadstool in bright pink. The really big moment of the ballet was undoubtedly Miss Ginner's valiant fight with the mists and then her ultimate death as the lights faded, although the effect of this was marred for Noël by the fact that she seemed so much larger and better developed than the mists which vanquished her.

The Times of June 26th 1912 noted that 'Miss Joan Carrol and Mr Noël Coward as the Toadstool and the Mushroom headed delightfully a little troupe of various small and engaging fungi'. It failed to note, however, that Master Eric Coward was also to be seen, though credited in rather smaller type, as one of the small and engaging fungi, and that the Savoy Hotel dinners advertised in the theatre programme had risen monstrously to 5/6d.

By October Noël was back with Hawtrey, this time at Oswald Stoll's London Coliseum in a sketch, number eleven on the current variety bill, entitled *A Little Fowl Play*. It ran for four weeks although Noël was only allowed to play the matinées as the Bow Street magistrate had refused to licence him for the evening performance in which he wouldn't have appeared until eleven at night. Hawtrey nevertheless insisted on paying him the full salary while using the assistant stage manager for the evening performances, and Coward would stand nightly in the wings watching and learning. The rest of the bill changed from week to week, so he was able at various times to see George Robey, a Wild West show, and, since one-act plays and 'straight' actors were frequently to be found on variety bills, Pauline Chase in J. M. Barrie's *Pantaloon*.

After *A Little Fowl Play* Hawtrey re-engaged Noël for his original part in *Where the Rainbow Ends,* which for the Christmas of 1912 had moved to the Garrick Theatre. 'A plain little boy', said somebody watching Noël act at this time, 'but a pleasant personality'. The cast for *The Rainbow* was virtually unchanged and the run uneventful except for one memorable night when Philip Tonge, still playing Crispian walked with Noël to Baker Street tube station after the show. On the way Philip decided to tell Noël the facts of life, and Noël returned home in a state of high hysteria. 'Mother', he announced, in a tragic voice, charging into her bedroom, 'I have lost my innocence'. Mother laughed gently, broke it to him that he had done nothing of the kind, and made the cocoa. She also suggested that if he was going to be an actor it was probably as well that he had learnt about 'life' as early as possible.

In the spring of 1913, by which time Noël had acquired a bicycle and a gramophone together with several records from a new friend called Parker-Jarvis who lived in Ealing. Italia Conti wrote offering him a three-week engagement with the Liverpool Repertory Company at the inevitable two pounds a week. Noël was to play at Liverpool and Manchester in a new production by a young Basil Dean of Gerhart Hauptmann's *Hannele*. His mother saw him off from Euston for the trip to Liverpool; on the train were about ten other children due to appear in the production, one of whom instantly caught Noël's attention.

> She wore a black satin coat and a black velvet military hat with a peak, her face was far from pretty, but tremendously alive. She was very *mondaine*,

carried a handbag with a powder-puff and frequently dabbed her generously turned-up nose. She confided to me that her name was Gertrude Lawrence, but that I was to call her Gert because everybody did, that she had been in *The Miracle* at Olympia and *Fifinella* at the Gaiety, Manchester. She then gave me an orange and told me a few mildly dirty stories, and I loved her from then onwards.

Noël appeared with Gert and Roy Royston and Harold French, all angels in Hannele's dream sequence; he then played a schoolboy and reverted to an angel at the end of the piece but failed to enjoy any of it very much. He wore short tunics and bare feet and remained deeply homesick throughout, although things did liven up a bit on a trip to New Brighton when Gert hit Miss Conti's sister over the head with a rounders bat. Miss Lawrence remembered Noël as 'a thin, unusually shy boy with a slight lisp' and recalled that on one occasion during the tour of *Hannele* the two of them were given a large box of peppermints on condition that they shared it with the rest of the cast:

> Noël and I managed to forget this admonition and to eat most of the sweets ourselves in the taxi on the way to the theatre. Soon I began to feel queer. When we went on in the heaven scene, the other celestial beings seemed to float and bob dizzily around me. I stole a glance at Noël. He was positively green. Presently the audience was permitted an unexpected vision of heaven in which two small angels were being violently sick.

After a week in Liverpool the *Hannele* company moved to Manchester where a local magistrate refused to licence the children unless they went to school every day during the week. Accordingly Noël spent four days feeling miserable and hating a large red board school in the Oxford Road; relations with Basil Dean were also somewhat strained. 'If ever you speak to me again in that tone of voice', Noël announced from the stage in the course of one particularly fraught rehearsal, 'I shall go straight home to my mother.'

While Noël was away, the family left their Battersea flat and moved to a maisonette called 'Ben Lomond' on the south side of Clapham Common. The rooms were bigger than those in Battersea, and Clapham Common had a splendid pond where Mr Coward sailed his model yacht in the weeks when he wasn't travelling for Payne's pianos. After the move, and after a few more gloomy weeks hanging around the agents' offices, Noël found himself at what was then Charles Gulliver's London Palladium in the prologue to a bizarre spectacle entitled *War in the Air*. The programme described this (item ten on the bill for the week of June 23rd 1913) as 'a spectacular object lesson designed to Arouse the National Consciousness to a sense of its Hovering Peril.' The Hovering Peril was attack from the air, and Noël appeared in the prologue as an airstruck child praying. 'Please God, Bless Mummy and Daddy and Violet and make me a great big aviator one day.' There followed a massive aerial battle, at least until the third performance when one of the planes swung on a wire into the auditorium, got hitched on to the front of the upper circle, and remained there for three hours with the 'great big aviator' on board. For the rest of the week the management abandoned that part of the entertainment.

But looking back to the programme of this production, the author Frank Duprée seems to have been alarmingly prescient. Writing in 1913, he listed the synopsis as follows:

> The time: 1915.
> Scene 1: The Air Office.
>   The Declaration of War.
>   Britannia must rule the air.
> Scene 2: Interior of the Conning Tower.
>   The forged despatches.
>   The invading fleet.
>   The destructive bomb.
> Scene 3: The great flight for home and country.
>   The wireless message.
> Scene 4: Top of the Central Aerial Station.
>   The war in the air.
>   Poor old London.
>   The timely rescue.
>   The coming of 'The Conqueror'.

All in all it was an instructive time for Noël who shared the bill with Cissie Lupino ('Speciality Dancer'), Nellie Wallace ('Quintessence of Quaintness') and Sie Tahar's Oriental Zienats ('War tumblers of World-Wide Repute, introducing Marym Sie Tahar, the only real Arabian Lady Tumbler').

After the Palladium *War in the Air* also made brief appearances at the Willesden Hippodrome and the Shoreditch Olympia, where Noël would get into costume and make-up as early as possible so that he could stand in the wings watching George Robey, Phil Ray and Beattie and Babs higher up the variety bill which they all shared with a good many performing animals; on one occasion Noël let loose a whole basket of snakes between the matinée and evening performances, to the consternation of Madame Alicia Adelaide Needham and her Ladies Choir.

3

1913–1915

I never cared who scored the goal
Or which side won the silver cup,
I never learned to bat or bowl
But I heard the curtain going up.

After *War in the Air* ended its brief tour in the summer of 1913 Noël, now an established if out-of-work actor, wrote around to various theatres in the West End demanding free tickets to their current shows for himself and his mother. Not entirely surprisingly, the request (written on visiting cards printed with the words 'Master Noël Coward, Mr Charles Hawtrey's Company') was frequently turned down, but some theatres made a practice of giving 'comps' to resting actors and in this way the Cowards managed to see a good deal of what London entertainment had to offer. 'Common, dear, and very silly', was the not infrequent verdict of Mrs Coward, but Noël, as ever, watched, listened and learnt.

For their holiday that summer, Noël's aunts Vida and Borby took a cottage at Lee-on-the-Solent, and the whole family went down there for a month. In the absence of Uncle George's Concert Party Noël allied himself with 'The Poppy Pierrots' who played twice daily on the end of the pier and allowed him to join them for a couple of songs on benefit nights. By now his musical talent was developing, although untaught, fairly rapidly:

I was born into a generation that still took light music seriously. The lyrics and melodies of Gilbert and Sullivan were hummed and strummed into my consciousness at an early age. My aunts and uncles, who were legion, sang them singly and in unison at the slightest provocation. By the time I was four years old 'Take a Pair of Sparlking Eyes', 'Tit Willow', 'We're Very Wide Awake', the 'Moon and I' and 'I Have a Song to Sing-O' had been fairly inculcated into my bloodstream. My mother and father were both musical in a light, amateur sense but their gift was in no way remarkable. My father, although he could improvise agreeably at the piano, never composed a set piece of music in his life … I had no piano lessons when I was a little boy, except occasionally from my mother who tried once or twice, with singular lack of success, to teach me my notes. I could, however, from the age of about seven onwards, play any tune I had heard on the piano in the pitch dark. To be born with a natural ear for music is a great and glorious gift. It is no occasion for pride and it has nothing to do with will-power, concentration or industry. It is either there or it isn't. What is so curious is that it cannot, in any circumstances, be wrong where one's own harmonies are concerned.

In August 1913, while the Cowards were still at Lee-on-the-Solent, a postcard arrived from Charles Hawtrey inviting Noël to audition for the part of Buster in *Never Say Die,* a new comedy that was going into the Apollo. Mrs Coward, realizing there had been a delay in forwarding the card, which had been written four days earlier, hurried Noël into a London train and took him straight to the theatre. There they discovered that Hawtrey, in the absence of any reply from the Cowards, had cast Reginald Sheffield for the part. Noël's bitter disappointment was only partly assuaged by the offer of understudying the character at two pounds ten shillings a week. However, he was still in no position to refuse work and spent the next few months at the Apollo fervently hoping that Reggie Sheffield would fall under a bus, which he didn't, and in the meantime eating what was left of the asparagus devoured nightly on stage during the second act. At this time money was still desperately tight in the Coward household, and his father was doing rather less successfully in the new piano business than when first he joined Metzler's; but Noël and his mother managed to make a very little go a long way. Their success at this is vouched for by Gertrude Lawrence, who decided mistakenly when she first met Noël that 'his people were in a position to give him educational advantages – they were comfortably situated', though she added graciously that 'Noël wasn't snobbish about this.'

In November 1913, Coward left Hawtrey's company for the third time and, having already played twice in *Where the Rainbow Ends,* now joined the cast of the other great children's classic, *Peter Pan.* For this engagement, which involved playing 'Slightly' for a season at the Duke of York's and then a lengthy tour of outer London and the provinces until the end of March, Mrs Coward managed to beat the director up thirty shillings and Noël's salary scaled new heights at four pounds a week. The director was Dion Boucicault, then married to Irene Vanbrugh, and Peter Pan was played by Pauline Chase.

That Christmas *Peter Pan* ran for matinées only, a new arrangement which led the critic of *The Observer* to enquire rather prematurely 'Is this the beginning of the end?'. He did, however, see 'an excellent Slightly in Mr Noël Coward'; another critic wrote 'The immortal Slightly as acted by Master Noël Coward, is quite a young boy and his grave pretence at wisdom is all the funnier.' Also in the production, acting with Noël for the second and in fact the last time was Micheál MacLiammóir; he was less keen on the latter's performance:

I remember thinking that Noël was too intelligent for the part. Slightly is the moronic boy, you know, who fell out of his pram or something. But Noël gave his usual rhythmic, debonair, mother-of-pearl brilliance to the part, and he shook the imaginary thermometer much too smartly – I'm sure Slightly would have bungled it. Noël always seemed completely, as they say in the West of Ireland, 'fit for any emergency from pitch and toss to manslaughter'. He could have done anything. Yeats' description of Aubrey Beardsley once reminded me of Noël when Yeats said Beardsley was not only a brilliant artist in that very confined black and white world of his, but that he could also have been a great writer, a great statesman, a great politician. One felt that about Noël. Another extraordinary quality was his intense loyalty, even then, to the theatre; it gave Noël everything in the world he dreamed of or wanted. I wanted vague things beyond, and I went in quest of them and got lost, while he remained perfectly assured; perhaps in his innermost soul he does have moments of doubt, but I can't really imagine Noël doubting anything.

He was always quite certain of everything: I remember on the tour of *Peter Pan* in Glasgow. Noël once told me the facts of life in a dressing-room. And the next week I learned them quite differently from somebody else, so I went back to Noël and we had some giant sticks of Leichner grease-paint which had just been invented and I remember shaking one at Noël rather in the classic way he waggles his own finger at people and saying 'It just isn't true, Noël.' He looked at me for a moment and then murmured, 'It's no use your waggling that extremely suggestive piece of greasepaint at me, what I've told you is the exact truth.' But I don t think it was.

Noël really wasn't like a child at all – he lacked the quality. I don't mean he was an unnatural, preposterously precocious, forward or unpleasant child at all. But to other children he seemed totally grown-up. He was decidedly puckish, witty, dry, clipped and immensely competent. I remember once during *Peter Pan* Noël and I were asked to tea by a horrible old man who lived in Earls Court and I said I didn't want to go much; Noël said nor did he, but he thought we ought to because it was good for business to be invited out. I looked at him with a kind of religious terror: at fourteen he knew it all.

When the run of *Peter Pan* ended in London, Mrs Coward managed to attach herself to the tour and to get her fares paid by agreeing to look after, as well as her own son, a boy called Donald Buckley who had taken over as 'Michael'. Buckley shared digs with them in Glasgow, Edinburgh and Birmingham, and also managed to liven up a dull week in Newcastle by catching some sinister lice in his head to Noël's huge and smugly clean delight. After the provinces the company toured some of the London suburbs – Wimbledon, Hammersmith and then Kennington, which was near enough to the Cowards' home in Clapham for the entire cast to be invited there for tea after one of the matinées. Of that gathering Noël remembered only that he sang at his guests for some considerable time and that Pauline Chase arrived with her friend, who played the Mermaid, in a sparkling new yellow roadster. The tour ended in March and for the next nine months Noël was out of work. He spent the time developing two friendships, the first he had achieved outside the family, one of which remained vitally important to him for many years to come. The first was with an artist called Philip Streatfield, then about thirty, who had a studio in Chelsea and in whom Noël found all the Bohemian charm that he expected of a painter. The second was with an older acquaintance, the girl who had played Rosamund Carey in the first production of *Where the Rainbow Ends*, Esmé Wynne. During the run of *The Rainbow*, when they appeared together and when Noël stage-managed the matinée of Esmé's first play, the two had taken a hearty dislike to each other; but by early in 1913 this was all forgotten and they built up a long and loyal friendship which led to their both writing consistently, for the first time in their lives – poems in her case, short stories in his. It could perhaps be said (and has been by Esmé) that she started Noël on his writing:

> We quickly formed a brother–sister relationship (I was an only child and he only had a young brother) and from that time onwards until some time after I was married, we were close but entirely platonic friends, having mutual ambitions, acting and writing together, and enjoying each other's company more than that of any other of our friends. We wrote curtain-raisers in which I acted on tour: I wrote lyrics which he put to music and we collaborated on an unpublished book of short sketches.

Noël, for his part, admitted a considerable debt to Esmé:

> She egged me on to write …and she was the spur to my acting ambitions because I was madly jealous of her playing the lead in *The Rainbow* when I only had a small part.

So far from finding her 'pompous, stodgy and slightly superior', as he had during rehearsals, Noël now found in Esmé a devoted friend with whom to walk, talk, daydream, and even do some light shoplifting while Esmé watched disapprovingly. She remarked later:

> At that time, Mrs Coward left Noël alone a lot – she didn't blame him for anything, though she knew that he used to shoplift a bit, but instead of backing me up and telling him that he'd be put in prison and have his career ruined, she just used to laugh. She was an amusing, sharp-faced, brave little lady who doted on Noël; to keep him and the family she took on a lodging-house, and I think Noël inherited her tenacity while from his father he acquired a blind devotion to music.

Esmé and Noël had more than a little in common; both child actors (Esmé's mother had been on the stage and her Aunt Mona still was), both romantics, both addicted to exploring the still intimate and often village-like suburbs of London, they were ideally suited to one another. So much so that their friendship even survived the time that Esmé spent in a Belgian Convent and the appalling, self-inflicted nicknames of Poj (Noël) and Stoj (Esmé). To say that they were inseparable would be putting it mildly:

> We even had baths together for the simple reason that we didn't wish to waste a moment's companionship and because it seemed affected to stop short in the middle of some vital discussion for such a paltry reason as conventional modesty.

Esmé Wynne later married, left the stage and became an ardent Christian Scientist; she was also a determined believer in the power of imagination, and writing in the January 1966 issue of *The Layman* she noted:

> I have personally witnessed this power (of imagination) in action in the case of an associate of my childhood who became the most famous man of the theatre of his day. I was with him when, during a country walk, he clearly formulated his desire in imagination and expressed it to me in the words 'I am going to have the whole theatrical world at my feet.' At that time he was fifteen years of age, plain, with no financial resources except meagre earnings as an actor, a good ear for music, and an ability to play by heart but no knowledge of the theory; his chief asset being a brilliant sense of humour. Yet long before he reached the age of forty he had achieved his ambition and was triumphantly at the top of his world.

This vision of Noël in mid-countryside at the age of fifteen seeing his entire future in one sudden, blinding moment of truth may seem a little romantic in retrospect. All the same, both children were by now clearly aware of where their futures lay; Esmé's wish was to 'know the truth' about life, as she herself later described it, while Noël was to be a success, though at the time he was still far enough under Esmé's woodland influence to be writing short stories about Pan. But the most important thing about their friendship was the boundless mutual admiration and encouragement it afforded. Esmé did, however, find one subject over which even their friendship could never come to terms:

> My interest in religion was tabooed. Noël was totally uninterested in the subject and didn't want to discuss it. He also felt that any doubts cast on Orthodoxy reflected on the intelligence of his adored mother who, like my own parents, was firmly, unquestioningly and irrationally Church of England. Eventually, to avoid the quarrels that resulted from any attempt on my part to speak on this fundamental interest, we drew up a Palship Contract one clause of which forbade the discussion of religion.

Noël's other teenage friendship, with Philip Streatfield, matured during a holiday in May 1914, when they took a car and drove through the West

Country for a fortnight, stopping at farms along the coasts of Devon and Cornwall while Philip painted and Noël walked across his beloved beaches. Later that year they were in Cornwall again, staying in a cottage in Polperro, when on the fourth of August war was declared. Immediately, Noël was sent back to London: Philip put him on a train at Truro and gave him into the charge of a fellow-passenger, the novelist, Hugh Walpole, who treated Noël to lunch and gave him half a crown when they reached London.

The war, in its first three years, had no effect on Noël's teenage life whatsoever; the autumn of 1914 was spent looking for a Christmas engagement which totally failed to materialize, possibly because he had just reached the awkward age: too old and too large for the boy parts and not yet a 'young juvenile'. But just after Christmas a telegram arrived from Dion Boucicault announcing that A. W. Baskcomb, who was playing his original part of Slightly in *Peter Pan,* had been taken suddenly ill. A day later, Noël was back in the theatre as Slightly at the Duke of York's for the second year running, with this time Madge Titheradge as Peter and Holman Clark as Captain Hook. Rival entertainments in London that Christmas included Oscar Asche as a Zulu Chieftain, Beerbohm Tree as Micawber in *David Copperfield,* and Gerald du Maurier as Raffles at Wyndham's. On the allied front near Wimcreux, Seymour Hicks and Ellaline Terriss were giving war concerts while at home the Scala was showing a new film programme entitled *With the Fighting Forces of Europe.*

After the London run Noël did not work again until the very end of 1915. This was not, though it could well have been, because there weren't any offers; rather it was because he developed a hacking cough which, a doctor discovered, was caused by a tubercular gland in his chest. Dr Etlinger, an old friend of the family, took Noël into his sanatorium at Wokingham where he lived in the doctor's own house and for the first of two occasions in his life (the second was the 1939–45 war) came into contact with a lot of men who did not have long to live. Noël was not seriously ill at this time; but he learnt enough about tuberculosis, he said later, 'not to be fooled by false illusions when the time comes for me to face the truth of dying.' At the sanatorium he wrote some one-act plays which he persuaded the staff to perform, and by the summer he was stronger and healthier than he had ever been before.

After a few weeks he left the sanatorium, and, to keep his mother happy, had himself confirmed; the ceremony was severely endangered by Esmé, who plagued the Clapham Vicar with unanswerable questions until he was eventually forced to demand of Mrs Coward that she keep the girl away until Noël was safely confirmed in the faith.

Confirmed but not noticeably more spiritual, Noël went off to stay with some friends of Philip Streatfield in Rutland; the holiday was an unqualified success except for the departure when Mrs Coward, who was seeing Noël off at St Pancras, left her bag on the Tube with what little money she still had after scraping together enough for his ticket. To pay the fare she had to pawn her wedding ring, but luckily her bag was later recovered. Noël spent a few happy weeks in the country where his hostess was a Mrs Cooper who had the unnerving habit of lying flat on her back on a mattress in front of the fire and shooting off witticisms in a kind of petulant wail. Even so the time passed amiably enough, and before long Noël started thinking about Christmas and the 1915/16 revival of *Where the Rainbow Ends,* now on its fifth consecutive season with only a few of the original company still playing. But Esmé Wynne and Philip Tonge were still in the company and Noël, too old to play the page-boy again, was cast as The Slacker, a cross between a man and a dragon; it was a short, showy part with an 'exit, laughing hysterically' which Noël enjoyed hugely and which usually brought a round of applause from the audience.

4

1916

I was a talented child, God knows, and when washed and smarmed down a bit, passably attractive. But I was, I believe, one of the worst boy actors ever inflicted on the general public.

By the spring of 1916, the effect of the war was at last becoming noticeable in the theatre; entertainment tended to centre on light musicals, as in the second war, or on plays of unassailable patriotism, for which category *Where the Rainbow Ends* was well qualified. There were more revivals than usual, and the two leading actor-managers of the time had already leapt into the patriotic breach; Beerbohm Tree revived *Drake* and Frank Benson was giving his *Henry V.* But most patriotic of all were Boots the Chemists who took a page in the *Stage Yearbook* for that year to announce 'No more German Greasepaint! Leichner is completely superseded... Boots British Greasepaint is the best we ever used.'

It was at about this time that Noël's father, still a traveller with Payne's Pianos, made one of his rare pronouncements concerning his elder son. In the course of a lengthy conversation with Mr Dunkley, a piano maker in Clapham High Street, Coward père announced that in his view the boy was going to be clever. Meanwhile Noël was persevering with *The Rainbow*, with his friendship with Esmé, and with the occasional poems:

> I can only assume that the compulsion to make rhymes was born in me. It cannot have been hereditary for neither my mother nor my father nor any of my forebears on either side of the family displayed, as far as I know, the faintest aptitude for writing poetry or verse... There is no time I can remember when I was not fascinated by words "going together"; Lewis Carroll, Edward Lear, Beatrix Potter, all fed my childish passion, in addition to all the usual nursery rhymes that the flesh is heir to, beginning, to the best of my belief, with 'Pat-A-Cake, Pat-A-Cake, Baker's Man'. I can still distinctly recall being exasperated when any of these whimsical effusions were slipshod in rhyming or scansion.
>
> Some years later when I was rushing headlong towards puberty I wrote a series of short couplets under the general heading *Vegetable Verse*. These, I am relieved to say, have disappeared completely... I can recall only two tantalizing fragments:

> In A Voice Of Soft Staccato
> We Will Speak Of The Tomato

and

> The Sinful AspaRAGus
> To Iniquity Will Drag Us

Later in his teens, inspired and at the same time slightly irritated by the feverish industry of his friend Esmé Wynne, Noël decided after a few competitive failures to strike out on a line of his own with songs rather than poems. Being a natural musician, he found it easier to write to tunes jangling in his head than to devote himself to mastering iambics, trochees, anapaests, or dactyls. If a tune came first he would set words to it; if the words came first he would set them to music at the piano, which almost invariably meant changing the verse to fit the tune.

This process also infuriated Esmé who unwisely allowed Noël to take one of her rather soulful love poems, beginning:

> Our little love is dying:
> On his head droop lately crimson roses faded quite

and set it to music. Noël's song began:

> Our little love is dying on his head ...

But in spite of this their friendship thrived as they began to act more together – first in 'The Rainbow' and then in a spring 1916 tour of *Charley's Aunt* which lasted four long months. This also gave them the time for a collaboration called *Le Rêve de Pierrot* (words, Esmé Wynne; music, Noël Coward) that included the memorable stanza:

> Ah, see the world. All I hold dear
> Heigh Ho, it is a merry din,
> The rivers still are running clear
> The world's still living in its sin.

Esmé remembered Noël as a plain, chubby and curiously bumptious child to whom she was devoted, mainly because he made her laugh. Theirs was an entirely unromantic alliance, though when Esmé first became a friend of his, she went to one of his birthday parties in Battersea where they played hide-and-seek together:

> We hid in the same room and while we were waiting to be found he dared to peck at my cheek. When he'd done so we both shrieked with laughter and that was the end of any sentiment between us. But we stayed very

great friends for a long time and we share marvellous memories of a time when life was easier and more fun. It was so much better to have been friends than lovers.

I think the first real sorrow in his life was when his voice broke – before that I remember him leaning up against the grand piano in Philip Streatfield's studio in Chelsea singing 'There is a Green Hill Far Away'. You'd have thought he was an angel from heaven if it hadn't been for the conversation that went before and after it. But he was seldom really sad – he's always had a natural ebullience and a flippancy that guards him from most of the sorrows of the world.

Both his mother and I had every confidence in his talent and his humour; we knew that he could do whatever he wanted, and it was all so carefully planned – even his refusal to discuss religion with me was I think partly because if he wanted to get where he was going, it was essential that he should keep an open mind. A religious man wouldn't have written half the things that Noël has. Even the war didn't concern him very much, though we were both pacifists of a kind; we neither smoked nor drank during our friendship, and we were rooted in Bernard Shaw who said that the majority are always wrong. We felt that about the war and we used to tell our friends who were old enough to enlist that they should be conscientious objectors. We'd never heard of sedition, but I suppose that's what it was… On the tour of *Charley's Aunt* we had terrible rows, but they were over in a flash, usually because he couldn't bear to be alone, although I didn't mind it, and there was nobody else in the company that he could talk to.

The tour was, by all accounts or at least by those of Esmé and Noël, a deeply gloomy affair, characterized by endless meals of minced haddock and baked beans in chilly boarding-houses. They played Amy and Charley at salaries of two pounds and two pounds ten a week respectively, though for that money Noël was required to provide his own clothes. He discovered early in rehearsal that of all the characters in Brandon Thomas's farce, Charley was the one who worked hardest and who got for his pains the least laughs. Neither the play nor the rest of the cast appealed to Noël even remotely; it was produced by J. R. Crawford, who also played the Colonel, and who, Noël remarked later, 'directed rehearsals with all the airy deftness of a rheumatic deacon producing *Macbeth* for a church social.'

The tour ground on through provincial England from February to June 1916 playing in chilly theatres with an even chillier atmosphere backstage: in Peterborough they performed during a blizzard to precisely six people, rather less than were in the cast; in Bristol Noël had a brief bout of religious mania which arrived one afternoon during a matinée when he thought inexplicably that he was going to die, and left as abruptly the next morning when he found to his amazement that he hadn't; and in Wolverhampton he was nearly knocked out by the leading juvenile after a series of rows about the state of the bath in their shared digs. Otherwise the tour was an uneventful one, marked only by Noël's delight at coming to the end of it.

Coward spent the summer months working with his Aunt Kitty on a series of impersonations of famous stars with which it was his intention to play the halls while Aunt Kitty played the piano. They went to a number of auditions but as the most they were ever offered was a trial week at their own expense in a particularly sombre seaside resort, Noël reluctantly abandoned that idea and went off to Cornwall to stay with a new friend, John Ekins, whose father was the rector of Rame. John was a year older than Noël, also a child actor and, if anything, even more stagestruck. He had once played Crispian, the part that Noël always wanted in *Where the Rainbow Ends,* and after their Cornish holiday he got a part in a melodrama called *The Best of Luck* which opened at Drury Lane with Madge Titheradge in September. Noël, out of work, used to walk on at the Lane to give himself the illusion of having a job, and he and Esmé remained devoted friends of John Ekins until he died suddenly of spinal meningitis (the disease that had killed Noël's elder brother) while training for the Air Force in 1917.

Later in 1916 Noël was hired by Robert Courtneidge to play a small part in a new musical comedy called *The Light Blues,* but before that went into rehearsal he completed the first successful full-length song of which he was both composer and lyricist. It was called 'Forbidden Fruit' and the first three lines ran:

> Ordinary man
> Invariably sighs
> Vainly for what cannot be.

This world weary theme ended on a note of bitter disillusion:

> For the brute
> Loves the fruit
> That's forbidden
> And I'll bet you half a crown
> He'll appreciate the flavour of it much, much more
> If he has to climb a bit to shake it down.

In sheer self-defence Noël later pointed out that although the bet of half a crown did rather let down the song's tone of sophisticated urbanity, it was about all he could afford at the time. Also, it rhymed with 'down'.

The Light Blues was a comedy about May Week in Cambridge, written by Mark Ambient and Jack Hulbert who had recently come down from that University; it opened at the Shaftesbury Theatre with a cast led by Albert

Chevalier, Shaun Glenville and Jack Hulbert together with his wife of a few weeks, Courtneidge's daughter Cicely. Noël, in an insecure false moustache that seems to have entirely vanished before the gentleman from *Play Pictorial* arrived to take the pictures, played a dude called Basil Pyecroft who became deeply involved in a sub-plot about a necklace that disappeared and then mysteriously reappeared in a banana skin at the end of Act Two. He was also allowed to understudy Mr Hulbert, and set off for a three-week tour of Cardiff, Newcastle and Glasgow in high hopes that Hulbert would have the grace to drop dead or at the very least fall ill before the West End opening on September 16th. Mr Hulbert did neither, but when the tour reached Glasgow Noël had one of the most painful experiences of his young theatrical life.

In the show he had one brief scene with Shaun Glenville, who, to put it mildly, was prone to an occasional impromptu remark on stage. Noël, nothing if not a willing lad, used to laugh at these on the principle that laughing at the leading comedian could hardly fail to improve his standing in the company. Courtneidge however thought differently and, summoning Noël to the front of the stage during one morning rehearsal, told him that quite apart from being a very young and a very bad actor, it was practically criminal of him to accept a salary of four pounds a week for fooling about on the stage and giggling at other actors. 'Young man,' added Courtneidge, 'I pay you to amuse the public, not yourself.' Noël, deeply humiliated, rode out the storm and was only slightly cheered to hear Cicely murmur at the end of it 'You mustn't mind Father.' She recalled later that Noël was:

> A thin, pale-faced youth who seemed to know everything and infuriated me because he was always right. During rehearsals he consistently aired his views, although he was never asked, and if he did not agree with the way a scene was being developed, even though he was playing the smallest part, he would say so. This made him difficult to like, particularly when my father repeatedly said 'that young man is going to make a name for himself one day' and especially when Father never once said anything like that to me or Jack.

A fortnight before the opening of *The Light Blues,* Oscar Asche started a run of some two thousand performances in *Chu-Chin-Chow* at His Majesty's. The same cannot be said for the cast of the Ambient-Hulbert musical, which was to fall very short of Asche's theatrical landmark and in fact lasted only a matter of days. The public stayed away from *The Light Blues* in droves, perhaps because the first of the Zeppelin raids on London had coincided with the opening night; in less than two weeks the musical was out of the Shaftesbury and Noël was out of a job.

As the legitimate theatre had nothing else to offer for the moment, Coward turned his mind to other ways of making a living and became, briefly, a professional dancer. Although, as he admitted later, 'my adolescence was too apparent, my figure too gangling and coltish to promote evil desire in even the most debauched night-club habitués', he was nevertheless employed during October 1916 to dance with a Miss Eileen Denis at the Elysée Restaurant which later became the Café de Paris and later still the home of Mecca Dancing in Leicester Square.

Noël was billed, quite untruthfully, as 'direct from the London Opera House' and it was announced that during Dinners he would make his first appearance in 'New Costume Dances'; these apparently were performed as part of 'a pierrot fantasia' at the insistence of Miss Denis's mother. The programme was described as 'a new innovation' and during afternoon teas the customers were treated not only to Noël and Miss Denis but also to 'La Petite Doria – the Wonderful Child Character Dancer'. The whole episode was rather a disappointment to Noël, who had exotic visions of being asked to leap naked out of pies at private supper parties; the invitations failed to materialize and by Christmas he was back in the theatre, a little older and none the wiser but largely unscathed by the experience.

5

1917–1918

I was paid, I think, a pound a day, for which I wheeled a wheelbarrow up and down a village street in Worcestershire with Lilian Gish. The name of the film was Hearts of the World, *and it left little mark on me beyond a most unpleasant memory of getting up at five every morning and making my face bright yellow.*

The Christmas season 1916–17 found Noël still on the fringe of the faintly cloying realm of children's plays; he turned up in a red-and-white striped blazer and a pillbox hat playing a Sandhurst cadet, Jack Morrison, in *The Happy Family* by Cecil Aldin and Adrian Ross at the Prince of Wales. This was a bizarre entertainment in which the entire cast, barring Mimi Crawford and Noël, turned into animals during the second act. Noël was thus left to sing a rousing military number, 'Sentry Go', backed by a chorus consisting entirely of ducks and pigs. He was however delighted to be dancing and singing again for the first time on stage since *The Goldfish,* and one of the more obscure weeklies did have the generosity to note that 'Mr Coward combines the grace and movement of a Russian dancer with the looks and manner of an English schoolboy.' For some time afterwards, Noël carried a yellowing copy of that notice in his jacket pocket.

The Happy Family was to be remembered briefly by Noël about eight years later, mainly because its first act contained an over-cheerful number which began:

> Isn't it awfully jolly
> Doing a little revue?
> Never could be a more happy idea,
> It's nobby and nutty and new.

At the end of a twenty-seven hour dress rehearsal for *On with the Dance* in Manchester during March 1925, Noël sang this in its gruesome entirety to his producer, an unamused Charles Blake Cochran.

After *The Happy Family* Coward didn't get work in the theatre again until the August of 1917, a state of affairs which depressed him immeasurably. But in his own eyes Noël was no longer only an actor; he was now a writer as well, and in the meantime he continued to turn out lyrics and some one-act plays, frequently in collaboration with Esmé Wynne. Their friendship had progressed far beyond the stage when their favourite pastime was to dress up in each other's clothes:

> I shall never forget [wrote Esmé later] the sight of Noël dashing across Clapham High Road after a large straw hat which the wind had blown from his head, his short dark hair protruding ridiculously from the hole in his girl's wig, his large patent-leather shoes flapping wildly below the knee-length skirts of my blue gingham dress.

All that transvestism in Clapham was by this time a thing of the past. Noël had written a number of verses, short stories, plays and even a full-length novel in the many spare moments of his life as a child actor, but the first of these to achieve any success at all was a one-act curtain-raiser written with Esmé called *The Last Chapter* and later renamed *Ida Collaborates.* It was a light comedy about the unrequited passion of a charwoman's daughter for a distinguished author, and it was first presented by a touring management at the Theatre Royal, Aldershot, on August 20th 1917. Esmé herself played Ida and *The Stage,* while declining to comment on the play itself, noted that 'the piece gives Miss Esmé Wynne full opportunities of showing her talents, and she does not fail to take advantage of them.' She had perhaps learnt, as did Noël shortly afterwards, that there's a lot to be said for writing a play with yourself in mind for the leading role.

The rest of Noël's early work as a writer is shrouded not so much in forgetfulness as in secrecy:

> There are indeed a great number of prose exercises of my own written between the ages of eleven and seventeen which are locked away in trunks and strong boxes and which I am determined will never see the light of day in my lifetime. After I am dead is quite another matter... in the meantime however, these early immature whimsies will be left to gather the dust they so richly deserve for so long as there is breath in my body.

If 1917 was the year in which a play of Noël's was first presented on the stage, it was also the year in which he played his first part in a film. David Wark Griffith, fresh from the triumph of his *Birth of a Nation* and the financial debacle of *Intolerance,* came to Europe to make *Hearts of the World,* a propaganda film about the German occupation of a French village which had Lilian and Dorothy Gish in the cast. As it was designed to arouse anti-German feeling around the world (and *Birth of a Nation* had shown how suitable was the new silver screen for propaganda purposes), *Hearts of the World* was made with the full co-operation of the allied governments. D. W. Griffith himself was taken on a lengthy tour of the French and Belgian battlefronts, at the end of which he remarked memorably that 'viewed as drama, the war is in some ways disappointing.'

The film did its best to be beastly to the Germans, with Erich von Stroheim as a villainous Hun and such captions as 'Month after Month piled up its legend of Hunnish crime on the book of God'; after it opened in June 1918 the British Board of Historians acclaimed Griffith as 'the greatest of war historians'. Noël was engaged to be an extra pushing a wheelbarrow in some of the French village sequences which were in fact filmed amid the comparative safety of Worcestershire. His sole contribution to the picture was the suggestion that he should push the barrow towards rather than away from the camera, and he remained largely unimpressed by his luck at getting to work with the great Griffith so early in his career. He does, however, recall that Mrs Gish and her daughters were 'remarkably friendly and kind', and that they invited him to lunch whenever he was on the location.

Hearts of the World was not rapturously received by the critics, who considered it maudlin, biased and essentially mediocre. For Noël too the film was a somewhat unrewarding experience; although he enjoyed meeting the Gish family, he felt he did not have enough to do in the picture and also that the elaborate mechanics of silent filming had involved a disproportionate amount of his time for so brief an appearance on the screen. Another seventeen years of his life were to elapse before he next appeared before the cameras.

In August 1917, Noël went to Manchester for the Gaiety Theatre's production of *Wild Heather,* a social drama by Dorothy Brandon in which he played a fairly aimless character called Leicester Boyd with Helen Haye as his mother. Leicester Boyd drifted in and out of the action until the end of the second act, when he drifted out altogether thereby allowing Noël to catch the second half of the variety bills at the Palace or the Hippodrome. One week he went every night to watch Ivy St Helier and Clara Evelyn playing pianos back to back at the Palace, and afterwards made them agree to spend the next afternoon listening to him playing his songs, in the hope that they might buy one or two of them. Miss St Helier listened politely, showed Noël some basic chords which were good for the opening of almost any song, and in that one afternoon Coward learnt almost as much about being 'an entertainer at the piano, from her as he had about acting from Charles Hawtrey.

He did, however, fail to sell them any of his songs. To Miss St Helier 'he seemed a very shy boy, and I tried to help him with his technique a bit. I remember telling him "never apologize to an audience; when you sit at the piano, do it with authority and above all don't just play the notes – arrest them"'.

Charles Hawtrey's influence reappeared in Noël's life, while Coward was playing at the Gaiety, in the unlikely shape of Gilbert Miller, a young American impresario. Hawtrey had suggested Coward for a part in *The Saving Grace,* a new comedy by Haddon Chambers which he and Miller were to present jointly at the Garrick in the autumn, and Gilbert had come to Manchester to see Coward for himself. He liked what he saw, offered Noël the part over dinner after the show, and told him he would be one of an otherwise all-star cast led by Hawtrey himself. 'By this time,' wrote Noël later, 'I was so dazed that I should only have given him a languid nod if he had told me that Ellen Terry was going to play my baby sister.'

The part in *The Saving Grace* was the breakthrough that Noël had been hoping for, working for and waiting for. Yet it came virtually out of the blue, a reflection of the faith that Hawtrey had in his talent rather than of the talent itself. The rest of the small cast were players of the calibre of Hawtrey, Ellis Jeffreys and Mary Jerrold, and if it seems strange that an unknown seventeen-year-old was in their midst one might remember that at the end of 1917 juvenile actors old enough to have some experience but young enough not to be fighting for their country were few and far between. A combination of Coward's talent and his luck got him into a part which could not but do him good.

When *Wild Heather* was in its last week at Manchester, the two men who were to lead the British musical theatre from the 1920s into the 1950s met face to face for the first time. Ivor Novello was seven years older than Noël and at that time considerably more successful; he was in Manchester with *Arlette,* a musical comedy which he had written and was now watching on its way to London. Novello, already widely known as the composer of 'Keep the Home Fires Burning', had written the scores for other West End shows before *Arlette* and was in a position deeply envied by Noël who was hoping to achieve the same kind of early success, but unable at that time to see much chance of doing so. Coward was nevertheless reassured to discover that when they first met, with a mutual friend, Bobby Andrews, outside the Midland Hotel, Novello was 'wearing an old overcoat with an Astrakhan collar and a degraded brown hat, and if he had suddenly produced a violin from somewhere and played the 'Barcarolle' from *The Tales of Hoffman,* I should have given him threepence from sheer pity.' Esmé Wynne, who knew them both early in their long careers, remembered that 'Noël was infinitely more intelligent, and certainly more talented as an actor, but Ivor was much more affectionate and sweet.'

But comparisons between Novello and Coward are largely futile, since their talents, superficially the same, were in fact widely different; Novello's music came from a native Welsh sense of melody that flowed through innumerable lilting songs whilst Noël's was a more careful, studied, staccato style of composition which depended for its effect as much on the words as the music. They had in common a great love of the theatre, and a sort of wary mutual respect; 'if', Noël once said to Novello, 'anyone ever tells you that I've been rude about you behind your back – believe them.' It seemed to Coward that Novello had everything going for him; his looks were considerably better than Noël's and, in their music, what came almost instinctively to Ivor only came to Noël after endless hard work; though in their acting if anything the reverse was true. 'Ivor', said Bobby Andrews, 'admired Noël's talent – whereas Noël admired Ivor's flair.'

The Saving Grace ran in the West End for several months through the worst Zeppelin raids of the war, which nightly coincided with a tender love scene that Noël played with Emily Brooke. Coward in fact had found some difficulty with the part, since it was the first time he had tackled the intricate art of light comedy as an adult, but once again the presence and careful direction of Hawtrey came to his assistance and he made the first real success of his career as an actor. Noël was now playing a good part in a distinguished production and beginning to be recognized in the street for the first time; things were going in precisely the direction he wanted.

In his home life too, times were changing; Mrs Coward, bored and depressed by life in a maisonette on Clapham Common, decided to move back into central London and to return to the lodging-house business. As her sister Borby had died in the meantime, Noël's mother took Vida with Noël and Eric to live at 111, Ebury Street, across the road from where Aunt Ida had been successfully running a lodging-house for many years. Payne's Pianos had now entirely given up and Noël's father was left in early and enforced retirement to make and sail his model yachts on the Serpentine while his wife cooked for and coped with the lodgers. It was hard work, but life ran fairly smoothly for the family until January 1918. Then with the run of *The Saving Grace* over and Noël in rehearsal for a new play, a small grey card arrived: Noël was summoned instantly to an Army medical at the Camberwell Swimming Baths.

6

1918–1920

My career in the British Army was brief and inglorious.

It is perhaps fair to say that a summons to the Camberwell Swimming Baths is not the most auspicious beginning to a career in the armed forces; and for Noël, the nine months of 1918 that he spent on totally inactive service in and around Romford were one long disaster. A look at his writing and performance during the Second World War shows that he was not by any means an unpatriotic man; nor was he un-courageous. But as an admittedly self-centred young actor whose main priority in life was to get some money into the family and to get his mother out of the lodging-house as soon as he could, the war until 1918 meant very little to him. When it started he had only been fourteen, and now that it did at last affect him personally the national feeling of optimism and determination had degenerated into an overwhelming sense of futility and loss that Noël felt more keenly than any of the hope which had preceded it. In the last winter of the war it was hard to see that any good could come of the fighting, and the massive loss of life already seemed too high a price to pay for a still-distant peace. Noël would not, perhaps, have been afraid to fight; but he felt there was nothing he could usefully contribute to the war, while on a more domestic level there was a great deal to be done: 'the needs of my King and Country seemed unimportant compared with the vital necessity of forging ahead with my own life.'

As it happened, the King and Country took a similarly dim view of the usefulness of Noël to the war effort. From Camberwell, where the medical officer heard of Noël's earlier bout of tuberculosis, he was sent straight to a Labour Corps at Hounslow. There, only marginally reassured by the fact that the other fifty men drafted with him looked as though they could barely make it back to Camberwell, let alone to the front, Noël spent one uneasy night and a few hours next morning learning the elementary parade drill. Then, assisted by a ten-shilling note placed swiftly into the right hands, he managed to see the commanding officer and to get a day's leave of absence on the pretext of having to settle his affairs at home. Once back in the centre of London he went straight to the War Office, having prepared on the train a short list of influential officers who might help him get out of the Labour Corps as rapidly as he had fallen into it. At the tender age of eighteen Noël already had a few friends – if not actually at Court yet, then at least in the War Office.

Getting hourly more frantic, Noël worked his way through the list drawing a total blank every time, until the very last man on it suggested that he should see a Lieutenant Boughey. And here, finally, Noël got lucky. Boughey agreed that he was now perfectly fit and therefore had no right to be in a Labour Corps, telephoned the Hounslow C.O. to tell him so, and promised to get Coward a place in the Artists' Rifles, Philip Streatfeld's old regiment, after first letting him off for a couple of weeks' leave.

The Training Corps of the Artists' Rifles was then stationed in the middle of Gidea Park, near Romford in Essex. Life there was certainly a good deal better than with the Labour Corps at Hounslow, but it was still army life and Noël hated every regimented moment of it. He also snored, which failed to endear him to the other inhabitants of his hut. He was not a soldier, he was patently never going to be a soldier, and as his medical grading was B2 he was unlikely ever to see active service. Thus the long hours that he spent marching around Gidea Park were an exercise in total futility, though Noël himself was the only one to appreciate this fully. He developed a deep-seated loathing of the army that was to be matched only by his devotion in later years to the navy.

It was while he was forced to stay at Gidea Park that the second of Noël's one-act collaborations with Esmé Wynne, *Women and Whiskey* was produced on a provincial tour; this brought from a columnist in the *Daily Sketch* the fairly surprised comment that 'Noël Coward is not only an actor – he is something of a dramatist as well.'

The training session at Gidea Park came to an abrupt halt one morning when, running along a wooden path, Noël tripped on a slat and went crashing to the ground giving himself severe concussion which lasted until he awoke in the First London General Hospital to hear his mother explaining tearfully that he'd been unconscious for three days. In spite of a number of sceptical doctors, convinced that the whole thing was a hoax, Noël spent six weeks in the hospital where he was surrounded by shell-shock cases and given far too long to wonder whether he had a brain tumour or not. As it happened, he hadn't; the headaches got less frequent and soon he was well enough to sit up in bed reading the newly published first novels of G. B. Stern and Sheila Kaye-Smith. He wrote ardent fan letters to both ladies and, in the case of Miss Stern, succeeded in introducing her to her future husband, a young New Zealander called Geoffrey Holdsworth who befriended him in the hospital.

As well as reading a good many novels at this time, Noël also managed to write one, which, he said later, 'taught me two things – one was that it wasn't good enough for publication, and the other was that I had the knack of bright dialogue.'

When Noël was at length discharged from hospital he was given a week's leave before being ordered back to Gidea Park. In one of the more eccentric episodes of his life, he spent that week as chaperone on a kind of pre-honeymoon in Devon organized by Esmé Wynne and her future husband, Lynden Tyson. Esmé herself explained later:

> Lynden and I were so terrified of having children that we took Noël away with us on a holiday just before we got married. Lynden was paying for it all and, much as I loved him, I think he got rather jealous because I spent all the time talking to Noël; whenever I had to choose between them I chose Noël because mentally we got on so well together – with Lynden it was a much more physical thing.

Nevertheless the *ménage à trois* seems to have worked out except for one moment of crisis when Esmé and Noël were discovered by Lynden as they sailed simultaneously out of the bathroom. For Lynden this was almost the last straw:

> I knew that intellectually Noël and Esmé were very close, and though I wasn't able to understand their non-sexual relationship, I was getting a bit jealous of Master Noël. He spent most of the time with my fiancée and when one morning I saw both of them coming out of the loo together that, for me, was the end. I decided to break everything up and push off to London and leave them to it. But being very much in love with Esmé I didn't catch the train – I conveniently missed it, so I was there when she and Noël came back from their walk and after that Esmé and I had a hell of a row and then we made it up in the usual way and decided to get married anyway.

After Esmé and Lynden got married, Noël came up trumps again; he managed to get a friend of his in the Air Force to ensure that Lynden stayed in London for the last few months of the war.

Back with the Artists' Rifles Noël was put on light duties and spent a few gloomy weeks polishing everything in sight and cleaning out the latrines. Soon, and perhaps not surprisingly, the headaches began to recur, and eventually he said they became so bad that he could barely stand up. This time he was sent to the Colchester Hospital and placed, inexplicably, in a ward where all the other patients were epileptics. The alarming thing here was not so much their fits as the fact that none of them knew they were epileptic; Noël, not unnaturally began to wonder whether he too was epileptic without knowing it. For twenty-four hours, every ten minutes, he checked off squares in an exercise book; he did this twice a week for three weeks, and only then, looking back over all the squares safely filled in, could he be sure. After two months, in which he learnt among other things how to prevent an epileptic from leaping off his bed and out of the window, Noël was finally given a total discharge from the British Army and awarded a pension of seven-and-sixpence a week for six months. One suspects that he would happily have paid them rather more than that for his freedom.

> His breakdown [said Esmé Wynne] came at a very convenient time – and thank Heaven it did. I dreaded that Noël, like Saki who was then our great hero, would be killed in that dreadful war. In those days one's awareness was always of the waste and the sorrow… we hadn't learnt to talk of 'mopping-up operations', and death was something that happened daily to people we knew.

Once discharged, Noël started a lengthy round of auditions at which, dressed in a blue suit with a shirt, tie and socks to match (it took him some months to learn that the height of fashion was not necessarily to wear everything in the same colour) he would give them a brisk rendering of his own songs including his first, 'Forbidden Fruit', and a sentimental ballad called 'Tamarisk Town'. While he was waiting for work in London he also appeared with an amateur concert party entertaining wounded troops in Rutland; a lady who was at Oakham with the Women's Legion at that time remembers Noël singing a song of his which began:

My name's Elizabeth May
And no one takes liberties with me.

'I have never', noted the lady rather sadly, 'heard this since'.

By now Coward was always accompanying himself on the piano, a talent more or less self-taught; to his death he found it difficult to read music and almost impossible to write it down – when he played he did so by ear rather than eye, and in the years when he was composing regularly, he would either sing, whistle or hum the tune, often over the phone, to somebody who could transcribe it for him. But this limitation does not seem to have hampered his talent too severely; years later he reflected:

> I have only had two music lessons in my life. These were the first steps of what was to have been a full course which Fred Astaire and I enrolled for at the Guildhall School of Music, and they faltered and stopped when I was told by my instructor that I could not use consecutive fifths. He went on to explain that a gentleman called Ebenezer Prout had announced many years ago that consecutive fifths were wrong and must in no circumstances be employed. At that time Ebenezer Prout was merely a name to me (as a matter of fact he still is, and a very funny one at that) and I was unimpressed by his Victorian dicta. I argued back that Debussy and Ravel used consecutive fifths like mad. My instructor waved aside this triviality with a pudgy hand, and I left his presence for ever with the

parting shot that what was good enough for Debussy and Ravel was good enough for me. This outburst of rugged individualism deprived me of much valuable knowledge, and I have never deeply regretted it for a moment. Had I intended at the outset of my career to devote all my energies to music I would have endured the necessary training cheerfully enough, but in those days I was passionately involved in the theatre; acting and writing and singing and dancing seemed of more value to my immediate progress than counterpoint and harmony. I was willing to allow the musical side of my creative talent to take care of itself. On looking back, I think that on the whole I was right. I have often been irritated in later years by my inability to write music down effectively and by my complete lack of knowledge of orchestration except by ear, but being talented from the very beginning in several different media, I was forced by common sense to make a decision. The decision I made was to try to become a good writer and actor, and to compose tunes and harmonies whenever the urge to do so became too powerful to resist.

In one respect Coward resembled Irving Berlin, born eleven years earlier; both men were to become prolific composers of light music while themselves remaining only able to play it in limited keys and experiencing throughout their lives considerable difficulty in either writing or reading it. Perhaps for this reason both wrote songs that were melodically very simple and successful precisely because the tunes were easy to pick up and repeat; both also managed to reflect in their music the changing pattern of life in England and America between the wars, though in this Berlin was the more consistently accurate.

At about this time Noël also began to paint; Edna Mayo, with whose family he used to spend week-ends at Braintree, remembered that: 'he would share my paint-box and produce some pretty startling results. I was also fond of music and at that time the song 'The Rosary' was very popular – Noël had a beautiful voice and sang it like an angel. Then he would improvise at the piano for hours, going through the scores of the current musical comedies – all of which he seemed to know by heart.'

But the talent that was so apparent in other people's drawing-rooms went largely unrecognized at auditions, as management after management decided that they could do without the theatrical services of Mr Coward. His luck, however, seemed about to change with the arrival in England of Jerome Kern's musical *Oh, Boy!*, which for the benefit of un-American audiences was later retitled *Oh, Joy!* Auditions for this were held at the Shaftesbury Theatre, and it was only when Noël, wearing the routine blue suit with his audition smile frozen on to his face, was half-way through his song that he realized George Grossmith and Mr Laurillard, who were presenting the show in London, were so deep in conversation in the stalls that they had entirely failed to notice his presence at the piano. Pausing until the silence became so loud that even Grossmith and Laurillard broke off their chat to wonder what was happening, Coward then informed them that unless they were prepared to listen he was not prepared to sing to them. Mr Grossmith, overcome with remorse, not only listened but then insisted that Noël be hired, at a salary of twelve pounds a week, to play a part that would be decided on when rehearsals began in a few weeks' time.

Secure in the knowledge that he was about to be employed again, Noël decided the time had come for a holiday; this he managed to combine, albeit not very successfully, with his first actual meeting with G. B. Stern, the novelist to whom he'd been writing ardent fan letters since his illness in the First London General Hospital. Miss Stern happened to be staying at St Merryn in Cornwall as the guest of a family called Dawson-Scott, and she suggested that Noël should join them. In reply to his enquiry, Mrs Dawson-Scott told Noël that she would be happy to put him up for a fortnight if he could pay two pounds a week for his bed and board. Noël decided to go, and in one of the most unwise of the many telegrams he scattered over the world in his lifetime he told the Dawson-Scotts "ARRIVING PADSTOW FIVE-THIRTY TALL AND DIVINELY HANDSOME IN GREY". The recipients were not amused; Mrs Dawson-Scott, a large lady given to writing earthy novels in the Mary Webb tradition, was nervous that her beloved 'Peter' Stern would settle for Noël instead of Geoffrey Holdsworth, his old acquaintance from hospital whom the Dawson-Scotts far preferred as a future husband for her. On top of that, Noël's already acutely theatrical background and what Miss Stern called his 'young ferocity' did not blend well with the bleak existence led by the family in the depths of Cornwall. That the holiday was going to be a disaster became apparent on the very first evening after Noël's arrival, when he suggested that they should call him by his christian name. 'I think, Mr Coward', said Mrs Dawson-Scott, 'that we would rather wait a little.'

But Noël did succeed in his main objective, which was to develop his friendship with Miss Stern; leaving their hosts to mutter darkly about Noël's theatrical decadence, he and 'Peter' would set off for long walks along the cliffs. On these Noël kept threatening to dispose of the Dawson-Scotts, a threat he failed to pursue, and also sang Stevenson's 'Lad That Is Gone' persistently and apparently rather well. Miss Stern later published other memories of Noël on that tricky holiday:

> Bare legs, flannel bags rolled up, an old grey sweater splashed with ink, silk handkerchief knotted tightly around his head, wistful as the eternal Pierrot, mischievous as the faun he so curiously resembled... through a sea fog which lasted five days Noël talked gaily and incessantly and wrote plays and read them to us and read them to us and read them to us... I still don't know how he survived our irritation.

Shortly afterwards, Noël acted as best man when G. B. Stern married Geoffrey Holdsworth, the fellow-patient whom he had first introduced to her. It is said that in the vestry after they signed the register, he managed to delay the happy couple for some minutes while he read to them the first act of a new comedy. Later still, G. B. Stern was to dedicate her novel *Mosaic,* 'to Noël Coward, with as much respect as affection, which is saying a very great deal'. For his part, Noël remembered that on those Cornish cliff-top walks 'she permitted my Ego to strut bravely before her… never once did she trot out the 'Jack-of-all-trades-master-of-none' bugbear from which even at that age I had suffered a great deal.'

Never one to waste money, and he had paid the four pounds in advance, Noël stuck out the full fortnight in the face of continued hostility from the Dawson-Scotts. He then returned to London with a view to starting the rehearsals for *Oh, Joy!* But after the Cornish holiday a sharp attack of influenza kept him in bed for a week and when he did eventually report to the theatre for rehearsals it was to discover that the role in *Oh, Joy!* which Mr Grossmith had assured him would give full rein to his talent happened to be as one of a large number of gentlemen in the chorus. Livid, Coward took a taxi to the offices of Grossmith and Laurillard in Golden Square; there he banged on the desks until Mr Laurillard calmed his fury by agreeing that there really wasn't anything suitable in *Oh, Joy!* and instead offering Coward a part in *Scandal,* a new play which Arthur Bourchier and Kyrle Bellew were to do at the Strand in December.

Noël now had another enforced holiday, waiting for the rehearsals of *Scandal* to begin and in the meantime working on the beginning of a lush novel called *Cherry Pan* about a daughter of Pan who, by Coward's own admission, managed to be arch, elfin and altogether nauseating for nearly thirty thousand words, at which point she petered out owing to a lack of enthusiasm on the author's part and a lack of stamina on hers. Just before work started on *Scandal,* Armistice Day 1918 found Noël at the Savoy listening to Delysia singing the *Marseillaise* over and over again; the First World War had been, for Noël, little more than a gloomy background against which he grew through his teens:

> When it began I was too young to realize what it was all about, and now that it was over I could only perceive that life would probably be a good deal more enjoyable without it.

By the late autumn of 1918 the ambitions to be a composer, lyric-writer, novelist, actor and playwright, about which he'd talked endlessly to G. B. Stern on those Cornish cliffs, were crystallized in Noël's mind though his actual achievement to date was not so spectacular. Nevertheless, he had written a good many songs and sketches in collaboration with Esmé Wynne, as well as a couple of unfinished novels and some lyrics for the tunes of Doris Joel and Max Darewski. One of the latter, at least, was in the classic war-song mould of the time:

> When you come home on leave I'll still be waiting
> Waiting to greet you with a smile
> To charm away your pain
> And make you feel again
> That life is going to be worth while.

'Good old pot-boiling words,' said Noël, recalling them almost fifty years later, 'but what of it?'

Another of Coward's lyrics, for a song entitled 'Peter Pan' with music by Doris Joel, found its way into an André Charlot musical entertainment called *Tails Up* which opened at the Comedy Theatre in June of that year. Until this minor triumph Noël's relations with Charlot, the leading impresario of the time, had been disastrous. After trying unsuccessfully to get an audition with him on a number of occasions, Noël struck up a casual friendship with Beatrice Lillie, who was already working with Gertrude Lawrence in the Charlot revues. He then persuaded Miss Lillie to take him into Charlot's office, where sitting at a piano one day in 1917, Noël rapidly sang and played his way through his 'Forbidden Fruit'. Charlot listened in silence, bade him a polite farewell, and then rounded on Bea: 'How dare you', he demanded, 'bring that untalented young man into my office? He plays the piano badly and sings worse. Kindly do not waste my time with people like that ever again.' By the time of *Tails Up,* though Charlot had relented to the extent of buying Noël's lyrics, he still refused to allow him to sing them.

Noël also managed to sell a few magazine stories at this time and through the help of Max Darewski, he landed a three-year contract to write lyrics for the music-publishing company then run in the Charing Cross Road by Max's brother Herman. For this he got fifty pounds the first year, seventy-five the second, and a hundred the third; but the firm were deeply uninterested in the work that Coward produced for them in the first few months, and after a while Noël stopped going to their offices at all, except of course to collect the annual cheque which was paid promptly and charmingly, without any feeling of rancour, at the end of December. Some time after this Darewski's business went bankrupt, 'a fact', noted Noël ungratefully, 'that has never altogether astonished me.'

The part of Courtney Borner in *Scandal* was limited to two brief scenes in one of which Noël was got up, inexplicably, as Sir Walter Raleigh; perhaps because his part was not exactly crucial to this marital drama, Noël rapidly got bored of the play and its production, and his behaviour around the theatre left a good deal to be desired. His stock was particularly low among the middle-aged character ladies in the cast, one of whom complained with a certain amount of justification that Noël made clucking noises behind her back whenever she appeared on the stage; he was also unwise enough to remark in the hearing of a comedienne called Gladys Ffolliot that her dog smelled. A plea of truth did not help, and Noël soon discovered that his only friends in the company were Kyrle Bellew and Bourchier himself. Not long after they opened at the Strand, it was Bourchier who sent for Noël and warned him that as he was about to be sacked by the management, it might save a good deal of humiliation for Noël if he were to shoot off a letter of resignation that night. This Coward did, explaining with a certain evil delight to Grossmith and Laurillard that 'owing to the peculiar behaviour of the old ladies in the cast' he would have to give a fortnight's notice. The management, however, went one better, and when Noël arrived at the stage door the next evening he was given the rest of his salary and just half-an-hour to get his things out of the dressing-room.

At the very end of 1918 Noël was out of work and there was no immediate sign of anything on offer; there was, however, *The Last Trick*, a melodrama about revenge in four acts which he had written inside a week and now took to Gilbert Miller, the impresario who had cast him in *The Saving Grace* a year earlier. Miller liked the play, recognized in the nineteen-year-old Coward a 'man of many talents, over-sure of himself but a very hard worker' and agreed to take the play back with him to New York, to see if he could arrange for its production. Miller also taught Noël a few basic rules of playwriting that he'd learnt from months in Paris studying the well-made plays of Sardou and his contemporaries, remarking that though Coward's dialogue was fairly good the construction of his play was not; 'the construction of a play', said Miller, passing on some invaluable advice that had once been given to his father Henry, 'is as important as the foundation of a house – whereas the dialogue, however good, can only be considered as interior decoration.'

Coward never forgot this, and forced himself to become an architect as well as a decorator of plays.

After his ignominious departure from *Scandal,* Noël failed to get back into the theatre until the August of 1919, eight months later. In the meantime, boosted by the enthusiasm of Gilbert Miller, he wrote three more plays in rapid succession of which only the third, *The Rat Trap*, survived to achieve production, albeit eight years later and then only for twelve performances at the Everyman Theatre in Hampstead. The play was first published in 1924, with a dedication to 'the dear memory of Meggie Albanesi'. In the introduction to the third volume of his *Play Parade*, Coward described it as:

My first attempt at serious playwriting. As such it is not without merit. There is some excruciatingly sophisticated dialogue in the first act of which, at the time, I was inordinately proud. From the point of view of construction it is not very good except for the two principal quarrel scenes… I think it will only be interesting as a play to ardent students of my work, of which I hope there are several.

The play does have moments worthy of a later Coward, and a few characteristic traits are already recognizable, such as the passion for proper names; but by far the most important thing about *The Rat Trap* was that when Coward had finished it he felt, 'for the first time, with genuine conviction, that I really could write plays.'

But Noël still had ambitions to be a songwriter as well as a playwright and one frequent visitor to the room where he worked in Ebury Street was Lynden Tyson:

> I used to go into the front room where the grand piano was, and hear him banging away until he'd gradually built up a tune; then he'd say to Esmé 'Give me words to fit in with that' and Esmé would write down a lot of tripe but it fitted in with the tune and Noël would build on that. He never could put music on to paper, so he'd go off round the corner to someone who would transcribe it for him while he played: he could read music then, though he hadn't much of a voice for it. As an actor he was up against it because he was very young and provocative, and the older stage people used to give him a good bit of hell. I remember him saying to me once 'They don't like me; they've got no time for me, but I'll have them eating out of my hands before I've finished.'

At this time, the generosity of the Darewskis and the occasional magazine sales were enough to keep Noël in clothes and to help out with the rent; his stories, no longer concerned with the whimsies of Pan, 'dealt almost exclusively with the most lurid types; tarts, pimps, sinister courtesans and cynical adulterers whirled across my pages in great profusion.' When he wasn't working he spent as many week-ends as possible at large country-houses, enjoying every moment of an atmosphere that was to him quite new and attractively wealthy. He also made a good many new friends, among them Lorn Macnaughtan; she later became Lorn Loraine and for forty-four years until her death in November 1967, she remained Noël's secretary, representative and most devoted ally.

As his social contacts widened, Noël moved from his attic room at 111, Ebury Street to a larger room on the top floor; there he would give tea parties for his friends, most of whom tended to mistake his father for the butler, understandably enough since it was he who served the tea. Gertrude Lawrence reappeared in Noël's life at about this time, and Harold French recalls them dancing together, impeccably, at a place called Martan's which had opened in

Old Bond Street just after the war; 'but', said French, 'as early as this we were in slight awe of Noël – he had a very serious application to work which the rest of us failed to share; he was always very friendly, yet somehow slightly removed from the rest of us actors.'

And all the time, in the background, encouraging and helping Noël was his mother; 'a small, very gentle woman', said Lynden Tyson, 'extremely kind and so unlike the usual stage mother.'

In the August of 1919 Nigel Playfair offered Noël the part of Ralph in a production of *The Knight of the Burning Pestle* with which he was opening the sixth autumn season at the Birmingham Repertory theatre. Noël accepted Playfair's offer delightedly and went into rehearsal with Betty Chester, later a Co-Optimist and one of his greatest friends. But this production got off to a bad start, and failed to improve later; there was not much time before rehearsals began so Playfair suggested that Miss Chester and Noël should spend the few days staying in Oxford where they could learn their lines rapidly and in peace and quiet. All might have been well had they not elected to hire a punt and to learn the script while gliding down the Cherwell; predictably, the punt capsized, and two copies of *The Knight of the Burning Pestle* sank rapidly to the bottom leaving Noël and Miss Chester to return shamefacedly to London with only a passing knowledge of the lines. 'There was', said Noël later, 'a quality of fantasy about the whole engagement', possibly because of Playfair's rigid loyalty to the Elizabethan atmosphere of the original. To signal the interval, it was decided that a performing bear should climb up a pole; Maud Gill was thus inserted into a bearskin (the real animal being unavailable) and forced to sit on the pole while Noël and Miss Chester, whose aim was faultless, hurled buns into her mouth. For all that, Coward did not really enjoy *The Knight of the Burning Pestle* much; he failed to understand the play in particular or Elizabethan comedy technique in general, and felt that Playfair, who in his view 'directed with more selfishness than authority', had not really done quite enough to help his own performance: 'I mouthed and postured my way through it with little conviction and no sense of period' – a self-analytical verdict with which most of the critics agreed.

The three weeks in Birmingham were however considerably enlivened by a cable from Gilbert Miller, announcing that an American producer called Al Woods would pay five hundred dollars for an option on *The Last Trick*. Astounded, pleased and considerably richer, Noël returned to London where he and his mother stood gloatingly at the counter of a bank in the City while the money was counted out to them. Feeling for the first time that he really could afford to spend, Noël dined at The Ivy, went to innumerable theatres with Albanesi or Gertrude Lawrence, and ordered a number of backless waistcoats of the kind currently made fashionable by the novelist Michael

Arlen, one of a growing collection of writers, painters and actors whom Noël could now call his friends.

When 1919 was nearly over, Gilbert Miller returned from America, sent for Noël, and continued the lesson in playwriting that he had begun some months earlier. This time he also gave Noël the title and plot outline of a light comedy that he wanted written for Charles Hawtrey. 'I was then', said Noël, 'as I remained, extremely chary of writing based on somebody else's idea.' But, hardly in a position to refuse, he had *I'll Leave It to You* completed within three days; it was an amiable, innocuous, deeply unpretentious little comedy and Miller was fairly pleased with it, though not as entranced as was Noël himself. After negotiating a few alterations Miller returned to America having promised that he would stage it for trial production at the Gaiety Theatre in Manchester during the following April.

Noël, without any work in the meantime, was not best pleased by the delay; but he had at least the foresight to make sure that one part had his own name written all over it, thus guaranteeing that when the play was eventually produced he could claim payment as an actor and as author. By now it was the January of 1920 and the beginning of the decade with which Coward was to be constantly and inevitably associated.

7

1920–1921

I cannot think off-hand of anyone who was more intimately and turbulently connected with our theatre in the Twenties than myself.

The decade that began for Noël with *I'll Leave It to You* and ended with *Bitter-Sweet* did not, theatrically, get off to a very good start. The early Twenties were bleak and unproductive years for plays and the beginning of 1920 saw the London stage moving in no recognizable direction, though undoubtedly the days of the actor-managers were numbered. 'We have nobody', remarked Sir John Martin-Harvey sourly, 'who will sacrifice himself for the benefit of the higher drama in London by maintaining on his own shoulders the great traditions of the past.'

For Coward the decade was to be a highly productive and tremendously successful one, though he went into it with nothing certain beyond the April production of *I'll Leave It to You* in Manchester. In retrospect, it is tempting to see in Noël the spirit of the Twenties; in fact they were simply the first ten years of his adult working life, though to get them into that perspective would take him another quarter of a century:

> Between 1920 and 1930 I achieved a great deal of what I had set out to achieve, and a great deal that I had not. I had not, for instance, envisaged in those early days of the Twenties that before the decade was over I would be laid low by a serious nervous breakdown, recover from it, and return to London to be booed off the stage and spat at in the streets. Nor did I imagine, faced by this unmannerly disaster, that only a few months would ensue before I would be back again, steadier and a great deal more triumphant than before.

Having nothing better to do until rehearsals began for *I'll Leave It to You,* Noël made his first trip abroad early in the next year. He went, with a friend called Stewart Forster, to stay at the Ritz Hotel in Paris – for one night, after which, seeing the bill, they moved in to a small hotel in the Rue Caumartin for the rest of the week. It was on this first visit to Paris that Noël announced to Bobby Andrews, whom he found in a café by the Gare du Nord, that he would not, for all the world, have a settled income: 'Why?' asked Andrews. 'Because', murmured Noël, 'it would take away my determination to succeed.'

Back in England in the spring of 1920, Noël was soon to experience for the first time something of the success he so passionately desired. *I'll Leave It to You* opened in Manchester on May 3rd; at the end of the play there were cheers from the audience and Noël, pushed forward by Kate Cutler, made the first of the curtain speeches that were to be a feature of his first-nights for the next twenty years.

The following morning an early profile of Noël appeared in the *Daily Dispatch:*

> There is something freakish, Puck-like, about the narrow slant of his grey-green eyes, the tilt of his eyebrows, the sleek backward rush of his hair. He is lithe as a fawn; and if you told him, with perfect truth, that he was one of the three best dancers in London, his grieved surprise at hearing of the other two would only be equalled by his incredulity.

The play itself does not bear very close scrutiny now, nearly eighty years after its first performance, but then as a light comedy of its time one could hardly expect that it would. *I'll Leave It to You* seems to be the first example of Noël's supreme talent for giving the public what they want when they want it, though one suspects that the critics' enthusiasm for the play might not have been warmed by the author, who told them casually that it was written in a mere three days – 'whereas many of my plays take a week'. This was technically true, and a device that Noël would often use in later years to impress journalists with the speed at which plays and lyrics poured off his typewriter. It is, perhaps, only fair to add, as Noël never did, that before those three days he had spent some considerable time thinking out the play in detail – thus the time given only reflects his rate of typing, not that of composition. 'The comedy is finished', said Richard Brinsley Sheridan in a similar context, 'it only remains to write it.'

At the end of a successful first week in Manchester, Mrs Gilbert Miller and Mrs Charles Hawtrey arrived from London to inspect the play on behalf of their husbands. To Noël's barely disguised fury they appeared in his dressing-room after the last act to remark sadly that in their view the play didn't have a hope of success in London, and that they were off to cable their husbands accordingly.

Not so easily defeated, Noël completed the Manchester run at the end of the third week in May and returned to London where he found somebody prepared to take a more active interest in the production of his play: Lady Wyndham, the actress Mary Moore. As the widow of Sir Charles Wyndham, Miss Moore then managed that chain of theatres (Wyndham's, the Criterion and the New) which her husband had established and which her grandson, Donald Albery, inherited. She agreed to give *I'll Leave It to You* a London production at the New Theatre when Matheson Lang's *Carnival* went off on tour in the middle of July. As Noël himself was still six months under age, his father signed the contracts.

I'll Leave It to You opened in London on July 21st, 1920 to reviews that were generally good but of little use at the box-office. It lasted only thirty-seven performances and has seldom been professionally revived since, though Noël did manage to sell the amateur rights to Samuel French for a 'comfortable sum', and it appeared some time later in a production by the Hong Kong Amateur Dramatic Club. The play, dedicated to his mother, was also the first of Noël's to be seen in the United States: it opened in Boston in 1923 and then disappeared somewhere on the road to New York.

Nevertheless, *I'll Leave It to You* did Noël a great deal of public good; journalists assembled for his first press conference, at which it was announced that Noël was related to the distinguished organist James Coward. Indignant at being presented on the merits of someone else, Noël replied sharply, 'I am related to no one except myself.' The papers were filled the next morning with 'boy author makes good', and Lady Wyndham described him to the *Daily Express* as a 'British Sacha Guitry'. But her enthusiasm for the new Guitry waned a bit when she saw the weekly box-office returns, and the gloom of the company's fifth and final week at the New Theatre was darkened still further by Lady Wyndham's determination to limit her losses by having the stage lighting cut to half. Noël arrived at the theatre to find the stage in darkness and most of the arc lights being carried round the corner to Wyndham's where her ladyship felt they'd be more useful. Demanding their return, he refused to appear on stage without them; the audience were kept waiting for twenty-five minutes while Noël and the stage manager argued. There were not a great many people in the theatre at the time and the customers were fairly happy to be left talking amongst themselves. Finally, the lights were returned, the curtain went up, and Coward had learnt a good deal about his own strength in the theatre.

The play still closed a few nights later, but the publicity made it all worthwhile from Noël's point of view, if not from Lady Wyndham's. *The Glasgow Bulletin* described him as an 'amazing youth', the *Sunday Chronicle* considered him an 'infant prodigy', and Noël himself began to give the first of innumerable interviews in the press. To *The Globe* he admitted:

> The success of it all is a bit dazzling. This may be an age of youth but it does not always happen that young people get their chance of success. I have been exceptionally lucky. I made up my mind I would have one of my plays produced in London by the time I was twenty-one, which will be in December. I hope to be a manager by then, too.

For the record, he did not go into management until he was in his thirties. The *New Witness* predicted that within a year Noël would be enjoying the same success as Somerset Maugham in the theatre and the *Daily Mail* let Coward divulge the way he wrote:

With *I'll Leave It to You* I wrote the first and last acts in a day, working from nine in the morning to about five in the afternoon with, of course, intervals for meals. The second act took me two days – it was very much harder, I roughly schemed out the plot, and then I let the play take its own way.

I find all the technical details of entrances and exits and so on just work themselves out. I write at white heat, and during my work I occasionally read a book the style of which is different from what I am writing to get a kind of literary refreshment. I altered hardly a line of this play after I had written it.

This last habit was one that was to stay with Noël through most of his writing.

Looking back, one realizes that his first London production as an actor-dramatist gave Noël more than encouragement; in the faintly unpleasant children of *I'll Leave It to You* it is possible to see rough drafts for Sorel and Simon in *Hay Fever* four years later.

After *I'll Leave It to You* closed, Coward spent the August of 1920 working on two projects that were later abandoned: a play called *Barriers Down* which, he said later, 'was awful', and the lyrics for an opera called *Crissa*.

The rest of the summer and early autumn, if not immediately productive months, were not entirely uneventful for Noël; in the best traditions of a 'young man about town' he was caught by the police in the act of removing a number of flower pots and a hideous sun-blind from outside a row of houses in Kensington. The adventure cost him a few uneasy hours in a police station, forty shillings in cash and a sharp reminder from Esmé Wynne that a police record would not help the start of a promising career.

In November, by which time money was again an urgent problem, Nigel Playfair luckily decided to revive *The Knight of the Burning Pestle,* this time at the Kingsway Theatre in London. Noël was re-engaged for Ralph, and they opened to tepid enthusiasm on November 24th. Noël's hopefully Don Quixotic performance was considered 'a little too Mayfairish for a Jacobean grocer's son', though *The Illustrated London News* thought that 'he wandered about delightfully'. At one performance Mrs Patrick Campbell caused vast excitement backstage when she was seen in the audience, until it was realized that she had slept soundly throughout. Noël sent her a sharp note commenting on the rudeness of her behaviour, and the next night Mrs Campbell was back in long white gloves, clapping wildly every time Noël appeared.

Just before Christmas, playing in *The Knight of the Burning Pestle,* Coward developed a temperature of a hundred and two; deciding in the best traditions of the theatre that it was his duty to carry on (a song of his some thirty years later was to be called 'Why Must the Show Go On?') he succeeded in giving one or two terrible performances and sixteen of the company mumps before he too retired to bed. Playfair himself took over 'Ralph' for a while, but generally bad business and the mass attack of mumps closed the production very soon afterwards.

By the year's end Noël had recovered sufficiently to sign a contract with Gilbert Miller for an American comedy, *Polly with a Past,* which was due to open at the St James's in March 1921. In the meantime, Coward set off for a winter holiday at the Casino Hotel in Rapallo. It was not a success, as Noël had little money, less Italian and no friends there. After a few days he retreated to Alassio where his rich friend Mrs Cooper was staying at the Grand Hotel and only too happy to put him up. By now, thanks to *I'll Leave It to You,* the Coward name meant something even in Alassio, if not to the natives then at least to the members of the English Club there who asked him to play the piano and sing at one of their annual concerts. In the audience on that occasion, and giggling openly to Noël's indignation, was a young English woman who was to design almost all of Noël's major successes in the theatre from *The Vortex* onwards, Gladys Calthrop:

> Alassio was then a little village, and I was staying there with my parents; the Club was minute – a kind of church hall, I remember – and the man introducing Noël got his name wrong, which started my giggles and also infuriated Noël. But we became firm friends after that – mainly I think because we seemed to be the only two people in Alassio under thirty. Also Noël had what was politely known as a continental stomach for which I managed to find a cure at the local chemists. One night after that, being particularly rowdy, we managed to wreck the English Club by smearing the walls with black paint. Quite soon afterwards we went back to England, separately, and began to see each other a great deal in London.

Polly with a Past, an American farce that had done well in New York in the wartime conditions of 1917, opened in London at the St James's Theatre on March 2nd four years later. It was, by all accounts, not a very good play; but it did provide parts for Edna Best (as Polly), Edith Evans, Helen Haye, Noël and Henry Kendall as well as for two men who later became stalwarts of the English gentlemen actors' colony in Hollywood – Claude Rains and C. Aubrey Smith. Noël himself got £20 a week for what he considered to be an unrewarding feed part, but found a firm friend in Henry Kendall:

> Noël was a very high-spirited young man in those days, and a frightful giggler on stage. We used to catch it, all except Edith Evans who would get furious with us. In the end it got so bad that the stage manager cabled Gilbert Miller, who had gone off to New York after we opened at the St James's, saying that the younger members of the company were ruining the play by bad behaviour and back came Gilbert's reply: 'Sack them'.

All concerned were saved from this embarrassment by a coal strike, which paralysed transport, killed theatre business and put an end to Polly and her past.

But a hundred and ten performances in a year when nearly fifty productions lasted less than a month was not exactly shaming, and Noël (as was his custom when playing small parts) managed to elaborate the character as much as possible, to the fury of Rains and Kendall who were left to struggle for their laughs against a barrage of Coward business. Noël also achieved a good deal outside the theatre during this run:

> Songs, sketches, and plays were bursting out of me far too quickly and without nearly enough critical discrimination.

One rather better than the rest was *The Young Idea,* a sub-Shavian comedy in three acts about a couple of precocious children who reunite their estranged parents. The title came from Thomson's poem *The Seasons,* and the play owed a good deal to *You Never Can Tell;* perhaps for that reason the Vedrenne management sent it to Bernard Shaw, who then had *Heartbreak House* going into production at the Royal Court. Nevertheless Shaw took the time and the trouble to write to Noël about *The Young Idea,* suggesting that it was unwise to try to repeat the success he'd had with the twins in *You Never Can Tell,* but adding a word of encouragement:

> I have no doubt that you will succeed if you persevere… never fall into a breach of essential good manners and, above all, never see or read my plays. Unless you can get clean away from me you will begin as a back number, and be hopelessly out of date when you are forty.

While *The Young Idea* was doing a more than usually fruitless round of managers' offices, Noël again found time on his hands between the undemanding performances of his role as Clay Collins in *Polly with a Past.* The result was a book called *A Withered Nosegay,* illustrated by Lorn Loraine, dedicated to Esmé Wynne-Tyson and published in the following spring by Christopher's. This was a slim volume sending up the current vogue for romantic pseudo-historical character studies; it consisted of ten character sketches from the unforgettably named Sarah, Lady Tunnell-Penge through to Julie de Poopinac. Reading them now it is uncertain whether the satire hit any target at all, and it is difficult to judge the success of the parody. Few critics reviewed it at the time, though there were gossip-column items remarking yet again on Noël's versatile youthful talents, and the only reader's comment to hand is one inscribed on the fly-leaf of a copy given as a birthday present: 'I think this book rather rude,' writes the sender, 'but you were once an admirer of Noël Coward.' Coward himself felt, in retrospect, that *A Withered Nosegay* was written with too much zest and personal enjoyment and that it consequently fell a good way short of success: 'I have often regretted that the idea didn't come to me a little later, when I should have been more aware of its pitfalls and better equipped to grapple with it.' The book earned a grand total of £15 once the printing costs were paid, and Noël's share of the final profits was £7 10s.

About halfway through the run of *Polly with a Past,* after the show one night, Coward met Jeanne Eagels at a party given by Ivor Novello in the flat he kept above the Strand Theatre. Fresh from her triumph on Broadway in a play called *Daddies,* Miss Eagels radiated an aura of American magic that made Noël decide instantly it was time he visited New York where surely countless actresses like her were eagerly awaiting the arrival of his acting and playwriting talents.

Another inducement to go was Jeffery Holmesdale, then a captain in the Coldstream Guards, later Lord Amherst and throughout his adult life a close friend of Noël's. He was leaving for New York at the end of May, en route for Massachusetts and the centenary of Amherst College; as he was booked on the Aquitania, Holmesdale suggested that Noël should sail with him. Already able to recognize and share the passionate love of success nurtured by all true Americans, Noël decided that his dream of 'promising playwright conquers New World' would have more chance of reality if he were to arrive aboard the Aquitania rather than the freight steamer that was economically within his reach. The Aquitania would cost £100 one way; Noël had about half this in the bank, thanks to *Polly,* and he made the rest by selling two songs to Ned Lathom, a friend and benefactor who didn't actually want them but was charitably disposed and also very rich. Coward then persuaded Gilbert Miller's London office that he should be released from the last few performances of *Polly* and at the end of May, he set off for New York with Jeffery, a bundle of manuscripts and seventeen pounds in sterling.

8

1921–1924

*My faith in my own talents remained unwavering, but it did seem unduly optimistic
to suppose that the Americans would be perceptive enough to see me immediately in
the same light in which I saw myself. In this, I was perfectly right. They didn't.*

The Atlantic crossing on the Aquitania was a peaceful one, in spite of the
need to polish up *The Young Idea* and of a ship's concert at which Noël
had to accompany the Chief Steward while he sang the living daylights out of
Mandalay. On his arrival ('New York looks', Coward wrote on a post-card to
Esmé Wynne-Tyson, 'like I've always imagined Babylon must have looked.'),
and in spite of a certain homesickness for his mother, Noël found that the city
lived up to Jeanne Eagels' promise – at least for the few days that Jeffery stayed
there with him. In New York they embarked on a frantic sightseeing rush from
Washington Square uptown to Harlem by way of such sights as the Woolworth
Building, Coney Island and Fanny Brice singing 'Second-Hand Rose' in the
Ziegfeld Follies. They were also invited to spend a week-end with Averell
Harriman, on whose estate they were able to watch the rich playing polo.

But after Jeffery left, Noël found less to like about New York. It is, as
Moss Hart once said, not a city in which to be poor or unsuccessful; and Noël
was both. He also found that all three impresarios to whom he had letters of
introduction – Al Woods, Charles Dillingham and David Belasco – were on
their way out of the city for the summer, though Woods did pause long
enough to tell Noël that he had reluctantly abandoned, after a number of
unsuccessful rewrites, all plans to stage *The Last Trick* in America.

Fighting off the temptation to return to England, which wasn't difficult as
he did not have the fare, Noël settled in an apartment in Washington Square
South that was leased by Gabrielle Enthoven. Mrs Enthoven, who later gave
her name and a vast amount of material to the Victoria and Albert Museum's
Theatre Collection, was a vague acquaintance of Noël's who fortunately had
not only a spare room but also enough money not to be too worried about
Coward's share of the rent.

Noël's one success at this time was to sell to *Vanity Fair* for a very few
dollars indeed some of the burlesqued character sketches from *A Withered
Nosegay.* This was encouraging, but it was all; for the next four months, getting
daily more depressed as he wandered from Washington Square to Central
Park and back, Noël failed to do anything as an actor or a writer except to

realize how far down on his luck he was. There was overwhelming apathy on the part of managers and agents, and Noël's life was not made any easier at this time by the Theatre Guild, who, given his plays to read, had promptly locked them up for the summer months making it impossible for Coward to arouse the interest of any other prospective backers. Moreover he was now alone in the apartment, Mrs Enthoven having fled the heat of July in New York. He began to get slightly nervous about the neighbourhood; the discovery of large bed bugs and a broken lock on the front door was only partly offset by a friendly neighbourhood cop who left Noël a gun in case of any trouble.

But in these weeks Coward did manage to make a few friends, among them Tallulah Bankhead, Ronald Colman whom he'd first met in England, and George Kaufman who with Moss Hart later wrote (in *The Man Who Came to Dinner*) the only lastingly funny parody of Noël himself. Miss Bankhead, asked what Coward was like at this time, replied 'frustrated' and added, rather unexpectedly 'he was living on herbs and wild berries.'

The beginnings of two Coward plays, the second vastly better than the first, are also to be found in that New York summer. After Noël saw Molnar's *Liliom* on Broadway with Eva Le Gallienne and Joseph Schildkraut, he instantly began to write (with them in mind and remembering also a fiesta that he and Gladys Calthrop watched in Alassio the year before) a drama called *Sirocco*. He finished it quickly and had no cause to regret it until 1927 when it appeared for the first and last time, slightly retouched, with Ivor Novello and Frances Doble at Daly's.

The other play was an altogether happier affair, and though not actually written out until some time after Coward returned from America, it stemmed from a number of evenings that he spent at Riverside Drive as a guest of the actress Laurette Taylor and her husband Hartley Manners. To be a guest of the Manners' was evidently an altogether unnerving experience. They were a highly-strung family, deeply theatrical and prone to elaborate word games which always ended in hysteria and the entire family abandoning their guests to cope as best they could. Given eccentricity on this histrionic scale, and considering the unusually large number of authors on Miss Taylor's guest list, it was inevitable that someone would realize there was a play here somewhere; to Noël's great good fortune none of them thought of *Hay Fever* before he did.

One Sunday evening at Riverside Drive, Noël again met Lynn Fontanne, an actress he'd known slightly in London, who was now living in New York with Alfred Lunt:

> Noël, who was then still precocious but somehow very brilliant, came to see Alfred and me with the script of *The Young Idea*. I introduced him to Helen Hayes who would have been good casting for it but wouldn't touch

it; still, we tried very hard and I also introduced him to some publishers including Condé Nast. After that Noël dined with us almost every night because he couldn't afford to eat anywhere else, though we weren't so damn rich either.

Alfred Lunt, himself an actor six years older than Noël and also unemployed for the summer months:

> Noël made no kind of success on his first visit to America, though he was very likeable and through us got to know a great many people in the theatre. A gentleness and at times a deep sadness marked his character then, though the determination to succeed and preferably rapidly at that was never far away.

Noël's firm friendship with the Lunts was the beginning of a three-cornered alliance that lasted throughout their long working lives. The plans they made for themselves that summer included a success for Lynn in her new play, marriage for Lynn and Alfred soon afterwards, world stardom for all three of them, and ultimately a three-character play to be written by Noël and performed by the trio. Each of those four plans worked out impeccably, starting with Lynn Fontanne's triumph in the title role of *Dulcie;* at the first night Noël and Alfred, both unemployed and realizing that they depended on Lynn for their next meal, sat in the stalls 'praying that Mother would bring home the bacon'. She did.

Lynn's success as Dulcie was matched only by Noël's continuing failure to make any money in New York until he was eventually forced to borrow twenty dollars from her. It was not by any means the only time in either past or future that Noël had to borrow money from a friend, but it was the time that hurt the most.

It was also the end of Noël's poverty, not because twenty dollars went very far or lasted very long, but because the next morning brought a letter from the editor of a magazine called *Metropolitan* who had been given a copy of *I'll Leave It to You* to read. The editor now suggested that if Coward would turn his play into a short story for the magazine he'd pay five hundred dollars. 'For five hundred dollars', replied Noël, 'I would gladly consider turning *War and Peace* into a music-hall sketch.'

Harold French, the boy actor contemporary of Coward's was already doing rather better than Noël in New York:

> When Noël first came over we used to knock about a bit together; he was very broke, living down in the Village, and he used to pop into the Algonquin to see me, whether I was there or not. But the last time I saw him there he'd just sold his short story to *Metropolitan,* and he gave us all a big party at Delmonico's.

With the autumn, theatres opened again and Noël was able to retrieve his manuscripts from the Theatre Guild; he also managed to convert *The Young Idea* into a short story for *Metropolitan,* using the proceeds to move back into an hotel and visit a number of Broadway shows, in most of which he found a verve, attack and pace then altogether lacking in the West End. At the end of October, thanks to a lady called Gladys Barber who befriended Noël and whose husband was an executive with a shipping line, Coward got himself a free cabin on the *SS Cedric* bound for Liverpool. He left New York with a certain regret, already glamorizing in his memory the gloomier moments of his stay; after five months in America, he had precisely seven pounds more than he'd brought with him. The voyage home was peaceful, marked only by long conversations in the ship's tearoom with a fellow passenger and passionate theatregoer called Marie Stopes.

Back in Ebury Street, where George Moore was now one of a number of literary neighbours, Mrs Coward's delight at having Noël home failed to hide the fact that with his father out of work there was still no money, and that life there had recently been very depressing indeed for his family. Noël was at first unable to help; though he returned to the round of managers' offices, he now found himself in a tricky position where his name was too well-known for the offer of small parts and yet not distinguished enough for the offer of larger ones. The general despondency and total lack of work carried over into the beginning of 1922, but then Noël did manage to sell a couple of songs as well as the hack adaptation of a French play by Louis Verneuil, which had originally been called *Pour Avoir Adrienne.* The English version, commissioned for a hundred pounds by Dennis Eadie, was never produced, and characteristically Noël bought back the script some years later.

But without the prospect of any other work on the horizon, once Eadie's money ran out Noël was again forced to ask for a loan. This time he got £200 from his friend Ned Lathom who had been generous enough to pick up a number of his bills in the past, and who now insisted on making it a gift as he believed a loan might spoil their friendship. Using some of this money, Noël decided to find his mother a cottage in the country where she could stay for a few months to get over an illness and recover from the strain of coping with the family and the lodgers. Athene Seyler lent her house at Dymchurch to Noël and Gladys Calthrop who was helping in the search, and after a week of bicycling through Kent villages they found a four-roomed cottage next to a pub at St Mary in the Marsh for a rental of ten shillings a week.

Noël and his mother settled there for the spring while Mr Coward looked after the lodgers in Ebury Street; she recovered some of her lost health and her son spent the time writing a Ruritanian romantic melodrama of the kind later to be indelibly associated with Ivor Novello. It was eventually entitled

The Queen Was in the Parlour, and the fact that Noël wrote the whole play propped against a tombstone in the churchyard of St Mary's does not seem to have made it any gloomier than countless other plays of the period about the high life in middle Europe.

But it was a depressing time for Noël, and in the first six months of 1922 his beloved London seemed every bit as eager to ignore his work as had New York the previous summer. Yet two productions served briefly to keep his name before the public; first the Newspaper Press Fund matinée at Drury Lane in May, when Nelson Keys and George Grossmith did a brief duet of Noël's called *Bottles and Bones,* and then the Little Theatre's Grand Guignol series which, improbably enough, ran twenty-nine performances of a one-act comedy called *The Better Half* that Noël had written just before he went to America. This came last in a macabre bill which included a play about a deaf mute trying to kill himself before his sister could murder him, and Noël's light, acid look at marriage and separation seems to have been oddly out of place.

In his review, *The Morning Post* critic regretted that: 'Mr Coward is cursed with fatal facility, that failing of the young writer; he seems to think all his geese are swans and writes them down without waiting to see if anything better could be found in their place.'

Meanwhile Noël's father was running the lodging house in Ebury Street with a success that surprised him almost as much as it did his long-suffering guests; with Eric no longer in school, money was at last becoming a little easier for the family. By the end of June Noël and his mother had returned to London armed with a letter from Robert Courtneidge agreeing to present *The Young Idea* for a six-week trial run round the provinces. In Sholto, the juvenile lead, Noël had again written a part ideal for himself; but this time he had considerable difficulty in getting Courtneidge, who was also directing, to let him play it. Courtneidge felt, though he subsequently lost the battle, that the role should be played by someone younger and less sophisticated than Noël.

With nothing to do until rehearsals started in September, Coward was delighted to get an invitation from Lady Colefax who had decided that he would be a conversational asset to a week-long house-party she was giving at a stately, albeit rented, home near Oxford. Throughout the first half of the Twenties, Noël spent a large amount of his spare time in varying degrees of poverty among the very rich; they found him amusing and he revelled in their patronage, partly because of a certain inherent snobbery and mainly because he found them excellent copy for current work. Socially he was by now an ideal and near-professional house guest; by a careful development of his native wit and charm he made himself indispensable to a large number of hostesses who in return could offer living conditions vastly superior to Ebury Street.

Moreover, at a time when the aristocracy and the more successful members of the theatrical profession were becoming closely allied, sometimes even by marriage, it gave him the chance to make a few useful professional contacts.

With Lady Colefax, at a dinner party in London, Noël met Elsa Maxwell. Not yet the hostess with the mostest, Miss Maxwell nonetheless came up with an offer to pay all his expenses if he would accompany her and a friend, Dorothy Fellows-Gordon, on a fortnight's holiday in Venice. There the redoubtable Miss Maxwell even got him into a party for the Duke of Spoleto over the metaphorically dead body of its hostess; the rest of the holiday consisted for Coward of a couple of enchanting weeks on the Grand Canal and the realization that the life of a discerning gigolo could be very pleasant indeed.

The Young Idea opened at the Prince's Theatre in Bristol during the last week in September. The state of Noël's bank balance at the time can be judged from a letter written from the Prince's to Nelson Keys:

> I feel awful about the £50. I can't possibly pay it back until I've been working a little – I've been existing on credit for such ages – can you wait until November? I'm sure to make something on this tour because we're doing marvellous business... please forgive me for not paying you back before but you do understand, don't you? I am eternally grateful to you for lending it.

For *The Young Idea* and for Noël as author the provincial reviews were generally encouraging and business was excellent, though in spite of the play's 'sparkling dialogue, abounding humour and unexpected situations' (*Glasgow Citizen*) a London theatre couldn't be found for it until the Savoy became free when the Christmas play season ground to a halt in February. Until then the company disbanded, and Noël took the chance of a winter holiday in Davos where his benefactor Ned Lathom was recuperating after a bout of tuberculosis. He arrived there to find that Lathom had organized a massive welcome at the station with a reception committee and a friend dressed as the local Mayor to present Coward with the keys of the town. Noël was then driven through Davos on a sleigh, waving graciously to the mystified residents.

Settled into an hotel where (as the skiing season had not yet started) he and Lord Lathom's sister were the only two people not suffering from tuberculosis, Noël found Davos slightly macabre though somehow not depressing. Lathom seemed to be getting better; he was tremendously stagestruck, had already backed the Charlot revue *A to Z*, and now demanded to hear some of Noël's material. Realizing that there were enough songs by

Coward to support a revue, Lathom instantly summoned André Charlot to Davos. There the three men began a series of conferences from which, nine months and much sweat later, emerged a revue entitled *London Calling!*

Once the basic idea for the revue had been formulated by the three of them in Davos, Charlot returned to London leaving Noël to start work on the sketches: he had already agreed that Gertrude Lawrence, Maisie Gay and Noël together with one other comedian should head the bill. Coward worked hard on the sketches until Christmas came, turning Davos into one long party with such resident guests as Clifton Webb, Elsa Maxwell, Edward Molyneux, Maxine Elliott and Gladys Cooper. Someone else in Davos that Christmas, though not as part of the group, was Micheál MacLiammóir:

> Noël was with a very big, smart party and I used to see him in a white jersey riding around on a horse-drawn sled. I still thought then that he would do well, because without any effort or feeling of strain or social climbing he was always fond of fashionable, smart people. But at that time I'd developed a rather artificial hatred of the theatre and those kind of people; my idea of a good writer was somebody like Yeats, and I thought Wilde had already done everything that Noël could possibly do. I even used to run away and hide when I saw him, in case he recognized me.

Gladys Cooper, staying at the same hotel, also had uneasy recollections of Coward in Davos:

> He was unbearably smug then... I remember once over dinner suggesting to him that instead of writing countless plays which nobody ever produced he should find a really good writer like Edward Knoblock and collaborate with him. Noël looked horrified, and replied that as Shaw and Barrie and Maugham never collaborated he failed to see why he should. So I told him how conceited he was, and left it at that.

One should perhaps add here that in spite of that rough start, Dame Gladys and Mr Coward remained good friends for the rest of their lives.

Christmas over, Noël returned to London where *The Young Idea* opened to reviews that were even better than those for *I'll Leave It to You.* They heralded a run of just over seven weeks. Again the critics hailed a brilliant young writer's prodigious achievement, and again the audience stayed away in droves. But St John Ervine, writing in the *Observer,* was not altogether happy about the few who were already Noël's vociferous supporters:

> Mr Coward has not quite conquered his habit of writing plays as if they were charades, but he has wit and invention and if he can only restrain the enthusiasm of his friends and acquire a sense of fact, he will probably write a very good comedy. I was unfortunately wedged in the centre of a group of his more exuberant friends who greeted each of his sallies with

'That's a Noëlism!' and 'What a marvellous line!' even when Sholto referred to someone as possessing hands like wet hot-water bottles.

Still, to balance Ervine there was *The Sunday Chronicle* describing *The Young Idea* as the best farcical comedy to hit London since *The Importance of Being Earnest* thirty years earlier, and the *Royal Pictorial News* voting Noël 'the best-dressed young wit in London'. One wonders who were the runners-up.

The run was a brief but fairly happy one, improved for Noël by another satisfactory sale of the publication rights to Samuel French and by a telegram of heady praise from C. B. Cochran. With his mother safely re-installed in the lodging house, where his father continued to cope with the lodgers while she dealt with Eric and Aunt Vida, Noël set off with Gladys Calthrop to visit the hospitable Mrs Cooper, this time at Cap Ferrat where they would have stayed rather longer had it not been for the arrival of a Dominican Prior who took an instant dislike to both of them. As there was a strong possibility that Mrs Cooper, forced to choose who should remain with her, would have settled for the Prior anyway, Gladys and Noël swiftly moved on to Italy. There they holidayed until their money ran out, which it did alarmingly quickly, whereupon they returned to London and Charlot's production of *London Calling!*

In view of Coward's total inexperience where revue was concerned, and because Charlot was less than enthusiastic about some of the material that Coward had given him, Ronald Jeans was brought in to help with the book and Philip Braham with the music. Tubby Edlin was cast as principal comedian with Gertrude Lawrence and Maisie Gay, though there was now some doubt as to whether Coward himself would appear in the show. Charlot was only offering him a weekly £15, less than half what the others were getting and £5 a week less than Noël had been given for playing in *The Young Idea*. The salary did not therefore appeal to Coward, who held out for rather more on the grounds that he was anyway risking his prestige as a straight actor by appearing in revue. Charlot, unmoved, refused to go over £15 and decided to find someone else for the job. He had, however, overlooked a clause neatly inserted in the contract by Noël, guaranteeing himself as part-author the right to approve or veto all major casting. For the next few weeks Noël regularly and solidly objected to the suggestion of every juvenile lead in the business. Finally, with *London Calling!* now on the brink of rehearsal, Charlot was reluctantly forced to suggest a figure of £40 a week, an offer that Noël was graciously pleased to accept with the demand only that he be given the right to escape after six months.

This granted, Noël began work on his singing and dancing, talents that had been left unpractised since his days as a child actor. Enlisting the help of Fred Astaire, who at that time was conveniently enough appearing with his sister Adele in the London production of *Stop Flirting*, Noël learnt enough to get through such numbers as 'Other Girls' and 'You Were Meant For Me' in which he sang and danced with Gertrude Lawrence to arrangements by Astaire himself. Through its music, *London Calling!* saw the beginning of a long alliance between Noël and Elsie April, a bird-like lady given to wearing remarkable hats who, while refusing ever to compose anything herself, would solemnly transcribe any note Noël ever sang at her. This, as Noël himself could not then write music down on paper, proved an invaluable aid. Miss April, who later joined Cochran's staff as a chorus mistress, was to be involved in all of Noël's musical work between 1923 and the beginning of the second war; in that she transcribed and arranged his songs throughout these years it is fair to assume that hers was a major influence on the harmony of Coward compositions.

After two postponements for alterations and more rehearsal, *London Calling!,* with costumes by Edward Molyneux, opened cold with a matinée at the Duke of York's on September 4th 1923; the matinée was Charlot's idea, his theory being that as the entire company of artists and technicians were already exhausted by four long, hard and difficult weeks of rehearsal, the matinée (to which no critics were invited) would tire them even further, thus ensuring that the first evening performance, played entirely on raw nerves, would be remarkable for its nightmarish vivacity. In this Charlot proved absolutely correct; the first night, though it ran just over three hours, went superbly.

This first edition of the revue included twenty-six numbers of which half were solely composed by Noël; most of the numbers were published eight years later in his *Collected Sketches and Lyrics,* though only 'Parisian Pierrot', sung in the revue by Gertrude Lawrence, managed to outlive its original setting. This was the first successful song Noël ever achieved, and he had written it during a brief holiday in Germany.

> The idea of it came to me in a nightclub in Berlin in 1922. A frowsy blonde, wearing a sequin chest-protector and a divided skirt, appeared in the course of the cabaret with a rag pierrot doll dressed in black velvet. She placed it on a cushion where it sprawled in pathetic abandon while she pranced round it emitting gutteral noises. Her performance was unimpressive, but the doll fascinated me. The title *Parisian Pierrot* slipped into my mind, and in the taxi on the way back to my hotel, the song began.

Of the show itself, Noël notes: 'I appeared constantly, singing and dancing and acting with unbridled vivacity, and enjoyed myself very much indeed.' But the critics at the first night of *London Calling!* tended to be unimpressed by Noël's musical gifts: 'Mr Coward cannot compose', said the *Sunday Express,* 'and should sing only for his friends' amusement.' The number that provoked this comment was *Sentiment,* written by Coward himself and performed with a dance staged by Fred Astaire.

I bounded on [recalled Noël] at the opening performance fully confident that I was going to bring the house down. It certainly wasn't from want of trying that I didn't. I was immaculately dressed in tails, with a silk hat and a cane. I sang every couplet with perfect diction and a wealth of implication which sent them winging out into the dark auditorium, where they fell wetly, like pennies into mud.

Months later, in New York, Coward was to watch Jack Buchanan bringing the house down nightly with precisely the same number. At first, Noël told himself it was because Buchanan appeared so effortless where he had patently been trying as hard as he could; ultimately though he admitted, generously if a little reluctantly, that it was simply because Buchanan's whole revue technique was vastly superior to his own.

But the reviews for *London Calling!* were not all bad, though most critics felt it was a little long and that Noël himself was better at writing sketches than performing them. Two papers offered dubious personal tributes to Noël: one referred to him as the 'most promising amateur in the West End', and the other noted that he was 'unmistakeably talented, though not yet a Jack Hulbert'. Nor indeed was he as well known; a newspaper photograph of Coward that summer in a boat on what looks suspiciously like the lake at Battersea Park was captioned simply 'Gladys Cooper and A Friend'.

One number in *London Calling!* brought in a good deal of welcome publicity for Noël. This was *The Swiss Family Whittlebot*, an accurate if uncharitable send-up of a family of contemporary poets called Hernia, Gob and Sago; predictably a large number of critics thought they recognized a parody of the Sitwells. The result was an irate letter to Noël from Osbert, and the beginning of a bitter feud that only ended some five years later with a curt typewritten note from Edith Sitwell to Noël reading simply 'I accept your apology.'

However, the sketch caused such a furore, and the work of the fictional Hernia Whittlebot became so widely known that Noël was invited to speak her verse from the brand new 2LO Wireless Station; he made his first ever broadcast in a fifteen-minute reading of Miss Whittlebot's poems, sandwiched in between Chamber Music and a talk by the secretary of the Folk Dance Society on *The Sword Dance Through the Ages*. Later Miss Whittlebot herself began to make regular appearances in the gossip columns, to which Noël would feed such information as 'Hernia is busy preparing for publication her new books, *Gilded Sluts* and *Garbage*. She breakfasts on onions and Vichy water.' The strained relations between Coward and the English family Sitwell were not improved by a recital they gave at the Aeolian Hall 'from which', Osbert told Noël, 'you might get a few ideas.' In the middle of it Coward rose ostentatiously to his feet and left the building. The cause of Noël's passionate distaste of Miss Sitwell's free verse is not hard to find; she had abandoned the one thing Coward held most important in all his work, a strict sense of form.

London Calling! settled into the Duke of York's for a lengthy run in spite of the critics and in spite of Osbert Sitwell who just after the opening remarked spitefully that as he was going to be out of town for a few days he would miss the revue altogether. Noël retorted that he would be delighted to put a stage box at Mr Sitwell's disposal to hold Osbert, his sister, brother and all their followers and admirers any time they cared to come. But Noël was currently in a success for the first time in his adult career and although *London Calling!* got very much nastier notices than either *I'll Leave It to You* or *The Young Idea,* it ran a great deal longer. Curiously, within a few weeks of the revue's opening, Charlot decided to remove Gertrude Lawrence as well as the stage manager and a large number of the chorus and put them into André Charlot's *London Revue of 1924* which with three of Noël's original numbers was to open at the Times Square Theatre in New York early in January. Joyce Barbour successfully replaced Miss Lawrence in the London production, but with the rest of the company depleted *London Calling!* began to fall apart at the seams.

Noël rapidly lost interest in the show though the money was still useful, and it did give him the time to write two plays as well as a number with Melville Gideon called *There May Be Days* for the seventh edition of Gideon's *The Co-Optimists.* The two plays were later to emerge as *Fallen Angels* and *The Vortex,* a drama which had its origins, Coward later explained, in a chance meeting:

> A friend of mine was a guards officer, and he had a problem mother, a lady whose lovers were men of her son's age. One evening, I was in a supper club, the Garrick Galleries I think, with my friend when his mother walked in. 'Look over there', someone said, 'at that old hag with the good-looking young man in tow'. I tried to imagine what her son must have been thinking, and the incident gave me the idea for *The Vortex.*

After Christmas, Charlot returned from New York, where Beatrice Lillie and Jack Buchanan had opened his revue with tremendous success, and decided that *London Calling!* could do with a second edition. But by then Noël's six-month contract was up and he took the chance to escape the routine of grinding out a tired revue eight times a week. Now just twenty-four, Noël decided that the time had again arrived for him to try his luck in New York.

Before leaving for America, out of the £250 Noel had saved from *London Calling!,* he rented his mother a cottage at Dockenfield in Surrey where she could again escape the gloom of Ebury Street. This cottage, which cost only forty pounds a year, was discovered by Noël in a thick January fog which led him to believe that it was ideally situated in mid-countryside. In February his mother took possession, whereupon the fog lifted to reveal a large number of semi-detached villas across the road. By this time however, Noël was en route for America.

His visit to New York was partly a holiday, partly a celebration of the fact that he could now afford to spend his time in uptown New York rather than on a park bench in the Battery, and partly an attempt to collaborate with Jerome Kern on a new musical. That the attempt never got off the ground failed to depress Noël unduly, and he spent a few happy weeks hanging around Broadway reviving old contacts until he decided that it was time to go back to London where Gladys Cooper had suggested that she might be interested in doing *Fallen Angels* with Madge Titheradge under her own management at the Playhouse Theatre.

While Noël was in America a revised version of *A Withered Nosegay* called *Terribly Intimate Portraits* brought from the New York reviewers an overwhelming lack of enthusiasm. But one critic at least recognized in Coward something out of the ordinary – Alexander Woollcott, writing in a New York paper about Coward's imminent departure for London:

> It ought to be fairly easy to get up an endurable ship's concert during the next voyage of the Olympic. When she sails on Saturday her passenger list will bristle with such names as D. W. Griffith, Mary Garden, Douglas Fairbanks, Mary Pickford and the like. Then, if the luckless wight on whom pressure is brought to manage the concert is really bright, he will be careful to exhume from his cabin one Noël Coward, a young and sprightly English comedian who wrote the words and music of three of the best numbers in the *Charlot Revue*. Coward seems to have been born into the world just to write songs for Beatrice Lillie…

Noël had a pleasant voyage home basking in the reflected glory of Mary Pickford and Douglas Fairbanks, whose travels were accorded the kind of press coverage achieved in later years only by Elizabeth and Richard Burton. But back in London, Coward went into another period of deep gloom; the weather was horrible, *London Calling!* was still playing in a tired, mechanical routine, and Charlot refused to let Noël put some new life into it. Worse still, Madge Titheradge and Gladys Cooper found that they would never be free at the same time to do *Fallen Angels,* while *The Vortex* was still on an unsuccessful round of managers' offices. Noël fled London and settled into the cottage at Dockenfield outside Farnham, with his mother and an anaemic maid called Iris. There, visited occasionally by his father and Eric, Noël and Mrs Coward led a peaceful life only interrupted when, in the garden one afternoon, Coward remembered Laurette Taylor and his idea for a light comedy based on a week-end in a dotty theatrical household; he completed it within the next three days and called it first *Oranges and Lemons* and then on second thoughts, *Hay Fever.*

At this time Noël was not altogether happy with the play, but he took it to London where he got an appointment to read it to Marie Tempest in the hope that she might play Judith Bliss. In her drawing-room, with Miss Tempest's husband William Graham-Browne dozing quietly in the corner, she listened politely as Noël read the play aloud and then, equally politely, refused to do it. It was, she explained, yet another comedy at a time when she was looking for a drama; there was no emotion in it and though Judith might be a good part for her, the play was too light, too plotless and altogether lacking in any kind of action. All of which was true and did not prevent *Hay Fever,* with Miss Tempest in the lead, running for just 337 performances a year later. But at this time, though she felt that Noël was 'as clever as a bag of monkeys' and admired his perseverance (he in turn felt that 'when she steps on to the stage a certain magic occurs and this magic is in itself unexplainable and belongs only to the very great') she was sure that the play was not right for her, in spite of all that Noël had done to persuade her in his reading; it was Gladys Cooper who later remarked how much she hated having Noël read his own plays aloud to her: 'He makes them seem so much better than they really are.'

Undeterred by Marie Tempest's refusal, Noël added *Hay Fever* to *The Vortex* and *Fallen Angels* on the tour of managerial offices and himself returned to Dockenfield. There he turned out yet another play, a drawing-room drama called *Easy Virtue* which owed a certain amount to the tradition of Pinero and *The Second Mrs Tanqueray* but which was destined to do rather less well than the other three Coward plays hanging fire at this time.

The beginning of summer brought a letter from one manager, H. M. Harwood, expressing at last some interest in *The Vortex*. He said he was considering a production of it at the Ambassadors, provided only that Noël himself would not play Nicky. Noël, who had written the part expressly for himself, not unnaturally refused the offer.

In July, back on the 'extreme poverty among wealthy friends' circuit, Noël accepted an invitation from Ruby Miller to stay with her at Deauville for the rest of the summer. At her villa he met Sir James Dunn, an industrialist who decided at four o'clock one morning that Noël was a genius needing only the patronage that he could provide to the tune of a hundred pounds a month for the next five years in return for twenty per cent of Noël's earnings over that period. The details were to be agreed on their return to London, and would have been but for the fact that Noël returned first and related the scheme to Gladys Calthrop; she disapproved so heartily of the idea, and of Noël committing himself for five years to a 'strange financier', that he was ruled by her and never signed. Almost immediately, Noël's financial situation improved drastically.

In the autumn of 1924 the Everyman Theatre in Hampstead, once a drill hall, then a theatre and now a cinema, was being run by Norman Macdermott as a testing-ground for new plays, some of which went on from there to the West End. As soon as Noël returned from Deauville, Macdermott sent for him, said that he had enjoyed reading both *Hay Fever* and *The Vortex* hugely, and that his only problem was in deciding which should be staged in November at the Everyman.

9

1924–1925

The Vortex was an immediate success and established me both as a playwright and as an actor, which was very fortunate, because until then I had not proved myself to be so hot in either capacity.

T*he Vortex* is a near-melodrama that reaches its climax in a mid-Twenties adaptation of the closet scene from *Hamlet,* with an uneasy mother-son relationship further complicated by the fact that the son takes drugs and that the whole crisis erupts during a stately weekend in the country. It was in many ways a very strong play indeed and would have found little difficulty in winning any contemporary award for the Play of the Year but for one other: 1924 also happened to be the year of Bernard Shaw's *Saint Joan.*

As it was, *The Vortex* succeeded in good company with Shaw; from a production born amid a certain amount of technical and intellectual chaos emerged the success that gave Coward as actor and as playwright his name, his reputation and his future.

Once Norman Macdermott had shown interest in either *Hay Fever* or *The Vortex* for the Everyman at Hampstead, Noël talked him rapidly and firmly into doing *The Vortex* for the obvious reason that it contained a whacking great star role for Noël himself where *Hay Fever* offered nothing of the kind. Persuaded, Macdermott went ahead enthusiastically with *The Vortex* though casting proved something of a problem, mainly because the top salary for acting at the Everyman was five pounds a week. If a play transferred from Hampstead to the West End, actors could hope for more usual salaries; but in the meantime they had to be prepared to work for very little and not everybody was. However, a cast was finally enlisted, with Kate Cutler in the lead as Florence Lancaster and Noël as her addicted son Nicky. Macdermott, though hesitant about it at first, ultimately agreed to the author's demand that the sets and costumes should be left in the hands of a comparative newcomer to the business, Gladys Calthrop:

> It was the first play I had ever designed so I was terribly excited, though there was nowhere to paint the sets except outside the theatre in Hampstead High Street, and the costumes all had to be made in a kind of basement there.

But with the sets under way, all the contracts signed and rehearsals due to start in four days, Macdermott asked to see Noël in his office. From here on, the story of the first production of *The Vortex* takes on most of the qualities of the backstage sagas perpetrated by Hollywood in the Thirties, the only differences being that this was for real and that the end-product was vastly superior. The Everyman, Macdermott announced, was on the verge of bankruptcy and unless Noël could find a backer in the brief time available, *The Vortex* would not after all see the light of day.

Noël was faced with the need to raise capital in less than a week; not, this time, a small personal loan to get him through a bad month, but instead the comparatively vast sum of two hundred pounds. Ned Lathom, Coward's first thought, had already been over-generous in the past and to ask him again for money would be unthinkable. Few others, though, were enthusiastic enough about the theatre in general or Noël in particular to back *The Vortex* to that extent. Luckily for Coward, he found one of them; not exactly a friend, more of an acquaintance, but a young Armenian novelist called Dikran Kouyoumdjian who had recently been in the same penniless situation until his success earlier in the year with a best-seller called *The Green Hat* and the altered name of Michael Arlen. Over lunch at the Ritz, without asking any questions or setting any terms for repayment or even wanting to read the play, Arlen wrote Noël a cheque for two hundred and fifty pounds and went on recounting the plot of his new short story. Rehearsals of *The Vortex* went ahead as planned, for about two more weeks. Then Kate Cutler, putting an abrupt end to the friendship with Noël that dated back to the days of *I'll Leave It to You,* announced that the part of Florence (though written with her in mind) was not after all satisfactory and that, with the first night less than a week away, she would be leaving the company.

Her motives for walking out, and for bringing *The Vortex* to the verge of another ignominious halt, have never been entirely clear, and in retrospect from Miss Cutler's point of view it must be considered one of the great mistakes of her career. On the other hand one suspects that what worried her at the time was not so much her own part, which after all she had agreed to play some weeks earlier and remained now virtually unchanged, but rather Noël's which during rehearsal had changed considerably. This was particularly apparent in the last act, the confrontation between mother and son on which the rest of the play depended; during the second interval *The Vortex* undergoes a swift change from comedy to tragedy, and to make this viable Noël realized in rehearsal that his own part in Act Three would have to be greatly enlarged. Miss Cutler was not pleased at the prospect of sharing the dramatic highlights of the last act with the author, and perhaps for this reason above all others she left. Noël's position must have been a tricky one; as actor and as author he stood to gain a great deal by the changes in the last act, but as actor and as author he also stood to lose the entire play by the departure of Miss Cutler.

Nor was the quarrel made any easier by Noël's belief that, as an author, he was motivated by the best literary intentions while Miss Cutler held that, as an actor, he was simply trying to get himself a better part. To have given in to her, and to have reverted to the last act as originally written, would have been the easy way out; Noël chose the difficult one and began looking for a middle-aged actress who could take on a difficult and possibly unrewarding part with under a week's rehearsal.

Any actress even remotely suitable for the part was, understandably enough, unavailable at such short notice; it became within a few hours a search for someone available rather than someone suitable and on this basis Lilian Braithwaite was approached. It was, on the face of it, casting bizarre and possibly disastrous. Miss Braithwaite was a tall, dark grande dame of the theatre accustomed to presiding over gracious tea-party scenes in comedies at the Haymarket; Florence Lancaster was a small, fair, flamboyant neurotic. Unmoved by these considerations or indeed any others, Noël and Gladys Calthrop hastened round to Miss Braithwaite's flat in Pelham Crescent the morning after Kate Cutler's ultimatum, to read her *The Vortex*. She liked the play, and saw the challenge of the part; her career at this moment in time was not all that it might have been, and though she was about to accept a large salary for playing a small part in *Orange Blossoms* she had not actually signed the contract. She agreed, therefore, to take the risk of a fortnight in Hampstead with *The Vortex* provided only that Noël would return to Kate Cutler and give her one last chance to change her mind about giving up the role.

Noël, who had by this time decided that risk or not he would rather have Lilian than Kate Cutler for the part anyway, went back to Miss Cutler's flat where he blithely allowed her to talk herself irrevocably out of one of the best opportunities of her career, noticing in himself only the very slightest twinges of guilt.

Macdermott, who had been away for the week-end and had therefore missed all this, returned to his theatre on the Monday morning to find Miss Braithwaite in full rehearsal having already learnt most of the part. He was not pleased, partly because he felt her to be suicidal casting and mainly because he had not been consulted in the first place. He threatened to abandon the production entirely, until reminded by Noël that as the costs were now being met by Michael Arlen's cheque the production was no longer his to abandon. He was still nominally the director, but by this time the production was firmly in Noël's hands which, one suspects, was precisely the way Coward had wanted it all along. Macdermott suffered one further defeat when he attempted to take programme credit for Gladys Calthrop's Act Two setting, to which he had contributed one sole fireplace. Forced by Noël and Gladys to remove his name from this part of the programme, Macdermott also removed his fireplace from the set, leaving a nasty hole upstage on the first night.

The last week of rehearsal, in a November so icy that even driving up to Hampstead proved difficult, consisted exclusively of hard work and deep depression, though Miss Braithwaite proved a tower of strength while all collapsed around her; a further cast change had been forced when Helen Spencer developed diphtheria and had to be replaced at the last minute by Mollie Kerr as the young flapper. In the midst of all this theatrical hell the then Lord Chamberlain, Lord Cromer, decided that the play's theme was far too unpleasant for him to grant it a licence; though whether it was Florence's nymphomania, Nicky's drug-addiction or the son's passionate devotion to his mother that caused such alarm is not evident. But His Lordship was ultimately persuaded, by Noël, on the morning of the first night, that so far from being unpleasant *The Vortex* was in fact designed as a moral tract of the highest order, and on that understanding it was licensed for public performance. In his determination to get the play a licence, Coward had threatened to serialize the script in a national paper and let the public judge its moral suitability.

The day of the final dress rehearsal was endless and gloomy, enlivened only by the theatre cat excreting on stage centre during a run-through of the second act. That night the play was watched in absolute silence by two people: the journalist George Bishop and Miss Braithwaite's daughter, the actress Joyce Carey:

> It was shattering… I'd never seen anything like it on the stage in my life, and the last act left one literally shaking with excitement – both my mother and Noël were fantastically good. I was never encouraged to give my opinions (at least not by my mother) but afterwards I went backstage and found them huddled round a stove like Russian emigrés looking terribly moody, so I had to say how marvellous I thought it was and how I was sure that it would be the most tremendous success. My mother and Noël, I remember, both looked thoroughly surprised but they did cheer up a bit after that…

The first night, as Miss Carey had predicted, was nothing short of a triumph. Lilian's performance was steady as a rock and Noël, who had spent the whole day on his hands and knees with Gladys and the stage manager finishing off the set, got away with a nerve-strung histrionic tour de force that in later weeks he was able to refine and discipline into a more subdued but perhaps no more effective reading of the part.

Until then, by virtue of being his own director, he had not found time to do much about his acting. But the tension of his performance on the opening night at the Everyman was increased by the fact that in sweeping a collection of bottles from a dressing-table in the last act he managed to cut his wrist quite badly, which then bled effectively throughout his curtain speech. Blood, like children and dogs, could usually be relied on as an applause-raiser though on this occasion the play would unquestionably have survived without it.

Beyond doubt *The Vortex* came as a severe shock to its fashionable first-night house ('among the audience in this intriguing and barnlike little theatre were Lady Curzon, looking lovelier than ever, Michael Arlen, Lady Louis Mountbatten with Captain Mackintosh and Captain Dawson, Mr Eddie Marsh, Lady Carisbrooke, the Cochrans, Lord Lathom and all the regular theatrical enthusiasts of le beau monde'), precisely the kind of audience who presumably spent their weekends at country house-parties like that established in the first act. They had made the perilous journey to Hampstead, and a number of columns the following morning carried sharp footnotes describing the dangers of London Transport, on the strength of Noël's reputation as a writer of light comedy. But here, instead of another comedy, was a play of his about drug-addiction at a time when alcoholism was scarcely mentioned on the stage; it came as considerably more of a surprise to that audience, than would the curses of Jimmy Porter before another one on the theatrical outskirts of London almost thirty years later.

Now, in cold print, Nicky's outburst against his mother and the depraved world around her has echoes of the hilarity of Bea Lillie's 'Maud, You're Rotten to the Core'; but on the stage in 1924, its message, without even a backward glance at Pinero, came over as original and very startling indeed. 'If I had written that,' said Michael Arlen, going back-stage after the first night, 'I should have been so very proud.'

In fact *The Vortex* is a curious and sometimes uneasy mixture of the nineteenth and twentieth centuries; its form and its content are not always in perfect harmony. At the time of its first production, critics recognized a kind of fashionable depravity in Nicky's drug-taking and in the social gossip about the private lives of the week-end house-party set, to which it was widely believed that Noël already belonged. But it was left to St John Ervine alone among the original reviewers to realize that *The Vortex* is a very moral play, dedicated to the old-fashioned virtues of hard work and clean living, by which most of the characters are judged and found wanting. Here as in so many later plays from *Post-Mortem* to *Suite in Three Keys* Coward is concerned with standards – with what is done and what is not done in the best moral code of values; one is made constantly aware of the dignities of life, and of how these are being abused. 'It doesn't matter about death', Nicky tells his mother at the end of Act Three, 'but it matters terribly about life' – and, by implication, about the way we choose to live it.

But with the melodrama of this final confrontation still to come, the first act of *The Vortex* is misleading to say the least; it gives the impression that here is a precious, fairly innocuous comedy not far removed in style or content from the light, well-made pattern of *The Young Idea*. *The Vortex*, however, takes a turn for the better at roughly the same moment that its leading character takes a turn for the worse, and from then on reviewers looking for a point of reference were forced to turn to Maugham's savage *Our Betters*, seen in London a year before, rather than to the earlier and flimsier work of Coward himself.

In fact, there was now a feeling (shared by Lilian and Noël himself as well as most critics) that the wunderkind had come up with some-thing solid for the first time, a play that would ensure him success as a dramatist more lasting than the brittle and rather precarious social triumphs of the earlier comedies.

Enthusiastic reviews and a public titillated by the murmur of something faintly immoral assured for *The Vortex* a rapid transfer to the West End. Eight managers went to Hampstead to bid for it, reviving as they did so the old argument for a try-out theatre like the Everyman (which had also staged *Outward Bound* for the first time) to be given some kind of financial security as a form of insurance for playwrights and managers alike. In the event, *The Vortex* left Hampstead at the beginning of December after only twelve performances; a few days later, under the management of Limpus and Kenyon which had made Noël the most attractive offer, it opened at the Royalty Theatre to run there and subsequently at the Comedy and Little Theatres for a total of 224 West End performances. Superficially the resemblance between Noël and Nicky Lancaster was too great for Noël ever to escape the 'well-groomed, witty and decadent' label of the neurotic misfit that he had created for his play. But to have argued with all the publicity would have been ludicrous. If that was the picture of him Fleet Street wanted to purvey, then Noël was only too happy to go along with it; the results at the box-office were tangible, and he was astute enough to realize that the truth about him might prove a great deal less interesting to the public at large. At a time when the advertising industry was in its infancy and television had yet to be developed, his was an early example of the image becoming the reality.

On Coward's home life the effect of *The Vortex* was electric:

With this success came many pleasurable trappings. A car. New suits. Silk shirts. An extravagant amount of pyjamas and dressing-gowns, and a still more extravagant amount of publicity. I was photographed, and interviewed, and photographed again. In the street. In the park. In my dressing-room. At my piano. With my dear old mother, without my dear old mother – and, on one occasion, sitting up in an over-elaborate bed looking like a heavily doped Chinese Illusionist. This last photograph, I believe, did me a good deal of harm. People glancing at it concluded at once, and with a certain justification, that I was undoubtedly a weedy sensualist in the last stages of physical and moral degeneration, and that they had better hurry off to see me in my play before my inevitable demise placed that faintly macabre pleasure beyond their reach. This attitude, while temporarily very good for business, became irritating after a time, and for many years I was seldom mentioned in the Press without allusions to cocktails, post-war hysteria, and decadence.

The first night of *The Vortex* at the Royalty was December 16th 1924. Noël's twenty-fifth birthday; at the end Noël made a restrained, tactful curtain speech hoping that the West End would enjoy the play as much as had audiences up at the Everyman. They did, and the critics were again enthusiastic in the main, though Basil Macdonald Hastings for the *Daily Express* felt that it was a 'dustbin of a play'; James Agate, in the *Sunday Times,* after a good deal of praise ended rather sharply: 'The third act is too long, there is too much piano playing in the second, and ladies do not exhale cigarette smoke through the nose.' Still, the majority view was that of Ivor Brown who wrote that 'as actor and as author', Coward 'drives at reality.' Noël was again acclaimed, by critics though not necessarily the gentlemen themselves, as the new Sacha Guitry and/or Somerset Maugham.

The play also included for the first time, in the role of Helen, a worldly-wise friend to Florence, the character who reappears in different guises in most of Coward's post-*Vortex* plays as a kind of chorus; sometimes it is a man, and if so usually an author, sometimes a woman, but in either case planted there to watch the action from the sidelines and to utter the thoughts that come closest to the playwright's own detached and often cynical view of whatever the situation happens to be.

With the success of *The Vortex,* which was published soon after its West End opening and dedicated 'to Gladys Calthrop with a good deal of gratitude', Noël was everywhere in demand; not least by the *Evening News,* a paper mentioned by one of the characters in the play and which soon afterwards commissioned Noël to write for them on 'The Young Playwright's Problem'. Reading his article now it is something of a shock to find that Coward wrote it in much the same terms as those of his critics who, thirty years later, were to blame him vitriolically for perpetrating drawing-room comedies at the expense of progress towards realism in the theatre:

> Looking at the various difficulties that confront the modern dramatist, perhaps the most disheartening is the desire of the British public to be amused and not enlightened. The problem arises: is the theatre to be a medium of expression setting forth various aspects of reality, or merely a place of relaxation where weary business men and women can witness a pleasing spectacle bearing no relation whatever to the hard facts of existence, and demanding no effort of concentration?
>
> Those men are the lasting hope of the theatre who, placing the public intelligence at its highest, express accordingly their genuine convictions, and present the very real problems of life in dramatic surroundings.

One man who disagreed violently with Noël's desire at that time to portray 'reality' on the stage was Sir Gerald du Maurier, who was already alarmed by new trends in the theatre and saw in Noël's generation a challenge to his own supremacy. Soon after the opening of *The Vortex,* he published a scathing attack on contemporary stage morals:

> The public are asking for filth... the younger generation are knocking at the door of the dustbin... if life is worse than the stage, should the stage hold the mirror up to such distorted nature? If so, where shall we be – without reticence or reverence?

Much later in his life it is clear that Noël would have agreed with Sir Gerald wholeheartedly – indeed, he was to write a series of articles for the *Sunday Times* along markedly similar lines in 1961. But in 1925 Coward, together with Arnold Bennett and Edward Knoblock, leapt to the defence of the 'new drama'. Noël's reply to Sir Gerald was published by the *Daily Express:*

> Sir Gerald du Maurier, having – if he will forgive me saying so – enthusiastically showered the English stage with second-rate drama for many years, now rises up with incredible violence and has a nice slap all round at the earnest and perspiring young dramatists.
>
> This is awful; it is also a little unwise. Art demands reverence much more than life does – and Sir Gerald's reverence so far seems to have been entirely devoted to the box-office.
>
> To say that this age is degenerate and decadent is supremely ridiculous – it is no more degenerate and decadent than any other age; the only difference is that the usual conglomeration of human vices have come to the surface a little more since the war, and there is mercifully a little less hypocrisy about.
>
> Speaking for myself I should like to say that I intend to write as honestly and sincerely as possible on any subject that I choose, and if the public do not like it they need not pay to come and see it. Theatre-going, when all is said and done, is optional.
>
> When the self-advertising denouncers of the stage describe the English theatre as being 'in a disgraceful state', they speak a bitter truth without being aware of it – for a theatre-going public which cheerfully tolerates such false and nauseating sentimentality as has been handed out to them recently can hardly be acclaimed as judges of what is right or wrong, moral or immoral, in the theatre or out of it.

The success of *The Vortex* separated firmly and for about a quarter of a century Noël's public persona from the reality of his private life. To the press, since it was right for his *Vortex* image and was having a decidedly good effect at the box-office, Coward let it be known that he was a pampered, dilettante, casual playwright prone to knocking off a play like *The Vortex* in a few days and then lucky enough to get it put on in London. The truth, that he was a hard-working and dedicated playwright who had persevered with his plays over a long period of time uninterrupted by anything so chancy as luck, was of little interest to interviewers in search of lively copy, and was therefore suppressed by Noël who at that time was nothing if not obliging where journalists were concerned:

> I was wide open to them all, smiling and burbling bright witticisms, giving my views on this and that, discussing such problems as whether or not the modern girl would make a good mother or what I thought of current books and plays.

There seems to have been little doubt that *The Vortex* had already begun to change the climate of the London theatre from the whimsicality of Barrie to the hard-hearted cynicism of Lonsdale; there were, however, a few dissenting voices, in particular those of a critic who noted in *The Graphic* that 'the fault, dear Noël, lies not in our Ma's but in ourselves that we are slaves to dope', and of Hannen Swaffer who began long years of published attacks on Coward with a full page article for *The People*. In the course of this, Mr Swaffer deprecated the 'most decadent plays of our time', regretted that Coward's 'most promising of upbringings should have ended in this demi-mondaine disaster', and added, sorrowfully if a trifle inconsequentially, that 'this is not the sort of play you would like intelligent Indians to see.'

Elsewhere though it was generally accepted that *The Vortex* was beyond all others the play which typified the less attractive characteristics of the mid-Twenties; it also achieved a footnote in the history of the London theatre as the first major production in which the cast took curtain calls only at the end of the play and not between each act.

A profile of Noël at this time, combining moments of perception with a rather trusting repetition of the impression that he wished to convey came from the pen of Hesketh Pearson:

> Like Wilde, Noël Coward has a good deal of the showman in him... it takes the form of charm, plus excessive volubility. He is 'charming' to everybody, and as a consequence he has a host of admirers. Also no one who can entertain folk with an endless stream of persiflage is ever likely to want for company, and Noël's life is almost passed in a prolonged procession through applauding parties.

With *The Vortex* settled in to a long London run, Noël lent his musical talent to a couple of charity matinées and then started work almost at once on a number of new projects, among them the commission to write silent-screen titles for some films then being made by Michael Balcon at Gainsborough Studios. Difficult though it is to assign precise authorship to these, it is believed that one of Noël's titles, introducing an evil Count in an Ivor Novello–Isabel Jeans opus called *Return of the Rat* read:

THE COUNT, A MAN OF MORE CASH THAN
CONSEQUENCE, WHO KEPT HIS HEART IN
HIS TROUSER POCKET ALONG WITH HIS
OTHER SMALL CHANGE.

But film titles were not the full extent of Noël's literary occupations at this time. He also started to work on a revue, *On with the Dance,* which marked the beginning of a partnership with the impresario Charles B. Cochran that was to last for the next nine years. Coward wanted the authorship of the whole revue to be in his own hands; Cochran, uncertain still about Noël's musical gift, agreed that he should do the book and lyrics but gave the music to Philip Braham who had written some of the numbers for *London Calling!* In the event Noël so contrived the book that most of the music led directly into or out of his sketches, and therefore, had to be his own, allowing the long-suffering Mr Braham only three self-contained contributions. The revue starred Alice Delysia, supported by Douglas Byng and Hermione Baddeley; they were due to open at the Palace in Manchester on March 17th 1925, just three months after *The Vortex* transferred to the Royalty. Of the many Coward numbers in the show, one particular sextet in the revue seems to have been inspired by Noël's memories of his childhood at the Chapel Royal School; it began 'We're six dirty little choirboys, with really frightful minds…'

Rehearsals for *On with the Dance,* as so often for a Cochran revue, were held at the Poland Rooms in Soho and Coward kept a careful eye on them between performances of *The Vortex.* Apart from his and Braham's numbers there were also two brief ballets in the revue staged by Diaghilev's choreographer, Leonide Massine. One of these, 'Crescendo', was a modernistic interlude in which Massine and his puppet-like dancers 'jig to the tune of cocktails and jazz until, willynilly, they are swept up to a frenzied climax of impressionistic movement and it seems to have found its echo in the 'Twentieth Century Blues' sequence that ended Coward's *Calvalcade* five years later.

To be in Manchester for the opening of *On with the Dance* Noël took two nights off from *The Vortex;* he left the part of Nicky, after one rehearsal, in the hands of his understudy, a young, nervous but enthusiastic actor by the name of John Gielgud who had until recently been in repertory at Oxford. Prior to *The Vortex* Gielgud had first met Noël with Betty Chester at a party near his home in South Kensington, where he found Coward 'dreadfully precocious and rather too keen to show off at the piano.' Later, seeing *The Vortex* for the first time, Gielgud found himself bowled over by it, and was delighted when Noël interviewed him at the theatre and gave him the chance to understudy. But he had not expected to be thrown into the part quite so soon:

There are few occasions more nerve-racking than playing a leading part in the absence of a principal. Before I went on that evening, some kind person knocked at my door to tell me that several people had asked for their money back because they saw the notice posted at the box-office announcing that Noël was not appearing. But audiences are extraordinarily fair and well-disposed towards young understudies, especially if the play is an interesting one, and at the end of the evening the applause was just as warm as it had been on other nights…

Meanwhile in Manchester all was not going so smoothly; on his arrival there Noël discovered that his name was nowhere to be found on the hoarding above the theatre. Instead, in huge neon letters were the words 'Charles B. Cochran's Revue' which, considering that Noël had written three-quarters of the score, all the lyrics, all of the book, and directed the sketches as well as some of the numbers, seemed to him a slight overstatement of Cochran's involvement. Worse was to come; Cochran had also decided that in view of the show's inordinate length (the dress-rehearsal lasted just twenty-seven hours) the 'Poor Little Rich Girl' number would have to go. In the course of an irate confrontation in the Midland Hotel, throughout which Cochran remained draped solely in a bath towel and dripping wet, Coward managed to get his billing improved and, more important, to ensure the survival of 'Poor Little Rich Girl' which became the revue's only lasting memory unless of course one counts the existential vision of Douglas Byng and Ernest Thesiger as two old ladies going to bed in a Bloomsbury boarding-house. 'Poor Little Rich Girl', three verses and a refrain of rather moralistic advice, originally sung to Hermione Baddeley by Delysia, was played for the next forty years in most of the palm courts and on almost all the piers our coastlines possess; it also became a permanent part of Noël's piano repertoire. The song already showed signs of the clipped, economical phrasing that was to become the hallmark of so many of Coward's later compositions, and it managed to set to music the essence of the warning that he was nightly passing on to his stage mother in *The Vortex:*

Poor little rich girl,
You're a bewitched girl.
Better beware!
Laughing at danger,
Virtue a stranger,
Better take care!
The life you lead sets all your nerves a-jangle,
Your love affairs are in a hopeless tangle,
Though you're a child, dear,
Your life's a wild typhoon.

In lives of leisure
The craze for pleasure
Steadily grows.
Cocktails and laughter,
But what comes after?
Nobody knows…

For that song, as for 'A Room with a View', 'Mad Dogs and Englishmen', 'Someday I'll Find You', 'Mrs Worthington', and 'I'll See You Again', the royalties always arrived in rather larger cheques than for any of the other 281 that Coward later published.

Further down the cast-list for *On with the Dance,* playing assorted waiters and passers-by, was a young actor who years later turned impresario and presented Noël in a cabaret season at the Café de Paris, Donald Neville-Willing:

> Noël at the time of *On with the Dance* was very cryptic; he would look at us through those half-closed eyes and one never quite knew what he was thinking, though I suspected it was nothing very favourable where most of us actors were concerned… One realized that there was something different about Noël; he knew precisely what he wanted, and was ruthless about getting it where the show was concerned. He was also a tremendous leader, in that we all tried to follow the way he dressed and talked because we knew it was fashionable. He was a very old young man: important and powerful but fantastically kind in private. In the show one always worked for him, not the audience. His approval was all that mattered. Though he was our age, he knew it all; he was the first of the bright young things…

It was originally planned to open *On with the Dance* on the Monday night in Manchester; in the event, the dress-rehearsal ran from Monday morning until a few hours before the curtain went up on Tuesday, when the show opened to rapturous if unexpected acclaim.

Already the theatrical name of the season, Coward was now fêted accordingly: to say that all this success did not change him would be the oldest cliché in theatrical journalism, and at least partially untrue. But if ever a man was ready and prepared for success it was Noël; so far from it catching him unawares he had been conscious of his own talent since his days as a child actor, and in his view it had always been only a question of time before critics and audience alike endorsed that talent, which now, vehemently, they did. He had become a celebrity and what he enjoyed about it above all else was that it allowed him to indulge his passion for meeting other celebrities; membership of the Pen Club brought him into contact with Galsworthy, Wells and Arnold Bennett, and he was to be found at most of the literary gatherings which were then as much a feature of Bloomsbury as of Hampstead. Arriving at one of these, dressed in a suit and straight from the theatre, he discovered that everyone else present was in evening dress. Noël held up his hands for silence: 'Now,' he announced magnanimously, 'I don't want anyone to feel embarrassed.' But because of a penetrating gift for confident though curiously not often cocky self-appraisal, success did not change Noël beyond all recognition; it merely confirmed what in him had been tentative, allowed him more freedom in what he said and in where he went, and above all released him and his family from the need to wonder ever again where the money would come from. The confidence remained unchanged, but now there was something tangible to justify it.

10

1925

Success took me to her bosom like a maternal boa constrictor.

If Noël himself didn't change unrecognizably after *The Vortex,* people and places around him did; success altered the face of London for him. At home, he found the small room at the top of the lodging-house in Ebury Street could no longer contain him and the friends he now entertained; thus he moved to a larger room on the floor below and for some years to come, until he moved out altogether, it was true to say that as he moved up in the world he moved down in his mother's house, so that ultimately he was occupying the whole of the first floor.

Away from home he persevered with the parties and the rich social life of London in the mid-Twenties, but now there was one vital difference: he was there in his own right, as a celebrity, and no longer a vaguely disliked hanger-on. His immediate friends now included most of the young actors and writers in the English theatre, and Noël himself indulged a passion for celebrities which until the end of his life never left him. After the show at night his life centred on the Fifty-Fifty Club, then run by Constance Collier and Ivor Novello as a kind of licensed green-room; their idea had been to provide somewhere cheap for actors to meet and drink after their shows, but it soon became so fashionable that the actors themselves found it hard to prise the tables away from countless celebrity-spotters. Ultimately Novello reserved a corner table for his own especial friends and there, night after night, Noël would sit asking Constance Collier to tell him stories about the theatre of her youth. Before *The Vortex* she remembered him being 'a little bitter, as if aware that he had a much better brain than many of his more successful contemporaries.' But with his own success, she said, he became gradually more gentle: 'It made him kinder, more sympathetic.' By now Gladys Calthrop and, when he was in England, Jeffery Amherst were Noël's constant companions, as was Lorn Loraine who had worked for Meggie Albanesi until her death and then, during *The Vortex,* become Coward's personal secretary; another close friend in these years continued to be Betty Chester of the 'Co-Optimists'. She and Noël were remembered by Joyce Carey as 'continually together and very noisy indeed, particularly in restaurants.'

One friend, though, had by now disappeared almost entirely from Noël's life: Esmé Wynne-Tyson. The days of their close companionship were at an end.

This was not so much because of her marriage to Lynden, of whom Noël approved thoroughly, but rather because of her developing interest in Christian Science which gradually became the ruling factor in Esmé's life. Noël couldn't cope with this at all; told on one occasion by Esmé that there was really no such thing as pain, he is said to have stuck a pin into a friend's behind and, as he let out a piercing howl, to have asked Esmé how she explained that then.

On the principle that success breeds other successes, once *The Vortex* was an established hit both *Hay Fever* and *Fallen Angels,* which had previously been turned down by almost every management in London, went into rapid production; by June of 1925 Noël had all three and *On with the Dance* running simultaneously in the West End.

1925 was a good year not only for Coward but for the London theatre in general: Sean O'Casey made his name in England with *Juno and the Paycock,* Lonsdale offered *The Last of Mrs Cheney* and John Barrymore played *Hamlet* at the Haymarket. On the musical front *Rose Marie* opened at Drury Lane a week after *No, No, Nanette* at the Palace, while at the Empire Leicester Square, Sybil Thorndike and Lewis Casson staged a production of *Henry VIII* in which the Second Serving-man was played by Laurence Olivier.

Fallen Angels, which went into rehearsal during April, had lain idle since the plans for it to be played by Gladys Cooper and Madge Titheradge collapsed almost a year earlier. As a play it has always seemed a faintly unsatisfactory affair, perhaps because it is constructed as a vehicle for two stars on whom the whole thing depends; the second act is almost exclusively a dialogue for their two voices, while the first and third seem in a curious way to have been tacked on in order to expand into a full-length play what is essentially a revue sketch about two respectable middle-class ladies getting progressively drunker while they wait for the return of an old and common flame. The parts, in this case, are better than the play.

Edna Best and Margaret Bannerman were originally cast as Jane and Julia, the angels of the title, but during rehearsals Miss Bannerman gave way to a nervous breakdown and had to be replaced just four days before the opening night by Tallulah Bankhead.

Yet nothing in those somewhat fraught rehearsals or in the play's reception on the first night prepared either author or cast for the moral indignation and fury of most reviews the following morning. For though in retrospect *Fallen Angels* marks a return from the near-melodrama of *The Vortex* to the stream of light comedies that ran through Coward s work from *I'll Leave It to You* to *Nude with Violin* some thirty-six years later, it happened to come in the midst of the 1925 row over 'sex plays' to which du Maurier had already added the weight of his disapproval. In this climate of almost hysterical morality, *Fallen Angels* was deplored not as a bad or even an unfunny play, which would have been a tenable if uncharitable view, but rather as 'degenerate', 'vile', 'obscene', 'shocking', 'vulgar' and 'nauseating'.

The admission that both Jane and Julia had a pre-marital affair with the same man was leapt upon as conclusive proof that Noël had this time ventured too far into the realms of degradation. Drugs yes, sex no, seems to have been the general critical opinion with regard to Coward; and one gathers it was the prospect of ladies getting drunk (and upper-middle-class ladies at that) which visited upon him the wrath of Hannen Swaffer among many other critics.

The following Sunday, James Agate provided a less heated appraisal of Coward at this point in his career:

> Mr Coward is a very young playwright of quite extraordinary gifts who at the moment can no more be trusted with his talent for playwriting than a schoolboy can be trusted who has stolen a piece of chalk and encounters a providentially blank wall… he is too rapid, his tongue is too constantly in his cheek, and the circle of his characters is not wide enough.

In the *Evening Standard* a few days after *Fallen Angels* opened, Noël told a reporter:

> I may say I really have a frightfully depraved mind. I am never out of opium dens, cocaine dens and other evil places. My mind is a mass of corruption.

Lest there should be any lingering doubt in readers' minds, the interview was headed 'Author Jokes'.

Though the box-office takings for *Fallen Angels* were excellent as a result of all this publicity, opposition to the play persisted right up to the last performance when a Mrs Hornibrook, late of the London Council for the Promotion of Public Morality, rose from her seat at the end of the second act to deplore the sordidness of the whole affair. The orchestra rapidly drowned her out with a rendering of 'I Want to Be Happy', though not before Mrs Hornibrook had given it as her opinion that the work of Mr Eugene O'Neill was also undesirable, and that London playgoers did not go to see plays with 'sordidness, immorality and sexuality as their theme.'

Coward himself answered his critics in a wide-ranging, almost Shavian preface to three of his plays:

> I certainly deny very firmly the imputation (made by several) that I wrote *Fallen Angels* in order to be 'daring' and 'shocking'. Neither of these exceedingly second-rate ambitions has ever occurred to me.

He then proceeded to defend the free discussion of sex in the theatre:

> Rocks are infinitely more dangerous when they are submerged, and the sluggish waves of false sentiment and hypocrisy have been washing over reality far too long already in the art of this country. Sex being the most

important factor of human nature is naturally, and always will be, the fundamental root of good drama, and the well-meaning but slightly muddled zealots who are trying to banish sex from the stage will find on calmer reflection that they are bumptiously attempting a volte-face which could only successfully be achieved by the Almighty...

From that Coward moved to more general thoughts about the shape of the English theatre in 1925:

The actual cause of the very definite decline of our drama is that at least ninety per cent of the people at present concerned in it are mentally incapable of regarding it as art at all. I think, perhaps, that the public are still suffering from the complacent after-effects of winning the War, and have not yet regained the little discrimination they had a few years ago, otherwise they would not accept so cheerfully the somewhat tawdry efforts of our commercial managers to amuse them. One cannot, of course, blame the managers; they have their living to make and their wives and mistresses to support, but it certainly is regrettable that these noble and natural aspirations should be achieved so easily and at the cost of so little intellectual endeavour.

All of which can hardly have endeared Coward to the gentlemen in offices above Shaftesbury Avenue.

Just a week after the opening of *Fallen Angels* in London, Cochran brought *On with the Dance* into the Pavilion on Piccadilly Circus where, under his banner, it ran for 229 performances. For the first night, stalls were boosted to an unthinkable twenty-seven shillings, and the queue for standing-room started at five in the morning. Herbert Farjeon reviewing for *The Sphere* found space to worry about Coward:

When you consider his present output compared with the output of other writers for the theatre; and when you consider that he's also acting six nights a week and two afternoons; and when you consider, moreover, that in addition to all this he has his own public life to live, and lives it – well, you begin to realize that something is likely to get a little skimped now and then. It must be hard work throwing off a couple of lyrics before breakfast, setting them to music by eleven o'clock, finishing the big scene in Act II before dashing off to The Ivy Restaurant, appearing in a matinée, talking business with Mr Curtis Brown between Acts I and II and letting off gas to an interviewer between Acts II and III, sketching a new revue and practising the latest step before the evening performance, gathering copy and declaring that everything is just too marvellous or just too shattering at the Midnight Follies or the Gargoyle; as I say, it must be hard work, and I hope that Mr Coward will not suffer from a nervous breakdown as the result of it.

The breakdown forecast or at least feared by Farjeon came fifteen months later; in the meantime Noël was heavily photographed, notably by the glossy weeklies above such captions as 'Most versatile writer' and 'Best-known man of his generation'. One published a hilarious picture of him having breakfast in a rococo bed and talking animatedly on the telephone at the same time, wearing a dressing-gown apparently made out of material rejected by a bad tour of *The Mikado*.

With *On with the Dance, Fallen Angels* and *The Vortex* running simultaneously throughout the spring, Noël was still not too busy to bring out a further slim volume of poems by Hernia Whittlebot, the elaborate Sitwell parody which showed as yet no signs of palling.

By now *The Vortex* had made its final move, from the Comedy to the Little Theatre where Noël had first appeared on the stage in *The Goldfish* fourteen years earlier. His hatred of long runs was beginning to tell, and with business declining, the play drifted on into the boredom of daily repetition enlivened only by Seymour Hicks who stood on his seat cheering wildly after one matinée, by Bernard Shaw who left the theatre murmuring 'wonderful, damnable', and later by Madge Titheradge who was so moved by the whole affair that she fainted in Lilian Braithwaite's dressing-room afterwards. As Farjeon had suggested, Noël's social life (which consisted of nightly dinners at The Ivy and appearances at nightclubs dancing impeccably with Betty Chester or Gertrude Lawrence) as well as his other commitments in and around the theatre now took up so much of his life that he barely managed to arrive at *The Vortex* on time. John Gielgud, then still his understudy, used to stand at the stage door, looking down the street with a stick of make-up in his hand, ready to rush off to Coward's dressing-room and make up if he should fail to appear. But Noël never did.

Before the run of *The Vortex* ended in June, Charles Kenyon, who was then in management with Alban Limpus and looking for a vehicle that would suit Marie Tempest, remembered *Hay Fever,* the play that had almost been produced at Hampstead instead of *The Vortex*. He approached Coward, who pointed out that though *Hay Fever* had indeed been written with Miss Tempest in mind, she had turned it down a year before. 'I think', replied Kenyon, 'that she will like it now.' Influenced perhaps by the successes that Noël had achieved in the meantime, Miss Tempest decided a few days later that she would be happy to appear as Judith Bliss in *Hay Fever* at the Ambassadors Theatre, provided only that Noël himself would direct.

The prospect appalled Noël, as she was reputed to be a daunting lady not tremendously fond of directors telling her how to act. In the event, he need not have worried; early in rehearsals Miss Tempest summoned him on to the stage and announced that as Noël had written one particularly difficult scene the very least he could do would be to show her how to play it. This he did, and the two of them got along very well from then onwards; she later wrote of Noël in her diary: 'he is the most stimulating and exciting personality that has come into my life in the last ten years.'

Hay Fever (a meaningless title substituted at the last minute for *Oranges and Lemons* when a short story of that name was published in 1925) is a comedy of bad manners which starts with the arrival of four guests, invited independently by different members of the Bliss family for a week-end at a country house near Maidenhead. In a Twenties version of Albee's memorable parlour game *Get the Guests*, the visitors are then alternately ignored, embraced, embarrassed, humiliated and ultimately abandoned to slink away by themselves during a blazing family row, a curtain device echoed later by the end of *Private Lives*. As a play it offers some characteristic examples of Coward's wit: 'She goes about using Sex as a sort of shrimping-net', and 'You should wash, darling – really it's so bad for your skin to leave things lying about on it.'

It has been the mistake of countless amateurs and innumerable local theatres to assume that because *Hay Fever* is a comedy with few characters in one set it must therefore also be easy to perform. Coward himself knew better: '*Hay Fever* is far and away one of the most difficult plays to perform that I have ever encountered.' Played to perfection, as it was in a National Theatre production during the autumn of 1964, it becomes one of the great light comedies of this century; played with anything less than total perfection, as many other West End revivals, an audience can become suddenly and painfully aware that there is remarkably little action and that the lines are only funny if said dead right. Coward, asked in the Thirties to introduce his favourite play for a publisher's anthology, unhesitatingly chose *Hay Fever;* in view of *Private Lives* this seemed a strange choice, but the play's technical symmetry still appealed to him:

> It's quite extraordinarily well constructed. And as I did the whole thing in three days I didn't even rewrite. I enjoyed writing it and producing it, and I have frequently enjoyed watching it.

So, on the first night in June 1925, did most of the critics; though in some of their notices one detects the beginning of a curiously patronizing attitude which dictated that in almost all reviews of Coward comedies in the next forty years the words 'flippant' and 'trivial' were to recur with alarming frequency, implying by comparison that in some strange way the other comedies of the time were deeper and imbued with all kinds of significance denied by Coward to his audiences. Looking through the work of his contemporaries among writers of comedy, who range in style from Maugham through Lonsdale and Rattigan to Neil Simon, it is hard to find any who treat their themes with more weight or underlying seriousness than Coward, yet only he stood, until very recently, consistently accused of flippancy. Perhaps it was because the brittle, flash nature of his writing distracts attention from what his characters leave unsaid. As John Russell Taylor wrote in 1966:

> His comic creations do live as people, and their lives go on behind and under and around what they are saying; the text provides only the faintest guide lines to what is really going on between the people on the stage.

To go further, it is a fair test of acting in Coward plays to say if the characters' thoughts speak louder on stage than their words, then all is as it should be.

By the time *Hay Fever* opened, *The Vortex* was in its closing weeks and Noël had been replaced once again by John Gielgud, leaving him free to make a curtain speech at the end of *Hay Fever* in which he noted, with half an eye on the critics who had attacked *Fallen Angels,* that even if the new comedy was dreary they would have to admit it was clean as a whistle. This they did, and *The Era* went so far as to hail it as 'the gayest, brightest and most amusing entertainment in London.' James Agate for the *Sunday Times* was less ecstatic:

> There is neither health nor cleanness about any of Mr Coward's characters, who are still the same vicious babies sprawling upon the floor of their unwholesome crèche… Mr Coward is credited with the capacity to turn out these very highly polished pieces of writing in an incredibly short time; and if rumour and the illustrated weeklies are to be believed, he writes his plays in a flowered dressing-gown and before breakfast. But what I want to know is what kind of work he intends to do after breakfast, when he is clothed and in his right mind.

With *Hay Fever* launched into a year's run and *Fallen Angels* and *On with the Dance* still paying handsome royalties, Noël had a holiday through July; in the meantime he had been considering a number of offers from rival New York managements who wanted him to take *The Vortex* over to Broadway that autumn, and eventually he settled for Messrs Dillingham and Erlanger since they were willing also to have Lilian Braithwaite and Alan Hollis from the original cast. Basil Dean, arguably the leading director of the time and the man who'd directed Noël in *Hannele* at Liverpool in 1913, was brought in to produce *The Vortex* for New York, as Noël didn't want the double burden of acting and directing it again. It was also agreed with Dean that *Easy Virtue,* written before Noël's success with *The Vortex* but still unproduced, should be taken over with a view to doing it on Broadway later in the season. As well as these, *The Queen Was in the Parlour,* Noël's Ruritanian answer to the novels of Anthony Hope and the sentiment of Ivor Novello, was offered as a vehicle for Nazimova, while under a different management Laura Hope Crews planned to do *Hay Fever*. The Americans were in for a Coward winter.

Noël sailed for New York in August, but not before Hannen Swaffer had fired a parting shot: 'I hope *The Vortex* is a failure in New York. I should not like to think that America thought this typical of English life or the English character.' Arriving in New York in a blaze of publicized glory, Coward and his mother moved into the Plaza Hotel and then, seeing the bill for their first few days, promptly moved out again. They settled instead into an apartment on the upper East Side and Noël began rehearsals while Mrs Coward coped with America. After a few days Erlanger, one of the two producers, sent for Noël. Mother love, he explained, was kind of a sacred thing in America and his paying customers wouldn't go for all that shouting and abuse by the son in the last act. However, added Erlanger, this was only a minor problem and with some careful rewriting which he was himself willing to do while they rehearsed, *The Vortex* could be heaved into some kind of shape for New York. To Erlanger's amazement, Noël was not only unwilling to alter a line of the last act, which had after all proved not unsuccessful in London, but was also unwilling to allow Erlanger anywhere near a rehearsal. Writers, in Mr Erlanger's experience, were not expected to behave like that. Basil Dean, eager to smooth the whole thing over, suggested that with a little tact Erlanger could be managed. 'I have not', replied Noël, 'travelled three thousand miles to manage Mr Erlanger, but for him to manage me.'

Soon after that brief meeting, Erlanger and Dillingham withdrew their backing for *The Vortex* which was subsequently presented in Washington and on Broadway under the joint management of Sam Harris and Irving Berlin. After three weeks' rehearsal the play, now with a partially American cast, opened in the sweltering heat of Washington in mid-September. The first night there was not helped by a massive thunderstorm which drowned out most of Act II, nor by a moment in the last act when Noël was sobbing hysterically on the bed and Lilian Braithwaite strode to the window where she flung out the box containing the dope. A stagehand, unfamiliar with the play, tossed it straight back to her. Reviews in the Washington papers were not good; the 'unwholesome' label was dragged out again, most critics considered the play disappointing, and one paper added that 'if Mr Coward is the white hope of the English theatre, God help it.' Returning to New York at the end of the week in deep despair, Noël spent the few days before his New York opening night moving with his mother out of their first apartment, which had proved unsuitable, into a slightly larger one owned by Mae Murray and decorated in a style described by Noël as 'early Metro-Goldwyn' complete with wrought-iron doors, mock-Italian Gothic ceilings and a stained-glass window which lit up at night. Lilian Braithwaite, it is said, spent the few days prudently arranging a ticket for her return journey to England, convinced that *The Vortex* would not last out the week.

In fact, from the round of applause that greeted her first entrance onwards, the Broadway reception was nothing short of tumultuous. They cheered the end of each act and at the very end of the play Noël and his cast got a standing ovation the like of which they had never seen before and were seldom if ever to see again. That night, Noël maintains, he gave the best performance of his career.

The notices were generally excellent, though one or two critics objected to 'Mr Coward's hysterical collection of oversexed, overdressed, overnerved and overwhelmed neurasthenics.' But New York took to Noël in much the same way as had London a few months earlier.

Socially Noël was invited everywhere, in particular to a series of deeply unrelaxing week-ends on Long Island, which he found considerably harder work than his eight performances a week as Nicky Lancaster, but which in later years provided him with invaluable copy for a short story called *What Mad Pursuit?*

The night before *The Vortex,* the dramatization of Michael Arlen's *The Green Hat* had opened on Broadway to equally ecstatic reviews, and Coward and Arlen found themselves, as they had been in London a few months earlier, the twin social and intellectual heroes of the season. Inevitably it was rumoured that Arlen was tremendously jealous of Coward's success, though since he still had a considerable investment in *The Vortex* this was patently unlikely. However, the rumours persisted until he and Noël decided to scotch them and prove their friendship by meeting for dinner once a week at a night-club in New York. Thereafter it was rumoured that their relationship was, to put it mildly, unusually close.

But their friendship survived that too, and they remained for some years afterwards mutually admiring and fairly devoted. Arlen also showed something of Noël's deprecatory sense of humour: 'I am', he once remarked, 'every other inch a gentleman.' On the subject of themselves, Arlen once wrote to Noël that 'the difference between us is that you give the impression of escaping conceit when deep in your heart you are the most conceited man on earth, while I make people think I am awfully stuck on myself when that front is only the protection for a timid soul.'

Soon after *The Vortex* opened on Broadway, *Hay Fever* went into rehearsal with Laura Hope Crews and an otherwise undistinguished cast brought together under a curious managerial policy of first casting the parts and then reading the play. One lady hired in this way to play Myra, the sophisticated English flapper, had a heavy Brooklyn accent and a passion for chewing gum. When Coward tentatively suggested to her that she was not perhaps ideal casting, she spat the gum at his feet and remarked 'Accent hell – I gotta contract.'

The production was by Noël himself and Miss Hope-Crews, who decided that in the face of some pretty uninspired support the best thing she could do would be to overact the hell out of Judith Bliss, on the understandable theory that if she didn't *Hay Fever* would reach a total standstill somewhere in the middle of Act One. For her pains she received a severe roasting from all the critics except one who couldn't resist the temptation to head his notice *'Hay Fever* Nothing to Sneeze At.' Not altogether surprisingly, Noël's comedy was a resounding flop.

11

1926

Noël Coward died here.

Although the American *Hay Fever* collapsed after about six weeks of desultory business and a note by Alec Woollcott reading 'Noël Coward as an industry is still in its infancy', the Broadway run of *The Vortex* was cast-iron and kept Noël in New York throughout the winter of 1925–6; his mother and Gladys Calthrop stayed there with him, and they were joined by John C. Wilson, a young, dark and handsome American with the looks of an early film star. Wilson had been groomed by his family to go into the stockbroking business but instead he chose to attach himself firmly to Noël, becoming first his business manager then his partner and remaining for the next twenty years his closest friend and lover.

While *The Vortex* played on to near-capacity even when Noël was off for a week with a virus infection, *Easy Virtue* (the second of the plays brought over to New York in partnership with Basil Dean) went into rehearsal with Dean again directing and Jane Cowl heading a large cast. Coward had written it, with Constance Collier originally in mind for the lead, immediately after *Hay Fever* in the autumn of 1924, and it was to be the first of his plays premièred in the United States. In both theme and form *Easy Virtue* is a conscious throwback to the well-made drawing-room dramas of Pinero and Maugham which Noël remembered with affection and whose form he acknowledged with gratitude. Though times had changed since the days of Pinero, Coward noted, they had not necessarily changed for the better.

> The narrow-mindedness, the moral righteousness and the over-rigid social codes have disappeared, but with them has gone much that was graceful, well-behaved and endearing. It was in a mood of nostalgic regret at the decline of such conventions that I wrote *Easy Virtue*.

So far, so good; a young playwright tactfully acknowledging what he owed to the masters of the past by writing a play in their convention as a kind of valedictory salute. But it didn't work out quite like that; precisely because things had changed since 1880, writing in 1924 Coward had to create a different sort of play, giving almost psychological reasons for attitudes which forty years earlier would have passed without question. In updating a Pinero theme for the Twenties, the rigid convention had inevitably to be broken.

The critics unsurprisingly found the whole venture rather old-fashioned ('an ancient whangdoodle' in George Jean Nathan's phrase), but *Easy Virtue* settled comfortably into the Empire Theatre where it ran through the winter. Noël continued to play Nicky in *The Vortex* and spent some enjoyable months bathed in the cosy aura of success that New York in general and Sardi's in particular bestows on its theatrical favourites of the season; he was to be found with Jack Wilson at most of the right people's parties, occasionally playing the piano alongside such distinguished fellow-composers as Richard Rodgers and George Gershwin who apparently worried that Coward was unable to play nearly as well as he composed:

> Dear George Gershwin used to moan at me in genuine distress and try to force my fingers on to the right notes. As a matter of fact he showed me a few tricks that I can still do, but they are few and dreadfully far between. I can firmly but not boastfully claim that I am a better pianist than Irving Berlin, but as that superlative genius of light music is well known not to be able to play at all except in C major, I will not press the point.

Coward also found some old friends in Charlot's 1926 *Revue,* now in New York with Gertrude Lawrence, Jack Buchanan and Beatrice Lillie who sang 'Poor Little Rich Girl' and one or two of Noël's other compositions. Living up to the success of *The Vortex* and *Easy Virtue,* Noël bought himself a huge Rolls Royce which earned its keep with a number of publicity pictures in which Noël was to be seen clambering into the back of his chauffeur-driven limousine with a cigarette dangling from the lips and a slouch hat, looking curiously like one of the subsidiary gangsters in an Edward G. Robinson picture. The fact that Coward frequently had to clamber out again on the other side and hail a taxi, because the Rolls failed to start, went happily unrecorded by the New York press.

After five months of *The Vortex* in New York, Noël and Lilian Braithwaite and most of the Broadway company set off on a road tour which included weeks in Newark, Brooklyn, Cincinatti, Chicago and Cleveland. Noël found the tour deeply depressing, and indeed swore during it that he would never again play one part for more than six months, ideally three in London and three in New York. As an actor, a longer run might have seemed attractive, but as a playwright he realized it would destroy both the inclination and the energy needed to write something new. Nevertheless, this tour started off well enough, with the impetus of the play's Broadway success, and at first the out-of-town audiences, though not as exciting to play to, were at least there in sufficient numbers to fill the theatres. Noël was travelling with his mother and Jack, Gladys having left them to become art director of Eva Le Gallienne's newly-formed Civic Repertory Company.

The Vortex tour remained bearable until Chicago; in that city, supposedly the best date of them all, Coward reached what he considered to be the nadir of his professional career. *The Vortex* was booked to play Chicago for six weeks and Noël had ordered the Rolls to be driven from New York to meet him there. They opened at the Selwyn Theatre on George Washington's birthday, February 22nd, 1926, to a capacity audience who sat in stony silence through the jokier moments of the first act, and then fell about with laughter at the sight of Noël in his pyjamas upbraiding his mother at the play's hitherto serious climax. Noël had only been prevented from packing it in at the end of the second act, and from telling Chicago's theatregoers precisely what he thought of them, by Lilian who hissed in his ear the immortal words 'Remember You Are English!'

The season in Chicago was swiftly cut back from six weeks to two and even that seemed too long, though socially Noël enjoyed himself hugely with Iris Tree, Diana Cooper and Judith Anderson (all of whom were also playing in Chicago) on daily excursions to the local riding club. His friendship with Lady Diana was comparatively recent, and had begun on an uneasy footing after she announced to Noël at a party in London that she had not laughed once throughout *The Young Idea*. 'How strange', mused Noël, 'when I saw you in *The Glorious Adventure* I laughed all the time.'

Coward also used his free time in Chicago to write a play called *Semi-Monde* which was set over a number of years at the Ritz Hotel in Paris. The play was never professionally produced in his lifetime, perhaps because certain sexual abnormalities among the leading characters failed to convince the Lord Chamberlain that it deserved a licence; in Germany a translation of *Semi-Monde* by Rudolf Kommer stood a good chance of production by Max Reinhardt until the advent of Vicki Baum's *Grand Hotel* made its theme redundant.

When the two weeks in Chicago came to an end the company moved on to their final date, Cleveland, though not before the Master – as he was to be known in the years to come – had inscribed 'Noël Coward Died Here' in indelible ink on the wall of his dressing-room at the Selwyn; thirty years later the inscription was still there. After Cleveland Noël took his mother back to New York ('the two of them are so devoted to each other', remarked Jane Cowl, 'that they behave like newlyweds) where they made plans to sail back to England together with Jack Wilson on the Olympic. New York was still besotted by Noël: 'Coward excels at Charleston!' exclaimed one paper, and he himself made the affection a mutual affair:

> I had always felt [Noël told the *New York World*] that if I could only make a hit in America I should feel that I had done something quite wonderful. Success is tremendously important to me... I get a kick out of being

recognized and feeling that I matter. Life is pleasanter now, but I always felt that success would come. I didn't mind waiting for it and I'm not self-conscious about having achieved it.

Back in London with his mother and Jack and the Rolls in the spring of 1926, Noël found that he had nothing to do until the English production of *Easy Virtue* went into rehearsal in May. There were of course, the usual parties: 'I don't suppose you'd remember me', said an acquaintance to Noël at one of these. 'Of course I do', answered Noël, using his stock reply in time of social crisis, 'and how's Muriel?'

Then, as always when he could think of nothing else to do, Noël travelled; this time through the South of France and on to Sicily and Tunis. The result of the journey was a new comedy, *This Was a Man,* written in Palermo and dedicated to Jack Wilson; Noël himself considered it to be 'primarily satirical and on the whole rather dull', but when he got back to London he showed it to the ubiquitous Basil Dean who liked it enough to suggest putting it into production immediately after *Easy Virtue.* With this in mind, Noël sent it to the Lord Chamberlain's office where Lord Cromer, still in residence, took an even dimmer view of *This Was a Man* than had its author. It was, decided Cromer, totally unsuitable for public presentation, and though the Lord Chamberlain was never obliged to give reasons for refusing to license a play, it is fair to assume that his disapproval had something to do with a scene in the last act where the husband, told that his wife has committed adultery with his best friend, merely laughs. Infidelity was not, in the official view, a laughable affair and although *This Was a Man* was staged in New York later in 1926, then with rather more success in Berlin in 1927 (again translated by Kommer) and finally in Paris in 1928, it remained unproduced in this country. There is no doubt that if anyone wanted to produce it in England they could later have done so, though by the time official standards of morality had crumbled sufficiently to allow it, the play itself had become so out of date as to make the whole undertaking pointless.

But *Semi-Monde* and then *This Was a Man* were not the only causes of Coward's brush with censorship in 1926; early in May *Easy Virtue* started rehearsals in London with Jane Cowl and most of the original American company again under the direction of Basil Dean. When the play arrived in Manchester the local Watch Committee, while allowing the play itself, felt they could not permit so risqué a title; thus it was billed for the week as 'A New Play in Three Acts by Noël Coward' and played to large audiences next door to a cinema where the current attraction was shamelessly billed as *Flames of Passion.*

But the Manchester Watch Committee was at most a minor irritation; Noël's real quarrel lay with the Lord Chamberlain himself who, apart from

Coward's recent plays, had also banned such diverse classics as *Six Characters In Search Of An Author, Desire Under The Elms, L' École des Cocottes* and *Young Woodley*. Noël unburdened his fury to the *Sunday Chronicle*:

> I protest with all the energy I can summon up after an exceptionally strenuous season against this fantastic condition of affairs. Almost any day the law courts and police courts reveal the details of some unorthodox human alliance or intrigue. Yet no one makes a shout about it. But let a variation of these same circumstances be translated to a stage play that even sets out to show the wickedness of the thing, and see what an uproar they evoke. See how the Censor will arise in his wrath to smite with his blue pencil ... what I am calling for is a freer stage but at the same time I am not advocating licence for any one to come along and produce a play whose only point is its indelicacy... If we must have a Censor, at least let us have one that is able to discriminate between vulgarity and wit.

'A New Play in Three Acts By Noël Coward' moved from Manchester to the Duke of York's Theatre in London on June 9th 1926, just over six months after its first appearance in New York. In London the Coward name under the title (now permitted to revert to *Easy Virtue)* drew over three thousand applications for first-night tickets, and Miss Cowl took ecstatic curtain-calls amid an orgy of flowers ; but the critics the next morning were again uncertain about the value of the play. The *Telegraph* felt that it was 'a good piece of theatrical mechanism, unworthy of Mr Coward's promise', and the *Daily Express,* using a line that had already become a cliché where reviews of Coward were concerned, announced 'Play from an author not yet grown up.' There remained a quality in Noël that G. B. Stern described, not intentionally unkindly, as 'perpetually promising.'

At the box-office business was good, helped not inconsiderably by King George V and Queen Mary who made the first of innumerable royal visits to a Coward play, and *Easy Virtue* ran on well into the autumn.

Soon after the first night Noël took Jane Cowl to meet his family; it was an uneasy tea party not helped by his father who, turning to the already subdued actress, remarked 'Here, have a tongue sandwich: that'll make you talk.'

Six weeks after *Easy Virtue* opened, the Coward/Dean partnership put *The Queen Was in the Parlour* into rehearsal with Dean directing a cast headed by Madge Titheradge, Herbert Marshall and Lady Tree. This was the Ruritanian melodrama that Noël had written in the spring of 1922 when he was living with his mother in the cottage at St Mary in the Marsh. Originally titled *Nadya*, it was then called *Souvenir* and only reached its final title during these rehearsals. Odd as it must have seemed for Coward, then considered the most modern of playwrights, to be writing about Ruritania, *The Queen Was in the Parlour* did in fact predate *The Vortex* by more than a year. It adopted the full escapist flavour of lush romantic costume drama, with characters like Nadya, Queen of Krayia, who forsook her lover for her country in a plot that would not have disgraced Novello's *King's Rhapsody* thirty years later.

Yet Coward did not intend to parody, or even to mock, the Ruritanian form; he wrote the play, his only expedition into this limited terrain, because:

> Anthony Hope had blazed the trail and what was good enough for Anthony Hope was good enough for me. Ruritania is a dangerous country where romantic clichés lurk in every throne room but at that time I was young and eager and valiantly oblivious of them. I thought, with an arrogant naiveté at which I can now smile tolerantly, that my brisk modern mind could fill old bottles with heady new wine.

It couldn't and it didn't; but due largely to the acting of Madge Titheradge, *The Queen Was in the Parlour* held the St Martin's as a modest but steady success, and with *Easy Virtue* still at the Duke of York's Coward again had more than one play running in the West End. He was also writing more sketches at this time, and then there were the songs; none at this time very memorable perhaps, but still written frequently on an ad hoc basis:

> I just go on with the business of living, like other people do, until a song occurs to me. It may be while I am at dinner or on a bus or even while I am having a bath. If I am anywhere near a piano I fly to it, and play the tune with one hand. That 'fixes' it as a photographer would say, and I can proceed with the rest in a more leisurely way.

In Noël's private life the weeks after the opening of *The Queen Was in the Parlour* were a time to anchor and to try to estimate his rapid, frenzied success on both sides of the Atlantic in the last twenty months. In England he had become a star with *The Vortex,* and the play's success on Broadway had only served to bolster a steadily enlarging reputation when he returned to London. Added to this there was the success of *On with the Dance, Fallen Angels, Hay Fever* and, more recently, *Easy Virtue* and *The Queen Was in the Parlour* which though not ecstatically received had swept along on a general tide of enthusiasm for Coward and on the rather prurient hope that he might be again as outrageous as he had been in *Fallen Angels.* 'Consider his dialogue,' wrote Beverley Nichols in a 1926 Coward profile, 'smooth, hard, swift pebbles of thought thrown disdainfully against the glass windows of the houses in which we have ensconced ourselves.'

In short, Coward had not had a failure since before *The Vortex* unless one counts, as only he did, that play's disastrous visit to Chicago. He was now twenty-six, had formed himself with Gladys Calthrop and Jack Wilson into a limited company for tax purposes, and was financially secure if not yet hugely prosperous. In the last six years London had seen seven full-length Coward plays plus two revues; New York had seen four plays and there were three others from those years (*The Rat Trap, Sirocco* and *This Was a Man*) which had still to be staged. Apart from this enviable rate of strike as a playwright, Coward had made his name in the theatre as an actor, lyricist and composer, and in London and New York society as a generally presentable if slightly risqué wit, suitable for all invitations. Like Cole Porter, already a friend and the songwriter who of all Americans came closest to Coward in the meticulous arrangement of his lyrics, Noël straddled the gap between show business and the social aristocracy.

But now, in the autumn of 1926, Coward began to realize that he faced problems unthought of before he took *The Vortex* to America. For no longer was he the struggling, hopeful, promising young playwright of whom critics could confidently forecast great things: now, in their eyes, he had arrived and would henceforth be judged not on his potential but on his ability to maintain a rapidly acquired position near the head of his profession, a position which was already under fire from those who had disliked the plays that gave Coward his lead in the first place.

Though nobody was ever more confident about success than Noël, it had all happened very fast and this was really the first moment he'd had to step aside and think it all over. After *The Queen was in The Parlour* the next project was to be an American production of his latest play, *This Was a Man,* which had been banned for England by the Lord Chamberlain. But first, while he had the time, Noël decided to abandon the cottage at Dockenfield which had never been a great success anyway, and instead to find a larger house further out in the country for himself and his family as well as those of their friends and relations who were likely to turn up at week-ends. What he found, since there was now the money to pay for it, was Goldenhurst: a farmhouse near Aldington in Kent which became Coward's country home until some years after the second war.

But before they moved in, and before Coward had really found the time to think in general terms about what to do and where to go next, Basil Dean came up with a new offer; he wanted Noël to appear as Lewis Dodd in his production of Margaret Kennedy's *The Constant Nymph* at the New Theatre. Coward was not keen; he was still very tired, it was a long and potentially unrewarding part, and in any case he could only play it for a month prior to leaving for New York and the production of *This Was a Man.* In spite of that Basil Dean and Edna Best, who was to play Tessa, managed to bully Noël into creating the part. A few days later, lunching in The Ivy, Coward met John Gielgud and told him what he had agreed to do next. Gielgud replied that he would be very good as Lewis Dodd, and the two men parted. It was not until some weeks later that Coward discovered Basil Dean had originally promised the part to Gielgud, who until that meeting in The Ivy, still thought it was his. In the event Gielgud agreed to take over the part when Coward went to America, since by this time following Noël was nothing new to him, and the part of Lewis Dodd seemed too good to miss even at secondhand.

In the meantime *Easy Virtue* was coming to the end of its run after nearly five months at the Duke of York's because Jane Cowl wanted to go home to New York. When this was publicized Mrs Patrick Campbell wrote to Noël asking if she could play the part since she was, she said, badly in need of work. It had been decided however that the play should close, because business by then had begun to get a little shaky anyway; but Mrs Campbell was not pleased. 'All Noël Coward's characters', she remarked at a party soon afterwards, 'talk like typewriters.'

To replace *Easy Virtue,* Dean transferred *The Queen Was in the Parlour* from the St Martin's, and there was a suggestion that the Duke of York's should continue in this way to be a permanent Noël Coward theatre. No one seems to have doubted then that there would always be a Coward play in the West End capable of filling it, and his career as a playwright had moved at such a rate that already he was being revived: a few months before his twenty-seventh birthday the 'Q' Theatre resuscitated his first produced play *I'll Leave It to You.*

Abroad, *The Vortex* and *Fallen Angels* were running side by side in Berlin, though in The Hague performances of the latter play were banned by the city's Burgomaster on the grounds that it was 'obnoxious and below the standards of the Dutch Theatre.' Even without such drastic reaction from overseas, Noël remained good copy for the gossip-columns:

> He is still the same simple-hearted cheery boy he was when he got his first job in a revue chorus (sic)... unlike the other successful moderns, Noël has not taken a luxurious flat in Mayfair... he still lives at home with his people, of whom he is very fond... he will tell you with pride that whatever success he may have gained he owes entirely to his little mother, his greatest pal, who goes everywhere with him. When he was a small boy, she was the only one to recognize the spark of genius in Noël.

But Coward was to be seen from time to time out of his mother's company, usually with Jack Wilson though on one occasion in a theatre bar talking to a girl described in all seriousness as, 'very modern, favouring the Eton crop and long ear-rings, and recently returned from the Antipodes.' The item was headed, improbably, 'Noël Coward to Wed?'

Just before Noël went into rehearsal for *The Constant Nymph,* Michael Balcon announced that his thriving Gainsborough Pictures would be the first to film a Coward play as they had bought the rights to *Easy Virtue.* Balcon was delighted:

British production [he said] has been reproached with making films on American lines, with having failed to develop a national characteristic as the Germans have done. *Easy Virtue* is the answer: a country-house play with county people... the future of the cinema lies in the hands of the young writers and Mr Coward, as one of the most brilliant of them all, is a notable newcomer to British films.

For *The Constant Nymph,* which Basil Dean himself had adapted from Margaret Kennedy's best-selling novel about the Sanger family, Noël was required to grow his hair long, wear glasses and ill-fitting suits, smoke a pipe and generally to behave on the stage as he never had before. The part of Lewis Dodd demanded more of him as an actor, since it was less like him as a man, than anything he had ever played in the theatre and it is fair to say that he hated every single moment of it. Dean was determined to get him away from the 'Noël Coward mannerisms' that had already become over-familiar to London audiences: the result was not without difficulties for Noël, who had never smoked a pipe or worn his hair long in his life, and who consequently spent a fair amount of rehearsal time setting fire to his hair along with the tobacco. Asked why he had agreed to play the part, Noël told the *Daily Express:* 'Because I want to see if I am any good as an actor in other people's plays.' He hadn't acted in a play by any other author since *Polly with a Past* in 1921, and in return for getting him to do so now, Dean had to agree to act in a play of Noël's at some future date. Coward did not hold him to that promise.

At the end of a long and tough rehearsal period in which Noël threatened to give up the part roughly three times a week (with Gielgud constantly standing by to take over at a moment's notice), Mrs Patrick Campbell rang up and begged for dress-rehearsal tickets since, she said, she was now a poor, lonely, unwanted old woman who couldn't afford to buy them for the first night. She arrived at the final run-through slightly late, bearing in her arms her small Pekinese which yapped throughout.

The next morning, only hours before the first night, she rang Noël again with the news that she had enjoyed the play greatly and thought Edna Best quite good. As for Noël himself though, she told him that he was entirely miscast for Lewis Dodd, that he lacked the necessary glamour and should anyway be wearing a beard.

Unencouraged by the views of Mrs Patrick Campbell, Noël staggered through a mechanically difficult opening night involving innumerable scenes and at least three quick-changes from sports clothes to full evening dress and back. The play took nearly three and a half hours to perform but the reviews next morning were excellent for the play, for Edna Best, and for Noël. Even his old enemy, Hannen Swaffer, was forced to conclude:

Noël turns his face against the back wall, drops his voice and does everything that would make David Garrick very, very angry, yet by sheer triumph of personality he holds up every scene in which he appears. You may like his plays or you may not, but this tribute you must pay him – there has been in our memory no stage personality who has achieved such success in so many branches of his art as this youth of twenty-six.

After the first night, *The Constant Nymph* became technically easier to play, though at the end of the third performance the mood of Edna Best's tragic death on stage was shattered by a broken windowcord. Noël, having lifted her on to the bed, was supposed to fling up the window and utter the last line: 'Tessa's got away; she's safe; she's dead.' On this occasion, as the window crashed back on to his fingers, it became 'Tessa's got away; she's safe; she's – ow!' Whereupon the dead Tessa sat bolt upright on the bed and the curtain fell amid hysterical audience laughter. After that all went well for about a fortnight, but Noël did not complete the month that he had agreed to play Lewis Dodd; early in the third week his nerves, which had been considerably strained by the frenetic work of the past two years, finally snapped and he broke down. He played one entire performance in floods of uncontrollable tears to the bemused horror of cast and audience alike, and was then injected with a minute amount of strychnine by a doctor who ordered him to bed for a week in severe isolation. John Gielgud, who was rehearsing to follow Coward into the part a week later, took over at the matinée on the day after Noël's collapse. He, too, was unhappy in the role, hampered again in his interpretation by the memory of how Noël had spoken the lines, and not pleased by the fact that throughout the twelve months he played the part, photographs of Coward were left hanging in the lobby of the New Theatre.

Gielgud remembers that he imitated Noël terribly:

> It was the best thing to do since *The Vortex* and *The Constant Nymph* were his kind of plays. But following him made me very nervous, and I think it delayed me in finding a style of my own. When you start as an actor, though, you do need a model, and Noël was mine; he knew how to hold the stage, and I felt he was a great star even then.

A week after his collapse Noël, feeing well enough to ignore the advice of his doctor, caught the first boat to New York.

12

1926–1928

I can hardly wait
Till I see the great
Open Spaces,
My loving friends will not be there,
I'm so sick of their
God-damned faces,
Because I'm world weary, world weary,
Tired of all these jumping jacks,
I want to get right back to nature and relax.

In October 1926, while Noël was on his way to New York, the new Raymond Massey management at the Everyman. Theatre in Hampstead staged a rather belated production of his first serious play, *The Rat Trap*. Written eight years earlier, this was the account of marital disaster in a novelist's household which Gilbert Miller had tried without success to sell in New York before suggesting that Noël might have better luck with the plot of *I'll Leave It to You*. But if the Hampstead theatre hoped to repeat the success they'd had with Coward's *The Vortex* a few seasons earlier they were severely disappointed. In spite of a distinguished cast led by Robert Harris and Massey himself together with his future wife Adrianne Allen, and some intermittently witty lines, the production lasted a meagre twelve performances and has seldom been professionally performed since.

Arriving in New York, and believing that the nervous breakdown had departed as rapidly as it had arrived a fortnight earlier, leaving no tangible after-effects beyond a general feeling of physical and mental exhaustion, Noël began to cast the American production of *This Was a Man*. Though Lord Cromer had deemed this unsuitable for the consumption of English audiences, there could be no objection to its appearance in New York, where the conditions governing the presentation of plays related to the normal laws of libel and obscenity rather than to the arbitrary moral scruples of any single official – a system that England was only to adopt some forty years later. Francine Larrimore was cast as Carol, more for the power of her name at the box-office than for her suitability, which was dubious; supporting her were Auriol Lee and two stalwarts from the brigade of English gentlemen, Nigel Bruce and A. E. Matthews. Rehearsals, under Basil Dean's direction, went badly; Matty remembered being constantly uneasy, particularly at the dress rehearsal when Dean kept shouting 'Louder and funnier, Matthews'. Miss Larrimore was efficient but apparently miscast, and Noël dismissed the whole thing as 'that dreariest of dreary productions', being inclined to put the blame for its failure squarely on to Basil Dean: 'if the writing of *This Was A Man* was slow, the production was practically stationary. The second-act dinner scene between Francine Larrimore and Nigel Bruce made *Parsifal* in its entirety seem like a quick-fire vaudeville sketch.'

The first night audience at the Klaw Theatre in New York, presided over in the stage box by Noël, Jack Wilson and Gladys Calthrop (who had done the sets), was scarcely more enthusiastic and during the evening a crowded, fashionable auditorium gradually thinned out until after the second interval only a few small bands of the faithful remained dotted about the stalls. Talking to a reporter just before the opening night about the English ban on the play, Noël had said, 'I shall in future concentrate on New York where I am taken seriously as a serious writer, whereas in England people think I am out for salacious sensations. I shall from time to time write a pleasant little trifle for London.' The difficulty with this play was that it was neither one thing nor the other; serious perhaps in its intent, but essentially trifling in its execution, it lasted in New York for only thirty-one performances.

Noël, who had not been in exactly rude health when he arrived in New York, did not improve with the failure of *This Was a Man;* for a while he stayed in the city, where 'melancholia enveloped me like a thick cloud, blotting out the pleasure and the colour from everything.' Then, in an attempt to escape it, he took Jack Wilson with him for a fortnight's holiday in the Virginia mountains at White Sulphur Springs. But even there, far from anywhere familiar, he was unable to rest; by now he was so keyed up that he could not begin to cope with the meaning of a holiday, and instead wrote an eighteenth-century joke called *The Marquise,* a play which he had long promised for Marie Tempest. Unable to face the English winter or the effort of casting and rehearsing another new comedy, he merely sent the script back to London with a few production notes and decided to travel on to Hong Kong, keeping Jack with him as far as San Francisco.

Coward's hope was that time, together with the sight of new landscapes and a complete escape from routine and friends, would fend off the absolute mental and nervous breakdown that he now felt to be imminent. Leaving Jack unwillingly on the quayside at San Francisco, Noël sailed for China aboard the *SS President Pierce* on Christmas Day 1926. He only actually got as far as Honolulu before the breakdown caught up with him.

In the week that it then took to reach Hawaii from the West Coast, Noël got progressively worse; all the tension and the sweat of the last two years, which had been suppressed by the sheer force of continuous work, began to overtake him at last. In the throes of a severe nervous breakdown he became almost suicidally gloomy, was unable to sleep, and felt convinced that he was already spent – that at just twenty-seven he would never be able to write another word. But the illness was not purely mental; by the time the *President Pierce* docked in Honolulu, Noël's temperature ran to a hundred and three. On arrival, he was met by the chauffeured car of the Walter Dillinghams, one of the five patrician families who controlled through their land and their fortunes the social life of the islands before Hawaii achieved statehood, and who remain to this day a considerable influence on the political and economic shape of the fiftieth state. Mrs Walter Dillingham had planned a large and celebratory lunch to welcome Noël at her home on Diamond Head; in the middle of it the collapse that he'd been fighting for about six weeks finally arrived, and Noël went out cold.

When he woke up some hours later in a bed at the Moana Hotel in Waikiki, Honolulu's beach resort, a doctor was telling him that he had a slight fever. The 'slight fever' persisted for about a week, at the end of which Noël was strong enough to visit the doctor's surgery for a complete check-up. Finding no other visible cause for the fever, the doctor ultimately settled for Noël's long-healed tubercular scar and diagnosed that he had again, this time far more seriously, contracted tuberculosis. It was an alarming possibility; but Noël, who remembered the symptoms from his visits to Ned Lathom in Davos, knew enough about the disease to realize that in all probability he didn't have it. Still, he had something, and it was patently going to take a long time to go away even though his temperature was already back to near-normal.

The Dillinghams offered Noël their ranch at Mokuleia on the other side of the island, complete with its French caretaker, for as long as he wanted to stay there and recuperate. He stayed for about six weeks, untroubled by visitors or indeed anybody except the caretaker and his wife. He swam, slept and read, resolutely refusing to work though a tune did occur to him as he lay one morning on the beach; he did nothing about it at the time, but it stayed in the back of his mind until nearly a year later when it emerged as 'A Room with a View'.

He also used the time to reflect, to realize that he had tried to do too much too quickly, and to swear that in the future he would pace himself more carefully, doing less and ceasing to be the instant, adaptable, all-singing, all-joking, all-talented Noël Coward, available, neatly dressed and carefully rehearsed for all occasions. Instead he would do only what he wanted to do, and that with more care and selectivity.

At last, though, the loneliness combined with a certain yearning for home and his mother became too much for Noël; by now fully recovered and burnt black by the sun, he returned to Honolulu from where he sailed back to the mainland and then travelled home to England, collecting Jack and Gladys in New York on the way.

Meanwhile, at the Criterion Theatre in London, Marie Tempest had opened in *The Marquise;* the production had been rushed into rehearsal when another vehicle for Miss Tempest failed to run, but she wrote reassuringly to Noël in America: 'I may tell you that no library, picture gallery, antique furniture or silver shop has been overlooked to have everything period and correct... Your writing of the play is, to me amazing... I cannot tell you how much I love it all.' With her in the cast were her husband, William Graham-Browne who also directed, Frank Cellier, Robert Harris and a youthful Godfrey Winn. Press reaction to this 'boulevard farce in picturesque dress' had been largely favourable; 'amusing and well-constructed' was the general feeling, and thanks presumably to the expertise and enchantment of Miss Tempest the critics failed to notice that the *The Marquise* was in fact a slight domestic comedy with an unwieldy plot set in a curiously incongruous period. As a dramatist, Noël moved his career neither forward nor backward with *The Marquise,* but found a way of marking time pleasantly, innocuously and profitably enough, while (as Desmond MacCarthy noted) the success on this occasion belonged to Miss Tempest.

Noël himself went to see *The Marquise* on his first night back in London and was delighted with it. It had been composed, he wrote later:

> With Marie Tempest speaking every line of it in my mind's ear. To see her play it was for me obviously an enchanting evening, and it has made me forever incapable of judging the play on its merits. If, with intense concentration, I could detach myself for a moment from Marie Tempest's personality and performance, I might perhaps see what a tenuous, frivolous little piece *The Marquise* is... I might, bereft of her memory, read with disdain the whole play; sneer at its flippancy; laugh at its trivial love scenes and shudder at the impertinence of an author who, for no apparent reason except perhaps that pictorially the period is attractive, elects to place a brittle modern comedy in an eighteenth-century setting. But I am not and never shall be bereft of the memory of Marie Tempest [who made] *The Marquise* gay, brilliant, witty, charming and altogether delightful.

In retrospect, it is tempting to see in the toast by Esteban which opens Act One of *The Marquise* something of the Coward philosophy of life in general and playwriting in particular:

ESTEBAN: Children, my very dear children, if I were a magician the gift I
 would bestow on you would be Lightness of Touch. But being just an
 ordinary man, I can only whisper to you a little advice: enjoy yourselves as

much as possible, it will pass the time pleasantly and lead you into old age with a few gay memories to cheer you – and don't ask any more than that.

Noël spent the spring and summer of 1927 living with Jack Wilson at Goldenhurst, the farmhouse in Kent which Coward had bought and where his mother and Auntie Vida also now lived. Stripping away the wallpaper and tiled fireplaces they had found a perfectly preserved seventeenth-century building which with some subtle conversions made Goldenhurst an ideal country house. In these otherwise uneventful months Noël wrote a night-club sketch called *Pretty Prattle* for a charity matinée to raise money for Lilian Baylis and her Sadlers Wells Fund. At this time Coward also sold the film rights of *The Vortex* and *The Queen Was in the Parlour* to Michael Balcon, who already had *Easy Virtue* going into production with Alfred Hitchcock directing a cast led by Isabel Jeans and Franklyn Dyall. Balcon announced that Ivor Novello, who was then under contract to him, would star in *The Queen Was In The Parlour,* and that Noël himself, who had made some satisfactory screen tests for Gainsborough, would play his old part in the film of *The Vortex*; but Novello proved unavailable for *The Queen Was in the Parlour,* and in the end it was he who starred in *The Vortex* instead.

Noël was also becoming something of a cult among students, notably at Cambridge where undergraduates at King's College said that in an attempt to bring some reality to the acting of Shakespeare they would in future present his plays 'in the modern manner of Mr Noël Coward, with telephones.'

With work on the redecoration of Goldenhurst almost finished, Noël and Jack travelled to Vienna for the Austrian première of *The Marquise* which, they were more than a little surprised to find, being played by a large German lady in a modern red leather motoring coat. It was apparently a wildly funny performance, but not in quite the way the author had intended.

In the weeks while Noël had paused to consider his playwriting career, the critic St John Ervine had been doing precisely the same thing, and in the summer of 1927 Ervine published his findings in that unlikely organ of theatrical thought, *Good Housekeeping*. His view of Coward at this stage in Noël's development was twofold; firstly that he was undoubtedly the most interesting figure to have appeared in the English theatre since the war, an accomplished dramatist and composer and an actor who 'does all the wrong things and yet contrives to get the right effects.'

As a man [said Ervine], the young Coward is brilliant, loyal to his friends, generous and unaffected in his behaviour; he remembers those who were kind to him when he was in need of kindness, and he is full of courage and decision. He knows his mind and is not afraid to express it. He is sincere and simple and modest. His wits are quick and he has an uncanny knowledge of stagecraft. He writes good 'theatre'; his plays click; his big scenes come off… but a dramatist cannot live on technique. He certainly cannot live on tricks and the danger in which Mr Coward now is, or so it seems to me, is that of a man who has learnt one trick very well and is content to repeat it. Mr Coward is now at a turning point in his career. There is evidence in his work of sincerity, but one feels that it is in him rather than in his plays. Behind the flippancy and (the word is a harsh one but it is not used harshly) the ignorance of Mr Coward there is a fine, flexible and sensitive mind questing for truth. He writes too quickly and too much. Mr Coward is more than twenty-five, and he must now, if he is to maintain the high position he has so brilliantly won for himself, begin to think like an adult. The stuff is in him; he has only to bring it out.

Whether or not he admitted it, one suspects that Coward himself would have been forced to agree with almost every word of Ervine's appraisal.

Early in the summer Noël finished a new comedy, *Home Chat* and though he was not entirely happy about it he sent the script to Madge Titheradge who had made a success of his *The Queen was in The Parlour* a year before. She liked it, as did the ever-present Basil Dean, and it was decided to put it into rehearsal during the autumn at the Duke of York's. In the meantime Noël had a brief holiday on the Lido outside Venice with Mr and Mrs Cole Porter. Returning to Goldenhurst, he then played host to Alfred Lunt and Lynn Fontanne who brought with them a new play by S. N. Behrman called *The Second Man* which they had acted on Broadway and now suggested that Noël should act in London; on the Lunts' recommendation Noël agreed with the English producers, MacLeod and Mayer, that he would do it early in the following year.

The opening night of his own comedy *Home Chat* on October 27th 1927 was altogether ghastly and the first of two disasters in rapid succession that Noël was to endure that autumn. Somehow *Home Chat,* a mild comedy of supposed marital infidelity, was simply not up to what the audience had come to expect of Coward; at the first performance Nina Boucicault, nervous after her long absence from the stage, dried up frequently thereby making an already slow production filled with over-meticulous business seem a great deal slower. The audience, some of whom had queued for ten hours to get in, grew restive and at the final curtain there were boos from the gallery and the stalls. Noël, deciding that attack was the best form of defence leapt up on to the stage whereupon the booing grew a great deal louder. One shout rose above the rest: 'We expected a better play!' 'And I,' retorted Noël, 'expected better manners.'

With that the curtain was lowered to avoid further hostilities, and Noël was left to reflect that *Home Chat* 'is a little better than bad but not quite good enough and that is that.' Not, however, as far as the critics were concerned; their reviews the next morning were little short of vitriolic.

Home Chat staggered along for a bare month, at the end of which it was withdrawn from the Duke of York's. Basil Dean, undaunted, went straight on to the production of another Coward play, *Sirocco,* the Italian fiesta drama that Noël had written in America early in 1921; for this he cast Frances Doble as the wife and Ivor Novello as the lover. It was to be the only time that Coward and Novello worked together in the theatre; Novello at that time had made a considerable name for himself as the star of several silent films, but he still lacked much experience of playing leading roles on the stage, as indeed did Miss Doble, who was getting her first big chance. Dean however was optimistic and Noël was in no doubt that *Sirocco* was rather better than most of the other entertainment being offered by London theatres of the time.

Rehearsals for *Sirocco* started immediately after the first night of *Home Chat,* and Dean took infinite care over the big scene, the fiesta, which was mounted as a full scale production number. But on the first night at Daly's, where Noël was to be seen sitting in a stage box with his mother opening telegrams before the curtain rose, both Novello and Frances Doble found difficulty in developing or even sustaining two long parts that would have taxed actors of much wider experience. The gallery, though jammed with Novello's film fans, began to grow restless and during the second act when he tried to play the love scene with Frances Doble they started to laugh. G. B. Stern, sitting at the back of the stalls, reported to Noël that by the end of the second act they too were getting pretty bored. The last act was nothing short of a catastrophe, with jeers and catcalls in the gallery and an attempted polite hushing from the dress-circle below. Noël began to feel, perhaps rightly, that the jeering was directed at him rather than the play; that people tiring of his 'casual' triumphs were only too pleased to be present at a Coward failure. Certainly *Sirocco* was no worse than *Home Chat,* and perhaps no worse than other plays running more peacefully in London at that time; on the other hand it was not noticeably any better, and the reaction might purely have arisen from a feeling that Coward, who had shown his talent so young, could and should be doing better than this by now. In the chaos that followed the final curtain, two people failed entirely to grasp what was going on: Mrs Coward, who being slightly deaf turned to her son in the stage box murmuring, 'Is it a failure, dear?' and Basil Dean who, following his usual practice, had not been in front for the opening. Returning backstage after a quiet dinner he stood in the wings smiling happily, convinced that the noise he could hear out front was frenzied cheering. Noël, rushing backstage, found him happily raising and lowering the curtain while the cast took some of the most unnecessary curtain calls in the history of the English theatre.

Coward decided that the least he could do would be to join his cast on the stage; this, predictably, increased the fun of the audience. After about five minutes, when they showed no sign of going home and were still shrieking their protests, someone began to call for Frances Doble. The call was taken up and Miss Doble moved to the front of the stage to acknowledge some scattered but friendly applause; Noël, ushering her forward, was greeted with a cry of 'Hide behind the woman, would you?' In that moment of emotion, all Miss Doble could think of was the speech she had learned in anticipation of a less calamitous evening:

'Ladies and gentlemen,' she began, 'this is the happiest moment of my life.' On stage Ivor and Noël, unable to contain themselves any longer, began to giggle; this brought even louder catcalls as the curtain fell for the last time. But the evening was not quite over; as Noël left Daly's, an unsuitable theatre which for many years had housed only musicals but which appeared to be the only one free when *Sirocco* was looking for a home, there were a number of people waiting outside the stage door. As he got into his car several of them spat at him.

All of which suggests one of two possibilities; either audiences then were a great deal more fervent in their theatrical likes and dislikes than they have ever been since, or else Noël himself was capable of provoking rather more violent reactions to himself than almost any of his contemporaries. He personally remained convinced that public opinion had turned against him as a reaction to his rapid and early success, and that it was not solely motivated by the inadequacy of this one play. For their part the critics, who might have been more gentle with a less successful or self-assured writer, fairly slaughtered the play and its author. *Sirocco* was an unmitigated disaster, provoking notices that were probably the worst since the Archduke Ferdinand had been shot at Sarajevo. Hannen Swaffer in the *Sunday Express* was beside himself with glee:

> At last the public seem to appreciate the truth of what I have said now for over three years in season and out of season – that Noël Coward has nothing whatever to say, that he has no wit, and that his sneers at ordinary respectable people are irritating to the point of painfulness.

Edgar Wallace published 'a defence of Noël Coward', but it came too late to save *Sirocco*; though the house was sold out for three days, by lunchtime on the morning after the first night more than half the tickets had been returned. Suppressing a desire to leave England on the first boat, Noël decided to put a brave face on it; he appeared at The Ivy for lunch with Jack and Gladys where he discovered that Novello, surrounded by his coterie, had made the same decision. To their amazement they found themselves treated with sympathy rather than hostility, and Ivor went on to play *Sirocco* for every one of its twenty-eight performances. Noël took Jack Wilson to Paris for a short visit, moving on to Neuilly where they spent a few days with the designer Edward Molyneux who did his best to reassure Noël that by the time they returned to England the *Sirocco* fiasco would be entirely forgotten; Noël remained unconvinced, largely because every time he went out to buy an English paper he found yet another reference to the disaster of a few weeks ago. Indeed Noël became so convinced that editors were being unnecessarily spiteful in flogging what he hoped was a dead horse that he promised never again to write an article for an English newspaper, a promise that he kept unbroken for more than thirty years. He did however publish a few last thoughts on *Sirocco:*

> The reason given for its depressing reception have been varied and interesting. Some contend that the theatre was too big, others that the play was too small. The Press with a few kindly exceptions found it dull, unreal, immoral, stupid, over-produced, over-acted, under-produced and under-acted; the few kindly exceptions found it vital, significant, moral, dramatic, exquisitely produced and acted, and profoundly interesting. The Public, I regret to say, hardly found it at all.

Coward already belonged to a long line of ultra-English performers, unrelated only by blood, who believed that to give in to failure of any kind was unnecessary and unforgiveable. Unaffected by these London disasters, the Komódie Theatre in Berlin had a considerable success with an adapted and altered version of *This was a Man*; meanwhile New York managements still working their way stolidly through the Coward canon had arrived at *Fallen Angels* and *The Marquise*. Both these comedies opened on Broadway in the autumn of 1927; neither achieved huge success but *The Marquise* avoided the fate of *Fallen Angels* which was an undoubted flop. Both productions received kindly if not sparkling reviews: 'light but well-made comedies with some good ideas spread rather thinly' summarized the views of most New York critics on each occasion.

Before *Sirocco,* Noël had been contracted to do *The Second Man* in London early in 1928 and also to write a new revue for Cochran; after the deluge ('I hope you enjoyed the French Revolution', he wrote to the people who'd sent him *Sirocco* first-night cables) he offered both managements the chance to cancel the contracts and to extract themselves from what must have seemed extremely unattractive ventures in the current climate of anti-Coward feeling. Neither did; it was agreed that rehearsals for *The Second Man* would start soon after Christmas, and Cochran had merely laughed when Coward suggested he should abandon the revue. Instead they agreed to go ahead with it early in the new year; Noël was to write all the music, the book and the lyrics as well as supervising the production, and the cast was to be led by Jessie Matthews, Sonnie Hale, and Maisie Gay with a young Viennese dancer called Tilly Losch who was a discovery of Cochran's. By the time Noël and Jack returned to England after their stay with Molyneux, and a brief skiing holiday with Michael Arlen at St Moritz, Coward had learnt the whole of *The Second Man* and also written at least one of the songs for the Cochran revue – a number called 'Dance, Dance, Dance Little Lady' which continued the 'Poor Little Rich Girl' philosophy.

He had also found time to put the events of his immediate past into some kind of perspective:

> On looking back over the past few years during which I have achieved a certain amount of success as a playwright, it has depressed me a little to perceive in peaceful retrospect that my greatest success seems to have been as a public nuisance. I appear by quite unintentional means to have aroused many members of the Press, Church and Public to frenzies of irritation and rage. Elderly Clergymen in Norfolk have burst into print accusing me of sordid licentiousness, decadence, immorality and second-rate sensationalism. Outraged matrons have protested that young virgins visiting my plays are pretty likely to fling aside their hitherto closely guarded virtue forthwith and dive headfirst into lives of unspeakable corruption. The Press in their criticisms have deplored my upholding of vice and belittling of virtue, and in their gossip columns and paragraphs have frequently used my name as a label for any peculiarly unpleasant social type who happened to be in the news at the moment.

13

1928–1929

Youth is fleeting… to the rhythm beating in your mind.

NOËL rehearsed *The Second Man* through the January of 1928 under the careful direction of Basil Dean; the comedy was to open cold at the Playhouse on the embankment at the end of the month with Zena Dare. Ursula Jeans and Raymond Massey as the only other members of a distinguished cast. The author, S. N. Behrman, was then a New York journalist and critic largely unknown in England, though he had already written a trio of plays for Broadway. His *The Second Man* was a Lonsdalian comedy concerned, like *On Approval,* with the mixing and ultimate matching of two couples; Noël's character, Clark Storey, was a second-rate author with the detachment to know it, and the part allowed Noël to impersonate throughout the press caricature of himself: removed, cynical, flippant and periodically very witty. At the beginning of the third act, though, there was an uneasy moment of post-*Sirocco* truth when Noël, as Storey, had to hurl one of his own manuscripts into a wastebasket murmuring 'trash, trash, trash'. Coward warned Behrman that the audience were liable to react wildly to this; in fact they never did.

Behrman's play suggested a basic grounding in English drawing-room comedy that came incongruously from an American journalist, though it perhaps explains why *The Second Man* did considerably better in London than when it was staged in New York with Alfred Lunt and Lynn Fontanne. The characters were strong, the play had an almost perfect symmetry together with a powerful scene in which Ursula Jeans announced that she was carrying Coward's baby, followed almost instantly by another in which Ray Massey tried to kill Coward for maiming Miss Jeans, and on top of all that a fairly happy ending was the final guarantee of the play's instantaneous success in London. Even so, Noël had been deeply apprehensive; rehearsals were not altogether smooth and he remembered only too vividly his reception on the last occasion that he had appeared on a stage, as the author of *Sirocco*. This time however it was all a great deal better, from the applause that greeted his first entrance to the curtain calls which told the cast that they were in a success. Yet Noël could not altogether forget *Sirocco*: 'through the applause', he said later, 'I was listening ironically to crueller noises'. Hannen Swaffer of the *Daily Express* went backstage to make his peace with Noël: 'I have always said', murmured Swaffer in the dressing-room, 'that you act much better than you write.' 'How odd', replied Noël, 'I'm always saying the same thing about you.'

Other critics next morning were in firm favour of the play and of Noël's performance, their main thesis being that what Noël had lost on the swings he was now making up on the roundabouts: 'The world', according to the *Sporting and Dramatic*, 'will readily lose an unequal dramatist for a player of such quality'.

But not all the reviews left it at that; two or three critics decided that as they had never heard of S. N. Behrman, he must be a pseudonym for Coward himself who doubtless had not wanted to risk his name under the title after the catastrophes that were *Sirocco* and *Home Chat*. The mistake was a tempting one, if only because so much of the dialogue of *The Second Man* was in the well-turned, superficially brilliant mould of mid-Twenties Coward, and with the wisdom of hindsight one could almost see it as a dry run for the quartet-crossing of *Private Lives*. But as a matter of record, not one word of *The Second Man* was the work of Coward, who was appearing purely as an actor; though from the end of *The Second Man* to the beginning of *The Apple Cart* a quarter of a century later, all his subsequent London appearances were to be in plays or revues of his own. During the rehearsals and run of *The Second Man,* Noël got along excellently with Sam Behrman who found him 'the most entertaining companion in the world and one of the most generous spirits I know.'

In February 1928, soon after the opening of *The Second Man,* Noël's first play-into-film opened at the Pavilion; it was an Anglo-German co-production of *The Queen Was in the Parlour* with Lili Damita as Nadya and Paul Richter in the part for which Ivor Novello had originally been cast. It was not a critical success, largely because lengthy subtitles played havoc with the flow of Coward's drama and with the talents of the title-writer who seems to have had some difficulty spelling words like aspirin. 'An excuse for bad bed, bathroom and ballroom scenes,' wrote Beatrice Curtis Brown of the film in *The Graphic*, 'do let us be rid of this arty suggestiveness.' A month later the silent film of *The Vortex*, with Novello and Frances Doble directed by Adrian Brunel, opened to better but still mixed reviews at the Marble Arch Pavilion.

Late in March the Hitchcock silent version of *Easy Virtue* opened at the Stoll; it was considerably less faithful to the play, introduced various court sequences, but achieved much better reviews. By this time Michael Balcon at Gainsborough had decided that Noël might be commissioned to write directly for the screen; the result was the script for a romantic costume piece called *Concerto,* designed as a vehicle for Gainsborough's leading star of the time, Ivor Novello. But when Noël gave him the script, Balcon realized that although the story was good enough in itself, it simply would not work in silent film terms since 'it cried out for music'; although he had commissioned it for £1,200, most of which had already been paid, Balcon now asked Noël to call off the deal. Noël agreed, and even returned the money he'd received for it; but *Concerto* was not a total loss for him. A year later, threads of the plot turned up in *Bitter-Sweet*.

While he was playing in *The Second Man*, Coward's still-banned drama *This Was a Man* was performed to tepid reviews but huge audiences by the English Players in Paris where the Lord Chamberlain's ban did not of course apply; extra police were called out to control the crowds on the first night. Some of the English papers reviewed it there, though most suggested that London audiences were not missing a great deal. The Players kept it in their repertoire for the next five years, acting it on tour in Belgium, Holland, Germany, Monaco, Egypt, and South America. In England the Lord Chamberlain's edict appeared still more pointless in March 1928 when Martin Secker published the play in a Coward collection that also included *Home Chat* and *Sirocco*.

Most critics at this time were prepared to accept Coward as an actor after his success in *The Second Man,* but still unwilling to allow that he might again be a good playwright; an exception here was Ivor Brown, who had already managed to get Noël into some kind of historical perspective as a writer:

> Ten years ago we were all looking for that 'new world after the war'. Everybody had his eyes on the horizon and scanned it for the rising walls of a New Jerusalem. We had grand hopes of peace and plenty, of democracy fired by a common sympathy, of a new and kindly social order. People trumpeted the word 'Reconstruction' as though it were magic. We have had our disillusion. Reconstruction withered where it grew. New Jerusalems never rose from their fanciful foundations. Bravery of thought was replaced by bitterness of mood. It was easy to doubt everything: hard to find acceptable faiths. The younger generation may have been dismayed; but at least it could dance. It turned its back on solemn creeds. It was light of toe, light of touch. Of that period and temper Mr Coward is the dramatist… what he has done is to record the laughing way of a generation which is hiding its disenchantment under a smile.

A guest at Goldenhurst on one of the week-ends during *The Second Man* was Noël's old friend G. B. Stern, now back from Italy and making some quick money out of short stories and articles for which Noël berated her thoroughly. Her talent, he claimed, was too great to dissipate; but Miss Stern suspects that what really annoyed her host over the week-end was that of the nineteen rounds of croquet they played on the lawn in front of the house she won nineteen. It was some time before she was invited to Goldenhurst again. Another guest at what was rapidly becoming the most highly populated country-house in Kent was Dorothy Dickson, the American actress and dancer who was already living and working in England. Though later a friend and admirer of Noël's, she had found him unimpressive on a first acquaintance: 'Noël Coward?' she queried. 'Back home where I come from they grow on trees.'

Meanwhile, with *The Second Man* in the middle of a profitable run, Noël started auditions for the Cochran revue which remained without a title until, on its pre-London tour, Lorn Loraine brilliantly christened it *This Year of Grace*. This time Noël did not give up his role in London to be in Manchester on the opening night, though he and a relatively new friend, the novelist Arnold Bennett, did go up for the Sunday dress rehearsal. It was another all-night affair, but rather less gloomy than the final run-through of *On with the Dance* at the same theatre almost exactly three years earlier.

The revue ('a form of entertainment', wrote Ronald Jeans, 'so designed that it doesn't matter how late you get there') was in the best Charlot/Coward/Cochran tradition of no-expense-spared entertainment destined to be taken only after a large and rather good dinner. Not all of the twenty-four numbers were winners, but *This Year of Grace* did give its audience two new Coward songs that were the stuff theatregoers dreams were made of: Sonnie Hale and Jessie Matthews sang 'A Room with a View' and then, in the second half, Hale chanted 'Dance, Dance, Dance Little Lady' to Lauri Devine surrounded by the grotesque, grinning masks of Oliver Messel. Lovers of the kind of revue that used to be described as 'intimate', where the word signified an almost incestuous devotion to proper names, stage jokes and theatrical gossip, were kept more than happy by a number called 'Theatre Guide' which parodied in single-line blackouts some of the current West End plays (Douglas Byng turned up as a bizarre Young Woodley) ending with 'Any Noël Coward Play' in which an actress stepped forward amid raucous boos to announce that this was the happiest night of her life.

The morning after the dress-rehearsal Noël returned to London and *The Second Man,* and that night the opening of *This Year of Grace* went splendidly; during the week ticket agency representatives, hearing glowing reports of the revue, travelled to Manchester to do an advance sales deal with Cochran. Their request that he should remove Coward's name from the London billing as 'it might deter family audiences' was indignantly refused.

This Year of Grace opened at the London Pavilion on March 22nd 1928; the first night curtain rang up at eight, an hour before *The Second Man,* which meant that Coward was able to watch most of the first half and then, by persuading the other three in *The Second Man* to play at about double their usual pace, he got back to the Pavilion in time for the finale. His revue collected, faintly surprisingly, some of the best notices of Coward's career; surprisingly not because it was a poor revue, which it wasn't, but because it was in many respects run-of-the-mill where much of Coward's subsequent work showed rather more striking originality and theatrical courage. St John Ervine, for the *Observer,* went alphabetically overboard in writing what Terence Rattigan later called 'the best notice ever written anywhere by anyone about anything':

This Year of Grace is the most amusing, the most brilliant, the cleverest, the daintiest, the most exquisite, the most fanciful, the most graceful, the happiest, the most ironical, the jolliest, the most kaleidoscopic, the loveliest, the most magnificent, the neatest and nicest, the most opulent, the pithiest, the quickest, the richest, the most superb and tasteful, the most uberous, the most versatile, the wittiest...

and there happily he was stopped by the impossibility of the letter x. Reviews don't come like that very often. All this, so soon after the *Sirocco* attacks, seemed almost like compensation.

1928 was not an altogether exciting year in the light theatre and certainly the revue which earned Coward a thousand pounds a week in royalties was the best of its kind in town. Noël's double triumph in *The Second Man* and *This Year of Grace* was already being written about in terms of the greatest theatrical comeback yet recorded, and the seal was put on his new success by the then Prince of Wales, who had the orchestra play 'A Room with a View' no less than nine times at the Ascot Cabaret Ball. Virginia Woolf, too, was a keen if unlikely fan of *This Year of Grace*. In a letter to Noël she wrote that some of the numbers 'struck me on the forehead like a bullet. And what's more I remember them and see them enveloped in atmosphere – works of art in short... I think you ought to bring off something that will put these cautious, creeping novels that one has to read silently in an arm chair deep, deep in the shade.'

These were the years of the café society, which, contemporary press reports suggest, had been invented jointly by Noël and Prince Edward. In fact its roots went back further, to the marriages which linked the Gaiety Girls and Cochran's Young Ladies to the aristocracy, making the theatre suddenly socially acceptable; the arrival of Diaghilev's Russian Ballet in high society further destroyed the barriers that separated the peers from the players, and such hostesses of the time as Sibyl Colefax gave young actors like Coward and Gielgud the chance to meet not only the aristocracy but, more valuably, novelists and sculptors and other artists in a kind of latter-day salon. But this process of social change, the abolition of rigid formality in entertainment and an uneasy nightclub fusion of the decaying aristocracy and the advancing democracy could hardly be attributed to Noël, though certainly he took part in it and benefited from it in terms of the new opportunities it offered.

Early in the summer of 1928 *The Second Man* came to the end of a successful if not over-long run, and Cochran with his American partner Archie Selwyn began trying to persuade Noël that he should take a second company of *This Year of Grace* to New York, led by himself and Beatrice Lillie, leaving intact the London Company which was still playing to capacity at the Pavilion. While Noël was trying to decide whether he wanted to appear in revue again, he went with Gladys Calthrop to spend a week-end with her family solicitor in Surrey. On the Monday morning, just before they left, the solicitor's wife played them a new recording of *Die Fledermaus,* and on the way back to London Noël found himself thinking about how and why romantic operettas had virtually disappeared from the London stage, to be replaced by the slick, fast, funny American musicals of the Twenties. Out of a sense of nostalgia for the sentimental escapism of the old Daly's musicals, the idea for *Bitter-Sweet* began to form in Noël's mind.

He started to write it on a trip to New York where he went with Cochran in July to scout out possible talent for the Broadway production of *This Year of Grace*, having now decided that he would like to play the revue there for three months in the autumn. He and Cochran didn't find many revue performers of the kind they were looking for, but they spent an enjoyable expense-account fortnight on Broadway seeing such old friends as Fred and Adele Astaire in *Funny Face*. By the time they returned to England the first act of *Bitter-Sweet* was complete and Cochran had agreed to present it in the spring of 1929.

The rest of the summer was taken up with minor family crises; by this time Mrs Coward had sold the lease of the house in Ebury Street (though for a while Noël kept on his rooms there, using them as a flat and an office) and moved the entire family down to Goldenhurst. There, enjoying the full luxury of Noël's success for the first time, she bought herself a new car and drove it smartly through the plate-glass window of the grocer's shop in Ashford. Her other son, Eric, was now twenty-three and not finding it easy to be Noël's younger brother; he was by all accounts a likeable man who seemed in contrast to Noël amazingly ineffectual, a characteristic inherited from their father rather than their mother. As Eric wanted to travel, and as he could find no immediate prospects of any work in England, the family packed him off to Ceylon where he became a tea-planter in the hills outside Colombo. Meanwhile Goldenhurst was proving a trifle cramped as the permanent home of Noël, his parents and Auntie Vida as well as such regular guests as Jack, Gladys, Lorn and Jeffrey Amherst, so Jack came up with a plan which involved converting the barn into a home for all the family while Noël kept the house for himself and his visitors. The family rebelled, fearing that they were being turfed out to make way for Noël's 'grand theatrical friends', and Coward himself proved unequal to the struggle; his family stayed where they were and when the barn was converted it was Noël and Jack who went to live in it.

Soon after they moved in, Noël made plans to spend a few days on holiday in Paris: hearing of this, Alec Woollcott and his friend Harpo Marx decided they would be there first to give Coward a surprise at the railway station. When his train pulled in, Harpo was on the platform heavily disguised as an impoverished musician, complete with violin and upturned hat. 'Hello, Harpo,' remarked Noël as he walked up the platform, stopping only to throw him a coin, 'where's Alec?'

The second lavish and sentimental act of *Bitter-Sweet,* complete with such songs as 'Dear Little Café', was written in the unromantic and unlikely surroundings of a London nursing-home where Noël was recovering from an operation for piles in the late summer; Marie Tempest proved one of his more faithful and informative sick-bed visitors. Earlier Noël had taken the precaution of having a few dancing lessons before embarking on Sonnie Hale's numbers in *This Year of Grace,* and he'd also made his first records, five songs from the revue recorded with the Carroll Gibbons orchestra and released by HMV. Once out of the nursing home he went straight into rehearsal with Bea Lillie for the American production of *This Year of Grace.*

Coward still felt that he was not entirely at home in a revue of this diverse kind, and he wasn't altogether reassured by a ghastly try-out week in Baltimore when he and Miss Lillie ploughed through a series of tumultuous rows about the show and their own parts in it: 'for that one week we loathed each other with every quivering fibre of our beings.' Though he blamed Bea for Baltimore, Noël knew he lacked the elusive revue talent of Jack Buchanan or Sonnie Hale, and felt that he had to work much harder to achieve the same debonair effect. Nevertheless, the opening night at the Selwyn Theatre on Broadway was a riotous success, with stalls going for fifteen dollars on the black market and reviews the next morning that might have been written by Coward himself; Bea Lillie took the town by storm again, something she was to do at roughly five-yearly intervals from then on, their quarrels were instantly forgotten, and according to Robert Benchley in *Life*:

> Noël Coward has proved himself nothing short of a wonder-man in the concoction of *This Year of Grace...* it is the kind of revue that one might dream of writing for a completely civilized world and, so long as people crowd in to see it as they are doing now, we are prepared to retract everything we have ever said against Mankind. If Mankind wishes we will even endorse it – blindfold. But unless someone in America is able to do something that approximates Mr Coward's feat we shall always feel that it was a mistake to break away from England back there in 1776.

George Jean Nathan led a small rearguard action by less anglophile critics who couldn't see much to enjoy about *This Year of Grace,* but they were heavily outnumbered and the revue was obviously all set to be as much of a triumph in New York as it had been in London. The following night Gertrude Lawrence opened in George and Ira Gershwin's *Treasure Girl* at a theatre a few blocks away, and although this was considerably less successful, the Coward-Lawrence-Lillie trio became the most popular of the Broadway stars that season, appearing not only on stage but also at an endless series of charity and social functions where they were called upon to repeat ad nauseam the better-known parts of their musical repertoire.

Coward had originally contracted to play for just twelve weeks in New York, but in view of the packed houses he agreed to stay on through the winter in *This Year of Grace*. In these extra months he revived a number of old friendships, notably among the Alexander Woollcott set which, ranging from Ethel Barrymore through Harpo Marx to Thornton Wilder, gathered every Sunday morning at Alec's apartment for breakfast and backgammon. In December Woollcott devoted five pages of the New Yorker to a loving profile of the Master entitled 'Heureux Noël', and Coward himself published three plays (*The Queen Was in the Parlour, Sirocco* and *Home Chat*) that were as yet unknown in America. This edition carried an introduction from Arnold Bennett describing Coward as 'boyishly ingenuous, yet the most comprehensive man of the theatre in London today.'

Early in 1929 Noël too wrote an introduction, one of the first of dozens that he was to pen over the years; this was to Constance Collier's autobiographical *Harlequinade,* and it ignored a bitter quarrel they'd been through a few seasons earlier when Miss Collier had wanted to play in *Easy Virtue*. Noël managed, in paying tribute to Miss Collier's character, to pinpoint the qualities that he admired in and demanded of an actress: 'She is one of the few people I know who has concentrated heart and soul on her job and who has never for an instant wished for any laurels other than those legitimately earned in her profession... Nor has she ever doubted that for her as for all of us who belong, the theatre is the most adventurous, exciting and glamorous life in the world.'

In spite of the nightly demands of *This Year of Grace* and a large amount of socializing in and around New York, Noël found time that winter to complete *Bitter-Sweet*. Alfred Lunt suggested the title, and the rest of the music progressed smoothly once the main tune, 'I'll See You Again', had established itself firmly in Noël's mind during a traffic jam on the way home from the theatre. His first idea about Sari – the character who starts the operetta as a dowager Marchioness in London and then, in a flashback to the Vienna of 1880, drops fifty years to become the tragic romantic heroine who loses her lover in a duel – had been that Gertrude Lawrence should play it; but in New York during the winter both he and she came to realize that her voice was not strong enough or operatic enough to carry so lengthy and demanding a role as a singer. So Coward cabled Cochran in London, asking him to find a theatre and also to approach Evelyn Laye with a view to her playing Sari. But Miss Laye was not at that moment best pleased with the Cochran management. Her marriage to Sonnie Hale had recently broken up, according to rumour, because of his devotion to Jessie Matthews whom he later married; and it was after all Cochran himself who had just presented Miss Matthews and Mr Hale together as the co-stars of *Wake Up and Dream*.

In a mood of some bitterness Miss Laye turned down Cochran's offer, and *Bitter-Sweet* was still without a leading lady.

Then, shortly before Coward was due to leave New York, he literally ran into the American actress Peggy Wood in the lobby of the Algonquin Hotel. Alec Woollcott had suggested that she might be right for the part of Sari; Noël rapidly auditioned her in his studio apartment at the Hotel des Artistes, and within a matter of days she had signed the contract to play it in London, though Cochran was to have severe doubts about her looks and her faint American accent. A few days later Noël returned to London, leaving Bea Lillie to take *This Year of Grace* on to Philadelphia with Billy Milton as his replacement, and *Bitter-Sweet* went into rehearsal on the stage of the Scala Theatre at the end of May 1929.

> It was [wrote Noël afterwards] a musical that gave me more complete satisfaction than anything else I had yet written. Not especially on account of its dialogue, or its lyrics, or its music, or its production but as a whole. In the first place, it achieved and sustained the original mood of its conception more satisfactorily than a great deal of my other work. And in the second place, that particular mood of semi-nostalgic sentiment, when well done, invariably affects me very pleasantly. In *Bitter-Sweet* it did seem to me to be well done, and I felt accordingly very happy about it.

Noël's first venture into the world of operetta was a lavish return to the Viennese past in three acts and six scenes, and its score represents Coward at his closest to Ivor Novello, with lilting, unashamedly sentimental numbers like 'Zigeuner' and 'If Love Were All' as well as the classic 'I'll See You Again' which over the years proved to be one of the greatest song hits he ever had. Not surprisingly, it retains a very special place in his musical affections: 'Brass bands have blared it, string orchestras have swooned it, Palm Court quartettes have murdered it, barrel organs have ground it out in London squares and swing bands have tortured it beyond recognition... and I am still very fond of it and very proud of it.'

In the gloom that followed the General Strike, Coward had decided the time was right for a little romantic escapism and *Bitter-Sweet* was just that. It is true that in numbers like 'Ladies of the Town' and 'Green Carnation' there were signs of a wittier, more pointed and less schmalz-ridden musical, but by and large he seemed happy to surrender himself to the charm and the emotion that had filled Daly's so successfully for so many years; if *Bitter-Sweet* was not one of the original tales from the Vienna Woods, then it was a very passable imitation.

With Peggy Wood engaged, the rest of the characters proved easier to cast; Ivy St Helier was playing the part of the love-lorn *diseuse,* Manon la

Crevette, which Noël had written with his old friend in mind, and George Metaxa (who had only recently abandoned a promising career in the Romanian Ministry of Agriculture for the comparative insecurity of the stage) was cast as the music teacher Carl Linden. A young Robert Newton played Sari's priggish fiancé, and Alan Napier turned up as the Marquis whom she ultimately married. Cochran left Coward totally in charge of the production after an initial squabble over who should design the sets; Noël had wanted Gladys Calthrop to do them all, but Cochran insisted reasonably enough that if the second act, which took place in the Vienna café, was to stand apart from the English scenes before and after, it should be designed by a different artist. Accordingly he brought in Ernst Stern, who had done the sets for Reinhardt's production of *The Miracle,* to design the second act while Gladys did the first and third. Expert help was also sought from Tilly Losch, who came in to choreograph one of the dance sequences.

In rehearsal, Coward managed a company of nearly a hundred people, among them Sean O'Casey's future wife Eileen Carey, with tact and efficiency; Billy Milton, who had taken over from Coward in the New York production of *This Year of Grace,* now returned to London to play Vincent Howard, the young lover at the beginning of *Bitter-Sweet.* Coward's instructions at rehearsal were deep, characteristic: 'Play it very quickly, very clearly – and don't give them a chance to think.' Milton remembered Coward in rehearsal as kindly but somewhat distant 'like visiting royalty, gracious, lofty and always looking as though he were about to bestow some tremendous honour on one of the company'. One morning Ivy St Helier, having a little trouble with her part, heard a voice from the back of the dress-circle reminding her of something she had told Coward in a Manchester hotel room twelve years earlier: 'Never apologize to an audience!'

A great deal was at stake here – not only in terms of the tens of thousands of pounds that Cochran was spending on *Bitter-Sweet* but also because this was Coward's first major work as a composer and the first big show for which he alone could be held totally responsible as writer, composer, lyricist and director. By the nature of revue, *This Year of Grace* had been a far more fragmentary affair. With Elsie April, Geraldo and Cochran's resident orchestrator, de Orellana, looking after the notation of the music, rehearsals went remarkably smoothly; both Peggy Wood and Ivy St Helier had effective if highly emotional moments which they worked hard and carefully to bring to life, and when Cochran came to the final rehearsal in London he was incoherent with joy at the effectiveness of it all. That run-through was, decided Noël later, the most exciting performance of *Bitter-Sweet* that the cast ever achieved; as it finished Cochran found his voice, 'I would not,' he told the company, 'part with my rights in this show for a million pounds.'

Again Noël decided to use Manchester for a fortnight's try-out before bringing *Bitter-Sweet* into His Majesty's Theatre in London, and so its first public performance was at the Palace on July 2nd 1929. A few hours before it, Coward sent Cochran a telegram:

DEAR COCKY I HOPE THAT TONIGHT WILL IN SOME SMALL MEASURE JUSTIFY YOUR TOUCHING AND AMAZING FAITH IN ME. WITH MY DEEPEST GRATITUDE I WISH YOU SUCCESS. YOURS AFFECTIONATELY NOËL COWARD.

Cochran's amazing faith was indeed justified. The opening of *Bitter-Sweet* proved to be a riotous success and the reaction from both audience and press in Manchester, where on opening night they actually stood on their seats to cheer it, made the London opening ten days later seem something of an anti-climax.

Where Manchester had been lyrical in its praise, London was grudging; after a glittering first night, attended by Prince George, Lilian Braithwaite, Lady Mountbatten and Ivor Novello among innumerable others, the reviews were something less than ecstatic. *The Times* considered it 'a rather naive medley for a man of Mr Coward's talents', and though the tabloids were slightly better, awarding most of the acting honours to Ivy St Helier as Manon, the general temperature of the reviews was greatly and inexplicably cooler than for *This Year of Grace*. The fact that Coward had achieved a one-man English operetta unequalled in scope since the demise of Gilbert and Sullivan seemed to go largely unnoticed except by James Agate, who observed that it was a 'thoroughly good light entertainment'.

Nevertheless Madge Garland noted at the first night, that 'tiara'd women clapped till the seams of their gloves burst; the older generation could say with more complacency than truth that this was the way they had fallen in love, and the younger generation were wondering if in rejecting romantic love they might not have missed something.'

The journalistic estimate was that *Bitter-Sweet* would run at His Majesty's for about three months; in fact it lasted there for eighteen, then transferred to the Palace Theatre and ended its run in April 1931 after playing to cut-price audiences at the Lyceum. All in all nearly a million people saw it during more than seven hundred and fifty performances in London, and counting the subsequent French and American productions as well as the film rights and song royalties, it would be fair to assume that *Bitter-Sweet* made its author richer over the years by something in the region of two hundred and fifty thousand pounds. The published script was dedicated by Noël to Cochran, 'my help in ages past, my hope in years to come'.

14

1929–1930

My body has certainly wandered a good deal, but I have an uneasy suspicion that my mind has not wandered nearly enough.

IN the autumn of 1929, Cochran was planning a Broadway production of *Bitter-Sweet* in partnership with Archie Selwyn and Florenz Ziegfeld whose theatre it was to occupy. Once the London company with Peggy Wood were settled into His Majesty's, Noël took ten days off and went to stay in Avignon with William Bolitho, the author of *Twelve against the Gods,* whom he had first met at one of Woollcott's levées in New York the previous winter. Then, early in September, Noël began without much energy or enthusiasm to direct the second company for New York. Again he worked at the Scala, where rehearsals that had become repetitive and unexciting beyond belief were enlivened by the enthusiasm of Evelyn Laye, who was at last playing Sari having in the meantime seen *Bitter-Sweet* and realized the appalling mistake she had made in turning down the original offer. Cast opposite her as Carl was an incoherent Italian tenor called Alexandro Rosati, who had been engaged by Noël largely on the strength of his operatic voice but who then had to be abandoned in Boston on the way into New York when it was realized that hardly a word he spoke could be understood by the other actors, let alone the audience.

Evelyn Laye, who had never worked with Coward before, gave a broader performance than Peggy Wood and found it an enjoyable if daunting experience:

> In rehearsal Noël would give precious little actual direction, but he came up on the stage and acted some of the scenes with me and then suddenly I realized how they had to be played; he lit up everything and everybody around him at those rehearsals. I was always rather nervous of him offstage, and of that set of people like Gladys Calthrop and Jack Wilson who were always with him, but he was easy to work for because he seemed always so dedicated to it all. His music for *Bitter-Sweet* was remarkably easy to sing if you had a trained voice, and yet somehow it was unexpected. Like Noël himself, the tunes go off abruptly in a new and different direction when you are least ready for it. Like Richard Rodgers and Cole Porter, Coward demanded discipline in his music, and he was the most terrifying man to see in an audience, because his criticisms are ruthless and invariably accurate.

The try-out of *Bitter-Sweet* in Boston was fraught with technical problems, quite apart from the need to replace Rosati by Gerald Nodin at the last minute and the extra work that this entailed; on the opening night Miss Laye was to be heard hissing instructions at him under her breath on stage. Ziegfeld himself washed his hands of the whole production in a fit of pique after Noël had refused his offer of twelve lovely leggy showgirls to brighten up what he considered to be a sub-standard chorus line. But by the end of the Boston fortnight *Bitter-Sweet* was in presentable shape again, and the word of mouth from there ensured a glittering opening night on Broadway, with floodlights outside the theatre and tickets going for anything up to two hundred dollars a pair. A few moments before the curtain rose, Noël appeared in Evelyn Laye's dressing-room with a small mechanical bird in a cage. 'I wanted,' he said, 'to be the first to give it to you.' Miss Laye put the songs over that night with a vitality and charm which amazed even Coward, who had only caught a glimpse of her power in rehearsal and on the road. The show went marvellously; Noël made his by now traditional curtain speech at the end, and as he spoke, wrote Laurette Taylor, 'wreaths of laurels bearing inscriptions like "Duty", "Perseverance" and "Believe in your Star" seemed to be hanging from either arm.'

The reviews next morning went overboard for Evelyn Laye, and were only slightly less enthusiastic about Noël's operetta. Even the stock-market debacle on Wall Street did not prevent *Bitter-Sweet* playing to a weekly gross of fifty-five thousand dollars. It was published in an American edition with *Easy Virtue, Hay Fever* and a preface by Somerset Maugham who gracefully acknowledged that:

> For us English dramatists the young generation has assumed the brisk but determined form of Mr Noël Coward. He knocked at the door with impatient knuckles, and then he rattled the handle, and then he burst in. After a moment's stupor the older playwrights welcomed him affably enough and retired with what dignity they could muster to the shelf which with a sprightly gesture he indicated to them as their proper place… and since there is no one now writing who has more obviously a gift for the theatre than Mr Noël Coward, nor more influence with young writers, it is probably his inclination and practice that will be responsible for the manner in which plays will be written during the next thirty years.

Other writers, however, were less enthusiastic about Coward's talents. T. S. Eliot, writing at this time a *Dialogue on Dramatic Poetry* noted rather forlornly, 'I doubt that Mr Coward has ever spent one hour in the study of ethics', and Sean O'Casey was soon to publish his *Coward Codology,* a scathing tripartite attack on both Noël and his admirers.

But in New York, Coward suddenly found himself in huge demand again, be it to write a musical for the Astaires or to direct and compose background music for a projected season of lavish Cochran Shakespeare. Neither plan came to anything though, and by the end of November Noël was off on his travels again. Before he left, one notice for *Bitter-Sweet* above all the others pleased him in that it explained and justified precisely what he had tried to do; it came from William Bolitho, the novelist with whom Noël had been staying in Avignon earlier in the year. Discussing the essence of *Bitter-Sweet* in the *New York World,* Bolitho wrote: 'You find it faintly when you look over old letters the rats have nibbled at, one evening you don't go out; there is a little of it, impure and odorous, in the very sound of barrel organs, in quiet squares in the evenings, puffing out in gusts that intoxicate your heart. It is all right for beasts to have no memories; but we poor humans have to be compensated.'

In England, *Bitter-Sweet* was still playing to huge audiences at His Majesty's (one old lady went every Wednesday afternoon to sit entranced in the stage box clutching a bunch of violets) and early in 1930 a French adaptation, *Au Temps des Valses,* opened in Paris with Jane Marnac. Later in that year when Peggy Wood had to leave the London cast for a brief rest, Evelyn Laye flew back from America to take over the part of Sari. By this time the transatlantic production had closed after New York and a brief visit to Detroit, but in England *Bitter-Sweet* was still doing well enough to have a new brand of marmalade named after it. Max Beerbohm, already the sage of Rapallo, returned to London briefly and while he was there Cochran commissioned him to do a portfolio of drawings of the cast called 'Heroes and Heroines of *Bitter-Sweet*', which included an uncharacteristically portrait-like sketch of Noël to whom Max took a great liking. When the drawings were published, Beerbohm added to them a note about the everlasting nature of sentimentality, something that must have prompted Coward into writing *Bitter-Sweet* in the first place. 'Sentiment,' wrote Beerbohm in 1930, 'is out of fashion. Yet *Bitter-Sweet,* which is nothing if not sentimental, has not been a failure. Thus we see the things that are out of fashion do not cease to exist. Sentiment goes on unaffrighted by the roarings of the young lions and lionesses of Bloomsbury.'

Soon after *Bitter-Sweet* opened in New York Noël felt that the time had again come for him to travel; he caught a train from New York to Los Angeles, where he spent ten hair-raising and somehow unlikely days amid the frenzy of Hollywood, dining and gossiping with the likes of Gloria Swanson and Charlie Chaplin until he could no longer be certain which were the film sets and which the real houses. Escaping north to San Francisco, he caught a boat to Yokohama at the beginning of a journey that was to take him half-way around the world before he arrived back at Goldenhurst six months later.

These periodic voyages, almost total breaks from work and friends alike, were really the only private life Noël achieved until quite late in his life, and to get them he was having to travel further and further afield. The reason for them was a simple one; Noël had begun to take tremendous care of himself, and was the first to realize that if he wanted to carry on working at his particular rate then he would have to pace himself assiduously.

> I am neither stupid nor scared [he once wrote] and my sense of my own importance to the world is relatively small. On the other hand my sense of my own importance to myself is tremendous. I am all I have to work with, to play with, to suffer and enjoy. It is not the eyes of others that I am wary of, but my own. I do not intend to let myself down more than I can possibly help, and I find that the fewer illusions I have about me or the world around me, the better company I am for myself.

One suspects that, though for most of his life he had been closely surrounded by a small band of loyal friends, Noël enjoyed his own company enormously; certainly at the beginning of this voyage he was painfully aware that for the last three years he had been living in a crowd of people and events which had not really given him any time to think clearly beyond the next first night. On the boat, sailing away from San Francisco, he found that time; he also began to realize that, though he was back on top after the *Sirocco* fiasco, he had no way of knowing how long his success would hold out this time or, worse still, whether it was at all justified. He still could find no measuring-stick by which to assess whether his talent for playwriting, the one most important to him, was a real and lasting talent or whether it was (as most critics were suggesting then and for many years to come) a superficial gift of the glib gab which made possible rapid and early success but not the chance to develop, mature and expand as a writer. Noël simply did not know what his ability was, or where its limits lay, and he could think of nobody objective or perceptive enough to tell him.

In one way, this journey was an attempt by Noël to assess his career and to find out for himself where he could go from here. Looking back over the recent successes on both sides of the Atlantic, he couldn't escape the feeling that 'most of my gift horses seemed to have bad teeth' and that if they were to represent the height of his theatrical achievement then the accusations of superficiality would have had rather too firm a foundation in fact. In the past Noël had always been able to account for bad notices with the theory that critics were influenced by his over-rapid and apparently facile success: now, for the first time, he began to wonder if the plays had also been influenced by that same success. On the boat, as seldom elsewhere until after the war, Noël turned himself mentally inside out and began to consider himself almost objectively. For the rest of the time, as Ivor Brown has said, 'one knows everything of what Mr Coward does and nothing of what he is'; it is possible that except on such rare occasions as this, the ignorance about himself was shared by Noël too. His total obsession with whatever work was in hand led

St John Ervine to remark that 'Coward's entire existence has been spent in a corner of the theatre, remote from the general contacts of everyday life. I am amazed and disturbed at the slenderness of his intellectual resources… we might well wonder whether he has ever read a great book, seen a fine picture or a notable play, listened to music of worth, observed a piece of sculpture or taken any interest in even the commonplaces of a cultured man's life… his political, social and religious interests are negligible or non-existent.'

It seems unlikely that the journey around the world gave Noël a chance to catch up on all that, and one doubts whether he returned to Goldenhurst with a political, social or religious awareness that was noticeably more acute than when he left, but it was at least a beginning: this journey also gave Noël a chance to think ahead and to involve himself in issues greater and more important than the need to write a little something for the next Cochran revue. It was to supply one classic light comedy, but also a play that was both angrier and more committed to a point of view than anything else Coward ever wrote.

On this therapeutic voyage as on the last in 1927, Noël's first destination was Hawaii. This time he stayed only a few days, again as a guest of Walter Dillingham on Diamond Head, and then returned to the ranch at Mokuleia on the other side of the island where Noël had spent so long in convalescence on his first visit. Again Coward was overwhelmed by the already legendary hospitality of the Hawaiians, only this time he was in a fit state to enjoy it; he found time for a fish-spearing exhibition off the Oahu beaches, which were in those days comparatively unadopted by the tourist trade, and he also managed a vast amount of bathing before it was time to board the Tenyo Maru, a rather shaky steamship bound for Yokohama.

In the eight days that it took to reach Tokyo's maritime port from Honolulu, Noël set to work on a lengthy novel called *Julian Kane* which soon became so boring that he decided neither he nor any future reader would ever have the energy or the will-power to finish it. Instead he began to think about a new play, one that he had promised to write for Gertrude Lawrence as a consolation prize for not giving her the part of Sari in *Bitter-Sweet*. But no theme of any kind presented itself to his imagination, and all that Coward managed before the ship docked at Yokohama was the resolution never again to promise a play to anyone without first having something definite in mind.

Arriving in Japan, Noël discovered that Douglas Fairbanks and Mary Pickford had been there before him. Moreover they had arranged for him to be met by a massive official welcoming party on the quayside at Yokohama. Accordingly a launch was sent out to intercept his boat in the harbour and bring him ashore; but it pulled away from the Tenyo Maru rather too sharply with the result that the Japanese dignitaries were given their first sight of Noël flat on his face on the deck.

From Yokohama Noël travelled less precariously overland to the Imperial Hotel in Tokyo, where he was to meet his old friend and travelling companion Jeffery Amherst. According to a plan the two men had formulated at Goldenhurst almost a year earlier, Amherst, who had given up his job on the *New York World* to travel through the South Seas, would join up with Noël in Tokyo and together these two compulsive tourists would journey on to Peking, Angkor, Shanghai, Hong Kong, Indo-China, Singapore and back home via Colombo and the Suez Canal. That, at least, was the plan. Checking in at the Imperial, Noël discovered that Jeffery would be three days late; Noël spent the time sightseeing around Tokyo, which in 1929 he found flat and tremendously ugly, 'a sad scrap-heap of a city, rather like Wembley in the process of demolition.' Then, on the night before Jeffery was due to arrive, he went to bed early in the hope of waking up in time to greet him off the boat. But he failed to get much sleep:

> The moment I switched out the lights, Gertie appeared in a white Molyneux dress on a terrace in the South of France and refused to go again until four in the morning, by which time *Private Lives,* title and all, had constructed itself. In 1923 the play would have been written and typed within a few days of my thinking of it, but in 1929 I had learned the wisdom of not welcoming a new idea too ardently, so I forced it into the back of my mind, trusting to its own integrity to emerge again later on, when it had become sufficiently set and matured.

The next morning Jeffery arrived, and with him Noël spent three weeks viewing Japan before they moved on through Korea and Manchuria to Peking and then Shanghai. Paradoxically, Noël was able to find absolute peace and quiet in his life only when travelling; by some curious temperamental reversal of the nerves he was at his most tranquil when moving, and he travelled not for the pleasures of leaving or arriving or returning, nor yet for those of sightseeing, but for the sheer joy of finding himself on the move again. These were the only moments in his youth and middle age when time and place were absolutely immaterial, when he felt totally relaxed, and they resulted in some of his best writing.

The very end of 1929 found Noël and Jeffery at Mukden in Manchuria, where they celebrated the arrival of the Thirties with the understandably homesick members of the English Club before travelling on by train to Shanghai. En route Noël and Jeffery kept a gramophone and a large supply of Sophie Tucker's records in the train compartment, and left it only occasionally at stations when a local delegation would greet them with a few halting words of English. The sight of two travelling Englishmen – one an aristocrat at that

– was still rare enough in many parts of the far east to warrant an effusive reception committee, and in some places Noël's name was already vaguely familiar. Earlier, travelling by train through Korea, they had been flattered to find a huge crowd at one station and Noël was already shaking hands and launching into an impromptu speech to thank the Koreans for turning out in such force to meet him along the way when Jeffery saw out of the corner of his eye that a coffin was being unloaded from the other end of the train. It gradually became apparent that the Korean dignitaries were on the platform to meet and mourn the body of a distinguished local general.

After they reached Shanghai Noël spent a week in the depths of influenza, followed by a further fortnight's convalescence; wrapped in an uncharacteristically hideous flannel dressing-gown, he spent the time sketching out in some detail the three acts of *Private Lives* which he now considered to have matured sufficiently for the whole lot to be put on paper. The actual writing of what is perhaps his best comedy, and certainly the one which provides his safest claim to posterity, took him barely four days. He then cabled Gertrude Lawrence in New York telling her to keep the autumn of 1930 free, and put *Private Lives* away in his suitcase for a few more weeks before revising and typing a final draft.

Now totally recuperated, Noël stayed on for a further week in Shanghai where he and Jeffery met and made friends with a group of young naval officers who got permission from their captain for the two men to travel as passengers aboard *HMS Suffolk* on the journey down river from Shanghai and on to Hong Kong. It was, for Noël, the first of countless voyages as a guest of the Royal Navy; their traditions, the routine and discipline of the ward-room, the relentless Englishness of naval officers and their habit of dressing nightly for dinner while a marine band struggled through *Bitter-Sweet* as a well-meant tribute to their distinguished passenger, all struck in Coward a loud chord of sentimental attraction and devotion. Apart from his deep love of the sea, he found in the permanent activity of a cruiser, so long as it did not directly involve him, precisely the kind of relaxation in transit that caused him to travel in the first place. Better than any place on earth, Noël liked being on board a well-run ship and preferably one of the Royal Navy. In the fifteen years between that first voyage to Hong Kong and the end of the second war, he managed to go to sea frequently and almost always with the navy; by way of recognition and gratitude he wrote *In Which We Serve* which for all its emotional patriotism perhaps captured the spirit of the wartime navy better than any other film of the period.

At Hong Kong Noël and Jeffery reluctantly disembarked, leaving *HMS Suffolk* to sail on without them, and stayed for a week at the Peninsula Hotel in Kowloon. There Noël typed the final draft of *Private Lives* and posted copies of it to Gertrude Lawrence and Jack Wilson, with instructions that they should cable him in Singapore or Colombo with their reactions. That done, he and Jeffery caught a foul and filthy French cargo boat which happened at that time to be the only vessel leaving Hong Kong for their next chosen port of call, Haiphong. After five indescribably gloomy days at sea in a ship resembling the *Suffolk* only in so far as it travelled reasonably successfully over the water, they docked at Haiphong in what was then Indo-China and hired a car to drive inland. Their first stop was Hanoi, then capital of the French colony of Tonkin and in the throes of a minor revolution infinitely quieter and less devastating than the war which was to tear it apart thirty-five years later. Noël and Jeffery stayed overnight in Hanoi and then, hiring another car this time complete with driver, drove south through what is now Vietnam to Saigon. It took them a week, and Noël used the time to compose without pen, paper or piano, a song which had more than a passing relevance to his current occupation:

Mad Dogs and Englishmen
Go out in the midday sun,
The Japanese don't care to.
The Chinese wouldn't dare to,
Hindoos and Argentines sleep firmly from twelve to one,
But Englishmen detest a siesta.

The night before they were supposed to reach Saigon, Noël and Jeffery and their driver were staying in the rest-house of one of the villages developed along the route by the French colonizers when Jeffery became violently ill. During the night Noël took his temperature and, deciding not to tell Jeffery that it was over a hundred and four, woke the driver to make the last lap of the journey to Saigon as rapidly as possible. There Amherst was diagnosed, wrongly, as suffering from nothing more acute than a minor complaint of the liver. Nevertheless the doctor kept him in hospital in Saigon for over a month, leaving Noël on his own to explore a city that then claimed to be the Paris of the Orient. Coward found Saigon in 1930 'a very small town, well-arranged with several cafés and a municipal opera house, but not very like Paris.'

After the month was up, Jeffery, though still painfully thin and drawn, seemed to be better so he was allowed to leave hospital and with Noël travelled on to Angkor and then over the Siamese border to Bangkok. From there they caught a Danish freighter to Singapore, and on board Jeffery was again taken severely ill. From the boat Noël got him into a hospital in Singapore and was already beginning to think about how he would break the news of his old friend's death to the Amherst family in London when a local doctor diagnosed, correctly this time, that Jeffery had a bad case of amoebic dysentery which if treated correctly would keep him in hospital there for a month but no longer.

Faced with another enforced delay, Noël wondered what to do with his time in Singapore; it didn't take him long to find a group of English actors in the town, members of a troupe of strolling players called The Quaints whose strolls, organized by James Grant Anderson, took them all over India and the far east in the late Twenties and early Thirties. Currently they were playing at the Victoria Theatre in Singapore with a company which included Betty Hare and a twenty-two-year-old John Mills, and their repertoire was catholic enough to comprise *Hamlet, Mr Cinders, When Knights Were Bold* and R. C. Sherriff's triumphant war play *Journey's End.* Noël spent the whole of that month with The Quaints, first as a friend and then as an actor when (having temporarily lost one of their leading men) they persuaded him to play Stanhope for the three performances they were giving of *Journey's End.* Coward, having nothing better to do while Jeffery was still in hospital, agreed to try the role and according to what was almost standard procedure for The Quaints he learnt the part in two days and went through it at just three rehearsals before the first performance.

To an audience made up of the social elite of Singapore, who had seldom had the opportunity to see an actor of Noël's distinction in their corner of the world, Coward played Captain Stanhope in an intense, undisciplined, neurotic performance strongly reminiscent of the way he had acted in the early days of *The Vortex.* The local press were keen about John Mills as Raleigh and respectful towards Noël, all save the critic on the *Straits Times* who found the nerve to point out that Noël was unlikely casting for the gallant, tight-lipped officer and that his portrayal of Stanhope as 'a whimpering neurotic prig' was not really what the author or he, the critic, had in mind. Looking back on it Noël found himself forced to agree, adding only that with a little more time he might have improved in the part.

After *Journey's End,* with Jeffery now out of hospital, Noël abandoned The Quaints to continue their tour of the far east without his services as an actor, and together again he and Jeffery set off on the penultimate stage of their journey. This took them by way of Kuala Lumpur and Penang to Colombo where they were met by Noël's brother, Eric, who was still working as a tea planter nearby. It was, though he could hardly have been expected to realize it, the last time that Noël was to see his brother in good health. He and Jeffery spent a few days at Eric's bungalow in the hills above Colombo before returning to an hotel in the town itself where they found Linda and Cole Porter, also on a world tour, among the other guests. It was there that Noël received the first of about thirty telegrams from Gertrude Lawrence on the subject of *Private Lives.* It read, simply if unnervingly:

YOUR PLAY IS DELIGHTFUL AND THERE'S NOTHING THAT CAN'T BE FIXED.

Noël, outraged, cabled back:

THE ONLY THING TO BE FIXED WILL BE YOUR PERFORMANCE.

It appeared, however, from subsequent wires that what needed fixing in Miss Lawrence's view was not the play but her commitments to André Charlot. After she had suggested in successive cables that Noël should postpone *Private Lives* until the following spring, that he should in the meantime do a revue with her for Charlot, that she was contracted to Charlot forever, and then that she perhaps wasn't committed to Charlot at all and a team of international lawyers were trying to sort it all out, Noël not for the last time in his life lost patience with her. Gertrude Lawrence was still for Coward the artist who 'of all the actresses I know can, when she is playing true, give me the most pleasure' but he was not yet prepared to embroil himself in the incredible complexities of her private life and other involvements. He sent one final cable announcing that in view of her indecision he intended to stage *Private Lives* with another actress (an apparently foolhardy gesture until one remembers the number of other actresses who have played Amanda over the years with reasonable success) and before there was time for her to reply to that one, Noël and Jeffery had boarded an elderly P & O steamship heading back through the Red Sea and the Suez Canal to Marseilles.

On this final stage of the journey, having brusquely refused the inevitable deck tennis and quoits invitations, Noël shut himself up in his small, stuffy and deeply uncomfortable cabin to begin another play. At the time, Sherriff's *Journey's End* was still very much in his thoughts, not because of his own performance as Stanhope which he was rapidly trying to forget, but because the general theme of the play had moved and impressed him deeply. Left to himself on the ship he wrote what might almost have been a sequel: a look at life in 1930 seen through the eyes of a dying soldier who could well have been a character in *Journey's End*. The play was *Post-Mortem,* a strange, angry polemic about the betrayed promises and false illusions that came after the war to end all wars; it is a play unlike any other that Noël ever wrote, and one that was not to be professionally staged until after his death. As a vilification of war and of some contemporary attitudes to it, *Post-Mortem* offers some of Noël's best writing as well as a fair amount of his worst; its technique of jumping forwards and backwards in time, together with a tendency for every scene to turn rapidly into a discussion with no visible action, for years made it an impossibility for a professional stage director, though there was once a suggestion that Guthrie McClintic would attempt it. It has since been staged by captured British soldiers at a prison camp in Germany in 1944, by a school in Thame in 1966, and more recently at the King's Head Theatre in 1990. As a play it would seem to be ideally and almost uncannily suited (in form if not now in content) to the confines and altogether different demands and possibilities of a television production; realizing this, the producer Harry Moore included a shortened version of *Post-Mortem* as one in a series of plays called 'The Jazz Age' on BBC television in the autumn of 1968, and there was a professional stage premiere in London some twenty years later.

In *Post-Mortem* Coward does not so much write as explode on to paper; the play has a violence that is to be found nowhere else in his work, and he wrote it to release some evidently pent-up furies that could hardly have been allowed to escape into light comedies or period musicals. The result of all the rage in *Post-Mortem* was much the same as the effect created by Noël's performance as Stanhope: under-prepared, hastily conceived, hysterical, often chaotic but frequently very powerful nonetheless. In the fury of his play Coward hits out wildly at the church and state in general and at press barons and socialites in particular; one is aware yet again of the didactic moral preacher in Coward, occasionally fighting its way to the surface and having here a field day. In one tremendously long speech Perry, a character who survived the trenches but is now about to commit suicide (and who perhaps owes a certain amount to Noël's friendship with William Bolitho), describes the England of 1930:

> There are strides being made forward in science and equal sized strides being made backwards in hypocrisy. People are just the same, individually pleasant and collectively idiotic. Machinery is growing magnificently, people paint pictures of it and compose ballets about it, the artists are cottoning on to that very quickly because they're scared that soon there won't be any other sort of beauty left... Religion is doing very well. The Catholic Church still tops the bill as far as finance and general efficiency goes. The Church of England is still staggering along without much conviction. The Evangelists are screeching as usual and sending out missionaries. Christian Science is coming up smiling, a slightly superior smile, but always a smile. God is Love, there is no pain. Pain is error. Everything that isn't Love is error... Politically all is confusion, but that's nothing new. There's still poverty, unemployment, pain, greed, cruelty, passion and crime... The competitive sporting spirit is being admirably fostered, particularly as regards the Olympic Games. A superb preparation for the next War, fully realized by everyone but the public that will be involved. The newspapers still lie over anything of importance, and the majority still believes them implicitly. The only real difference in Post War conditions is that there are so many men maimed for life and still existing, and so many women whose heartache will never heal... The War is fashionable now, like a pleasantly harrowing film. Even men who fought in it, some of them, see in it a sort of vague glamour, they've slipped back as I knew they would...

It is tempting to dismiss *Post-Mortem* and its conclusion that 'life is a poor joke' with the thought that the artist and craftsman in Coward have here been defeated by the man with a message, but there is perhaps rather more to it than that. When the play was first published in 1931 with a dedication to Bolitho, *The Times* felt that 'an overpowering theme has trapped Mr Coward into losing his style and his head'; and technically it is true that *Post-Mortem* is unsatisfactory, as a stage play. But its theme ('if the men who died in the trenches could only come back now and see how little we have done to justify their sacrifice') was a perfectly valid one and the fault seems to lie with Coward's choice of medium, not with that of his message.

The play when published attracted some surprised reviews, mainly from critics who were forced to withdraw Coward from the pigeon-hole marked 'superficial satirist' or 'playboy of the west-end world' and to reconsider him in the light of *Post-Mortem*; but most came out in firm favour of it as a treatise if not as a play, and one man thoroughly impressed by it was T. E. Lawrence, then passing as 338171 Aircraftsman Shaw, a disguise that Noël sent up sky high in his reply ('Dear 338171, or may I call you 338...'). Lawrence of Arabia found *Post-Mortem* 'a really fine effort, which does you great honour as a human being... you had something far more important to say than usual, and I fancy that in saying it you let the box-office and the stalls go hang... as an argument it is first rate... people won't like you for being quite so serious as you are in this, but it gave me a thrill to read it.'

15

1930–1931

Private Lives was described variously as 'tenuous, thin, brittle, gossamer, iridescent and delightfully daring'. All of which connotated to the public mind cocktails, evening dress, repartee and irreverent allusions to copulation thereby causing a gratifying number of respectable people to queue up at the box office.

EARLY in the summer of 1930 Noël was back at Goldenhurst after his travels, and arrangements for the production of *Private Lives* that autumn were already in hand. To his amazement he had discovered when he got home that all the problems surrounding Gertrude Lawrence and her intricate commitments to André Charlot had vanished, and that she was not only available to play Amanda but was already over from America, staying at Edward Molyneux's luxurious villa at Cap d'Ail in the South of France, learning the lines. Noël decided to join her there, and wrote accordingly to Miss Lawrence:

> Mr Coward asks me to say that there was talk of you playing a small part in a play of his on condition that you tour and find your own clothes (same to be of reasonable quality) and understudy Jessie Matthews whom you have always imitated. Mr Coward will be visiting the South of France in mid-July and he will appear at Cap d'Ail, whether you like it or not, with Mr Jack Wilson on the 20th. If by any chance there is no room at the rather squalid lodgings you have taken, would you be so kind as to engage several suites for Mr Coward and Mr Wilson at the Hotel Mont Fleury which will enable same Mr Wilson and Mr Coward to have every conceivable meal with you and use all your toilets for their own advantage. Several complicated contracts are being sent to you by Mr Coward on the terms you agreed upon – i.e., £6 10s 0d a week and understudy.

On the way to Cap d'Ail with Jack, Noël stopped in Paris to see Sacha Guitry, the playwright and actor to whom he was still most frequently compared; the two men discovered reluctantly that they did have a fair amount in common, in their approach to the theatre in general and to light comedy in particular, and there was even a suggestion that after its London run Coward should do *Private Lives* in translation at Guitry's Théâtre de la Madeleine in Paris. Guitry also volunteered to write a play for Noël which he would then act in French in Paris, but this association of two actor-authors never came to anything, though three years later Coward did write *Conversation Piece* as a vehicle for Yvonne Printemps, the second of Guitry's five wives.

Leaving Paris for the South of France, Noël and Jack arrived at the Molyneux villa and there, with Gertie, Noël began to rehearse the main scenes of *Private Lives*. Writing later about that summer, Miss Lawrence remembered: 'every evening we arranged and rearranged the furniture in the drawing-room for a rehearsal. My other guests – among them G. B. Stern and William Powell – wandered in and out, amused themselves as they wished, and looked on Noël and me as two quite pleasant but quite mad creatures.'

At the end of July Noël and Gertie returned from Cap d'Ail and went into full rehearsal of *Private Lives* in London with Noël himself directing and Gladys Calthrop designing the sets. The rest of the casting was now complete: Victor was to be played by a young, moustached Laurence Olivier and Sibyl, the other protagonist in Coward's mixed doubles, by Adrianne Allen; Everley Gregg played the only other character, a maid with one brief appearance in Act III but to all intents and purposes there were anyway only two people in the entire play – Elyot Chase, played by Noël, and Amanda Prynne, played by Gertrude Lawrence. For Miss Allen and Mr Olivier were playing parts that, by Coward's own admission, existed solely as 'extra puppets', feeds to supply himself and Miss Lawrence with the motivation they needed to launch into lengthy duologues, one of which lasted for the whole of the second act. Victor and Sybil were considered by their creator to be 'little better that ninepins, lightly wooden and only there at all in order to be repeatedly knocked down and stood up again'. That Coward was aware of this from the very beginning explains the casting of Olivier in what must seem one of the more unlikely parts in Sir Laurence's long and distinguished career. Victor had to be attractive enough for Amanda to have married him, and from Noël's point of view to have a bad part played by a bad actor would have been too great a risk; on the principle that only exciting actors can ever play bores successfully, Coward approached Olivier whom he'd seen a year before in *Paris Bound*, knowing that he was sufficiently in need of a success (he had given up the chance of playing Stanhope in the original West End production of *Journey's End* to go into a disastrous *Beau Geste*) to accept the part of Victor.

For Olivier it was to be an instructive time; Noël sent for him to come to Ebury Street, where he found Coward sitting up in bed having breakfast:

> He told me I could ill afford to turn down the shop window of a London success at this point in my career; and he was, not arrogantly but in a matter-of-fact way, quite certain that *Private Lives* would be a triumph. I went away, read the play, and returned to tell Noël in all seriousness that I'd rather play Elyot – he nearly died with laughter. Then he told me not to be a bloody fool, that he'd get me fifty pounds a week for playing Victor, and that we'd start rehearsing in a fortnight. In rehearsals, in his own practical way, Noël was a great mind-opener and very inspiring to

work for... he was probably the first man who took hold of me and made me think... he taxed me with his sharpness and shrewdness and brilliance, and he used to point out when I was talking nonsense which nobody else had ever done before. He gave me a sense of balance, of right and wrong. He would make me read; I never used to read anything at all. I remember he said, 'Right, my boy, *Wuthering Heights, Of Human Bondage* and *The Old Wives' Tale* by Arnold Bennett. That'll do, those are three of the best. Read them.' I did... Noël also did a priceless thing; he taught me not to giggle on the stage. Once already I d been fired for doing it, and I was very nearly sacked from the Birmingham Rep. for the same reason. Noël cured me; by trying to make me laugh outrageously, he taught me how not to give in to it. My great triumph came in New York when one night I managed to break Noël up on the stage without giggling myself.

With Olivier cast and rehearsals well under way, the Lord Chamberlain (still Lord Cromer) announced that he was unhappy with the love-scene in the second act, which by the standards of 1930 and considering that the participants were technically divorced and remarried to other partners seemed altogether too risqué. Noël repaired instantly to St James's Palace where he read the play, acting out all the parts in front of His Lordship who was then persuaded that with some dignified direction the scene would after all be passable without any cuts. Rehearsals continued until, on August 18th 1930, *Private Lives* had its world première presented by Charles Cochran at the King's Theatre in Edinburgh. It was the first time that Coward and Gertrude Lawrence had appeared together in a straight play since *Hannele* at the Liverpool Rep. in 1913.

Private Lives almost certainly represents Coward's greatest claim to theatrical permanence; though it is the lightest of light comedies it has about it a symmetry and durability that have assured it near-constant production in one language or another from that first tour to the present day. It is in many ways a perfect light comedy, arguably the best to have come out of England in the first half of the twentieth century; and though at the time of its first production it seemed to many critics that *Private Lives* could only survive for as long as Gertrude Lawrence and Coward himself played it, the comedy has in fact been almost consistently successful ever since, a guaranteed copper-bottomed audience-puller that has temporarily rescued countless reps. from the throes of a bad season. Suitably enough *Private Lives* was also the play which, given a 1963 London production by the Hampstead Theatre Club, launched in his own lifetime a 'Noël Coward Renaissance'. It was also the keynote production at the Royal National Theatre for the Coward Centenary in 1999.

Yet *Private Lives*, though it has far outlived its original production, is a play that even more than most of Coward stands or falls by the way it is acted.

On paper, one discovers, there is almost nothing there: brief lines, the occasional aphorism ('women should be struck regularly, like gongs') and duologues that read dully but are designed to be spoken, whereupon, said right, they take on a sparkling life of their own that is quite invisible on the printed page. The dialogue in this comedy of manners is theatrically effective rather than naturalistic; there is virtually no action beyond a fight at the end of Act II and another at the end of Act III; there are no 'cameo' characters to break up the duologues except the maid at the end, and there is really no plot to sustain the actors if their own talents start to fail them. It is, in fact, a technical exercise of incredible difficulty for two accomplished light comedians.

After Edinburgh, *Private Lives* toured Liverpool, Birmingham, Manchester and finally Southsea where one night Amy Johnson was to be found among the audience. Reviews on the tour had been generally excellent, though in this last week *Private Lives* ran into some high moral outrage from a local Southsea critic:

> The play, with the exception of a certain amount of smart backchat, consisted of large buckets of stable manure thrown all over the great audience for two hours... Twenty years ago such a production would have been impossible; of course these four players in their own private lives may be quite moral and respectable. I know nothing about them and don't want to...

In London, where Noël's *Bitter-Sweet* was now well into its second year at His Majesty's, *Private Lives* opened the new Phoenix Theatre with a glittering high-society première. The reviews next morning were mixed, many more good than bad but none exactly raves: most critics offered something of the grudging patronage with which Allardyce Nicoll was later to dismiss Coward in his *World Drama*: 'amusing, no doubt, yet hardly moving farther below the surface than a paper boat in a bath-tub and, like the paper boat, ever in imminent danger of becoming a shapeless, sodden mass.'

One point about *Private Lives* that went almost entirely unnoticed was that, for a comedy, it is based on a very serious situation: Amanda and Elyot are unable to live apart, yet equally unable to live together – they love each other too much and are only too aware of it. Because of this, there is an underlying sadness about the major love-scenes which belies the general impression of a light and flippant comedy. But what the critics thought of *Private Lives* was on this occasion a matter of supreme irrelevance; the combination of Coward and Gertrude Lawrence would have filled the Phoenix to capacity for a season in 1930 if they had chosen merely to read *The Church Times* at one another.

In the brief London run Coward's partnership with Gertrude Lawrence was widely considered to be the best thing that either of them had ever achieved on the stage. Together they created a potent theatrical magic, and there was an indefinable chemistry in the public meeting of their two personalities which ensured that each inspired the other to be infinitely better. Coward himself, writing of Miss Lawrence a few years later:

> Everything she had been in my mind when I originally conceived the idea [for *Private Lives*] in Tokyo came to life on the stage: the witty, quick-silver delivery of lines; the romantic quality, tender and alluring; the swift, brittle rages; even the white Molyneux dress... Gertie has an astounding sense of the complete reality of the moment, and her moments, dictated by the extreme variability of her moods, change so swiftly that it is frequently difficult to discover what, apart from eating, sleeping and acting, is true of her at all... her talent is equally kaleidoscopic. She is the epitome of grace and charm and imperishable glamour. I have seen many actresses play Amanda in *Private Lives,* some brilliantly, some moderately and one or two abominably. But the part was written for Gertie and, as I conceived it and wrote it, I can say with authority that no actress in the world ever could or ever will come within a mile of her performance of it... Yet she can play a scene one night with perfect subtlety and restraint, and the next with such obviousness and over-emphasis that your senses reel. She has, in abundance, every theatrical essential but one: critical faculty. She can watch a great actor and be stirred to the depths, her emotional response is immediate and genuine. She can watch a bad actor and be stirred to the depths, the response is equally immediate and equally genuine. But for this tantalizing lack of discrimination she could, I believe, be the greatest actress alive in the theatre today.

Coward's devotion to Gertrude Lawrence had to survive a few backstage rows during *Private Lives*; on one occasion Everley Gregg was unwise enough to try to break up a fight between them, whereupon as at a given signal both Noël and Gertie rounded on her instead. A week after *Private Lives* opened at the Phoenix, Heinemann published the text of the play, thereby allowing the literary critics to have a go at it. *The Times* found it 'unreadable' while their Literary Supplement considered with rather more justification that the plot was 'so light as to be almost non-existent'. After years in which Noël had been compared relentlessly to Sacha Guitry, J. K. Prothero found a new comparison:

> Mr Coward, brilliant and rootless, emerges more and more as the Aldous Huxley of the theatre. With the same genius for the preposterous, he seizes unerringly on the exuberances and affectations of the moment, but for the purposes of recording only. His satire is not corrective, nor his wit creative. There is the same fundamental lack in his latest as in his earliest plays. He is neither constructive nor combative.

Aircraftsman Shaw, T. E. Lawrence, writing in private to Noël, was impressed by the economy of style in *Private Lives*: 'For fun I took some pages and tried to strike redundant words out of your phrases – only there were none.'

Although Noël claimed that he was unable to write anything while he was playing, during the autumn of 1930 he did, in fact, begin to work somewhat hesitantly on a new play. After the intimacy of *Private Lives* he wanted to try something on a much larger scale, to test his ability to write and produce a show big enough to fill the stage of the London Coliseum. Cochran was enthusiastic about the idea, and Noël began to think over the various possibilities, scouring history from the collapse of the Roman Empire through the French Revolution to a pageant of the Second Empire in his search for a suitable setting. But nothing he could find offered the right combination of crowd scenes and intimate characterization, lavish spectacle and manageable drama, until one afternoon, browsing in Foyles bookshop, he happened almost by accident upon some old bound volumes of the *Illustrated London News*. In one of these there was a full-page picture of a troopship leaving England for the Boer War. Instantly, though he never discovered quite why, Noël knew that this was the period he was looking for. He bought the magazines, hurried back to the new studio flat he had leased in Gerald Road, and began to go through the tunes of the time remembered from his earliest childhood, primarily 'Soldiers of the Queen' and 'Goodbye Dolly Gray'. He had invited Gladys Calthrop and G. B. ('Peter') Stern for tea, and in *Monogram* Miss Stern recalled:

> I had gone down late one afternoon to see Noël Coward at his studio in London and found him in a state of excitement, surrounded by a litter of old illustrated volumes of reference: 'Peter, do you know anything about the Boer War?', for he had just had the idea of writing a revue on a big scale that would cover the events of the first thirty years of the twentieth century. He was going to take one family, he said, and their servants, and show the same people going through it all, and I had ten years start of him, for he was only just going to be born when the Boer War broke out. I told him about the newsboys down the street, about the siege of Mafeking, about Bugler Dunne... We found the title that same evening. I kept on saying 'You want something like Pageant or Procession' – and then Noël shouted 'Cavalcade'!

Cavalcade was ultimately dedicated 'to Peter... in gratitude for a friendship maintained through many of its years', but its publication was still some way into the future. For Noël realized that although he had now crystallized the idea, he wouldn't be able to get it into any kind of shape until after he had finished playing *Private Lives*; only then could he give to *Cavalcade* the vast amount of time, concentration and research that it so obviously needed.

Therefore he outlined the story in brief to Cochran, and promised it vaguely for the middle of 1931.

Meanwhile *Private Lives* was coming to the end of its run at the Phoenix; before those early rehearsals at Cap d'Ail, Noël had made it clear in a letter to Cochran that he was not prepared to let the play run for more than three months in London and three on Broadway: 'If I play the same part over and over again for a long run, I become bored and frustrated and my performance deteriorates; in addition to this I have no time to write. Ideas occur to me and then retreat again because with eight performances a week to be got through, there is no time to develop them.' True to this limit, Noël closed the play in London in mid-December and went down to Goldenhurst to spend Christmas with Jack and the family. Cochran was already preparing his 1931 *Revue* and during that Christmas week Noël wrote four numbers for it; two of them, 'Any Little Fish' and 'Half-Caste Woman' he later recorded himself, and both became if not spectacular hits then at least reasonable and respectably-selling song successes.

The American production of *Private Lives* was due to open at the Times Square Theatre on Broadway at the end of January; Robert Newton was now to understudy Noël, and as Adrianne Allen was committed elsewhere to a film, her part was taken over by Jill Esmond, the actress who a few months earlier had married Laurence Olivier. Soon after Christmas, having given himself a little more time to think carefully about *Cavalcade*, Noël sailed for America on board the *Europa*.

Coward's original idea for *Cavalcade* had been that the thirty years of English history should be traced and dramatized through characters who would be the bright young things of the Nineties, giving birth in their turn to the equally vapid flappers of the Twenties. But on the boat to New York he began to realize that in *The Vortex* and in songs like 'Poor Little Rich Girl' and 'Dance Little Lady', in self-appointed roles as prophet and historian of the Bright Young Things, he had exhausted his anger about the rich, young and trendy of the time; the only trace of that moral finger-wagging at the ways of the modern world to be found in *Cavalcade* is the closing number, 'Twentieth Century Blues'. For his leading characters Noël chose to create a family called Marryot who perhaps for the first time in his work take on a life of their own (later the same was to be true of the family in *This Happy Breed*) and who exist in their own self-perpetuating right, not merely as personifications of something that Noël wished to state. Though still in embryo, the Marryots of *Cavalcade* were to become the quintessential English Family, every bit as archetypal as Dodie Smith's in *Dear Octopus* almost a decade later, and of course the models for the television series *Upstairs Downstairs.*

Arriving in America, Noël hired a penthouse on the corner of West 58th Street, looked up such old New York friends as Alec Woollcott and the artist Neysa McMein, and interrupted his researches on *Cavalcade* for long enough to re-rehearse *Private Lives*. It opened at the Times Square Theatre to reviews that were nothing short of ecstatic even from the less Anglophile critics. On Broadway as in London the Coward–Lawrence partnership worked like a dream; Richard Aldrich, the American producer who years later was to meet and then marry Gertrude Lawrence, saw her for the first time on the stage during the Broadway run of the play: 'I can think of no two people who have given Broadway a more sparkling and memorable evening than Gertrude and Noël in *Private Lives*. Each demanded the best from the other, and always received it; together they seemed the very essence of teamwork.'

Walter Winchell thought it 'something to go silly over', and in one memorable notice *Variety* summarized the plot: 'Mr Coward and Miss Lawrence are a couple of cooing meanies... Coward seems kinda grouchy over the scrapping... he goes to the piano and starts to sing'. The press reaction elsewhere was good enough for Metro-Goldwyn to put in an immediate and excellent offer for the screen rights.

Private Lives played on to packed houses in New York for the twelve weeks to which Coward had again limited himself, and on non-matinée days he locked himself up in the penthouse to plough through all the old volumes of the *Illustrated London News* that he had brought with him in the continuing search for *Cavalcade* material. Some of it, of course, he was old enough to remember: the 1910 beach scene was drawn accurately enough from his memories of Uncle George's Concert Party on the sands at Bognor, and as a South Londoner he could recall all the activity of Victoria Station when the troop trains pulled out for the First World War. Armistice Day he remembered, too, and the frenzy of a night-club in the early Twenties: all that and much more went into *Cavalcade*.

In March, Noël gave an interview to the *New York Herald Tribune*:

So far as I am concerned, posterity isn't of any frightful significance; I think if it were I'd become self-conscious and wouldn't be able to work at all. I could no more sit down and say 'Now I'll write an Immortal Drama' than I could fly, and anyway I don't want to. I have no great or beautiful thoughts. More than anything else I hate this pretentious, highbrow approach to things dramatic. The primary and dominant function of the theatre is to amuse people, not to reform or edify them.

In six years Coward had radically altered his ideas about the purpose of the medium in which he worked.

While *Private Lives* was still running in New York Cochran cabled from London that the Coliseum would not after all be available for *Cavalcade*, since *White Horse Inn* was going in there, but that he could get the Theatre Royal,

Drury Lane if Noël would commit himself to a definite opening date. Reluctantly, not really knowing whether or not he would be able to get it ready in time, but realizing that the Lane was too good to miss, Coward agreed to an opening date in September 1931. *Cavalcade* was already very clear in his mind, but he had only just begun to realize the amount of work involved; Cochran had also asked for production details, and Noël cabled in reply:

PART ONE SMALL INTERIOR

TWO DEPARTURE OF TROOPSHIP

THREE SMALL INTERIOR

FOUR MAFEKING NIGHT IN LONDON MUSIC HALL NECESSITATING PIVOT STAGE

FIVE EXTERIOR FRONT SCENE BIRDCAGE WALK

SIX EDWARDIAN RECEPTION

SEVEN MILE END ROAD FULL STAGE BUT CAN BE OPENED UP GRADUALLY AND DONE MOSTLY WITH LIGHTING

PART TWO ONE WHITE CITY FULL SET

TWO SMALL INTERIOR

THREE EDWARDIAN SEASIDE RESORT FULL SET BATHING MACHINES PIERROTS ETC.

FOUR TITANIC SMALL FRONT

SCENE FIVE OUTBREAK OF WAR SMALL INTERIOR

SIX VICTORIA STATION IN FOG SET AND LIGHTING EFFECTS

SEVEN AIR RAID OVER LONDON PRINCIPALLY LIGHTING AND SOUND

EIGHT INTERIOR OPENING ON TO TRAFALGAR SQUARE ARMISTICE NIGHT FULL STAGE AND CAST

PART THREE ONE GENERAL STRIKE FULL SET

TWO SMALL INTERIOR

THREE FASHIONABLE NIGHT CLUB FULL SET

FOUR SMALL INTERIOR

FIVE IMPRESSIONISTIC SUMMARY OF MODERN CIVILIZATION MOSTLY LIGHTS AND EFFECTS

SIX COMPLETE STAGE WITH PANORAMA AND UNION JACK FULL CAST NECESSITATES ONE BEST MODERN LIGHTING EQUIPMENT OBTAINABLE

TWO COMPANY OF GUARDS

THREE ORCHESTRA FIFTY

FOUR FACILITIES FOR COMPLETE BLACKOUTS

FIVE FULL WEEK OF DRESS REHEARSALS

SIX THEATRE FREE FOR ALL REHEARSALS

SEVEN ABOUT A DOZEN RELIABLE ACTORS THE REST WALKONS A FEW STRONG SINGERS

EIGHT FOG EFFECT INDIVIDUALS NECESSARY

ONE FRANK COLLINS STAGE SUPERVISION

TWO DAN O'NEILL STAGE MANAGEMENT

THREE ELSIE APRIL MUSIC SUPERVISION

FOUR CISSIE SEWELL CROWD WORK

FIVE GLADYS CALTHROP SUPERVISION OF COSTUMES AND SCENERY AND YOUR OWN GENERAL SUPERVISION

THIS SYNOPSIS IS MORE OR LESS ACCURATE BUT LIABLE TO REVISION PLEASE TAKE CARE THAT NO DETAIL OF THIS SHOULD REACH PRIVATE OR PARTICULARLY PRESS EARS REGARDS NOËL.

It says a great deal for Cochran as an impresario that he flinched only slightly on receipt of that cable; the placing of the actors at seventh on the list of priorities came as a firm hint, as if one were needed, that what Coward had in mind here was not so much a play as a spectacular.

Early in May 1931 Noël played Elyot in *Private Lives* for the last time and sailed back to England, delighted that he would at long last be able to start the actual writing of *Cavalcade.* But it was *Private Lives* which was to live on, and to remain at the centre of Noël's career; it also forged a vast number of links that led into the future – both Adrianne Allen and Laurence Olivier made Noël the godfather to their first children, and almost forty years later it was Adrianne's son Daniel Massey who played the part of his godfather in *Star!*, the film of Gertrude Lawrence's life. Noël and Gertie worked together in only one other production, *Tonight at Eight-Thirty* five years later, but for many theatregoers they were never again to be quite as magical as they had been in *Private Lives*: that one comedy lies at the heart and the basis of their reputation both joint and single.

'Sometimes,' said Noël, 'in *Private Lives* I would look across the stage at Gertie and she would simply take my breath away.'

16

1931–1932

The first night of Cavalcade *will remain forever in my memory as the most agonizing three hours I have ever spent in a theatre.*

More than thirty-five years after the first full stage production of *Cavalcade*, Coward found himself at a fork lunch in London the only man in possession of a knife. 'But, of course, dear boy,' he explained to an impressed reporter, 'after all I did write *Cavalcade*.' And indeed if Noël is to be considered in the light of any single technical achievement in the theatre, then *Cavalcade* is undoubtedly the one. Not because it is a very remarkable play, nor because it offers to the literature of the theatre any new or staggering thoughts, nor yet because it has much of a chance of survival (its size and scope have so far defeated most thoughts of professional revival on the stage) but purely because of the massive, almost numbing scale on which it is conceived. From Noël's one ambitious idea, confirmed and clarified by that single picture in a back number of the *Illustrated London News*, grew a grandiose show in three acts and twenty-two scenes that was to cost an almost unprecedented thirty thousand pre-war pounds, and that was to keep a cast and backstage crew of well over four hundred people employed at the Lane for more than a year, playing to a total box-office take of around three hundred thousand pounds. It was, in short, an epic.

Noël returned from New York with the intention of starting work on it immediately, but almost as soon as he landed his mother had an acute attack of appendicitis, and work on *Cavalcade* was put off for a while when it seemed that she might be even more seriously ill. Noël's devotion to Mrs Coward was such that concentration on anything else became impossible when she was ill; she had always been a steely lady on whom he could rely absolutely, and who knew with crystal clarity what was good for Noël and what was not. Now, suddenly, their roles were reversed for a time and Noël found it an uneasy experience; but soon she recovered. When she was better Noël returned to London from Goldenhurst, and together with Gladys Calthrop and the assembled heads of the various technical departments he carried out a long and detailed inspection of the facilities at Drury Lane: the depth of the stage, the width and height of the proscenium arch, and the various lighting and flying effects that were possible. They decided to use all the six hydraulic lifts to move actors and scenery in and out of the action, and settled on an

171

incredibly complicated stage and lighting plot which involved, for the first time in the English theatre, the use of collapsible footlights. Already it was apparent that one of the major headaches for the *Cavalcade* crew was going to be the amount of waiting time between each scene while sets were struck and others built at breakneck speed. Noël and Gladys planned it with the stage staff so that, in theory, there should never be a pause of more than half a minute between scenes, and then having cleared all the estimates with Cochran the two of them went down to Goldenhurst for ten days of intensive work.

From eight in the morning until five every evening with an hour off for lunch, Noël worked upstairs on the script while in the garage Gladys created the designs for the hundreds of costumes and dozens of sets. While *Cavalcade* was in preparation, *Bitter-Sweet* was coming towards the end of its two-year run and had reached the Hippodrome at Golders Green. On an impulse Noël decided to see it there one night, but at the box-office he found himself faced by a formidable lady who told him that there were no tickets to be had and no standing room either. The house was full. Patiently, Noël explained that he had written the book, music and lyrics for the show. For good measure he added that he had also directed it. There was a pause. Then the lady spoke: 'Proper little Ivor Novello, aren't you?'

The London theatre of the very early Thirties was in a fairly desperate condition, not only because the after-effects of the General Strike and the Depression had severely limited the amount of money people were able or prepared to spend at box-offices, but also because the cinema, now an all-talking, all-singing, all-dancing attraction, was offering cheaper and often considerably better entertainment. For the theatre it was a far from vintage time, and most critics found it hard to quarrel with the American George Jean Nathan who, on a visit to London early in 1931, remarked that 'your stage is unworthy of your country.'

Work on *Cavalcade* continued through the summer; in August, with the script typed and all the designs complete at last, Noël and Gladys had a break while the scenery and costumes were being made. They took themselves to a beach in the South of France where the weather was marvellous and the sea warm, but where they never managed to escape *Cavalcade* or to stop thinking for a moment about the gigantic technical problems that still lay ahead.

Back in England at the end of the month they finished casting the show: Mary Clare and Edward Sinclair were to play the Marryot parents and the company also included such Coward stalwarts as Moya Nugent, Arthur Macrae and Maidie Andrews as well as two newer friends from the Singapore 'Quaints', Betty Hare and John Mills. When it came to the auditions for crowd and walk-on parts, over a thousand actors and actresses applied; roughly three for every one job that Noël was able to offer. He found these auditions deeply depressing; not only because so many people had to be turned down at a time when unemployment in the theatre was even higher than usual, but also because he realized that many of the 'lucky' ones, getting barely thirty shillings a week for non-speaking roles, had themselves been playing major parts on that same stage at Drury Lane not so very long before. Early in the rehearsals Coward discovered to his horror that Cochran had promised three stage-struck society-girls walk-ons in the show; after a long argument Noël only agreed on condition that for each of them two extras were taken on from the ranks of those who really needed the work.

Early in September, rehearsals started in earnest; for the first ten days. As the stage was still full of engineers installing the two extra hydraulic lifts which the technicians had discovered *Cavalcade* would need, Noël rehearsed with the principals in one of the bars. Many of the scenes had been rearranged or altered or simply abandoned in the months since that first detailed cable to Cochran from New York, and although the Edwardian beach had survived intact, Noël had reluctantly to jettison the idea of having the sunbathers drenched with rain at the end of it, not because Drury Lane couldn't provide the necessary sprinklers but because the water would damage sets and make the next scene-change impossible. This was the first scene Noël had to rehearse with the full company, and when the engineers had finished building the lifts he found four hundred people on the stage patiently waiting for his first instructions. Daunted by the sheer number of them, Noël found a way of simplifying the production; he divided the crowd into units of twenty people, each with its own leader, and then gave everybody a colour and a number. The captain of each unit took charge of the others, and in blocking the larger scenes Noël was able to call out from the dress-circle: 'Would number seven red kindly cross down to number fifteen yellow-and-black stripe and then shake hands?' At first, in spite of all that organization, the whole thing was unutterably chaotic and Noël was severely tempted to leave four hundred people mingling inanely on the stage and go home to his studio in Gerald Road.

But he forced himself to stay, and gradually out of the confusion some sort of order emerged. Noël encouraged the crowd to improvise their own bits of business, forbidding only any marked over-acting, and the result was the gradual emergence of a whole stage-full of cameo performances that somehow managed to be near-perfect in period and style, whether for the beach scene or Queen Victoria's funeral or the scene at Victoria Station which was complete with a full-scale if recalcitrant steam engine. George Grossmith, then managing director of the company that ran the theatre, attended one of these rehearsals and announced that he was worried because *Cavalcade,* unlike most shows at the Lane, did not have much to offer the children at Christmas time. 'We shall,' replied Noël, 'be putting in a Harlequinade.'

After a week of endless, crisis-ridden dress rehearsals, *Cavalcade* had its first public performance at Drury Lane on October 13th 1931, soon after Britain came off the gold standard and a few days before the General Election threw out the Labour Party to return a true-blue National Government in a mood of near-hysterical patriotism. In the light of such fervour, Coward had a hard time explaining afterwards that the timing of *Cavalcade* was nothing more that a happy coincidence, and that he had not written this ultra-jingoistic epic to cash in on the national mood of the moment. Quite apart from the fact that *Cavalcade* had been conceived a full year earlier, Noël had been so involved in its elaborate production that he was barely aware of the election at all, let alone the likely result of it. He was, as always, bleakly uninterested in politics of any kind.

From *Cavalcade*'s opening toast 'To 1900' it followed the lives of the Marryot family and their servants through to the New Year's Eve of 1929, when another toast was offered:

JANE: Now, then, let's couple the future of England with the past of England.
     The glories and victories and triumphs that are over, and the sorrows
     that are over, too. Let's drink to our sons who made part of the pattern
     and to our hearts that died with them. Let's drink to the spirit of gallantry
     and courage that made a strange Heaven out of unbelievable Hell, and
     let's drink to the hope that one day this country of ours, which we love
     so much, will find dignity and greatness and peace again.

But *Cavalcade* did not end there; instead Coward returned to the bright young things of the Twenties, now ageing somewhat and in a night-club 'dancing without any particular enjoyment; it is the dull dancing of habit.' A singer begins to intone the only contemporary song that Coward wrote for *Cavalcade*:

Blues, Twentieth Century Blues, are getting me down.
Who's escaped those weary Twentieth Century Blues?
Why, if there's a God in the sky, why shouldn't he grin?
High above this dreary Twentieth Century din,
In this strange illusion,
Chaos and confusion,
People seem to lose their way.

The last scene of all, which followed that, was a darkened stage on which different sound and lighting effects gave a general impression of complete industrial and social chaos until it all faded and at the back of the stage a single Union Jack shone through the darkness. Thereupon the lights rose again slowly on the entire company singing 'God Save The King', and the curtain fell on the first night to tumultuous scenes of theatrical and patriotic fervour, amid which Noël addressed the audience from the stage: 'I hope this play has made you feel that, in spite of the troublous times we are living in, it is still a pretty exciting thing to be English.' The cheering redoubled, and as the curtain fell for the last time half the orchestra were reprising songs from the show while the other half were doggedly re-playing 'God Save The King'.

The first night of *Cavalcade* was an unquestionable triumph and the cheers that rang through Drury Lane are still remembered by people who were there. But for Noël, sitting in the stage box, the evening had come within a hair's breadth of being a total disaster. Early in the first act, during the first complicated scene-change, too many of the cast crowded on to one of the downstage lifts and it jammed; there followed a delay which was timed backstage at four and a half minutes, but which felt to most of the audience like four and a half hours. Dorothy Dickson was in the stalls:

> The orchestra kept playing a repetitive period waltz ['Lover of My Dreams'] that Noël had written as a parody of the popular tunes of 1900, and then they played some of the old war songs. People began to sing them softly – then they stopped, embarrassed lest the people sitting next to them should think that they were old enough to remember them. We all turned to watch Noël in the stage box, to see if he knew what was happening, and then the gallery became restless and started to clap derisively.

Many years were to pass before Noël could listen to that music again without shuddering. But during the wait in the box, knowing they were being watched, neither Noël nor Gladys dared to move; Jack Wilson, sitting directly behind Noël, put a hand on the shoulder of Coward's dinner-jacket and discovered it was already soaking wet with sweat. Backstage Danny O'Neill's crew were struggling frantically with the lift, and someone estimated it might take up to two hours to work it free. Then, just as Noël was about to walk down on to the stage and make some kind of announcement, the lift freed itself and *Cavalcade* went ahead. But the delay, and in particular the feeling of suppressed panic that it caused among the company, affected the rest of the performance to such an extent that at the end of the evening, in spite of all the applause, neither Coward nor Cochran were at all certain that they had a success. Cochran, in fact, went to bed convinced that the whole undertaking had failed, and that the reviews next morning would be terrible. He was wrong. By ten o'clock in the morning, when Cochran tried to phone the box-office at Drury Lane to see if they were doing any business, all the phones were busy and a queue already stretched out of the foyer down towards the corner of the Aldwych.

Coward had a triumph, but not perhaps for the reasons he had hoped. *Cavalcade* was hailed as having great patriotic appeal rather than as a good play: the reviews all carried such headlines as 'Coward's Call to Arms' or 'A Message to the Youth of the Nation'. In this context, Noël's curtain speech about it being 'a pretty exciting thing to be English' only added to the general impression and misconception that this was what *Cavalcade* was all about. In fact, Coward had intended there to be rather more to it than pure patriotism; but the audience had chosen to see his play in a different, more jingoistic light and Coward was still the first and the quickest to adapt to what was wanted of him; hence his curtain speech on the opening night.

Nearly seventy years later, with Coward no longer the *Zeitgeist,* it is possible to see that *Cavalcade* was dedicated not to pure patriotism but to the wider concept of Duty that runs through most of Noël's work: duty not only to country but to family, friends, talent, circumstances, ideals – a duty, in fact to behave correctly in all situations, a duty that Coward always saw as a condition of life itself.

Two weeks after the opening of *Cavalcade,* on the election night of October 28th 1931, King George V with Queen Mary and the entire Royal Family went to Drury Lane. The performance ran smoothly, Coward was presented to the King in the Royal Box during the second interval, Mary Clare was cheered by stalls and gallery alike when she spoke the final toast, and at the very end the entire audience rose to join the cast in singing 'God Save The King': during the applause that followed,

> The Queen drew back a little, leaving His Majesty in the front of the box to take the ovation alone. He stood there bowing, looking a little tired, and epitomizing that quality which English people have always deeply valued: unassailable dignity.

Noël had been in the theatre for almost exactly twenty-one years, and in that time he had come a long way to this night. It was even rumoured that, as a result of *Cavalcade,* a grateful monarch would bestow a knighthood on him, perhaps during the interval of that election-night performance. Nothing of the kind happened though, and over the years a number of theories ranging from the implausible to the unprintable have been put forward to explain why Coward only in 1970 became Sir Noël. One school of thought suggested that Noël, offered a knighthood during the run of *Cavalcade,* had jokingly told a friend that 'for a success like *Cavalcade* the least one should get is a peerage.' Apparently his remark got back to the Palace officials and that was the end of that. A more likely solution (apart from his homosexuality) lies in Coward's reaction when, on another occasion, he was offered the honorary rank of Lieutenant-Commander, R.N.V.R.... and decided to turn it down: 'I felt strongly that my name, my reputation and my friends alone would get me wherever I wanted to go.'

Noël Coward at two

At five

At seven

The programme for Coward's first public appearance

As Cannard in *The Great Name* with Lydia Bilbrooke and Charles Hawtrey, Prince of Wales Theatre, London, September 1911

With Esmé Wynne in *I'll Leave it to You* (The first Coward play to be produced in London), New Theatre, July 1920

Coward (second from left) with Henry Kendall, Donald Calthrop, Edith Evans (seated), Alice Moffat and Edna in *Polly with a Past*, St James's Theatre, London, March 1921

With Lilian Braithwaite in *The Vortex*, Everyman Theatre, Hampstead, 1924

'The legend of my modesty grew and grew. I became extraordinarily unspoiled by my great success. As a matter of fact, I still am.' London, mid-Twenties

As Lewis Dodd in *The Constant Nymph*, New Theatre, London, September 1926

Noël Coward in four numbers from *This Year of Grace!*, Selwyn Theatre, New York, November 1928

Noël Coward, drawn by Max Beerbohm for 'Heroes and Heroines of *Bitter-Sweet*', 1929

Private Lives, Phoenix Theatre, London, 1930 and Times Square Theatre, New York, 1931.

LEFT With Gertrude Lawrence
BELOW With Laurence Olivier

OPPOSITE:
ABOVE With Gertrude Lawrence
BELOW With Gertrude Lawrence, Laurence Olivier and Adrianne Allen

'Throughout the 1930s I was a highly publicised and irritatingly successful figure, much in demand.'

Troopship departure, 1900. One of 22 scenes from *Cavalcade* at the Theatre Royal, Drury Lane, October 1931

Noël Coward as Leo, Alfred Lunt as Otto and Lynn Fontanne as Gilda in the last act of *Design for Living*, Ethel Barrymore Theatre, New York, January 1933

Noël Coward as Paul and Yvonne Printemps as Melanie in *Conversation Piece*, His Majesty's Theatre, London, February 1934

Red Peppers

Red Peppers

With Gertrude Lawrence in three of the plays
from *Tonight at Eight-Thirty*

Ways and Means

Shadow Play

Noël Coward in a scene from *In Which We Serve*, 1942

With troops in Malta, August 1943

With Norman Hackforth and the 'little treasure', the Arakan, 1944

At Blue Harbour, Jamaica, 1953

Rehearsing for cabaret at the Desert Inn, Las Vegas, June 1955

With Mary Martin in *Together with Music*, the first CBS colour special, networked coast-to-coast in October 1955

As Hugo Latimer in
A Song at Twilight

As George Hilgay in
Shadows of the Evening

As Verner Conklin in
Come into the Garden Maud

Suite in Three Keys, Queen's Theatre, London, 1966

Receiving his degree as Hon. Doctor of Letters from the Chancellor of Sussex University in July 1972 (Richard Attenborough, left, was Vice-Chancellor)

But even Noël began to be alarmed by all the fervour surrounding *Cavalcade;* he realized that somewhere under it his play had almost entirely disappeared from view, and worse still he realized that it was his own curtain-speech about England which had encouraged audiences to start off on this wrong track; instead of a play about family life with two or three restrained, understated, brief but well-written scenes like that aboard the Titanic, it was being acclaimed as a theatrical rendering of 'Land of Hope and Glory' by all save a few critics in the intellectual weeklies who saw the whole thing as an unnecessary descent into jingoism, a wily commercial trick conceived, written and produced by Coward in a spirit of cynical mockery with his tongue firmly planted in his cheek.

To escape the blame and the over-effusive praise alike, Noël decided that the time had again come for him to sail away; with Jeffery Amherst, his perennial travelling companion, he set off on board ship, bound this time for a lengthy exploration of South America. There seemed, at that moment, nothing else to do; Noël was sure of his purely theatrical motives in writing *Cavalcade,* and though evidently nobody else was, it still seemed unlikely that in terms of stage success he could ever hope for anything better in his career than the night the King had come to *Cavalcade*. And so what now? Coward had not the remotest idea, but at any rate the journey through South America would provide a rest, another change of pace, and a chance to think again about his career; already he realized he had been a daring young man for so long that the trapeze was entirely stationary.

Coward was out of England for nine months, and while he was away St John Ervine again turned his *Observer* theatre column over one Sunday to a discussion of roughly the same thoughts that had begun to trouble Noël as he sailed from Boulogne aboard a German–Spanish cargo boat on a leisurely journey to Rio de Janeiro. Did Coward, in his work, have a distinct philosophy that went beyond the desire to entertain, and if so what was it? In the last two decades he had written twenty-three plays and revues, most of which had further involved him as either an actor or a director or both. For Ervine, Coward was then 'a figure of his age, a faithful representative of a part of the spirit of his time. If we wish to understand some of the youth who grew to manhood in the War, we must take a good look at Mr Coward, in whom the gaiety and the despair of his generation are exactly mingled... what our dramatist has is an emotion about life, the emotion of an exceedingly sensitive and generous nature. That is all. He has no faith, at present, in life here or hereafter: he is a hedonist who has no hope of finding what he diffidently seeks – enough excitement to pass the time... he will do well to guard against the allegory by Mr Max Beerbohm in which a man became like the mask of himself because he had worn it too long.'

But Noël's moments of introvertive doubt were ever short-lived, lasting usually until whatever ship he happened to be aboard reached the next port of call. From Rio de Janeiro he and Jeffery travelled overland through South America and for the first few weeks Noël was happy not to have to think about another play or indeed anything beyond the brief lyric for a song that more or less explained his present condition:

> The world is wide, and when my day is done
> I shall at least have travelled free.
> Led by this wanderlust that turns my eyes to far horizons.
> Though time and tide won't wait for anyone,
> There's one illusion left for me
> And that's the happiness I've known alone.

Reaching the Argentine early in 1932, Noël's sightseeing and his peace of mind were simultaneously interrupted by a telegram from Alfred Lunt and Lynn Fontanne in New York:

CONTRACT WITH THEATRE GUILD UP IN JUNE WE SHALL BE FREE WHAT ABOUT IT?

'It' was a plan that Coward and the Lunts had first formulated all those years ago in New York. One day, they had said, when they were all stars in their own right and happened to be simultaneously free, they would act together in a play of Noël's:

> We had met, discussed, argued, and parted again many times, knowing that it was something that we wanted to do very much indeed and searching wildly through our minds for suitable characters. At one moment we were to be three foreigners. Lynn, Eurasian; Alfred, German; and I, Chinese. At another we were to be three acrobats, rapping out 'Allez Oops' and flipping handkerchiefs at one another. A further plan was that the entire play should be played in a gigantic bed, dealing with life and love in the Schnitzler manner. This, however, was hilariously discarded after Alfred had suggested a few stage directions which, if followed faithfully, would undoubtedly have landed all three of us in gaol.

But now, at long last, the Lunts were free, Noël was free and the venture was possible; the only snag was that Noël still had not the vaguest idea about a play of any kind. For the rest of his travels with Jeffery through Patagonia, Chile, Peru and Colombia he tried desperately to think of a situation for their three characters, and failed dismally. No period, no place, no event offered the right setting for them until, sailing on a Norwegian freighter from Panama north to Los Angeles, Noël suddenly found the idea he was looking for; it then took him ten days, working mornings only, to write *Design for Living*.

Back in England, soon after the opening of *Cavalcade* and in good time for the Christmas book trade, Hutchinson published a volume of Coward's *Collected Sketches and Lyrics*. It was prefaced by some general reflections on the nature and the problems of being one of Cochran's revue writers, constantly at the mercy of a flexible running order and so:

> Usually dragged, protesting miserably, into a cold office behind the dress circle and commanded to write then and there a brief but incredibly witty interlude to be played in front of black velvet curtains by no more than four members of the cast (the principals all being occupied with quick changes), without furniture as there is no time to get it on and off, and finishing with such a gloriously funny climax that the audience remain gaily hysterical for at least a minute and a half in pitch darkness.

At the beginning of February 1932, the Hollywood film version of *Private Lives* reached the Empire in Leicester Square. This, the first Coward 'talkie', was not, according to *The Times,* a suitable play for the screen – if only because there was no way of pre-judging an audience's laughter in the cinema, so the film's timing was invariably just wrong. Those members of the audience at the press preview who noticed how very closely Norma Shearer and Robert Montgomery resembled Gertrude Lawrence and Noël in their playing of the balcony scene might not have been surprised to learn that during the New York run of *Private Lives* the stage performance had been photographed, as had *Cavalcade* in London, for the benefit of actors and producers in Hollywood.

In America the film of *Private Lives* had already proved so successful at cinema box-offices that when Noël got back from South America to Los Angeles and hence Hollywood, he found no difficulty in selling to the Fox Film Corporation the screen rights to three more of his plays: *Cavalcade,* (which fetched a hundred thousand dollars) *Hay Fever* (which was never made) and *Bitter-Sweet* (which was not in fact filmed in Hollywood until ten years later, and then by MGM, though there was an earlier English version). On that profitable visit to Hollywood Noël also sold to Paramount the rights to make a talking picture of *The Queen Was in the Parlour.*

17

1932–1933

*Throughout the Thirties I was a highly publicized and irritatingly successful figure,
much in demand.*

R eturning to England in the spring of 1932 Noël found himself, not entirely
accidentally, on the same transatlantic boat as Alexander Woollcott,
who later described the experience in a letter to Beatrice Kaufman:

> Noël is the only gamester I ever knew with my own wholeheartedness.
> We played backgammon or Russian Bank all the way over. I had never
> before crossed the Atlantic without once laying eyes on the darned thing.
> The other passengers were mysteriously angered by this singleness of
> purpose. They would stop by and say: "Don't you two ever tire of that
> game?" or "Still at it?" or, in the case of the German passengers they
> would merely say "Immer?" to each other in passing. We finally devised
> an effective rejoinder, merely singing in duet:

> We hope you fry in hell
> We hope you fry in hell
> Heigho
> The-merry-o
> We hope you fry in hell.

While he was waiting for the Lunts to be ready for *Design for Living,* Noël
went back to Charles Cochran with the idea for another revue, this one to be
made up of the songs and sketches that he had written since *This Year of Grace*
four years earlier. They included 'Mad Dogs and Englishmen', 'Children of
the Ritz', 'Mad About the Boy' and a wealth of material that he had written
during the nine months he'd been out of England. But Coward was determined
that this next production would be all his own work: not the usual amalgam
of writers, composers and lyricists all brought together under Cochran's ample
banner, but instead a one-man revue of which he would be sole author,
composer, lyricist and director. The numbers would not include the traditional
ballet or slapstick set-pieces, nor the usual lavish panoramas of old Spain or
New Mexico; instead they would be intimate, unspectacular and witty with
rather more concentration on the words than the sets. But even that did not
guarantee enough autonomy for what Coward had in mind; he decided also
that the cast would include no stars of the Lawrence/Lillie calibre, whose

special talents demanded special material which they then moulded into their own peculiar style, but instead less celebrated actors and actresses who could be shaped by Noël into what he wanted for each number. The only other artist involved with Noël in the creation of this revue would be Gladys Calthrop, who was again to design the sets and costumes.

Cochran was understandably appalled; quite apart from the realisation that it would no longer be his but Coward's 1932 *Revue*, he genuinely believed that the best revues were not the work of one man but of several: he was also worried that many of the numbers Coward showed him (in particular the sketches about radio and the press, the two songs in the 'Poor Little Rich Girl' vein – 'Children of the Ritz' and 'Debutantes' – and a mournful ditty about the wife of an unsuccessful touring acrobat) were either too downbeat or else too satirical to form the basis of a successful revue in the early Thirties. But Coward at this moment in his career, with *Cavalcade* still running at Drury Lane and the successes of *Private Lives* and *Bitter-Sweet* still fresh in the public memory, was in a very strong position indeed; Cochran realized that in spite of his many doubts the offer of a new Coward revue was one that no sane impresario could then afford to turn down.

Gradually the new revue was cast, with Ivy St Helier, Joyce Barbour, John Mills and the American comedian Romney Brent leading a company of almost a hundred people that also included in two very minor parts a young South African singer called Graham Payn who was to become Noël's constant companion in the years to come. The revue still lacked a title, though 'Here's to Mr Woollcott, God Bless Him' had already been suggested by Coward's recent fellow passenger; in the end it was called simply *Words and Music*.

At the end of July it went into rehearsal and a month later, like all the Coward–Cochran revues, it opened for an out-of-town trial at the Opera House in Manchester. Throughout the rehearsals Noël had worked frenetically but systematically to ensure that every gesture, every move in every number was orchestrated to the overall theme that he wanted; in this way he superimposed a precise pattern on to every aspect of the production which guaranteed *Words and Music* the absolute unity he had never managed to achieve in past revues. Arriving for the first rehearsal, the company had been amazed to find that, contrary to all revue practice, the running order of *Words and Music* was already planned and typed as were the scripts for all the sketches. From then on, it was rehearsed to all intents and purposes like a play, with none of the usual last-minute alterations in the placing and timing of numbers.

Because of this the first performance went smoothly enough, and the notices next morning glowed with an almost unanimous enthusiasm. The Manchester critics liked the unity of *Words and Music,* and they all welcomed the satire, not a commodity that had hitherto been very apparent in Cochran's revues. But the chaos and confusion so conspicuously lacking from this first night arrived rather unexpectedly on the second, when, shortly before the curtain was due to rise, the conductor and musical director of *Words and Music* abruptly resigned after a disagreement with the management. At ludicrously short notice, as there was nobody else who could possibly do it, Noël was faced with conducting an orchestra for the first time in his life through a long and difficult score. The fact that he had written the music did not make conducting it very much easier, but he and the orchestra managed to struggle through, though not without some casualties; Noël took the number 'Something to do with Spring' so fast that its singers, Joyce Barbour and John Mills, found it quite impossible to keep up. Eventually, giving up the unequal struggle, they staggered off into the wings cursing and exhausted.

After two weeks at the Opera House, *Words and Music* moved to the Adelphi Theatre in London, not the smallest of theatres and possibly ill-suited to what was (despite the size of the cast) essentially an intimate revue. Brian Howard wrote in his diary after the first night 'I have always felt that Coward's music could have been written by some tremendously shrewd bird', but the London notices were generally ecstatic, and it was David Fairweather in *Theatre World* who summarized the case for the show: 'this revue strikes a definitely new note in conception and execution; where others rely on big "names" who struggle valiantly to overcome the handicap of uninspired material, this one takes a few clever people little known to the general public, and makes them into stars through the brilliance of the sketches and songs entrusted to them. In short, *Words and Music* is an overwhelming success of brains in a desert of mediocrity.'

But audiences were not so sure; perhaps because it came under the Cochran banner they found the revue unexpected and not always the escapist entertainment they were looking for. Business was very good for the first few weeks but then it began to fall away badly and *Words and Music* survived for barely twenty weeks. It was the first of the joint Cochran–Coward productions not to show a profit, and although they got some of their money back on a brief post-London tour, Cochran's original doubts about the financial success of the revue had proved to be justified.

Once *Words and Music* had opened, Noël had very little more to do with it; instead he spent the early part of the autumn working on *Spangled Unicorn,* a fairly innocuous parody of modern verse which still affords a few laughs and would not at the time have disgraced an issue or two of *Punch.* But it betrayed signs of hasty preparation and suggested that for its author the joke had run out shortly before the end of the book. To go with the cod biographies of his 'poets', Noël used an unbelievable batch of old photographs which he had bought some years earlier in a London junkshop. But he had failed to realize that though the people involved would obviously now be dead, their families were still very much alive and not best pleased to find photographs of their dear departed adorning a mocking parody of this nature. It was with some difficulty and a certain amount of payment that he avoided actual lawsuits.

Soon after the publication of *Spangled Unicorn* Noël did voluntarily involve himself in a legal action over *Oranges and Lemons,* the sketch about two old women going to bed in a boarding house that Coward had written for *On with the Dance* in 1925. He claimed, successfully, that though he had given permission for it to be used in a variety bill called *Non-Stop Revels* in the summer of 1932, he had not realized that the script would be altered to include 'unpleasant suggestions and some unsavoury wording such as to damage the reputation of the author.' The sketch was put back to its original form for the rest of the run.

Oranges and Lemons was not, fortunately, the only example of Coward's work to be revived during 1932. Gatenby Bell formed a touring repertory group known as 'The Noël Coward Company' whose intention was 'to present the work of this brilliant author under his own supervision'. During August Noël approved the casting of a troupe that was led by Kate Cutler and included a young, moustached and generally unknown actor called James Mason. The company opened at the Malvern Festival Theatre early in September with a repertoire that included *Private Lives, Hay Fever, Fallen Angels* and *The Vortex,* presented at the rate of two plays a week. Noël wrote an introduction to the company in their first programme:

> The Noël Coward Company sounds strangely important and significant to me… The repertory includes most of my work of the last fourteen years, and when I remember all those rehearsals, and dress rehearsals, and first nights, and the cheers and boos, triumphs and failures, nostalgic tears dim my old eyes and a certain hoary tenderness wells up in my heart, not only for the plays themselves, but for the people who are going to act them. I do hope that they and the public will enjoy them as much as I did.

The Noël Coward Company toured the provinces until the end of the year, when it disbanded never to re-form; but for Coward to have written enough successful plays by the age of thirty-two to justify the founding of an entire company devoted solely to his work was a not insignificant achievement, and one that could then only be claimed by two other playwrights in the English theatre: Shakespeare and Shaw.

In September, after a run of eleven months in which it had played to around seven hundred thousand people, *Cavalcade* closed at Drury Lane; Coward was at the last performance together with Adrianne Allen and her husband Raymond Massey, and as the cheers died away he made a short, sad speech of farewell to the company. Six months later *Cavalcade* was to reopen as a film at the Tivoli, but as a play the last words on it came from a critic who was at that final performance: 'It may not have read very well, but by God *Cavalcade* played well!'

In private as in public, Noël's life was still totally bound up in the theatre; the explanation of his long and close friendship with Gertrude Lawrence is that in many ways he was very like her, and it has been said of Miss Lawrence at this time that she only really came alive when she was acting on a stage. One suspects that for Noël too the only real existence lay in a theatre, whether he was there as actor, director, composer, lyricist, playwright or merely as a compulsive member of almost every first-night audience in London, Paris and New York. At this time more than later, his life and his home were in the theatre. True there was Goldenhurst, where Coward spent most weekends entertaining innumerable friends and playing a mean game of croquet, and there were his mother and his close friend Jack Wilson, but they and everything else around him in these years came second to his overpowering and all-consuming interest in the theatre. His friends, with the exception of such already distinguished novelists as Rebecca West and G. B. Stern, were equally tied to show-business in one form or another, and though Noël was prepared to take time off (primarily to read and to travel) he admitted that he was nowhere else remotely as happy as in a theatre. In a romantic, artistic, financial and practical sense he belonged to the theatre, and there were times in the Thirties when one could have been forgiven for thinking that it belonged to him.

Mrs Coward, with the lodging house in Ebury Street already far behind her, began to enjoy the richer life of Goldenhurst; one of Noël's pilot friends from the local flying club took her up one afternoon in his two-seater plane for a trip over Kent. When they landed, after looping the loop, Noël asked his mother nervously whether she had enjoyed an experience that would have made stronger and younger women flinch: 'Enormously, dear. I always used to swing quite high as a girl.'

Words and Music left a legacy of song royalties in 'Mad Dogs and Englishmen' and 'The Party's Over Now' which continue to benefit the Coward Estate today, but long before it closed at the Adelphi Noël had already turned his mind back to the comparatively legitimate confines of *Design for Living*. At the end of 1932 he returned to New York and started to work on it with the Lunts.

Design for Living is perhaps the closest that Coward has ever come to writing a black comedy; it is a curious, untypical, amoral and often touching drama which lies outside the mainstream of Coward's comic writing because it is simultaneously more philosophic and less carefully structured than any of his other major comedies. And yet there are similarities: like *Fallen Angels,* like *Hay Fever* and like *Private Lives, Design for Living* is about a group of people who find it impossible to live together and equally impossible to live apart. In this case they are a threesome, Gilda, Otto and Leo, who discover that contrary to popular belief, a trio is company and indeed the only way that they can survive. Noël constructed his play on a strictly three-cornered basis: Gilda loves Otto and Leo, both of whom love her and are devoted to each other. Any attempt by Gilda to exclude either Otto or Leo or both is doomed to failure, and at the final curtain all three realize that their design for living has inevitably to be triangular. Coward himself describes their problem vividly if a trifle fancifully:

> These glib, over-articulate and amoral creatures force their lives into fantastic shapes and problems because they cannot help themselves. Impelled chiefly by the impact of their personalities each upon the other, they are like moths in a pool of light, unable to tolerate the lonely outer darkness, and equally unable to share the light without colliding constantly and bruising one another's wings.

But because the idea of a triangular alliance has about it something vaguely immoral, though the most that these three characters do together onstage is to laugh uproariously at the final curtain, American reaction to the play was somewhat guarded. About the acting of the Lunts and Noël though, there was no doubt whatsoever: Richard Lockridge in the *New York Sun* found it 'as happy a spectacle of surface skating as one might hope to see. They skate with fantastic swoops and little nonsensical shouts and a fine abundance of animal spirits, sometimes on very thin ice.' One or two critics came close to describing it in the words of Gilda's wronged husband as 'a disgusting, three-sided erotic hotch-potch', but Brooks Atkinson for the *New York Times* could see that though *Design for Living* might be decadent, it was also a play of 'skill, art and clairvoyance, performed by an incomparable trio of comedians.'

As if to ward off the accusations of immorality that he knew would come, Coward makes it clear that his characters are artists (Otto paints, Leo writes plays and Gilda decorates interiors) living in a world of their own that has little in common with, and cannot be invaded by, ordinary mortals. But their world does allow them to tilt at some already familiar Coward windmills, notably London theatre critics, inane journalists, the problems of 'second-hand people' to be found at country house-parties, and the fatuity of polite conversation at social gatherings of the upper classes. Above all else, this vehicle for three players, all known intimately to the author and all cast by him long before the actual play was written, is simply about three people who happen to love each other very much.

In the character of Leo, the playwright who suddenly has a success, Noël wrote himself a part that bore a more than passing resemblance to his own character and to the way he lived his life in the years immediately after *The Vortex:*

LEO: It's inevitable that the more successful I become, the more people will run after me. I don't believe in their friendship, and I don't take them seriously, but I enjoy them... They'll drop me, all right, when they're tired of me; but maybe I shall get tired first.

After one initial row over who should have which dressing-room (each was determined that the other should have the best) Noël and the Lunts got along as superbly as they always had; 'there was no rivalry between us,' said Alfred Lunt, 'but nor did Noël really try to direct either of us – we moved around different places on the stage from night to night.' To relieve the tension of the first night, as Miss Fontanne was waiting in the wings to go on at the beginning of the play, Noël crept over to wish her luck. 'If the enemy were at the gates of Goldenhurst,' remarked Miss Fontanne, 'you'd send your own mother out to face the guns.'

Design for Living was an immediate success on Broadway, though as it played in one of the seasons following the slump people were not too keen to hand over good money at the box-office. Alfred Lunt, asked by the box-office manager whether it was all right to accept cheques, decided against it; 'but,' he added, 'we'll take anything else in payment – chickens, turkeys, eggs, whatever they've got.'

Playing together night after night, Noël and the Lunts found they were so precisely tuned in to each other's wave-lengths that they could alter lines and even the whole mood of a performance without disconcerting the others in the least. One night, in the drunk scene that ends Act Two, Noël and Alfred began to speak each other's lines, at first unintentionally; rapidly they realized their mistake, but having made it they continued through to the end of the act in each other's parts without disturbing either the play or the audience in the least.

During the time that Noël was in America with *Design for Living,* his brother Eric had returned to England and was living with their mother at Goldenhurst. She found him drawn and emaciated by an intestinal disease that he had contracted in Ceylon and from which he never managed to recover. After a prolonged and painful illness he died in the spring of 1933 at the age of twenty-eight; his death came as a great blow to Mrs Coward who retained for the less successful of her two sons a deep devotion. Noël, told of Eric's death while he was playing in New York, arranged for his mother and her sister Vida, now nearly eighty, to join him there after the funeral; but Coward himself could not feel great sorrow for a brother whom he had barely known in adult life and with whom he had had remarkably little in common.

Design for Living closed on Broadway at the end of May 1933, and because the Lunts were committed elsewhere Noël abandoned any immediate plans to take it to London. At the end of their last matinée on Broadway, the infinitely painstaking Lynn Fontanne told Noël with some delight that after months of experiment she had finally discovered the correct way to execute a particularly tricky piece of business in the last act. 'Isn't it a little late for that now?' queried Noël. 'Not at all,' replied Miss Fontanne, 'there's always tonight.'

Coward's stock in America at this time was very high indeed; apart from the Broadway success of *Design for Living* which made him something in the region of £12,000, the Hollywood film of *Cavalcade,* already billed as 'The Picture of the Generation', was proving an enormous success at cinemas all over the country. In Pittsburgh it broke the local record by taking nearly sixteen thousand dollars in a single week. The film was an amazingly accurate reproduction of the play, with Diana Wynyard and Clive Brook now playing the Marryots and some of the original cast still intact.

In New York Noël was given a thousand pounds to sing on his own ten-minute radio show, and the offer was not an isolated one; but in spite of his heady commercial success he decided to return to London soon after *Design for Living* closed, having first sold the film rights to Paramount. English theatre enthusiasts were already able to read the play in its published version, but it was to be six years before they could see it on the stage and then without either Coward or the Lunts. Just before Noël left New York, for one memorable Sunday-night performance, he and Lynn and Alfred Lunt were to be found as the guest stars at the Ringling Brothers' Circus. They rode once round the ring, seated regally on massive elephants, waving graciously to a faintly bemused audience.

By the time Noël got back to England with his mother and Aunt Vida, two films of his plays were on simultaneous release there: *Cavalcade,* which in its first three London weeks played to a hundred thousand people, and *Tonight Is Ours,* an ultra-romantic Hollywood concoction which had Claudette Colbert and Fredric March embroiled in a lush screenplay that bore a vague, passing resemblance to *The Queen Was in the Parlour.* Noël even managed to recognize a few of his original lines in it. *Cavalcade,* which had been filmed by Fox at a cost of three hundred thousand pounds, was ecstatically if jealously reviewed in London: C. A. Lejeune for the *Observer* complained that it was 'the best British film that has ever been made, and it was made in America... Our own producers ought to go into corners and kick themselves. Why in the world couldn't we have produced it in our own studios?' Fears that Hollywood would tamper with the play proved entirely groundless, though Noël was not always so lucky in this respect.

All his life, Coward once complained, he had been plagued by reporters demanding why he had never repeated the success of *Bitter-Sweet.* It was not for want of trying; twice in the Thirties he attempted lavish, romantic and escapist musicals set in the not-too-distant past, but neither achieved anything like the lasting success of *Bitter-Sweet.* The first attempt was made soon after *Design for Living* when Noël, back home at Goldenhurst in the summer of 1933, began to think about a possible vehicle for Yvonne Printemps, undisturbed by the fact that at that time she spoke barely a word of English. Watching her on the stage in Paris, Coward had been enchanted by her singing voice, and he felt sure that she could learn enough of the language to cope with whatever plot he could come up with. The result, some months later, was a romantic, sentimental comedy with music set in Regency Brighton and called *Conversation Piece.* But the score did not come without a struggle:

> I was working at Goldenhurst. I had completed some odd musical phrases here and there, but no main waltz theme, and I was firmly and miserably stuck. 1 had sat at the piano daily for hours, repeatedly trying to hammer out an original tune or even an arresting first phrase, and nothing had resulted from my concentrated efforts but banality. I knew that I could never complete the score without my main theme as a pivot and finally, after ten days of increasing despair, I decided to give up and, rather than go on flogging myself any further, postpone the whole project for at least six months... I felt fairly wretched but at least relieved that I had had the sense to admit failure while there was still time. I poured myself a large whisky and soda, dined in grey solitude, poured myself another, even larger, whisky and soda and sat gloomily envisaging everybody's disappointment and facing the fact that my talent had withered and that I should never write any more music until the day I died. The whisky did little to banish my gloom, but there was no more work to be done and I didn't care if I became fried as a coot, so I gave myself another drink and decided to go to bed. I switched off the light at the door and noticed that there was one lamp left on by the piano. I walked automatically to turn it off, sat down, and played 'I'll Follow My Secret Heart' straight through in G flat, a key I had never played in before.

While *Conversation Piece* was still unfinished on the piano and the typewriter, the British and Dominion Film Company released a screen adaptation of *Bitter-Sweet* directed by Herbert Wilcox who had cast his wife, Anna Neagle, as Sari. The film abandoned the last act of Coward's play entirely, but left the petite Ivy St Helier in her original part as Manon; when, some time later, Miss St Helier broke her leg in two places it was inevitably Noël who enquired 'Did it have two places?'

The film opened simultaneously in New York and in London, where it was introduced at the Carlton cinema by a stage show of almost unprecedented inanity in which a gentleman in fancy dress, who had recurring trouble with his shoulder straps, strode around the stage declaiming inferior couplets which eulogized Noël and made vague allusions to the story of *Bitter-Sweet* while behind him the pages of an enormous programme were slowly and mechanically turned. The male ushers of the Carlton then strode on dressed as Austrian soldiers to proclaim in cracked voices their undying affection for Tokay.

But the film, considered as such and not as an adaptation of Noël's play, was less terrible than might have been expected, and although Coward was not exactly happy with it at the time, he thought back almost fondly to it a decade later when he'd seen what the combination of Hollywood, Nelson Eddy and Jeanette Macdonald managed to do with the same basic material.

18

1933–1935

Czar of all the Rushes.

Just before Christmas 1933, with *Conversation Piece* virtually complete, Noël took the script with him to Paris; there he and the actor Pierre Fresnay, who was later to marry Yvonne Printemps, spent day after day going through the play with her, teaching her the English language in general and her part as Melanie in particular. Often, she came close to giving the whole thing up; her English was too bad, she said, for her ever to be able to get through the part in public. But Fresnay persisted, patiently teaching her the words and the music while Noël offered suggestions and encouragement whenever he could; *Conversation Piece* had been written expressly for her theatrical charms, and Coward realized that to do it without her would be all but impossible. While they were in Paris, Noël and Yvonne also sang together for the then French President and Madame Lebrun at an embassy ball; a day or two later, leaving Fresnay to reassure his friend and to work with her, Coward returned to England with plans to start full rehearsals early in January.

In the meantime, while Yvonne was still suffering huge doubts and writing incessantly to Coward asking him to abandon the whole project or at the very least to release her from it, Noël turned his attention briefly to another song. This one was not intended for *Conversation Piece* at all, and in fact it remains one of the few lastingly popular Coward songs that did not have its origin in one of his shows. Instead it was a light but nonetheless heartfelt reply to the countless eager mothers whose endless letters, now reaching Noël at the rate of almost one a day, begged him to find parts for their respective daughters in whatever he happened to be staging next. In an open reply to one for all, he wrote:

Regarding yours, dear Mrs Worthington,
Of Wednesday the 23rd,
Although your baby,
May be,
Keen on a stage career,
How can I make it clear,
That this is not a good idea?
For her to hope,
Dear Mrs Worthington,

Is on the face of it absurd,
Her personality
Is not in reality
Inviting enough,
Exciting enough
For this particular sphere.

Don't put your daughter on the stage, Mrs Worthington,
Don't put your daughter on the stage,
The profession is overcrowded
And the struggle's pretty tough
And admitting the fact
She's burning to act,
That isn't quite enough.

But though the song, which Noël recorded soon afterwards, sold well enough and served him admirably for cabaret appearances during and after the war, as a plea it was a total failure: so far from discouraging maternal ambitions it actually encouraged dozens of other Mrs Worthingtons to write in about their daughters, each letter dismissing the song as a gay little joke before going on to ask about the chances for their own girls, and each mother equally convinced that the song couldn't possibly be intended for her at all. 'The road of the social reformer,' remarked Noël sadly as the letters continued to pour in, 'is paved with disillusion.'

In the first week of 1934 Yvonne Printemps at long last found the courage to sign for Melanie in *Conversation Piece,* and Noël began rehearsals in London almost at once. The large cast included two men who subsequently became Hollywood stars, Louis Hayward and George Sanders, and one of the ladies of the chorus was Valerie Hobson. Noël himself directed, and the costumes and sets were as almost ever in the hands of Gladys Calthrop. Rehearsals were more than usually fraught, not only because Yvonne was still in grave trouble with her English, but also because Romney Brent, who played opposite her, became more and more convinced as the days went by that he, a youngish American comedian, had been hopelessly miscast as the middle-aged, bitter and cynical French adventurer whom Coward had created in the character of Paul, Duc de Chaucigny-Varennes. Eventually, only a few days before they were due to open cold at His Majesty's Theatre, Brent insisted on being released. He returned to America and Noël, against the advice of Cochran and a fair number of his friends, took over the part himself.

To consider any of Coward's plays on paper rather than in performance is usually to underestimate his theatrical achievement, and nowhere is this more apparent than with *Conversation Piece*: it appears to be the loosely-

organized, slackly-written saga, which was once uncharitably described as
'Son of *Bitter-Sweet'*. But in production *Conversation Piece* stemmed from and
then revolved around the performance of Yvonne Printemps, who like Evelyn
Laye in the American *Bitter-Sweet* carried it through on the first night to a
tremendous success which started on a personal level and then radiated from
her to encompass the rest of the company. Without her, it is doubtful whether
Conversation Piece would have survived at all; the plot is less conspicuous than
in Coward's earlier musical romance and rambles still further, the songs
(with the memorable exception of 'I'll Follow My Secret Heart') are also not
up to the standards of *Bitter-Sweet* and there was little that the other members
of the cast could have done to fill in their underdeveloped characters. As
Paul, Noël was efficient but wooden; he himself later admitted this and also
that his plot bore some pretty remarkable anachronisms, not the least of
which was an English packet-boat sailing blissfully for the French coast in the
middle of the Napoleonic wars.

But the reviews that mattered at the box-office, the ones in the popular
dailies, were all excellent and before long *Conversation Piece* was breaking
the theatre records and playing to standing-room only at almost a thousand
pounds a night. Yvonne Printemps' English did not improve spectacularly
during the season, but it was no mean tribute to her that by the end of it the
rest of the company spoke fluent French. About eight weeks into the run,
Noël began to suffer his usual restlessness at playing a single part night
after night for any length of time, and he decided temporarily to leave the
cast. He was replaced by Pierre Fresnay, who had the advantage of correct
nationality for the part and an already close friendship off-stage with his
leading lady; by all accounts he gave a considerably more relaxed portrayal
of the Duc de Chaucigny-Varennes.

Meanwhile Noël, who had by this time added a taste for management to
his passionate involvement in every other aspect of theatrical production,
decided that in future he would present his own plays and others in a new
partnership with his friend Jack Wilson. But to make himself a more
independent and, finally, an entirely self-contained unit as actor-author-
manager-composer-lyricist-director he had first to break away after nine years
from the man who, perhaps more than any other, had helped his career in the
English theatre – Charles Cochran:

> My dear Cocky,
>
> If you were a less understanding or generous person this letter would
> be very difficult to write; as it is, however, I feel you will appreciate my
> motives completely and without prejudice.
>
> I have decided after mature consideration to present my own and
> other people's plays in the future in partnership with Jack. This actually

has been brewing up in my mind over a period of years, and I am writing to you first in confidence because I want you to understand that there would be no question of forsaking you or breaking our tremendously happy and successful association for any other reason except that I feel this is an inevitable development of my career in the theatre.

Particularly I want you to realize how deeply grateful I am for all the generosity and courage and friendship you have shown me over everything we have done together... but above all, dear Cocky, I want to insist upon one important fact which, sentimental as it may seem, is on my part deeply sincere, and that is that without your encouragement and faith in me and my work it is unlikely that I should ever have reached the position I now hold in the theatre, and that whatever may happen in the future I feel that there is a personal bond between us which has nothing to do with business or finance or production. Please understand about all this and continue to give me the benefit of your invaluable friendship.

Yours affectionately, Noël.

For Cochran, Coward's decision to break away meant a considerable financial loss for the future; but he took it well, and ended their partnership by presenting Noël with a Georgian snuffbox inscribed, in what must have been the understatement of the year: 'For Noël, in memory of a not altogether unsuccessful association.'

The new management was formed in John C. Wilson's name, and involved him and Noël with the Lunts in a partnership that was launched in March 1934; their first production was an American comedy by S. N. Behrman called *Biography*. Like Behrman's *The Second Man* in which Noël had played during 1928, this was a smooth, literary and sometimes cynical comedy of American manners; and although Noël had doubts about the play and no intention of acting in it himself, he did seem a natural and obvious choice to direct it. Ina Claire repeated her original Broadway performance, and opposite her, as the editor who persuades her to write her autobiography and so provides the driving-force for the rest of the action, Noël cast Laurence Olivier. With a company that also included Frank Cellier they opened during April to reviews that were mixed; none was altogether bad, but a fair number of critics were uncertain about what to make of a light comedy which had been so evidently designed primarily for a Broadway rather than a West End audience. Noël's name on the posters was not an advantage, since the critics came expecting a Coward comedy and found something rather less effervescent. The result was luke-warm press criticism and an altogether disastrous run; by the end of the first week the cast were on half salaries, and a few weeks later *Biography* closed, having signally failed to live up to its original success on Broadway. The John C. Wilson management was off to a depressing and deeply unprofitable start.

It is some indication of Noël's standing in the profession at this time, and of how far he had come since the days when the press set him up as the angry young rebel against du Maurier's grand old man of the theatre, that when Sir Gerald died in April 1934 Coward was asked to replace him as President of the Actors' Orphanage. Noël held the job until 1956, twenty-two years in which his work for the children involved the planning of innumerable garden parties and midnight matinées to raise funds, and also, when the war came, the organization of the wholesale evacuation to America of those who were under fifteen.

Thus Coward was already a distinguished member of the stage establishment; the fury of the mid-Twenties, when in prefaces to his plays he had campaigned for theatrical reform with a zeal that would not have shamed Bernard Shaw, had already been mellowed by time and success into a kind of benign endurance. When, in London and New York during 1934, the first volume of his collected *Play Parade* was published, the preface merely offered a gentle snub for the critics, delivered as from a very great height:

> I find it very interesting nowadays, now that I have fortunately achieved a definite publicity value, to read criticisms and analyses of my plays written by people of whom I have never heard and whom I have certainly never seen, and who appear to have an insatiable passion for labelling everything with a motive. They search busily behind the simplest of my phrases, like old ladies peering under the bed for burglars, and are not content until they have unearthed some definite, and usually quite inaccurate, reason for my saying this or that. This strange mania I can only suppose is the distinctive feature of a critical mind as opposed to a creative one. It seems to me that a professional writer should be animated by no other motive than the desire to write, and, by doing so, to earn his living.

Apart from the appearance of this, the first of seven *Play Parades* that Noël was to publish over the next thirty years, 1934 also saw the arrival in London of the Ernst Lubitsch film of *Design for Living*. In an adaptation for the screen by Ben Hecht, the three central characters were played by Miriam Hopkins, Gary Cooper (in the Coward part) and Fredric March; the result was successful but unfaithful to Noël's original script. The Coward plot might have seemed ideally suited to Lubitsch's own style of pointed screen comedy, but Hecht's adaptation abandoned most of the lines in the play and broadened a sophisticated comedy into what sometimes became near-farce. Lubitsch was unrepentant: 'I offer no apologies to Mr Coward for altering his play... he knows as well as I do that no picture ever lived up to a stage reputation if taken word for word.' Coward was not pleased, but as he'd been paid ten thousand pounds for the screen rights he was able to get over it; the unkindest cut of all was perhaps Hecht's, who was reported by one paper to have said,

'There's only one line of Coward's left in the picture – see if you can find it.' Noël refused even to find the picture.

In July Noël went back, as he had promised Cochran that he would, to the part of the Duc de Chaucigny-Varennes in *Conversation Piece* which Fresnay had been playing in his absence. But after only a dozen performances he was rushed to hospital with acute appendicitis and Fresnay returned to finish the run which had in fact only a few more weeks at His Majesty's before the entire production was moved to New York for the autumn.

Recuperating at Goldenhurst after the successful emergency operation to remove his appendix, Noël wrote a new play which he intended as a vehicle for the Lunts and called *Point Valaine*. Then, as there was no chance of producing it before Christmas since Lynn Fontanne was also meant to be resting for her health, and as Noël had to direct another play for the Wilson management in London early in the autumn, he decided to take the chance of a brief holiday aboard a yacht that he'd chartered from Claude Grahame-White. The outcome was disastrous; Noël took a new friend, the actor Louis Hayward, with him and together they sailed down the coast of Italy to Ile Rousse off Corsica, where the yacht was anchored while they went ashore for a couple of days. During one night a storm blew up and the yacht was thrown against some offshore rocks where it broke up. The next morning Noël and Hayward waded out to it and managed to retrieve a few of their possessions, in Noël's case his typewriter, his passport and the manuscript of his first autobiography, *Present Indicative*, which he had just started to write. He lost all of the clothes that were on the yacht as well as about three hundred pounds in cash.

Returning to London after this rather traumatic holiday, Noël started the production of another Broadway comedy for the Wilson management; this one was *The Royal Family*, a comedy by George Kaufman and Edna Ferber about a family of celebrated but hysterical American actors not a million miles removed from the Barrymores. In England, for obvious reasons, the play had to be retitled and was therefore rechristened *Theatre Royal* by Noël. Rehearsals for this most theatrical of comedies proved chaotic, initially because even after they had started there was some doubt about who was to play the male lead. Brian Aherne had been Coward's original choice, but an overrunning film in Hollywood meant that he wouldn't be available for another month at least; in the meantime Laurence Olivier agreed, as a favour to Noël and for £100 a week, to rehearse and play the beginning of the pre-London tour, leaving Aherne to take over before it went into the Lyric Theatre. But Olivier, though not pleased at being cast as a kind of provincial understudy, turned in a performance of such splendour in the John Barrymore role and became so popular with the rest of the cast on tour that it was soon clear Aherne would find his act an almost impossible one to follow. Aherne decided, rather than put his head into that particular noose, that he'd accept an alternative offer to play Mercutio on Broadway; thus after considerable persuasion by Coward it was Olivier who opened in London as well, and who played throughout the run of *Theatre Royal*. With him, as the older generations of the Cavendish family, were Madge Titheradge and Marie Tempest; they were a distinguished and mutually devoted company in a play that had already proved a cast-iron success in New York.

Coward, directing Olivier for the third time in four years, had a firm understanding of and liking for his performance in a comedy which was, after all, not so very far removed in theme from Noël's own *Hay Fever*. But the rehearsals, even when Olivier was established in the part, were neither as smooth nor as straightforward as one might have expected of that cast and director; Noël himself developed another intestinal inflammation soon after his appendicitis, and had to spend alternate days in the theatre and in a London nursing-home.

By the time *Theatre Royal* opened in Glasgow, however, Noël had totally recovered and from that first week of the tour onwards the play was an evident success; when it reached Edinburgh, an observant theatre-goer at one performance noticed that the Indian servant who makes a brief appearance in the comedy bore that night a striking resemblance to Mr Coward himself: 'he had dressed rather sketchily for the part, his turban askew, and he uttered a long string of pseudo Hindu words. It took the cast some seconds to realize what was happening, then there was a sudden pause followed by a few aborted giggles whereupon Coward vanished offstage as surprisingly as he'd arrived.'

In London the reviews for *Theatre Royal* were almost all good, and business was even better. Noël had latched eagerly on to the eccentric theatrical exaggerations of Broadway's 'royal family' and in his production, the generations of highly-strung actors clinging desperately to their artistic temperaments were played up for all they were worth. Their moves, their meals, even their baths were all timed and produced for major effects, and it turned out to be a play in which all Coward's deep-rooted instincts for the theatre theatrical could be expressed on stage. Discussing the acting, one critic said that even allowing for the subject matter it still seemed far too hammy; 'all acting,' replied Noël, 'worth the name is ham. We rehearse for weeks to hide it, but it has to be there all the time.' For Coward, the lasting pleasure of *Theatre Royal* was the chance to work again with his beloved Marie Tempest:

She has more allure and glamour and charm at seventy than most women I know who are in their twenties and thirties. Her dignity is unassailable and I have a strong feeling that it always was; I think what impresses me most about her is her unspoken but very definite demand for good behaviour.

For Marie Tempest, Noël at that time was still the *enfant gâté* of the theatre:

At his birth two godmothers sat over his cradle, the benevolent one who gave him one superb gift, and the malignant one who tossed in a handful of gifts almost as good. She disappeared with a cackling laugh. Noël is aware of these gifts and he feels that he must exploit them all. That is the trap which was laid by the malignant godmother. This is just my Victorian way of saying that I do not think he will ever quite fulfil his great promise if he does not curb his versatility. He is spending his gifts too lavishly. When one is a considerable person it is not wise to do anything below the standards set by one's best. As an artist he is extraordinarily generous in his praise of others. His spontaneous appreciation of other writers and other actors shows the bigness of his heart. And he has never grown beyond the friends who were kind to him before he was successful. On no one has success sat more lightly; he has warmed himself in it, and he has mellowed.

With *Theatre Royal* safely launched in a production that was to run comfortably and profitably through the winter, Noël turned his attention briefly to an appearance as a guest singing some of his own songs on Henry Hall's radio programme, and then to the casting of *Point Valaine* for New York. In the meantime *Conversation Piece* had opened on Broadway with Yvonne Printemps, Pierre Fresnay and almost exactly the same cast that had played it in London earlier in the year. Cole Porter's cable to Noël after the first night read 'I have just left *Conversation Piece*. It's a Wow!' but the Broadway critics were less flattering.

Though it played to weekly returns of over ten thousand dollars for the first couple of weeks at the 44th Street Theatre, business soon fell away badly and *Conversation Piece* lasted rather less than two months in New York.

A few weeks after *Theatre Royal* had opened in London, Noël left England to join the Lunts at their home, in Genesee Depot, Wisconsin; by the time he arrived there they had read *Point Valaine,* liked it, and were keen to do it on Broadway. It was agreed that, with Noël directing but not on this occasion playing any of the parts, they would rehearse in New York through December before opening on Christmas night 1934, at the Colonial Theatre in Boston. In the cast were Philip Tonge, Noël's old child-actor friend, and his mother Lilian. It could scarcely be said of Noël that he ever failed to find work for old friends.

Before rehearsals started, Noël went to spend a week-end with Alec Woollcott at his Neshobe Island home; there, after dinner one night, Coward announced that he would read *Point Valaine* to the assembled company.

'Where?' asked Woollcott, icily; as the room where they were sitting was the only possible location, the reading was indefinitely postponed.

But *Point Valaine* proved on this its first outing to be one of Coward's least successful plays, and none of its subsequent revivals has done anything to rehabilitate a drama which the author himself admitted is based on a theme 'neither big enough for tragedy nor light enough for comedy'. It is perhaps not entirely coincidental that *Point Valaine* should be dedicated by Noël to Somerset Maugham: in its characters and theme the play is unlike anything that Noël ever tried to do before or afterwards, and in its murky way the plot echoes Maugham at his most lugubrious. Indeed some of the characters in *Point Valaine* seem to have drifted in from a road company of *Rain*.

For Noël, it was an attempt to break entirely new ground, and in that if nothing else he was successful. Evidently he was experimenting with the creation of new moods and feelings, above all trying to find ways to convey a sense of impending horror on the stage without, until the bitter end, being forced to give any actual reason for it. As a short story it might have worked very well indeed; as a play it failed to work at all. Neither the mood nor the plot are alone enough to sustain *Point Valaine,* and the characters are a vaguely defined and deeply unattractive lot who seem to deserve all that they ultimately get.

The opening night in Boston was a gloomy way to spend Christmas, and it is not surprising that this production marked the low watermark in Coward's enduring friendship with the Lunts. They became as depressed about the play as Noël himself, and the result was a mutual irritability that started in rehearsals, and lasted through Boston, where a rain machine flooded the stage and all the sets were found to be too big for the scene-changes. The Broadway opening in January was disastrous. The audience, who had come in the expectation of a light Coward comedy, were reduced to stony indifference and the reviews were quick to point out that as a play it was well below Coward's best. Brooks Atkinson put his finger on one of the main reasons for the disappointment that greeted the play: 'Coward's gifts are so multitudinous, his range is so bewildering and his success has been so dazzling that we are all inclined to expect too much of him. When we come to one of his new plays we are feverishly prepared as for a sign from God.'

Point Valaine lasted less than eight weeks at the Ethel Barrymore Theatre on Broadway, and financially it represented another considerable loss to Noël's management. It was also the greatest failure that the Lunts ever had.

On the credit side of John C. Wilson Ltd, *Theatre Royal* was still making good money in England, and *Design for Living* had been sold as *Sérénade à Trois* for France, but the losses sustained by first *Biography* in London and now *Point Valaine* in New York were very heavy. At the beginning of April 1935 Lorn Loraine wrote to Noël's mother at Goldenhurst:

We have got to go very, very easy on money and economize rigidly wherever it is possible. Mind you, I am pretty sure the shortage is only temporary and would never have arisen if *Point Valaine* had done better and if it were not for the fact that half of all Noël's personal earnings have to go into a special tax account as soon as they are received. Still, the fact remains that money is definitely tight and has been for some months. Both the bank accounts have overdrafts and there is very little coming in just now – a good deal less than has to go out.

Noël, still in New York after *Point Valaine* closed, realized the need to make some money rapidly. He agreed therefore, for the first time in the seventeen years since he had worked for D. W. Griffith, to make a film; his sole celluloid appearance in the meantime had been in a disappointing screen test with Gertrude Lawrence during the run of *Private Lives*. The new film's title was *The Scoundrel,* and it was one of a series of three independent productions written and directed jointly by Ben Hecht and Charles MacArthur who in an attempt to escape the professional bondage of Hollywood were making low-budget pictures in their own Astoria Studios on Long Island. For Noël the money, around five thousand dollars, was only a fraction of what he could have earned by going to Hollywood, but by this time he was interested in the script and the promise that he'd be playing opposite Helen Hayes who later became Mrs MacArthur. But at the last minute she was unable to make the film and her part was played by Julie Haydon; Noël did, however, have one old friend in the cast in the massive shape of Alexander Woollcott, who noted that throughout the studio Coward was known colloquially as the czar of all the rushes.

The Scoundrel was made quickly and efficiently, but even so Noël found the business of filming a confusing and irritating affair, and seeing the film afterwards he felt that both he and it should have been considerably better than they were. Critics in New York and London disagreed: they found it an adventurous, off-beat morality tale with Noël ideally cast as the cynical publisher who comes back from the dead grasping a bunch of seaweed to proclaim that salvation can be found in altruistic tears. It was, for its time, a very modern, impressionistic and indirect film which failed to appeal to the mass of audiences outside London who were already acclimatized to the more orthodox fare of Hollywood, but which nevertheless achieved a considerable artistic success.

In New York *The Scoundrel,* perhaps because it was unlike any other film of the period, became something of a cult; the writers, Betty Comden and Adolph Green, then still in their teens, held parties at which they would act out the entire script before their long-suffering friends, and Miss Comden subsequently went so far as to hold her wedding luncheon in the restaurant where Noël and Julie Haydon had filmed a highly-charged love-scene.

As soon as *The Scoundrel* was safely in the can, Noël left New York for London, travelling by a route that was less direct though infinitely more picturesque than the North Atlantic. He went home via Japan, Hong Kong, Singapore and Colombo. It was while he was in Singapore that he heard of the death of his friend T. E. Lawrence. 'It is ironic,' Noël told a reporter from the local paper, 'that a man of his genius, courage, strength of purpose and vision should have been snuffed out in one blinding, noisy moment on that idiotic motor-cycle.'

On his way around the world, his old and ever-present wanderlust briefly allayed, Coward worked on *Present Indicative,* the autobiography which he had promised Nelson Doubleday in New York for the autumn. In idle moments he also began to think about the construction of not one but nine new plays.

19

1935–1937

The critical laurels that had been so confidently prophesied for me in the Twenties never graced my brow, and I was forced throughout the Thirties to console myself with the bitter palliative of commercial success which I enjoyed very much indeed.

When in the late summer of 1935 Gertrude Lawrence went to stay with Noël, now back home at Goldenhurst, he was able to show her the basic layout and most of the scripts for a new and elaborate vehicle that he had erected for their respective talents: a series of nine one-act plays ranging in mood from slapstick comedy to high tragedy, in all of which they would both appear, to be played in first London and then New York as alternating triple bills under the omnibus title *Tonight at Eight-Thirty.*

The success of *Private Lives*, together with Noël's fervent belief in the star system, had made him think deeply about another way to bring himself and Gertrude Lawrence together again on the stage in parts that would allow them to display their varied acting and singing talents to the best possible advantage. *Private Lives* had, in his view and that of many of the people surrounding him, proved that the combination of Gertrude Lawrence and himself conjured up a box-office magic which could be invoked again given the right vehicle. But he needed to write something that would be varied enough to let them both work in their own individual ways, and also exciting enough to overcome the very real boredom that he found in nightly repetition of the same part; given those requirements, it very soon occurred to him on his way around the world that three plays would be better than one, and by the same token, nine would be better than three.

In the first quarter of this century, with a few distinguished exceptions among the works of Bernard Shaw and J. M. Barrie, the one-act play had fallen on hard times; in the provinces some were still presented as undercast, ill-produced curtain-raisers, but in general the form had disappeared as a result of a widespread managerial belief that the public did not come to see double- or triple-bills because they felt paradoxically they would be getting less value for money. But for Coward, the one-act play, 'having a great advantage over a long one in that it can sustain a mood without technical creaking or overpadding, deserves a better fate, and if by careful writing, acting, and producing I can do a little towards reinstating it in its rightful pride, I shall have achieved one of my more sentimental ambitions.'

With some of the *Tonight at Eight-Thirty* plays already virtually complete in his mind, Noël had returned to England in mid-June for the annual theatrical garden party which he and a distinguished committee of actors ran to raise money for the eighty children who then lived in the Actors' Orphanage.

When he was at Goldenhurst, working on the rest of *Tonight at Eight-Thirty*, Noël had a cable from Alfred Lunt saying that rather than be a partner in the John C. Wilson management he had decided to accept an offer to become a director on the board of New York's Theatre Guild. Noël's cabled reply ran:

CONGRATULATIONS DEAR GRANDPA DO BE GOOD AND SWEET AND READ EVERY SCRIPT CAREFULLY AND SEND US ALL THE ONES THE GUILD TURN DOWN THEY ARE USUALLY THE BEST.

Later in the summer Noël was involved for the second time on the outskirts of a lawsuit. This one was brought against Cochran by the Parnell-Zeitlin management who charged that by selling Hollywood the film rights of *Cavalcade* and allowing the film to be shown in the English provinces, Cochran had broken a contract which gave them the sole rights to present *Cavalcade* outside London. Not unexpectedly, the film's success had hit touring profits badly for the stage show, and Cochran together with the Drury Lane Theatre Company had to pay Parnell-Zeitlin damages of five thousand pounds.

By the end of August Noël had finished all nine of the *Tonight at Eight-Thirty* plays and it was decided that, after rehearsing first with Gertie at Goldenhurst and then with the full company in London, they would open under the banner of the Wilson management at the Opera House in Manchester in mid-October; then, after a nine-week tour of the provinces and a brief Christmas holiday they would open in London at the Phoenix Theatre early in the January of 1936.

During the various provincial, London and Broadway runs of *Tonight at Eight-Thirty* the sequence and arrangement of the plays was altered frequently in a kind of permanent repertory, and even the title went through such local variations as *Tonight at Seven-Thirty* for theatres outside London and *Today at Two-Thirty* for matinées. But the triple bill that launched the whole series in Manchester consisted of *We Were Dancing* followed by *The Astonished Heart* and then *Red Peppers*. Of these, *We Were Dancing* was really no more than a curtain-raiser, an acid little comedy about a woman deciding in the cold light of dawn that she will not after all be eloping from her marriage. It was set on the veranda of the country club at Samolo, a mythical island in the South Seas that Coward invented for this play and then used again as the setting for a musical, *Pacific 1860*, for a later comedy, *South Sea Bubble*, and also for his novel *Pomp and Circumstance*. The last play, *Red Peppers*, was the least ambitious of the three but in many ways the most popular and the most successful of all the plays that made up *Tonight at Eight-Thirty*. Here Coward managed with accuracy, tinged by a certain sentimental affection, to recapture the flavour of tacky music-hall acts struggling to survive in bad touring dates; not only the words of Lily and George Pepper but also their musical numbers ('Has Anybody Seen Our Ship?' and 'Men About Town') suggest that Coward had a very sharp eye and ear for the routines of the old music-halls and that he was able to recreate them evocatively.

Halfway through the first week of *Tonight at Eight-Thirty* in Manchester Coward brought in the second triple bill; this started with *Hands Across the Sea*, a light comedy about the confusion of a London socialite when she is suddenly faced with the arrival of two colonial guests and a Maharajah who might have religious objections to Douglas Byng. It was designed primarily as a vehicle for Gertrude Lawrence, and Coward was always unable to think of the play, 'without remembering the infinite variety of her inflections, her absurd, scatterbrained conversations on the telephone, her frantic desire to be hospitable and charming, and her expression of blank dismay when she suddenly realized that her visitors were not who she thought they were at all. It was a superb performance in the finest traditions of high comedy, already now over and done with forever but as far as I am concerned never to be forgotten.' In the play she was married to a naval commander, and although Coward denied that the characters of Lady Maureen and Commander Peter Gilpin were in any way based on his old friends the Mountbattens, there were, to say the least, certain superficial similarities.

Fumed Oak, the second play in this cycle, was set in the suburban surroundings of a very different social milieu; it was a comedy of domestic revolt based on the 'worm will turn' formula that had proved both useful and successful for Maugham in *The Breadwinner*. In Coward's play the worm was Henry Gow, an ageing, moustached, down-trodden and browbeaten family man who finally abandons his overbearing wife, snivelling daughter and bullying mother-in-law to start a new life abroad. For Noël, Henry Gow was unlike any other character he had ever attempted to write or play, and perhaps for that reason he enjoyed doing *Fumed Oak* more than any other play in the repertoire.

Taken together with his later full-length play *This Happy Breed, Fumed Oak* serves as a useful reminder that Coward was not solely capable of writing about the rich and glamorous predecessors of the Beautiful People among whom the vast majority of his early plays were set. Nevertheless the last play in this second *Tonight at Eight-Thirty* collection was a return to romantic musical fantasy called *Shadow Play* in which Noël and Miss Lawrence, impeccably dressed, danced in the moonlight and generally exuded overpowering charm through a rather transparent account of a marriage being retrieved from the brink of collapse. 'It is very much easier to be witty if you are writing about educated people,' Coward once told a journalist who accused him of being a playwriting snob, 'and besides the British public have always rather liked things about the upper classes', a fact of theatrical life that Wilde discovered before him. But class-consciousness apart, *Shadow Play* (though not by any means the best of the bunch) retains a certain technical interest for Coward's use on the stage of such highly cinematic techniques as flashbacks and disconnected scenes played quickly in pools of light to make up the theatrical equivalent of a montage.

These then were the first six plays of *Tonight at Eight-Thirty*, and alternating them Coward toured the provinces throughout the autumn of 1935. In Birmingham, their last date before Christmas and London, *We Were Dancing* was replaced by *Family Album*, a mock-Victorian comedy about a missing will which provided a few good laughs and some better parts for those members of the cast who had until now fared rather less well than the two principals. At the end of a tour which had made just over twenty-six thousand pounds at the box-offices, the *Tonight at Eight-Thirty* company broke up for Christmas.

Noël, taking Jeffery Amherst with him, went for a brief Scandinavian holiday first to Stockholm, where they met Greta Garbo, and then on to Copenhagen where he accidentally crushed one of his fingers in the door during a New Year's Eve party given by Prince William; when at the beginning of January Noël opened in *Tonight at Eight-Thirty* at the Phoenix Theatre in London it was with a heavily-bandaged hand. Nevertheless, the two triple bills, opening in successive weeks, were rapturously received by glittering first-night audiences that included the Prince of Wales and Mrs Simpson. The reviews varied from the disappointed to the besotted; the majority were excellent for the stars but scathing for the plays.

To both Coward and Gertrude Lawrence the plays offered countless opportunities for virtuoso solos and duets which they clutched with both hands, but for Coward as author and director and composer and lyricist as well as actor it was beyond doubt the best showcase for his varied talents that he has ever managed to build. *Tonight at Eight-Thirty* seemed dedicated to the idea that there was nothing in the theatre that Coward couldn't do; 'I wonder,' mused one member of the audience after seeing him in all six plays at matinée and evening performances on the same day, 'what he is like on the tightrope?'

Early in the London run of *Tonight at Eight-Thirty* the death was announced of King George V; he had come to the throne as Noël was rehearsing *The Goldfish*, and the twenty-five years of his reign had spanned the whole of Coward's professional career. Theatres were closed on the night of his death, and the atmosphere of deep mourning in which they reopened made the jokes about bereavement in *Family Album* seem in execrable taste; it was therefore hauled out of the repertory and replaced by *We Were Dancing*, the play that had originally been a part of the first bill on tour.

Later in the run Noël found time to involve himself more closely in the affairs of the Actors' Orphanage; on close inspection he had discovered some curious discrepancies and legal irregularities in the way the Orphanage was run and, not content to be a nominal President involved only in the annual garden party, Coward organized a boardroom putsch which in spite of some severe opposition from other members of the committee, succeeded in putting the Orphanage on to a basis of business efficiency rather than sentimental charity. The whole manoeuvre took about a month and a vast amount of energetic lobbying; but by the end of it Coward was so caught up in the atmosphere of the boardroom that he wrote *Star Chamber*, a vindictive and highly satirical account of a committee meeting at which leading actors and actresses try to organize a nameless charity, constantly breaking off the discussion to pose for press photographs or to sort out the chaos caused by the collision of their own egos. The play was added to *Tonight at Eight-Thirty* in place of *Hands Across the Sea*, but it only survived for one matinée performance in the course of which Coward discovered that what had been funny and outlandish and true in real life was signally less hilarious when transposed to the already unreal atmosphere of the stage, where the over-theatrical chaos seemed merely normal.

After the first two cycles of *Tonight at Eight-Thirty* had been playing for twelve weeks, Gertrude Lawrence was taken suddenly and violently ill and the theatre had to be closed for the rest of the month of April because (as in *Private Lives*) Noël found himself unable to continue playing without her. For Miss Lawrence, the months surrounding *Tonight at Eight-Thirty* were among the most difficult of her life. Shortly before rehearsals began she had been declared bankrupt, and although her friend Robert Montgomery lent her the money to invest in the plays so that she could hope for a reasonable share of the profits, that alone did not bring in enough to get her out of the woods. So while she was appearing with Noël she also accepted a film offer from Alexander Korda to play opposite Charles Laughton in *Rembrandt*. The strain of filming every day and then acting at night in different plays proved too much for her, and led to the breakdown which briefly closed *Tonight at Eight-Thirty*. Gertie persistently refused to recognize the implications and inconveniences of bankruptcy; after one particularly expensive shopping spree during the run of the Coward plays her agent, Bill O'Bryen, asked Noël if he and Jack Wilson would join him in a joint attempt to explain to Gertie the facts of a bankrupt's life. They all arranged to meet for supper after the show one night at O'Bryen's house. 'Gertie,' predicted Noël, 'will be in one of three moods. Either she'll be very angry and break all the furniture, or she'll be very tearful and make it all wringing wet, or she'll just sit there with her hands on her lap and say that she doesn't understand. I only hope to God she doesn't understand.' In the event, she failed to show up at all.

When *Tonight at Eight-Thirty* reopened, Joyce Carey joined the cast in place of Alison Leggatt who had also been taken ill; but when Gertrude Lawrence had fully recovered and returned, the two other plays that Noël had written were rehearsed and added to the repertoire in early May, forming with the reinstated *Family Album* three cycles of three plays each of which was then played alternately until the end of the London run with the cast slogging through two different cycles on matinée days. One of the new plays, *Still Life* was to reappear in an extended version ten years later as Noël's screenplay for one of the best British films of the immediately post-war period, *Brief Encounter*. As a matter of record, of the nine plays in *Tonight at Eight-Thirty* all but three were later filmed in one form or another.

With the repertory at last complete, *Tonight at Eight-Thirty* ran on at the Phoenix Theatre until the end of the third week in June, to achieve a total of just over a hundred and fifty London performances. Ivor Brown, summing up for the *Observer*, noted that Coward, 'the man who used to write very slight long plays, has now composed very full brief ones.' Sir Seymour Hicks, in the audience for one of the last performances, had been so impressed by Noël's achievement that he presented him with one of his most treasured possessions, a sword which once belonged to Edmund Kean.

For Noël, the stage partnership with Gertrude Lawrence had again been a magical if intermittently tempestuous affair; their acting together was a kind of private relationship in which the audience were allowed to participate sometimes, almost vicariously, and there was no competition between them though there were the occasional rows. During February he had cabled his friend Jack Wilson in New York:

EVERYTHING LOVELY STOP CRACKING ROW WITH GERTIE OVER HANDS ACROSS THE SEA LASTING SEVEN MINUTES STOP PERFORMANCE EXQUISITE EVER SINCE

And in March, by which time it had been arranged that Wilson would also present the plays on Broadway in the autumn, another cable from Noël, in mock-fury, ran:

VERY SORRY FIND MY ENGAGEMENTS WILL NOT PERMIT ME APPEAR UNDER YOUR BANNER IN AMERICA UNLESS I GET FURTHER 58 PER CENT OF THE GROSS FOR ARDUOUS TASK RESTRAINING MISS LAWRENCE FROM BEING GROCK BEATRICE LILLIE THEDA BARA MARY PICKFORD AND BERT LAHR ALL AT ONCE.

By now Coward was already deep into an almost lifelong habit of sending frequent telegrams in verse winging around the world via Western Union to mark various occasions in his and friends' lives that ranged from the festive to the unprintable. In the middle of June 1936, to take an example from the former category, the University of Wisconsin bestowed an honorary doctorate of letters on the distinguished American actress Katherine Cornell:

DARLING DARLING DOCTOR KITTY
THOUGH QUITE REASONABLY PRETTY
THOUGH UNDOUBTEDLY A STAR, DEAR
PLEASE REMEMBER WHO YOU ARE, DEAR.
WHY, IN LIEU OF ALL YOUR BETTERS,
SHOULD YOU HAVE DISTINGUISHED LETTERS?
THIS COMES FROM THE JEALOUS SOUL
OF YOUR SOMEDAY DOCTOR NOËL.

At the end of June 1936, with *Tonight at Eight-Thirty* finished in England and his Orphanage theatrical garden party safely behind him, Noël agreed that in the lull before taking *Tonight at Eight-Thirty* to America he would direct a new play in London for the John C. Wilson management. This was *Mademoiselle*, a comedy originally written for the French theatre by Jacques Deval. It opened at Wyndham's in mid-September to a reception that was something less than rapturous, but managed to run successfully through the autumn until the Abdication knocked the bottom out of theatre business all over London.

That summer, not for the first time in his adult life, Noël had been seized by a fervent desire to paint; the results were not always artistically triumphant, but he did manage to sell at least one of his works to G. B. Stern:

Noël sold me the painting for £1 18s 6d. The sum shows clearly enough that bargaining took place, and that his original valuation was two pounds. He demanded, further, that it should be insured for not a penny less than £4,000. It really might be a good deal worse: a rather solid yet Whistlerish effect of dark blue archways across the Seine at night. He called it 'Where the Bee Sucks'.

Immediately after *Mademoiselle* opened in London, Noël left for New York and the American production of *Tonight at Eight-Thirty*. Just before their Boston opening, Noël decided as a joke to send Gertrude Lawrence a good luck telegram signed Fiorello La Guardia, then Mayor of New York. Accordingly he dictated it over the phone, ending with the signature.

Telephonist: But are you really Mayor La Guardia?
N.C.:　　　No.
Telephonist: Then you can't sign it Mayor La Guardia. What is your

real name?
N.C.:   Noël Coward.
Telephonist: Are you really Noël Coward?
N.C.:   Yes.
Telephonist: In that case you can sign it Mayor La Guardia.

After the tour, Noël brought *Tonight at Eight-Thirty* in to New York where the reviews were remarkably similar in tone to those in London almost a year earlier; the general critical feeling was again that Coward and Gertrude Lawrence were quite superb but that the plays were rather less of a triumph. The New York première was an eventful first night, not only because of the usual crowds who turned out to welcome the Coward–Lawrence partnership back to Broadway. Lucius Beebe, a reporter with the *Herald Tribune*, agreed as a publicity stunt for a Fifth Avenue jewellers to wear a diamond gardenia in his lapel worth fifteen thousand dollars. During the first interval it was stolen, not in fact for publicity purposes, by a kleptomanic English lady of noble birth who only returned it after considerable police persuasion.

Soon after *Tonight at Eight-Thirty* opened at the National, a cable from Lorn in London about the King's abdication caused Noël to issue on behalf of his company a brief and dignified statement of unswerving loyalty to the Crown. But privately the news depressed him greatly; Edward VIII had been if not a close friend of Coward's then at least more than a casual acquaintance, and in private life the ex-Prince of Wales had stood for that section of high English society with which Noël had long been associated. The King's abrupt departure from the throne seemed therefore to fragment a social order whose members had until now found no reason to suppose that it would not be secure, for some years to come.

Early in 1937, while Noël was playing *Tonight at Eight-Thirty* in New York and living in the apartment on 52nd Street and the East River that he'd only recently bought from Alexander Woollcott, the *London Sunday Express* began to serialize his autobiography *Present Indicative,* and a few weeks later the whole book appeared in both London and New York. Covering the period of Noël's life until the end of 1931, it was, wrote St John Ervine in the *Observer,* 'the book of a man who according to his capacity has taken the measure of life and does not shrink from coping with it'; a number of other critics wrote of Coward admiringly if improbably as 'the richest man in the English theatre today'. But Cyril Connolly, reviewing for the *New Statesman,* took a less flattering view of Coward as revealed by himself in the book; after dismissing *Present Indicative* as 'almost always shallow and often dull' Connolly went on to wonder:

> What are we left with? The picture, carefully incomplete, of a success; probably of one of the most talented and prodigiously successful people the world has ever known – a person of infinite charm and adaptability

whose very adaptability however makes him inferior to a more compact and worldly competitor in his own sphere, like Cole Porter; and an essentially unhappy man, a man who gives one the impression of having seldom really thought or really lived and who is intelligent enough to know it. But what can he do about it? He is not religious, politics bore him, art means facility or else brickbats, love, wild excitement and the nervous breakdown. There is only success, more and more of it, till from his pinnacle he can look down to where Ivor Novello and Beverley Nichols gather samphire on a ledge, and to where, a pinpoint on the sands below, Mr Godfrey Winn is counting pebbles. But success is all there is, and that even is temporary. For one can't read any of Noël Coward's plays now... they are written in the most topical and perishable way imaginable, the cream in them turns sour overnight – they are even dead before they are turned into talkies, however engaging they may seem at the time. This book reveals a terrible predicament, that of a young man with the Midas touch, with a gift that does not creep and branch and flower, but which turns everything it touches into immediate gold. And the gold melts, too.

In the March of 1937 the strain of playing nine parts in as many plays within a repertoire that often entailed acting no less than six of them on a single matinée day finally took its toll on Noël; like Gertrude Lawrence in London a year before him, he collapsed. At first he was only off for six performances, but then three days after he returned to the theatre he broke down again directly after a performance, and this time his New York doctor refused to let him go back to the theatre. *Tonight at Eight-Thirty* was closed at once, almost a month before it was due to end its Broadway run, and Noël left for a holiday in Nassau.

From Nassau, Coward sailed on to Bermuda before returning to New York and then London in time for the coronation of King George VI, by which time he had entirely recovered from the second nervous breakdown he'd suffered in ten years. But he did not intend to risk a third; back home at Goldenhurst he told the press that he would not be working again as an actor for at least two years, and as events developed it was, in fact, six years before he again appeared on the stage in a play.

For the Coronation, after lacerating his hands by pulling every string in sight, Noël managed to procure for Lorn and himself two seats on the Royal Household stand outside Buckingham Palace. Then, after a few weeks in comparative idleness at Goldenhurst, he reached an agreement with Hugh ('Binkie') Beaumont of H. M. Tennent whereby he would direct Gerald Savory's new comedy *George and Margaret* for New York in the autumn, though as a result of various backstage disagreements and the sacking of one director he was only to be involved in the last week of rehearsals in Manchester prior to the company leaving for Broadway. In his view the play's Broadway chances were not good; from the ship on his way to New York he cabled Jack Wilson:

SEE VERY LITTLE POSSIBILITY NEW YORK SUCCESS BUT
HOPE AT LEAST I HAVE AVERTED SCANDALOUS FAILURE AS
REGARDS BILLING UNOFFICIAL GOSSIP INEVITABLE BUT
PREFER MY NAME HAVE NO OFFICIAL CONNECTION WITH
PRODUCTION WHATEVER BOTH FOR PLAY'S SAKE AND MY
OWN SUGGEST NO DIRECTOR'S NAME BE MENTIONED WILL
BE VERY CAREFUL WITH PRESS AND ONLY MENTION
BUYING LARGE CASTLE IN GEORGIA.

By the end of the Atlantic crossing Coward's cables to Wilson were getting
even more urgent:

ABSOLUTELY REFUSE HAVE MY NAME OFFICIALLY
CONNECTED WITH GEORGE AND MARGARET HAVE MERELY
REDIRECTED CAST NOT ENGAGED BY ME AND TIDIED UP
AS MUCH AS POSSIBLE THIS DEFINITELY NOT MY
PRODUCTION.

Although, or perhaps because, Noël had altered the play slightly for an
American audience, *George and Margaret* failed to repeat its overwhelming
London success in New York; it suffered by being seen in the same Broadway
season as another English comedy, Rattigan's *French Without Tears*, and ran
for barely two months. While Noël was with the play in New York his father
died, peacefully and not altogether unexpectedly, at Goldenhurst; Lorn Loraine
looked after his funeral arrangements, and Noël stayed out in America to
visit first Alec Woollcott in Vermont and later the Lunts in Wisconsin. Then
in October, he decided to return on the *Normandie* to England because, as he
cabled Lorn from New York:

I CAN'T WORK OUT HERE AND I AM LONGING TO GET ON
WITH IT.

20

1937–1940

For me, the pre-war past died on the day Mr Neville Chamberlain returned with such gay insouciance from Munich.

Noël's telegram from New York about 'getting on with it' referred to an idea for a new production that had occurred to him while he was staying in America; he now had it in mind to write a musical comedy called *Operette* which, he told Peggy Wood on his way home, would be 'rather *Bitter-Sweet* in atmosphere but later in period.' Back at Goldenhurst he worked on the idea throughout the October and November of 1937, and by Christmas he was ready to start thinking about a cast. In the meantime Gertrude Lawrence had opened on Broadway in *Susan and God*, the first straight play she had done for some years. 'LEGITIMATE AT LAST,' cabled Noël, 'WON'T MOTHER BE PLEASED.'

Though the London theatre had seen nothing of Coward's work in 1937, in the provinces Sybil Thorndike and Lewis Casson were touring with their own company in two plays from *Tonight at Eight-Thirty* (*Fumed Oak* and *Hands Across the Sea*) to which they added Bernard Shaw's *Village Wooing* in a triple bill. 'Two of my plays and one of his,' Coward remarked, 'that fairly puts Mr Shaw in his place.'

In *Operette* Noël had written parts for Peggy Wood, hoping that she might repeat her *Bitter-Sweet* success, and also for the Viennese singer Fritzi Massary whom he brought out of a five-year retirement to play Liesl. Noël planned to direct it himself, and it was arranged that the John C. Wilson management would present it at the Opera House in Manchester for a month from mid-February, prior to bringing it into His Majesty's Theatre in London where both *Conversation Piece* and *Bitter-Sweet* had played. By the end of the year the book for *Operette* was complete, and Noël had written the score of a dozen songs including 'Where Are The Songs We Sung?', 'Dearest Love' and, most memorably, 'The Stately Homes of England'.

Operette was the second and last attempt that Coward made to follow the nostalgic success he'd had with *Bitter-Sweet* almost a decade earlier, but it was one of the least successful musicals Coward had ever written. It told the story of an imaginary Gaiety Girl in the early nineteen-hundreds who achieved stardom overnight but then had to sacrifice her love life to her career, and within its two acts and seventeen scenes Coward left no cliché of backstage life unturned. There was the understudy who took over at a few minutes notice after the star had a tantrum, the actress in love with the young aristocrat whose stiff-backed dowager mother told her to give him up, and the star who staggered on with the show in the face of overwhelming grief and in response to lines like 'Go on and act... act better than you have ever acted in your life!'

But from Coward's point of view the main trouble with *Operette* was that it was overwritten and undercomposed, so that in production the plot became an elaborate and top-heavy affair which the songs were unable to carry. This is where the structure that had served *Bitter-Sweet* so well tended to collapse, and with the exception of 'The Stately Homes' there were no musical show-stoppers at all. The action of *Operette* switched rapidly between the play-within-a-play and the backstage lives of those involved in it, a device which confused theatre-goers in Manchester quite considerably. On the first night there Coward leant out of his box to see bewildered playgoers furtively striking matches and rustling their programmes in a frantic effort to find out where they were supposed to be and what the hell was going on.

But by this time it was too late to perform any drastic rescue operation on *Operette,* and though Noël did manage to simplify it considerably before London, it opened at His Majesty's a month later to notices that were almost uniformly bleak. 'I can stand any amount of criticism,' said Noël, 'as long as it's unqualified praise.' On this occasion it wasn't. The magic of Coward's name on the posters was still potent enough to give *Operette* a run of just over four months, but the musical did little for the esteem in which he was held by theatre-goers. Nevertheless, 'The Stately Homes' later came in useful for Noël's cabaret repertoire and a couple of other songs were salvaged from the wreck for use again in two of his post-war musicals.

Within a few days of the London opening of *Operette,* Coward left for the Mediterranean; he had been asked by Louis Mountbatten to do some work on behalf of the Royal Naval Film Corporation which had been founded by Mountbatten earlier in the year. Its object was to equip the Navy with enough projectors to make the showing of feature films a regular part of off-duty life for all ranks in the senior service, and Coward's job was to travel around the Mediterranean fleet asking sailors what kind of films they would most like to see on board ship, and relaying their answers back to the Corporation in London. It was a task that he enjoyed hugely, as it allowed him to renew his old affection for the life of the wardroom. It also laid him wide open to Emmanuel Shinwell, who popped up in the House of Commons to enquire with untiring regularity why Mr Coward should be conveyed around the seven seas by ships of the Royal Navy at vast cost to the British taxpayer.

When Noël got back to England in the early autumn of 1938, he and Jack Wilson decided to rehash *Words and Music* as a revue for Beatrice Lillie to play on Broadway under the title *Set to Music*. Some of the songs that Coward had written for *Words and Music* six years earlier were left in the new show, and the added numbers included 'The Stately Homes of England' which was put into the revue since there was not now much likelihood of *Operette* being seen in America. Coward also put in 'Marvellous Party' for Bea, a song he had written the previous summer after Elsa Maxwell invited him to come 'just as he was' to an informal beach party in the South of France. When Noël arrived, just as he was, he found about a hundred people in the last stages of evening dress expecting him to entertain them.

> I've been to a marvellous party
> With Nounou and Nada and Nell,
> It was in the fresh air
> And we went as we were
> And we stayed as we were
> Which was Hell.
> Poor Grace started singing at midnight
> And didn't stop singing till four;
> We knew the excitement was bound to begin
> When Laura got blind on Dubonnet and gin
> And scratched her veneer with a Cartier pin,
> I couldn't have liked it more.

Elaborate plans for the Broadway staging of *Set to Music* went ahead throughout September with Noël at Goldenhurst and Jack Wilson in New York exchanging cables daily if not hourly; the dialogue that Noël carried on in this transatlantic fashion began in the usual theatrical terms:

SUGGEST YOU ENGAGE EIGHT REALLY BEAUTIFUL SHOWGIRLS MORE OR LESS SAME HEIGHT NO PARTICULAR TALENT REQUIRED ALSO NEED CLOSE HARMONY TRIO.

But then, as the pre-Munich situation worsened, the cables got more agitated:

GRAVE POSSIBILITY WAR WITHIN NEXT FEW WEEKS OR DAYS IF THIS HAPPENS POSTPONEMENT REVUE INEVITABLE AND ANNIHILATION ALL OF US PROBABLE.

With Neville Chamberlain back from Munich bearing his piece of paper the gathering storm seemed to have subsided, at least for the moment; but Noël, not normally a man who could care one way or the other about affairs even remotely political, felt violently that the bid for 'peace in our time' had been a grave mistake, and that his beloved country had now been severely compromised.

After a brief holiday in Rome where he watched a parade led by Mussolini, looking 'like an over-ripe plum squeezed into a white uniform', Coward left Europe for New York aboard the *Normandie* with Gladys Calthrop, who was going to design *Set to Music,* and Cole Lesley whom Noël had taken on as a valet during the run of *Tonight at Eight-Thirty*: 'Coley' was to stay with him as his personal secretary for the next thirty years with only a wartime break. Noël was also involved at this time in complicated negotiations for the presentation by the Wilson-Coward management of *Dear Octopus* during the same New York theatre season as *Set to Music*. It was some time before both the play and the revue emerged from the chaos of transatlantic casting and planning into some sort of shape for rehearsals in the late autumn.

Set to Music opened in Boston on Boxing Day 1938 to a considerably more enthusiastic response than had greeted the world première of *Point Valaine* in that city four years and one day earlier. From there it went to Broadway where the reviews were excellent for Bea Lillie, if rather grudging about Noël; for most critics Bea was the show and it became an evening with Beatrice Lillie rather than another Coward revue. There was praise too for Richard Haydn, the young English comedian, who made an appearance in the second half as Edwin Carp, 'the phenomenal fish mimic', holding forth in some imaginary, demented vaudeville programme. On the opening night in New York, as the 'five minutes' was called, Noël burst into Haydn's dressing-room:

> I just came by [he said] to remind you not to be nervous; all you have to remember is that the entire thing depends on you.

Almost immediately after the first night, with business for the revue looking very satisfactory indeed, Noël decided to travel again; this time to Pago-Pago by way of his beloved Honolulu. On the way he stopped off to visit Cary Grant in California, and briefly joined the frenetically social Hollywood round.

At the very beginning of 1939, fully six years after Coward himself had played it in America with the Lunts, *Design for Living* opened at the Theatre Royal, Haymarket, with an English cast. Beyond doubt the play suffered from the six-year gap which separated its writing from its first London production, and the climate of the Thirties had changed fast enough for the comedy to belong already to a different and dated era.

After his brief holiday by the Pacific with Cary Grant, Coward decided that he would not after all be visiting Pago-Pago; instead he planned to stay with the Dillinghams in Hawaii and while there to write himself a new play for London in the autumn. But even that plan was subject to change; after Noël had been in Honolulu for a few days, he found that he was not writing a play at all but instead the first of the many short stories that were to make up a major part of his output as a writer in the later stages of his life. Coward found the short story, lying in form as it does somewhere between a novel and a play, an absorbing experiment in disciplined writing which combined the advantages he had already found in the one-act play with none of the disadvantages of the inevitable compromises over casting or production.

In this first collection that Coward wrote while he was in Hawaii and titled *To Step Aside* there were seven short stories, some of them distinctly Maughamesque in their flavour but all written in a spare, dry, witty style which suggested that Coward, had he not been first and foremost a playwright, could have earned a decent living as a writer of fiction. Maugham himself, to whom Noël subsequently sent his stories, had reservations about only one of them:

> I have just finished *To Step Aside* and should like to tell you how much I enjoyed it… but I m sorry you have wasted 'Aunt Tittie' on a short story; you had material there for a great picaresque novel which probably no one but you could write and it is a shame to have squandered thus such a wealth of splendid stuff. Heaven knows I'm all for concision, but no one in the world could cram *Tom Jones*, say, into a couple of columns of an evening paper.

Among the other stories that made up *To Step Aside* one was distinctly autobiographical: 'What Mad Pursuit?', written in a fit of retrospective fury after Noël had spent one of the most frantically uncomfortable week-ends of his life in what he had been told by his hostess would be a 'restful' house on Long Island. Coward's account of a hectic and altogether ghastly American social scene is in many respects the prose equivalent of his 'Marvellous Party' song.

Within the month in Honolulu he had completed all the stories and, feeling on the good authority of almost every newspaper in sight that another European crisis was imminent and this one worse than the last, he returned home in the early spring of 1939. While Noël was passing through New York, Jack Wilson tried to persuade him to stay and join the cast of *Set to Music,* as business for the revue had fallen off badly during the winter. But Coward was determined to refuse, partly because he didn't want to risk the prestige of his name on Broadway by trying to bolster a shaky show well into its run, and mainly because he honestly felt that at a time of such world uncertainty he wanted to be at home. He did, however, stay in New York for long enough to attend the 1939 World's Fair; the organizers had promised him the honour of a 'Noël Coward Evening' there and he arrived with Constance Collier to find a massed band at the gates proudly playing selections from Jerome Kern's *Show Boat,* until they realized their mistake and switched rapidly if discordantly to *Bitter-Sweet*. Inside the gates, Noël discovered that the prospect of an evening in his honour had singularly failed to attract the fair-goers, most of whom had by now gone home. Followed by a few embarrassed officials Noël took to stopping people on the sidewalk and begging 'Please, can I give you my autograph?' Later he was given a ceremonial dinner in a huge and otherwise totally empty restaurant, by which time both Noël and Miss Collier were in fits of hysterical laughter; but their evening was finally vindicated by a visit to the amusement area of the fairground where Noël was gratifyingly mobbed, albeit none too soon.

Noël got back to Goldenhurst to find waiting for him some crippling tax bills and the threat of early action by the Inland Revenue; but within a few days Jack Wilson was able to reassure him from New York that M.G.M. had agreed to pay eighty thousand dollars for the film rights to all the plays in *Tonight at Eight-Thirty*. With that new financial crisis overcome almost as quickly as it had arrived, Noël settled back at Goldenhurst to the writing of two new and totally contrasting plays; *Present Laughter* (which was originally entitled *Sweet Sorrow*) and *This Happy Breed,* in both of which he planned to appear in London during the autumn, alternating the two on successive nights with the same company. While he was writing them he was evidently aware that long before the autumn, world events might well make the whole venture ludicrously optimistic and improbable, but bathed in the general glow of governmental optimism Coward was prepared at that stage to believe that his country might yet last out the rest of 1939 in peace.

With both plays virtually complete and another theatrical garden party successfully presided over in an even more exalted social atmosphere than usual, due largely to the arrival of his friends the then Duke and Duchess of Kent, Noël attempted to cheer up Jack Wilson (who had just been forced by declining business to close *Set to Music* on Broadway) with the news of his two new plays which, he now believed, would be ready to open in Manchester on September 11th 1939. In the meantime, as a holiday before starting rehearsals, Noël decided to try to see for himself the current condition of Europe; inside six weeks, and with help from a friend at the Foreign Office, he planned to visit Warsaw, Danzig, Moscow, Leningrad, Helsinki, Stockholm, Oslo and Copenhagen in the late summer.

In Warsaw, he found amid the rampant feudalism of country house-parties a fatalist conviction that war was imminent, but also an absolute confidence that it would be won by the allies without a Nazi invasion of Poland; Lawrence Durrell, then stationed in Danzig, later reported that German agents, already suspecting that Noël was a spy, became thoroughly convinced by his fleeting visit. From Poland Coward travelled on to Moscow where, despite the fact that he arrived in the midst of a carnival week, he discovered an overwhelming and deeply depressing lethargy among the citizens. He had hoped to meet some of the leading Russian actors of the time, most of whom had been enthusiastically described to him by the Lunts, but to his amazement he discovered that the ones who weren't actually out of the capital on summer tours were unwilling to receive him in their houses, since he was visiting Russia on his own initiative and not through Intourist. He was, however, taken on an alarmingly official tour of Moscow's highlights, including the huge marble underground stations which gave him the impression of 'a series of ornate gentlemen's lavatories.'

After a brief visit to Leningrad he left Russia gladly vowing never to return and experiencing:

> A sensation of despair, of utter hopelessness for the future of a world in which a political experiment of apparently immense social significance should, in order to achieve its obscure ends, have to be based primarily upon enforced ignorance; the denial of personal freedom, even of thought; and the organized debarring of an entire race from the slightest contact with any ideas of life other than those arbitrarily imposed upon it by a self-constituted minority.

From Leningrad Noël crossed over to Finland which he found by contrast quite enchantingly pleasant; the one uneasy moment of an otherwise highly enjoyable visit occurred when a local journalist announced to Noël that Sibelius, who lived a few miles outside Helsinki, was so looking forward to meeting him that he'd be bitterly hurt if Noël returned to England without paying his fellow-composer the courtesy of a brief visit. Impressed and flattered, Noël travelled out to a small Finnish village where he found a bald, startled old gentleman who spoke no English, had never heard of Coward, and who was consequently mystified and irritated by this disruption of his peace. Sibelius did, however, supply tea and biscuits, and smiled on the one occasion when it became clear to him that Noël was about to leave.

Coward travelled on through Scandinavia and then back to England, making a detour to spend what he correctly believed would be his last week on holiday in the South of France for many years to come. This was, in effect, the last gathering of the pre-war clans on the Riviera; Noël was surrounded by old friends, among them Joyce Carey, Marlene Dietrich, Somerset Maugham and Alan Webb; it was in some ways a melancholy occasion, made almost unbearable by the realization when he visited Maxine Elliott at her Villa above Golfe Juan during her last illness that both he and she knew they would never see each other again. As Noël's boat pulled away from the jetty below her Château de l'Horizon he looked up to see her on her balcony, a classically beautiful figure in a white nightgown and flowing hair, waving at him. She died within a few months.

Back in England during the August of 1939, Noël had already started rehearsals for *Present Laughter* and *This Happy Breed* when a man called Sir

Campbell Stuart telephoned and insisted on meeting him at midnight on the same day at the studio in Gerald Road; he also asked mysteriously whether Coward happened to like Paris. Noël, with some help from his friend Robert Boothby who knew that Sir Campbell was a director of *The Times* and had been involved in propaganda in the First World War, guessed that Stuart was about to offer him a job in the Information Service in the event of war, for which he would presumably be based in Paris.

As it happened, Boothby, who had been lunching at Goldenhurst on that day, was returning to London by way of Winston Churchill's house; he suggested that he should take Noël with him, for dinner at Chartwell, and that Coward could then ask Churchill what he should do about Stuart's offer. In spite of the plays Noël was keen to start some kind of war work as soon as possible, since it was obvious that the actual declaration could now only be a matter of days away. His first inclination, before hearing from Stuart, had been to suggest himself for work as some sort of entertainments officer in the navy, since he already had good contacts in that direction through Mountbatten and his work for the Royal Naval Film Corporation. But in many ways that solution seemed too comfortably easy, and Coward felt that possibly even he could do more for his country in time of crisis than see to it that sailors were properly entertained.

Coward put his problem, which essentially came to a choice between the navy that he knew and a possibly more rewarding post with the as yet unknown Stuart outfit, to Winston Churchill at Chartwell a few hours before the meeting with Stuart. After insisting that he should sing 'Mad Dogs and Englishmen', Churchill offered Noël advice that was unequivocal, if not very helpful: 'Get into a warship and see some action! Go and sing to them when the guns are firing – that's your job.' Noël, given an answer he neither expected nor wanted, bitterly reflected that if the morale of the Royal Navy was at such a low ebb that the sailors were unable to go into battle without him singing 'Mad Dogs and Englishmen' at them, then the country was in even more trouble than he'd realized. Apart from that, although singing while the guns fired sounded like resolute and courageous action, it would in fact be pretty impracticable; during a naval battle all sailors would be at action stations, and Noël would thus be left singing to himself in the wardroom.

The few hours that separated Churchill's advice and the meeting with Stuart in London were crucial to Noël; he was faced, finally and after much theoretical argument, with the urgent need to decide what he was going to do in the war. On the one hand, he understood Churchill's point; he was an entertainer, and there would undoubtedly be many occasions in the next few years when he would find himself singing merrily to the troops. On the other hand, he genuinely believed that as an intelligent and able writer he perhaps had more to offer in the field of propaganda. Eventually, for that reason, he chose to ignore Churchill's advice, for which Winston, who had never liked Coward as much as his songs, did not readily forgive him.

But Noël's patriotism at this time was a vital if sometimes overstated affair; he was now thirty-nine, and it had been twenty-one years since he'd abruptly left the army with a mixture of illness and relief at the end of the first war. At that time his career, and the need to get his mother out of the lodging house in Ebury Street, were considerably stronger forces in his life than the needs of King and Country. But now, with Mrs Coward safely installed at Goldenhurst and his career secure enough to withstand a wartime gap, Noël threw himself into war work with an ardour that made it seem almost as though he wanted to compensate in the second war for not having done quite enough in the first.

His travels through Europe in 1939 had given him at least a fleeting glimpse of the way of the world outside England and America, and in twenty years of adult life he had developed a devotion to his own country which was not diminished because it was often a sentimental and almost theatrical feeling. But more important to him, even in the late August of 1939, than any considerations of King or Country, of victory or defeat in war, was the crystal-clear realization that if he bungled the meeting with Stuart, or if he failed to get himself into some useful kind of war work as rapidly as possible, whatever books or plays he lived to write in the future 'would be inevitably and irrevocably tainted by the fact that I had allowed to slip through my fingers the opportunity to prove my own integrity to myself.'

At the meeting in Gerald Road, Sir Campbell Stuart outlined to Noël what he had in mind; if and when war came, Coward was to go instantly to Paris and there set up a Bureau of Propaganda which would operate in conjunction with the French Ministry of Information, then run by Jean Giraudoux and staffed by André Maurois among others, to 'disseminate propaganda in neutral territory.'

Coward agreed to do it. For the next two weeks, while rehearsals carried on for both *This Happy Breed* and *Present Laughter,* he spent almost every evening at secret briefings for the Paris assignment given by either Stuart or his deputy, Colonel Brooks. Then, on the first of September 1939, the Germans invaded Poland and it was obvious that the war was only hours away; Noël cancelled his two plays, disbanded the company and within a week he was installed at the Ritz Hotel in Paris. What he found when he got to France was a disillusioning mixture of apathy and absolute ignorance on all sides; few people knew who Noël was or why he was there and fewer still cared. Moreover, given the ludicrous conditions of absolute secrecy in which he was supposed to be operating, the prevailing atmosphere in Paris at the outbreak of war, and the apparent lack of any official support for him from either government, it was virtually impossible for Coward to start doing anything at all. To make things worse, whereas the German propaganda machine was already dropping lurid and effective anti-British cartoons into France, Coward knew that British intelligence was merely bombarding Germany with copies of the speeches of Neville Chamberlain and Lord Halifax. 'If', Noël wrote in an acid memorandum to Stuart, 'it is the policy of His Majesty's Government to bore the Germans to death, I don't believe we have quite enough time.'

But gradually, given at last the help of the Director of Military Intelligence, Coward's role sorted itself out; with the assistance of his own Chief of Staff, Viscount Strathallan, Noël found an office and set it up as the British propaganda headquarters in Paris. With Cole Lesley he'd also found himself a flat opposite the Ritz in the Place Vendôme, and by the end of 1939 he had an office staff of no less than five. None of them was entirely clear about what precisely they were supposed to be doing, but they did spend a fair amount of their time conceiving, minuting and suggesting ideas for propaganda, while a vast amount of it was also taken up in the endless reading of stupefyingly boring official documents. Still not enough, however, to dispel a distinct feeling of anti-climax and irritation. Nothing whatsoever seemed to be happening; the Maginot Line was apparently impregnable, and at times during that winter in Paris it was hard for Noël to realize that there was a war on at all.

About once a month Coward managed to get back to England on the pretext of having something vital to discuss with Stuart; then he would stop off at Goldenhurst for a weekend with his mother and Lorn and Joyce and Gladys and those friends who were still around, before returning to Paris and the frustrating realization that the work he was doing there was sadly lacking in either importance or utility. He did, however, use the time in France to embark on two training courses which he felt might prove useful to him in some as yet unimaginable contingency; first he found a teacher to improve his already adequate knowledge of the French language, and then he persuaded one of the men in his office to teach him the basic principles of radio operation.

Not a mechanically-minded man at the best of times, Noël did nevertheless manage to learn enough about the working of wireless transmitters to pull off the one solid achievement of his seven months in charge of the Paris office: the closing of Radio Fécamp in January 1940. Fécamp was a small commercial radio station in northern France which was continuing through the winter of 1939 to broadcast independently, in defiance of an agreement between the English and French governments that in the event of war all radio broadcasts in France would be centrally controlled and operated only on certain wavelengths, to avoid the danger that stations in the north like Normandie and Fécamp could provide radio cross-bearings for enemy aircraft on their way up the English Channel. Noël, in the face of considerable official apathy from those above him, launched his office into a hard-fought campaign to get the station closed down at once. This in itself was no simple task, as a number of leading French politicians of the time had financial interests in keeping it open. But after taking the problem to his own boss and then as high as Churchill's son-in-law, Duncan Sandys, and signally failing to get any help, Noël found a dishonest but thoroughly successful way round the difficulty. He went to Jean Giraudoux at the French Information Ministry and, lying through his teeth, told him that he had heard privately through certain political and journalistic sources that an almighty public scandal was about to break over the French government's involvement in Radio Fécamp and the dangers it posed to allied aircraft. Forty-eight hours later Radio Fécamp was closed down for the duration of the war.

While Noël was in Paris, a telegram from Adrianne Allen (whom he had not nicknamed Planny Anny for nothing) and her second husband Bill Whitney suggested he ought to put to Chamberlain and to the then French leader Edouard Daladier the proposal that they should demand an explicit statement of moral support for their two countries from President Roosevelt. Noël's cabled reply was brisk:

DARLING PLANNY THOUGH INTERNATIONALLY BOSSY I AM NOT YET INTERNATIONALLY AUTHORITATIVE FEAR GENTLEMEN YOU MENTION MIGHT CONCEIVABLY RESENT MY TELLING THEM HOW TO READ THEIR LINES.

Noël's frustration and boredom at the lack of anything to do in Paris returned once the Radio Fécamp episode was closed, and he felt badly out of touch with England where in the theatre at least his friends seemed to be carrying on much as before the declaration of war. In fact three of his numbers from *Set to Music* were currently being performed by Bea Lillie and Bobby Howes in a new Tennent revue at the Queen's Theatre called, somewhat prematurely, *All Clear*.

Because a veil of secrecy had been drawn over Noël's activities, or lack of them, and as he himself had been told by Stuart to give no interviews, a number of English papers began to wonder in print what he was doing in Paris, spending good tax-paid money to no obvious or apparent end. Both the *Daily Telegraph* and the *Sunday Pictorial* announced that Noël had been seen 'sauntering along the rue Royale in Naval uniform' and asked what right he had to wear it. Patently he had no right at all, as although he had been offered the honorary rank of a Lieutenant Commander in the R.N.V.R. after his work for Mountbatten's Royal Naval Film Corporation, he had turned it down; then, when war came it was decided that he would be far more useful and more mobile as a civilian than as an officer under orders.

In fact the press reports from Paris were untrue; Noël had never been seen in uniform, nor (as another report suggested) had he been seen in the Ritz bar 'hissing unutterable secrets into the ear of a beautiful Polish spy.' But as he was officially forbidden to offer any convincing explanation for his civilian presence in Paris, the stories were left uncorrected and probably did Coward's image a fair amount of damage in the eyes of those who actually were wearing uniforms and indeed fighting in them.

In March 1940, by which time the only useful thing that Noël had done since the closing of Radio Fécamp was to sing with Maurice Chevalier at an Anglo-French troop concert in Arras, he was getting desperate to leave France. His occasional suggestions for propaganda, such as showering Berlin with sticky confetti printed in Union Jack patterns after the German had boasted that the RAF never flew over their cities, were rejected out of hand by his superiors as either too frivolous or too fanciful, while the few ideas that London was prepared to accept were then modified to a point of absolute ineffectuality.

On one of his monthly visits to London, Noël pointed out to Stuart that the Paris office was now set up and running smoothly, and that his only use there was as a kind of figure-head. The office, he suggested, could be run rather better and more efficiently in his absence by Strathallan. Stuart accepted Coward's passionate request for a change, and offered him six weeks in America; though officially on leave, Coward's unofficial brief would be to travel around the States talking to leading politicians and newspaper editors and proprietors in an attempt to assess broadly the climate of opinion in America towards the war in Europe. Leaving David Strathallan to look after the office and Coley to look after his flat in the Place Vendôme, Noël left for America in the middle of April with the firm belief that he would be back at the Paris office by the beginning of June.

21

1940–1941

I behaved through most of the war with gallantry tinged, I suspect, by a strong urge to show off.

In the few weeks before Noël left Paris for New York in the spring of 1940, the atmosphere there changed considerably; after the German invasion of Norway and Denmark the 'phony war' seemed to be over and Noël, believing that his job in Paris might at last begin to come alive, was no longer so sure that he was right to leave it. He had already decided, with tight-lipped patriotism, that for the duration of the war he would renounce all creative impulses and devote himself entirely to the service of his beloved country, and in this mood of self-sacrifice he was entirely prepared to remain in Paris if anybody would actually tell him what to do there. But Stuart still wanted him to go to America in an attempt to assess the feeling across the States about the start of a more active war in Europe; so Coward duly travelled by train to Genoa and then from there, aboard the *Washington*, he sailed to New York, only slightly unnerved by Stuart's firm belief that Nazi agents might try to intercept him on the way in an effort to uncover the 'secrets' of what Coward had been doing in the Paris office. But either the German intelligence was already aware of Noël's almost total ineffectuality in Paris or else they remained bleakly uninterested in whatever he had been doing. In any event he was allowed to board the *Washington* unintercepted, and did not even have to resort to the dramatic precaution, suggested by his London superiors, of locking himself in a cabin for twenty-four hours before the ship sailed.

As soon as he landed in New York, where Jack Wilson was waiting for him as ever, Noël got involved with his old friend in planning the cabaret for a massive Relief Ball at the Astor Hotel, designed to raise money for the allies; elsewhere in New York he found the American theatrical and social scene almost totally unchanged. The war was still three thousand miles away, and Broadway life continued in much the same way as it had on his last visit a year earlier. From New York Noël travelled on to Washington, where in dinner-party conversations with such distinguished political commentators as Joe Alsop and Walter Lippmann he found to his considerable relief that the isolationist views expressed publicly by many Americans at this time were not necessarily shared by all. Although there were those Americans who still believed that whatever happened in Europe was no concern of theirs,

Coward noted and related back to London a strong feeling among the few leading politicians he met in Washington that their country's ultimate participation in the war was inevitable, and moreover that they would be fighting not to solve some distant internal European squabble but for an issue which affected the future of world peace in general and of western civilization in particular.

In Washington, Coward was invited to see F.D.R. himself who was charming, non-committal, but entirely prepared to summarize for Noël the conflicting emotions in America both for and against the isolationism that was rampant there at that time. Like Churchill on Coward's evening at Chartwell a few months earlier, Roosevelt also insisted that Noël should sing 'Mad Dogs and Englishmen' to him. Noël was fast beginning to think of that song in much the same way that a brush salesman thinks of brushes: useful as a door-opener but ultimately unrewarding after years of close and repetitive contact.

The song was, however, destined to achieve almost international significance a few years later when, at a dinner party given by Churchill on board *HMS Prince of Wales* in honour of President Roosevelt on the evening following the signing of the Atlantic Charter, the two world leaders became involved in a heated argument as to whether 'In Bangkok at twelve o'clock they foam at the mouth and run' came at the end of the first refrain or at the end of the second. It was Roosevelt who got it right; told later by Coward that he'd been wrong, Churchill murmured, 'England can take it.'

Before he returned to New York, Noël ran into Richard Casey, the Australian Minister whom he'd first met with a delegation of Dominions visitors at Arras when he was singing there in the concert with Maurice Chevalier during the winter. Casey now suggested, though at this time without any firm or practicable plan, that Noël should do a concert tour of Australia, singing out there for the Red Cross and for troops in training. In principle Noël agreed, though he was still unwilling to commit himself to the role of the forces' entertainer and in any case he seriously doubted whether Stuart would ever allow him to go even if he really wanted to; Australia was then even further removed from the front line than the United States.

Back in New York, Noël took time out from his quasi-official duties to persuade a dithering Gertrude Lawrence that it would in fact be a good thing if she went into the Moss Hart–Ira Gershwin–Kurt Weill musical *Lady in the Dark*, a bit of friendly finger-wagging which cannot be said to have altogether harmed Miss Lawrence's theatrical career, as *Lady in the Dark* ran almost uninterrupted throughout 1941 and then well into 1942.

In the early morning of the day that Wilson's huge Allied Relief Ball was scheduled, May 10th 1940, news reached New York that the Germans had invaded Holland; sickened and frightened and worried, Noël and Jack decided nevertheless that they had no alternative but to go ahead with it. Among the guests that night were Vivien Leigh and Laurence Olivier, who had just opened *Romeo and Juliet* on Broadway to some of the worst reviews either of them ever received. 'My darlings,' murmured Noël in welcome, 'how brave of you to come.' The next morning Coward wanted to return directly to the Paris office, but a cable from Strathallan there told him that everything was still under control, and another from Stuart in London told him that he might well be of more use if he stayed in America and continued to report back from there. Obediently, if reluctantly, Noël stuck to his orders and travelled on through Chicago and the midwest to San Francisco and Los Angeles talking all the time, tapping public and private opinions and compiling a furtive list of those Americans definitely opposed to a policy of isolationism.

Meanwhile the war news from Europe got progressively worse until, in the midst of meetings in California, Noël could bear it no longer. A week before the evacuation of Dunkirk he flew back from Los Angeles to New York, intending despite Stuart to return to his Paris office. But waiting for him in New York Coward found a telegram from London informing him that with the coming of Churchill's new coalition government Sir Campbell Stuart had been ousted from his job, and that Stuart's intelligence organization was now in the charge of the new Minister of Information, Duff Cooper. Noël cabled Cooper, whom he had known for some years, asking what he should do; the reply was non-committal, suggesting that Coward should make up his mind for himself about whether or not to return, but adding that in Cooper's opinion he might possibly be of more use where he was. Despite their long friendship, Cooper retained throughout the war certain doubts about Noël's usefulness in any capacity even faintly outside the realm of pure entertainment, and he was by no means alone among officials in this.

Noël, after considerable thought, decided that without explicit official backing from the British government and without any specific assignment from Cooper, there was really very little more he could do in America. After some frantic string-pulling he got himself on to a Clipper leaving for Europe at the beginning of June. In the meantime, faced with mounting press and radio hysteria about the future of his native land, Coward found time amid the comparative peace of New York to reconsider his position. He wanted so much to return to England, he decided, partly because of the desire to be near his mother and at least some of his old friends in a time of considerable peril, but mainly on account of a deep, emotional, thoroughly sentimental and totally unquenchable patriotism for England, his country right or wrong, and everything that it stood for:

> I loved its follies and apathies and curious streaks of genius; I loved standing to attention for 'God Save The King'; I loved British courage,

British humour, and British understatement; I loved the justice, efficiency and even the dullness of British Colonial Administration. I loved the people – the ordinary, the extraordinary, the good, the bad, the indifferent – and what is more I belonged to that exasperating, weather-sodden little island with its uninspired cooking, its muddled thinking and its unregenerate pride, and it belonged to me whether it liked it or not. There was no escape, no getting round it, that was my personal truth and facing up to it, once and for all, I experienced a strong sense of relief.

A couple of days after the evacuation of Dunkirk, Noël found himself back at the White House for dinner, again at the invitation of President and Mrs Roosevelt. While he was there, F.D.R. questioned him deeply about the national characteristics of the British, their resilience and their blind faith in the impossibility of being conquered by the Germans. None but the British, Roosevelt told Coward, could have transformed a full-scale military defeat like Dunkirk into a shining spiritual victory.

Then, a day later than scheduled, Noël left La Guardia on the Clipper bound for Lisbon. In mid-flight the captain told them that Italy had entered the war; on arrival in Lisbon, Noël still planned to catch the first train to Paris and then wait for instructions from London unless he had to evacuate his staff from the Place de la Madeleine right away. As there were no trains out of the Portuguese capital until the SudExpress the following morning, Noël spent the night in a Lisbon hotel. The next morning, as he was leaving for the station, he was summoned to the office of Sir Walford Selby, then British Ambassador to Portugal. Selby explicitly forbade Coward to return to Paris; his embassy, he said, had been unable to contact their French equivalent for ten days and the situation in Paris was obviously very grave indeed. Selby added that he would get Coward on the first available flight to London, and that from there he could return to Paris and help with the evacuation of his office; but for Noël to try to get into France overland would be directly opposed to his express and official advice and highly dangerous into the bargain. Noël took Selby's advice, and the SudExpress left Lisbon that morning without him. It arrived in Paris just twenty-four hours before Hitler.

Noël stayed in Lisbon for the next two days awaiting a London flight, and while he was there the ambassador persuaded him to speak to the British Club; Noël gave them an impassioned speech about how England would survive, ending perhaps a shade over-dramatically with the toast from the end of *Cavalcade*. He departed for London the next morning; en route his plane touched down at Bordeaux, where he learnt that the Germans had entered Paris. Noël suppressed an immediate, lunatic desire to board a train to the capital and find out what had happened to his office and his flat, to Strathallan and to Coley; instead he rejoined the plane and left France on the last civilian flight out of the country for five years. A few months later, Jerome Kern and Oscar Hammerstein dedicated to Noël a song entitled 'The Last Time I Saw Paris'.

Back in London, Coward discovered that when the Germans were within a couple of days of Paris both Coley and Strathallan, together with the rest of the office staff, had managed to get out; though Coley took with him everything he could manage to carry, he had to abandon most of the contents of the flat in the Place Vendôme where, as Coward thought, they remained for the benefit and possible edification of the occupying Germans. It was not until after the war ended that Noël discovered his faithful French maid had cleared out the entire flat and taken all his belongings to her own home where she walled them up in one of the bedrooms before swearing a statement in front of the local notary to the effect that if anything happened to her, Mr Coward should be informed that his possessions were safely hidden and could be had for the ripping down of a wall.

In the month that followed, Noël traipsed round London looking for a job; with the fall of France his intelligence posting was obviously at an end, and nobody, it seemed, had anything else to offer him apart from a couple of B.B.C. wartime broadcasts to America. Duff Cooper suggested that he should return to the States in an unspecified role just looking for information; other friends suggested he should become an entertainments officer, take a minor desk job at the Ministry of Information, or go into the R.N.V.R. as an information officer. All were perfectly viable possibilities, but in none did Coward feel that he would be used to the best of his potential wartime value; and though he tried every friend in a high place that he could possibly find, none of them could or would do any better for him.

Eventually, when nothing else seemed possible and it became apparent that no official in wartime England was exactly crying out for the services of Mr Coward, he decided to take Duff Cooper's suggestion as the best of a bad bunch. At the beginning of July he went back to America armed with nothing more than a hazy and unspecific Ministry request that he should try to elicit more opinions from American politicians and newspaper editors.

But during the five weeks that he'd spent in London Noël had not only been trying to sort out his own future; he had also persuaded his mother and Aunt Vida to move out of the city to the comparative safety of North Devon, and then managed to get most of the Goldenhurst furniture into storage before his house was taken over by the army. An equally pressing problem in these weeks had been the question of what to do with the sixty children in the Actors' Orphanage who were then under fifteen and who, the Orphanage committee had decided, should be evacuated to either America or Canada. Noël managed to rally a group of the English colony in Hollywood, led by Dame May Whitty and the likes of Ronald Colman, Douglas Fairbanks,

Cary Grant and Alfred Hitchcock, who discovered that although California did not offer the immediate hope of a home for the children it would be possible to find them a billet somewhere on the east coast. One of Noël's more clearly defined tasks on his arrival in New York was to sort out precisely where the children were to go; another far easier one was to find and congratulate his beloved Gertrude Lawrence who, on July 4th 1940, had married Richard Stoddard Aldrich, the manager of the Playhouse at Dennis on Cape Cod where she had recently been playing in a summer stock revival of *Private Lives*. Noël, hearing of the marriage, cabled her from London:

DEAR MRS A. HOORAY HOORAY
AT LAST YOU ARE DEFLOWERED!
ON THIS AS EVERY OTHER DAY
I LOVE YOU, NOËL COWARD.

Coward sailed from Liverpool for New York on the *Britannic*, which was already crammed with evacuee women and children; on his arrival he went straight to Lord Lothian, the British Ambassador to Washington, since his one definite instruction from Duff Cooper had been to see about the possibilities of forming some kind of organization to counteract the anti-British propaganda which the Nazis were then attempting to spread throughout America. But Lothian considered that any such organization would be out of the question for the time being, and at his request Noël returned to the social round, interviewing senators and journalists and arguing about isolationism with usually courteous hosts. He sang songs, went to endless Rotary luncheons, told stories about England in wartime, and generally made himself as pleasant as possible since that seemed to be the most important part of an image-building assignment.

Only once did his façade of unremitting charm come close to cracking, and that was when, in California, he was treated to a fifteen-minute diatribe about the awfulness of the English by ex-President Herbert Hoover. Restraining the impulse to reply in similarly outspoken terms about America's uninvolvement in the war, Noël travelled on through the rest of the summer from city to city on a bland, fact-finding and deeply frustrating tour which he was the first to recognize as inordinately futile. He did, however, manage one definite achievement: the Orphanage children were settled blissfully into the Gould Foundation just outside New York, where they were treated throughout the war with such care and devotion in surroundings of such unknown luxury that, come the end of the war, many of them were highly reluctant to return to England; of those that did, a fair proportion later returned to marry Americans.

One weekend during his American travels, Noël went to stay with Alexander Woollcott at his summer home on Lake Bomoseen in Vermont;

there he found Moss Hart, still negotiating with Gertrude Lawrence over *Lady in the Dark*. Later Hart recalled:

> Noël had been to bombed London and back since our last meeting, but it was not of war he spoke as he stepped out of the launch and we shook hands. 'Gertie signed the contract yet?' he asked quickly. 'No,' I answered, and the amount of emotion I apparently managed to get into that one word sent him roaring with pleasure up the path and into what I can only describe as a tribal war dance.

As the summer passed, Noël began to recognize a modification in the American attitude; the invasions of Norway, Denmark, Holland and Belgium, the retreat from Dunkirk and then the fall of France had resulted in a flurry of American activity leading up to the autumn election that reinstated Roosevelt on a platform of increased wartime aid for Britain. In October, by which time Noël was again wondering what he could possibly be going to do next, his friend Richard Casey the Australian Minister in Washington made a firm offer to send him out to Australia and New Zealand as a guest of the Dominion governments to make broadcasts there about the British war effort and to give concerts for training camps, the Australian Red Cross and war charities. It was the first firm offer of a job that Noël had been given since Sir Campbell Stuart had sent him over to Paris thirteen months earlier, and the first chance of an official and dignified wartime posting he'd yet had; Noël, after first checking with Lord Lothian at the embassy in Washington who seemed almost immoderately relieved to be losing him to the other side of the world, leapt at the Australian opportunity.

Before leaving America, he returned briefly to New York and prepared to install his mother and Aunt Vida in his apartment on East 52nd Street; at Noël's request they had now left England altogether and evacuated themselves to New York. Then, in mid-October, he travelled overland to San Pedro in California where Marlene Dietrich, already an old friend, saw him sail away on board the *Monterey* in the general direction of Australasia; he had decided to travel there by boat rather than plane in order to give himself the time to write a series of wartime broadcasts for the Australian Broadcasting Commission.

After Honolulu, the *Monterey* made an unexpected detour via Japan and the China Sea before docking at Sydney; the Pacific was not yet at war and their crossing was supremely peaceful until they reached Yokohama. There the Japanese immigration office refused to allow any of the English passengers on the *Monterey* to go ashore; Noël, an inveterate sightseer, was not prepared to be deterred from that even in wartime. Disguising himself apparently quite plausibly as an American seaman, he spent an uneventful evening ashore with the crew exploring the night-clubs and brothels of Yokohama before returning safely to the ship and the realization that he had, in fact, run an unnecessary risk which was not only foolhardy but would have made some pretty salacious copy for those English newspapers that were already gunning for him.

In England, where Bea Lillie and Vic Oliver were now touring Army camps with some of the *Tonight at Eight-Thirty* plays, sections of the press had started to enquire how Noël had managed to spend so much of the war so far in the comparative safety of first America and now Australia; a number of articles (later there was to be one by John Gordon in the *Sunday Express* entitled 'The Wandering Minstrel') hurt Noël deeply by suggesting that he was pulling rather less than his wartime weight, which was debatable in view of his public relations efforts and of the apparent unwillingness of the Information Ministry to let him do anything more. Curiously, the one criticism of Noël's wartime activities which could have been levelled with fairness and accuracy was the only one that no paper actually raised; in his speeches all over the world urging help for the British war effort, Noël was preaching the self-sacrifice that he personally had signally failed to practise when himself a soldier in 1918. The defence for that lay only in the way that Noël's character and conscience had matured and developed in the twenty-one years that separated the end of the first war from the beginning of the second.

From Yokohama the *Monterey* sailed to Shanghai, where Noël made a defiantly anti-Japanese broadcast and then stayed overnight in the Cathay Hotel suite where he had written *Private Lives* almost exactly eleven years earlier. Between Shanghai and Manila he then got down to writing the series of broadcasts he was to give from Sydney and Melbourne. These were later published in Australia and England under the collective title *Australia Visited 1940* and, as so often with his own work, it was Coward himself who provided the most accurate review of them: 'they were simple in style, not pompous, injected with a little humour here and there, generally innocuous and I fear a trifle dull.'

In fact there were a total of eight major broadcasts, ranging in themes from 'The World at War' to 'The Spirit of England'; they tended to be sententious and often didactic, yet they were undoubtedly heartfelt and buried in them among the finger-wagging, the sentiment and the sometimes hopeless idealism was a great deal of common sense about democracy, propaganda and the shape of things past, present and to come, all of which suggested that Coward had not kept his head as firmly buried in the sand throughout the nineteen-thirties as had many of his English theatrical contemporaries.

Arriving in Sydney in November at the start of an Australasian tour which was to last until the beginning of February 1941, Noël got a rapid indication of the kind of work he was in for over the next few months; 'at his first reception', reported the *Sydney Telegraph*, 'Mr Coward shook hands with 794 women and 21 men.' To launch his tour, which now had the official blessing of both the Governor-General, Lord Gowrie, and Prime Minister

Menzies, Noël gave a press conference in Sydney at which he came up instantly, though not for the first time, against the problem of a public identity which had dogged him persistently and irritatingly since his first great success with *The Vortex* in 1924. The gulf that separated Coward himself from the image that the press had given him was, in peacetime, unimportant and often highly profitable; if reporters wished to think of him as a well-groomed, witty, sophisticated, occasionally decadent and neurotic but undoubtedly talented playboy who was given to tossing off aphoristic light comedies before breakfast, dressed only in a silk dressing-gown and a cigarette holder, then that was all right by him and usually quite acceptable at the box-office. But now, in wartime, it did not sit so lightly on his shoulders; the *Sunday Express* had already suggested that 'his flippant England – cocktails, countesses and caviare – has gone, and a man of the people more in tune with the new mood of Britain would be a better proposition as a roving ambassador', and the *Daily Mirror* had accused Coward in no uncertain terms of being 'stilted and undemocratic'.

Although he could discount most of these press attacks, Coward himself desperately wanted to be taken seriously by the Australians:

> No matter [he told them] how light and flippant it is frequently my profession to be, now, when we are fighting so grimly for the freedom of civilization, the desire to make a contribution – however small – towards our ultimate victory is stronger in me than any other incentive I have ever known.

In the seven weeks that Noël spent in Australia before travelling on to New Zealand, he visited Adelaide, Perth, Fremantle, Canberra, Brisbane, Launceston, and Hobart in Tasmania, as well as Sydney and Melbourne. With him went a secretary, a road manager and an accompanist whom he had picked up in a Sydney night club. Apart from broadcasts, and hospital and club visits, he did a series of concerts all over south and western Australia which raised a total of nearly twelve thousand pounds for war charities and the Red Cross. Most of the shows went excellently, and Coward's fears that the Australians mightn't take kindly to some of his more sophisticated, nightclub-oriented songs proved unfounded save in one training camp for soldiers outside Melbourne where the diggers, raised to heights of anti-British fury by the two local newspapers that opposed Menzies' pro-allied government stand, jeered Coward before he had even managed to belt out the opening words of 'Mrs Worthington'.

After a final concert in Sydney, which raised an additional two thousand pounds for the bombed-out victims of the London blitz, Noël had a brief Christmas holiday in Canberra with the Governor-General and Lady Gowrie, and then sailed on to New Zealand early in the January of 1941.

If Noël had learnt anything from these, the first of countless troop concerts that he was to give all over the world in the course of the next four years, it was that although obviously happier with the more urbane and mixed audiences to be found in the theatres and cinemas and church halls of town and cities, he could actually cope with an audience consisting solely of servicemen in a camp. For them, he was hardly a routine entertainment; a blithe, middle-aged Englishman with no real voice and a red carnation in his buttonhole must have come as a fair shock to troops already used to blonde singers and good, bawdy comedians as their wartime entertainers. But Coward found that he could, given average luck, hold most of them for up to an hour though he never really discovered for his own peace of mind whether this was a tribute to his dynamic stage presence or to the natural courtesy and good-humour of most servicemen.

New Zealand, despite a visibly slower national tempo and the assignment to Noël of a desperately jocular A.D.C., was an almost equal triumph for him; there were highly receptive military and civilian audiences, streets lined with cheering people and packed receptions at town halls on both islands. The only minor disasters were the Lady Mayoress of Wellington who drove Noël, white with fury, out of her official reception by telling him that in her view 'The Stately Homes of England' was unpatriotic and an insult to the British people, and, later on the tour, an over-enthusiastic mother who stuck her baby through the open window of Noël's moving car to have him kiss it, thereby coming within a hair's-breadth of breaking the child's back.

From Auckland, Noël travelled back to America and overland to Washington, where Sir William Stephenson, the Canadian millionaire whose British Security Co-ordination represented British Intelligence in the U.S., offered him a new secret service assignment. However, within a few hours of Noël's acceptance, this was nipped in the bud by Churchill himself who decided to alter Stephenson's entire plan and to have it executed without Noël. 'A greater power than we could contradict,' Stephenson told Coward, 'has thwarted our intents.' At the beginning of 1941, therefore, Noël found himself back in London with yet again no idea of what he could possibly be going to do next, and worse still with no indication from sources official or otherwise that anybody much cared. The day after he returned, Noël gave a press conference in Gerald Road to tell reporters precisely what he had been doing abroad since war broke out, and to remind them hopefully that whereas they were entirely at liberty to criticize his abilities as an entertainer, they really had no right at all to criticize his private character as 'unsuitable for war work' without some kind of proof.

A few days after Noël had re-installed himself in Gerald Road, the whole of his office there and most of the studio apartment at the side of it was blown to bits in a blitz. Noël, returning from a dinner party in time to pick up a few of the pieces, realized that it would be some time before he could live there again, and therefore moved rapidly into a room at the Savoy. When, three nights later, another bomb blew in the doors of that hotel's Grill while he was dining there, it was Noël, together with Judy Campbell, who leapt up on to Carroll Gibbons' bandstand to entertain the bemused customers with spirited renderings of 'Mad Dogs and Englishmen' and 'A Nightingale Sang in Berkeley Square'. The other diners, faced with a choice of staying to be sung at or leaving to face the blitz, not unnaturally stayed where they were and enjoyed themselves hugely. In gratitude, the Savoy moved Noël next day into a river suite for the same price that he had been paying for a single room.

Early in May, after a sad visit to Goldenhurst to see how the army were looking after it, Noël and Joyce Carey travelled down to Portmeirion for a week beside the seaside in that mock-Italian village on the coast of North Wales. But the 'holiday' was not, in fact, anything of the kind. Although at the outbreak of war exactly twenty months earlier Noël had sworn that he would not write another play until it was all over, he had soon begun to think that this was, though undoubtedly patriotic and well-intentioned, perhaps a rather meaningless gesture. By the time he sailed for Australia in the previous year he had already been working intermittently in America on an unproduced and generally unsatisfactory comedy called *Time Remembered*. A few months later he had said in one of the Melbourne broadcasts 'of course I cannot guarantee that a time will not come in the war when suddenly something goes snap and cascades of bright witticisms tumble out of me like coins from a fruit machine when the three lemons come up together'.

By now, it had been two years since Coward had completed anything at all on paper except memoranda and the *Australia Visited* broadcasts, and in talking to Joyce Carey the first morning on the beach at Portmeirion the three lemons suddenly came up together. The result, six days of solid writing later, was the completed script of *Blithe Spirit* which, when put into immediate rehearsal and production ran just three short of two thousand performances in the West End: a record for its time and for many years afterwards.

In Noël's original concept of the play, Madame Arcati had been a small part designed for his beloved friend Clemence Dane who at that time expressed a vague desire to act; but in the actual writing of *Blithe Spirit* the character developed to the point where this eccentric medium became central and crucial to the comedy. Apart from that major development, once the play was committed to paper in those six days at Portmeirion Noël made no changes in the first draft whatsoever beyond the correction of typing errors, and in production only two lines of *Blithe Spirit* were ever cut. The fruit machine had paid out rapidly and in full.

22

1941–1942

This is the story of a ship… and of the Fleet in which we serve.

Returning to London from Portmeirion with Joyce Carey and the completed script of *Blithe Spirit*, Noël immediately began to think about casting. He believed it was probably the best comedy he'd yet written, and found little difficulty in negotiating a co-production by H. M. Tennent and the John C. Wilson management; their plan was that Noël himself would direct an English cast going into the bomb-damaged but still serviceable Piccadilly Theatre, while Wilson would present and direct an American company in New York early in the fall. For Charles Condomine, the henpecked author at the constant mercy of wives living and dead in *Blithe Spirit*, Noël cast Cecil Parker; Elvira, his first wife and in many ways the best part of them all, was played by Kay Hammond, a superb and glamorous light comedienne who had established her reputation in *French Without Tears* a few seasons earlier. Fay Compton created the part of Condomine's second wife, Ruth, and Margaret Rutherford, in one of the most successful and characteristic roles of her career, played the zany, improbably psychic, bicycling Madame Arcati.

While *Blithe Spirit* was in rehearsal, the M.G.M. film of *Bitter-Sweet* opened in lurid technicolour at the Empire in Leicester Square. It was, in Noël's considered opinion, 'vulgar, lacking in taste and absolutely untrue to my original story'; all of which was fair comment but did not prevent the Nelson Eddy–Jeanette Macdonald vehicle making a vast amount of money and killing for the next two decades all the hopes that Noël had nurtured of reviving the original.

After two out-of-town weeks in Manchester and Leeds, *Blithe Spirit* opened in London on July 2nd 1941 to loud acclaim. The only dissenting voice came from the dress-circle, when an indignant lady announced that it was rubbish, rude to spiritualists and should be taken off immediately. Though Graham Greene for the *Spectator* found it 'a weary exhibition of bad taste' the rest of the reviews were exuberant, and the feeling was that here Coward had written an ideally escapist entertainment, flippant and careless about death yet funny and sturdy enough to be a constant source of joy and hilarity to wartime theatre-goers. Not for the first time in his career, though perhaps for the last, Noël had written a play which was exactly what the theatre-going public wanted at precisely the moment they wanted it most.

In fact, judged purely at the box-office, Coward was probably right in thinking of *Blithe Spirit* as the most successful of all his plays, and even Allardyce Nicoll accepted it as 'a minor comic masterpiece of the lighter sort'. But it lies well outside the mainstream of Noël's earlier comedies, if only because we are not here faced with a closed, self-perpetuating group of central characters coping with themselves and an alien world around them. The end of the Thirties, the coming of the war and the two years that Coward had spent away from any prolonged stints at the typewriter seemed to have changed if not his style then at least his sense of development; there is more of a plot in *Blithe Spirit* than in any of his comedies of the late Twenties and Thirties, and it undoubtedly marks the beginning of a new period in his work as a playwright. From now on his plays were to have much less in common with each other; all the old recurrent themes, the immorality and ultimate futility of the bright young things, the witty central characters battling almost incestuously with each other and fending off an unamused and disapproving outside world, all ended with the Thirties. Instead, Coward's comedies of the Forties and Fifties all exist, whether successfully or not, independently and (with the exceptions of *Relative Values* and *Quadrille*) in their own right, without back-references to current social mores or the accepted conventions of high-society behaviour.

Soon after *Blithe Spirit* opened at the Piccadilly, Noël was standing on the platform of a London railway station on the morning following a particularly bad blitz:

> Most of the glass in the station roof had been blown out and there was dust in the air and the smell of burning. The train I was waiting to meet was running late and so I sat on a platform seat and watched the Londoners scurrying about in the thin sunshine. They all seemed to me to be gay and determined and wholly admirable and for a moment or two I was overwhelmed by a wave of sentimental pride. A song started in my head then and there and was finished in a couple of days. The tune was based on an age-old English melody that had been appropriated by the Germans and used as a foundation for "Deutschland über Alles", and I considered that the time had come for us to have it back in London where it belonged. I am proud of the words of this song; they express what I felt at the time and what I still feel:

> In our city darkened now, street and square and crescent,
> We can feel our living past in our shadowed present,
> Ghosts beside our starlit Thames
> Who lived and loved and died
> Keep throughout the ages London Pride.

While Noël was still staying at the Savoy wondering what to do or where to go next in the war, he was approached by Filippo del Giudice, the Italian producer who a few years later was to set up the film of Olivier's *Henry V.* Del Giudice, together with Anthony Havelock-Allan offered Noël the chance to make any film he liked; if he would agree to write and act in it for them, their Two Cities film company would give him complete control over subject, cast and director as well as putting up all the money needed to finance it. Noël was not unnaturally flattered that the film men should set such store by the value of his name, but he had grave doubts; his experience of filming had so far been limited to *The Scoundrel* and a youthful appearance in Griffith's *Hearts of the World*, neither of which he'd been entirely happy about, and as an author he considered that his work (with the possible exceptions of *Cavalcade* and *Private Lives*) had been totally destroyed by transference to the silver screen.

Nevertheless, he could hardly fail to have appreciated the opportunity that was being offered to him; he told del Giudice that if he could find a suitable theme for a film then he would certainly think hard about it. Neither Coward nor del Giudice had long to wait; the following evening, dining with Louis Mountbatten who had just returned to England after the sinking of *HMS Kelly* off the island of Crete, Noël became fascinated by the story that Mountbatten told of his command. Coward began to realize that here, if he could only write it honestly and without too much sentimentality, was the storyline for a film which could combine a patriotic wartime salute to the navy with a drama involving a cross-section of humanity under severe pressures: the kind of human mosaic that he knew he had been able to put together with considerable accuracy and success in *Cavalcade* twelve years earlier, with, this time, the added advantage that he could draw deeply on his considerable knowledge of and love for the workings of the Royal Navy. Thus was born the idea for *In Which We Serve,* the film which was to take almost all of Coward's time and energy for the next twelve months and which ultimately became the only other product of Coward's working life to equal the ambition, the scope and the eventual patriotic success of the epic that was *Cavalcade.*

This time, however, the problems were even greater; in the first place neither Mountbatten nor the navy wanted the story of the film to be identifiable with him or the *Kelly* in any way at all, since the Admiralty would obviously take a poor view of that kind of publicity and individual glorification in wartime. Mountbatten and *HMS Kelly* did, of course, inspire *In Which We Serve,* and the character that Noël played in the film, Captain Edward Kinross, bore some pretty close resemblances to the then head of Combined Operations (Noël even wore Mountbatten's old cap in some sequences) but officially the film was to be the story of no one man and no one ship; instead *In Which We Serve* was to be a generalized, dramatized, fictionalized account of 'a destroyer' and its crew from commissioning to sinking. On those conditions, realizing the film's potential propaganda value to the navy in time of war, Mountbatten agreed to give all the help he could; he even allowed survivors from the *Kelly* to appear in the film and to act as technical advisors.

Without Mountbatten's help, it is doubtful whether *In Which We Serve* would ever have got further than Noël's typewriter; as soon as it was announced that Coward was to start work on a naval film, gossip columnists began to wonder in print whether he was exactly the right man to do it considering that he'd never been in the navy, and there was a good deal of early unrest in government and film circles. But the navy itself, prodded into helping by Mountbatten's evident enthusiasm, offered Noël considerable technical and logistical help in the planning of it; without their anonymous support *In Which We Serve* might well have lost the authenticity and realism which made palatable the film's more fervently patriotic moments.

Noël started work on the first draft of a script right away, and within a very few weeks there was already enough on paper to let del Giudice's Two Cities company start setting it up; Noël was to co-direct the picture himself, as well as writing it, composing the music and playing the lead; the other director was to be the young David Lean, on his first major film assignment.

During this preparatory stage, long before it got anywhere near the studio floor, *In Which We Serve* was almost totally defeated by Jack Beddington, Director of the Films Division at the Ministry of Information. He it was who read Noël's first draft outline and decided that as naval propaganda the story was thoroughly unsuitable, since it showed a British ship actually being sunk by the enemy. The fierce pro-British patriotism and the absolute confidence of naval invincibility in the face of utter disaster that permeated every line of Noël's script had apparently eluded Mr Beddington, who also found it impossible to accept that a serving officer would pardon a man guilty of desertion in the way that Coward's captain pardoned the young stoker in the film – even though Noël assured him that this episode was not wholly fictitious.

But threatened with this ministerial disapproval, the first of countless official hurdles that the film had to overcome at various stages in its production, Two Cities were tempted to abandon the whole venture. Fortunately for Noël, Mountbatten happened still to be in England:

> When everything was going wrong I rang Mountbatten to ask for his help. He told me to come straight round to his house. When I got there he was in the bath, so I sat on the lavatory seat and told him all my problems. He then sorted them out.

Mountbatten instantly got official Admiralty clearance for the film from Sir Tom Phillips, the then First Sea Lord's immediate deputy. Armed with that, it was not difficult for Noël to put Mr Beddington in a very uncomfortable position indeed, and the objections withered rapidly; Mr Beddington did, however, write to Noël when *In Which We Serve* first opened in London, to assure him that the film was both effective and moving. Coward did not reply.

By the end of September 1941 *In Which We Serve* was well under way. Gladys Calthrop was supervising the design and building of countless sets including the life-size replica of a destroyer on Stage Five at Denham Studios, which would become *HMS Torrin* for the film, while Noël had already started to cast a company of actors chosen primarily from the theatre. Celia Johnson was to play his wife Alix and among the members of his crew were John Mills, Bernard Miles, Richard Attenborough and Michael Wilding. Although shooting was not due to start for another four months, Coward had already seen enough of the workings of the British film industry in wartime to realize that the only hope for his picture was absolute efficiency and clarity of purpose at all times; he decided therefore to do a second draft of the script incorporating all shooting instructions, set requirements and other contingency planning so that the final version looked not unlike the plans for a major nautical manoeuvre. But before starting on it he wanted a brief holiday to absorb once again the atmosphere of the navy.

During the next three or four weeks, he visited first *HMS Nigeria* and then *HMS Shropshire* where he saw if not enemy action then at least the continuing naval traditions of bridge and wardroom and mess. The atmosphere of relaxed formality which Noël had found so attractive on his visits to the navy during the Thirties had, not unnaturally, now disappeared into the grim activities of war but he could still see the navy's appeal for a writer; on board ship, even now, there was a complete, isolated and artificial community with every social stratum represented in microcosm. The feeling was of a small country town whose inhabitants were now bound together in a common endeavour springing not from a grandiose concept of 'King and Country' but rather from a much simpler and more immediate need to preserve their community at all costs; and that feeling of a ship's inherent unity was the most important theme of Coward's script for *In Which We Serve*.

His memories refreshed and he himself again deeply imbued with the atmosphere and spirit of the navy, Noël went back to his studio in Gerald Road, which had at long last been cleared of its bomb damage, to start the final draft of the film script. In the meantime the Lunts had resolutely turned down the American production of *Blithe Spirit*, but with a cast headed by Clifton Webb, Peggy Wood, and Mildred Natwick as Madame Arcati, it had toured and opened to considerable success on Broadway where it was to last for the next eighteen months. Noël himself had also been heard in America at this time singing such numbers as 'London Pride' and his new Home Guard parody 'Could You Please Oblige Us With A Bren Gun?' at the special request of Henry Morgenthau Jr on a coast-to-coast radio programme sponsored by the U.S. Treasury. During the preparation of *In Which We Serve,* that programme, together with occasional troop and station concerts in England, was to be the extent of Noël's war work; because of the film he had reluctantly to decline, at least for the moment, an offer from Field-Marshal Smuts to do a series of troop concerts in South Africa. The shooting schedules made this an impossibility until the end of 1942 at the earliest, and in fact various later projects delayed his arrival in Johannesburg until the beginning of 1944. In the meantime he struggled on with the script for his film.

One morning soon after his return to Gerald Road, Coward's work on *In Which We Serve* was interrupted by the arrival of two police officers bearing summonses from the Finance Defence Department. In a state of some shock, Noël learnt from them that he was liable to be fined a possible total of over twenty thousand pounds for having broken currency regulations by keeping and spending money in the United States after August 1939 when new laws had made it compulsory to declare any money held overseas to the Treasury and illegal to spend any of it without prior permission. Noël claimed then, and maintained until the end of his life, that he knew nothing of any such laws and had never been told of them by his accountants in either England or America. He had kept a dollar account in New York since the days of *The Vortex,* and the royalties from his plays and songs, together with money from the current Broadway production of *Blithe Spirit* were still being paid into it by Jack Wilson; moreover when Noël had been in the States on unofficial business for the Ministry of Information in 1940 he had spent thirty thousand of his own dollars travelling around the country because he had nothing else to live on. But his ignorance of the law seemed a pretty thin defence at first, and Noël was only too aware of the damage that a well-publicized court case, whatever its outcome, would do to his relations with Mountbatten and the Admiralty over *In Which We Serve.* The charges could not, in short, have been made at a worse time.

Immediately after the policemen left his studio Noël got himself a lawyer, the eminent Dingwall Bateson, who advised that he should plead guilty; the maximum fine if he pleaded innocent and was found guilty could go up to over £60,000 but Bateson thought that with a plea of guilty Coward could get away with the minimum of £5,000. Noël, deciding that the publicity would be unsavoury either way, was about to accept Bateson's suggestion when, out of the blue, he received a letter from George Bernard Shaw pointing out that whatever the lawyers and the judge had to say, 'there can be no guilt without intention' and ending 'therefore let nothing induce you to plead Guilty.'

Coward, severely opposed by Bateson and his barrister, Geoffrey ('Khaki') Roberts, stuck to Shaw's advice; the case came up at the end of the month, and after an unsuccessful attempt by the prosecution to prove that Noël had been in America solely for his own enjoyment and safety rather than for any unofficial ministerial business, the judge grudgingly let him off with a fine of only £200 which, as the minimum assessment had been £5,000, was taken by the defence to be more of an award than a penalty.

But Noël was not through yet; a week later he was summoned to appear before a court at the Mansion House to answer related charges about keeping undeclared dollars in the United States. On this occasion he was fined a further £1,600 before finally being released; but the two trials were, surprisingly enough, played down in the press and they did no lasting harm to *In Which We Serve*. They did, however, cause Noël to get his business affairs into rather better order by sacking one firm of accountants and drastically reorganizing the terms of his partnership with Jack Wilson. At the end of it all he cabled Bernard Shaw:

DEAR GBS THE RESULT OF MY HAVING FOLLOWED YOUR ADVICE IS ONLY TOO APPARENT STOP I AM ETERNALLY GRATEFUL TO YOU NOT ONLY FOR YOUR WISDOM BUT FOR THE DEEP KINDNESS THAT PROMPTED YOUR MOST OPPORTUNE AND VERY REAL HELP.

A number of his friends wrote to Noël at this time expressing indignant sympathy for what had happened to him; among them was Rebecca West: 'I can't quite see what more you could do for your country, except strip yourself of all your clothes and sell them for War Weapons Week, after which your country would step in and prosecute you for indecent exposure.'

Meanwhile *Blithe Spirit* was continuing to prove itself a gold mine, not only in London but also in America. Noël at this stage was firmly refusing all Hollywood offers for the film rights because, as he cabled Jack Wilson:

ALL MY PLAYS EXCEPTING CAVALCADE HAVE BEEN VULGARIZED DISTORTED AND RUINED BY MOVIE MINDS AM NOW MIDDLE-AGED AND PRESTIGE AND QUALITY OF MY WORK ARE MY ONLY ASSETS FOR THE FUTURE THEREFORE HAVE DECIDED HENCEFORWARD NEVER TO SELL FILM RIGHTS UNLESS I HAVE ABSOLUTE CONTROL OF SCRIPT DIALOGUE CAST TREATMENT DIRECTOR CAMERAMAN CUTTER AND PUBLICITY CONVINCED PRESENT UNAVOIDABLE LOSS IS FUTURE INEVITABLE GAIN.

But Noël's refusal strained relations between himself and his partner, and the legal need to reorganize the affiance with Jack Wilson on a more businesslike footing didn't make them any easier; on top of that, Jack was also having to cope with Noël's mother who was still in New York but now determined to get back to England and her beloved son. Wilson did all he could to help, as did Noël from the other end, but transatlantic travel for private reasons in the winter of 1941–2 was not easy to arrange. So Mrs Coward, now seventy-eight, stayed on in New York, suffering acutely from the loneliness and homesickness which were beginning to affect her health. Soon after the court cases, when Noël was still worried about their effect on *In Which We Serve* and struggling to get the script ready for the first day of shooting, Mrs Coward had written to him from New York suggesting that he should join her there and stay well clear of England until after the war, especially after 'the way the government had behaved' over his finances. Noël's letter in reply to hers was furiously indignant, but it was also the closest he came to an actual statement of his wartime beliefs. The letter was posted the morning before Pearl Harbor, and it ran in part as follows:

> You don't seem to realize why I have done what I have done since the War began. The reason I want to do all I can for my country has nothing to do with governments. One of the privileges which we are fighting for is to be able to grumble about our governments as much as we like… I am working for the country itself and for the ordinary people who belong to it. If you had been here during some of the bad blitzes and seen what I have seen or if you had been with the navy as much as I have, you would understand better what I mean. The reason that I didn't come back to America when I really could have if I'd tried hard enough, or go to South Africa in September as the South African Government wished, was that in this moment of crisis I wanted to be here experiencing what all the people I know and all the millions of people I don't know are experiencing. This is because I happen to be English and I happen to believe and know that if I ran away and refused to have anything to do with the war and lived comfortably in Hollywood as so many of my actor friends have done, I should be ashamed to the end of my days. The qualities which have made me a success in life are entirely British. *Cavalcade, Bitter-Sweet, Hay Fever,* everything I've ever written could never have been written by anybody but an Englishman… I feel very ashamed of many of the people I know in America for their attitude over this war. It is theirs as much as ours and they have allowed us to fight it for them for over two years… if I didn't feel that in every way I was doing my best to help in what we are fighting for, I would never forgive myself and would probably never be able to write another good play in all my life… England may be a very small island, vastly overcrowded, frequently badly managed, but it is in my view the best and bravest country in the world.

During the endless and depressing winter that followed the bombing of Pearl Harbor and America's entry into the war, Noël became totally wrapped up in his work at Denham Studios. As soon as the two currency cases were over, and he found to his vast relief that they were not going to affect the future of *In Which We Serve*, Noël moved into a damp cottage near the studios and, with Gladys Calthrop who went to join him there, he continued to work intensively on the elaborate and often tricky preparations for the picture. By now steeped in an atmosphere of naval heroism, he was invited by the Green Room Club to propose the toast to Esmond Knight at a special matinée staged in London during January 1942 to mark Knight's courage and the partial loss of his eyesight in the action between *HMS Hood* and the *Bismarck*.

During these weeks, when Gladys was living and working side by side with Noël in the same artistic relationship they had built up during the preparations for *Cavalcade* a dozen years earlier, she heard of the death of her only son Hugo who had been killed fighting in Burma. She had been devoted to him, but demanded no pity. Without even a pause, she continued her work with Coward, now perhaps even more fervently than before.

Coward was in no doubt of his film's potential importance to both himself and the navy: 'it will', he wrote to his mother, 'be the best thing I have ever done... a naval *Cavalcade* that is absolutely right for this time.' On February 5th 1942, after seven months of punishingly hard work drafting different versions of the script, testing the actors and make-up and complicated technical effects, arguing about a total budget of only £200,000, and wondering whether the whole project would ever get off the ground, shooting started on *In Which We Serve*. For the next twenty weeks Coward, together with his cast, crew and technical advisers from the navy, sweated through the picture from seven-thirty in the morning until after eight at night. Some days, two hundred and fifty sailors on loan from the Admiralty would appear on the set to play the crew of the Torrin; other days Noël and Bernard Miles and John Mills would spend up to their necks in a tank of oily water filming the sequences that involved the Carley float. These provide the backbone of the film, for it is while the captain and the few survivors of his crew are clinging to the float for dear life in the hope of being picked out of the sea after the Torrin has been torpedoed, that they remember their families and their private lives which have until now been dominated by their ship. As they hang on, exhausted and wounded, the film flashes back to show them with their loved ones and then to show through the eyes of her crew the ordeals and the achievements of *HMS Torrin* from the time of her commissioning until the disastrous end to this her last battle.

The ship and the crew are archetypal, and in Coward's film they stand as obvious symbols for the eternal, indomitable fighting spirit of his beloved navy, 'the fleet in which we serve'. In one of the film's early montage sequences Noël does, however, allow himself a moment in which to get his own back on the Beaverbrook press, which had in recent months been particularly disparaging about his war efforts. Soon after Chamberlain's declaration of war is heard on the soundtrack, *HMS Torrin* is pictured steaming out of harbour fresh from her commissioning. A tracking shot moves slowly down the side of the ship to the muddy water below, where floats a tattered copy of the *Daily Express* bearing its headline 'No War This Year'. With this one shot Noël made an implacable enemy of Lord Beaverbrook, then in the war cabinet and determined not to have his newspaper mocked in this way. In the next few months Beaverbrook tried, consistently but unsuccessfully, to have the film banned.

At the time of *In Which We Serve* Richard Attenborough was still a student at RADA, and this was his first film: 'I arrived on the set for my first day's shooting, well-nigh terrified. No one seemed to know who I was or what I was meant to be doing; then this figure approached. 'Good morning,' he said, 'you're Richard Attenborough, aren't you? You won't know me, my name's Noël Coward.'

As an actor, Coward still found the business of filming a repetitive and irritatingly fiddly affair, but as the film's producer he ran the set with an iron efficiency and a constant will to work that thoroughly disturbed some of the more union-minded members of his crew, who found their tea breaks severely threatened. One day during April, with half the film already in the can, the King and Queen with their daughters Elizabeth and Margaret were brought down to Denham by Mountbatten to inspect the production. Noël was thrilled by their presence, and performed the whole of his captain's 'Dunkirk' speech in three short takes while the royal family stood at the side of the set to watch. The King had already read the script of *In Which We Serve,* and he told Coward that in his view it was 'a very good and appealing way of dealing with the subject... although the ship is lost, the spirit which animates the Royal Navy is clearly brought out in the men, and the procession of ships coming along at the end to take its place demonstrates the power of the Navy.'

By late June the whole of the picture was in the can save one last shot of Noël standing on the bridge which proved in the event to be near-fatal for him:

> A replica of the bridge of the destroyer had been placed on the edge of the large outside tank at Denham Studios. Above it, a few hundred yards away on a scaffolding, were perched the enormous tanks filled with thousands of gallons of water. On a given signal a lever would be pulled, whereupon the tanks would disgorge their load down a chute, and overturn and capsize the bridge with me on it... I looked at the flimsy structure on which I was to stand and then up at the vast tanks and said 'No'... In no circumstances would I either do it myself or allow any living creature to stand on the bridge until I saw what the impact of water would do to it. Finally, after some grumbling at the time waste, they gave

in to my insistence and ordered the signal to be given. The whistle blew and we all stood back and watched. There was a loud roar as the water came hurtling down the chute, and, in a split second there was nothing left of the bridge at all. It was immediately obvious that anyone standing on it would have been killed instantly.

But by the end of the month even that shot was safely on film, and apart from some dubbing and post-synchronization during July Noël had come to the end of *In Which We Serve*.

A few months earlier he had decided that after nearly a year inside the frustrating routine of a film studio, he would like above all else to get back into the live theatre; and as there was no sign from any official quarter that his services might be needed anywhere for anything, he agreed with Binkie Beaumont of H. M. Tennent to spend the autumn and winter touring the provinces with a repertoire of three of his own plays: *Blithe Spirit*, which had not so far been seen outside London, and the two he had been forced to abandon in rehearsal at the outbreak of war, *Present Laughter* and *This Happy Breed*. He had not appeared on the stage as an actor since his nervous breakdown had ended the run of *Tonight at Eight-Thirty* in New York so abruptly during the March of 1937, and to feel his way back into the routine he agreed that during the August of 1942 he would replace Cecil Parker for two weeks in the London production of *Blithe Spirit* at the St James's.

Noël was delighted to be back in a theatre; the joy of acting out a whole play to a receptive audience, and of hearing laughter and applause again after months of playing disconnected scenes to the dispassionate technicians on a studio floor, more than compensated for the vague pangs of guilt with which he acknowledged that his determination at the outbreak of war not to act again until it was all over had wavered and cracked in less than three years. His ideas about performing 'useful wartime tasks' had all been officially frustrated, and after some unrewarding brushes with the administration and the press in his quasi-diplomatic roles he was only too happy to be back in command of his home territory in a theatre. He even managed to persuade himself that his original wartime plans had been ludicrously over-patriotic and that he was really being most useful by simply carrying on with his peacetime occupations to the best of his ability.

Early in the fortnight that Noël played for Cecil Parker at the St James's, he heard that the Duke of Kent had been killed in an air crash in Scotland. It came as a bitter shock; the Duke had been a close friend and perhaps lover of Noël's from the time when he went backstage after *London Calling!* in 1923, and in the last few months Coward's cottage near Denham had been very close to the Kents' country home and Noël had been a frequent visitor there. Coward was ill-prepared for this sudden news; between the wars he had been lucky enough never to lose a close friend through death and he had forgotten, in the years since Philip Streatfield and John Ekins had died, how much pain it could cause him. It was with considerable difficulty that Coward played on through *Blithe Spirit,* with its light treatment of death, for the rest of his short stay in the London production.

In the meantime, while Noël was casting and rehearsing a company to appear in his three plays on tour, and campaigning on the side for a committee who wanted to get London's theatres open on Sundays, Jack had cabled him from New York that his mother was still chafing to get back to him in London. She had, however, flatly refused to travel by boat, and was instead on a permanent standby waiting for a place on a Clipper that might take her as far as Lisbon. Often during the summer of 1942 she would set out for the airport, only to return dejected to her apartment the next morning after failing to get a seat. Wilson did, however, send more cheerful news about *Blithe Spirit* which had won the American drama critics' award for the year and also a 'best performance' award for Mildred Natwick as Madame Arcati. Roughly half the producers in Hollywood were still bidding for the film rights in spite of Noël's veto, and a New York radio station announced they would like to use the character of Elvira as the heroine of a new soap opera which they planned to run for several years with Janet Gaynor in the lead. Coward's reply was curt:

IN NO CIRCUMSTANCES WHATSOEVER STOP SUGGEST THEY GET SHAW'S PERMISSION TO USE SAINT JOAN.

After innumerable false starts Jack managed to get Mrs Coward on to a Clipper bound not for Lisbon but better still for Ireland, and she was back in London with her son just before he started off on the provincial tour in September. As she wanted to stay in London, and as Goldenhurst was in any case still requisitioned, Noël settled her with her sister Vida into one of the old mansion flats that border Eaton Square, and that became her home until she died a decade later.

During the week of September 20th 1942, Noël and his company opened *Blithe Spirit* in Blackpool at the start of a tour which was to take them from Inverness to Bournemouth via twenty-five different theatres in the next six months. Of the three entertainments that made up this travelling *Play Parade, Present Laughter* was by far the most self-indulgent; like *Hay Fever* it is a comedy about the 'theatricals' that Noël still knew and loved so well, but this time written with the sole intent of providing, in Garry Essendine, a whacking star role for its author. Over the years the play has nevertheless proved a well-oiled and perfectly satisfactory vehicle for a number of other actors, among them Nigel Patrick, Peter O'Toole, Tom Conti, George C. Scott and Sir Donald Sinden. Essendine is in many ways the middle-aged projection of the dilettante, debonair persona first accorded to Coward after the success of *The Vortex* in 1924; he is a witty, tiresome, self-obsessed, dressing-gowned figure who struts through the play like an educated peacock. But at the end of the first act there is a revealing moment when Essendine, and through him Coward himself, is called upon to give some advice to an angry young playwright:

GARRY: ...to begin with, your play is not a play at all. It's a meaningless jumble of adolescent, pseudo intellectual poppycock. It bears no relation to the theatre or to life or to anything... If you wish to be a playwright you just leave the theatre of tomorrow to take care of itself. Go and get yourself a job as a butler in a repertory company if they'll have you. Learn from the ground up how plays are constructed and what is actable and what isn't. Then sit down and write at least twenty plays one after the other, and if you can manage to get the twenty-first produced for a Sunday night performance you'll be damned lucky!

From the West End sophistication of *Present Laughter* to the South London suburbia of *This Happy Breed* was a very long jump indeed, but one that Coward made as playwright and as actor with consummate agility. *This Happy Breed* was a domestic *Cavalcade*, the saga of one lower middle-class family and their various personal trials and successes through the twenty years that separated the Armistice from Munich. From his childhood, Noël had known Clapham commoners like these ('I was born somewhere in the middle of the social scale, and so got a good view of both upper and lower reaches') and a tendency in his writing to make them over-articulate was more or less offset by the accuracy with which he depicted the changing pattern of their family life through one generation; *This Happy Breed* is a microcosmic impression of what England was like for one family at one time, in which action comes second to dialogue and in which the ultimate heroine is England herself.

In a dramatized and faintly sentimentalized form, this play goes to the root of Coward's social instinct ; though blithely uninterested in politics, and actively hostile to politicians through the late Thirties and early Forties, he retained an unshakeable faith in the ability of his fellow-countrymen to muddle through whatever befell them, led only by common sense and their own natural instinct for survival.

At the end of the first week of Coward's tour, by which time *This Happy Breed, Blithe Spirit* and *Present Laughter* had all been seen for two nights each in Blackpool, Noël and Gladys and Joyce returned to London for the world première of *In Which We Serve*. The reviews were ecstatic; Dilys Powell in the *Sunday Times* felt it was 'the best film about the war yet made in this country or in America', and when it opened in New York a few weeks later, critics there were equally impressed. Bosley Crowther for the New York Times thought it 'one of the most eloquent motion pictures of these or any other times.' In the Academy Awards early in 1943, Coward was given a special Oscar for his 'outstanding production achievement on *In Which We Serve*', and as a first venture for him as a film producer it was beyond doubt a remarkable triumph both technically and artistically. With that one patriotic film, made of and for its uneasy time, Noël cleared himself of the suggestions that his war work had been less than adequate. The picture became, as Mountbatten had always known it would, the navy's most successful piece of wartime propaganda.

23

1942–1944

I saw much homesickness and loneliness but no bitterness; much suffering but no despair, and shining through it all the same unconquerable spirit.

The tour that had started in Blackpool in September ground on through the autumn and winter of 1942; each of the three plays, *Present Laughter, This Happy Breed* and *Blithe Spirit*, was performed for two days in every town, and on the seventh day the whole company piled themselves and their sets and costumes into such civilian trains as were running on wartime Sundays and trekked on to the next date.

They were received everywhere with open arms and excellent reviews, and it is evident that the standard of writing and production in these three plays was considerably higher than that of most entertainments on prolonged tours of Great Britain at the beginning of the fourth year of the war.

For Noël it was a wearing but happy period in his working life, though he still had vague doubts about whether rolling them in the aisles in Newcastle was a sufficient contribution to the war effort. He was, however, faintly reassured to discover that a great many other actors were doing much the same thing, and indeed the English provincial theatre has never again been as active as it was between 1939 and 1945. In some towns, notably Inverness, the Coward troupe played in un-converted cinemas, and at others the size of the theatres varied from only a couple of hundred to well over a thousand seats. The performances started as early as six in the evenings to let audiences catch their last buses home, and at the end of each play Noël would give a brief but apparently riveting curtain-speech about the dangers of careless talk in wartime. This he would illustrate with gruesome examples, entirely of his own imagining, about the terrible things that could happen if people talked too much.

Later on, as the tour moved slowly south through England, he and Judy Campbell, still dissatisfied with what they were doing for the war effort, decided to give a series of hospital and munition factory concerts in each town they visited. These were not a success; arrangements were perfunctory, microphones failed, audiences were often sparse, the songs were over-sophisticated and often deeply unsuitable, and worst of all the factory performances had to be scheduled for the lunch hour, at which time there was nothing the ravenous girls wanted to do less than listen to a couple of London cabaret singers in concert. After a few weeks Noël realized he could not carry on doing the lunch-hour concerts as well as eight performances of three plays a week, and as the concerts were seldom rapturously received they were hardly worth the nervous breakdown he felt sure they would provoke in him before very long; by Christmas he had therefore abandoned them, though he did do a few troop concerts in Scotland early in 1943.

By this time *In Which We Serve* had gone on general release all over the country and was doing Noël a power of good; there was even the suggestion, as there had been after *Cavalcade,* that the film would win Coward a knighthood. But the court cases over his American currency, coming at the precise and embarrassing moment that they did, possibly scotched any of those hopes. The film's value as propaganda was, however, taken for granted, and the Ministry of Information which had originally been so opposed to the whole affair now began to wonder whether Noël could repeat its success with a film dedicated this time to the glory of the army. David Niven, then seconded to the Director of Public Relations, approached him with the idea of a military film along similar lines, but Coward realized at once that to attempt to repeat the success of his beloved *In Which We Serve* would be foolhardy, and that a failure so soon afterwards might considerably harm his now glowing celluloid reputation. There was little doubt that he had made the best film yet released about World War II; its triumph had even managed to obliterate the memory of *We Were Dancing,* a ludicrously romantic saga starring Norma Shearer and Melvyn Douglas which M.G.M. had based vaguely on Noël's play of the same name, and which they had released a few months before *In Which We Serve.*

For his old friend Alexander Woollcott, misquoting fervently from *Private Lives, In Which We Serve* marked the highest achievement of Noël's career:

New York City, November 12, 1942.

Dear Noël,
There isn't a particle of you that I know, remember, or want. But my hat is off to you after seeing *In Which We Serve.* I've seen three or four good movies in my time. This is one of them… a really perfect thing. There was no moment of it from which I drew back or dissented. I went away marveling at its sure-footedness and realizing that all the ups and downs of your life (in particular the downs) had taught you to be unerring for your great occasion. All your years were a kind of preparation for this. If you had done nothing else and were never again to do anything else they would have been well spent.

Such was Woollcott's enthusiasm for the picture that he volunteered to broadcast a series of radio trailers for it, turning over his fee from United

Artists to the British War Relief. But this was to be the last letter that Noël ever received from Woollcott, who died suddenly after a heart attack in New York on January 23rd 1943. Their last meeting, at Alec's home on Lake Bomoseen early in 1941, had been a friendly if rather wary occasion; both men were by then fully accustomed to being stage centre at all times, and each found a certain difficulty in having to share the attention of the other guests. For all that they remained on excellent terms, and after a friendship that had lasted nearly twenty years, Alec's death came as a severe shock to Coward.

Meanwhile other tributes to the film were pouring in by almost every post; Richard Hillary, to whom Noël had written in praise of *The Last Enemy*, replied that *In Which We Serve* was the best film he'd ever seen and a splendid piece of propaganda as well; Brendan Bracken at the Information Ministry found it 'a rousing success'; Anthony Eden at the Foreign Office wrote that it made him 'moved, proud and ashamed – proud of the Royal Navy, ashamed to be sitting at a desk myself, and moved because I damned well couldn't help it'; and for Jan Masaryk at the Czechoslovak Foreign Ministry it was 'everything that we needed so badly at this very moment.'

Considerably cheered by all that, Noël continued his tour through a bitterly cold winter; when the company got to Hull at the end of November there was no heating in the hotels and Noël had to get a doctor's certificate before the manager would allow him to light a fire. But by the time they reached Leicester early in the New Year he had solved that problem too; an entry in Harold Nicolson's diary for February 20th 1943 reads:

> Noël Coward was staying at the Grand Hotel having a new play (sic) tried out at the Leicester Theatre. I entered his sitting-room as he was having his bath. A valet was opening endless scent bottles and folding clothes. There was a large apparatus in the corner in front of which Noël, clad only in a triangulo, seated himself with an expression of intense desire and submitted himself to five minutes of infrared, talking gaily all the while. So patriotic he was, so light-hearted, and so comfortable and well-served. He is a nice, nice man.

From Leicester the company travelled down to Southsea and Noël was able to stop off on the way to collect his mail from Lorn Loraine; among the post was a telegram from Ray Goetz in Hot Springs, Arkansas, suggesting that he and Gertrude Lawrence would be so very pleased if Noël would write the life of Sarah Bernhardt as a play for Miss Lawrence. Noël cabled in reply:

DEAR RAY TERRIBLY SORRY UNABLE TO WRITE LIFE OF SARAH BERNHARDT FOR GERTRUDE LAWRENCE AS BUSY WRITING LIFE OF ELEANORA DUSE FOR BEATRICE LILLIE.

The twenty-fourth week of a tour only occasionally interrupted by air raids was played in Exeter, where Noël suddenly acquired a temperature of 104 and a vehement attack of jaundice during the first performance there of *This Happy Breed*. Dennis Price took over for the rest of that week and the next in Bournemouth, but the final week in Plymouth had to be cancelled altogether.

Before jaundice confined him for some days to an alien hotel bed, Noël had agreed with H. M. Tennent that he would play an eight-week London season of *Present Laughter* alternated nightly with *This Happy Breed*. As this was not due to start until the end of April, Noël had six weeks in which to recover; he went first to the Imperial Hotel in Torquay and then to a clifftop hotel at Tintagel in Cornwall where he spent the next month thoroughly depressed but gradually recuperating.

He then returned to London, having decided that as soon as the Haymarket season was over he would like to go abroad again for a series of troop and hospital concerts; but he resolutely refused to have these sponsored by ENSA. Noël found the whole concept of actors entertaining in uniform somehow ludicrous; he felt that Basil Dean's organization was not always as efficient as it might be, and above all he had learnt from the months in Paris and America early in the war to steer well clear of any kind of officialdom whenever possible.

On April 29th 1943, nine days after his mother had celebrated her eightieth birthday in London, Noël opened *Present Laughter* at the Haymarket and followed it the next night with *This Happy Breed*. Both plays drew more good than bad reviews, though the national critics were happier with *Present Laughter* because Noël himself seemed more at home in its urbane surroundings than in those of *This Happy Breed*. W. A. Darlington, however, found that Noël was here writing 'for the first time with sympathy, understanding and admiration of the common man.'

During the eight-week run of what was billed simply as 'The Coward Season' at the Haymarket, Noël rejoined the David Lean/Ronald Neame/Anthony Havelock-Allan unit which had made *In Which We Serve*. After the world-wide success of their first film together, the four men now planned to transfer both *Blithe Spirit* and *This Happy Breed* to the screen. The first of these was only in its earliest planning stages while Coward was playing in London, but *This Happy Breed* went into production as a film during his Haymarket run with an entirely different cast led by Robert Newton, Celia Johnson, Stanley Holloway and John Mills. Noël was nominally the producer, though in fact he had little direct control over the picture and was happy to leave most of the production details to Lean and Havelock-Allan.

When 'The Coward Season' was over, Noël sadly took leave of the actors with whom he'd been playing for almost a full year, and sailed from Plymouth aboard *HMS Charybdis*, a light cruiser bound for Gibraltar where he was to start a troop tour of the Middle East that would take him from the middle of July until the beginning of October 1943.

The night before he left England, Noël did a forces' broadcast for the BBC; introduced as 'nothing less than a national figure' he sang a selection of his songs, including one new number which provoked a considerable furore. Entitled 'Don't Let's be Beastly to the Germans', it was an acid comment on those who were already suggesting that when the war ended in an allied victory the Nazis should be treated with generosity and mercy:

> Let's help the dirty swine again
> To occupy the Rhine again
> But don't let's be beastly to the Hun.

was the general tone of the parody, and when Noël first sang it at a private party on the stage of the Haymarket to mark the end of the season there, Churchill had liked it enough to demand three reprises. But now, public reaction was vastly less enthusiastic; dozens of radio listeners entirely missed the point of the satire and believed that Noël was genuinely calling for gentle forgiveness of the enemy. The result was a sackful of abusive letters, a vitriolic article by Spike Hughes (who had once worked for Coward as the orchestrator of *Words and Music*) in the *Daily Herald* accusing him of 'appalling taste and mischievous disregard for public feeling', and joint panic by the BBC and HMV who first disowned and then suppressed Noël's recording of his song for the rest of that year.

Coward himself, happily oblivious to all this, was by now halfway to Gibraltar and delighted to find himself back amid the dignity and discipline of the Royal Navy. It was the first time he had been on board ship since the preparations for *In Which We Serve,* and it was with some difficulty that he restrained himself from giving a repetition of his valiant Captain Kinross performance when the *Charybdis* ran into trouble with enemy aircraft and a submarine in mid-crossing. His stock was high with the ship's company, for whom he did a couple of special concerts below decks, and he was formally invited to become 'godfather' to the ship. He agreed, and was to be seen standing proudly on the bridge as *HMS Charybdis* sailed into Gibraltar harbour with the marine band solemnly playing the waltz from *Bitter-Sweet.*

In Gibraltar Noël stayed at Government House, where he found Anthony Quayle acting as an A.D.C. to the Governor; together they spent a happy evening watching Beatrice Lillie, Vivien Leigh and Leslie Henson leading a travelling concert party on its way home from North Africa. After a few days on the rock, Noël flew to Oran and from there on to Algiers where he was to give the first three of nearly a hundred troop concerts on this twelve-week tour. In Algiers he met, between performances, Douglas Fairbanks, Harold Macmillan, General Eisenhower and André Gide, all of whom welcomed him with some enthusiasm. The efficiency and common sense of the American leader impressed Coward hugely; 'I devoutly hope,' wrote Noël in his diary for August 5th 1943, 'that after the war Eisenhower's voice will be heard in the United States.'

After the concerts in Algiers, Noël sailed on to Malta with a convoy of small destroyers; halfway across the Mediterranean they ran foul of enemy submarines which sank one of their number, but Noël's destroyer reached harbour without mishap and on the way he gave another performance of his songs for the sailors on board, this time without a pianist or indeed a piano. In Malta Noël sang his songs at an average of three concerts a day, mostly in hospitals where he never ceased to be overwhelmingly impressed by:

> The sheer endurance of those soldiers, sailors and airmen, and their capacity for overcoming, or at least appearing to overcome, desolation, boredom, homesickness, pain and discomfort. They lay, day after day, week after week and sometimes month after month, with nothing to do but swat flies if they happened to have an uninjured hand to do it with, and I seldom heard them complain. Many of them had snapshots of their wives or mothers or girlfriends or children always close at hand so that they could look at them whenever they could bear to. Most of them hadn't been home for two or three years; some of them would never go home again. It was only after I had left them that any sadness came into my mind. In their presence their own good manners made any display of sympathy impossible. I could only hope that by just chatting to them for a few minutes I had at least temporarily mitigated their boredom and given them something to talk about in their letters home.

Just before he left Malta Noël ran into Randolph Churchill, an old acquaintance who was currently serving in North Africa; their tenuous friendship was to survive until the end of Churchill's life, relatively unharmed by Noël's remark that 'the thing I like best about dear Randolph is that he remains so unspoiled by his great failure'. After a few hours spent in Sicily with the R.A.F., coincidentally on the day the Germans finally decided to evacuate it, Noël took off in a DC3 for an uneventful flight to Cairo. There he was met by Jeffery Amherst, now a wing-commander in the Air Force, who guided him through a city almost untouched by the war. The pre-1939 life of the 'international set' seemed to survive there in its own exclusive way under Farouk, and for Noël the brief stopover was a pleasant moment of absolute relaxation, though he felt the atmosphere to be unnecessarily escapist and in fairly bad taste at that particular moment in the war. From Cairo he went on to talk and sing to patients at the hospitals of Beirut, Baghdad and Basra, in all of which he had cause to be grateful that he'd recently done a six-month tour of the English provinces; without it he would never have been able to answer in eyewitness detail all the questions about conditions in various home towns put to him by countless injured servicemen. Coward also did a couple of troop concerts in Basra, where apart from the usual problems of bad acoustics and eccentric lighting to which Noël and his long-suffering accompanist were now immune, they had to contend with all the noises of a railway shunting yard beside which they had been allocated their make-shift stage.

When news of the Italian surrender came at the end of the first week in September, Noël was back in Cairo for six more hospital concerts and then a tour of the canal zone; there he sang for the troops and also gave them occasional renderings of such patriotic verse as Clemence Dane's 'Plymouth Hoe' and the Agincourt speech from *Henry V.* Between the shows he stayed with Richard Casey, the ambulant Australian politician who had sent Noël on his first wartime tour in 1940; and it was while he was with Casey again that Coward received another invitation from the government of South Africa to do a prolonged tour there early in the following year. He accepted, after first reassuring himself that he would get two months at home in London between the end of these concerts and the start of the next series. Then he went on to play at hospitals and camps in Alexandria and Tripoli, where he found hospital wards crammed with victims of the recent Salerno landings and a sadly seedy town with 'the foolish pathos of an expensive tart who has allowed herself to go to seed.'

The producer Peter Daubeny, in hospital at Tripoli having just lost an arm in the fighting, was among the audience at one of Noël's concerts there:

> I was beset by anxiety lest Noël, who was disguised as a Desert Rat and had managed to give his disguise a Cartier finish, should exasperate this audience still numbed and battered from the Salerno beach-head... Noël was revealed, sleek, over-trim and debonair as usual, grinning from ear to ear... but it was an extraordinary triumph of personality over environment... if the audience were not to be wooed lightly, by the sorcery of Noël's talent, they were to be bludgeoned into a state of attentive submission by his vitality and determination... like a child being kissed goodnight, Noël used every flattering artifice to keep us with him.

After that particular concert, Noël visited Daubeny in his ward, where a man in the next bed was also a Guards officer who had lost an arm in the fighting:

> It was heartening talking to those two boys, both of them a million per cent English, both of them Guards officers and both so utterly different from each other and so unmistakable in type... between them they created an atmosphere of well-bred, privileged England at its best. I had a mental picture of sycamores, tennis-courts, green lawns and rather yellowing white flannels.

From Tripoli Noël returned to Algiers for more concerts and then finally to Gibraltar, where he rounded it all off with one last broadcast of his songs. He was left in little doubt that his tour had been a success, at least from the troops' point of view; officers had, understandably enough, been sometimes reluctant to spend their valuable time organizing transport and facilities for a lone entertainer not even backed by the official blessing and resources of ENSA, and from time to time Noël had found to his righteous indignation that he was being classified and treated quite simply as a nuisance. But the soldiers, sailors and airmen of all allied countries to whom he had played in hospitals and camps had proved receptive, appreciative and only too delighted to have Noël take their minds off the grim realities of their situation for an hour or so.

After his last broadcast Noël had hoped to sail back to England on *HMS Charybdis*, but she was given a sudden change of orders and the last Noël saw of his 'godship' was her silhouette leaving Gibraltar harbour on the evening tide. A fortnight later, by which time Noël had flown back to London on a Dakota, *HMS Charybdis* was sunk in action off the coast of France.

Back at his studio in Gerald Road, Noël found a telegram from Field-Marshal Smuts confirming that he was expected to start a three-month tour of South Africa early in the new year. He arranged with the Ministry of Information that he should travel via New York, where Henry Morgenthau at the Treasury had asked him to do a couple of government broadcasts, and Noël was therefore due to sail from Glasgow on the Queen Elizabeth in barely eight weeks' time. In London before he left again, Noël did find the time to visit those of his friends and relations who had not either evacuated themselves or been posted abroad, and he also started discussions with David Lean and Ronald Neame about the filming of *Blithe Spirit* which, now that *This Happy Breed* was virtually complete, Lean intended to put into production at Denham. As a play, *Blithe Spirit* was still running in London to near-capacity, though it had by now transferred from the St James's to the smaller Duchess Theatre. For the film, Coward approved Lean's casting of Rex Harrison, Constance Cummings and (from the original stage company) Kay Hammond and Margaret Rutherford.

In these autumn weeks Noël rather unwisely decided to publish the diary that he had kept of his recent Middle-Eastern tour. This appeared on the bookstalls a few months later, in a version heavily cut by the censor for 'security reasons', to be greeted by widespread critical derision. Coward had intended the diary to be both a recollection of and a tribute to the fighting men he had met on his travels, but reviewers found Noël's day-to-day jottings superficial, glib, condescending and flippant in turn; they gave an unflattering impression of Noël as a gossipy traveller perhaps over-concerned with his own creature comforts in wartime, and the diary was not helped by self-consciously grand footnotes graciously informing the lay reader that 'Dickie and Edwina' were in reality Lord and Lady Mountbatten. In the *Observer* Ivor Brown noted with a certain accuracy that:

> Coward remains a puzzle. He sees so much – and so little. He has travelled far more than most men of his age and yet, when he writes, it always has to be of the same little world. Dump him anywhere, on any island of the seventeen seas, and he would certainly at once run into somebody known as Tim or Tiny, Boodles or Bims, and be dining with an Excellency or an Admiral twenty minutes later. If there were natives on the island he would hardly notice. God put them there, no doubt, to serve dinners to Excellencies.

But far worse was to follow; the *Middle East Diary* was also published in America, where readers took exception to a paragraph describing some Americans in hospital at Tripoli after the Salerno landings; it ended, 'I was less impressed by some of the mournful little Brooklyn boys lying there in tears amid the alien corn with nothing worse than a bullet wound in the leg or a fractured arm.' The people of Brooklyn were bitterly offended by what they considered a gratuitous and apparently anti-Semitic insult; Fiorello la Guardia delivered a vituperative broadcast against Noël, and there was even a club 'For the Prevention of Noël Coward Re-Entering America'. It was Beatrice Lillie who thoughtfully procured a membership card and posted it to Noël.

But that particular storm didn't break until Noël was deep into South Africa; in the meantime he sailed from Glasgow for New York at the beginning of December 1943, having first made sure that Norman Hackforth, who was to be his pianist on the tour, would join up with him in Pretoria early in January. Hackforth, known in later years as the mystery voice in innumerable broadcasts of *Twenty Questions,* had been an accompanist for Bea Lillie and in 1943 had been touring the Middle East as the pianist for a troop show. Meeting Noël there, he offered to play for him on the rest of his wartime tours. The third member of Coward's troupe for South Africa was to be Bert Lister Noël's old dresser who (while Cole Lesley served in the R.A.F.) acted as his valet and a kind of travelling secretary; a witty, volatile Londoner, Lister was to stay with Noël throughout the South African tour, cheering him through his concert appearances and criticizing him in no uncertain terms when he felt that Noël's performance was not up to standard.

On the crossing aboard the *Queen Elizabeth,* Noël pranced through his repertoire at the inevitable concert for the passengers; otherwise the journey was uneventful, and when the ship docked in New York five days later Jack Wilson was waiting on the quayside. Noël spent the next three weeks staying at his flat and visiting old friends on and off Broadway. He had not been in the city since early in 1941 when America had still been at peace but even now, with the country at war, he saw very little sign of it in New York itself; theatres and restaurants were as crowded as ever, blackouts and rationing and air-raid sirens were still unknown, and Noël rapidly became very irritated by a city 'intolerably shiny, secure and well-dressed, as though it was continually going out to gay parties while London had to stay at home and do the housework.'

In New York Noël did the Morgenthau broadcasts and also an extra one on Christmas Day for the Free French. He had then planned to fly on to South Africa right away, but a bout of flu while he was staying with Jack left him tired and not altogether fit; Bill Stephenson, his old friend from early wartime tours of America, who was then running a secret service agency with headquarters rather surprisingly located in an office overlooking the skating rink at the Rockefeller Centre, insisted he should take an extra fortnight out to rest and recuperate in Jamaica on his way south. Stephenson had already arranged to have the beginning of Coward's South African tour postponed, acting on the reasonable theory that this would cause far less trouble in the long run than if Noël were to break down midway through it. Thus it was early in the January of 1944 that Noël found himself in Jamaica for the first time; he became instantly addicted to the island, its people, its scenery and above all its climate, and for the next two decades he managed to spend at least three months of almost every year there.

On that first visit to Jamaica Noël stayed in retreat at a house high above Kingston where within a few days he had fully recovered; but remembering Stephenson's warning about the dangers of a collapse in mid-tour, he stayed on for the second week to be absolutely sure of his health and used the time to write a joky number about a relapsed missionary called simply 'Uncle Harry'.

Then, browned by the sun and already determined to return to Jamaica as soon as possible after the war, Noël flew on to Trinidad where he did a couple of concerts at the naval base before continuing his flight with the American Air Force to Natal. There, during a brief touchdown for refuelling, Noël just had time to have dinner and sing 'I'll See You Again' even more rapidly than usual to the faintly surprised guests at a dance in the local officers' mess before he rejoined the plane for the flight to Accra. From there after various delays and changes of aircraft he got himself to Khartoum where Bert Lister was waiting with most of the luggage and a nasty attack of tonsilitis. This delayed everything still further, and the two men didn't reach Pretoria until the beginning of February, almost a month after the tour had originally been due to start.

Once in Pretoria, Noël started again on the punishing routine that had become so familiar to him in Australia three years earlier: an endless succession of rehearsals, performances, broadcasts, official luncheons, bazaar openings, dinners, arrivals, departures and civic receptions, interrupted only very occasionally by a quiet week-end between engagements. Almost as soon as he arrived, Coward decided that since he was there as an official guest of Smuts and the South African government he would do well not to refer to his heartfelt dislike of segregation and racial intolerance, a resolve he kept with amazing self-control throughout the tour. He was greeted everywhere with a fervour that had not been equalled on any earlier tour; there were special carriages on trains, town hall receptions jammed to the doors, and policemen to guard him from the crowds lining the streets wherever he went; for Norman Hackforth it all resembled nothing so much as a royal tour by a popular and much-loved monarch.

In actual performance, Noël had no doubts about his abilities as a solo entertainer, though he knew full well that he and Norman could not carry much more than an hour on the stage; nevertheless, he was horrified to discover on arrival in Pretoria that Myles Bourke, the officer who was organizing the tour for the government, had arranged for him to be accompanied throughout by an air force band complete with their resident crooner. Noël had no intention of having to follow another singer in his shows, nor did he fancy competition of any other allied kind. He would, he told an aghast Bourke, expect to be preceded whenever he sang in city theatres by the full Cape Town Symphony Orchestra which would have to play for the first half of the programme. 'That,' Noël told Hackforth privately, 'will bore the bejesus out of the audience and then we can go on for an hour in the second half and they'll be only too delighted to see us.'

When he was singing for the troops, Noël told the organizers, he would manage just with Hackforth; he also rearranged the whole of Bourke's scheduled itinerary for the tour and insisted that Smuts himself together with his full cabinet should attend the opening concert in Cape Town. With Hackforth, Noël then began to rehearse in earnest; their plan was that after the interval they would launch together into a selection of Coward songs, after which Noël would give a brief patriotic rendering of Clemence Dane's 'Plymouth Hoe' and his own 'Lie in the Dark and Listen'. From time to time he would also slip in the Agincourt speech from *Henry V* and the closing commentary from *In Which We Serve* for good measure. During the poems, Norman would leave the stage to return refreshed at the end and play a five-minute medley of Coward tunes known affectionately to their composer as 'scrambled father':

> This medley would allow me to retire to my dressing-room and decide whether or not to shoot myself. Then, provided the audience was still present, I would come back on and round off the evening with the strongest comedy numbers in my repertoire.

After a week of rehearsals, they tried out the performance at a number of army camps around Pretoria and then travelled down to Cape Town by train, stopping briefly on the way at Paarl where a bewildered Afrikaans-speaking Mayor attempted a rather halting speech of welcome to Noël's intense but regally suppressed embarrassment.

Arriving in Cape Town in mid-February, Noël was driven through thick crowds of welcome, waving graciously from an open car; he was only mildly surprised to find that many thousands of people should have been at a sufficiently loose end to turn out and cheer him in the middle of a weekday morning. A reception committee at the station had been led by Marie Ney, the actress who some forty months earlier had been at the railway station in Melbourne to greet Noël on his arrival there, thus giving him the pleasant but curious impression that, in the Dominions at any rate, Miss Ney must be omnipresent. His Grand Opening Concert at the Alhambra Theatre in Cape Town was given in aid of Mrs Smuts' Comforts Fund, and it was packed with people who'd paid up to five guineas for a ticket. The Symphony Orchestra took care of the first half of the programme, and Noël bounced on, sweating with fear, after the interval. He sang upwards of a dozen of his own songs as well as a topically rewritten version of Cole Porter's 'Let's Do It', all of which went very well indeed, though he and Norman and Bert realized that a bad attack of nerves had prevented him from being anything like as good as he could be and would be again later in the tour.

At thirty-eight other concerts in and around Cape Town during the next three weeks Noël sang this repertoire of his numbers over and over again, together with such additions as 'Surrey With The Fringe On Top' from the new Rodgers and Hammerstein Broadway hit *Oklahoma!* At one of these concerts the critic of the *Cape Argus* noted 'though Coward has none of the usual equipment of the chanteur (he has little looks, no natural charm and little sympathy with his audience) such is his consummate craftsmanship that each crisp, clear song sparkles with a very acceptable brilliance.' In fact Noël's stay on the Cape would have been an unqualified success but for the aptly named Mr Sauer, who demanded in parliament to know why private carriages on trains and other special facilities were being accorded to 'this English music-hall crooner'. Smuts himself came to Noël's defence, explaining that as he was there on the government's business it was their duty to provide him with all the help available. Sauer pressed his point no further, but the fracas made a good story for those English newspapers (notably Beaverbrook's) which were still far from charitably disposed toward Coward's wartime activities.

Noël spent a fair amount of his spare time in Cape Town dodging a hectic round of private social activities which he felt would leave him far too exhausted to get through his innumerable performances adequately; he did, however, succumb to one nightmarish weekend built around a lavish dinner party at which Noël, as the guest of honour, was solemnly expected to eat each course at a different table, tête-à-tête with six of the more socially acceptable ladies of the district. At a moment during this routine when he was left unguarded, Noël managed to slip away and ring the ever-faithful Bert Lister who duly arrived half an hour later with his car and garbled messages about an entirely mythical but apparently urgent telephone call awaiting Noël at his hotel: with that the two men disappeared rapidly into the night, never to be seen by that particular hostess again.

From Cape Town Noël took his entourage on by train to Durban, arriving there a day too early for the full official reception which meant that he had to hide out at Umdoni Park for the next twenty-four hours and then reappear nonchalantly on the Monday morning to be greeted by an overwrought Deputy Mayor while a Ladies' Orchestra scratched through *Bitter-Sweet* in what felt like its entirety. Coward then gave a series of concerts at Ye Playhouse, a large cinema decorated incongruously like a medieval castle. Here Noël started on the busiest section of his tour, which involved concerts in towns, army camps and air bases from Bloemfontein and Kimberley to Pretoria and finally Johannesburg. Along the way Noël also inspected, with truly royal fervour, bazaars and flower shows, art exhibitions, cadets of all descriptions, hospitals, gold mines, boys' clubs and on one surprising occasion the ladies' lavatory at a Victoria League hostel.

The concerts all seemed to go reasonably well, some obviously rather better than others, though Noël remained convinced that of all the hundreds of performances he'd given in the course of the war so far, only about a dozen had been much more than adequate. Hackforth was constantly amazed by Noël's perfectionism and his ox-like stamina on the tour, but they were both relieved to think that their travels were slowly coming to an end after the long, hard three-month slog. On his last day in South Africa Noël went to bid farewell to Smuts and his wife Ouma, whom he found living in cosy chaos in a ramshackle ex-British Army barracks in Pretoria. Then after one last broadcast Noël and Norman and Bert went on to Southern Rhodesia, where they had agreed to do nine shows in as many days in and around Bulawayo and Salisbury; when they were over, there were more concerts to be done in Nairobi and Mombasa, after which the three men intended to fly home, exhausted but happy, by way of Cairo. While they were in Bulawayo, however, a cable from Lord Mountbatten put a rapid end to that idea. Mountbatten wanted Noël to fly direct to his headquarters in Ceylon after he finished in Mombasa, and from there to go on to Assam and Burma, specifically to entertain the Fourteenth Army, who were, said the cable, badly in need of a little light relief.

Noël felt he had no alternative but to agree; the South African tour had unquestionably been a success, over twenty thousand pounds had been raised for the Red Cross and Mrs Smuts' Comforts Fund, yet for all that he was well aware that he'd been working far away from any front line, among people for whom the war was still a very distant reality. Now Mountbatten was offering Noël the chance to sing for men who were in far greater need of entertainment; Coward immediately cabled Mountbatten that as there was no direct flight available he'd travel on a ship from Mombasa, and he then left Southern Rhodesia after firing a brisk parting shot at an insistent lady reporter from one of the local papers who kept asking whether he had anything to say to the *Star*: 'Yes,' replied Noël, as his train pulled out, 'Twinkle.'

24

1944–1948

The theatre must be treated with respect. It is a house of strange enchantment, a temple of dreams. What it most emphatically is not and never will be is a scruffy, ill-lit drill hall serving as a temporary soap-box for political propaganda.

After one farewell performance in Mombasa, Noël sailed in a convoy for Ceylon aboard the destoyer *Rapid*, having first arranged for Norman and Bert to fly direct to Cairo and wait there until he found out when and where he would next need them. On his arrival in Ceylon, Noël was briefed by Mountbatten about the tour that lay ahead; his old friend warned him that he would be singing to groups of weary, embittered, disgruntled, depressed, homesick and often frustrated 'forgotten army' soldiers at the height of the monsoon season. In addition, Mountbatten foresaw trouble for Noël from 'Vinegar Joe' Stilwell, the American Army General then in command of North-Eastern Burma, who did grudgingly allow Coward to sing to his troops along the Ledo Road but later refused to allow him near his front line. This tour started early in June at Chittagong, where Noël was rejoined by Norman but not by Bert who was trapped in Alexandria with a mild attack of typhoid fever. Equipped only with a small elderly upright piano known lovingly as the 'Little Treasure' and an A.D.C. seconded to them by Mountbatten, Noël and Norman travelled slowly along the Arakan Front doing up to five troop shows a day and sleeping in damp bamboo huts at night. Occasionally a telegram would filter through from Lorn Loraine in London, telling Noël that she had moved his mother out to the comparative safety of Malvern after three houses within twenty-five yards of her flat had been razed to the ground by flying bombs, or (in more cheerful vein) that the film of *This Happy Breed* had opened to a universally excellent press. Alternately depressed and buoyant, depending on the cables and how well or badly the last show had gone, Noël ploughed on through the Imphal Valley to Comilla, visiting field hospitals and troop divisions often only a matter of yards from the Japanese lines.

Retaining an absolute, rock-hard sense of professional duty, and secretly rather glad to be seeing some action after the almost guilty tranquillity he had sensed in South Africa, Noël refused to let the misery of the hospitals or such considerations as exhaustion and the heat, snakes and bedbugs, in any way deter him or even crack that faintly glazed smile which was by now fixed permanently to his face. Colonel Williams-Wynne, D.S.O., was commanding one of the units that Noël visited a few miles inland from the Arakan coast of Burma:

> We had not had any entertainment at all for nearly two years... we were over a hundred miles from a one-horse railhead and separated from it by one of the bumpiest roads in the world... even ENSA had failed to find us and it seemed highly improbable that Noël Coward would ever get to us through the monsoon... each hour a shower as heavy as Niagara poured down on to us, battering our shelters and turning every gully into a raging torrent. The temperature and humidity were dead-heating for a hundred... but Coward did arrive, exactly on schedule, and we built him a stage made out of a few boards raised just high enough to keep the piano out of the water. At first his songs seemed too sophisticated, intimate revue stuff a bit beyond most of our troops; but gradually he won them over and, with short intervals to gulp some water and change his shirt, he sang on for two hours: everything from 'London Pride' to a much-encored finale of 'Mad Dogs and Englishmen'. Then we gave him a mug of chlorinated tea in the officers' mess and he and Hackforth drove off to do two more shows further along the front that night.

Noël's rigid sense of his duty to try and entertain the troops, come what might, only let him down once on this tour; after five shows in a single day he was exhorted to do a sixth by a jovial C.O. who then ignored his songs entirely and passed a series of mildly filthy pictures around for the perusal of the rest of that small audience. Noël, in high fury, stormed off the stage and out of the camp. But all the rest of his shows went rather better, at least until he and Norman reached the Ledo Road where they began playing to all-American audiences. There, one particular contingent of Negro troops who had never heard of Coward by reputation found themselves also unable to hear him in person since he was belting out the songs from a platform built right beside the Road itself, along which lorries and heavy transporters thundered continually. That particular afternoon was the last occasion on which Noël ever got the bird. For Norman, fighting a losing battle to keep his 'little treasure' out of the water which threatened to engulf it and him, the performance was an equally ghastly experience, but it made everything else on the tour seem almost comfortable by comparison.

A few days later Noël developed a mild dysentery which forced him to leave the platform periodically during performances while Norman filled in with tactful interludes at the piano until Coward was able to reappear and carry on with the show. But this part of the tour was now virtually complete, and leaving the advanced forces they soon returned to Calcutta for a brief pause before setting off on a more comfortable if less rewarding round of Delhi, Madras, Bombay and Bangalore. On this the last stage of his last wartime tour, Noël found the Empire spirit still rampant in India; the war even at that stage had done little to alter the Blimpishness of the old-guard Indian Army Officer about whom, during the break in Calcutta, Coward wrote a number called 'I Wonder What Happened to Him?'

The morning after Coward's first performance in Bombay he narrowly avoided being killed when his car was in a violent crash with a naval lorry; the collision left an already tense man thoroughly shaken and totally unable to move his right arm for some days.

Resolutely imbued with the 'show must go on' spirit, he completed the final fortnight in India and then collapsed totally under delayed reaction to the crash as soon as he got back to Ceylon. There he stayed in a hotel bed for a week, slowly recuperating but dejected that he'd had to cancel all the dozen shows he'd originally promised to do for Mountbatten's special forces in and around Kandy. He did eventually manage three rather strained farewell performances at the naval base in Trincomalee, and then returned to the doodlebugs in London after tours which had in the end kept him away from England for almost a year.

Back home after some of the most strenuous months of a not uneventful life. Noël took the rest of 1944 comparatively quietly; he read a lot, mostly novels, and gradually eased himself back into the routine of film and theatre work. The Coward–Lean–Neame unit, by now christened Cineguild, had another success with *This Happy Breed*; it had played to a consistently good box-office ever since the gala première which, while Noël was in India, had been presided over by his mother. It was already on general release when Coward returned, and the filming of *Blithe Spirit* by Cineguild was in its final stages at Denham. As soon as he felt he'd got his health back, Noël began to work on yet another film for them; this was to be a screen adaptation of *Still Life*, originally one of the *Tonight at Eight-Thirty* plays and now expanded by Coward into the script for *Brief Encounter*. For a time he did no more war work, though after his return from Ceylon Noël was appointed to the largely honorary post of an advisor to the BBC on the content and quality of their forces' broadcasting.

In spite of renewed attacks from the doodlebugs, Noël found that by the year's end life in London was gradually getting back to normal, and he started to make plans for the peace which he felt could not now be more than a few months away; his ideas ranged from a new and romantic operetta (the determination to repeat the success of *Bitter-Sweet* died hard) through American productions of *This Happy Breed* and *Present Laughter* to a post-war revue for London, though only the third of these materialized in the immediate future.

In December 1944 Noël agreed, although he still deeply disliked and distrusted the whole organization, to do some work for ENSA; together with a motley crowd of strolling players led by Bobby Howes and Josephine Baker, he sang first at the Marigny Theatre in Paris, then in Versailles and lastly at a huge music-hall in Brussels. It was in the course of one of these concerts that Frances Day solemnly presented her drawers to Field-Marshal Montgomery, who behaved with commendable decorum.

In Paris, after the first joys of the liberation, Noël found an uneasy atmosphere of recrimination, shame and bitterness at what had happened in the years of the Nazi occupation. Sacha Guitry was only one among many figures of the prewar French theatre who were now accused of collaboration with the Germans; 'worse things than bombardment', wrote Noël in his diary, 'can happen to civilians in wartime', and from that thought grew the idea for *Peace in Our Time* a play which Coward wrote in the following year about what might have happened to Londoners under an imagined Nazi occupation of the city.

While he was in Paris Noël started to get his flat in the Place Vendôme back to order; soon after the liberation a friend had written to him describing the way it looked after four years of use by the Nazi High Command:

> The place has been occupied by what must have been a particularly unpleasant pair of Gestapo hounds, never properly housebroken. The filth is indescribable... the carpets in the dining room bear an historical and chronological record of the gastronomic, alcoholic and purely colic history of the inhabitants... there are too some remarkable stains on the bed, notably on the brown satin headboard which, if my deductions are correct, are a remarkable commentary on the acrobatic agility of the occupants... I might add that there are also three pictures missing.

Having made his peace at least temporarily with Basil Dean and ENSA, Noël returned to London from Brussels and did a similar patching-up job at the Stage Door Canteen, a servicemen's entertainment centre presided over by Dorothy Dickson on the derelict Lyons' site next to Simpson's in Piccadilly. Noël had originally refused to have anything to do with this, pleading that he was too busy elsewhere, but on Christmas night 1944 he suddenly appeared there and sang his way through the best part of an hour. He was also still doing the occasional broadcast, either talking about some aspect of his tours or singing songs over the transatlantic circuit to America.

In their last issue of the year, the weekly *Time and Tide* published the results of a literary competition in which readers were asked to elect an English Academy of forty members to compare with the Académie Française. The historian G. M. Trevelyan polled the most votes, followed closely by H. G. Wells, E. M. Forster, John Masefield, Somerset Maugham and most of the Sitwells. Towards the bottom of the list, with a total of eighteen votes each, came a group which consisted of H. E. Bates, James Agate, Lord David Cecil, his father-in-law Desmond MacCarthy, C. S. Lewis, Harold Nicolson and Noël Coward.

By the middle of January 1945, Noël had decided to shelve the idea of a Drury Lane operetta, at least for the moment, and to concentrate on the revue which he planned to stage the moment that peace was declared. With this in mind he went back to Tintagel in Cornwall where he'd found absolute relaxation after his bout of jaundice two years earlier, and began slowly to work out some of the numbers. He had found a title, *Sigh No More*, but little else, by the time he had to return to Paris to inaugurate a new stage door canteen there in an opening gala which also featured Maurice Chevalier and Marlene Dietrich.

Then, at the beginning of May, with the surrender of Germany only a matter of days away, Noël dined privately one night with Winston Churchill and Lady Juliet Duff: 'Emotion submerged us and without exchanging a word, as simultaneously as though we had carefully rehearsed it, we rose to our feet and drank Mr Churchill's health.' Less than a week later, on May 8th 1945, Noël celebrated V. E. Day at home in London with his mother and with the cast of *Blithe Spirit* which was still playing at the Duchess.

1945 was to be a rather mixed year for Coward; it got off to a bad start with the film of *Blithe Spirit* which *The Times* described as 'no more than a coloured photograph of the play' and which came as a considerable disappointment after the excellence of the same production team's *In Which We Serve* and *This Happy Breed*; nor was the film any more successful in America, where it was subjected to some misleadingly sexy posters and an orgy of tasteless publicity. In the gossip columns there still lingered a certain distaste for Coward's wartime activities though J. B. Priestley was among those who took the trouble to defend him in print. Noël himself, though convinced in his own conscience that throughout the war he had in fact done the right things both artistically and patriotically, was now in his own mind uncertain about what to do next. He realized, sooner perhaps than did many other actors and playwrights returning from the war, that the demands and conditions of his profession had altered drastically; the world of 1939 was already a long way into the past, and what had been good enough for the theatre then might well be a disaster six cataclysmic years later. On the other hand, Coward had both *Blithe Spirit* and a glossy revival of *Private Lives* with John Clements and Kay Hammond still running successfully in London as nightly proof that a little light escapism never did anyone any harm at the box-office; believing, therefore, that in revue also the mixture as before might still prove a tonic, he staged *Sigh No More* as an only slightly modified version of the pre-war Cochran–Charlot revues.

A few weeks after the end of the war in Europe, the allied authorities in Germany published copies of a Nazi blacklist which named those people in England who'd been marked down for arrest and probable execution if the German invasion had succeeded. High on a distinguished list of political and literary figures were the novelist Rebecca West and Noël himself. 'Just think,' wrote Miss West on a postcard to Coward the day after the list was made public, 'of the people we'd have been seen dead with!'

During the third week of August, *Sigh No More* moved from Manchester, where it had opened, into the Piccadilly Theatre to reviews that were no more than mildly favourable in the main; where Coward was concerned the critics seemed to be marking time, uncertain where if at all he would fit into the pattern of the post-war theatre and unwilling to commit themselves so soon.

It had been at the first dress-rehearsal of this particular revue that Noël had taken the choreographer Wendy Toye on one side to remonstrate with her about a young dancer who'd inadvertently forgotten his codpiece; 'for God's sake,' Noël told her, 'get that young man to take that Rockingham tea service out of his tights.'

But if the reviews for *Sigh No More* did not exactly offer the enthusiastic welcome home that Noël might have hoped for, those for *Brief Encounter* a few weeks later were more than adequate compensation: in short they were raves. C. A. Lejeune for the *Observer* considered it 'not only the most mature work Mr Coward has yet prepared for the cinema, but one of the most emotionally honest and deeply satisfying films that have ever been made in this country.' Celia Johnson, making her third Coward film in as many years (*In Which We Serve* and *This Happy Breed* had been the first two) played the middle-aged housewife who accidentally meets and falls in love with Trevor Howard as an equally married family doctor; the film is the story of their brief, subdued and ultimately hopeless affair, played out mainly in the waiting-room of a dingy small-town station against an atmosphere of stifling provincial conformity.

Brief Encounter was perhaps the best example of Coward's technique of writing against the action, in that his characters said one thing and patently meant something quite different; one love scene was played with the doctor talking throughout about preventive medicine until Laura abruptly said 'You suddenly look much younger', which cut right through the barriers and forced them to talk about themselves at last. The tight-lipped, understated and terribly English anti-romanticism of Coward's dialogue laid itself wide open to a hilarious American parody by Mike Nichols and Elaine May some ten years later, but in retrospect David Lean's sensitive direction and the performances of his two stars has assured the film a place among perhaps less than a dozen classic love stories of the screen. Viewed now, *Brief Encounter* commands interest and admiration for the naturalism of its acting and its photography; the screen historian Roger Manvell has noted that in this film for the first time English audiences were faced with people on the screen who looked and behaved more or less as they would in real life, and Lean's technique set a pattern of post-war realism in the English cinema which was to be followed for some years to come.

Early in the run of *Sigh No More* its star, Cyril Ritchard, developed laryngitis and Noël did his now familiar if still unnerving leap into the breach to play his sketches and sing his songs for two September performances while Ritchard was recovering his voice. But once that brief excursion on to the boards was over, Noël spent the rest of 1945 amid the comparative peace of White Cliffs, a house overlooking and indeed practically in the sea at St Margaret's Bay, near Dover, which he bought to live in until Goldenhurst became habitable again; successive requisitions had wreaked a certain havoc on Noël's old home, and it was not until five years after the war ended that he managed to get the money and the permits to put Goldenhurst back into shape. As soon as he was demobilized from the R.A.F. Cole Lesley returned to Noël's service, acting now as his secretary. Mrs Coward was still living at the flat in Eaton Square, but Gladys Calthrop bought a house directly above White Cliffs and with Joyce Carey and Clemence Dane coming down for most weekends, Noël's private life eased back into the same routine created by the same people who, in the years before the war, had surrounded him at Goldenhurst. Only Jack Wilson was missing; during the war he had established a career for himself as a successful producer and director in America, and he now found it impossible to leave it behind in order to return to Noël in England.

By the end of 1945, with *Sigh No More* doing less than adequate business at the Piccadilly where it survived only a few more weeks, Noël was already hard at work on a new romantic operetta: it would be his third since *Bitter-Sweet*. This now had a title, *Pacific 1860*, and was taking hesitant shape as a love story about a world-renowned singer falling in love with a younger man on Samolo, the mythical island in the South Seas that seems to have owed a certain amount to his memories of both Hawaii and Jamaica. During the winter Noël took the time out to work on some of the short stories which eventually made up his *Star Quality* collection, but it was *Pacific 1860* that occupied most of his working life at this time. Originally he had planned the operetta for His Majesty's, a theatre that would have been ideally suited in size for the kind of entertainment that Noël had in mind. But when His Majesty's proved unavailable, Prince Littler offered Coward the chance to reopen the Theatre Royal at Drury Lane, which since it was bombed in 1940 had only been used as the headquarters of ENSA.

Though it was technically far less suited to *Pacific 1860* than His Majesty's, Noël realized that Drury Lane was not a theatre to be turned down lightly even if it did mean expanding his operetta to a larger scale and running the risk that the Lane's bomb damage would not be repaired in time to re-open in the autumn of 1946. It was now clear that his score would once again need a leading woman singer capable of carrying most of the numbers in the way that Peggy Wood (in *Bitter-Sweet*) Yvonne Printemps (in *Conversation Piece*) and Fritzi Massary (in *Operette*) had carried the Coward operettas of the past. But this time the need was for a different kind of star: still a romantic heroine, but one capable of playing in a lighter and rather more cheerful convention. Before long Noël's choice fell firmly on to Mary Martin; after some hectic transatlantic negotiation she agreed to make her London début in *Pacific 1860*, and Noël, together with Gladys Calthrop who was once again his designer, began to tailor the production to their newly-acquired star.

Work on *Pacific 1860* continued at White Cliffs throughout the spring and summer, but Noël had to greet Mary Martin and her entourage at Southampton with the gloomy news that a permit to repair the bomb damage at Drury Lane had been unexpectedly refused; that there was now little likelihood of opening there before the very end of the year at the earliest. By approaching Aneurin Bevan in person, Noël did manage to get the permit through, but he still had to delay all rehearsals for a month.

At the beginning of November Noël started to direct a company of nearly a hundred in *Pacific 1860*, now due to open at Drury Lane on December 19th; but from the first week of rehearsal onwards almost everything that could possibly go wrong with the show proceeded balefully to do so. In ideal conditions *Pacific 1860* would not have rated as the best of the Coward musicals, but many better productions would have collapsed similarly under the problems it faced that autumn at Drury Lane. Rehearsals were constantly interrupted by the need to repair and replace various parts of the stage, the seats were only put back into the auditorium three days before the first night, and Coward's ambitious plans for a full week of dress-rehearsals (which had been feasible for *Cavalcade*, his only other production at the Lane) had to be abandoned as totally impracticable; nor was it possible to open *Pacific 1860* anywhere outside London in the hope of polishing some of its rougher moments during a tour, as provincial theatres were already into the beginning of their pantomime season.

Worse still, during the last week of rehearsals Noël and Mary Martin gradually began to realize simultaneously that even for an entertainer of her undoubted and flexible talent she was hopelessly miscast, and was having to struggle with a part originally constructed for a heavier and older soprano. Rows about costumes developed into more serious arguments about the show itself, and a feeling of impending doom began to permeate Drury Lane. In the bitter cold, since permits to reinstall the theatre's heating system had been held up, the company struggled through two hasty and sketchy dress-rehearsals which served only to leave a frozen and depressed author-director with the conviction that there were a thousand things still wrong with *Pacific*

1860 and that he had neither the time nor the opportunity to get even a dozen of them right in the few days before the first night. But if Coward was chilled in the stalls, the company on stage, dressed as for a light-hearted love story set in the tropical heat of the South Seas, could barely manage to make themselves heard through the chattering of their teeth.

For Noël, the last few days of rehearsals were one of the unhappiest periods he had ever known in the theatre, and the notices after the first night bore out his premonitions of absolute disaster. *Pacific 1860*, which might have scraped by in easier times, had everything going against it including the icy weather which made any enjoyment at Drury Lane distinctly hard to find. Nor was the operetta helped by great expectations; this was, after all, the show that was to reopen London's finest theatre after a six-year gap, and audiences were expecting something pretty splendid. What they and the critics got was an innocuous, vaguely pleasant entertainment, strong on its score (which was another determined attempt by Coward to return the light musical theatre to some of its former glory) but rather weaker on its book, lyrics and performances. The songs had an undeniable, deliberately nostalgic charm, but reviews of *Pacific 1860* were hallmarked by disappointment. The most that any morning paper could find to say of the music was that it was 'faintly reminiscent of Ivor Novello'. Nevertheless, the advance booking had been excellent, and for the first few weeks a respectable number of people turned up to shiver at Drury Lane each night; soon though, the notices and the fuel crisis began to take their inevitable toll and although Mary Martin played on doggedly through the next four months, the last two were in Noël's phrase 'more of a convulsive stagger than a run'. The production lost a total of twenty-eight thousand pounds.

Coward himself rapidly closed his mind to a resounding and unfortunate flop, a discipline that he had cultivated from his earliest days in the business, and decided to retrieve his reputation with a brisk revival of *Present Laughter* at the Haymarket in the spring. Soon after Christmas he treated himself to a winter holiday at Palm Beach in Florida, and by the time he returned to London it was clear from Prince Littler's office that *Pacific 1860* would have to be withdrawn in April. Although a failure, it had not done Mary Martin any lasting harm, and a few years later she was to draw capacity audiences into the same theatre with *South Pacific*; but Noël's post-war image had undoubtedly been tarnished by it. His reputation was suddenly made to seem both shaky and irrevocably dated, an irrelevant survival from a bygone era, and his work appeared only safe in revival. Though occasional new plays of his, most notably *Relative Values* and *Quadrille,* did achieve success in the Fifties, it seems reasonable to consider that the failure of *Pacific 1860* marked the beginning of a slump in Coward's professional standing from which he did not totally recover until the National Theatre revival of *Hay Fever* eighteen years later. But long before *Pacific 1860* Noël had become immune to most press reaction whether good or bad: 'if I had really cared about press notices,' he wrote to a friend in 1946, 'I would have shot myself in the Twenties.'

While he was again playing Garry Essendine in the revival of *Present Laughter*, Noël put the finishing touches to *Peace in Our Time,* the play about a German occupation of London which he had started to write the previous year. It was a curious drama, not strictly comparable to any other of Coward's plays though it shared with *This Happy Breed* a belief in the unconquerable common sense, patriotism and ultimate imperturbability of the British middle class: one of its characters even quoted the 'This England' speech at some length. Set constantly in the saloon bar of a Knightsbridge pub called The Shy Gazelle, *Peace in Our Time* was an attempt to telescope character-impressions of Britain under five years of increasingly harsh enemy occupation into two acts and eight scenes. Like *This Happy Breed* the new play was an episodic mixture of melodrama, sentiment and occasional comic relief; but the result was heavier and ultimately perhaps less satisfactory. A friend called Ingram Fraser who had been in Paris towards the end of the war advised Noël on the technicalities of a resistance movement, and in writing the play Coward was heavily influenced by what he personally had seen of Paris since her liberation:

> There was in post-war France an atmosphere of subtle disintegration, a certain lassitude and above all the suspicion of collaboration... there was an epidemic of malicious denunciation, some of it justified and a great deal of it not... I began to suspect then that the physical effect of four years' intermittent bombing is far less damaging to the intrinsic character of a nation than the spiritual effect of four years' enemy occupation. This in time led me to wonder what might have happened to London and England if in 1940 the Germans had successfully invaded and occupied us.

But the press did not take kindly to Noël's dramatic speculations; *Peace in Our Time,* directed by Alan Webb 'under the author's supervision', opened in Brighton during July 1947 and then after some drastic rewriting went into the Lyric Theatre a week later to generally terrible notices. Though Harold Hobson led a small band of determined admirers, Beverley Baxter in the *Evening Standard* was sure enough that they were wrong to head his notice 'Crisis for Coward'. A large cast headed by Elspeth March and Bernard Lee also included such names of the future as Alan Badel, Kenneth More and Dora Bryan, and on this occasion the actors emerged with considerably more credit than the playwright: 'It was,' wrote Alan Dent, 'like watching thirty-six competent swimmers paddling about in six inches of water.' The reaction from the critics was largely one of pained surprise; Coward was simply not expected to turn up with this kind of problem play, and his style seemed somehow ill-suited to its content. In the event, *Peace in Our Time* had an unspectacular but hardly shameful run first at the Lyric and then the Aldwych theatres. Its interest, like that of *Post-Mortem,* now lies in the light it throws on Coward as a writer of serious plays although this side of his work was still so little known outside England that Harold Clurman could solemnly write from New York in 1947: 'All Noël Coward's plays reveal a state of mind in which contempt and indifference to the world have been accepted as a sort of aristocratic privilege.' It would be difficult to find plays expressing less 'contempt and indifference to the world' than *This Happy Breed* or *Peace in Our Time,* which was actually running in London at the time.

As soon as *Peace in Our Time* had opened in London Noël left for America; his intention was to visit a number of old friends including Jack Wilson and the Lunts, to inspect Tallulah Bankhead who was touring the land with *Private Lives* and to negotiate a possible revival of *Tonight at Eight-Thirty*. In the meantime another of Coward's plays of the Thirties, *Point Valaine,* flickered briefly at the Embassy Theatre in Swiss Cottage; its first night there was enlivened by an indignant playwright called Townley Searle who insisted that Coward had stolen the title from one of his early dramas and who in retaliation showered the auditorium with leaflets of protest. Among generally bad notices was one by Graham Greene who raised the issue of Coward's handling of 'common speech'. This was a debatable point which could also have been related to both *This Happy Breed* and *Peace in Our Time*:

> Mr Coward was separated from ordinary life early by his theatrical success, and one suspects that when he does overhear the common speech he finds himself overwhelmed by the pathos of its very cheapness and inadequacy. But it is the sense of inadequacy that he fails to convey, and with it he loses the pathos.

The Embassy company, led by Mary Ellis and Anthony Ireland, wanted to transfer *Point Valaine* to the West End in spite of the notices, but in a cable from New York Noël firmly declined the offer: 'I HAVE,' he wired, 'NEVER REALLY CONSIDERED THAT THIS PLAY WAS QUITE GOOD ENOUGH.' While he was in America Noël also declined the offer to play opposite Gertrude Lawrence in the revival of *Tonight at Eight-Thirty,* although after some hesitation he did agree reluctantly to let Graham Payn play his parts. Coward himself was due to return to England early in October, but instead he stayed on in New York to take over the production of *Tonight at Eight-Thirty,* 'for the sake,' as he put it in a cable to Lorn Loraine, 'of all concerned.' This revival of six of his one-act plays, for a coast-to-coast tour which lasted through the winter of 1947–8, was in many respects ill-cast and ill-conceived; nevertheless, it brought Noël as director together again with his beloved Gertrude Lawrence and it gave his protégé Graham Payn the daunting opportunity to play the Coward parts under the author's own direction.

As soon as the tour opened Noël returned to London to spend Christmas with his mother and to be a guest at the wedding of Princess Elizabeth and Prince Philip. Then, early in January of 1948, he sailed back to America; this time he took Lorn with him and they caught up with the tour of *Tonight at Eight-Thirty* in San Francisco where Noël took over for a few performances while Graham was off with influenza. It was the last time he was ever to appear on the stage with Gertrude Lawrence. In February the tour came to an end and *Tonight at Eight-Thirty* opened at the National Theatre on Broadway; there it signally failed to repeat its original triumph at the same theatre in 1936. It was in fact the short-lived disaster that Coward must have foreseen when he originally refused to play in the revival, and four weeks later it closed amid deep company depression and swiftly falling business; the plays were simply out of tune with the post-war times, neither old enough to have a period charm nor young enough to have any contemporary relevance.

It had now been just three years since the end of the war in Europe, and of the six productions with which Coward had been connected in that time only the revival of *Present Laughter* could have been considered a success. The time had come, Noël decided, to return to Jamaica.

25

1948–1951

When the storm clouds are riding
Through a winter sky, Sail Away.

Noël had meant to return to Jamaica ever since the end of the war; now he did so, taking Graham with him in an attempt to cheer them both up after the collapse of *Tonight at Eight-Thirty* on Broadway. For the three months he planned to stay there Noël rented Goldeneye, the house that Ian Fleming had recently built overlooking the north shore on the old donkey race-track at Oracabessa. Like Coward, Fleming had also fallen in love with Jamaica during the last months of the war, and on the island over the later years a firm friendship developed between the two writers which was to last until Fleming's death in 1964. But their friendship grew despite Goldeneye rather than because of it; Noël found the house 'perfectly ghastly' and lost little time in renaming it 'Golden Eye, nose and throat'. Fleming charged him fifty pounds a week for the privilege of staying there through the spring of 1948, a rental which Noël considered:

> Altogether too much for bed and board in a barracks. There was no hot water in those days. Only cold showers. We were manly and pretended to like it. But I did get tired of the iron bedstead and the pictures of the snakes he had plastered all over the bedroom wall and the banquette you sat on at the dining table which was so narrow it bit into your bottom, and the cushions that felt as if they had been filled with chipped steel.

James Bond's ideas about creature comforts, it would seem, were not shared by his creator.

At Goldeneye Noël painted a good many blue Jamaican lagoons and also started work on *Future Indefinite*, the second volume of his autobiography which (leaving a gap of nine years after the end of *Present Indicative*) picked up his life again in 1939 and carried it through the war years to 1945. In the meantime his reputation as a revivable playwright in America had been retrieved from the disaster of *Tonight at Eight-Thirty* by Tallulah Bankhead who had by now made *Private Lives* resolutely her own eccentric thing and planned to take it in to New York during the autumn under Jack Wilson's management. Noël's own thoughts were turning back to films; he planned to star in an adaptation of *The Astonished Heart*, one of the few remaining *Tonight at Eight-Thirty* plays that had not yet been transferred to celluloid. But he was in no immediate hurry to return to

274

England, particularly as a falling lump of chalk from the Kent cliffs had made a nasty hole in the roof of the house at St Margaret's Bay; while they were waiting for that to be repaired, Noël and Graham stayed on at Goldeneye and looked around the island for a house to buy, since Noël by now had every intention of making Jamaica his winter home.

Finding nothing that they liked for sale in Jamaica, they eventually decided to have a house built about a mile down the coast from Goldeneye in the direction of Port Maria. Cash was short at the time, and to raise the money for the land Noël cabled Lorn Loraine to sell his ageing Rolls Royce which fetched the best part of a thousand pounds.

Noël returned via New York to England at the end of June to find an invitation from Herbert Morrison to join the planning council of the Festival of Britain projected for three years later; he accepted this unarduous committee task, and, once the annual garden party for the Actors' Orphanage was over, started to work on the expanded version of *The Astonished Heart*. But there was little likelihood of getting that into production before the middle of 1949, and in the meantime Noël, not noticeably one to shy at trying something new, decided to play in a French adaptation of *Present Laughter* which was due for production in Paris during the autumn. The French language did not present a grave problem for Coward, since he'd picked up enough of it during the months he was working there at the beginning of the war to master the adaptation of his play which had been made by André Roussin and Pierre Gay. They had translated it as *Joyeux Chagrins*, a direct rendering of the comedy's first English title (*Sweet Sorrow*) and it went into rehearsal in Paris at the end of September with Noël as both director and star.

Brave but not foolhardy, Coward planned to give the play and his accent a brisk try-out in Brussels before taking it in to the Théâtre Edouard VII in Paris early in November. Rehearsals were less fraught than he had anticipated, and encouraged by the thought that *Present Laughter* was also doing excellently in Australia while in New York Tallulah Bankhead had made a triumphant success of *Private Lives,* Noël worked on *Joyeux Chagrins* through October. Appearing on the French stage for the first time as an actor he got generous reviews for both his accent and his play, in which most critics saw the natural successor to the Boulevard comedies of their recent past. He played in *Joyeux Chagrins* through to Christmas and then set off again with Graham for Jamaica.

Arriving there at the end of a year in which detailed ground-plans had been airmailed back and forth across the world, they found a flat-iron shaped building duly erected on the land Noël had bought near Port Maria. With grave misgivings and a few desultory sticks of furniture they moved in to what became, with certain modifications and considerable improvements,

Noël's Jamaican home until his death. Money was still very scarce indeed, and even a cheque for three thousand pounds from his English account via Lorn Loraine in London did not seem to meet the costs of fitting and furnishing the new house. Noël cabled in reply:

DEAR KINDLY, GENEROUS AND LOVING LORN,
SO GRATEFUL AM I THAT I CANNOT SPEAK.
THAT YOU SHOULD YIELD SO MUCH FROM PLENTY'S HORN
I SHAN'T NEED ANY MORE TILL TUESDAY WEEK.

But *Private Lives* continued to prove a goldmine for royalties; while Tallulah Bankhead carried it through into 1949 on Broadway, Margaret Lockwood and Peter Graves took it on a fourteen-week tour of the English provinces. Even so, any money that it brought in to Noël was rapidly going out again on the cost of building in Jamaica, and Coward was already looking ahead keenly to the five thousand pounds that he'd been guaranteed for his work as the author and star of *The Astonished Heart*. He had also agreed some months earlier to write a new comedy for Gertrude Lawrence, and in the last few weeks of this Jamaican spring a play called *Island Fling* gradually took shape in his mind; in the event Gertie never starred in it, and seven years were to elapse before it reached London as *South Sea Bubble*.

Noël got back to England to find himself swathed in provincial revival: both *Private Lives* and *Bitter-Sweet* were on lengthy tours, although neither of them ever reached London. Noël himself started to work almost immediately on *The Astonished Heart*, which was also to star Celia Johnson and Margaret Leighton. By this time Cineguild, his old wartime film unit, had split up and Noël was left to make the film for Sydney Box at Gainsborough Pictures with Terence Fisher and Anthony Darnborough as co-directors. It was not a success, and one is left to reflect that it might have worked better had Coward been able to keep Cineguild intact.

Towards the end of 1949, with *The Astonished Heart* already in its editing stages, Noël went to Plymouth to see a revival of *Fallen Angels* with Hermione Gingold as Jane and Hermione Baddeley as Julia; he was deeply horrified by what he found. The Hermiones, at the suggestion of Peter Daubeny their producer, were sending up *Fallen Angels* sky high. Noël was not amused; but despite a furious confrontation backstage at the Plymouth Theatre he failed to persuade either of them to modify their performances or tone down the parody, and in his absence the two ladies settled into the Ambassadors' for an eminently successful London run of three hundred performances. That Coward did not take kindly to seeing his play mocked, altered and riddled with new double-entendres was understandable enough; on the other hand, as Miss Gingold was quick to point out:

Fallen Angels is not yet old enough to be revived as a period piece for its curiosity value, and yet its big scene where the two women get drunk no longer shocks or scandalizes as it did in 1925; so much of the punch has gone. We decided the play would only work if acted as a romp, rather than as a light comedy.

If Miss Gingold didn't have theatrical justice on her side, she was at least able to claim a precedent: in New York the Tallulah Bankhead *Private Lives* had been a similar send-up of the original, in which the audience were asked to laugh at rather than with the play. When Noël saw that production for the first time he admitted that it worked alarmingly well, though in this case also there is no doubt that if he'd realized how his play was going to be treated in time to stop it, he certainly would have done so. Indeed he went so far as to write a letter to the New York press agreeing with most of the criticisms of Miss Bankhead.

As there was little else he could do about them, Noël closed his mind to both revivals, took the royalties and went back to Jamaica where he celebrated his fiftieth birthday with Graham and Joyce Carey at Blue Harbour, the name now given to the house he had at last finished building on the north shore. There, through December and January, Noël worked on a new musical which he called *Ace of Clubs*. He seemed delighted with the result, and posted the finished script back to Gladys Calthrop in London so that she could start sketching the set and costume designs.

Early in February 1950 Noël returned from Jamaica by way of New York where *The Astonished Heart* opened to grudging reviews and initially rather disappointing business; back in London at the end of the month he heard that Val Parnell had turned down *Ace of Clubs* on the grounds that though the score was quite good enough the book really wasn't, a view entirely borne out by the critics when it was presented later in the year by Tom Arnold. All in all it was a depressing return for Coward, as the London première of *The Astonished Heart* at the Leicester Square Odeon in March provoked a further series of terrible reviews. John Gassner, however, began to see a parallel between Noël and the character he played in *The Astonished Heart*:

> [As a playwright] his values are those of a Harley Street doctor who knows that the old virtues of clean living and plain thinking – home, hearth, exercise and good diet – are the best no matter how often his profession keeps him in touch with the aberrations.

At the box-office Noël's name was currently something less than magic, but *Ace of Clubs* opened in Manchester in mid-May and then made its way slowly into London according to a familiar Coward pattern of excellent reviews on tour followed by a rather less enthusiastic critical welcome in the West End.

After *Bitter-Sweet* (Victorian), *Conversation Piece* (Regency), *Operette* (Edwardian) and *Pacific 1860* (Victorian-Colonial), *Ace of Clubs* was a determined effort by Coward to come up to date with a story full of gangsters, black marketeers, tough chorus girls and stolen jewellery. But as his first contemporary musical it was a considerable disappointment.

A few days after *Ace of Clubs* opened in London, Noël returned alone to Blue Harbour where he wrote the rest of *Star Quality,* his second collection of six short stories, and also started to work on a light drawing-room comedy which opened in London a year later as *Relative Values.* In less than two months at Blue Harbour he finished the stories and then flew back to New York, where Goddard Lieberson at Columbia Records had invited him to make a recording of his 1933 *Conversation Piece.* The recording was a success, once Noël had convinced a sceptical conductor and arranger that although he still couldn't write a note of music his ear was good enough to detect an oboe which was playing B flat when it should have been playing B natural.

With the Festival of Britain now only a matter of months away Noël's absence abroad forced him to resign from the organizing committee, though when he went back to Blue Harbour he did turn his mind to a song called 'Don't Make Fun of the Fair' which could hardly have been designed to cheer the hearts of the other committee members; his only other contact with the Festival had been to refuse unhesitatingly the offer of a festive revival of *Cavalcade* at the Harrow Coliseum.

Coward stayed on through the spring at Blue Harbour, where an otherwise peaceful and happy existence was shattered by the news from England that Ivor Novello and Charles Cochran had died within a few weeks of each other. Both men had been known to him since the very beginning of his adult career in the theatre, and their deaths early in 1951 marked for Coward the end not only of valued personal friendships but also of an era in the English theatre. A few years later he was to note that 'the worst thing about growing old is watching your friends die off' but already at only just over fifty Noël was beginning to feel out of touch with his country and its theatre. The failures of the last four years, from *Pacific 1860* to *Ace of Clubs*, had planted in his mind a fear that what the public wanted was no longer what he had to offer, and Novello's sudden death seemed to leave Noël alone, the last survivor of the theatrical triumphs of the Twenties and Thirties. 'There is a small measure of consolation,' Noël wrote from Jamaica, 'in the thought that Ivor died at the height of his triumphant career and will never know the weariness of age nor the sadness of decline.'

That spring, with *Relative Values* already virtually complete, Noël began to outline another light comedy which emerged three years later as *Nude with Violin.* In the meantime his *Star Quality* collection of short stories was published both in

London and New York to mixed reviews, more good than bad but generally less enthusiastic in England than in America where the unforgettably named Florence Haxton Bullock gave it the *Herald-Tribune*'s approval. Apart from his fascination with what was to Coward a comparatively new form of writing, short stories began to acquire an obvious advantage over plays for him:

> You sit there, on your balcony or wherever you are, and write a short story, and enjoy being able to do it and the pattern the story constructs for itself as it goes along; but you don't then have to go through the misery of casting, rehearsing and ultimately being panned by the critics for all your trouble. It's so lovely to be able to write it, send it to the publishers, correct the proofs, take out all those extra adjectives and then realize that there's an end to the whole thing.

At the beginning of June Noël returned to London with some of his Jamaican paintings which he showed at a charity exhibition in the company of such other untypical artists as Edward G. Robinson and the Duchess of Gloucester. Later in the month the usual garden party for the Actors' Orphanage was held in Chelsea, where number 42 on a programme listing the various attractions read simply 'Noël Coward at home: Admission Three Shillings'. Home in this case turned out to be a rather small tent where instead of his usual autograph-signing Noël had decided to sing his way through a medley of his old songs. This he did no less than a dozen times during the afternoon and evening, to considerable acclaim from audiences who had been queueing to see him for up to an hour in the teeming rain. His success that one day was to lead directly to the last major development in Coward's varied career; his emergence later in the year, to his own and everyone else's surprise, as a highly successful cabaret entertainer.

But before Noël could turn his mind to cabaret there remained the H. M. Tennent production of *Relative Values*, the new play that was to re-establish Coward in the eyes of a post-war audience as a writer of immaculate light comedy. Gladys Cooper came back from California to play the lead (curiously it was the first and only time that Coward worked with her, although they had been friends for over thirty years) and Noël himself planned to direct. But for the first time since *The Vortex* twenty-seven years earlier, Noël did not use Gladys Calthrop as his designer; she was away, and in her absence the setting for the play was designed by Michael Relph.

When Noël was casting *Relative Values* in mid-August, a severe hurricane hit the North Shore of Jamaica, leaving Blue Harbour unscathed but wrecking other houses around Port Maria and tearing up the beaches. Noël instantly cabled a hundred pounds to the governor, Sir Hugh Foot, as a token gesture of help for the disaster fund, and then waited anxiously until his many new friends in the area all reported that they were safe and comparatively well.

In London during that summer Beatrice Lillie opened a season in cabaret at the Café de Paris with Norman Hackforth as her accompanist; Noël was at her first performance and afterwards, remembering their wartime tours together, Hackforth asked him why he didn't venture a season in cabaret there himself. Noël thought it over carefully, agreed that for £750 a week and with Norman at the piano again he would try a month at the Café in the autumn, and then went back to work on *Relative Values*.

In September 1951, when he was just about to put the play into rehearsal, Noël at last found a buyer for White Cliffs which was now lying empty as all the furniture had been moved back to Goldenhurst; the buyer turned out to be none other than Noël's Jamaican neighbour Ian Fleming who, about to marry Anne Rothermere, was looking for somewhere for them to live at weekends when they were in England. Thus domestic negotiations between the two writers started again, and stretched on through the winter provoking a lengthy and sardonic correspondence about who was to pay for what.

Relative Values went through rehearsals smoothly enough, and there was already a feeling among the company that this was to be the play which could put an end to the run of theatrical failure from which Noël had not really escaped since *Pacific 1860* five years earlier. The cast, though not quite so heavily loaded with the old Coward brigade as usual, were all at home in his work and Gladys Cooper remained thoroughly enthusiastic about his play although she occasionally found Noël's direction too doctrinaire for her taste. 'It is ridiculous,' she remarked after one especially trying morning, 'Noël expects me to be word-perfect at the first rehearsal.' 'It is not,' retorted Noël, 'the first rehearsal I worry about so much as the first night.'

However, the play opened to considerable acclaim in Newcastle, and after the first week of the tour Noël felt confident enough to leave the cast to their own devices and return to London where he started getting his cabaret act into shape. He had, of course, a vast repertoire of songs to choose from; but he'd not sung many of them for more than five years and he was uncertain which were still topical and whether there were some that had gone well on the wartime tours abroad yet would turn out to be disastrous when sung to a peacetime audience at home. To discover all this, he did an experimental concert at the Theatre Royal in Brighton one Sunday late in October, and then, faintly reassured by his success with that but still highly nervous, he opened at the Café de Paris for the first time on October 29th 1951.

'The lights were lowered,' recalled Donald Neville-Willing who then managed the Café and was known to Noël as Major-Baby on account of his army rank, 'the orchestra struck up 'I'll See You Again', and very slowly a spotlit figure walked down the staircase to tumultuous applause from the crowded tables around the dance-floor. It turned out to be Norman Hackforth.'

Noël followed, however, and the result was one of the greatest personal successes in his career. 'For nearly an hour,' reported the *Evening News,* 'this quizzical, faintly oriental-looking gentleman with a shocking voice held spellbound an audience that included Princess Margaret and the Duchess of Kent.

Noël sang them a medley of his own songs from 'Mad Dogs and Englishmen' through the canon to 'The Stately Homes of England', with such occasional interpolations as an upbeat rendering of 'Loch Lomond' and his own rewritten version of Cole Porter's 'Let's Do It'.

The success of that first night in cabaret restored to the currency of Coward's name a value it had not held since the partnership with Gertrude Lawrence ended in the Thirties; suddenly the magic was back. The Café de Paris boosted his salary to a thousand a week and begged him to stay on for an additional fortnight making six weeks in all; Noël agreed, taking his last two weeks' salary in the shape of an enchanting Boudin that he found in a Bond Street art gallery.

While he was still appearing in cabaret, *Relative Values* ended its tour and went in to the Savoy Theatre; Harold Hobson considered that it was 'the best play Coward has written for several years', and Anthony Cookman for the *Tatler* found it 'a flawless piece of work'. Another critic, the young Kenneth Tynan, went to see Noël in cabaret at the Café de Paris:

> Forty years ago he was Slightly in *Peter Pan* and you might say that he has been wholly in *Peter Pan* ever since. No private considerations have ever been allowed to deflect the drive of his career; like Gielgud and Rattigan, like the late Ivor Novello, he is a congenital bachelor. He began, like many other satirists (Evelyn Waugh, for instance) by rebelling against conformity, and ended up making his peace with it, even becoming its outspoken advocate... to see him whole, public and private personalities conjoined, you must see him in cabaret... he padded down the celebrated stairs, halted before the microphone on black-suede-clad feet, and, upraising both hands in a gesture of benediction, set about demonstrating how these things should be done. Baring his teeth as if unveiling some grotesque monument, and cooing like a baritone dove, he gave us 'I'll See You Again' and the other bat's-wing melodies of his youth. Nothing he does on these occasions sounds strained or arid; his tanned, leathery face is still an enthusiast's. All the time the hands are at their task, affectionately calming your too-kind applause. Amused by his own frolicsomeness, he sways from side to side, waggling a finger if your attention looks like wandering. If it is possible to romp fastidiously, that is what Coward does.

To Douglas Fairbanks, who had cabled his congratulations on Noël's return to public grace and favour, Coward wired:

DEAR DOUG THANK YOU SO VERY MUCH FOR SWEET CABLE BUT TRIUMPH INCOMPLETE UNLESS YOU ARE HERE TO SEE THE ENGLISH MISTINGUETTE.

In fact London's answer to Mistinguette refused to prolong his season at the Café any further than mid-December, and although he was nightly bringing the house down there he still decided to reject a dazzling offer of more than five thousand dollars a week to do a cabaret tour of American hotels in the spring; Noël remained uncertain about whether his ultra-English material would go down as well on the other side of the Atlantic, and he did not intend to risk it at that moment. While he was playing at the Café he did however think back to certain other concert appearances abroad at an earlier and tougher moment in his professional life:

> In the luxurious intimacy of the Café de Paris I sometimes glanced at Norman sitting impeccably at the grand piano, and my mind flashed back to those rickety wooden stages, to the steaming heat, the wind, the rain, and the insects, and I saw him with sudden vivid clarity divested of dinner-jacket, red carnation and brilliantine, and wearing instead an open-neck, sweat-stained khaki shirt, with a lock of damp hair hanging over one eye, and hammering away at the Little Treasure as though he was at his last gasp and this was the last conscious action of his life.

After his first season at the Café de Paris came to an end, and having promised to play there again in the following year, Noël delayed his usual winter trip to Jamaica and instead stayed at Goldenhurst to work on a new comedy for Alfred Lunt and Lynn Fontanne. It was the first play he'd written for them since the ill-starred *Point Valaine* in 1934, but this by contrast was to be the lightest of romantic period comedies: entitled *Quadrille,* it opened in London during the autumn of 1952.

26

1951–1955

Let's hope we have no worse to plague us
Than two shows a night at Las Vegas.

With *Relative Values* running to near-capacity at the Savoy and his first triumphant season in cabaret at the Café de Paris drawn to a close, Noël continued to work with an almost religious fervour; *Quadrille* was still on the typewriter, there were more songs to be written for future cabarets, and there were negotiations in progress about the possibility of filming three of the original *Tonight at Eight-Thirty* plays as one composite film, since similar celluloid packages of stories by Maugham and O. Henry were proving successful at the box-office. While he was at Goldenhurst for the Christmas of 1951, Noël heard again from his old childhood friend Esmé Wynne-Tyson; in the thirty years that had elapsed since they went their separate ways she had become a fervent Christian Scientist, and she now wrote to ask whether Noël in his turn had developed any kind of mental or spiritual philosophy. His reply was predictably down to earth:

> You ask how I am thinking these days; do you know, the awful thing is I don't believe I am thinking very differently from the way I have always thought. My philosophy is as simple as ever. I love smoking, drinking, moderate sexual intercourse on a diminishing scale, reading and writing (not arithmetic). I have a selfless absorption in the well-being and achievement of Noël Coward. I do not care for any church (even the dear old Mother Church) and I don't believe there is a Universal Truth and if you have found it you are a better man than I am, Gunga Din. In spite of my unregenerate spiritual attitude I am jolly kind to everybody and still attentive and devoted to my dear old Mother who is hale and hearty, sharp as a needle and occasionally very cross indeed. I have built myself a little house in Jamaica on the edge of the sea where I eat bread-fruit, coconuts, yams, bananas and rather curious fish and where I also lie in the sun and relax and paint a series of pictures in oils, all of which I consider to be of great beauty but which, in reality, are amateur, inept and great fun to do... in the meantime, do you ever come up to London or are we never to meet again until I am on my deathbed and you appear with, I hope, not *extreme* unction?

Meanwhile the tenancy of White Cliffs was about to pass from Noël Coward to Ian Fleming who was still a year away from the publication of his first James Bond novel, *Casino Royale*; by now the two writers were old and close friends, since Coward had frequently offered the sanctuary of weekends at Goldenhurst to Fleming and Anne Rothermere during the more tempestuous moments of their friendship, and within months of the sale of White Cliffs Noël was a delighted witness at their wedding in Jamaica.

A couple of weeks into 1952 Noël, who in a recent interview had described himself as 'that splendid old Chinese character actor and writer', was able to wire the Lunts in New York:

QUADRILLE IS FINISHED I LOVE IT VERY MUCH AND ONLY HOPE THAT YOU WILL.

This, his latest play, was a romantic comedy in three acts based on a variation of the mixed doubles principle that had proved so successful with *Private Lives* just twenty years earlier; in this case it opened with lovers escaping their marriages and finding in a chilly Victorian railway buffet much of the same melancholy romanticism that had characterized Coward's other railway love-story, *Brief Encounter*. But the main asset of *Quadrille* was a couple of hefty star leads for the Lunts, and as a vehicle for their two performances (or rather for the single performance into which their remarkable talents had long since coalesced) it trundled along satisfactorily enough while lacking the sparkle of many of Coward's earlier comedies.

Having decided that with this play he might as well go the whole romantic hog, Noël invited Cecil Beaton to design some lavish period costumes and settings. It was the first time the two men had worked together, and Beaton's relations with Coward had been a trifle chilly ever since he had been told by Noël in the course of a transatlantic crossing from New York in 1930 that he was 'flabby, flobby and affected, with an undulating walk, clothes too conspicuously exaggerated, and a voice that is both too high and too precise.' Since then, however, he had established himself as a designer and photographer of considerable international repute, and Noël had revised his earlier estimation. Beaton was delighted to get the offer to design *Quadrille* and wrote in reply:

> I am utterly enchanted by the play; it has the charm, wit and frivolity of *The Importance* and is more tender and mature than anything you have ever written… it has always been my ambition to do scenery and costumes for one of your plays, and I feel that I am very lucky to have been kept for this particular occasion… nothing on earth that I know of would prevent me from doing the job.

In a similarly ecstatic mood, Beaton wrote to Lynn Fontanne about what fun it would be for them all to be working together on a play; Miss Fontanne replied that on the contrary, 'it will be a lot of hard work, anxiety, worry.

We will very likely fight to death, we will hope to win through to success, but it won't be fun.'

Towards the end of January 1952 Noël staged one special evening of cabaret at the Café de Paris which raised over two thousand pounds for the Actors' Orphanage. The annual Orphanage garden party was by now proving both over-costly and impracticable on account of the rain which invariably drenched it; so Coward's committee had voted to raise funds instead by occasional gala evenings at the Café and also by a midnight matinée to be given annually at the London Palladium in June. But one of the committee's new problems was the need to find a title for what eventually became the *Night of 100 Stars*, to the suggestion that this midnight benefit involving most of the actors in London should be called *Summer Stars*, Noël had replied quietly that 'Some are not'.

At the Café Noël had Mary Martin as a partner; she was by now back at Drury Lane playing Nellie Forbush in *South Pacific*, the squabbles with Noël over *Pacific 1860* had long since been forgotten, and in cabaret the Coward–Martin partnership had a considerable one-night-stand success which the two entertainers later repeated on American television in *Together with Music*. A couple of days after the Café appearance Noël left London for Jamaica, stopping briefly in New York to read *Quadrille* to the Lunts who were suitable impressed and also reassuringly optimistic about its chances of success.

At Blue Harbour Noël was kept fairly busy by a succession of visitors to Jamaica who that winter included the Lunts, Jack Wilson, Vivien Leigh and Laurence Olivier; he was also obliged to take delivery of a live alligator, sent express from Harrods by Bea Lillie who had tied a label around its neck reading simply 'So what else is new?' Early in May, with another season at the Café de Paris and the London production of *Quadrille* on the horizon, Noël left the alligator at Blue Harbour and flew back to England.

In the middle of June Noël opened at the Café de Paris and simultaneously put *Quadrille* into rehearsal; at the Café nightly except Sundays for a month he sang a selection of those of his songs from the Twenties and Thirties that had worn well or already acquired a period charm, adding to the repertoire some new numbers which included 'There Are Bad Times Just Around the Corner', a song dedicated to the belief that every cloud did not in fact have a silver lining. 'His personality,' said the Sunday Times, 'almost persuaded his audiences that he could sing.' Coward's opening night was as always a star-studded occasion, a night for journalistic drooling in the world of Paul Slickey, and it set Coward fair for the second record-breaking season of the four that he was to do at the Café in the early Fifties. 'In cabaret,' noted one critic, 'Coward is benign though slightly flustered, like a Cardinal who has been asked to participate in some frenetic tribal rite.'

With another Café season launched, Noël turned back to the rehearsals of *Quadrille* which he directed 'with grateful acknowledgement to Miss Fontanne and Mr Lunt', implying that a certain amount of the production originated with the Lunts themselves. While they were in rehearsal, Graham Payn opened in *The Globe Revue*, a new Tennent production which included two of Noël's songs; but the heyday of intimate West End revue, to which Noël had first contributed thirty years earlier, was now beginning to draw to a close and this was to be the last revue featuring any new Coward material.

A few days after Noël ended his season at the Café, *Quadrille* started an eight-week tour at the Opera House in Manchester. Reviews on tour were excellent for the Lunts and the Beaton décor, though somewhat more guarded about Coward's script.

On September 6th, six days before the London opening of *Quadrille*, a story in an evening paper told Noël of the sudden death of Gertrude Lawrence. He had last seen her in the previous May when he was on his way home from Jamaica; then they had lunched together in New York and talked about the possibility that she would at last play his *Island Fling* in London when the Broadway run of *The King and I* came to its end. Now she was dead, lights were dimmed that night outside theatres throughout London and New York, and Coward was left to collect a few memories of the actress who had been his loving and beloved friend both in the theatre and out of it for almost exactly forty years. This was for *The Times*:

> We first worked together as child actors in the Playhouse Theatre, Liverpool, in 1912; since then, whether we have been acting together or not, we have been integrally part of each other's lives... I wish so very deeply that I could have seen her just once more playing in a play of mine, for no one I have ever known, however brilliant and however gifted, has contributed quite what she contributed to my work. Her quality was, to me, unique and her magic imperishable.

The London first night of *Quadrille* brought for the Lunts a batch of rave reviews and for Noël some of the most vitriolic press reaction that even he had ever encountered; the *Daily Telegraph* found the play 'an empty trifle', and Kenneth Tynan remarked that it was 'comedy gone flabby, comedy swollen with sentiment, tugging at heart-strings which have slackened long ago with tedium. It is also comedy predictable, comedy suspenseless, comedy which is all situation and no plot. *Quadrille* suggests Oscar Wilde rewritten on a Sunday afternoon in a rectory garden by Amanda McKittrick Ros.'

It is difficult to discover precisely what in *Quadrille* beyond a reversion to the old critical distaste for the work of Coward led to this onslaught: though not by any means one of the great light comedies of our time, and rating somewhere below the best half-dozen of Coward's own, it is nonetheless carefully constructed and endowed with that tender, retrospective charm that has been the saviour of many lesser plays. Here for the first time Coward tried, with intermittent but sometimes considerable success, to contain within a play his deeply pro-American feelings. In the character of Axel Diensen, played by Alfred Lunt, is an amalgam of the characteristics that made America great in the late nineteenth century; a bearded pioneer of the railways. Diensen talks of his native land in lengthy speeches whose patriotic lyricism would not have disgraced Walt Whitman.

But in any case the reviews were bad only for Coward, not the Lunts; their magic remained untarnished by the notices and within days of the September opening at the Phoenix *Quadrille* was sold out until Christmas. Throughout the autumn Noël remained in England, deciding reluctantly that in spite of some more tempting offers from hotels in New York the time had still not come to try his cabaret luck in America. Within a week of the *Quadrille* attacks, he had come in for another batch of unenviable reviews on account of *Meet Me Tonight*, a rather shaky film package of three of his plays from *Tonight at Eight-Thirty*. In spite of a star-studded cast the film was generally considered to be an artistic disaster, perhaps because the best plays of the *Tonight at Eight-Thirty* bunch had already been filmed elsewhere and those that were left had proved more difficult to adapt; but contrary to popular belief at the time, Coward had not been involved in their conversion.

In the first week of 1953 Noël left London for his usual Jamaican winter, having first decided that in the spring he would return to the stage opposite Margaret Leighton in a Tennent production of Bernard Shaw's *The Apple Cart*. This would be the first time he had ever played in Shaw, and indeed the first time for more than twenty years that he had appeared on the stage in the work of any author other than himself. He treated the assignment with predictable thoroughness, and as soon as he arrived at Blue Harbour began to learn one of the longest parts in the Shaw repertoire: 'There is no seagull in Jamaica that does not now know that play by heart. They heard my lines daily for three months.'

While the seagulls and Noël were thus occupied, he also found time to finish the second of his autobiographies, *Future Indefinite*, and to entertain another visitor to Blue Harbour, Clemence Dane, the playwright and novelist who on account of her fondness for the ocean became affectionately known to the household as Moby Dane.

Returning to London early in April, Noël went straight into rehearsal under Michael MacOwan's direction for *The Apple Cart*; he arrived at the first reading word-perfect, thereby thoroughly disconcerting a distinguished cast. But, despite this head start, he did not find Shaw easy to play: 'I knew the words, but it took me a while to discover how to say them; playing Shaw is a question of remembering your scales, because you can't do a long Shavian speech in a monotone.'

Early in rehearsals a young actor playing one of the smaller parts told Coward that he was again reading *Present Indicative*; 'that's right dear boy,' replied its author, 'always keep abreast of the classics.'

After a trial week in Brighton *The Apple Cart* opened at the Theatre Royal in the Haymarket a month before the Coronation of Queen Elizabeth the Second. Coward's notices varied only from excellent to grudgingly good; it had been a bright idea to revive Shaw's comedy about the place of the monarchy in the scheme of things political at a time when people were for once actually thinking about the monarchy, and even the epilogue about America's desire to rejoin the Empire had a kind of relevance in the spring of 1953. The climate of critical opinion, particularly among the Sunday papers, suggested that Shaw had found an able interpreter in Coward, and *The Apple Cart* settled down to enviable business for the three months to which Noël had as usual limited his appearance. Early in the run, conducting a party of visitors back to the stage door after the show, Noël turned a corner to come upon the bearded Laurence Naismith, in his shirt-tails and little else, making a backstage phone-call; 'that,' Coward told his amazed guests, 'is our Miss Pringle – such a hairy girl.'

Later in May Noël returned to the Café de Paris where he sang after *The Apple Cart* every night for the four weeks on either side of the Coronation. On the night of the Coronation itself, after his appearances at the Haymarket and the Café, Noël also sang at a celebration ball given in the restaurant of the Savoy Hotel which was so gala that the menus were printed on white satin. As his appearance there was timed for only fifteen minutes after he was due to finish at the Café, and as Noël was convinced that at that hour the streets of London would still be thronged with crowds of merrymakers, he arranged for a car complete with police escort to get himself and Norman Hackforth from the Café to the Savoy in time. Accordingly they were solemnly transported from Leicester Square to the Strand with police outriders and sirens to blast them through streets by now totally deserted: they achieved the journey with roughly thirteen minutes to spare. Earlier in a long day, Noël had watched the Coronation procession making its way down the Mall, and in particular the hugely enchanting Queen Salote of Tonga who was sharing her open coach with a rather small attaché from the Tongan embassy. 'Who,' someone asked Noël as they watched, 'is that in the coach with Queen Salote?' 'Her lunch', he replied.

Later in June *Quadrille* came to the last of more than three hundred performances at the Phoenix, and soon afterwards Noël brought his own season at the Café de Paris to a close, though not before a memorable night when one of the diners at the Café was the musical comedy star Elsie Randolph. An old acquaintance of Coward's, she sent him a note hoping that he would join her for a drink after his performance and initialled it E.R. It was therefore with some uneasiness that Miss Randolph looked up a few moments later to find a party of the royal family at a table nearby.

At about this time an assessment of Noël written by Tynan for the *Evening Standard*, concluded:

> Coward has been accused of having enervated English comedy by making it languid and blasé. The truth, of course, is the opposite. Coward took sophistication out of the refrigerator and set it bubbling on the hob. He doses his sentences with pauses as you dose epileptics with drugs. To be with him for any length of time is exhausting and invigorating in roughly equal proportions. He is perfectly well aware that he possesses "star quality" which is the lodestar of his life. In his case, it might be defined as the ability to project, without effort, the outline of a unique personality which has never existed before him in print or paint. Even the youngest of us will know in fifty years time exactly what we mean by 'a very Noël Coward sort of person.'

After *The Apple Cart* closed, Noël started to work on a new project: a musical version of Wilde's *Lady Windermere's Fan*. The score for this occupied him for the rest of 1953, but shortly before Christmas he set off for Jamaica; there, at Blue Harbour, he completed the last of more than a dozen numbers which, together with what survived of Wilde's original play, made up *After the Ball*.

Coward did not, however, plan to produce *After the Ball* himself, and he remained in Jamaica while it went into rehearsal in London; then, at the end of March 1954, by which time *Future Indefinite* was due for publication, he returned to England. The autobiography of Coward's war years seemed to come as a vague disappointment to most critics though *The Economist* saw that throughout *Future Indefinite* Coward was making a consistently valid statement about his later self:

> He is painfully expatriated... success faithfully attends him, the eminent appreciate him, Royalty thanks him, audiences applaud him; but he remains somehow uneasily not 'in', not orientated, uncertain of his proper role; a figure at once more complex and more sympathetic than one would conjecture him to realize.

After The Ball had started its pre-London tour at the Royal Court in Liverpool on the first day of March 1954; for the next twelve weeks, as it wound its way around England to some pretty uncomplimentary reviews, the director Robert Helpmann and later Coward himself made some extensive alterations to the production, adding and cutting whole numbers, breaking it into three acts instead of two, getting a new conductor and rearranging the orchestrations. Then, in the middle of June, it reached the Globe Theatre in London to notices that were mixed roughly six to four against the show.

The real trouble with *After the Ball* seems to have been that Coward failed to find a way of inserting his songs into Wilde's tightly constructed plot without slowing the action down to a near-standstill. But his name at the box-office still proved a useful counterweight to the critics and his musical survived for a not entirely discreditable total of one hundred and eighty-eight performances.

Noël himself went on to the Café de Paris, where for one night only he introduced his already legendary friend Marlene Dietrich; he then planned to set off in early July for Cap Ferrat and a brief summer holiday at the home of another old friend, Somerset Maugham. But on the first of July Mrs Coward, who was now ninety-one and had been ailing for some time, died peacefully at her flat in Eaton Square. Noël who had remained singularly devoted to his mother throughout the fifty-four years of his life, was deeply distressed; although her death was an eventuality for which he had been prepared, it came as a great and bitter sorrow to him. 'She was always there when I wanted her,' Noël was later to say of his mother, 'and never when I didn't, which meant that I always wanted her. She was the one person who could always tell me outright when something I had written was bad. She never lied to me.' Coward was now left with no close relatives whatsoever.

Within a few days of his mother's death Noël was back at work, recording a new album of his Café de Paris songs for Philips; then, towards the end of July, he went for his delayed holiday with Maugham at Cap Ferrat. The 'old party', as Maugham had long since christened himself, was now eighty and Coward found himself one of a rapidly diminishing band of friends whose company Maugham still found tolerable; artistically, socially and in the pattern of their private lives the two writers had a great deal in common, and as Coward approached his seventies he even grew to look curiously like pictures of Maugham at the same age. They had first met as early as 1917, and at a time when Noël was just about to start his career as a playwright he found in Maugham 'one of my immediate gods of the theatre'. It is indeed arguable that Coward's debt to Maugham is considerably greater than to any other of his predecessors; in *Our Betters* it is possible to see the beginnings of *The Vortex*, in *The Breadwinner* the model for *Fumed Oak*, and a number of Coward's short stories seem deliberately based on the style of the writer who was called 'The Master' before him.

But although their careers and their ideas often overlapped, although they had similar beliefs about light comedy in the theatre, and although

Coward spent a fair amount of time at the Villa Mauresque over the years, he never really got to know Maugham very well:

> He was a complex man and his view of his fellow creatures was jaundiced to say the least. He of course had his friends and his loves, and I myself am indebted to him for nearly fifty years of kindness and hospitality, but I cannot truthfully say that I really knew him intimately. He believed, rather proudly, I think, that he had no illusions about people but in fact he had one major one and that was that they were no good... Willie had little faith in the human heart perhaps because, having started his career as a medical student, he was unable to regard it as anything but a functional organ.

Returning to England in September, Noël started the last of his four consecutive seasons at the Café de Paris, where Milton Shulman found him 'blinking in the spotlight and looking like a totem pole in a dress suit... here was an immaculate monument reminding the middle-aged audience not only of what they were but of what they had become.' For what proved to be Coward's farewell season in London cabaret (a year or so later the Café was taken over by Mecca Dancing) he sang his way through the repertoire that had been so well tried and tested down the years, adding to it only another rewritten version of a song by Cole Porter and a new song of his own about the redoubtable Mrs Wentworth-Brewster to whom life called in a bar on the Piccola Marina.

Early in November, while Coward was still jamming the tables at the Café, Alfred Lunt directed *Quadrille* for New York with himself and Lynn Fontanne playing their original parts. For the *Times* Brooks Atkinson found it no more than 'a pleasant charade', but Broadway audiences seemed to have little objection to mildness overtaking the Lunt–Coward partnership, and the American *Quadrille* ran on well into 1955.

At the end of his Café season Noël at last began to feel that he was ready to face an American nightclub audience; he had been offered $40,000 a week to appear at the Desert Inn, Las Vegas, for a month of the following year. While he was still thinking the offer over, although one suspects for that salary remarkably little thought was required, he stayed at Blue Harbour and began work on a new comedy about modern art which emerged two years later as *Nude with Violin*.

Early in 1955, while Noël was still in Jamaica, Lorn Loraine embarked on a lengthy series of meetings in London with Coward's lawyers and accountants in an attempt to sort out a tax position which had already become very nasty indeed, and which left Coward not for the first time in his life owing rather more to the Revenue than he actually had to hand at that particular moment. His theatrical disasters of the late Forties had indeed led to a bank overdraft that was currently running at around £19,000. Still, there was always the hope that Las Vegas would solve that problem, and by May the contract for the Desert Inn was already signed and sealed.

A month later Noël arrived in Nevada to start rehearsing with an American accompanist since the union restrictions there made it impossible for him to have Norman Hackforth to play for him again. In an effort to improve the condition of his voice Coward, a lifelong heavy smoker, even tried to give up cigarettes for a few days; finding though that this actually made him considerably more husky, he rapidly abandoned the attempt. Noël was apprehensive about how his ultra-English material would go over to an American gambling audience; but at forty thousand dollars a week he was getting more than Las Vegas had ever paid to an entertainer with the single exception of Liberace, and Noël noted sharply that 'for that kind of money they can throw bottles at me if they so choose.'

They didn't. With a repertoire of songs ancient and modern that was largely unchanged from his last stint at the Café, Coward opened his season at the Desert Inn on June 7th 1955; and although the first of fifty-six shows that he was to give there twice nightly for the next month was somewhat strained on account of his ferocious nerves, by the second house at midnight he had relaxed sufficiently first to ensure and then to enjoy one of the greatest personal successes of his life. A headline in *Variety* told the story in its own inimitable way: 'Las Vegas, Hipping, Shouts "More!" as Noël Coward Wows Em in Café Turn.'

At the age of fifty-five, armed with little more than that increasingly oriental face, some ageing songs and an irrepressible talent to amuse, the man once christened 'Destiny's Tot' by Woollcott had pulled off another major triumph. The only sadness was that neither Woollcott nor Gertrude Lawrence nor any of the other major figures from Coward's past were at Las Vegas to see the consummate artistry with which it was done.

27

1955–1958

The world has treated me very well – but then I haven't treated it so badly either.

Noël continued to sing twice nightly to what he later described as 'Nescafé Society' at Las Vegas for the next month, missing only a couple of performances when his voice began to give out and Gordon MacRae agreed to take over. Once he got his voice back Noël was determined to keep in good trim for the rest of the season, and took up a series of elaborate vocal exercises; other guests at the Desert Inn were surprised and occasionally alarmed to hear deep mooing sounds issuing from his suite before every performance. Coward found Las Vegas 'endlessly enthralling, like a vast cruise ship with everything so organized you never have to think for yourself' and his success there was almost unprecedented; Wilbur Clark, owner of the Desert Inn, told the local paper that 'until a couple of months ago I'd never heard of this guy Coward – but he's doing O.K.', something of an understatement in view of the daily queue for returns which stretched the whole length of the Inn. Even more important, from Clark's point of view, was the fact that Coward's audience tended to become a gambling audience later in the evening; a valuable characteristic, since earlier attempts to import 'legitimate' stars to Las Vegas had resulted in audiences who wouldn't be seen dead near a one-armed bandit.

In the middle of July 1955 Coward bade a fond farewell to Vegas and went home to Goldenhurst a considerably wealthier man than when he left it. During the summer, he stayed in England to turn in a brief, brisk and profitable performance as Hesketh-Baggott, the dapper head of the employment exchange who sends Passepartout to work for Phileas Fogg at the very beginning of the Mike Todd all-star film of *Around the World in 80 Days*. The dialogue for this scene was written by Noël himself. At this time he also negotiated a contract worth five hundred thousand dollars to do three coast-to-coast television shows for C.B.S. during the autumn and winter of 1955–6. Negotiations for these Coward spectaculars were carried out at some length with American television executives who used to write on paper headed 'From the Desk of… ' until Noël started replying 'Dear Desk'.

Coward also received two other offers at this time, both of which he turned down; one was the part of Professor Higgins in a musical to be called *My Fair Lady,* and the other was the part of an English soldier, subsequently played by Alec Guinness, in a film to be called *The Bridge on the River Kwai*. Perhaps not since Olivier turned down *Journey's End* a quarter of a century earlier had an actor chalked up such memorably misplaced refusals, but in retrospect Coward remained commendably calm and unremorseful; it was indeed he who suggested Rex Harrison to the producers of *My Fair Lady*.

In October Coward returned to New York to make his debut on American television in its first full colour spectacular, an event he shared with Mary Martin; their joint appearance was sponsored for C.B.S. by Ford and entitled *Together with Music*. Forty-one rehearsals went into the making of it, and even then Coward wasn't satisfied: 'We're still doing it on our nerves – I want it done on technique.' For ninety minutes, live and in colour, the two entertainers sang together and alone through most of Coward and much of Kern, Gershwin, Porter, Rodgers and Hammerstein. The show cost Ford a cool five hundred thousand dollars but was undoubtedly worth every cent of it; Margot Fonteyn and William Faulkner turned up in the studio to watch, and the *New York Times* considered that Coward, in spite of some initial stiffness, 'can write off this occasion as one of the triumphs of his career... it was a knock-out.' The next morning, after he had seen the notices and been rung up by what seemed like every viewer in New York, Noël cabled Lorn Loraine in London:

COMPARED TO THIS, LAS VEGAS WAS LIKE A BAD MATINÉE AT DUNDEE.

Via television, America had apparently rediscovered Coward at a time when in his own country he was a prophet without much theatrical honour.

After Christmas with Lorn in Jamaica, Noël flew back to Hollywood where he was to do the television version of *Blithe Spirit* for C.B.S. early in January; he himself played Condomine with Lauren Bacall as Elvira, Claudette Colbert as Ruth, and Philip Tonge, his old friend from early days as a child actor, playing Doctor Bradman. Rehearsals were somewhat fraught on account of Miss Colbert's difficulty in learning a lengthy part; reports from the studio floor offered the following star exchange:

Colbert: I'm sorry, I knew these lines backwards last night.
Coward: And that's just the way you're saying them this morning.
Colbert: If you're not very careful I may throw something at you.
Coward: You might start with my cues.

But *Blithe Spirit* was all right on the night, in spite of a certain nervousness on the part of its Ford sponsors who seriously considered some of the dialogue too racy for a television audience; predictably Coward refused to cut any more of his play than had already been sacrificed to a seventy-five minute time slot, noting sharply that 'People who object to the language in *Blithe*

Spirit are crackpots, and Mr Ford should be happy if they don't buy his cars. They would be a menace on the highways.'

From Hollywood Noël went back to Jamaica, stopping off on the way for a careful look at Bermuda; already it was becoming clear from Lorn in London that in spite of his recent American successes Coward was still in deep financial trouble at home, and his legal advisers were suggesting that to take up residence abroad might be the only way out. For tax purposes Bermuda was then more suitable than Jamaica, and accordingly on this visit Noël began to look around for a possible house. The one that he found, after considerable searching, was Spithead Lodge in Warwick, a house that had once belonged to Eugene O'Neill and had been the birthplace of his daughter Oonagh, later Mrs Charles Chaplin.

Before taking it over Noël returned to Jamaica, from where he wrote to Lorn instructing her to sell both Goldenhurst and the studio flat in Gerald Road, since two English homes for a man planning to settle in Bermuda were patently an extravagance he would have to do without. He also wrote to the Actors' Orphanage asking them, in view of his determination to live abroad, to release him from the Presidency that he had held without a break since April 1934. The Orphanage accepted his resignation reluctantly and elected Laurence Olivier in his place; Coward had been, in Tyrone Guthrie's words, 'not only a dignified figurehead but a man who regularly visited the children, made sure that the beds were clean, that the slops were emptied, the stairs swept, the meals adequate and that the orphans felt that their president really stood in loco parentis.'

While Noël was still abroad, *South Sea Bubble*, the play he had originally written for Gertrude Lawrence, opened at the Lyric Theatre with Vivien Leigh now in the lead; thirteen days later on May 8th 1956, John Osborne's *Look Back in Anger* opened at the Royal Court and launched a revolution which was to affect the shape of the English theatre for the next ten years. Osborne, in fact, was to shake up the theatre of the mid-Fifties in precisely the way that Coward had shaken up the theatre of the mid-Twenties with *The Vortex*, though of the two Coward's play probably came as the greater shock to his audience.

It was a critic on *The Times* who first saw a connection between the two writers:

> Widely acclaimed as the most exciting play of its year, John Osborne's *Look Back in Anger* appears very like *The Vortex* which established Mr Coward as the sympathetic voice of another post-war generation. It has the same air of desperate sincerity... the heroes of both plays are neurotics, but they suffer, and when an author can convey that suffering on the stage is genuine, it matters not how thin-spirited the sufferer; we are moved.

South Sea Bubble however, failed to move anybody much; *The Times* considered it 'a minor but not unpleasing Coward' while most of the other reviews jumped through the inevitable hoops labelled 'superficial', 'hollow' and 'brittle'.

In New York during May, Coward and Edna Best had a considerable success with the third of his C.B.S. television specials, *This Happy Breed*; Noël again played Frank Gibbons, in what the *New York Post* considered to be 'the most impressive performance of his career.' A few days later, after returning to Blue Harbour, he took part in Ed Murrow's *Small World* television hookup; the other guests were Siobhan McKenna in Dublin and James Thurber in New York, but the programme seems to have turned into something of an evening with Noël Coward. He talked to, or rather at, Murrow about his painting ('Touch and Gauguin'), his notion of comfort ('good books, agreeable people and first-rate plumbing'), his reflections on Las Vegas ('one of the most respectable towns I've ever known; people are so preoccupied with gambling they've no time for the major vices'), his thoughts about American television ('it is for appearing on, not for looking at. I don't trust ratings, which I'm sure I could boost if I had the forethought to marry Grace Kelly or commit a really thorough trunk murder before my performance'), and finally his reflections on the first fifty-six years of his life ('the world has treated me very well, but then I haven't treated it so badly either').

After the Ed Murrow show Noël returned to New York for a one-night stand with André Kostelanetz at Carnegie Hall, where he found the musical courage to conduct the New York Philharmonic in some of his own music; he then flew to his new home in Bermuda for the first time. In London, Lorn was selling up his property; his two cars had already been sold and at an auction during the summer a collection of seven paintings went for a total of just over ten thousand pounds. Goldenhurst proved far harder to sell than either the London studio or the paintings and eventually went for just over five thousand to the only man who'd put in a bid for it.

But in spite of all the sales, it was still not public knowledge that Coward had given up his English residence to settle in Bermuda; that particular storm did not break until the middle of September when Tennent's decided to present John Gielgud in the most recent of Coward's plays, *Nude with Violin*. Like *South Sea Bubble* this too had undergone a number of rewrites, as the choice of a leading player veered from Rex Harrison to Yvonne Arnaud before ultimately settling on Gielgud; it would be the first time that Sir John had worked with Coward since the days when he followed Noël into *The Vortex* and *The Constant Nymph* thirty years earlier. On this occasion Gielgud was also to direct the play, with a cast which included Kathleen Harrison and Patience Collier, on the understanding that Coward would 'supervise' the production during its pre-London run at the Olympia Theatre in Dublin.

The choice of Dublin was not made by chance alone; Noël's tax position was now such that although he owed nothing to the Commissioners, a single day on British soil could put him in their debt to the tune of about twenty thousand pounds. In the whole of 1955, although he'd only spent a total of eight weeks in England, his tax bill had come to just £27,000; he had paid it out of the Las Vegas earnings, but realized fairly swiftly that he could ill afford to go on like that. 'I am not a businessman,' he told the *Sunday Express,* 'my brain is my fortune and at fifty-six I have got to tread pretty carefully.'

Thus his decision to live outside England from now on, one which caused him a certain amount of pain, was based on the need to avoid taxation in the future (as an emigré he only became liable for forty per cent of his taxes) rather than to escape paying what he already owed, though that nice distinction rapidly disappeared in the hail of press abuse which rained down on Coward when the story broke at the end of September. A few days before the world première of *Nude with Violin* in Dublin, Coward left Bermuda for New York where in a brisk forty-eight-hour stopover he caught up with no less than five films including *War and Peace.* From New York he sailed to Paris and then joined a plane flying direct to Dublin, provoking as he did so a storm of journalistic protest. On what one can only assume to have been a slow news day the *Daily Sketch* took half of their front page to announce 'Coward Cocks Snook By Air' and followed it with a front-and-back page spread and a map to prove that every county Coward's plane flew over was saving him three thousand pounds in taxes. The implication throughout was that it was money already owed. Following hard on that, a Socialist member of Parliament solemnly rose in the House to utter one of the most remarkable non sequiturs of our time: 'Noël Coward has said he loves his England, but just can't afford to live in it. What about our wartime experiences?'

Within a day or two of Coward's arrival in Dublin the story had reached hysteria proportions. On independent television, Rediffusion's 'This Week' turned itself over to a ponderous discussion of whether or not Coward had the right to live how and where he chose.

Although across the whole spectrum of the press the attacks on Coward were marginally outnumbered by the letters and articles published in his defence, the attacks received more prominence and in a curious, insidious way they hurt him considerably. The decision to sell off all his property in England and to live abroad for the rest of his life had not been taken lightly or indeed willingly; it was not so many years since he had written 'I belong to this exasperating weather-sodden little island… and it belongs to me whether it likes it or not' and there is no reason to believe that an invidious tax position could have destroyed overnight the links that had been forged between Coward and his country over more than half a century. He was, and he remained, tremendously English; and to be told in so many words that he was 'disgracing his country' was not a charge that he found easy to shrug off.

On the other side of the coin, this massive bout of publicity could just be seen as a testimonial to Coward's continuing celebrity value, and it certainly did the business for *Nude with Violin* a fair amount of good; the cast played to standing-room only in Dublin after a rough first night at which the gallery showered the stage with paper darts made of the programmes. Noël stayed in Dublin for the two weeks that his play was there: 'I arrived to find that Gielgud had directed it with such loving care for my play that he'd forgotten his own performance, so I helped a little with that.'

Leaving *Nude with Violin* to complete its tour and go into London without him, Noël returned to Spithead Lodge in Bermuda; the tax authorities had accepted his decision to settle abroad, but stipulated that to show proof of his intention he should spend the rest of 1956 and virtually all of 1957 out of England. After that, he would be allowed up to twelve weeks a year in Britain without prejudice to his emigré status.

Nude with Violin opened in London at the Globe Theatre, a few yards up Shaftesbury Avenue from the Lyric where *South Sea Bubble* was still in residence, early in November 1956; the reviews tended to be good for Gielgud, who was making only his second stage appearance in modern dress since the beginning of the war, but chilly for Coward's play. 'Billed as a comedy,' said the *Evening Standard*, 'it emerged as a farce and ended as a corpse.' Noël was not missing much by remaining in Bermuda. Yet despite bad notices his play proved durable enough to survive three changes of leading man at the Globe and to last there for the next year.

For Christmas Coward went back to Blue Harbour; he stayed in Jamaica for the rest of the winter, working on a new play called *Volcano*, doing a fair amount of painting, and starting work on a novel which he set in Samolo, using some of the characters from *South Sea Bubble*. He also reached the decision to play Sebastien in *Nude with Violin* in New York before the end of 1957.

In London again early in June for the two weeks allowed him by the Inland Revenue, he planned to visit some old friends, and also to put Michael Wilding into *Nude with Violin* in place of John Gielgud who was leaving for Stratford-upon-Avon. 'I shall stay,' Coward told Alan Brien, 'in the Oliver Messel Suite on the top floor of the Dorchester. All that luxury is not really me but doubtless I shall be able to rise above it. Thanks to the vilifications poured upon my head in recent months I am now as famous as Debbie Reynolds, which is most gratifying.'

But back in England the shouting about his taxes seemed to have subsided at last, and the story of his finances was allowed to die a natural death. Relieved and delighted, Noël turned back to *Nude with Violin*; he did, however, have mixed feelings about the replacement of Gielgud by Wilding who, he noted later, 'brought to the play large audiences, immense personal charm and startling inaudibility'. While he was in London Coward also paid a visit to

Look Back in Anger at the Royal Court, which he found 'electrifying... Osborne's is a great gift, though I believe it to be composed of vitality rather than anger.'

Early in the autumn Noël started a pre-Broadway tour of *Nude with Violin* at Wilmington in Delaware, both directing and playing the lead. When the company reached Philadelphia, Coward offered a local reporter some thoughts on the gradual destruction by Americans of the English language: 'I ask you: words like "hospitalized" and "togetherness" and "trained nurse" – absurd. What in heaven's name would be the use of an untrained nurse?'

Nude with Violin opened on Broadway in November to generally tepid reviews; Walter Kerr started his *Herald-Tribune* review: 'It is delightful to have Mr Noël Coward back in the theatre. It would be even more delightful to have him back in a play.' Nevertheless they did reasonable business throughout that winter in New York, and in February Coward brought in *Present Laughter* to alternate with it. He then took the two plays out to California for a brief tour, but before the company left New York for San Francisco, the National Association of Plumbing Contractors solemnly presented Noël with a plaque 'for his kind words about plumbing on the Ed Murrow Show.'

Coward got considerably better reviews on the West Coast than he had in New York, and he played both his comedies to splendid business in San Francisco and Los Angeles until the end of March. Then he returned to Blue Harbour in Jamaica to start work in one of the few fields still entirely fresh to him: ballet. He had been commissioned by Anton Dolin to compose something new for the tenth anniversary season of the London Festival Ballet which was coming up in the following year. Dolin had left Coward with a wide and generous brief, asking only that the result should be fairly typical of England in general and of London in particular. Through the rest of the spring and early summer of 1958 Noël wrote the score for *London Morning*, a ballet set outside the gates of Buckingham Palace where, as the composer himself has said, remarkably little actually happens: 'soldiers and children and American tourists pass by, some rain falls because in London some rain always falls, some bells chime because in London bells always chime, and the Palace guard is changed because in London the Palace guard is always changed at precisely the same time on every morning of every day of the year.' The theme of the ballet, in so far as it had one, was that it was still exciting to go to London to see the Queen; but there were moments in *London Morning* when one might have been forgiven for thinking that the work had been commissioned by American Express rather than the Festival Ballet.

With *London Morning* almost complete, Noël started to work on a play; not, for once, a new play of his own, but instead an English version of a Feydeau farce, *Occupe-toi d'Amélie*, which Vivien Leigh had asked him to adapt as a vehicle for her. It was not a task which Coward much enjoyed; he found it difficult and frustrating to work with another playwright's plot, he was out of sympathy with the complex farcical convention in which Feydeau had worked it, and he admitted to Lorn Loraine in a letter that his adaptation was 'only barely limping along'. Later in the summer, leaving *Amélie* on the typewriter, Noël went to stay with some friends in the South of France; Winston Churchill was also on holiday there, and Noël discovered to his considerable relief that the old man did not share the feelings of the English press about his emigration to the West Indies; 'Save what you can' was Churchill's only comment.

Back in Bermuda and only a few months away from his fifty-ninth birthday, Noël began to consider his own position, both in the theatre and outside it:

> When I was one-and-twenty I was ambitious, cheerful and high-spirited. I had never heard of the Death Wish and was briskly unaware that I belonged to a dying civilization. Today this dubious implication is pitched at me from all directions. Despair is the new religion, the new mode; it is in the books we read, the music we hear and, very much too often, in the plays we see. Well, I am no longer one-and-twenty but I still have no preoccupation with the Death Wish. I am still ambitious and cheerful and not offensively high-spirited and still unaware that I belong to a dying civilization. If I do, there really isn't anything I can do about it and so I shall just press on with my life as I like living it until I die of natural causes or an H-bomb blows me to smithereens. I knew, in my teens, that the world was full of hatred, envy, malice, cruelty, jealousy, unrequited love, murder, despair and destruction. I also knew, at the same time, that it was full of kindness, joy, pleasure, requited love, generosity, fun, excitement, laughter and friends. Nothing that has happened to me over the years has caused me to re-adjust in my mind the balance of these observed phenomena. I do become increasingly exasperated however when in my own beloved profession all that I was brought up and trained to believe in is now decried. Nowadays a well constructed play is despised and a light comedy whose only purpose is to amuse is dismissed as 'trivial' and 'without significance'. Since when has laughter been so insignificant? No merriment apparently must scratch the set, grim patina of these dire times. We must all just sit and wait for death, or hurry it on, according to how we feel. To my mind, one of the most efficacious ways of hurrying it on is to sit in a theatre watching a verbose, humourless, ill-constructed play, acted with turgid intensity, which has received rave notices and is closing on Saturday.

28

1958–1962

*In the Sixties, regardless of evil portents, prophetic despair and a great deal too much
writing on the wall, I managed to write one or two fairly cheerful musical comedies.*

By early in the November of 1958 Coward had completed his adaptation
of the Feydeau farce, which in view of the obvious impossibility of *Occupy
Yourself With Amelia* he had retitled *Look After Lulu*; a mild bout of pneumonia
kept him in Bermuda for the rest of that month, but as soon as he had recovered
he left Spithead Lodge to start negotiations for the production of the farce on
both sides of the Atlantic. Noël went first to New York, where he saw Tammy
Grimes in cabaret and instantly persuaded her that she should star in the
American *Lulu*, and then to London where it was arranged that Vivien Leigh
would open in the English production at the Royal Court during July.

The choice of the Royal Court was a curious one; since George Devine
had taken it over in 1955 it had been essentially a writers' theatre, concerned
with the discovery of new talent and, since the success of *Look Back in Anger*
there in 1956, dedicated to a school of playwrights (Arden, Jellicoe, Simpson,
Delaney, Wesker, Livings) who in their theatrical style, ideas and intentions
stood about as far removed from Coward as was artistically and socially possible.
However the box office takings at the Court had been shaky of late, and Devine,
realizing that he needed a money-maker if he was to continue the experimental
work he wanted to do there, settled reluctantly for what looked like an assured
success. Later he grew marginally more enthusiastic about *Look After Lulu* and
having persuaded Tony Richardson, then the Court's other artistic director, to
produce it, Devine himself agreed to play one of the parts.

The other production of this Feydeau–Coward farce got off to a less
auspicious start: in spite of the joint and separate efforts of Coward and its
director, Cyril Ritchard, *Look After Lulu* opened in New York at the beginning
of March to a distinctly chilly reception and only lasted on Broadway for a
meagre thirty-nine performances. Undaunted by the experience, Coward flew
back to Jamaica. 'Remember me?' asked a woman he encountered at the airport,
'we once met with Douglas Fairbanks.' 'Madam,' replied Coward, 'I often find
it hard even to remember Douglas Fairbanks.'

Now that the furore over Noël's tax problems had finally subsided and
showed no sign of blowing up again, he was beginning to have second thoughts
about Bermuda as a place of residence; in the three years since he had bought

Spithead Lodge there he had discovered that it signally failed to hold for him the near-magical attraction of Jamaica, To Coward, Bermuda now appeared to be a tight and overcrowded little island imbued with the atmosphere of an English golf club and too many clipped hedges. When he also discovered that his house there had become a landmark for guides taking busloads of tourists around the island, he decided that the time had come to sell up and move again; thus while he was staying in Jamaica in 1959 he happily accepted an offer of just over twenty-seven thousand pounds for Spithead Lodge and signed away the Bermuda property forever. But the tax problem remained; Jamaica was still not feasible as the permanent foreign base that he needed to satisfy the Commissioners of the Inland Revenue, and accordingly Noël began to look through the property columns for another house in either Switzerland or the South of France.

Having sold Spithead Lodge Noël stayed at Blue Harbour for the rest of the spring, using his time in Jamaica to work on a new play about a group of actresses in retirement which emerged a year later as *Waiting in the Wings*. In April, with this already virtually complete, he agreed to play Hawthorne, the suave spymaster from MI5 in the film of Graham Greene's *Our Man in Havana*. Most of Coward's scenes were shot in Havana itself, where Noël was directed by Carol Reed in this his first film (with the exception of his guest appearance in *Around the World in 80 Days*) for almost a decade. Coward managed to steal a fair amount of the picture from its star Alec Guinness, and enjoyed the experience enormously:

> Although the theatre is my first love, I've found certain films fascinating and this was one of them. I had to unlearn all my stage technique; I'm not a very adroit film actor, not technically, and Carol had to stop me overdoing any of my facial expressions. 'Remember,' he would say, 'in this shot your lower lip is a foot wide.' I was still playing it all to the back of the gallery.

From Cuba, Coward flew back to London and completed his studio filming for *Our Man in Havana*. In June, looking through the property columns of the *Daily Telegraph*, he found the house he had been looking for, a highly suitable and attractive chalet overlooking Lac Leman just nine miles above Montreux at Les Avants, where Noël was now to stay for the best part of every year. Friends and near neighbours around Les Avants included Adrianne Allen, Joan Sutherland, Charles Chaplin and, slightly further up into the mountains, David Niven and the Burtons.

London Morning opened in London at the Festival Hall in the middle of July to a generally hostile press; Clive Barnes for the *Spectator* found it 'as predictable an entertainment as all-in wrestling... it takes place in front of Buckingham Palace and has everything except Christopher Robin who must have been saying his prayers when it was cast.'

But by the end of the fifties recent and bitter experience had made Coward glacially immune to bad notices; in any case by now his thoughts were far removed from the ballet and back with *Look After Lulu* which opened its pre-London tour at Newcastle a few days after the première of *London Morning.* During the London rehearsals for *Lulu,* John Osborne is said to have wandered into the Royal Court, seen Vivien Leigh rehearsing on its stage with Anthony Quayle and Max Adrian, and assumed that in some nightmarish way he had been suddenly transported from Sloane Square to the heart of Shaftesbury Avenue. The idea had been for the Court to conquer the West End; instead it seemed that the reverse had happened.

The morning after *Lulu* opened at the Royal Court, to bad notices and a certain amount of journalistic shrieking about the betrayal of avant-garde values in Sloane Square, Coward flew to Athens for a fortnight's cruising around the Greek Islands aboard an Onassis family yacht. Then, tanned and rested, he returned to London to find that *Look After Lulu* had survived its notices and that business at the Court had in fact been good enough to justify a transfer to the West End in September; there Lulu played to adequate business at the New Theatre, just one more in a long line of Coward comedies which nobody liked except the public.

In the autumn Noël went back to Switzerland with Cole Lesley and settled into the chalet at Les Avants which had been redecorated and furnished with the best of what still remained from Goldenhurst, the studio in Gerald Road and Spithead Lodge; one downstairs lavatory was entirely wall-papered with the sheet music of Coward's songs. In October, Frank Sinatra wired from Hollywood to ask Noël's price for a guest appearance on his network television show; 'ONE HUNDRED THOUSAND DOLLARS,' replied Coward, 'PLUS MY EXPENSES AND THE RETURN AIR FARE FROM GENEVA.' Mr Sinatra did not pursue that particular enquiry any further.

At the end of the year, on the verge of his sixtieth birthday Noël returned to London to do another film; this was *Surprise Package,* a gangster comedy produced and directed by Stanley Donen and scripted by Harry Kurnitz from an Art Buchwald story. With that parenthood and a cast led by Yul Brynner, Mitzi Gaynor and Coward himself as a benign if impoverished ex-King of Anatolia, the film should have been all right; it was, however, to emerge as one of the major celluloid disappointments of 1960. *Surprise Package* remains to date the sole film in which Coward sings and dances, albeit only in a rather halting title sequence shared with Miss Gaynor. To say that he steals the picture would imply that there was something of value in it to be stolen; at the very most, he was involved in petty pilfering.

Noël's arrival at the age of sixty, in December 1959, provoked from a New York paper the thought that:

There is a generation growing up which does not know Coward, which never knew the world he pictured and pilloried, which thinks the characters in his plays artificial and shallow. That in itself is evidence of his success, for that is exactly the world that Coward was showing us. He was writing better social history than they realize – perhaps better than even he realized at the time.

The birthday also prompted a few autobiographical thoughts from Coward himself:

I am now more of a perfectionist than I used to be; I take pride in being a professional. I don't write plays with the idea of giving some great thought to the world, and that isn't just coy modesty. As one gets older one doesn't feel quite so strongly any more, one discovers that everything is always going to be exactly the same with different hats on… if I wanted to write a play with a message, God forbid, it would undoubtedly be a comedy. When the public is no longer interested in what I have to write, then it will be brought home to me that I am out of touch: not before. Nowadays though I find that I rather enjoy my downfalls; to me it's acridly funny when something flops that has taken me months to write and compose. In private I suppose I am a tremendous celebrity snob, and by celebrity I don't mean Brigitte Bardot but people of achievement like Somerset Maugham or Rebecca West. Looking back through my life I find that my personality only really changed once, and that was when I was twenty-four and I became a star and a privileged person. Yet to my inner mind I'm much the same now as I was before *The Vortex*; I'm as anxious to be good as I ever was, only now time's wingèd chariot seems to be goosing me. It doesn't bother me that I don't write in England any more. I love England but I hate the climate and I have absolutely no regrets about having left… looking around me I deplore the lack of style and elegance in most modern plays; I long for the glamour of great stars who used to drive up to the stage door in huge limousines. In my younger days I was tremendously keen to be a star and famous and successful; well, I have been successful for most of my life, and if at this late stage I were to have another series of resounding failures I believe I could regard them with a certain equanimity.

Just after Christmas *Our Man in Havana* opened in London and New York to a press that had reservations about the picture but was universally delighted with Coward's part in it. Hawthorne was the first and the best of the roles that Noël played on the screen as a character actor: the highlights of a memorable performance included the solemn caution with which Coward closes a door made only of bamboo shoots in a futile attempt at security, the quintessential wagging of that distinguished left index finger as he recruits the recalcitrant Guinness in a Cuban gentlemen's convenience, and Reed's superb establishing shots of Coward striding through the back streets of Havana complete with furled umbrella and Eden hat, a figure at once correct, commanding and deeply absurd.

But Noël was already back at Les Avants when the film opened, and he stayed there through the rest of the winter working on the final chapters of *Pomp and Circumstance*, a light novel about the islanders of his beloved though mythical Samolo which had occupied him intermittently for the past three years. A bout of phlebitis early in the spring of 1960 kept him immobile at the chalet for six weeks ('my right leg turned bright pink and I had to be carried about like a parcel') but it did give him the time he needed to finish the book and to revise *Waiting in the Wings*. Then, fully recovered ('I am now scampering about the house like a sixty-year-old waiting eagerly for the first joyous signs of syphilis'), he arranged for the publication of this his first and so far only published novel, dedicated it to Nancy Mitford and sold the pre-publication serial rights across Europe and America for a solid fifteen thousand pounds. 'It is so light and insignificant,' he wrote to his publisher, 'that you will have difficulty in getting it between hard covers.' After a celebratory holiday in Morocco he flew back to London and there set up a production of *Waiting in the Wings*, with Sybil Thorndike, Lewis Casson and Marie Löhr for later in the year.

Waiting in the Wings marks the final development of Coward's talent as a playwright, and as such it belongs in a group with his 1965 trilogy *Suite in Three Keys*; after the light comedies of the Fifties, his latest play cut deeper and came closer to tragi-comedy: a curious, highly theatrical and often very effective blend of drama, pathos, humour and occasionally maudlin sentimentality. It was based on the gathering of a group of old actresses living out their enforced retirement at a home called *The Wings* in moods that ranged from open hostility, anger and bitterness at having to exist on charity, to contentment or at least fairly placid resignation. 'The play as a whole,' wrote Coward in an introduction to it, 'contains the basic truth that old age needn't be nearly so dreary and sad as it's supposed to be, provided you greet it with humour and live it with courage.'

The new play, Coward's fiftieth, was turned down by H. M. Tennent (the management which had presented virtually all of his work in London since the war) and when it eventually reached the Duke of York's in September under Michael Redgrave's auspices, it opened to cheers from the first-night audience followed by a mixed, sometimes vicious and for once generally unjustified press. Often in the past it could have been said that the critics were wrong about Coward, either because they failed to understand what he was trying to do or else because they failed to realize that the public would still want to see it; but they had often also erred on the side of generosity, and *Waiting in the Wings* is perhaps the only example of an important Coward play that was severely underrated by a large section of the press and that suffered at the box-office as a result. It is a comedy built on an essentially sad premise, and it proved perhaps for that reason not to be immune to critical attack in the way that *Private Lives* or even *Nude with Violin* had been.

In London the first night was little short of triumphant; curtain calls were taken amid loud cheers from a capacity house, and the only discordant note was struck by a *Daily Express* reporter who asked Noël as he left the theatre whether there was any truth in the rumour that he'd had his face lifted several times. Yet from the reviews that appeared in at least five papers the following morning, it seemed that the whole evening had been the theatrical fiasco of all time.

The journalistic objection is readily apparent; here at the beginning of the forward-looking Sixties, almost five years after the arrival of Osborne at the Court, was a drama by Coward who'd been around as a playwright for the last forty years about a lot of old actresses who'd been around for even longer. It is, however, a pity that only a handful of the Sunday and weekly critics bothered to look any closer. There are, it is true, moments when the play becomes undeniably mawkish; on the other hand there are also moments of near-Chekhovian dignity and a melancholy insight into the problems of growing old and lonely which far transcend the theatrical limits of *The Wings*. But it was perhaps the mixture of the two which made it such an unpalatable offering for most critics; in any case *Waiting in the Wings* played to capacity for its first three months on the advance booking alone, but then went into a sharp pre-Christmas slump from which it never really recovered. Including tours before and after the London run, it survived for a total of nine months on the stage.

The notices for *Waiting in the Wings* hit Coward very hard indeed; not since *Peace in Our Time* had any play involved both his intellect and his emotions so totally, and in the fourteen intervening years he really had managed to make himself almost as impervious to press criticism as he claimed to be. The seven plays and musicals written and produced in this post-war period had served with varying success to keep the pot boiling, but none of them had meant a great deal to him personally; they were part of a continuing, by now almost automatic professional process. In *Waiting in the Wings*, however, Noël was writing about characters he knew and loved well, members of a profession for which he retained an intense devotion. In Pirandellian fashion the borderline between truth and drama was blurred by the fact that a home for old actresses not unlike the one in the play did then exist at Ivor Novello's old house in Berkshire, and by the fact that one or two of the actresses with smaller parts in the play found themselves in real life facing alarmingly similar situations.

Ironically Noël emerged far better from the reviews for *Surprise Package* which opened in London a few days later; to an actor who had played Shaw's King Magnus and won, the role of an urbane ex-King in a Yul Brynner film was not exactly arduous. The general critical impression was that other actors should now be as cautious about sharing films with Coward as they had hitherto been about sharing them with children and dogs.

In October 1960 *Pomp and Circumstance* was published on both sides of the Atlantic. It was not rapturously received. Quentin Crewe for the *Sunday Express* saw it as final proof that Coward had 'signed off from the world around him' and most other English reviews echoed the feeling that it was hopelessly dated, though in America this was translated by critics into an endearing quaintness. In fact *Pomp and Circumstance* does not display Coward's prose in as favourable a light as many of his short stories whose format seems better suited to his particular brevity of expression; the novel's shape owes a certain amount to Nancy Mitford's technique of first-person narration, hence presumably its dedication, and it tells a story which though diverting enough would undoubtedly benefit enormously were the author to read it aloud in those measured, precise, mocking tones. To borrow a literary definition from Graham Greene, *Pomp and Circumstance* is not so much a novel as an entertainment.

Shortly after its publication in England, while both *Waiting in the Wings* and *Surprise Package* were running in the West End, Noël flew to New York where he defended the escapism of his novel at a literary luncheon:

> I am well aware of what is going on around me, but at a time when the present is overshadowed and the future less assured than ever, the gift to amuse is not to be dismissed too contemptuously… I do not wish to prove how sad life can be to those who already know it only too well.

By Christmas *Pomp and Circumstance* was already in the American best-seller list where it was to stay for the next twenty-six weeks, and Coward was back at Blue Harbour, where he allowed himself to be photographed in a red smoking jacket up to his ankles in the breaking surf clutching a cup of tea, a memorable picture which subsequently appeared in the New Yorker and elsewhere above an advertisement from the Jamaican tourist board expounding the joys of their island.

Early in the new year, having in the meantime declined the offer to play Humbert Humbert in the film of *Lolita*, Coward finally committed to print his growing distaste for the contemporary English theatre; three consecutive January issues of the *Sunday Times* carried diatribes in which he aimed first at the playwrights of the new wave, secondly at the actors of the 'scratch and mumble' school and thirdly at the critics who encouraged both. Coward's attacks were delivered as from a great height, in tones of near-papal authority, and their main argument was contained in the last paragraph of his first article:

> Consider the public. Treat it with tact and courtesy. It will accept much from you if you are clever enough to win it to your side. Never fear it nor despise

it. Coax it, charm it, interest it, stimulate it, shock it now and then if you must, make it laugh, make it cry and make it think, but above all, dear pioneers, in spite of indiscriminate and largely ignorant critical acclaim, in spite of awards and prizes and other dubious accolades, never, never, never bore the living hell out of it.

In the second article Coward switched his attack from the writers to the actors, laying into them for destroying the magic of the theatre by paying too much attention to the Method and not enough to their personal appearance offstage; and in a concluding onslaught he turned on the critics, his oldest enemies, whom he accused of:

Favouring dustbin drama to the exclusion of everything else. The prevalent assumption that any successful play presented by a commercial management in the West End is automatically inferior in quality to anything produced on a shoe string in the East End or Sloane Square is both inaccurate and silly. It also betrays an attitude of old-fashioned class-consciousness and inverted snobbery which has now become obvious to the ordinary playgoer.

Replies to this tripartite onslaught came from Bernard Levin ('like Canute, Coward howls for the wave to recede and leave his kind in peace'), Kenneth Tynan ('the bridge of a sinking ship is scarcely the ideal place from which to deliver a lecture on the technique of keeping afloat') and Robert Bolt who concluded the argument on behalf of the playwrights of his generation:

We are truly sorry our first effort at a vintage of our own should taste so nasty to a cultivated palate. It doesn't taste so good to us. But it can't be helped. We think that other bottle is quite, quite empty. It was Mr Coward who had the last of it.

John Osborne, asked for his view of Coward, was nothing if not magnanimous:

Mr Coward, like Miss Dietrich, is his own invention and contribution to this century. Anyone who cannot see that should keep well away from the theatre.

A few years later, when the shouting had died away, Coward was asked what had really prompted him to write those articles:

Well, I was getting awfully sick of this emphasis on the underprivileged and proletariat on account of it being entirely a misrepresentation of fact. No people in the world have a better time than the English. If you go round a few pubs in the East End or Chelsea, or anywhere you like, they have a ball. They come around and scream and enjoy themselves, and then we go to the Royal Court Theatre and we see people who lack communication with each other, who are miserable, who are trying to break through this terrible social barrier – they don't do any such thing. They're as merry as grigs, all of them. Obviously there is a certain amount of poverty and disease and unhappiness, but not nearly as much as in other countries. The Welfare State is doing very nicely, thank you.

Noël spent the rest of the winter at Blue Harbour working from six in the morning until midday every day on the words and music for *Sail Away*, his first original musical since the disastrous *Ace of Clubs* more than a decade earlier. By the end of February the score was complete, and he returned to New York to start auditions. While he was there, dining one night at Sardi's, two mid-western ladies stopped at his table and asked for an autograph; this, however, failed to enlighten either lady since his writing was not of the clearest. Finally, after considerable scrutiny, one of them made sense of it; 'Oh,' she told her friend in tones of ringing disappointment, 'it's only that guy who's always being photographed with Marlene Dietrich outside theatres.'

Sail Away was scheduled to open in New York during the autumn of 1961, the first of Coward's musicals ever to have an American rather than an English première and the first new musical of his to be seen in New York since *Conversation Piece* had opened on Broadway a quarter of a century earlier. In the intervening years first *Guys and Dolls* and subsequently *West Side Story* had changed the whole shape of the American musical theatre, and Coward was well aware that he was entering the most expensive, overcrowded and competitive field that Broadway had to offer. In these months he commuted between New York, London and Jamaica, rethinking different drafts of the script and inspecting other musicals of the time. While he was in New York he was taken to see *Camelot*, which he felt was 'like *Parsifal* without the jokes'.

In July *Sail Away* went into rehearsal in New York with Coward himself directing, and early in August it opened at the Colonial Theatre in Boston. The general impression after its first night was that the audience, which included Jacqueline Kennedy, the Lunts, Danny Kaye, Judy Garland and Richard Rodgers, sparkled rather more than the show in its current shape, and a vast amount of work was done to it on the road. Early in October the show arrived on Broadway, whose critics Coward had always felt would give the show a better chance of success than those in London:

I'll never write another musical for the West End, [he told the *New York Times*] the critics there never even notice the music. Here in New York they take their light music much more seriously, and the whole production expertise on Broadway is something we simply don't have in London. I know that if *Sail Away* were opening in England now the critics would insult me mercilessly, and why should I go through torture? At my time of life I don't need to, so can you blame me for gearing my new musical to a country where at least I am accepted on my merits?

A few weeks after *Sail Away* opened on Broadway to critics who were not all that kind, Noël departed for Jamaica with Graham Payn who had flown out to New York for the first night. While they were at Blue Harbour a cable told them of the death in New York of Jack Wilson, who had been Coward's manager and one of his closest friends in the central period of his life. That friendship, however, was now a thing of the past. Professionally Wilson's place had been taken over by the Charles Russell–Lance Hamilton partnership, though *Sail Away* proved to be the last Coward show managed by them before that friendship also collapsed in a welter of acrimonious financial and personal disagreements.

Back in England early in 1962, Noël was the guest of honour one Sunday at a dinner given by the Gallery First-Nighters' Club; beginning his speech 'Desperately accustomed as I am to public speaking,' he continued: 'You ask my advice about acting? Speak clearly, don't bump into people, and if you must have motivation think of your pay packet on Friday.'

29

1962–1966

This, dear boy, is the beginning of the Noël Coward Renaissance.

Under Noël's direction *Sail Away* opened its English run in Bristol at the beginning of June 1962, and came into London a fortnight later; the main musical opposition to it in the West End at the time was Lionel Bart's *Blitz* which, proclaimed Coward, was 'twice as long as the real thing and just as loud'. In many ways, and in spite of Coward's earlier doubts, *Sail Away* fared better in London than it had in New York and the notices, displaying an eagerness to welcome the increasingly rare sight of a stage musical by a home-grown composer, were marginally better than they had been on Broadway.

John Whiting, the playwright who was then also drama critic for the *London Magazine*, used *Sail Away* as the starting point for an affectionate essay about Noël:

> We have had him with us now for sixty glorious years: we had better accept him. That extraordinary piece of landscaping which he uses for a face, and the dying dove which he pretends is a voice, are always hinting nowadays that he is forgotten, old-fashioned and unloved. That he is forgotten is demonstrably untrue... that he is old-fashioned is another matter: *Sail Away* is the bluntest thing to have struck the West End theatre for many a year... but is he unloved? Speaking as one twenty years his junior, all I can ask is: who doesn't love his youth? For that is what Coward is to men of my age: *Private Lives, Conversation Piece, Operette, Tonight at Eight-Thirty, The Scoundrel* and all those songs we sang to our girls driving back in the red M.G. from the Thames pub on a summer night in 1936.

Sail Away did not, predictably, set the town on fire any more than it had in New York; but it ran on comfortably through the rest of 1962 while Noël went back to Switzerland to work with Harry Kurnitz on *The Girl who Came to Supper*, a new adaptation of Terence Rattigan's coronation year comedy *The Sleeping Prince*. This had already been unsuccessfully reincarnated once as a film called *The Prince and the Showgirl*, but Noël was now employed to supply it with music and lyrics for a Broadway production in 1963. In October, with more than half of that score already completed, Coward flew to New York en route for another winter in the Jamaican sun; while he was there, Somerset Maugham published in *Show* magazine some fairly unsavoury memoirs about his ex-wife Syrie. Garson Kanin noted Coward's reaction at the time:

Noël is one of the many who take the position that Maugham's behaviour is reprehensible and unforgivable. He declares that he, for one, wants nothing more to do with W.S.M. … he adds that a man who is capable of writing in this way about his former wife and about his daughter is capable of anything and might in the next week or month publish other material detrimental to others around him… 'The man who wrote that awful slop is not the man who has been my friend for so many years. Some evil spirit has entered his body. He is dangerous, a creature to be feared and shunned'…

It was the end of an old friendship, though Coward did visit Maugham once more before he died three years later: 'He was infinitely pathetic.'

Early in the spring of 1963, Noël flew to Paris for a few days to film a 'guest star' role in an altogether inadequate Audrey Hepburn–William Holden comedy called *Paris When It Sizzles.* Coward's performance in this suggests that he closed his eyes to the script, clenched his teeth and kept thinking of the money; although he didn't exactly save the picture it remains impossible to think of anyone who could have done so.

From Paris he went to London where, his views about contemporary playwrights having somewhat mellowed in recent months, he agreed to put up a thousand pounds to help back the film version of Harold Pinter's *The Caretaker.* Then at the beginning of May he set off for Australia by way of Hong Kong, writing the first of a new group of short stories as he travelled. 'What,' asked a reporter when Coward arrived in Melbourne, 'is your idea of a perfect life?' 'Mine.' Noël had not been back to Australia since his wartime tours in 1940, and on this occasion he only stayed there for a week to see an all-Australian cast safely launched in *Sail Away*; then, as he was leaving Melbourne to complete the round trip back to America by way of Singapore, a lady reporter enquired whether he'd tell her something he'd learned in Australia. 'Kangaroo,' was the reply.

When Noël reached Singapore he found a cable from Lorn Loraine telling him that *Ladies' Home Journal* had offered seven and a half thousand dollars for his latest short story, *Mrs Capper's Birthday*, and asking Noël to cable back his instructions. 'NO INSTRUCTIONS,' wired Noël happily as he set sail for San Francisco via Yokohama and Honolulu, 'JUST GRAB IT.'

While he was abroad, James Roose-Evans' Hampstead Theatre Club production of *Private Lives* transferred to the Duke of York's where it was to run for the rest of the year. In retrospect the 'Noël Coward Renaissance' which hit London in the following year can be seen to have started with the unexpected success of this revival, and there is something biographically satisfying in that, like the first production of *The Vortex,* it too should have been launched in Hampstead. A fair number of critics came to this production of *Private Lives* without having seen the play before (the last London revival had been the John Clements production in 1944) and their reaction was one of delighted if bemused discovery: 'Can it be,' wondered one critic, 'that we have underrated Coward all these years, and that *Private Lives* so far from being a badly dated relic is in fact the funniest play to have adorned the English theatre in this century?'

The Girl who Came to Supper opened in Boston at the beginning of October to good notices, travelled north to Toronto where the theatre was larger and the reception less enthusiastic, and then went into New York by way of Philadelphia early in December; while the show was on tour President Kennedy was killed in Dallas, throwing into horrifyingly tasteless topicality a number about royal assassinations which Coward had written for the musical and called 'Long Live The King – If He Can'. It was instantly hauled out of the show forever, and replaced by 'My Family Tree', a number that had first turned up as 'Countess Mitzi' in Coward's *Operette* almost thirty years earlier.

On Broadway *The Girl who Came to Supper* opened to a generally dismal press; Walter Kerr was of the opinion that Kurnitz and Coward should 'have let sleeping princes lie' and the *New Yorker* found that 'all the operatic foolishness of this piece is disheartening'. But the musical did have one triumphant, show-stopping sequence involving Tessie O'Shea as Ada Cockle, a character invented by Coward to belt over a medley of street songs that he wrote for her in an affectionate parody of the Edwardian music-hall. These songs represented Coward at somewhere very near his musical and lyrical best; but they were not enough to save an otherwise rather clumsily adapted show from a disappointing run on Broadway, and *The Girl who Came to Supper* remains the only one of Coward's eight musicals that has never had a professional stage production in England.

After the first night in New York, Noël flew to Jamaica where he spent Christmas at Blue Harbour working on the plans for *High Spirits*. Coward himself was to direct this musical version of *Blithe Spirit* (adapted by Hugh Martin and Timothy Gray) and he had already signed Bea Lillie for Madame Arcati and Tammy Grimes for Elvira. But it was, from the very beginning, readily apparent to Coward and everyone else involved that the production was destined to become another of those evenings with Bea Lillie; her rare, zany, remarkable talent found in Madame Arcati an altogether suitable vehicle and she proceeded to lift the show off the ground at each of her entrances, putting it back neatly where she found it as she left. *High Spirits* opened on Broadway at the beginning of April and ran on to almost capacity business for the rest of 1964.

During the summer Noël filmed short introductions to four of his plays (*Present Laughter, Blithe Spirit, The Vortex* and *Design for Living*) which were being revived on English television. Looking, he said, 'as though someone had sat on my head,' Coward delivered to the camera brief thoughts about each of the plays and why he wrote them; he also managed to work in cogent if defensive statements about the star system, the need for plays to have beginnings, middles and ends, and the advantages of playwrights who wrote hefty starring leads for themselves. But in private there were signs now that Noël had reached some kind of peace in his own mind; after all the attacks and defences of the past few years, when he seemed to stand alone in literate reaction against the theatrical avant-gardistes, he had at last satisfied himself that on his own behalf he had no cause for concern about posterity:

> It must not be imagined however that I was not beset by doubts... in my deep Christian subconscious there was the gnawing suspicion that I was nothing but a jester, a foolish, capering lightweight with neither depths nor real human understanding; that immediately after my death, if not a long while before, my name would be obliterated from public memory. I searched my mind, for long years I searched, to find a theme solemn enough on which to base a really important play; it was only a little while ago that, to quote Madame Arcati, 'it came upon me in a blinding flash' that I had already written several important plays... important because they had given a vast number of people a great deal of pleasure.

But if Noël himself had already accepted his place in theatrical history, it still needed some kind of official recognition. In the absence of a knighthood, he got the next best accolade: an offer from Sir Laurence Olivier to revive *Hay Fever* with the new National Theatre Company.

Olivier, who in 1926 had himself auditioned for a role in the first touring production of the play and been turned down, now saw in *Hay Fever* one of the minor twentieth-century classics that have always been a part of the National's catholic repertoire, and he invited Coward to direct it. 'I am thrilled and flattered,' wrote Coward in reply to Olivier's offer, 'and frankly a little flabbergasted that the National Theatre should have had the curious perceptiveness to choose a very early play of mine and to give it a cast that could play the Albanian telephone directory.'

Hay Fever, written just forty years earlier, was not perhaps the most obvious of Coward's plays for the National to honour; *Private Lives* is funnier and *Design for Living* more typical of the now time-honoured 'cocktails and laughter but what comes after' Coward myth. Yet of all his work *Hay Fever* is the best suited to a talented company playing together and off each other in perfect harmony; it offers one tremendous star lead, but unlike many of the other comedies it also offers five other parts that are very nearly as good. To have Coward direct it himself was a good idea; not only did he remember the style of the early Twenties with an accuracy that could be rivalled by few other directors still in the business, but he also understood better than anyone the elliptical twin-level technique which he had first perfected and which Harold Pinter had later adapted to his own darker dramatic purpose: the technique of having a character say one thing while thinking and meaning something entirely different. In retrospect it was now possible to see this as Coward's greatest contribution to stage comedy in the Twenties; after the carefully orchestrated epigrams of Oscar Wilde he brought to the theatre a style that was at once simpler and more spontaneous though less literary and no longer so explicit. A character in *Shadow Play*, written eleven years after *Hay Fever*, summed it all up: 'Small talk, a lot of small talk, with other thoughts going on behind.'

Early in October Noël flew to London to start rehearsals for *Hay Fever*; at the airport he was met by a reporter who suggested it was rather old hat for the National to be doing a revival like this in the mid-Sixties. Fixing him with that stare once described by Robert Benchley as 'the look of a dead albatross' Noël remarked acidly that if a comedy was intrinsically very good it would live over the centuries without becoming dated, like for instance *The School for Scandal* or *The Importance of Being Earnest*. 'Oh,' said the reporter, 'and are they yours too?'

Noël had not worked with Dame Edith Evans, who was playing Judith Bliss at the National, since they had acted together in *Polly with a Past* during the spring of 1921, and although he found her performance 'funny and true and fascinating', there were certain problems in rehearsal. One particular line which ran: 'On a clear day you can see Marlow', Dame Edith would always read as 'On a very clear day you can see Marlow'. Finally Noël could bear to have the rhythm of his line destroyed no longer; rising to his feet in the stalls he called out, 'Edith, the line is 'On a clear day you can see Marlow'. On a very clear day you can see Marlowe *and* Beaumont and Fletcher.'

With *Hay Fever* and the London production of *High Spirits* running simultaneously, Coward had come back with a vengeance. Less than ten years after the row over his emigration had threatened to exile him forever, and less than five years after the row over his *Sunday Times* articles had threatened to define him as a perpetually angry old outcast rejected by the theatre which he had helped to shape, he turned overnight into the grand old man of entertainment, an imposing theatrical figure demanding reverence for his longevity and admiration for the way his reputation had bounced back. Ronald Bryden summed it up for the *New Statesman*:

> The perennial shock of modernity is the amount of it which simply consists of old things looking different... who would have thought the landmarks of the Sixties would include a Nobel Prize for Sartre, a surge of historical interest in the Great War and the emergence of Noël Coward as the

grand old man of British drama? There he was one morning flipping verbal tiddlywinks with reporters about 'Dad's Renaissance', in that light, endlessly parodiable voice which sang 'Mad Dogs and Englishmen' and 'Mrs Worthington'. The next, he was there again, a national treasure: slightly older than the century on which he sits, his eyelids wearier than ever, hanging beside Forster, Eliot and the O.M.'s, demonstrably the greatest living English playwright.

As if further proof were needed of Coward's new establishment status, the B.B.C. approached him at this time and asked him to link their ninetieth-birthday tribute to Sir Winston Churchill, which Noël did on television at the end of November.

After their brief provincial tours, *Hay Fever* reached London a week before *High Spirits* and opened at the Old Vic to notices that were among the best Coward had ever received from the English press; even the younger tabloid critics wrote of 'a classic' and admitted to falling about with laughter at it. As Judith Bliss, Dame Edith Evans swept voluminously about the stage, sang in a voice which put Douglas Byng to shame, and dared her audience to realize that strictly speaking she was almost twenty years too old for the part; yet her outrageous theatricality was ideal. In Judith, it now became clear, lies the archetypal Coward mother-emblem exaggerated beyond life itself but possessing characteristics central to both Florence Lancaster of *The Vortex* and Jane Marryott of *Cavalcade,* while pointing the way to the Countess of Marshwood in *Relative Values* and even to Mrs Wentworth-Brewster for whom life called so vociferously in a bar on the Piccola Marina.

The rave reviews for *Hay Fever*, vastly better than those for the play's original production, did not encourage Coward to start arranging any laurels: 'Bad notices depress me for about an hour, but good notices cheer me up for only about an hour and a half. After that I want to begin working on something entirely new.'

Early in the new year Noël found that the Coward Renaissance in London had encouraged an American management to think of presenting three of his major comedies on Broadway under the direction of Edward Albee, yet another contemporary playwright who had long been a self-confessed Coward enthusiast. In fact the project failed to materialize, but Albee did write a glowing preface to a paperback reprint of some of the early plays:

Mr Coward writes dialogue as well as any man going; it is seemingly effortless, surprising in the most wonderfully surprising places, and 'true' – very, very true. He is, as well, a dramatic mountain goat; his plays are better made than most – but not in the sense of the superimposed paste job of form, but from within: order more than form. And Mr Coward's subjects – like ways we kid ourselves – have not, unless my mind has been turned inward too long, gone out of date... his work stands a very good chance of being with us for a long, long time.

While Noël was in Jamaica during the early months of 1965, in London Nigel Patrick directed and starred in a revival of *Present Laughter*. But already the critics' enthusiasm for rediscovering Coward had begun to wear thin, and the wit of *Present Laughter* which had sparkled and entertained hugely in wartime London seemed a trifle flat more than twenty years later. It had not yet acquired the 'period piece' flavour of *Hay Fever* yet in spite of disappointing reviews it still proved to be indestructible at the box office; it ran on at the Queen's for 364 performances.

Noël spent the first half of 1965 at Blue Harbour, where his many guests included not only Peter Sellers and Joan Sutherland but also, for one distinguished lunch party, the Queen Mother herself who repaid Coward's hospitality by having him to stay at Sandringham later in the summer. During his months in Jamaica, that year as in so many past, Noël slipped back into a rigid pattern of work at the typewriter from seven in the morning until midday. He was starting to draft a trilogy of plays set in a Swiss hotel, which was to emerge in the following year as *Suite in Three Keys*.

Early in the summer of 1965 Coward returned to England and accepted an offer from Otto Preminger to play Carol Lynley's seedy, perverted, lecherous old landlord in the thriller *Bunny Lake is Missing*. It was the first of three films (the other two were *Boom* in 1967 and *The Italian Job* in 1968) for which Coward was cast against type and allowed to escape at least temporarily from the smooth, svelte, impeccable image conveyed by the rest of his screen appearances. *Bunny Lake* starred Laurence Olivier, with whom Coward had last appeared in *Private Lives* in New York thirty-five years earlier, and the rest of a distinguished cast included Martita Hunt, Anna Massey and Keir Dullea, an actor who was not exactly overjoyed one morning to find Noël creeping up behind him on the set murmuring 'Keir Dullea... Gone Tomorrow.'

After his work for Preminger Noël returned to Switzerland where he finished *Suite in Three Keys*. Then, towards the end of November he decided that the time had again come for him to travel:

My passion for journeys is undimmed by the passing years. I'm always too late or too early, however; I arrive in Japan just when the cherry blossoms have fallen. I get to China too early for the next revolution. I reach Canada when the maple leaves have gone and the snow hasn't arrived. People are always telling me about something I have just missed; I find it very restful.

This time, Coward decided to visit the Seychelle Islands for no real reason other than that they were there and that he had never seen them;

the expedition was however something of a disaster. Almost as soon as he arrived in the Seychelles he caught a particularly virulent form of amoebic dysentery which drained him: 'I lay about, moaning and groaning, on a chaise longue thoughtfully supplied by Government House.' Then, in an increasingly desperate attempt to get cured he flew to Rome where an eminent specialist diagnosed chronic colitis, wrongly, and prescribed a useless diet of mashed potatoes to be taken every four hours. Soon after Christmas Noël was back in Switzerland, at a clinic in Geneva which diagnosed, correctly this time, that he had a spastic colon; there they managed to put an end to the dysentery with a series of drugs, though he was left at the end of it a very weak man indeed. In time most of his strength duly returned, but his health never entirely recovered from the battering that it took in those months.

In March 1966, against the advice of his Swiss doctors, Noël flew to London and started rehearsals with Irene Worth and Lilli Palmer for *Suite in Three Keys*. Of these three latest Coward plays, *A Song at Twilight* was the most important and also far and away the best; an earnestly moral drama, it concerned an ageing distinguished, petulant, bitchy and truculent writer who managed to conceal his homosexuality from the world at the cost of warping his talent and cutting off his human sympathies. Yet curiously enough *A Song at Twilight* started out in Coward's mind as a comedy; he had recently read David Cecil's biography of Max Beerbohm, which describes Constance Collier's visit to Max when they were both in their seventies and long after their friendship had ended; 'I thought how funny it was. There was Constance, Max's old flame, coming to see him again, only now she was still full of vitality and he of course wasn't, so she absolutely exhausted him.'

But gradually, as the play developed in Coward's mind, he realized that there could be more to it than just the meeting of a couple of Elyot and Amanda figures in their old age. What if the writer, unlike Max Beerbohm, had been homosexual for most of his life; and what if the woman brought with her letters that could incriminate him in the eyes of posterity? Slowly but surely this became the theme of *A Song at Twilight*; an old, queer author fighting a threat to his 'good name'. Given that plot, it is not altogether surprising that many critics took the play to be firmly based on Somerset Maugham, an allusion which Coward fostered by making up to look curiously like him on the stage.

But if Beerbohm and Maugham were the direct influences on the creation of Sir Hugo Latymer, there was also a certain amount of Coward himself in the character he had written and was about to play.

Those critics who saw a reference to Maugham in *A Song at Twilight* also saw a kind of poetic justice, remembering the way that Maugham had characterized Hugh Walpole in *Cakes and Ale*. But Coward's play was built on an issue at once wider and more subjective than that. His attitude to Maugham was one of retrospective pity rather than vindictiveness; reading the Beverley Nichols revelations, Noël's only comment had been 'how nice for dear Beverley to have found all that gold down in Somerset.'

Shadows of the Evening and *Come into the Garden, Maud* (the double bill which completed Coward's *Suite*) opened at the Queen's ten days after *A Song at Twilight* and then alternated with it until the end of July, so that on matinée days Coward would find himself acting all three plays in an eight-hour period, an experience which taxed his health, his strength and his memory quite considerably.

It was Peter Lewis for the *Daily Mail* who pinpointed the one component that held together all the parts of *Suite in Three Keys*:

> As the curtain fell last night I felt oddly elated, as if I had recaptured the flavour of an elusive drink that one tasted when young but which had never been mixed quite right since. I know the name of it... not mannerism, not bravura, not histrionics, but style.

The *Observer* saw these plays as a kind of Cowardian answer to Sartre's *Huis Clos* (similarly involving three characters in one room) bearing back the message that 'love, courage and consideration can prevent other people from being Hell' while Alan Brien for the *Sunday Telegraph* thought he had seen 'the greatest theatrical entertainer of our century desperately signalling to us that he has a message but is afraid he lacks the equipment to transmit it across the footlights.'

Throughout Coward's career his reputation went up and down like the mercury in some particularly unreliable thermometer, but with the success of *Suite in Three Keys* it was definitely moving upward and it is possible that Noël now decided to leave it there; in any event he was never to appear on a stage again, and it was tempting to see in the *Goodnight, Sweetheart* which ended *Suite in Three Keys* a more significant farewell.

30

1966–1969

It's terrifying how little time there is left; every day now is a dividend, and there is still so much I want to do... but my life up to now has left me with no persistent regrets of any kind. I don't look back in anger nor, indeed, in anything approaching even mild rage; I rather look back in pleasure and amusement. As for death, it holds no fear for me... provided it is not going to be a painful, lingering affair.

Suite in Three Keys ran on in London until the end of July 1966; having then reached his time-honoured three month limit, Noël ended the season in spite of the fact that they were still playing to near-capacity every night. The plays had severely strained his health and he knew it; there had been talk of producing them on Broadway in the autumn, but Coward's doctor ruled this out entirely and insisted that he should take the rest of his sixty-seventh year very quietly indeed.

Just before he left London to go back to Switzerland for the rest of the summer, Noël gave his name for a fee running into thousands of pounds to an advertisement for a new Gillette razor blade; he was asked simply to list those things which he believed still had 'style', and his reply was, in S. N. Behrman's phrase, 'echt-Noël':

A candy-striped jeep
Jane Austen
Cassius Clay
The Times before it changed
Danny La Rue
Charleston, South Carolina
'Monsieur' de Givenchy
A zebra (but *not* a zebra crossing)
Evading boredom
Gertrude Lawrence
The Paris Opera House
White
A seagull
A Brixham trawler
Margot Fonteyn
Any Cole Porter song
English pageantry

Marlene's voice
Lingfield has a tiny bit.

After *Suite in Three Keys* closed in London Noël went back to Les Avants and spent the next few months there, taking them almost as quietly as his doctor had asked; he did, however, start collecting together some of the verse he'd written over the last twenty years with a view to publishing it together with two new poems of near-epic length, *P & O 1930* and *Not Yet the Dodo*. But these did not give Coward any illusions about the lasting value of his work as a poet: 'those dear old fairies at my christening in St Alban's church, Teddington, endowed me with many rich gifts, but a true poetic sense was not one of them.' At Les Avants Coward also persevered with his painting, made fervent attempts to learn the Italian language from gramophone records, and edited the latest collection of his short stories which was to be published in the following year.

During the October of 1966 one remaining Coward play had its English stage première; this was *Post-Mortem,* the angry vilification of the First War which he had written in 1930 shortly after acting in *Journey's End* and which remains the most unfamiliar and least typical of all his published plays. Recognizing its limitations, Coward had never allowed it to be performed professionally; it had, however, been staged in a German prisoner of war camp in 1943, and the author now gave permission for it to be produced by sixth-formers under Gerard Gould's direction at the grammar school where he teaches in Oxfordshire. Gould had recognized that the play could work, given the fervent sincerity of a very young cast, and Eric Shorter for the *Daily Telegraph* saw in his production a play 'written in a tremor of youthful indignation – and much overwritten in places. But its rage is authentic, the fury is fresh, and the feeling in the writing is very considerable'. The play also came to light as somewhat belated support for the theory that within Coward a social historian, a moralist and a philosopher were forever asking to be let out. Coward however would have none of this: 'I have no deep thoughts about the human race, nor am I particularly interested in reforming it; indeed if I did there would be nothing left for me to write about. Anyway, I don't think perhaps I could.'

Towards the end of May 1967 Coward, by now almost fully recovered from the various illnesses which had dogged him over the past two years, flew to New York where he'd agreed to play Caesar opposite Norman Wisdom in a spectacular television musical version of *Androcles and the Lion* for which Richard Rodgers had written the score. While Noël was in New York he also agreed that his godson, Daniel Massey, should be the actor to play him as a young man in *Star!,* the film of Gertrude Lawrence's life which Robert Wise was then about to put into production as a vehicle for Julie Andrews.

At the beginning of the autumn Noël returned to London for the publication of both *Bon Voyage*, his short story collection, and the thin volume of his verse which took *Not Yet The Dodo* as its title; he also did his usual autumnal round of London theatres, dropping into the Royal Court where he found Alec Guinness and a painfully miscast Simone Signoret in *Macbeth*, a production which Coward subtitled 'Aimez-Vous Glamis'.

All four stories in *Bon Voyage* were concerned with age, loneliness and death, and they were greeted by the literary critics with that mixture of grudging admiration for the content and lofty distaste for the form which had marked most reviews of Coward publications since *To Step Aside* in 1939. *Not Yet The Dodo*, in many respects a companion volume, showed Noël in a gentle, Betjemanesque light (subjects included retirement to the West Country and a Battle of Britain dinner) using rhyme schemes that somehow looked as though they should have been set to music.

Later in the autumn Noël left London for Sardinia, where he'd agreed to play a male witch opposite Elizabeth Taylor and Richard Burton in what was then called *Goforth* but subsequently became *Boom*. The film was adapted by Tennessee Williams from his play *The Milk Train Doesn't Stop Here Any More* and directed by Joseph Losey, but neither they nor the Burtons managed to save a ponderous and pretentious picture from some terrible reviews. Of Coward it was said, as with every one of his screen appearances over the last fifteen years, that he'd stolen whatever there was to steal in the picture.

Towards the end of November, a few days after Coward had returned to Switzerland from Sardinia, Lorn Loraine died in London at the age of seventy-three. For the last forty-seven years she had been Coward's closest friend, confidante and adviser; a sensible, practical, tremendously kindly woman, she had organized his English affairs as both his manager and his secretary, running his professional life with a mixture of efficiency and devotion which he found both invaluable and irreplaceable. Above all she had taught him the permanent value of rigid self-criticism. Now, with Lornie dead, Coward's last great personal tie to England was broken; moreover he had lost one of the few deep friendships which had survived throughout his adult life. It is not that Coward was a difficult man to befriend; merely that he found lasting alliances hard to sustain:

> I am no good at love
> My heart should be wise and free
> I kill the unfortunate golden goose
> Whoever it may be
> With over-articulate tenderness
> And too much intensity.

But Coward still had Cole Lesley and Graham Payn as perpetually loyal and devoted companions, and with comfortably run homes for the three of them in Switzerland and Jamaica he was finding it increasingly hard to think of anything they missed by not living in England. Les Avants provided a base from which he could easily go to work anywhere in Europe, and Blue Harbour did the same for North America, while both places were ideal to live in at precisely the times when most people chose not to be there: Switzerland in the summers and Jamaica in the winters.

After Lornie's funeral, Noël flew back to Blue Harbour for the winter which, once the shock of her death had passed, he spent working on *Past Conditional*, the last instalment of his autobiography. Then early in the spring of 1968 Coward decided that once again it was time to travel; taking Coley with him, he set off from Blue Harbour via Bali and Bangkok for Hong Kong. There, surrounded by photographers, he solemnly but cautiously fired off the gun which he had immortalized in *Mad Dogs and Englishmen* thirty-seven years earlier:

In Hong Kong
They strike a gong
And fire off a noonday gun
To reprimand each inmate
Who's in late.

Early in March Noël was back in England, where he turned up briefly in *Don't Count the Candles*, a film about old age made for television by Lord Snowdon; 'fifty years ago', Coward remarked in this, 'at the age of fifty people had given up – now they're all taking rejuvenating shots. I tried some once: they had no effect at all beyond making me feel very sleepy.' Noël was also unimpressed by a Swiss doctor who specialized in the attempted rejuvenation of others: 'I believe he uses a bloody great syringe about the size of a rolling pin and he injects a horrifying solvent made from an unborn ewe. To judge from the effect on some of my friends, it's a very non-U ewe.'

Coward stayed in Europe for the rest of the year, travelling only as far west as Dublin where he spent a few summer weeks playing a majestic old lag in a film called *The Italian Job*. The director for this was Peter Collinson, whom Coward had first encountered as a particularly obstreperous youth at the Actors' Orphanage during the war; the star was Michael Caine, who noted that 'acting with Coward is rather like acting with God.'

Early in the autumn, Noël returned to London for a memorial service to his old friend Princess Marina, and then travelled on to Paris for an infinitely more cheerful occasion: the eightieth birthday of another old friend, Maurice

Chevalier. Meanwhile the Coward Renaissance still seemed to be at its height: in England the newly-formed Thames Television company ran a series of dramatizations of his short stories, in America a collection of his early songs and sketches was presented as 'Noël Coward's Sweet Potato', in Australia there was a festival of his plays, and in Paris a boulevard revival of *Brief Encounter*. Later in the year Coward himself recorded a lengthy television interview with David Frost, and just before Christmas two of his one-act plays were converted into a somewhat disastrous stage musical called *Mr and Mrs*. But what really kept Coward in the public eye during 1968 was the release, on both sides of the Atlantic, of *Star!* By choosing Daniel Massey (who as a child had played Coward's son in *In Which We Serve*) to play him as a young man, Noël had thoughtfully secured the services of a subtle and intelligent actor who knew his godfather well enough, paradoxically, to give an impression rather than an impersonation of him. Within these limits Massey built up a careful and altogether credible portrait of the young Noël which remained for many critics the best thing about an otherwise disappointing musical epic.

Nevertheless, it, too, will only serve to foster the Coward myth built up by journalists and the man himself in roughly equal proportions over more than forty years and now apparently indestructible; the witty young man with the clenched cigarette-holder and the silk dressing-gown is finally perpetuated on celluloid. In a way, one suspects that is how Coward himself wanted it; the rest of the story, and the work that went on behind that increasingly oriental façade, are far too complex for instant public recognition. In the Twenties Coward found himself suddenly the right man in the right place at the right time; he had what the public wanted and with surprisingly few interruptions he continued to give it to them for the rest of his life. If ever an author knew his market and wrote for it, then Coward was that author; luck has played its part in his success, but he was a man who made luck happen.

Usually, when a playwright dies, his work goes into a kind of instant oblivion from which it emerges after ten or fifteen years to enjoy renaissance and rediscovery. It was curiously typical of Coward that he should have gone through this process and remained alive at the end of it. His talent was for years overpublicized and under-estimated; now, perhaps for the first time, the estimates were getting closer to accuracy. Retirement always seemed unlikely; asked once how his friends would know when he had given up, Noël had replied 'they can follow my coffin.'

When *Star!* opened in London, Coward himself was at the première. On the screen a young man of seventeen, eager and efficient, started to entertain; looking from screen to stalls one realized that in more than fifty intervening years he had never really stopped:

But I believe
That since my life began,
The most I've had is just
A talent to amuse.

Epilogue

And that is the way it was at the beginning of 1969 when this book went to the printers for the first time: Coward was to live four more years, but they were by his standards remarkably inactive ones. No new plays written or produced, no more film appearances, no more short stories, no more songs: just a gentle retreat from professional life caused partly by increasingly ill-health and also I believe by the fact that he had at last lost the will to work, the will that had driven him so hard since the days of *The Goldfish* sixty years earlier.

While I was writing *A Talent to Amuse*, our first child was born and Noël became Hugo's godfather: every Christmas thereafter there would be a present in the post, except one year when a huge chauffeur-driven Daimler drew up outside our terraced house in Dulwich with, on the back seat in splendid isolation, an enormous teddy bear bearing a label reading simply 'love Noël'. Whenever he was in London we would meet to show him how his godson was ageing or how we were, and sometimes we would go out to Switzerland for marvellous weekends in the snow with Noël and David Niven and Joan Sutherland, who were among his starrier neighbours on the slopes above Montreux. He could not conceivably have been more generous either to us or about the book, and somehow its success seemed to warm and reassure him, proof at last that people did still want to know about his work. 'I am,' he said in a cable to me on the day of publication, 'simply wild about me.'

But for much of the year he was now staying under his beloved Jamaican sun with his devoted companions Cole Lesley and Graham Payn, and increasingly when I saw him back in London or Les Avants I was struck, as many must have been, by how quickly old age seemed to be catching up with him. When we first met he was a very young sixty-four, and when I last saw him he seemed to be an elderly seventy-two: a succession of illnesses chronicled in his own Diaries (and therefore not to be repeated here) had taken their toll, but health apart, these could not, I think, have been unhappy years for him.

His seventieth birthday in December 1969 was marked by a seven-day media celebration (christened by Coward himself 'holy week' or, alternatively, 'Dad's Renaissance') which included a season dedicated to his screen work at the National Film Theatre, a dozen of his plays on BBC radio and television, a gala midnight matinée at the Phoenix Theatre which we also called *A Talent to Amuse*, a televised banquet at the Savoy for which the after-dinner tributes to him came from the Lords Mountbatten and Olivier, and countless TV, radio and press features all of which led up to the news two weeks later that he had at last been awarded a knighthood in the New Year Honours of 1970.

Those celebrations, marking as they did the height of the Coward revival which had started four years earlier with the National's *Hay Fever*, were for Noël ample proof that he had returned to public grace and favour, both as an artist and as a man. With them, I believe, he saw a fitting end to his public and professional life, simply because there was no conceivable way they could be topped – and Noël was not a man who believed in anti-climax.

Broadway, not to be outdone by the West End, gave him a special Tony for Distinguished Achievement a few months later, and the University of Sussex gave him an honorary doctorate: suddenly everyone seemed aware of a national treasure for too long neglected, and revivals were now everywhere – *Brief Encounter* on stage in Paris, *Private Lives* on Broadway and *Blithe Spirit* in London. The comedies were, of course, vastly easier to revive than the musicals, many of which had badly-dated books but still contained a treasury of great songs. First in recital at such festivals like King's Lynn and Aldeburgh, then in a Toronto cabaret devised by Roderick Cook (*Oh! Coward*) and finally in a Mermaid Theatre anthology called *Cowardy Custard*, it became clear that these songs could however be rearranged into revue evenings of enormous charm and success.

By the beginning of 1973, Noël had *Cowardy Custard* and a Maggie Smith revival of *Private Lives* playing to capacity in the West End and *Oh! Coward* doing equally well on Broadway. After inspecting all three, and accompanying his old friend Marlene Dietrich to a New York gala, despite the fact that she had just announced to the press that she had decided not to spend Christmas in Switzerland with him 'because he might be dead before I get there', Noël travelled on to Jamaica for his usual winter in the sun.

And it was there, three months later, that he died: on the night of 25-26 March he had dinner as usual with his beloved Coley and Graham, and bade them goodnight from the threshold of Firefly, the house on the hill where he slept and worked. They walked back down the hill to the main house at Blue Harbour: when they awoke it was to a distraught houseboy bearing the news that Noël was suddenly very ill. By the time they got back to Firefly he had died, in bed, of a heart attack: his last words to them had been 'Goodnight my darlings – I'll see you tomorrow.'

The morning after his death, *The Guardian* in London noted that 'he died, as he had lived, with no self-pity and a ruthless instinct for the quick curtain', and throughout the lengthy obituaries that ran in press and television around the world there was the feeling that Coward's death, though undeniably sad for anyone who cared even remotely about the British theatre, had come with the perfect timing that had always been a feature of his life. Rebecca West, his lifelong friend, wrote of 'a very dignified man, dry but not dry like a desert, dry like a very good dry sherry.'

Noël was buried where he had always been happiest, in the garden at Firefly. His estate, valued in six figures, was left in the care of Cole Lesley and Graham Payn who returned to England for a memorial service at which Sir John Betjeman, the Poet Laureate, read Noël's last completed work:

When I have fears, as Keats had fears,
Of the moment I'll cease to be;
I console myself with vanished years,
Remembered laughter, remembered tears,
And the peace of the changing sea.

When I feel sad, as Keats felt sad,
That my life is so nearly done;
It gives me comfort to dwell upon
Remembered friends who are dead and gone,
And the jokes we had and the fun.

How happy they are I cannot know,
But happy am I who loved them so.

Of the greatest friends who outlived him, Cole Lesley, died suddenly in 1980; Graham Payn lives on in the house that was Noël's Swiss home for the last fifteen years of his life, while Firefly is preserved as a writers' retreat in Jamaica, thanks to loving neighbours.

When the playboy of the West End world, jack of all its entertainment trades (and Master of most) died, he was as old as the century and its most constant, if often controversial, show-business reflection. He left behind him over fifty plays, twenty-five films, hundreds of songs, a ballet, two autobiographies, a wartime diary, a novel, several volumes of short stories and countless poems, sketches, recordings and paintings, not to mention the memories of three generations of playgoers on both sides of the Atlantic for whom he had been the most ineffably elegant and ubiquitous of entertainers.

And in the twenty-six years since his death, his work has remained in constant revival: *Blithe Spirit* at the National Theatre in a production by Harold Pinter; *Private Lives* in the West End with Michael Jayston and Maria Aitken and on Broadway with Richard Burton and Elizabeth Taylor; *Design For Living* in London and New York; *Present Laughter* in the West End with Donald Sinden and on Broadway with George C. Scott; *Hay Fever* in London with Penelope Keith. Television documentaries have recalled and examined his career; record companies have reissued his scores. Cabaret pianists have recalled his long-lost early melodies; the actors' church in Covent Garden bears a memorial; his Diaries have become worldwide bestsellers; a musical called *Noël & Gertie* celebrates his private and professional partnership with

Gertrude Lawrence; his films are forever on television (*Brief Encounter* was indeed remade for it with Burton and Sophia Loren) and his songs are constantly on radio, while few repertory or amateur theatre companies go for more than a year without at least one of his plays. Even the epic *Cavalcade* has come back to life.

And then, on March 28th 1984, came the ultimate national accolade: in the presence of more than a thousand people, Queen Elizabeth the Queen Mother unveiled a memorial stone at Westminster Abbey. It reads simply:

Noël Coward.
Playwright, Actor, Composer.
6 December 1899 – 26 March 1973.
Buried in Jamaica.
A Talent to Amuse.

All that London lacks now is a Noël Coward Theatre, and I cannot believe it will be too long before we get one. His centenary in 1999 has been marked by lifesize statues unveiled in the foyers of the Theatre Royal Drury Lane and the Gershwin in New York; a major National Theatre staging of *Private Lives*; gala concerts at Drury Lane and Carnegie Hall; a New York revival of *Noël and Gertie* (retitled *If Love Were All*), starring Twiggy; and, in London, a new Coward revue as well as a Geraldine McEwin revival of *Hay Fever*. The National Film Theatre has put on a Coward retrospective season, complete sets of his plays and memoirs are back in print, and the University of Birmingham has inaugurated its Noël Coward Study Centre.

A BRIGHT PARTICULAR STAR

To Alexis and Juliet,
my own two starry ladies

Quotations

Sometimes, in *Private Lives*, I would look at her across the stage and she would simply take my breath away; I can think of nobody living or dead who ever gave to my work as much as she did.
  Noël Coward

Poor Richard Aldrich: he thinks he is marrying Miss Lawrence, but he will very soon find out that it's Myth Lawrence.
  Constance Collier

There did not seem to be a shy bone in her body.
  June, Lady Inverclyde

She was generous to the point of recklessness.
  Cecil Beaton

She spent money like an entire fleet of drunken sailors.
  Fanny Holtzmann

She could see a Maurice Chevalier film in the afternoon and play her entire performance that night as Maurice Chevalier; she was infinitely suggestible.
  Douglas Fairbanks

In the cerebral sense, she was scarcely an actress at all.
  Ronald Bryden

Her moral victory was that she learned how to act when she, above all women, could have been a successful actress without taking the trouble.
  Rebecca West

When she enters, the stage becomes visibly brighter.
  Cedric Hardwicke

It wasn't that my mother ever really intended to be unkind or difficult; it was just that she could never discover precisely what a mother was supposed to do. Our relationship was a disaster.
  Pamela Clatworthy

Vitamins should take Gertrude Lawrence.
  Harold Cohen

She can't sing, but who cares?
  Agnes de Mille

There was one element of a working relationship with Gertie that I have never experienced in working with any other actress, and that element was sheer unalloyed fun.
  Moss Hart

She was a light that danced and swayed, that burned not with a dull lamp's steady glow but with all the divine uncertainty of flickering candles on a Christmas tree.
  Daphne du Maurier

When Gertrude Lawrence has a good time, everybody has a good time. Or else.
  John Chapman

She regarded her own divorce and bankruptcy proceedings as accidents unrelated to her, like falling off a horse. It could have happened to anybody.
  Cole Lesley

She loved life, she loved people, she loved the theatre and she loved applause.
  Yul Brynner

Her features were irregular, with a strange blob of a nose, but she had beautiful eyes and hands, wore clothes like a dream, and danced with exquisite grace; although her voice was never very good (she wobbled if she had to sustain a high note and was frequently out of tune), she had learned to use it with beguiling charm.
  John Gielgud

She was a blazing great star, and we shall never see another quite like her.
  Laurence Olivier

Once you had worked with Gertie, you could work with anyone.
  Anne Leon

I am not what you'd call wonderfully talented, but I am light on my feet and I do make the best of things. All I really lack is a private life.
  Gertrude Lawrence

Preface

She may not always have been the best, but she was certainly the brightest. Others of her generation were better singers, better dancers, better actresses; Gertrude Lawrence was a better star. For her, the Gershwins wrote *Oh, Kay*; for her Noël Coward wrote *Private Lives* and *Tonight at Eight-Thirty*; for her Richard Rodgers and Oscar Hammerstein wrote *The King and I.* It was Gertrude Lawrence who first sang Coward's 'Someday I'll Find You', she who made hits out of the Gershwins' 'Someone To Watch Over Me' and 'Do, Do, Do', she who first sang Weill's 'Jenny' in *Lady in the Dark* and much of Cole Porter's score for *Nymph Errant.* For a brief but memorable time she was First Lady of the musical comedy stage on Broadway and in the West End.

She was a bright particular star who rose above the limitations and variations of her talent to personify the brittle glamour of a post-First World War generation which was hiding its disillusion under an often cynical smile.

When she died, suddenly and unexpectedly of undetected cancer in September 1952 at the age of only fifty-four, they dimmed all the theatre lights not only along Broadway, where until only a few weeks before she had been playing Mrs Anna in *The King and I,* but also in the West End, which, apart from one post-war appearance in a play by Daphne du Maurier, she had forsaken after the run of *Tonight at Eight-Thirty* in 1936. It was a unique tribute to an actress who had started out in 1911 at Olympia as one of a hundred and fifty child choristers in *The Miracle* and who was inclined to view her entire career from then onwards as something of a miracle in itself.

But by the time those lights were shining again, most traces of Gertrude Lawrence had disappeared; she died before television had begun to immortalize its artists on tape, before radio shows were regularly recorded, and though she made half a dozen films, her appearances in them are mostly undistinguished and give no clear impression of a radiance which could hold theatre audiences spellbound. True, there are a few recordings of her best-known numbers, but again they are inclined to emphasize her technical failings without giving any real idea to the present-day listener of what kept her close to the top of her profession for the best part of thirty years.

What follows, then, is an attempt to chronicle that career through her own words and the memories of those who knew and worked with her on both sides of the Atlantic and the war. Gertrude Lawrence left behind her just one brief and less than wholly trustworthy autobiography, published in 1945 as *A Star Danced*; a decade later, soon after her death, her second husband (the American theatrical manager-turned-diplomat Richard Aldrich) published an account of the time in which he knew her, a period from 1939 to 1952 interrupted by the four years he spent at war. But both these books have now been out of print for the best part of twenty years, and to them needs to be added the hitherto unheard evidence of her only child Pamela, who has been kind enough to give me much of her time and many of her recollections of a not always easy relationship.

The rags-to-riches life of Gertrude Lawrence often sounds like the script for a singularly appalling Hollywood musical (and once indeed it did become just that – a film called *Star!* for which she was impersonated by Julie Andrews, a lady bearing about as much resemblance to her as to Mickey Rooney); an active sex life led Gertie through two marriages and a series of affairs with the likes of Douglas Fairbanks Jr and Captain Philip Astley, and her lifelong inability to refrain from spending instantaneously any money that came to hand, and often a great deal that did not, led her at the height of her fame into a prolonged and, for its time, scandalous bankruptcy hearing.

Not always the most brilliant selector of scripts ('Nothing that can't be fixed' was her reaction to the first offer of *Private Lives*, to which Coward replied, 'The only thing to be fixed will be your performance') Gertrude Lawrence yet managed to attract the most distinguished composers, lyricists, lovers, playwrights, directors and managers of her day. 'Her quality was to me unique,' wrote Coward when she died, 'and her magic imperishable'; it is as a critical record and a pictorial celebration of her magic and her quality that this book is intended.

For all their help in putting it together, my sincere thanks must go not only to Mrs Pamela Clatworthy but also to the following: Mrs Philip Astley, Felix Barker, Peter Bull, Dr William Cahan, Constance Carpenter, Rosalind Chatto, Dorothy Dickson, Daphne du Maurier, Marlene Filers, Charles Evans, Douglas Fairbanks Jnr, Milton Goldman, Morton Gottlieb, Michael Gough, Cathy Haill, Radie Harris, Kitty Carlisle Hart, Alice Heggen, Raymond Mander, Joe Mitchenson, Timothy Morgan-Owen, Graham Payn, Jason Pollock, Pamela Webb, Arnold Weissberger and Evie Williams. I would also like to thank my editor at Punch, Alan Coren, for his customary generosity in giving me time away from the office to finish the book, and my publishers Weidenfeld & Nicolson in London, Colin Webb and John Curtis, as well as Beverly-Jane Loo at McGraw Hill in New York for their unflagging enthusiasm.

In further research I have as always been much helped by the staffs of the Theatre Museum and the Victoria and Albert Museum, the British Film Institute, and of the Billy Rose Theatre Collection at the New York Public Library, Performing Arts Research Centre.

1

BABE IN THE WOOD

Gertrude Lawrence was born, appropriately enough, on Independence Day: 4 July. The year was 1898, though later she was to put 1901 in the reference books, a practice not unknown in the theatrical profession. Her parents were then living in a less-than-desirable residence at 6 Bath Terrace, Newington, London. They christened her Gertrud Alexandra Dagmar and her father's surname was Klasen, though by the time of his only daughter's birth he was already working as Arthur Lawrence.

Gertie's father was a Dane whose family had moved from Schleswig-Holstein to London when he was two; there, in later years, he had begun to carve out a career for himself in the theatre, as Frederick Willis recalls:

> Marie Lloyd was always principal boy at the Crown Theatre, Peckham, but at Drury Lane she was always principal girl. At the Crown she'd have a first-class company to support her, and among the lesser lights there was Arthur Lawrence. He was Demon King for years at this theatre, and being a bass singer was usually billed as 'A bold bad demon with a bass voice in everything'. He delighted us with 'Asleep in the Deep' and other old favourites, and held us spellbound as he descended lower and lower down the musical scale. When he reached rock bottom he breathed a sigh of relief… He loved a drink, was very thin, very active, very social and always had a new story to tell. None of us had much hope that he would ever reach the top rank… and the last time I saw him was in the Strand (in 1905), when he told me that he was among the resident choir at the new London Coliseum, a novel and short-lived feature of that variety theatre in its early days.

Gertie's mother (born Alice Louise Banks) came from a faintly more 'genteel' family background: her father had been a master builder and there was considerable ill-feeling among the relatives when she ran off to marry a none-too-profound *basso profundo*. Moreover their worst fears about him were rapidly realized; though Arthur behaved well enough during his courtship ('We were never ever out together after ten o'clock,' Mrs Klasen proudly told her daughter, much of whose life and career was to be based on being out after ten o'clock), once married he took rapidly to the bottle. 'His gaiety,' remembered his daughter later, 'his charm, his blond good looks disappeared. He became ugly in disposition and demeanour. Mother left him soon after I was born, and I grew up with no memories and no real knowledge of him.'

When, in the late 1940s Gertrude Lawrence came to write a graphic and romantic but perhaps rather less than wholly factual account of her early life (which she called *A Star Danced*) she gave lengthy descriptions of a waif-like cockney London childhood. Few street corners in the Clapham district of the early 1900s appear to have been complete without a barefoot Gertie, dancing to the music of the barrel organs and singing, at the age of six, her first big number:

Oh, it ain't all honey, and it ain't all jam,
Walking round the ouses with a three-wheel pram,
All on me lonesome, not a bit to eat,
Walking about on me poor old feet.
My old man, if I could find im,
A lesson I would give.
Poor old me, I aven't got a key.
And I don't know where to live.

It was left to Noël Coward, Gertie's lifelong friend, critic and partner, to remark of his own similar South London childhood:

I was born in Teddington, Middlesex, an ordinary middle-class boy. I was not gutter. I didn't gnaw kippers' heads in the gutter as Gertrude Lawrence quite untruthfully always insisted that she did. But nor was our first memory the crunch of carriage wheels in the drive. Because neither of our families had drives.

After the departure of Arthur Lawrence, his wife remarried and entertained occasional gentleman callers. Family life for little Gertie was therefore not strictly uneventful, but nor was it a matter of abject and utter poverty. This legend grew in later years, notably in American press interviews where Gertie, realizing that journalists expected some kind of a story and never having been reticent with the press, was inclined to exaggerate a childhood of genteel lower-middle-class deprivation into one of near-starvation.

1898, the year of Gertrude Lawrence's birth, was also the year the United States took possession of Hawaii, the year Kitchener defeated the Dervishes at Omdurman, and the year Pierre and Marie Curie discovered radium. More relevant to Gertrude Lawrence's subsequent career, it was the year of the first-ever flashlight photograph. Bernard Shaw wrote *Caesar and Cleopatra* that year, Oscar Wilde wrote the *Ballad of Reading Gaol* and another notable star born in 1898 was Paul Robeson.

The British theatre at this time was led by Sir Henry Irving, and it was still the high summer of the actor-managers; melodramas were beginning a long, slow decline, and, in general, revivals were preferred to new plays by actors and audiences alike. W. S. Gilbert called the British dramatists of this time 'steady and stolid', while the critic J. T. Grein noted that 'so long as Shakespeare still draws the crowds… we need not bewail the poverty of our contemporary drama', though in fact both Bernard Shaw and, in Ireland, W. B. Yeats were writing prolifically by 1900, while Pinero and H. A. Jones were still at their height.

Quite what drew Gertrud Klasen into the theatre is unclear; she can have had only the vaguest notion of what her father did for a living, and though there may well have been 'something in the blood', by her own account she simply started with a concert party at the seaside at the age of six. The fact that she was beside the sea (in fact at Bognor) at all suggests that there was a little more money in the family than she later cared to admit, for in 1904 a Bognor holiday would not have been exactly routine for a family living in the depths of South London poverty. For Gertie's only daughter Pamela, there is still a certain mystery about how and with whom her grandmother was living in the earliest years of Gertie's childhood:

> I've an intriguing family group showing my grandmother with a whole lot of people in the back-yard of the house in Clapham, and by the time I went to live there years later Granny was sometimes known as Mrs Dewing and sometimes as Mrs Bentley. I know that she got her divorce from Arthur Klasen, who took to calling himself Lawrence off-stage as well as on, once the anti-German feeling started, but I've never been quite sure whether she then married both Dewing and subsequently Bentley or whether only one of them. I do remember Mr Dewing, a lovely man he was, with a yellowing moustache and a roll-top desk, and he used to take me on his knee and tell me that if my grandmother hadn't met him she'd have been a great lady.

Given that somewhat shadowy domestic arrangement, Gertie was herself less than forthcoming about the precise details of her early childhood; she did, however, once give a vivid account of her first professional engagement:

> The summer of my sixth birthday, my stepfather [presumably either Dewing or Bentley] must have had a streak of unusual good luck with the horses, because he took Mother and me to Bognor for the bank holiday. It was boiling hot, I remember, and the sands were crowded. I had never been to the sea before; the bathers, the picnic parties on the sand, the strollers along the front fascinated me. A concert party was entertaining, and Dad paid for us to go in. At the close of the regular bill the 'funny man' came forward and invited anyone in the audience who cared to, to come up on the stage and entertain the crowd. A push from Mother, and the command, 'Go on, now, Gertie, and sing your song,' was all the urging I needed. 'It ain't all honey and it ain't all jam,' I carolled lightly, twirling on my toes with my skimpy pink frock held out as far as it would stretch. The applause and the cheers were gratifying, even without the

large golden sovereign with which the manager rewarded me after a little speech.

One day some student of twentieth-century British theatre will research the influence of seaside concert parties in the first decade of this century; their habit of inviting talented (or simply shameless) children from the audience to leap up onto the stage provided not only a cheap and easy finale but was also the fore-runner of innumerable television talent shows of equally horrendous fascination.

In 1907, just three summers after Gertrude Lawrence's starring debut there, Uncle George's Concert Party, a pierrot troupe also working the sands, offered a large box of chocolates in a spontaneously-organized competition to see which of the children in the audience was willing to sing the whole of 'Come Along with Me to The Zoo, Dear'. The winner was a seven-and-a-half year old Noël Coward.

Back in London in the autumn of 1904, Gertrude Lawrence and her stepfather and mother, a lady who was not only Irish, Jewish and cockney but also ambitious for her daughter in an almost classic 'stage mother' fashion, took to a kind of involuntary tour of South London as Gertie later explained:

When times were good, we lived in rooms at Kennington Oval; but only as long as luck was with Dad on the horses. Then we'd move, as we frequently did. There was a regular ritual connected with these movings which varied only as we moved up or down in the economic scale. If the move was occasioned by good fortune, Mother added a piano to the furniture she ordered to be sent around to the new address. There was something undeniably genteel about a piano in the house, even if no one could actually play it.

If the move was in the other direction, a van drove up and men smelling of sawdust and beer carried away the piano and the rest of the furniture which we had on the hire-purchase plan... Mother was always on her dignity with them. She refused to be commiserated with, and the impersonal air with which she watched the men from the hire furniture company stagger down the front steps under the pseudo-Jacobean fumed oak dresser was a triumph of dramatic genius. As the rooms became emptier, you felt that Mother was merely clearing her decks for bolder action, and that when we had furniture again it would be on a nobler, more elegant scale.

Meanwhile Dad would have slipped round the corner and entered into negotiations with the neighbourhood greengrocer whose account had been paid up and whose friendship could therefore be relied upon. Not until after dark, when there would be no prying eyes, would Mother take down the window curtains and pack the few possessions rightfully our own... then, close to midnight, the grocer's boy would arrive with his cart.

Dad would tiptoe down the stairs with the parcels and baskets and pile them on the cart while the boy leaned on the railings and kept a lookout for 'nosey Parkers'. In all this there was nothing original; we were merely following a tradition long recognised in Clapham and other less-favoured districts. This manoeuvre was known as a 'moonlight flit'. Obviously it was a move to cheaper lodgings in another district where we and our straitened circumstances were as yet unknown. Equally obviously, it was without the landlord's knowledge. There must have been families whose moonlight flits were sad and shamefaced. Not ours. There was something daring and whimsical about this sort of move which challenged all that was adventurous in our three natures.

None of the three men in Gertie's mother's life seems to have enjoyed what might be called a steady income or a regular job, and by the time her daughter was ten there had been one too many of the moonlight flits. Mother decided therefore that the only answer was to get a job herself and this she did, in the back of the chorus for the Christmas pantomime at the Brixton Theatre.

That year, in 1908, it was *Babes in the Wood* and though the title characters had already been cast, it so happened that:

> The theatre manager wanted a child who could sing and dance with nine others in a troupe, and one who could he trusted to be on time for the show and not get into mischief. Mother promised she would take care of all that, and I was taken on. We children were little robin redbreasts in the forest ballet when the 'Babes' got lost in the wood. Dressed in brown tights, very wrinkled at the knees, our skinny bodies clad in musty feathers and with hats which had beaks in front, we covered the two unfortunate children with artificial leaves to keep them from the cold until they were rescued by Robin Hood and his Merry Men. Mother was one of the Merry Men.

So, little Gertie Klasen was already on the stage; not, at this time, due to any burning ambition or recognizable talent, but partly because it was worth the princely sum of six shillings a week and mainly because, encouraged by both her mother and her grandmother, she recognized in the theatre a kind of escape from a suburban South London world of genteel poverty and moonlight flits, one which had already claimed rather too many of her neighbours. The theatre was not at this time an especially 'respectable' profession except in its highest reaches: Irving had been granted his knighthood (the first ever given to any member of his profession) in 1895, but from *Hamlet* at the Lyceum to *Babes in the Wood* at Brixton was a considerable distance; if not geographically then certainly socially and professionally. Yet precisely because very few self-respecting families of the middle and upper classes would willingly allow offspring of theirs in through a stage door, the theatre was considerably more open to children a little lower down the scale or of professional families.

There was a constant demand for stage children in the early 1900s, since they were widely considered to be audience-pullers, and this demand could as often as not be met by those (both parents and children) in need of an escape from the reality of an unprofitable and unsuccessful existence. The stage was, after all, a place where anything could happen and sometimes did.

One pantomime does not make or even adequately launch a career, and it rapidly became clear to little Gertie and her mother that if she was to have any hope at all of a life on the stage, even for a decade or so until she was old enough to catch herself a financially suitable husband, she would first need some sort of training. Backstage at Brixton, there had been rumours concerning a lady called Italia Conti:

> Miss Italia Conti held a unique place in the world of the British theatre. She had a basement studio just off Great Portland Street where the boys and girls she accepted as pupils practised dance steps, did acrobatic exercises on the horizontal bar, and were taught elocution and the rudiments of the drama. The studio was a big room lined with mirrors in which you could see yourself from every angle, and at one end was a small stage with a piano. Mother had no money to pay for dancing and singing lessons for me. Dad had suffered a run of bad luck for months, and we had moved to cheaper and still cheaper lodgings. My education did not benefit by these flittings about Clapham and Brixton; whenever we moved into a new district it usually meant my entering a new school. It also meant finding myself one of a new group of children, who stood off and eyed me suspiciously. The boys and girls at Miss Conti's eyed each other too, but their glances were different. They looked at me critically, not at my clothes or where I lived, but for what I was able to do. Many of them had been born into theatrical families. All of them aspired to stardom. I sang and danced for Miss Conti, and she thought me sufficiently talented to offer to give me free lessons. On these terms I was enrolled one afternoon a week for a six weeks' trial period. If I showed promise, I had the opportunity of staying on as a pupil-teacher, thereby repaying my tuition.

She showed promise. Not a lot, at first, but enough to get into another Christmas show, and Reinhardt's Olympia epic *The Miracle* (as one of 150 child choristers), and then a fairy play called *Fifinella* which starred those two subsequent stalwarts of Hollywood character acting, Eric Blore and Estelle Winwood. Though rehearsals were held in London, *Fifinella* was to open at the Liverpool Repertory Theatre in December 1912, then under the direction of Basil Dean. Dean was (and remained for the next fifty years or more) a distinguished director but something of a martinet, and there was a widely held theory in the British theatre for most of the twentieth century that if as a child actor or actress you had started your career with Basil Dean, then there wasn't much else they could do to you in later life that didn't come as some form of a rest cure. A demanding and hard taskmaster, Dean was later to recall his first meeting with Gertrude Lawrence as uneventful:

> Among the lively pack of stage children supplied by Italia Conti was one, Gertrude Lawrence, a rather plain child with pigtails who seemed to feel the thrill even more than the rest of us, jumping in and out of stage trap-doors intended not for her but for the Demon King.

The success of *Fifinella* led Basil Dean and the Liverpool Repertory on to another show requiring a large number of children, Hauptmann's dream play *Hannele* with which Stanislavsky had enjoyed a considerable success in Moscow a few years earlier. By now it was the beginning of 1913, and one of the children cast for *Hannele* was Noël Coward, not in fact a Conti child (despite that lady's later inclination to claim him as one of hers) but already achieving a considerable reputation for himself as a boy actor after seasons in *The Goldfish* and *Where the Rainbow Ends.* The job in *Hannele* was, however, the first for which he would be required to leave London and the tender clutches of his adoring if ambitious mother. Noël wrote twenty-five years later:

> I was engaged at a salary of two pounds a week. In due course I was seen off by Mother at Euston, and in company of about ten other children and Miss Conti, travelled to Liverpool. It was a pleasant journey. We ate sandwiches and chocolate and played card games on a travelling rug stretched across our knees. Some of the children I already knew. Gracie Seppings and two sisters, Ivy and Dorothy Moody, had been in the *Rainbow* with me, and a very perky little boy in a yachting cap called Roy Royston I had met at one or two parties. The others were strangers, and still are, with the exception of Harold French and a vivacious little girl with ringlets to whom I took an instant fancy. She wore a black satin coat and a black velvet military hat with a peak, her face was far from pretty, but tremendously alive. She was very *mondaine,* carried a handbag with a powder-puff and frequently dabbed her generously turned-up nose. She confided to me that her name was Gertrude Lawrence, but that I was to call her Gert because everybody did... She then gave me an orange and told me a few mildly dirty stories, and I loved her from then onwards.

She was then fourteen; he had just turned thirteen. Privately, it was the start of a beautiful if sometimes stormy friendship. Professionally, it was the most important meeting of both their lives.

2

CHILD ACTRESS AND DANSEUSE

At some point in her Italia Conti schooldays, after 1910 and before the meeting on the train with Noël, Gertrud Alexandra Dagmar Klasen had become, for reasons not unconnected with posters and programmes and the then remote but just conceivable possibility of a name in lights, plain Gertrude Lawrence. Though she still never saw her father, his stage name had been the obvious one for her to adopt, and the Gertrud had acquired a final 'e' in the interests of sounding English (which she anyway was, at least by birth if not by parentage) at a time when to sound even faintly German was not the best of ideas.

As for the meeting with Noël, it is hard if not impossible to over-estimate its importance; until Gertie's death just forty years later, they were to remain privately and publicly a double-act of unique and imperishable talent and charm known simply as Noël and Gertie. Their interest in each other was everything save sexual; sometimes brother and sister, sometimes father and daughter, sometimes just tetchily good friends they travelled together and apart through four decades of British and American theatrical history. But for Gertie there would have been no *Private Lives*, no *Tonight at Eight-Thirty*; but for Noël she might have stayed forever in the mindless revues of the early 1920s.

In fact, Noël and Gertie were after their first shared production only to share the same stage in less than half a dozen other shows; but their partnership was not simply a matter of shared curtain calls. It informed and conditioned both their careers more deeply than (in her lifetime) either of them cared to admit. Already, at the time of *Hannele*, they had in common a similarly unglamorous South London childhood (true, Noël's family were slightly better off, running as they then did, a boarding house) and an early realization that the theatre could provide them simultaneously with an escape and a career. Noël's family had certainly never indulged in the moonlight flits which Gertie was to recall so vividly, and technically he may have been a notch or two above her in the social order; but there was, as she had already noted, a great levelling among stage children, whose hierarchy depended not on background or dress but on the size of the role then being played and the nearness to the footlights that was allowed them by the director. The director in this case was again Basil Dean, who wrote later:

> It was in my production of *Hannele* that Gertrude Lawrence and Noël Coward first acted together, appearing as members of the Angelic

344

Chorus in the dream sequences, although from their subsequent careers it does not seem that either of them was markedly influenced by the experience. Gertie was just over fourteen... and suffered her first professional heartbreak when she discovered that her surname had been spelt with a U instead of a W in the programme. Noël was a pimply, knobbly-kneed youngster with an assured manner.

Unlike Gertie who was already more independent, Noël's 'assured manner' masked a deep and desperate homesickness; things did, however, brighten up a bit when, after Liverpool, they played Manchester and Gertie hit Miss Conti's sister over the head with a rounders bat. In Gertie's view Noël seemed at that time to be 'a thin, unusually shy boy with a slight lisp.' There was the memorable night when the two of them were given a large box of peppermints on condition they shared it with the rest of the cast:

> Noël and I managed to forget this admonition and to eat most of the sweets ourselves in the taxi on the way to the theatre. Soon I began to feel queer, and when we went on in the heaven scene the other celestial beings seemed to float and bob dizzily around me. I stole a glance at Noël. He was positively green. Presently the audience was permitted an unexpected vision of heaven in which two small angels were being violently sick.

After the show each night Miss Conti's little band of stage children would return to a drab lodging house in Manchester's Acker Street, where Noël shared a room with Roy Royston and Harold French, who later remembered:

> One night after we three boys had undressed – last to bed turns out the gas – there came a subdued tapping from outside. Noël threw on a dressing-gown and gently opened the door. Standing there was Gertie and two friends. 'How about a little game of Nap?' they wanted to know. My pack of cards was produced and we settled down. The girls had brought their purses so it was money, not matches, we played for. After a while Noël, never an avid Nap player, opted for bed. Gertie too got bored and while Roy, the other two girls and I went on trying to win each other's ha'pennies, Noël and Gertie chatted – she sitting on the side of his truckle bed till far into the night. It was in that rather sordid little room in Manchester that Noël and Gertie started a friendship, deep and true, that was to last until she died.

Fourteen years later, the British theatre being a small world, it was the author of that memoir and Gertie who were together to sing George and Ira Gershwin's 'Do, Do, Do' in the first London production of *Oh, Kay!* But with *Hannele* closing at the end of its Manchester week, Gertie returned to London more than ever determined that it was to be an actor's life for her; she even spent some of her salary having a hundred cards printed:

LITTLE GERTIE LAWRENCE
Child Actress and Danseuse

If they did not immediately bring her in any more work they did at least confirm in print her new-found career.

At home things were not going too well; because there was no money and Miss Conti's generosity, though considerable, was something less than infinite, Gertie had to withdraw from further lessons. With no work forthcoming for herself, her mother or her stepfather, family life became a series of more or less bitter quarrels about the future; these were interrupted by the occasional joy such as a trip to the seaside at Brighton during which, if Miss Lawrence is to be believed, she invested in a penny-in-the-slot fortune telling machine which duly delivered her a card reading 'A star danced, and you were born', a message Gertie chose to interpret as meaning that she was already a dancer and would one day be a star.

To be a star, however, meant first getting herself back into the theatre, and although Harold French, Noël Coward and her other card-playing friends from *Hannele* were having little difficulty in carving out careers for themselves as boy actors because it was a career chosen by precious few male teenagers, for a girl it was considerably more difficult– there was no shortage of *them* whatsoever. For Gertie to get back into the theatre meant knowing somebody already there, and in a position to advise or introduce:

> Mother and I were out shopping one day when suddenly she stopped to read a poster stuck up on a wall... Heading the cast as the star appeared the name Arthur Lawrence. 'That's your father,' said Mother, pointing. I stared at the name, trying to accustom myself to the idea of a relationship between this man and me. No one had ever told me much about my father. I could not remember having seen him or heard of his taking the slightest interest in my existence... We walked on, and no more was said about my father. I would have liked to have gone to the theatre to see him and hear him sing, but Mother did not suggest it. I only had to look at her to realise the subject was closed. But the sudden discovery that I had a father who was a success in the theatre set me thinking... a plan began to develop in my mind... One evening several months later, when Mother was out, I decided to carry out my plan, and I packed a few belongings in a small straw portmanteau. I then collected all the empty bottles and jars in the house, returned them to the grocer's, and got the money I needed for the journey. Wearing my best coat and a large mushroom-shaped hat, and carrying the portmanteau, I took the tram to the theatre where I knew my father was appearing. A note left on the kitchen table told Mother of my decision to join my father, and that she was not to worry.

And Mother didn't; backstage at the theatre Gertie sent in her printed card and:

> Presently a man stood there – a very tall man who leaned forward to peer at me in the dim, flickering light. He was in his shirt-sleeves and collarless. One half of his face was smeared with grease and burnt cork. Out of the black face a pair of very blue eyes stared at me in utter incredulity. He spoke in a deep, quiet voice: 'Who are you? What are you doing here?' 'I'm Gertie,' I said, 'and I've come to stay.'

Viewed from the present distance, three-quarters of a century later, it is not easy to establish whether the early life of Gertrude Lawrence really did resemble one of the weepier penny-dreadful novels of the period, or whether those were merely the terms in which she later chose to recall it. Certainly she did at this time leave her mother for her father, certainly he was then singing in travelling variety shows. Whether she really said 'I'm Gertie and I've come to stay' only he and she would ever have known, but later evidence indicates that she was a character of remarkably limited imagination, immensely susceptible to anything she had recently read or seen or heard. Her life was to be lived out in a series of clichés, and her talent lay in either turning those clichés inside out or simply in rising above them. If anyone could have played that stage-door reunion with a father in those terms and got away with it, then Gertie would have been the one.

Life with father was, however, not a lot easier than life with mother had been; for six years now he'd been living with a chorus girl called Rose, who initially was understandably reluctant to take on the responsibilities of watching over a teenage girl as well as a drunken lover. Eventually, though, it was agreed that little Gertie would tour with them in her role as 'child danseuse', handing over any money she could make to her father and Rose in return for her keep. Father, meanwhile, had agreed to write a weekly letter to his ex-wife reporting on their daughter's progress and whereabouts, although as the drink slowly but surely got the better of him, these letters were more and more often written by Rose.

After a while, the endless routine of casting offices and stage-door tips about who was looking for whom in what sort of show led Gertie to another chorus-and-understudy job, this one in a touring revue (the first to attempt a kind of up-market vaudeville) called *Miss Plaster of Paris*. For fifteen shillings a week, most of which still went to her father, she was required to sing and dance a bit, sit atop a column in one tasteful tableau (a role she got by having the smallest bottom in the company) and above all understudy the leading lady, who happened to be married to the show's producer-star. On a Saturday night, after a few drinks, it was his custom to beat her up a bit, which usually meant that Gertie played the Monday night show while she recovered.

Miss Plaster of Paris bred a sequel, *Miss Lamb of Canterbury*, and by the time that tour came to its close a number of things had happened, not least the start of the First World War. This, like most wars, did nothing but good at the box-office; there had never been a greater need for entertainment, and within a year of Sarajevo the London acting community's unemployment problems had been cut by something like a half.

The war, however, impinged on Gertie's life a good deal less than a major family decision which she had recently reached in conversation with Arthur's hitherto faithful Rose. The two girls decided that so long as either of them were there to dry him out and bring home any kind of a salary, his drinking would only continue. The answer, they decided, for his sake as well as theirs, was to leave him to his own devices.

As it happened, they needn't have bothered; before they were able to announce their decision to him, Arthur told them both that he'd been offered a year-long tour of South Africa in a variety show which was also to feature a young Victor McLaglen, and that he would therefore be leaving in the morning.

Gertie was never again to live with either her father or her mother as a dependent, though she kept in touch with them both and, when times were good, sent money. She was now just sixteen, and alone.

For a while she lived at the Theatrical Girls' Club in Greek Street, leaving London to tour in any show that would have her in its chorus. Her experience was by now not inconsiderable; since *Fifinella* and *Hannele*, she had done the two revues, a musical called *All Aboard*, which rapidly sank, plus a show with her father called *The Little Michus* about a French pastry-cook and his troubles with twin daughters, one of whom was conveniently played by Gertie. Then, in 1916 came a disastrous engagement as a dancer in a touring company which ended in Shrewsbury, a country town not generally regarded as the centre of British theatrical activity. The company manager, affectionately known to the girls as 'old four-eyes' on account of his thick spectacles, was a shy man; so shy that when the money ran out before the end of the week, leaving him a bit short for the wages, he decided to return to London rather than get himself involved in any nasty verbal altercations with the cast. Thus he was able to keep most of the box-office takings.

Stranded quite literally penniless in Shrewsbury, Gertie got a job serving behind the bar in the hotel where she was already staying; luckily it was Shrewsbury's busy season, with the flower festival in full swing, and after a month behind the bar she had made enough not only to pay off her hotel bill but also to continue living there in reasonable comfort.

What she was waiting for was, of course, the arrival in the town of another touring company, and sure enough eventually one did come through, in need as always of a little local talent to take care of the roles for which they had not thought it worthwhile paying any actresses' train fares from London. Thus it was that each evening around 7 p.m. Gertie would leave the bar of the Red Lion, cross the road to the theatre and, dressed as a nun, sing 'My Rosary' as the prelude to a religious drama. By the time that run came to an end, she had saved enough to head back to London.

Now, with her father's departure for South Africa and the break-up of what had become her second family, Gertie received some parting words of advice from Rose:

> Go on your own. You've got something and I think you're going to get on. You're not exactly pretty, and you're too thin for everybody's taste, but you've got *class*. You need to be seen by the West End toffs.

Not that there were too many West End toffs to be found in Swindon, which was where Gertie went next with a show called *Money For Nothing*. As usual she was in the chorus, dancing a little and singing a little and understudying stars who were never ill, and hoping against hope that this would be the show which finally got her off the road and the outer-London circuit and into the West End. It wasn't; but it did get her noticed by people who were able, in the end, to do her a bit of good. To London in 1913 had come a celebrated American revue couple called Lee White and Clay Smith; during 1916 they decided to visit Swindon. Staying overnight, they also visited the local music hall and there, in *Money For Nothing*, they found Gertie.

Quite what they saw in her is not known; but something about her work that night, something about the moment or two in the show when she had a fraction of a song or dance to herself, impressed them enough to offer her dinner at their hotel. They wanted, they said, to help her and they believed that her talent would justify their interest; they made it clear that there was nothing on offer at the moment, but they would always like to know where she was in case anything came up.

Gertie, a prolific and constant postcard-writer then as later in life, took to sending Lee White and Clay Smith lists of her touring dates; later, when she was playing Yarmouth, there came a telegram:

WE HAVE RECOMMENDED YOU FOR A JOB IN NEW CHARLOT REVUE STOP COME AT ONCE.

Gertie was halfway to the station before a fellow chorus girl, chasing after her, pointed out that although there was nothing specific in writing to tie her to the present tour, if she left in midweek and headed for London only to find that Charlot couldn't use her, she would doubtless be replaced at Yarmouth and then find herself once again out of work. Caution prevailed, and she replied with another telegram: 'DOES YOUR WIRE CONSTITUTE A CONTRACT?' 'YES, IF YOU CAN COME AT ONCE,' came the answer. She did. Collecting the fare from some friendly soldiers who happened to be in training at Yarmouth and to have seen her show, she headed for London and *Some* in June 1916, one of a long line of revues presented by André Charlot. Though largely forgotten today (he was to die a sad and impecunious death in Hollywood after the Second World War) Charlot was the architect and founding father of the twentieth-century British 'intimate' revue and was once described by J. M. Barrie as 'the whole British theatrical profession in a nutshell'. While Flo Ziegfeld on Broadway was more concerned with the spectacle of large numbers of lovely ladies descending staircases very slowly, it was André Charlot who pioneered the concept of the 'intimate' revue in which elements of comedy, dance and song would be merged to provide an altogether more thoughtful and coherent spectacle. Where Cochran and Ziegfeld worked almost exclusively for the eye, Charlot worked also for the ear, giving in his shows as much importance to the words as to the music.

Some (an eccentric title partially explained by the fact that the words 'More Samples' were printed on posters and programmes directly below it, referring audiences back to an earlier show by the same authors, Grattan & Tate, which had been called simply *Samples*) opened at the Vaudeville Theatre in London on 29 June 1916. It was a company show with a cast of twelve, and the top billing was given to Clay Smith and Lee White together with an eighteen-year-old Toronto-born comedienne called Beatrice Lillie, It was specifically to understudy Beatrice Lillie that Gertie had been brought from Yarmouth, and *Some* was to prove the start of a professional partnership between the two women which continued well into the 1920s.

In the opinion of the then drama critic of *The Times, Some* was 'an evening of excellent fooling', which had an intriguingly original opening number in which the entire cast were seen outside their own stage door, desperately trying to get taxis home. After this, the revue was a mixture of songs, dance numbers and sketches, the latter including a satirical attack on the hopelessness of London's new telephone system ('always a fitting butt for good-natured banter' wrote one critic prophetically).

For Beatrice Lillie, just six weeks older than Gertrude Lawrence but already considerably further advanced in her stage career, having reached the West End within three months of her stage debut at the Chatham Empire in 1914, the arrival of Gertie at rehearsals for *Some* meant not only the grandeur of having her own understudy but also the discovery of a kindred spirit with whom to lark around backstage and sometimes even on stage:

I was young and callow enough to be elated over the acquisition of my first understudy, and a quick glance at her showed enormous blue eyes in a vivid, elfish face... after we had been running for several months at the Vaudeville, news came that America had entered the war. That April [1917] evening, a number of mine was cut so that our American star Lee White could sing a song which her husband Clay appeared to have composed in a matter of minutes. He stepped out from behind the curtains to announce his brand-new rouser, *America Answers The Call*; the front tabs were drawn and there stood Lee, tall and majestic, giving out in her strong contralto: America answers the call, America answers the call Tramp, tramp, tramp, tramp, tramp, The boys are marching...

There was no resisting the impulse. Standing behind the drop-curtain to hear what Clay had wrought, my feet began to feel a twitch. In a moment, I was marking time, then I started marching out myself to the beat of the drummer, to and fro behind Lee. Feeling the same impulse, Gertie fell into step behind me until the curtains were swaying as if in a high breeze.

Within seconds, an irate Clay Smith was backstage, accompanied by an equally irate 'Uncle' André Charlot. Both Bea and Gertie were immediately given ten days' notice to quit the show. It was not an auspicious start to Gertie's first West End engagement.

3

A STAR DANCED

The following morning, Charlot sent for the two girls and told them that they would not he dismissed after all: Bea, he said, was irreplaceable (a home truth in the comfortable knowledge of which Miss Lillie was to revel for the rest of her eccentric career) and Gertie had been reprieved at the special request of Clay Smith, who was not (at least at that time) a man to bear a grudge.

The reprieve did not, however, make either Gertie or Bea any better behaved backstage; they were like a couple of naughty schoolgirls and their relationship from this time forward was akin to that of two incurable pranksters let loose in a world which, already unreal enough, could easily be sabotaged with highly enjoyable results. A week or two after the saga of the 'Tramp, tramp, tramp' song, Bea noticed that Lee White (who like her husband Clay Smith had money in the show and therefore a considerable share of the solo numbers) was doing a song in the second half called 'Have You Seen the Ducks Go By?', which required a number of the chorus girls, including Gertie, to cross the stage behind a wall, revealing only their hats which were, suitably enough, in the shape of ducks. This was altogether too much of a temptation for Gertie:

> I couldn't help making my duck frisk about and behave as no properly drilled duck would ever do. Nor could I resist popping my head up over the wall in the wrong place, winking at the audience, and laughing when they laughed at me. Naturally Lee did not like this in the least. But Bea Lillie adored it, and would join us in the chorus and pop her head up over the wall, minus the duck head-dress but wearing a man's straw hat and a false moustache... finally both Lee and Clay stopped speaking to us at all.

Quite apart from the ingratitude shown by Gertie to the couple who, whatever their inability to share a joke, had actually taken the trouble to get her out of a second-rate touring revue and into the West End, to anyone used to the more formal atmosphere of present-day theatre, Bea and Gertie's lively behaviour on-stage must be rather surprising. The reason that they got away with it seems to have been that Bea was considered by Charlot as too important to dismiss, and Gertie too insignificant. To the question of motive, Gertrude Lawrence herself once came up with an eminently satisfactory answer:

> I suppose a psychologist could find a reason for the irrepressible impulse to play pranks which obsessed me for several seasons after I got started on the London stage. They were the kind of pranks that usually only

352

Gertrude Lawrence at ten

At twelve

As leader of the *Frolics*
at Murray's night-club in 1920

Child Stars no longer: Gertie and Noël Coward in his *London Calling!* And Gertie in two other numbers from the show…

'…Parisian Pierrot'

'…Poor Little Rich Girl'

'Fallen Babies': Gertie (*left*) and Bea Lillie in the Charlot parody of Coward's *Fallen Angels*

After the midnight first-night of *Charlot's Revue*, 1925: (*left to right, back row*) André Charlot, Joseph Coyne, Herbert Mundin, Peter Haddon, Jack Hulbert, Leslie Henson, George Grossmith, Noel Coward, Laddie Cliff, Henry Kendal, Jack Buchanan and Morris Harvey; (*third row*) Fay Compton, Phyllis Dare, Phyllis Monkman, Maisie Gay, Lillian Braithwaite, Violet Loraine and Zena Dare; (*second row*) Cicely Courtneidge, Gwen Farrar, Nora Blaney, Isabel Jeans, June, Heather Thatcher and Ivy St Helier; (*front row*) Rosaline Courtneidge, Irene Browne, Tallulah Bankhead, Beatrice Lillie, Gertrude Lawrence and Dorothy Dickson

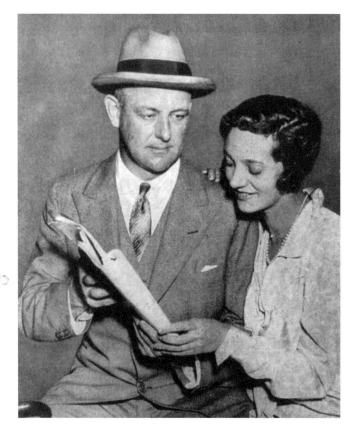

With P. G. Wodehouse during rehearsals for *Oh, Kay!*

Gertie, who had a long career in advertising, seen dining at Grosvenor House, London, with Doug and a well-known pale ale.

With Leslie Howard in *Candle-Light*, 1929

Noël and Gertie in 'Family Album', one of the nine plays from *Tonight at Eight-Thirty*, 1936

As Lisa, the *Lady in the Dark*, in Moss Hart and Kurt Weill's revolutionary Broadway musical, 1941

Star in battledress: Gertie as a driver for the American Red Cross

With Raymond Massey in *Pygmalion*, Broadway, 1949

Her last London appearance, in Daphne du Maurier's *September Tide*, 1949

'Shall We Dance?' with Yul Brynner in her final Broadway musical, *The King and I*, 1951

schoolchildren think are funny – fake telegrams, keyholes stuffed with soap, coat sleeves sewn up at the cuffs so that the victim found it impossible to make a quick change of costume. If it seems strange that I should have taken such liberties after I had been at such pains to get an opportunity in a London production, I can only explain these idiosyncrasies of mine on the ground that I must have been making up for those years when I had been working at a time when most children my age were playing games. Perhaps, it was just something I had to get out of my system. Perhaps, too, it was the not abnormal reaction of a girl who suddenly found herself made much of for the first time in her life. On looking back it seems to me extraordinary the patience which André Charlot had with me during those seasons. I must have been an unmitigated nuisance – to him and to all the other members of the company. What I needed was to have someone tick me off.

But that time was still to come. Meanwhile, her one-show engagement at the Vaudeville was turning into a permanent Charlot season; as *Some* came to the end of its run there, the decision was made to replace it with another Charlot revue. This one, which opened early in 1917, was called *Cheep!* and again it starred Clay Smith and Lee White. Harry Grattan was billed as sole author (though a footnote added 'Songs by Clay Smith, Bert Lee and R. P. Weston') and it was further announced in the programme that 'This show is staged by the Author because we could not afford a real producer.' The rest of the cast stayed much the same, with Bea Lillie getting billed now in thicker type than anyone save Lee White, and the critic of the *Observer* thought that 'this was without exception the wittiest, most amusing and prettiest revue to be seen in town.'

Gertie was still being used in the chorus and to understudy Bea, who had thus far not missed a single performance of either show; her freedom of manoeuvre on stage was (probably because of her behaviour during *Some*) severely curtailed, and Charlot made very sure that she would never again get the chance of the kind of disruption she had earlier managed to create with the ducks. As a result, she was getting thoroughly bored and looking for a way out of *Cheep!* when one unexpectedly presented itself. On 11 July 1917, from her shared dressing-room at the Vaudeville, she wrote to André Charlot:

I have heard today that *Some* is to go on tour in a few weeks' time, and I want to ask you if I might be allowed to join that company? You see, Mr Charlot, I feel an awful outsider in the show here at present, especially after all my little parts in *Some,* and as I have done a good deal of male impersonation I am daring to ask you – if you haven't settled on somebody else already might I take Miss Lillie's roles on the tour? Or failing that Billie Carleton's? The latter is a very easy task, and after having played Blanche Marie on tour in *The Little Michus* for eight months I think I am quite capable. Anyway, will you try me? I do so want to make good, and seem to be making very little headway here at present. Do answer this, or let me see you myself. Awaiting your reply, Yours very sincerely, Gertrude Lawrence.

Grasping the chance to separate Gertie and Bea at last, and perhaps also recognizing that there was indeed in Gertie something special which was not exactly being brought to the fore by a job in the back row of a chorus at the Vaudeville, Charlot agreed to send her out on tour doing the Bea Lillie material from *Some*.

By the time that tour ended and she was back in the chorus of *Cheep!*, certain things had become abundantly clear to Gertie. First, though she had enjoyed at last having a go at Bea's numbers, she had also discovered that there wasn't much point in starring in towns so obscure that nobody in the audience would ever be likely to do you any professional good. Second and more important, however, she had discovered that she could handle a star number. It had been nearly a decade since Italia Conti and the ballet mistress Madame Espinosa had first taken her into their classes, nearly a decade since some singing teacher had put a piece of paper under the strings of a piano and told her that was what her tinnily vibrating cockney voice sounded like, and that she would have to work on it if it was ever to sound even faintly musical.

Now it did, but who was to hear it? Back at the Vaudeville, Gertie put the problem to Beatrice Lillie, who quickly came up with her own brand of solution:

My understudy may have been a latent star, but she needed assistance to help her shine. She had to have a chance to prove herself to Charlot and the rest of the cast by playing for me. After a certain amount of soul-searching (was it the right thing to do, to put friendship ahead of my public, etc.?) I telephoned the theatre one morning. 'I'm in bed', I lied in a croaky whisper, 'with a temperature of a hundred and three. If it goes any higher, I'm going to sell.' So that night, with the same delicious feeling you get playing hooky from school, I took a busman's holiday and went to see Oscar Asche in *Chu-Chin-Chow*.

So for that one night in late 1917, Gertrude Lawrence made her starring debut in the West End 'due to the indisposition of Miss Beatrice Lillie.' By all accounts she did well enough, but Bea did not intend to stay phonily 'indisposed' for more than a single night, so the next day it was back to the chorus, which was where Gertie stayed for the rest of the run of that revue.

Away from the theatre, her life was becoming romantically active enough to take her mind at least temporarily off her boredom at the Vaudeville. Though she was still too far down the cast list to attract the attention of any of the wealthy admirers who would later be found at so many of her stage doors, she had briefly become engaged 'to a boy then serving in the balloon barrage which protected London.' That romantic wartime liaison finished however almost as rapidly as it had started, and Gertie had then met one of Charlot's dance directors, a Blackpool man by the name of Francis Gordon-Howley:

> Frank was twenty years my senior, and I was immensely flattered by his attention. Moreover he belonged to my world – the world of the theatre. He spoke my language – that of the theatre. He was a director, and he talked to me of his future plans in which I figured as his star. Other boyfriends had expected me to marry them and leave the theatre; Frank expected me to marry him and stay in the theatre.

And she did. By the beginning of 1918, without missing a single night at the Vaudeville, Gertrude Lawrence had managed to get herself married – and pregnant, though whether by Frank Howley or the 'barrage balloon boy' was never entirely clear. Howley was a modest and by all accounts charming character, no Svengali, and Gertie was by now certainly not some wilting Trilby; yet there's no doubt that their relationship both before and during their short-lived marriage was more one of father and daughter than of husband and wife. Quite apart from the twenty-year difference in their ages, Howley was – though never too successfully – a talent scout and a moulder of singers and dancers, and just as he recognized in Gertie 'someone to do something with', so she recognized in him a father she had never had and a manager who might do something to get her still uneventful career off the ground. The trouble, although it didn't become apparent until several months later, was that Howley (unlike Charlot) was not a man who would ever manage to become an all-powerful impresario.

For the time being, life proceeded reasonably calmly; Charlot had raised Gertie's salary from £3 to £4 a week at the Vaudeville, and she and Howley took a small flat in Carlton Mansions, Maida Vale, where they were soon joined by Frank's two brothers. Howley wasn't actually working at this time, or indeed at almost any time during their brief marriage, but the idea was that he would raise the money to form his own production company, which would then present shows in which Gertie would naturally be the leading lady. Quite where this money was to come from never became altogether clear, but before she had too much time to worry about that there was better news for Miss Lawrence (as she was still known). *Cheep!* was to be replaced at the Vaudeville in May 1918 by a third Charlot revue entitled *Tabs*. By now Clay Smith and Lee White had returned to America and the stars of *Tabs* were therefore to be Bea Lillie and a young singer-dancer with whom Gertie was to work frequently in the near future, Walter Williams. But the best news about *Tabs* was that there in the poster billing (admittedly in thirteenth place out of a cast of fourteen) was at last the name Gertrude Lawrence and, more important still, two of the twenty-two numbers in the show were to be hers.

Overall credit for the words and music of *Tabs* was taken by Ronald Jeans and an up-and-coming Welsh composer by the name of Ivor Novello, though Gertie didn't sing any of Novello's music; her two numbers were 'I Love You for Loving Me' (lyrics Ronald Jeans, music Bob Adams) and 'Dinkey Diddle-Ums' (Mills–Scott–Long), both of which appear to have sunk more or less without trace – certainly they were not exactly on the lips of every whistling messenger boy who passed the Vaudeville on his way up the Strand in that last summer of the First World War.

Tabs opened to the glowing reviews that Charlot had by now come to expect, but Gertie had begun to get more than a little careless about understudy rehearsals, with the result that Charlot had taken that job away from her and re-assigned it to a young girl named Jessie Matthews. As Bea Lillie was renowned for never being 'off', the whole question of who should understudy her seemed to Gertie more than a little academic. Luckily, however, her husband began to miss the extra pound or so a week which the understudying paid, and after a month or two convinced Gertie that she should go back to it which, with Charlot's benevolence, she did. And only in the nick of time.

One morning in July Bea Lillie, as was her wont, went out riding in Hyde Park as part of what one gossip column described as 'a merry group including Eileen Molyneux, Princess Clementine and Prince Napoleon.' Only that morning it wasn't quite so merry; Bea's horse threw her to the ground, resulting in medium concussion, a bent collarbone which had to be in plaster for the next month, and Bea's celebrated comment, 'The next horse I ride on, I'm going to be tied on.'

Gertie's big chance had come and not, in her view, a moment too soon. There was just one snag. She was by now seven months pregnant:

> My chance – the chance I'd longed for for years. The chance every understudy dreams about – the star suddenly ill, or meeting with an accident, and the little understudy having to step in and take her place. Now this had happened to me. As I stood there in Bea's dressing-room and her dresser helped me with swift, experienced fingers I thought 'The irony of it. It has happened to me just now when I'm feeling so ill'… In a couple of numbers Bea was doing male impersonations. For these she wore a white tie and tails. The black broadcloth suit was cut perfectly and fitted her slim, straight body like a glove. I held my breath while the dresser laced me up tightly; then I got into the trousers and white waistcoat… When my call came, I went on and for the first time in my life on the stage I knew anxiety. Bea was a tremendous favourite. Most of the audience had come on purpose to see her. Could I satisfy them? If I could hold that audience, if I could make them laugh and applaud and like Gertrude Lawrence, then the rest of my career was assured. If I failed…

But she didn't; when she finally came offstage two and a half hours later Charlot was standing in the wings grinning broadly. It was all Gertie needed to know and for the next two months, getting ever more pregnant, she played show after show until finally a message came from Bea: 'I don't know about the horse, but I'm fit for work again.'

It was agreed Bea would return to *Tabs* the following Monday; that Saturday, Frank went up to Liverpool where he had heard of a possible directing job. His two brothers were in the Maida Vale flat with Gertie, both in bed with influenza. Feeling distinctly queasy, she left alone for the theatre and played both houses; as the final curtain fell, she knew she was going to have the baby. Not in a matter of days or weeks, but in a matter of hours. Leaving the stage door, she decided the best idea would be to go home to mother, with whom there had been a sort of uneasy *rapprochement* since her marriage. Cabs were not in those days inclined to travel all the way to Clapham, especially since raging over London that night was one of the worst air raids of the war. Eventually she stopped a policeman who in turn bullied a cab driver; once arrived in Clapham she was bundled by mother straight into a nearby nursing home and by the Monday night, as Bea Lillie returned to her starring role in *Tabs,* her understudy was the proud possessor of a little girl called Pamela.

When, for the first and last time in her life, she became a mother (she eventually had an operation to prevent a recurrence of the event) Gertrude Lawrence was just twenty and had been married less than a year; the baby, she announced firmly in her autobiography, was in any case 'several months premature'. Though the drama of Pamela's birth nearly fitted the 'born in a trunk' cliché and neatly belonged to the scenario of the cut-price romantic novel within which so much of Gertie's life was already being lived, the arrival of a child broke the traditional requirements of romantic fiction by totally destroying rather than saving the already tattered Howley marriage.

Frank returned from Liverpool still jobless, pawned one of Gertie's rings to cover his expenses, and left her to settle the nursing home account. There being virtually no money at all now, the lease of the Maida Vale flat was given up and Gertie took the new baby home to Mother, leaving Frank to his own resources. After a spirited but all too characteristically unsuccessful attempt to kidnap his own child, Frank decided that enough was enough. He asked for one last meeting with Gertie, at the Lyons' Corner House where they had first planned to marry, and agreed that if she would give him all the money then in her purse, which came to about £5, he would go to live in Manchester and run a casting agency for pantomime dancers; which, until he took to running a boarding house there, was precisely what he did.

The failure of the marriage had not of course been his fault alone, as his daughter Pamela discovered some years later when, as an adult, she finally got to know him:

When my own eldest child, his grandson, was about three my father came down from Manchester to stay with us, and he brought his second wife, an ex-Tiller Girl, who had, unlike my mother, been able to make him very happy. It was only about the third time we'd ever met; once he'd come to visit me at Roedean and once when I was on tour in Manchester with a play he came backstage and bought me a hideous blue tulle evening dress, which, to be fair to Daddy, I chose myself because of the diamanté scattered over it like something out of *Come Dancing*. But when he came to stay with us he told me, and I believe it, that he had decided on purpose not to see me because he didn't want me to feel torn between two parents. He was very modest, very unassuming and I think that what went wrong with their marriage was quite simply that Mummy had begun to be a success and he hadn't. In those days if that sort of thing happened at all it usually happened the other way around, with the man getting bored of the wife he had married when times were hard, and then going off in search of something more glamorous when times got better. In this case it was the wife who outgrew the husband; my mother just left my father behind. It was as simple as that: he'd married an understudy and by the time I was born a few months later she'd taken over a starring role. She wasn't about to go back to the chorus, and she knew that he didn't have anything to offer that she hadn't already outgrown. I wasn't enough to keep them together, but what month-old baby ever could have been?

4

FORCED TO TOUR

So, as the First World War dragged to its November close, Gertrude Lawrence found herself at the head of a one-parent family; so far as she, none too regretfully, was concerned, there was to be no further contact with Howley and divorce proceedings were soon under way. She and her baby were now safely installed with mother in Clapham, and though the terraced house at 14, Lydon Road was less than glamorous, it did represent a kind of security.

Charlot, in recognition of Gertie's new-found status as a mother, increased her salary at the Vaudeville to £6 a week, but with Bea now fully recovered from her fall, Gertie found it difficult and depressing to return to her old chorus-and-supporting status. In December of that year, however, *Tabs* was replaced by a fourth Charlot revue entitled *Buzz, Buzz,* in which she was given not only such solos as 'Winnie the Window Cleaner' but also some straight romantic numbers with Walter Williams. Bea Lillie had by this time left the Vaudeville team, but Gertie was not her clear heiress apparent; certainly she had at last escaped the line of girl dancers, yet without managing to establish herself as the company's leading lady either.

The relationship with Charlot continued to deteriorate as, soon after the first night, Gertie returned to her old on-stage tricks in an attempt to alleviate what looked like the boredom of a long run and her depression at not having been allowed to step straight into Bea's shoes. Off-stage, however, her life took an altogether more cheerful turn: the little money she was earning was at least regular, and she soon realized that her mother would be happy to keep Pamela with her in Clapham even if she, Gertie, were not actually to return there every night. Early in 1919, she therefore took a share in a small Mayfair flat and proceeded, carefully and insistently, to work her way into high society. One of her Charlot understudies, June (later Lady Inverclyde) recalled:

> She was a wraith of a girl, not at all pretty but extraordinarily magnetic, who appeared to live on an inexhaustible fund of nervous vitality. Her sole mainstays were guts and gallantry and a driving determination to succeed. The men pouring back from the war were eager for carefree enjoyment and Gertie handed it to them in hunks. They filled the stalls and boxes of the Vaudeville and every night her chintzy little dressing-room housed bevvies of young officers. I used to see them lolling against the walls, lounging on the couch, and hear their laughing responses to

Gertie's saucy wit. There did not seem to be a shy bone in her body. She didn't care what she said or did in public, so long as it drew attention to her... I think she would have dyed her hair pink if she had felt the occasion warranted it. She adored playing to the public both on and off the stage. For her, the unwritten law that actresses should only be seen across the footlights did not exist. Gertie was seen everywhere: wearing a flying helmet or ludicrously swinging a tennis racquet at the newly-founded Hendon Flying Club; lunching in the best restaurants; dancing at the best nightclubs; peering into Cartier's windows. Her moods were mercurial and she began to cultivate a variety of accents; rowdy, county, blasé, – all to be used at the right time in the right place.

These were just beginning to be the years of the bright young things, the Café Society and Coward's poor little rich girls; the years when any reasonably attractive chorus girl who was half-way good in bed could be fairly certain of marrying, if not actually into the aristocracy (though that too often happened), at least into an altogether better social and financial circle than the one she had been born into. Theatre at this time was a social rather than an intellectual event, and it brought together as never before or since two totally separate worlds: most theatre people of the era came from backgrounds they were fast trying to forget, and were in any case the first generation not to be made to feel ashamed of their trade. Most of the young male aristocracy, already jolted by war, were having a hard time settling back into country life with girls who reminded them all too clearly of their mothers or sisters. For both teams of escapers, the stage door provided a meeting place, a kind of neutral territory where, safe from their own and each others' families, discreet liaisons could be formed and pursued through innumerable late-night suppers and Mayfair flats.

Moreover, at a time when progress in the theatre tended to be accidental and arbitrary, rather than the result of careful career-planning, a girl with the right friends, who turned up in the right nightclubs and therefore next morning in the right gossip-columns, was more likely to catch the eye of a producer than a girl who spent her spare evenings at ballet classes. To become a star in the theatre, unless an exclusively Shakespearian career was envisaged, you had also to become a star outside the theatre and it was, however sub-consciously, to that project Gertrude Lawrence now turned her attentions.

It led her at first into a good deal of trouble. In organizing for herself some sort of private life away from mother, the baby and Clapham, she turned first to her old child-actor friends; Noël was already hard at work in *Scandal* at the Strand Theatre, but he and Ivor Novello (whom she had first met as the composer of Charlot's *Tabs*) separately introduced her around and about to a whole new world of late-night suppers and discreet attachments, which, added to the strain of still doing eight shows a week at the Vaudeville, rapidly led her into a state of exhaustion. Pleading a combination of lumbago and tonsillitis, she persuaded the long-suffering Charlot to release her from *Buzz, Buzz* for a fortnight while she recuperated. All might have been well had she not agreed, towards the end of the fortnight (when she was already feeling distinctly better) to join a party Novello was making up to go to a new Ethel Baird opening night. As luck would have it, in the theatre seat next to hers sat André Charlot. And that was it. He'd put up with nearly three years of Gertie fooling about on stage and off, and his patience was now exhausted. She had been away from his show for more than six performances, which allowed him to cancel her contract, and the next morning she received a note from him in which he did just that. 'If you are well enough to go to other people's plays' his note ended, not unreasonably, 'you are well enough to come to your own.'

She was out of a job and, what was worse, in London's small and tight-knit theatrical community, every other management soon knew why. Codes of behaviour were at the time curious but distinct: no producer much minded what a young actress got up to in her spare time, but she was still expected to be on stage eight times a week. Already Gertie had broken that rule and was being considered 'unreliable'. Moreover her West End career had been solely in Charlot revues at the Vaudeville, which were a law, and a language, unto themselves. There was no reason to believe she could do anything else but Charlot revues, and it was from a Charlot revue that she had just been sacked.

Gertie was not one to take that sort of thing lying down; having rapidly discovered that stage doors were now barred to her, she looked around for another job and rapidly found one. One of the newer London landmarks of this time was a nightclub called Murray's; far-sightedly joining in the new cabaret craze, it began providing its upper-crust customers with the best floorshow in town, a carefully choreographed all-singing, all-dancing extravaganza, a miniaturised version of one of the Cochran or Charlot revues. Its over-riding attraction was that you could eat and drink, maybe even talk, during the entertainment and that its stars were expected (if not actually forced) to join your table for a little champagne afterwards.

Early in 1919 Gertrude Lawrence applied for a job there, and Murray's was to become her professional home for almost the whole of the next two years. It is difficult now to assess whether she or the club got the better deal. From the club's point of view, it acquired for the first time a 'legit' singer and dancer, somebody who had actually worked with Charlot and Bea Lillie at the Vaudeville instead of on the usual showgirl-club circuit. From Gertie's point of view, she was able to star (only, admittedly, in a forty-minute show) in the West End still, but was now able to get into direct contact with her admirers without having to run the risk that the most promising or desirable of them might not bother to make the journey round to the stage door.

It was at Murray's that Gertie caught the eye of the Duke of Kent and the future Edward VIII; it was there too that she began to be noticed, not only by the 'beautiful people' of her day but by journalists and by stars and directors from the legitimate theatre (still her first love) who, by dropping in to the club's midnight show on the way home from their dressing-rooms, were able to see and applaud Gertie as they never would had she been playing a show with the same curtain-times as theirs. In a social if not in a professional sense, her nightclub work at Murray's was the making of Gertrude Lawrence, for it was there that she was first seen by Captain Philip Astley.

The son of a wealthy country clergyman, Astley had been born at Chequers, the country house later given to the nation as a weekend residence for the Prime Minister of the day. Not only that, noted Gertie eagerly, but:

> He was christened in the robes of Oliver Cromwell, and educated at Eton and the Royal Military College, added to which he was desperately good-looking and had unparalleled charm. We had to fall in love with each other: it was as natural and instinctive to us as to breathe.

Though later each was seriously to consider marriage to the other (usually at different times), for the present there could be no thought of it; Gertie was still officially Mrs Gordon-Howley, and for Astley to have been involved in divorce proceedings would have ruined a promising career in the Household Cavalry. Astley fast became almost everything to Gertie: lover, escort, friend, adviser and above all tutor in the social ways of the world to which Gertie still most wanted to belong.

> Philip [recalled his last wife] was at that time the perfect young man about town: he was handsome, he was rich, he was experienced, he owned a positively enormous car complete with chauffeur, and his family had by now grown accustomed to him going out with actresses. There had been one before Gertie, and when Philip went to see his mother to tell her there was a problem she simply reached under her pillow and brought out an envelope full of pound notes and said, 'I think you'll find that will solve it.'

This time it was rather different; Philip was rapidly falling deeply in love with Gertie, and they were to stay together for the best part of the 1920s until, much to Gertie's regret and rage, he eventually married Madeleine Carroll. But Astley's influence on Gertie, and his importance to her, was as crucial in the social sphere as was Coward's in the theatre and it was Noël's friend and biographer Cole Lesley who once explained the significance of the Astley-Lawrence partnership:

> Gertie was taught everything by Philip, who guided her taste in clothes and everything else and she, monkey-quick, picked up from him every

trick of behaviour and social jargon until the girl from Brixton emerged during their long relationship as a perfectly polished product of Mayfair.

Gertie did not come of a generation who took pride in humble origins; she was genuinely ashamed of her social background, eager to forget both mother and daughter in Clapham and to rebuild herself in the image of the early 1920s lady about town, a fitting partner for Captain Astley and a guest who would not disgrace herself with the wrong fork at dinner with the Prince of Wales, for that was now the exalted circle in which the girl from Murray's was starting to move:

> I'll never forget dashing into my dressing-room one night to find the Duke of Kent seated before my mirror, trying on a wig of long, false curls... I was often invited (because of Philip) to the parties which the Prince of Wales gave in his apartment at St James's Palace, at which everyone sang and danced and did stunts. These parties were always informal and entertaining. You met people of all sorts and from every walk of life and profession, but never anyone who was dull or stuffy. He invited international tennis champions, the newest blues singer, a guitarist who was all the rage in Paris, as well as his own intimate set. It was amusing that all this fun went on late at night inside the solemn old pile, with the sentries keeping up their march along the pavement just outside... the Prince once took me on a tour of the state apartments in the palace. We paused at the window from which, according to the centuries-old tradition, every new sovereign is acclaimed on his accession to the throne. Each of us was thinking silently that someday the King's herald would proclaim from the balcony outside that very window: 'The King is dead – long live King Edward VIII'... at that time, during the early 1920s, no one in London had even heard of Mrs Wallis Warfield Simpson.

They were, however, beginning to hear about Gertrude Lawrence; her fame at Murray's was spreading to such an extent that even André Charlot came to see her there. She was good, he admitted, so good that it was high time she got herself back into the legitimate theatre rather than run the risk of becoming London's leading nightclub girl. Gertie saw that danger, as did Philip; but Charlot wasn't going to take her back even now, and no other West End manager who came into Murray's came clutching a contract for her.

To her credit (and perhaps also because of the increasingly sensible advice about her career she was getting from Astley) Gertie gave up a lucrative engagement at Murray's towards the end of 1920 and began to work her passage back into the straight theatre. At first all she could get was a touring revue called *The Midnight Frolics*, followed at Christmas 1920 by a job understudying Phyllis Dare as the Princess in *Aladdin,* that year's pantomime at the London Hippodrome. But part of the deal was that she would be allowed to play some matinées, which she did, and when that closed she spent the best part of 1921 touring music-halls in London and around the country as part of a double-act she'd formed with Walter Williams.

Williams was by now enjoying considerable success as the singer of 'K-K-Katie' and together, billing themselves as 'Straight from London' and using some of Charlot's old revue material without worrying too much about copyright fees, he and Gertie managed to get themselves some good top-of-the-bill bookings on the old Moss Empire circuit, Vaudeville experience that was to stand her in good stead when fifteen years later she came to play in Coward's *Red Peppers*.

But the touring life of a music-hall act did not suit Gertie's highly social domestic arrangements, and what she wanted was a show in London. When one did not materialize, she decided to take a few months off and (with a little financial help from Astley) rented a summer cottage by the Thames near Windsor. There, for the first time (and again at Astley's prompting) she began to get to know her now two-and-a-half-year-old daughter, whom she had invited along with her mother to stay with her. Gertie later recalled:

> Among our gay [an accurate description in its current usage] companions at that time was Lord Lathom, and several times he and Philip and the others would stop at Buck's Club, pick up a hamper of chicken, fruit, champagne etcetera and we would all roar down to the cottage and get mother out of bed to act as hostess... one night, we gave her a real surprise. We all arrived without warning, as usual, and routed her out of bed. Down she came, and we had supper. Suddenly she realised that there was a stranger in our midst and that we were calling him 'Sir'. Her gaze shot down the table, past his face, and fixed itself on my delighted grin; I nodded. I knew she had recognised the Prince of Wales.

Somehow it all seemed a long way from Clapham and the moonlight flits, but it was not advancing Gertie's theatrical career. Indeed she might have stayed by the river at Windsor giving gracious surprise supper parties for the rest of the 1920s (many ex-showgirls did) had it not been, in that late summer of 1921, for a magical and almost eerie repetition of events from her recent past.

André Charlot was again preparing a new revue to be entitled *A to Z* and, since it was destined for the Prince of Wales Theatre, it would have to be on an infinitely larger scale than anything he had ever done at the Vaudeville. A starry cast was to he headed by the famous American close-harmony Trix Sisters and Jack Buchanan; the other leading female role Charlot had given to his stalwart comedienne from the Vaudeville, Beatrice Lillie. In September they began rehearsing and by the end of that month Bea was in hospital with a recurrence of back trouble. *A to Z* had an opening date fixed for October, sets were built, musicians hired, and there was no way they could wait for Miss Lillie to return. Charlot thought back to the last time this had happened, and decided that if history was repeating itself then so would he; messages were sent to the riverside cottage and by the following morning Gertie was rehearsing Bea's numbers.

Though the best of the songs were supposed to go to the Trix Sisters, there was one, 'Limehouse Blues', which had somehow got away and was set up as a duet for Gertie and Jack Buchanan, who had not worked together before; later the song became one of her most constant and profitable hits on record. Written by Philip Braham and Douglas Furber, it began:

> In Limehouse, where yellow ladies dance and play,
> In Limehouse, you can hear those blues all day...

'Limehouse Blues' led *The Times* critic to describe *A to Z* as 'all Charlot, Charm and Chinatown.' The score also featured Novello's 'And Her Mother Came Too' as a solo for Buchanan. All in all, *A to Z* had so much going for it that they survived at the Prince of Wales for 428 performances, a run of fourteen months, which allowed Bea Lillie eventually to step back into the numbers that had originally been meant for her. The success of *A to Z* did both Buchanan and Gertrude Lawrence a power of good; while the programme was advertising *dîners dansant* and nightclub suppers for eight shillings a head, Gertie could relax in the knowledge that she was back in the real theatre at last.

Her friendships now divided into two distinct categories; there were her theatre friends – Noël, Bea, Buchanan – and then there were her 'grand' friends; and the two groups sometimes led her into considerable social uncertainty. Bea Lillie once recalled how she and Buchanan were being shown by Gertie around an especially palatial new flat she had rented:

> After she had taken us on a conducted tour of its splendours, Jack asked, 'Why do you need a place as big as this?' 'Oh, but wait,"'she said. 'You see, I now have a chauffeur and three mehds.' 'Three whats?' I said. 'Mehds.' I still didn't get it. 'How do you spell it?' 'Mehd. M-A-I-D. And then I have a butler, and...' I don't remember whether it was Jack or I who threw the first cushion at her. I know we knocked her down, literally. It did her good now and then. She was a darling, but she sometimes behaved like an Empress of China.

As she settled in to the Prince of Wales Theatre, where she was to spend almost the whole of 1922 happily engaged in *A to Z*, Gertie at last had the chance to get herself into some sort of order; with Philip Astley in almost constant attendance she was able to lead the kind of social and theatrical life that until now had been at best an ambition. In the West End she, Buchanan and Charlot were already part of a team, one that would go on soon to conquer Broadway as well; more important, they were working in a comparatively new theatrical form of 'intimate' revue, which perfectly caught the somewhat frenzied spirit of the times. 'Revue', wrote Herbert Farjeon, one of its greatest practitioners, 'is a form of entertainment so designed that it matters neither how late you reach it nor how early you have to leave it.' The sequence of songs, short comedy sketches and dance numbers, each more or less self-contained and unlikely to last more than a matter of minutes, was ideally suited to audiences who were apt to find their attention wandering. The 1920s were not a time of deep dedication to a single topic for a long period of time, which was why on balance revues usually did better business than straight plays. This was the era of revue, and of revue Gertrude Lawrence was now the newest and brightest star.

Privately, too, things were going very well: several years later stars as diverse as Madeleine Carroll and David Niven were to acknowledge the importance of Astley's friendship and advice, but Gertie was the first, best and most important of his 'creations'. It was because of him that her dressing-room was filled night after night not only with flowers but also with princes of the blood royal and, so linked at that time were stage and society, that the more fashionable she was off stage, the greater her box-office value was too. For all that, the mockery of Bea Lillie was a low price to pay. Gertrude Lawrence was now the flavour of the month and the problem became not how to make it, but how to make it last.

A to Z, apart from being among the very best of all Charlot's many revues, proved a splendid showcase for Gertie's now considerable talent. Whether doing the despair of ' Limehouse Blues'…

Poor broken blossom
And nobody's child,
Haunted and taunted
You're just kind of wild

…or the infinitely more upbeat and jolly double with Buchanan:

A cup of coffee, a sandwich, and you,
A cosy corner – a table for two…

she was proving night after night and twice on Saturdays that, unlike many better actresses, she had the gift for instant changes of mood, lightning switches from comedy to song to dance and back again. Moreover she was a quick study, able to accept new material suddenly thrown at her an hour or two before the show in an attempt to keep it topical through changing newspaper headlines. In an age before radio or television, when most London theatres were hermetically sealed with unchanging productions, revues were able to alter themselves from week to week according to changing public moods. They were of the moment for the moment, and so was Gertrude Lawrence.

After the show, the dinner parties were usually at Rule's in Maiden Lane, where Gertie later recalled:

> Walls lined with signed photographs of actors and actresses, boxing champions, cabinet ministers and marble busts of Shakespeare and Beerbohm Tree... the place was just the same as when Edward VII, then Prince of Wales, had given supper parties to Lillie Langtry in the private room upstairs. This was the room in which we had our parties and our young Prince of Wales sat where his grandfather had sat, enjoying our gay chatter.

Towards the end of the year Charlot took Gertie out of *A to Z,* giving Bea the chance she should have had a year earlier, and put her instead into an unenthralling but respectably successful Joseph Coyne musical comedy called *Dédé*, which ran through the winter at the Garrick; in Christmas week Charlot again moved her, with several other stars from shows of his all over London, to play in cabaret at the Hotel Metropole in *The Midnight Follies*, a task Gertie found considerably more sociable and therefore more enjoyable than working with Coyne at the Garrick. Then, early in 1923, it was time for another Charlot revue.

This one was to be on Charlot's home territory at the Vaudeville and was bizarrely entitled *Rats*, presumably in the hope that someone would then pronounce it a Rattling Good Show which several critics dutifully did. Its stars were Gertrude Lawrence and two male comedians, Alfred Lester and Herbert Mundin, and one of its more eccentric showstoppers was Gertie in full Ku-Klux-Klan costume singing a hymn to lynchings. Critics found the proceedings generally enchanting; 'Miss Lawrence', noted *The Times,* 'is dashing, full of assurance, extraordinary in facial expressions and with humour radiating from every limb and feature. It is high time she appeared in a stage comedy.'

5

PARISIAN PIERROT

O n a skiing holiday in Davos early in 1923 Noël Coward, Charlot and Lord Lathom worked out the basis for a revue which, in honour of the newly established British radio network, was to be known as *London Calling!* It was understood that the revue was to star Gertrude Lawrence, Maisie Gay and Noël himself together with one other comedian, but in view of Coward's total inexperience where revue was concerned, and because Charlot was less than enthusiastic about some of the material that he had already written, Ronald Jeans was brought in to help with the book and Philip Braham with the music – both men already tried and tested through countless earlier Charlot revues. Tubby Edlin was cast as the principal comedian, and there then developed some doubt as to whether or not Coward himself would actually appear in the show. Charlot was only offering him a weekly £15 – less than half what the others were now getting – and the salary did not therefore much appeal to Noël who held out for rather more on the grounds that, unlike the others, he was risking his prestige as a straight actor by appearing in revue.

Charlot, unmoved, refused to go over £15 and decided to find someone else for the job. He had, however, overlooked a clause neatly inserted in his contract by Noël, guaranteeing himself as part-author the right to approve or veto all major casting. For the next few weeks Noël regularly, politely and firmly objected to the casting suggestion of every juvenile lead in the business. Finally, with *London Calling!* on the very brink of rehearsal, Charlot was reluctantly forced to make him an offer of £40 a week, an offer that Noël was graciously pleased to accept with the demand only that he be given the right to escape after six months.

This granted, Noël began work on his singing and dancing, talents which had been left unpractised since his days as a child actor. Enlisting the help of Fred Astaire, who at that time was conveniently enough appearing with his sister Adele in the London production of *Stop Flirting*, Noël learnt enough to get through such numbers as 'Other Girls' and 'You Were Meant For Me' which he sang and danced with Gertie to choreography by Astaire himself.

After two postponements for alterations and more rehearsal, *London Calling!* (with costumes by Edward Molyneux) opened with no pre-London tour at a matinée on 4 September 1923 at the Duke of York's Theatre; the matinée was Charlot's idea, his theory being that as the entire company of artists and technicians were already exhausted by four long, hard and difficult weeks of rehearsal, the matinée (to which no critics were invited) would tire them even further, thus ensuring that the first evening performance, played entirely on raw nerves, would be remarkable for its nightmarish vivacity. The gamble worked; the first night went superbly and the reviews were ecstatic.

This first version of *London Calling!* included twenty-six numbers of which half were composed by Noël, although only 'Parisian Pierrot', which he wrote for Gertie and which, according to Cecil Beaton, she made into 'the signature tune of the late 1920s' managed to outlive its original setting. This was the first hit song Noël ever achieved, and he had written it during a brief holiday in Germany:

> The idea of it came to me in a nightclub in Berlin in 1922. A frowsy blonde, wearing a sequin chest-protector and a divided skirt, appeared in the course of the cabaret with a rag pierrot doll dressed in black velvet. She placed it on a cushion where it sprawled in pathetic abandon while she pranced round it emitting guttural noises. Her performance was unimpressive but the doll fascinated me. The title 'Parisian Pierrot' slipped into my mind, and in the taxi on the way back to the hotel the song began.

Of the show itself, Noël later recalled: 'I appeared constantly, singing and dancing and acting with unbridled vivacity and enjoying myself very much indeed.' But the critics at the first night of *London Calling!*, though still in love with Gertie, tended to be unimpressed by Mr Coward's musical gifts: 'He cannot compose', said the *Sunday Express,* 'and should sing only for his friends' amazement.' One number, 'Sentiment', staged by Fred Astaire, was particularly tricky for Noël:

> I would bound on stage immaculately dressed in tails, with a silk hat and cane and singing every couplet with perfect diction and a wealth of implication which sent the words winging out into the dark auditorium, where they fell wetly like pennies into mud.

Months later, in New York, Noël was to watch Jack Buchanan bringing the house down nightly with that same number, and had to admit ruefully to himself that Jack's seemingly effortless revue technique was then, as always, vastly superior to his own. But the reviews for *London Calling!* were not by any means all bad, though most critics found it a little long and Noël better at the writing than the performing. Two papers offered him, amidst all the praise for Gertie, dubious personal tributes. One called him 'the most promising amateur in the West End' and the other noted that he was 'unmistakeably talented, though not yet another Jack Hulbert.'

London Calling! settled into the Duke of York's for a lengthy run, despite Noël's rather grudging press and a celebrated feud with the Sitwell family who thought they recognized in one of the numbers, 'The Swiss Family Whittlebot', an all too accurate parody of themselves and their verse; just after the first night Osbert remarked acidly that as he was leaving town for the weekend he would have to miss the show, since it would doubtless have closed before he got back, to which Noël retorted that on the contrary they were in for a long run and he would be happy to place a stage box at the Sitwells' disposal from which they could see the show with *all* their supporters.

This was all good publicity, as were the full-length pictures that started to appear in the glossy weeklies of Gertie in her 'Parisian Pierrot' costume. She also had one or two numbers that required a certain amount of acting, not least 'Early Mourning', in which she played a society hostess hearing the awful news that her husband has just jumped off Waterloo Bridge, and then being told the even more awful news that he has not. But Gertie was still being thought of as a singer rather than an actress, and it was as a singer that Charlot was to take her to New York within a few weeks of the London opening of Coward's first revue.

No sooner was *London Calling!* safely away and running than Charlot had an even more ambitious idea. For the past year or two he had been casting vague glances over the Atlantic, made aware by the occasional offers that were reaching both him and his revue stars that Broadway had nothing quite like the kind of shows he had pioneered in London, and that it would pay well for them. In the autumn of 1923 he therefore decided to form a company of his own leading players, lift the best songs and sketches from his last half-dozen London revues, and take them all to New York.

This meant recasting *London Calling!* within three months of its opening (which did not much please Coward, who was left to play it on in London with a distinctly second-rate company) as Charlot took from the West End not only Gertie (who gave over her material in *London Calling!* to Joyce Barbour) but also Jack Buchanan and Beatrice Lillie to form the nucleus of his American company. Under the management of the American Archie Selwyn and Charlot together, they were to open on Broadway as *André Charlot's London Revue of 1924.*

Charlot himself had already been over to prepare the way and try to alert Broadway audiences to what they were to be asked to buy seats for:

When the American public is given a chance to see my London revue [he told the press] they will understand the difference between this type of show and vaudeville in America... over the years we have developed an intimate understanding between players and audience such as you do not know in this country. The mixture is hard to define since it depends not only on a company in which everyone – not just the principals – can sing and dance and act, but also on lighting and scenic effects which are simple but artistic. I intend to offer outstanding melody, humour, good taste and distinctive charm.

In short, Charlot was offering Broadway not just three unknowns, but three unknowns in an unknown kind of entertainment. Aware that he would therefore need all the help he could get, the first person he hired in New York was a press agent, Walter Wanger, later to be better known as the Hollywood producer of the epic Taylor-Burton *Cleopatra* and countless other films.

Wanger arrived in London, took a look at *London Calling!* and announced that though quiet good taste was all very well in its way, what Charlot would need for a Broadway hit could best be described as 'Oomph'. This he proposed to inject into the proceedings by arranging a talent contest to find 'The Most Beautiful Blonde In Britain', who would duly be given her chance to appear on Broadway in the chorus of the revue. Leaving nothing to chance, Wanger also selected the winner, a lady called Bobbie Storey who was then working as a barmaid at Rule's.

André Charlot's London Revue of 1924 did a week's English try-out (in what was still actually 1923) at the Golders Green Hippodrome where, noted the press, 'the Prince of Wales laughed as loudly as anyone else in the audience.' Carrying therefore an unofficial royal seal of approval, the company then set sail on the *Aquitania* for New York.

Both Gertie and Bea Lillie were leaving their small children with their grandmothers, but Bea seems to have felt rather more maternally deprived than Gertie, who was in any case now well accustomed to living apart from Pamela. The crossing was, by Bea's own account, a jolly one:

> Gertie and I made a shipboard friend of one of the season's glamour boys, Alastair McIntosh, who later married Constance Talmadge. When Gertie, Jack and I all told him that we had no idea where to stay in New York he ordered another drink all round and told us that he had a friend who owned the Ambassador Hotel on Park Avenue and that we'd be very happy there.

Lord Beaverbrook (then still Max Aitken) was also on board the *Aquitania,* where he christened Lawrence, Lillie and Buchanan 'the Big Three', a useful description which was to stay with them throughout their joint Broadway lives. The welcoming press conference held while they were still docking, was, however, less than successful for them; carefully briefed by Wanger, the gentlemen of the New York press and their photographers hurtled straight past the Big Three to get the story on Bobbie Storey, Britain's Most Beautiful Blonde Barmaid, who would now be appearing in the show as a result of the talent contest.

The others took it badly. Buchanan went down to the desk to ascertain what time the next ship was leaving for London, Bea felt 'that somebody had shot a hole in my middle' and it was left to Gertie to guide them both to the suites that had been reserved in their names at the Ambassador. It being still early morning, and Christmas Eve at that, Gertie ordered up the first editions of the evening papers:

> With cheeks that the mist and fog of London had tinted the colour of English roses [one report read] and with appearances as neat as the hedgerows in springtime, with eyes that glowed as brightly as the lights that illuminate Big Ben at night, and lips that laugh merrily, twenty-five beauties from the tight little isle across the sea who are due to appear in the André Charlot revue tripped lightly down the gangplank of the *Aquitania*.

One of those beauties was a totally unknown sixteen-year-old Jessie Matthews for whom the reality of New York was a little less than wonderful:

> I sat on my trunk in the customs shed and wondered what had hit me... it was nine o'clock on Christmas Eve and no one wanted me... a burly customs guard said 'You can always spend the night on Ellis Island, kiddo.'

Back at the Ambassador, things were going slightly better until Gertie ordered them a sizeable breakfast: 'sausages, eggs, slices of ham and bacon by the dozen; a bakeshop's fill of toast and muffins, firkins of coffee and glistening sections of a fruit none of us had set breakfast eyes on before called grapefruit.' The only thing wrong with that was the bill, which came to twenty-five dollars without the tip.

Guided by Buchanan's ever alert grasp of financial affairs, the three of them rapidly worked out that if twenty-five dollars was what the Ambassador was charging for breakfast, then none of them could afford to stay for lunch, let alone several weeks. The only solution was to leave, and leave fast. 'We shall need a cab, of course,' said Gertie. 'Can we afford it?' asked Jack. 'No', replied Bea, 'but you know Gertie.' This dialogue summarises almost too perfectly the characters and their relationships to each other. In the cab they headed straight for the Algonquin, which they had heard offered sanctuary to impoverished artists, writers and actors and had even in those early days a special affection for the British.

There was, after all, no indication yet that *Charlot's Revue of 1924* was actually going to succeed on Broadway, and in the meantime its stars could see little purpose in throwing money around even if there had been any to throw. Buchanan was at this time still walking down to the docks most evenings to enquire what times the boats left for London; Gertie and Bea, though faintly more optimistic about their theatrical chances, were less than reassured by their week's try-out in Atlantic City, where Bea overheard Selwyn himself muttering, 'Jeez – it stinks.'

By the time they got back to New York the entire cast was so enveloped in gloom that Bea didn't bother to unpack her suitcase, thinking she'd leave that task until she caught the boat home to England in what would doubtless only be a day or two. Nor were any of them much more reassured by their first glimpses of Broadway:

> Before our New York opening, [wrote Gertie later] Jack, Bea and I were taken to see all the shows on Broadway. We were very much impressed and rather frightened by the obvious lavishness of the productions in comparison with our intimate revue. As Jack said, 'It seemed to us that what New York wanted was hundreds of girls dressed in feathers, with tons of scenery studded with diamonds and ten-dollar bills.' We saw Grace Moore sing 'Orange Grove in California' for which song the entire theatre was perfumed by orange blossom. We wondered if we could compete, with our tiny show and our British humour.

That remained to be seen.

6

LILLIE AND LAWRENCE,
LAWRENCE AND LILLIE

In most, if not all, of her subsequent interviews for American papers, Gertrude Lawrence was to claim that she 'fell in love with New York on first sight.' The reality was something rather different; neither she nor Buchanan nor Bea Lillie had much cause to love their American impresario after Selwyn's celebrated remark about their show, nor had they much reason to believe – judging from the neighbouring shows they had already seen along Broadway – that what they had to offer would he of much interest or excitement to New York theatre-goers who then seemed to prefer the trappings of shows to the contents.

They therefore went into the Broadway opening of *André Charlot's London Revue of 1924* with a kind of resigned tolerance, genuinely anticipating rapid closure and already quite looking forward to a speedy return home. Only the young Jessie Matthews, understudying Gertie, was able to find much magic backstage:

> I used to stand out there in the darkened wings watching Gertie Lawrence rehearse a number. She was as lovely as a dream in her satin Pierrot costume, and I'd never seen such a beautiful stage picture as the set for 'Parisian Pierrot'. There were black velvet hangings and on the stage were masses of huge coloured velvet cushions... In my room at the Martha Washington Hotel, I'd scrape my hair under a tight handkerchief and pretend it was the little black skull cap that Gertie wore. I'd pull the pillows from the bed and lie on the floor like she did and sing 'Parisian Pierrot'. Every gesture that Gertie made I had practised, every movement I copied. By the time opening night arrived I was a little, undersized, immature carbon copy of Gertrude Lawrence, I knew every song, every dance, every nuance with which she held her audience in thrall.

Opening night was 9 January 1924; Selwyn had pleaded with Charlot and his company to 'Americanize' their material but they had all staunchly refused, preferring to keep to their original agreement, which had been to show Broadway the best of their London songs and sketches unchanged. And they were right. The sheer, unexpected originality of the *Charlot Revue* took the six Broadway critics (Heywood Broun, George Jean Nathan, Percy Hammond, Burns Mantle, Ring Lardner and Alec Woollcott) by storm; they had quite simply seen nothing like it in their entire theatre-going lives:

When André Charlot's company stepped out on the stage last night with their opening 'How do you do?' number, there was an immediate response between actors and audience. That cordial relationship continued throughout the evening and when the curtain fell, the fact was established that in *Charlot's Revue*, Broadway has something altogether new in the way of musical comedy.

What Woollcott and the others were experiencing was something which in London had been taken for granted, since there it had always been the rule for revues rather than the exception: the idea that an audience was composed of individual customers, guests in fact, who should he treated the way they would be treated by the best maître d'hôtel in the best restaurant in town. Buchanan above all, and to a lesser degree both Gertie and Bea, had stage presences which allowed them to play a number as if only to a single spectator at a time. The audience thus became a part of the show, just as diners become a part of a restaurant, and it was something no Vaudeville house had ever achieved. It was, in a word, intimacy.

Admittedly there was a certain anglophile snobbery in all this; Woollcott was then just making his name as a drama critic, and like all critics on the make he needed something to hang his hat on; fortunately for those involved with the *Charlot Revue*, he chose the English theatre and was to remain for the next two decades the best publicist any London actor or actress in New York could have desired. Besides, as became clear from Woollcott's very first column on the show, there was always a good story in the triumph of the underdog:

It is fair to suspect that Mr Ziegfeld and Mr George White (of *Follies* fame) must have fairly laughed themselves into a coma at the innocence of this London manager for thinking that any revue so airy and so unpretentious would not be trampled underfoot in New York. Why, the chorus was not half so populous as that of the *Follies*, and there wasn't so much as a yard of gold cloth in the whole thing.

Others were less amused; Walter Pidgeon, then an up-and-coming musical comedy star, told Michael Marshall that as the first-night curtain fell to tumultuous applause Irving Berlin was to be seen sitting motionless and ostentatiously refusing to clap. 'Sour grapes?' asked Elsie Janis; 'No', replied Berlin, 'I was just thinking that this entire production has cost less than the finale of one of my *Music Box* revues!'

Heywood Broun commented, 'Beatrice Lillie, Gertrude Lawrence and Jack Buchanan are worth a good deal more than their weight in gold cloth and velvet hangings' (another dig at Ziegfeld and White). By the time those notices hit the streets the Charlot team were the hottest performers in New York. It was from this moment that Gertrude Lawrence began to love the city which has always cherished its successes and cruelly rejected its failures.

Soon a little rhyme was to be on everyone's lips:

> Lillie and Lawrence,
> Lawrence and Lillie,
> If you haven't seen them,
> You're perfectly silly.

As the queues formed morning after morning outside the Selwyn Theatre, the cast settled down to a prolonged celebration. By staying at the Algonquin (which reminded Gertie, she said, of a really good cheap hotel in the Midlands) the Charlot stars found themselves in the midst of precisely the people who were most enjoying and most able to publicize their show. The present and future members of the Round Table there were all fervently pro-British, and were keen to promote something which seemed to rock the current Broadway establishment. Bea and Gertie (and to some extent Buchanan, though he was always more inclined to keep himself to himself, especially when abroad) became the Algonquin's favourite rebels, and it was there that they in turn met some of its greatest stars. The press were constantly requesting interviews; one morning the phone rang in the suite Gertie was still sharing with Bea and it was the latter who got to it first.

'Is this Miss Lillie from England?' asked a professional journalistic voice. 'This is the *New York Sun*. We'd like to be able to tell our readers, Miss Lillie, your feelings about the death of President Harding.'

'Who?'

'Our President, Miss Lillie, Warren Gamaliel Harding. He's dead. How do you feel about it?'

Even Bea was momentarily at a loss for words and Gertie, across the other side of the room, was no help either.

'Well,' Bea finally flustered, 'well, I mean, it's a great loss, isn't it? A man like that. What a terrible thing! How will you find another President now?'

There was a pause at the other end of the line. Then the reporter spoke again. 'As a matter of fact,' he said, 'President Harding died last August. I hope you will do better next time.' It was the American playwright Marc Connelly.

Despite the fact that due to an electrical fault on the neon sign outside the Selwyn their show was very often billed as *Harlot's Revue of 1924*, or maybe precisely because of it, tickets were by now virtually impossible to come by. No foreign artists, at any rate since Jenny Lind, had been welcomed quite like this and Woollcott took to claiming most of the credit – except that when he got too insufferably patronizing either Gertie or Bea would sidle up to him and enquire, 'Tell us, Uncle Alec, what is the Statue of Liberty actually there for?'

By now the two girls had moved out of the Algonquin and into a dup.. apartment on West 54th Street which was, wrote Percy Hammond, 'first among the famous places every visitor to New York should head towards.' Most did, and a good many of the residents too: Gertie once listed Dorothy Parker, Jeanne Eagels, Bob Sherwood, Richard Barthelmess, Laurette Taylor, Jimmy Walker, Oscar Hammerstein, Arthur Schwartz, Jerome Kern, Rodgers and Hart, Jascha Heifitz, George and Ira Gershwin, Clifton Webb, Vincent Youmans and Irving Berlin – and that was just at a single party, though it's unclear who got to the piano first.

After the first three months Buchanan returned to London; he had only signed for that long on Broadway as he had a West End show to go back to, and Charlot brought out the celebrated English comic Nelson 'Bunch' Keys to replace him. It is some indication of the concern that Charlot was causing rival Broadway managements, however, that on Keys' arrival in New York Ziegfeld tried to prevent him going on stage by claiming that he had a prior contract with the comic. He didn't, and Keys duly opened for Charlot. Gertie meanwhile had started giving long, gracious dressing-room interviews to the press, mostly about the struggles she had endured on her way to the top:

> I have been through the hardships, the unending torture of financial insecurity and the untiring labours that the Theatre demands... now of course I am a Star, but my struggles have made me all the more aware of the pleasures of success.

One can hear very faintly in the background through most of these press interviews the hysterical giggles of Bea Lillie, never one to take herself or her work quite so solemnly.

The English on Broadway could still do no wrong: papers published little notes explaining that 'Toodle-oo' and 'Cheerio' were synonyms for 'Goodbye', and one added that Miss Lawrence would be most grateful if aspiring American songwriters would cease sending her their material as she already had more than enough to read.

Originally the idea had been for *Charlot's Revue* to close on Broadway at the beginning of June, as was then the custom for most shows there; but business was so good that instead of closing at that time they simply moved from the Times Square Theatre next door to the larger Selwyn Theatre and played there right through to the end of August, thereby making Broadway history and setting a pattern which the other really big hit shows were, eventually, to follow. It was Robert Baral who finally summarized the importance of this first Broadway season:

> Gertrude Lawrence and her co-stars definitely dented the prestige of the *Ziegfeld Follies* and similar annual shows overnight, and set off a chain

reaction throughout Broadway. The girlie-girlie revues were now definitely passé after this first Charlot import, and the accent was now on wit. Beatrice Lillie and Gertrude Lawrence lit up the sky with their sheer versatility – Miss Lawrence alone had over twenty-five changes of character, from glamour to drab.

Jessie Matthews was still in that chorus, as was another young English girl called Constance Carpenter who, just twenty-eight years later, was to succeed after Gertie's sudden death to the Broadway role of Anna Leonowens in *The King and I.*

Through the summer of 1924 Gertie grew increasingly capricious; though her social life was still in the whirl she had grown both to love and to need, her sexual life was considerably less exciting. She was still deeply in love with Astley and he, three thousand miles across the Atlantic, with her; for this enforced separation they were to stay remarkably and almost entirely faithful to each other, but that didn't make Gertie any easier for the rest of the company to live with.

She would appear at the theatre every night (indeed she never missed a single New York performance) but began taking against certain numbers, notably 'Parisian Pierrot', which, though critically acclaimed, was curiously not a great applause-getter. In the heat of a Broadway July she began to get tired of it; sending the costume up to Jessie Matthews in the understudies' room, she would, once Jessie was dressed in it, decide that she would do the number herself after all. This happened two or three times until Jessie, who was just as headstrong an understudy as Gertie herself had once been, insisted that either she did the number or she didn't; Gertie, amused at such presumption, agreed that she would *not* be doing it, and for the rest of the New York run 'Parisian Pierrot' was duly sung by Jessie Matthews.

Early in September they finally closed at the Selwyn; business was still good, but Charlot had heard that there was even bigger money to be made on the road. Their last night on Broadway was, therefore, in the nature of a triumphal send-off; Bea played one entire number sitting in the lap of Alec Woollcott in the auditorium, and Gertie wrote:

After the finale the entire house rose and cheered us. They pelted us with flowers. When the orchestra struck up 'Auld Lang Syne' the audience and the company joined in the singing. Everyone took hold of the hand of the person next to him. The chain of friendly hand-clasps stretched across the stage, across the footlights, and continued throughout the house. When the audience was finally pushed out of the theatre several hundred of them merely adjourned to the stage door, where they formed such an imposing mob scene that traffic was clogged in 42nd Street. When Bea and I came out, laden with flowers, to get into our waiting taxi we found the roof of the vehicle packed with the more ardent revellers, who escorted us through the streets of New York singing our own songs to us.

The tour opened in Boston, where Gertie caught a severe cold; by the time they reached Toronto it was showing signs of turning into something much worse, but she refused to give up the show or (Toronto being Bea's birthplace) the inevitable parties which carried on most nights between the ending of the applause and the rising of the sun. By the final week of the Toronto booking, a doctor had diagnosed double pneumonia and a mild form of pleurisy, and as the company travelled on to Detroit she was left behind in a local hospital to reflect on the folly of her ways.

Reports that Gertrude Lawrence was 'dying' spread rapidly through the world's press, unnerving not only Philip Astley back in England but also Jessie Matthews on the tour who, though she had prayed like all understudies for her principal to fall ill, did not want an actual death on her conscience.

Gertie spent Christmas and a total of fourteen weeks recovering in that Toronto hospital, and early in 1925 Philip, who was now by her bedside, got a doctor's report to convince Charlot that she should not return to the tour. Joyce Barbour had (much to the fury of Jessie Matthews) already been brought out to replace her, and Philip took Gertie straight back to New York. From there they sailed for France where Philip, typically, had friends who would lend them a villa on the Riviera in which Gertie could complete her recovery. This she duly did, much helped by a leisurely springtime drive down to Sicily.

There was just one problem. Charlot wanted the British public to be well aware of the Broadway success of his 1924 revue; when it finally closed in the spring of 1925 it had lasted fully fifteen months, or rather longer if the British staging is included. He planned therefore to stage a massive homecoming for his American company, starting with a triumphal disembarkation at Southampton and climaxing in a gala midnight matinée before the cast went straight into rehearsal for his new 1925 revue. But of the three Broadway principals, Buchanan had long since been at work back in London, Gertie was sunning herself on the Riviera, and only Bea had soldiered on to the end of the tour. Though an impressive lady, she could scarcely constitute a gala homecoming all on her own. It was Philip Astley, in conversation with Charlot, who came up with the solution: he and Gertie would motor up from their Riviera villa to Cherbourg, and there join the *SS Olympic* on which the rest of the company had already sailed from New York. Photographers at Southampton a few hours later were therefore able to photograph 'Lillie and Lawrence, Lawrence and Lillie' leading the Charlot players triumphantly down the gangplank onto home soil. If you hadn't seen them, you were (in the words of the song) perfectly silly.

To welcome them back to London, from the most triumphant mission so far in twentieth-century British theatre, casts of all the other shows in town gathered at the Prince of Wales Theatre, now Charlot's London headquarters, for a midnight matinée which bore the proud title *Charlot's Revue as seen in America*. One critic wrote that the matinée was 'the greatest single event in the whole history of British stage revue.' Bea Lillie was more specific:

> The midnight show was the first of its kind in the modern London theatre. My dear, you should have been there. There were 31 – count them, 31 – stars of the stage and silver screen in the boxes and the stalls. Jack Buchanan, who later joined the show again, was typical, coming over from the Empire Theatre when his own musical was over. Like Jack, most of them just had time to change from theatre costumes into evening clothes. During the interval, they all trooped up on stage with us for a swallow of champagne. Noël, who'd written some of our new numbers, sat with Lilian Braithwaite who was playing his mother in *The Vortex*; John Barrymore was with Lady Diana Cooper (not to be confused with Gladys Cooper, *The Bohemian Girl*, also there) and Ivor Novello. George Grossmith, my leading man in a later Hollywood movie, appeared in a box sporting a monocle and so did his boxmate Heather Thatcher. Zena Dare wore black, and Tallulah Bankhead a mammoth bunch of orchids. There sat Fay Compton and Leon Quartermaine, Phyllis Monkman all in pale pink and gold tissue, and Fanny Brice in the flesh.

So good was all this home-coming publicity that Charlot decided not to risk closing his theatre while a new revue was prepared for the rest of 1925. Instead, the company would simply carry on playing the old material from Broadway, and then gradually feed in new numbers and artists as the time came for a change. Making a virtue of this financial opportunity, Charlot (now quite adept at publicity after a year in New York) then announced proudly that his revue would be the only one in town to 'change' every month, though he never specified exactly how much of it would change at any one time.

By the summer a good deal of new material had found its way into the revue; Gertie and Bea were now doing a 'Broadway Medley' and, inspired by what they had seen in New York of the Trix and Dolly Sisters, they were also doing a burlesque sister act as well as parodies of Fanny Brice and Sophie Tucker. Charlot was constantly at them to try something new: 'We have not', he told his two stars, 'come all the way back from America merely to rest on our laurels,' and it wasn't long before they had introduced their celebrated 'Fallen Babies' routine as two alcoholic one-year-olds falling about inside their prams, an oblique tribute to the West End success that Noël was now having with a grown-up comedy called *Fallen Angels*.

Late in the summer of 1925, by which time Buchanan had rejoined the revue and they had also taken on an unknown chorus girl by the name of

Marjorie Robertson (later to achieve fame as Anna Neagle), Charlot announced that it was time for the leading members of the company to start thinking once again about packing their bags. They could easily be replaced by other stars at the Prince of Wales, but Broadway expected once again to see the Big Three.

This time Gertie, Bea and Buchanan set sail in October aboard the *Caronia*; also aboard for that star-studded crossing were Michael Arlen, who had recently published *The Green Hat*, the playwright Frederick Lonsdale, ex-Prime Minister Lloyd George and H. G. Wells; though Gertie had again left both Pamela and Philip behind, Bea was now accompanied by both her son and her husband, Sir Robert Peel, in whose honour a mass band of pipers was assembled on the quayside in New York. When it was tactfully pointed out to them that neither Sir Robert nor Lady Beatrice Peel had any discernible Scottish connections whatsoever, the pipers looked a little disconsolate, until the ever tactful Jack Buchanan mentioned that he came from Scotland and they could therefore pipe him ashore instead.

By the time they all arrived in New York with the Charlot company, Noël Coward and Lilian Braithwaite had already opened on Broadway in *The Vortex*, as had the stage version of *The Green Hat*; the start of the first full-scale English invasion of the Great White Way had already happened, but Broadway theatre-goers didn't forget their first visitors and of the opening night of the new *Charlot's Revue of 1926* Aleck Woollcott was able to write: 'It was not a performance – it was a reunion.'

7

SOMEONE TO WATCH OVER ME

Charlot's Revue of 1926 opened on 11 November 1925 at the Selwyn Theatre on Broadway and by now, in New York even more than in London, the Buchanan–Lawrence–Lillie trio really were very big stars indeed; even before their new show opened, the box office had taken a $200,000 advance, and as a reflection of that the joint Charlot–Selwyn management was now paying each of them $2,500 per week. For Gertie, who less than five years earlier had still been getting £6 a week from Charlot back in London, it was at this point that money, fatally, began to lose much of its sense of reality. She began to spend, and she never really stopped.

Many of her contemporaries, not least Noël Coward, had come as she had from suburban London backgrounds, but the effect of sudden fame and wealth on Gertie was rather different. Noël, until the day he died, drew a kind of strength from his boarding house childhood; he was infinitely proud of his mother for having managed to support him and his father and brother through some difficult times, and equally proud that he had managed to rise above those origins and through his own considerable talent move into a much higher level of society. He never forgot his past.

But Gertie saw nothing in her childhood that was really worth remembering, drew no real sense of achievement from an equally rapid climb out of the suburbs. The past was never a source of strength or support, and it gave her none of the innate caution or sense of economic survival which it had given Noël. The present was all that ever mattered to her, and in that present as fast as the money came in she spent it. It was, in one sense, fool's gold.

Moreover, although Bea Lillie now had the support and love of her husband to keep her in touch with some kind of off-stage reality, Gertie only had her stardom. Philip Astley's duties with his regiment were as usual keeping him in London, which is also where Pamela was still living with Gertie's mother. Gertie was on the town.

For the 1926 revue she was still doing highlights from earlier Charlot shows in London and New York (audiences of the time had apparently little objection to seeing favourite sketches and songs done time after time), though it was now, for the first time, that Broadway saw her in two of Noël's numbers from *London Calling!*, 'Russian Blues' and 'Carrie'. She had also taken over his 'Poor Little Rich Girl', which Alice Delysia had done in London the previous summer as a number in a Cochran revue called *On With The Dance*.

But for Noël himself, still playing on Broadway in *The Vortex*:

> It was thrilling to see the three of them, Gertie and Bea and Jack, hailed as great stars by the whole of New York. It invested them, for me, with a new kind of glamour as though I was discovering them too and had never seen them before in my life. The appreciation of American audiences certainly gave an extra fillip to their performances. There was a shine on all of them, a happy gratification bursting through. I could swear that they had none of them ever been so good before.

Woollcott, still the most vociferous of the Charlot trio's American admirers, now singled out Gertie for special praise:

> She dances with magical lightness and her voice is true and clear; the personification of style and sophistication, she can also convulse an audience with a bit of cockney horseplay or bring tears to its eyes with a sentimental ballad. She is the ideal star.

Though she could hardly have known it at the time, this *1926 Revue* was to mark both the high-spot and the end of Gertie's partnership with the other Charlot stars; each was to be involved in later revues, for Charlot and for other managers, but the unique alliance of Bea, Gertie, Jack and André was now drawing to its close, having set a new financial and artistic standard for revues on both sides of the Atlantic. Not that Charlot himself was yet losing any of his old energy or acumen – no sooner had the revue opened at the Selwyn than he decided that there was a little extra money to he made if his company would also go into cabaret; after all, as the *New York Times* had already noted, 'the Charlot principals are now regarded by their audiences as good and personal friends.' How much better therefore to have them play not just across the footlights and orchestra pit but around dining tables as well. To this end, Charlot took a lease on the Rendezvous Club on West 45th Street and its opening was described in the *New York American* as:

> One of the most brilliant gatherings of the nightclub season... at New York's newest 'gin' [bootleg] club, where Jack Buchanan, Gertrude Lawrence and Bea Lillie made their cabaret debut, the scene was reminiscent of some New York millionaire's private party. Some of those present were Harpo Marx, Ethel Barrymore, Irving Berlin, Edmund Goulding, Elsie Janis, Marilyn Miller, Clifton Webb, Grace Moore and the William K. Vanderbilts.

Gertie and Bea were already being described as 'first ladies of Broadway' and though Bea was always more nonchalant about these honours, to Gertie they meant a great deal. America in general and New York in particular were now hers; there she was in this her twenty-eighth year, acquiring everything she had always longed for at home: money, fame and applause.

Though she remained reasonably faithful to Astley, she was seldom short of an 'escort', and somehow the longer she stayed out of England the more distant and unreal it had begun to seem to her. That, after all, was the past; America was the present and she was loving every single day of it. Nor had Charlot any intention of letting her return home, even had she wanted to: after the *1926 Revue* closed on Broadway in the early spring there was another coast-to-coast tour in the contract.

The new tour started in Detroit, made its way to Chicago and from there to Los Angeles where it opened in Hollywood's then new El Capitán Theatre in the middle of April. Though she was only destined to make one film there, and that a quarter of a century later, Gertrude Lawrence took to California on this first visit like a duck to water:

> I began to go about with bare legs, stockingless, which I found both comfortable and economical, and, as soon as it was announced in the press that Gertrude Lawrence was going around barelegged, the papers began to interview fashion experts and other actresses to get their opinion of the fad I had started. Marilyn Miller, when interviewed, expressed ladylike disapproval of the innovation and announced that she had brought back from Paris two hundred pairs of silk stockings which she had every intention of wearing. Carmel Snow, fashion editor of *Harper's Bazaar*, was quoted exclaiming in horror 'The idea is disgusting. It will never be done by nice people.'

The Hollywood run was a spectacular success until its closing night. As Gertie wrote later:

> Then we gradually noticed that all the big Hollywood stars in the front seats were leaving before the finale. This worried us terribly; we couldn't understand such behaviour. Well, Jack went on in his full Highland costume and sang the opening of the last song; I followed, dressed as Flora MacDonald; and then on came Bea as Bonnie Prince Charlie. By this time there wasn't a single Hollywood male star out front. We all sang bravely and laughed gaily, trying to carry off our dismay, when suddenly one by one onto the stage came the missing males. They all had their trousers rolled up to the knees; Valentino had on a Scots head-dress borrowed from the chorus girls; Charlie Chaplin had his dinner jacket tied round his waist like a kilt; Richard Barthelmess had a tam o'shanter on; the Marx Brothers all wore red beards; and Jack Gilbert carried a ladder, for what reason no one knew. They took over our whole finale; they made speeches and Chaplin, who at that time was refusing to do 'talkies', made his speech in dumb show.

Then it was on with the rest of the tour, by the end of which Gertie had come to certain decisions about her future. The first and most important was that she had had enough of revue; it had given her a marvellous start in London, and a superb introduction to America, but now she sensed, before any of the others, that its days were numbered. Despite glowing reviews, *Charlot's 1926 Revue* had actually done rather worse business both on Broadway and on tour than its predecessor.

Secondly, though she had every intention of returning to England for a summer holiday and to be with Philip and Pamela, she was still very much more enthusiastic about working in New York. London had always had other stars in her field; Jessie Matthews was now coming up fast, having replaced her in the London versions of *Charlot's Revue*, and though she could always be sure of getting good work in the West End there was at this time less enthusiasm for her on home territory. There, after all, she was just another 'local girl made good' on the stage; in New York she was something special, foreign, different. There was nobody else on Broadway quite like Gertrude Lawrence.

She therefore let it be known that if anybody had a show for her she'd be available on Broadway for the autumn of 1926, and meanwhile she returned to London for the summer. Her days with the Charlot team were over.

One thing might perhaps have changed those Broadway plans of Gertie's: back with Philip at a flat in Mayfair it occurred to her that he might now propose marriage. It would not be difficult to get her divorce, since she and Frank had been living apart for fully seven years. No proposal came, though Philip did change one aspect of Gertie's family life now and for the foreseeable future. He made it clear to her that no self-respecting mother could continue to leave her only child with a grandmother; Pamela was her daughter, and as such should live with Gertie wherever Gertie happened to be. That autumn, when Gertie returned to Broadway, Pamela went with her.

Among those who had heard that Gertie was looking for a Broadway show were George and Ira Gershwin, both admirers of hers from the Charlot revues, and Gertie's fellow-Londoner P. G. Wodehouse, who was already working then with Guy Bolton although at that time their usual composer was Jerome Kern, hence the legendary Broadway rhyme:

> This is the trio of musical fame
> Bolton and Wodehouse and Kern,
> Better than anyone else you can name,
> Bolton and Wodehouse and Kern.
> Nobody knows what on earth they've been bitten by;
> All I can say is I mean to get lit an' buy
> Orchestra seats for the next one that's written by
> Bolton and Wodehouse and Kern.

For their new show Bolton and Wodehouse planned to work with the Gershwins, and Bolton already had his eye on Miss Lawrence:

> I had seen her performing in the Charlot revues and had written her a note saying that I was willing to provide her with a straight comedy, a musical comedy or a revue, whichever she preferred. I slipped in a reference to my collaborator, Pelham Grenville Wodehouse. I thought that might fetch her. It did. She replied by telegram – twelve sheets of it, saying that as soon as she was free of Charlot she would put herself in my hands... but she had never played in a 'book' show and she wanted to be sure of her ground, of not making a mistake.

The play we wrote for her was a saga of those romantic days the Prohibition Era. It was laid at Montauk at the tip of Long Island with the Rum Fleet anchored twelve miles away, the hero's beach house boarded up for the winter, its cellars loaded with bootleg liquor, and Gertie, come ashore from her brother's liquor-laden yacht, bent on finding the man she had met for one magical evening and fallen in love with.

Apart from having to change his shirt three times every morning on account of the heat, Wodehouse recorded in his diary that he had a happy summer writing the new show with Bolton. They had already done *Have a Heart* and *Oh, Boy!* (or *Oh, Joy!* as it was known to non-American speaking audiences) and *The Riviera Girl* and *Sally* and *Leave It to Jane* among a dozen other shows so they were not exactly unaccustomed to the Broadway musical form, although, wrote Wodehouse, 'this time I shall have it easy. George Gershwin being the composer means that Ira Gershwin will write the lyrics, so that I shall simply be helping Guy with book as much as I can.'

While Bolton and Wodehouse were concocting their Prohibition plot, the Gershwins were at work on a vintage score; one which was to include 'Clap Yo' Hands' and 'Do, Do, Do' and 'Maybe' and above all, 'Someone To Watch Over Me.' When they went into New York rehearsals early in September 1926, all they lacked was a title. The show was variously known as *Mayfair, Miss Mayfair* and *Cheerio!* until, just before the Philadelphia opening, the authors decided to settle for the fact that it was developing into another of their *Oh!* shows. This one then became known as *Oh, Kay!* and of its first night at the Imperial Theatre on Broadway in November 1926 the *Herald Tribune* critic wrote:

> All of us simply floated away on the canoodling notes of 'Maybe' and were brought back to Broadway by such flesh and bony anthems as 'Fidgety Feet' and 'Clap Yo' Hands'.

But the show-stopping moment was when Gertie, alone on stage, sang a wistful number to a strange rag doll that George Gershwin had bought her, shortly before opening night, in a Philadelphia toy shop:

Won't you tell him, please, to put on some speed,
Follow my lead?
Oh, how I need
Someone to watch over me...

As a summary of Gertie's own off-stage needs at the time this was pretty accurate. *Oh, Kay!* was enough of a triumph to carry Gertie all through 1927 on Broadway and almost all through 1928 in London. Her first big starring musical could not have been better, either for her or for its audiences, and it established her away from Buchanan and Bea as a star all on her own, capable of carrying a Broadway show virtually single-handed, though she was of course in the best of all possible hands: 'The book of *Oh Kay!*', noted Burns Mantle simply, 'was written by Guy Bolton and P. G. Wodehouse, than whom there are no better librettists writing for our stage.' And the Gershwins weren't too bad either.

With Astley still in London, Gertie's need for someone to watch over her led her that winter with reasonable speed into the arms of an American lover, Bert Taylor. The scion of a wealthy American family (his sister was the legendary socialite Countess di Frasso) Taylor was a Wall Street banker, already living apart from a wife and two small children. It was, for Gertie, love at first sight all over again:

> Immediately my life changed... this tall, dark-haired, stunning-looking American was like someone one only reads about. With a snap of his fingers, a glance, a quiet word, he had the power to bring about miracles. Bert had been born with a golden spoon in his mouth. His father was President of the New York Stock Exchange and Bert had rolled up an enormous fortune of his own during those years when Wall Street was still holding carnival... he knocked me off my feet. From the moment of his entry into my life I began to live in a storybook world. While New York streets were glazed with ice and the sky sent down showers of sleet, my apartment was abloom with Spring and the fragrance of American Beauty roses. A banker in Bert's position could, and not infrequently did, make a profit of a hundred thousand dollars in a day's trading on the Stock Exchange and, exhilarated by this achievement, on his way up town to his club he would drop in at Cartier's and spend a part of the day's bag on a gorgeous bauble to please the lady of his heart.

Bert Taylor had little difficulty in sweeping off her feet a lady who, by her own admission, was there just waiting to be swept:

> From the start of my friendship with Philip Astley we had both known that we had no real future together. Circumstances to which we both had to submit (presumably Gertie's love for the stage and America, Philip's for the Guards and England) kept us apart, and although for several

years I had been happy with half a loaf, I was inevitably now getting both lonely and restless.

Gertie was, however, still very fond of Philip and well aware of all that he had done for her back in London; she therefore wrote to him with news of the Taylor affair. Philip took the next boat to New York and asked her to marry him. She refused. Had he asked in London a year or two earlier, Gertie later wrote, she would have been very happy to become Mrs Astley. But by now things had changed. Her love affair with New York (and America in the person of Bert Taylor) was at its height, and deep down she knew very well that what Philip was offering was not just marriage but a life away from the stage, a life in the country bringing up children; the life that so many of her London chorus-girl contemporaries had happily chosen as an escape from their own families or the grind of yet another Charlot revue. But Gertie was now no longer doing that; she was doing a Broadway musical by the Gershwins, and she loved it. What is more, she had begun to doubt if she was ever going to be able to be happy away from the theatre; from the age of ten, the theatre was all she had really known. Life outside the theatre usually meant trouble; trouble with husbands, mothers, fathers, children. It was unglamorous, uneasy and usually, in her case, unsatisfactory. In the greatest and oldest of the many backstage clichés in which Gertrude Lawrence lived out her life, she was only really happy once she got through a stage door. The endless fuss about the decoration of dressing-rooms (which was to become a feature of her later career) was not just the usual starry insecurity or temperament on display. She cared passionately about the decoration and state of her dressing-room because that was the only home she ever really wanted or understood or recognized. Her life had been and always would be the theatre, and, when Philip Astley finally offered her a different one, Bert Taylor became a wonderfully convenient excuse for not facing up to the fact that she could never successfully be Mrs anybody. It will doubtless be argued that she did eventually manage to become Mrs Aldrich, to which the only answer is that in a marriage which lasted twelve years he was at war for five and she was on the stage for seven.

Philip Astley, whose manners were as impeccable in defeat as in success, took Gertie's rejection of his proposal like the officer and gentleman he always was and caught the next boat back to England while Gertie stayed in New York to finish the Broadway run of *Oh, Kay!* With his departure, she lost not only a lover and a friend but also the only man who might have been able to see her safely through the 1930s:

Tell me, where is the shepherd for this lost lamb?
There's a somebody I'm longing to see
I hope that he
Turns out to be
Someone to watch over me.

8

OK WITH *OH, KAY!*

Although Philip had never managed to instil into Gertie any sense of the value of money, he had managed to persuade her to put a thousand pounds into a twenty-year trust fund for her daughter, one of the very few intelligent investments she was ever to make. But with Philip now back in England, mother and daughter weren't getting on very well together in New York, as Pamela later recalled:

I was suddenly taken out of this working-class Clapham environment where I'd grown up with my grandmother and there were constant soapsuds around the front door because Granny still boiled the laundry in the copper, and thrown into this frightfully sophisticated New York world where my only relationship with Mummy was being lined up next to her for photographs. She got me into a boarding school fairly rapidly, but there were still the holidays and I remember waking up every morning and asking Mummy's maid Dorothy what sort of mood she was likely to be in that day, and if it was bad then I'd just get out of the house as soon as possible. It wasn't that she ever really meant to he unkind or difficult, it was just that she had absolutely no idea of what being a mother really meant. How could she? Her own family had broken up when she was barely ten, and she had just never seen or known any kind of domestic life. She had no idea what mothers were supposed to do. She was terribly irritable with the staff she hired, kept firing people and then begging them to stay because she couldn't manage without them, but she never really knew where a daughter fitted in to the household or what she was supposed to say to me. I made her very uneasy; not because I was a good-looking child, or any kind of a threat to her, but simply because she had never really met a child before and had no idea what she was supposed to be doing with me. Later we got on better, because she could visualize herself as a kind of older sister offering advice, but in the early days she was constantly protected from me by servants and agents and she was never really there when you needed her, or if she was then her maid would say 'Don't bother your mother now, dear – she's tired.' Going to day school in New York meant being up early for breakfast in the dining-room, just me because Mummy was still asleep or having breakfast in bed, and then when I got back in the afternoons she'd be getting ready to go off to the theatre. I don't think she was consciously trying to avoid me, but our lives just never seemed to overlap except if there were holidays when she wasn't doing a play and I was home. But then we used to find that, because we'd been apart so much, we had nothing to say to each other.

As if aware of the gap that Philip's departure had left in her life, Gertie soon began to surround herself with other people; not just Bert Taylor but secretaries and maids; there was also Helen Downes, a wealthy New York lady who was to stay with Gertie for several years as a kind of unpaid aide. The only difference was that where it had been Gertie who had once listened to Philip, it was now all of the others who listened to Gertie; none of them really had the courage or the authority to check her spending, which was now reaching epidemic proportions, or her greater excesses of temperament; there were only two men who could ever do that, Philip and Noël, and they were both back in London.

For a while, none of that much mattered; the Wall Street crash was still nearly two years off, Bert was still around to pay some of the more expensive bills, and money was still a joy rather than a problem. Gertie's attitude was, then as always, one of 'easy come easy go'; she took considerable pride in the fact that she was not, unlike many of her friends and contemporaries, ever totally 'kept' by anyone. Though she had never objected to Philip, or now Bert, accounting for a certain amount of her living expenses, her own considerable theatre salary was never banked against a rainy day. It too went towards the ever-increasing cost of just being Gertrude Lawrence.

Oh, Kay! which had made Gertie the first British actress to star in an American musical on Broadway, ran on through to the midsummer of 1927, and the management then decided to move it and Gertie straight to London for the following autumn; after some slight anglicizing (notably the casting of Claude Hulbert as 'The Duke of Datchet') they opened at His Majesty's in late September to good business but some rather grudging reviews. Playing opposite Gertie now was her old child-actor friend from *Hannele*, Harold French:

> At the first reading we assured each other again and again how wonderful it was to be working together again. That lasted all of two weeks. Our scenes worked wonderfully, dance routines presented no problem, my body, legs, arms and feet found no difficulty in obeying the demands of the choreographer. But before we went into the dance, duets had to be sung. Great numbers, all of them – 'Maybe', 'Do, Do, Do', 'Someone To Watch Over Me'; Mr Gershwin was no slouch. We were into the third week when I first noticed it, 'it' being a slightly puzzled look on Gertie's face as we were singing our first duet together…
> I thought nothing of it until we had finished the dance and made our exit. Then, casually, she enquired 'Who's your singing teacher, Harold?'

It rapidly became clear that Harold French was going to have more than a little trouble with the numbers, and this was reflected in such first-night notices as 'he knows how to move about the stage but is no canary' from St John Ervine in the *Observer*. Indeed the whole experience of *Oh, Kay!* not only cooled the French–Lawrence friendship but also cured him of any further desire to work in musicals; from then on he was to have a distinguished straight-theatre career as a director, most notably of the plays of Terence Rattigan.

That apart, *Oh, Kay!* worked well enough in London: the full score still included a ravishing number called 'Dear Little Girl' which was then to disappear without trace for forty years, only to resurface as a piano duet for Julie Andrews and Daniel Massey in the otherwise appalling Gertrude Lawrence film biography *Star!* If the reviews found *Oh, Kay!* rather thin, they were at least marvellous for Gertie herself who, in the view of *The Times*, was:

> A brilliant and happy girl combining in the most remarkable manner a variety of talents. She has looks, grace, humour, voice, dignity, acting ability and immense charm. She can play the gamine and the lady; she can range in voice and gesture from the good-natured cockney slut to the well-bred woman; and she has an unfailing fund of invention that enables her to fill an empty phrase with fun. Her mere mumbles are comic, and she has that indefinable radiance which compels an audience to concentrate its attentions on her. In Miss Lawrence we possess an actress of genius.

As homecomings go, that one can't have been considered bad: Gertie was, as the song said, OK with *Oh, Kay!* Philip Astley, though no longer quite the devoted escort he had been, continued to drop into her dressing-room, and Gertie decided the time had come to get at least the rest of her private life into some sort of order; to this end she leased a large and costly flat in Portland Place from the Marquis de Casa Maury, installed Pamela along with André Charlot's similarly-aged daughter at a Catholic girls' boarding school near Margate, hired the ever-fashionable Sibyl Colefax to do some interior decoration at the flat, and set about getting her divorce in case Bert Taylor's thoughts might be turning towards a proposal.

The divorce itself wasn't too difficult to arrange; Frank had, after all, left her (admittedly with some encouragement) holding a month-old baby and that was now almost ten years ago. He was not, therefore, in the strongest position to contest Gertie's suit, and some tribute to the stunning performance she must have given in the witness box can he gleaned from press reports of the judge's summing up. Lord Merivale, noting evidence of Howley's adultery at a Hull hotel, said:

> This is one of the worst cases of which I have ever heard – in which a girl of nineteen was seduced by a man at a time when he was in a position of authority in the theatrical profession to which she belonged. They were married and a child was born, but the husband never maintained his wife and child. Apparently the view of the husband was that from that time onward he might live on the earnings of his wife. Naturally, therefore,

they did not live together for long. The petitioner has been abominably used, and now it seems she has prospects of making a new start in life. The divorce will be granted.

Gertie was thus foot-loose and fancy free, with a minimum of the unattractive publicity which was inclined to surround actresses' divorces in this period. Sure enough, Bert Taylor took the judge's hint; that summer he came to London and proposed marriage. Gertie accepted, though it was to remain a curious and ultimately unfulfilled engagement. For the next year or so, they were frequently to be photographed in each other's arms; on certain of these occasions Gertie would reveal to the press that she could hardly wait to become Mrs Taylor and that she was just longing to settle down and bring up his children in America as soon as the present production came to its close. On other occasions, beneath similar photographs, the caption would announce that regretfully Miss Lawrence and Mr Taylor had decided after all not to get married because, as Gertie would then explain at some length:

> I believe that the duty of a wife is to offer companionship to her husband. How can I, who must go to the theatre at night, be a companion to a husband who would be home from business at 5 pm? I would like to marry Mr Taylor very much, but I don't think it would be fair to him: he would expect me to retire, but I am now on the threshold of success for which I have worked for many years and I simply can't give it all up just for love.

Being engaged, therefore, seemed to provide the ideal solution; it kept Bert tied reasonably closely to her without committing either of them to a radical change in their lifestyle. It satisfied the rather eccentric morality of the time, whereby a leading female star was expected to have some sort of male in close attendance, but it left Gertie free when Bert was not visiting London to carry on her own life, still indeed seeing Philip Astley in whom the flame was far from totally quenched, and the same applied to Bert. Theirs was, in other words, an 'open' engagement and as such was to remain reasonably successful for the next couple of years.

Early in January 1928, with *Oh, Kay!* still running successfully at His Majesty's, Gertie took another and very important, though little publicized, step forward in her career. Dedicated and devoted as she was to the theatre, she had already begun to realize that the life of a revue and musical-comedy star was inclined to be a little shorter than she might one day wish. Looking around her in the West End that winter, it was not hard to recognize that the stars who had lasted – the stars who were still working well in their fifties and sixties and even seventies – were not as a rule the song-and-dance brigade. If Gertie's star was to last, she would have to make herself into a straight actress too.

Her chance came when Charlot, her old protector and manager, agreed to stage, as a charity show for the Actors' Orphanage, for one Sunday night Owen Davis's Pulitzer-prizewinning American drama *Icebound*, about the old Maine family squabbling over money and a wastrel son. Gertie played plain Jane, the poor relation, 'far removed' said one critic 'from the quips and nods and becks and wreathed smiles which have made her famous in musical comedy.' There was no question of staging *Icebound* for any longer than that one Sunday night, and few papers bothered even to notice it next morning; but what Gertie had done, quietly and firmly, was to alert the ever-watchful eyes of London theatre managers to the fact that she was now open to offers of work in the straight theatre as well as in revue.

Then it was back to *Oh, Kay!* for the rest of the winter and spring of 1928, and by the time that show eventually closed Gertie had already had another script from George and Ira Gershwin. This was *Treasure Girl*, last and least successful of the 'smart' Gershwin scores of the 1920s and one containing a song called 'I Don't Think I'll Fall In Love Today' which was intentionally or not, a remarkable summary of the current state of play concerning Gertie and Bert Taylor:

SHE: Just think of what love leads to:
　　Maybe to marriage – maybe divorce.

HE: Into a jam love speeds two;
　　It may be nature's course,
　　But we mustn't be
　　Like the other sheep.

SHE: Better far if we
　　Look before we leap.

BOTH: Perhaps it's better after all
　　If we don't answer Nature's call.

There was, however, no way of knowing, as Gertie once again packed her innumerable bags and set off for New York in the late summer of 1928, that *Treasure Girl* wasn't going to be another smash hit; indeed so confident was she of success, that she took Pamela with her, a maid, and two cars – a custom-built Bentley and, for when the traffic got really bad, a very small Austin Seven, which inspired one New York cop to shout as she drove past him 'Say lady, what do you do with it at night? Keep it under the bed?'

Bert was there to greet her on the quayside, where they gave one of their 'no we have no immediate plans for marriage' interviews to the assembled press. Gertie then established herself in a large apartment on

Park Avenue and went straight into rehearsal. The score for *Treasure Girl* was by no means a poor one, including as it did 'I've Got a Crush on You', 'Feeling I'm Falling' 'Krazy for You' and 'Got A Rainbow', but something was wrong here and it was very possibly the plot. Gertie's private life may have been going rapidly from grandeur to grandeur, but there was something about her stage presence which still invited and indeed demanded sympathy for the 'poor little rich girl'. It was indeed Coward himself who was the first to spot the increasing gap between the lady Gertie thought she was and the lady she really was; that previous summer, following the run of *Oh, Kay!*, they had met up again in London just after Gertie had come back from a brief holiday on the French Riviera. She told him the stories of yachts, and parties, and grand friends, and then added that she would have to get back there as soon as possible, preferably in December or January, as she certainly couldn't stand the thought of ever having to live through another English winter. 'No, darling, I'm sure you couldn't,' agreed Noël, 'especially after all those childhood years in sun-drenched Clapham.'

Now audiences, too, wanted to reassure themselves that Gertie was never really as grand or as distant as she could somehow seem; they wanted to be able to warm to her, and *Treasure Girl* gave them no chance, telling as it did the story of a girl so avid for money and position that she would even double-cross her lover. Despite a strong supporting cast (led by Clifton Webb) and a lyrically good score, Broadway rejected *Treasure Girl* and two months later, wrote Ira Gershwin, 'we were all taken off to Cain's Warehouse' which was where scenery from Broadway flops was traditionally stored.

Too proud to return to London with news of her first real New York disaster, Gertie stayed on in New York hoping that something might turn up. What did turn up by about Christmas, was not another show (since in those days there were precious few mid-season openings and casting for the new season would not therefore begin again until the summer) but instead the offer of her very first film. It came from Paramount, but not from Hollywood; instead, at their comparatively modest studio complex out on Long Island they were starting out on a picture first called *The Gay Lady* and then rapidly retitled *The Battle of Paris*. Initially the film had a good deal going for it, including not only the co-stars Gertie, Charlie Ruggles and Arthur Treacher, but the first two songs ('Here Comes the Bandwagon' and 'They All Fall in Love') ever to be written for the screen by Cole Porter. There was however not much of a script, indeed so little that the director threatened to resign. Held to his contract by Paramount lawyers, he returned to the studios on Long Island to discover that all the good daytime had been booked and floorspace was in such short supply that he and his company would have to work between eight at night and five in the morning.

Uncharitably described by one film critic as a 'floperetta', *The Battle of Paris* turned out to be a curious and now long-lost little musical comedy about a girl called Georgie who, struggling to make a living as an artist in pre-First World War Paris, falls in love with an American soldier and then takes up nightclub singing in an effort to secure his love. The plot here was something less than crucial, though one critic did wonder how, just before the Armistice, Miss Lawrence had managed to assemble in Paris an entire male-voice choir from the American army, and another critic added that 'if all Miss Lawrence wishes to do is wear lovely clothes, then some plot device might have been found to alleviate the boredom of watching her steal dress after dress from mannequins in store windows.' But *The Battle of Paris* did at least give Gertie the chance to sing her way through six numbers, and a note from Paramount's head office to its distributors said 'Sell strongly on songs and clothing of G. Lawrence', which they dutifully did. This may have been a less than spectacular or distinguished screen debut, but as such it was to be in almost perfect keeping with the rest of her film career.

By staying around New York, and commuting each morning to Paramount's Long Island sound stages, Gertie had the chance to keep her ear close to the Broadway ground and therefore to position herself carefully for the cream of the autumn show offers. Her unexpected and rather alarming failure in the last Gershwin musical indicated to her that a change of direction was called for. Rather than risk another musical, she was keen to try her luck in a straight play and rumour from England had it that Yvonne Arnaud had just opened there in a play which would perfectly suit Gertie on Broadway for the fall of 1929. It was a Viennese comedy called, in London, *By Candle-Light*. But as the adapter for New York of *Candle-Light* (as it became) was Gertie's old friend and author from *Oh, Kay!*, P. G. Wodehouse, there wasn't a lot of difficulty. Indeed when Gertie first saw the play, on her annual summer holiday in England after the filming of *The Battle of Paris,* she knew at once that it was the play in which she wanted to make her straight-theatre debut on Broadway. Noël cabled when he heard of her plans:

LEGITIMATE AT LAST. WON'T MOTHER BE PLEASED?

9

ENTER AMANDA

For the Broadway production of *Candle-Light* in the autumn of 1929, Gilbert Miller (who was both producer and director) decided to assemble a largely English cast, indeed so English that the three principals – Gertie, Reginald Owen and an up-and-coming matinée idol called Leslie Howard – did most of their rehearsing in London that summer and even played a trial week in Southampton before travelling down to the docks there and taking the boat back to New York. Wodehouse noted in his diary that his friendship with Gertie now became a little strained, largely because he was so confident of her success in his play that he chose not to hang around in New York but instead to travel on to California for a Hollywood scripting job. By the time he got back to Baltimore, where *Candle-Light* was now being tried out before American audiences, he therefore got 'a distinctly chilly reception from Gertie before being taken back into the fold.'

The Broadway opening was triumphant, and in their first week at the Empire Theatre they took just over $18,000 which meant a healthy $1,800 into Gertie's bank balance. Her reviews had admittedly been a little less than wonderful; the *New York Times* found her 'as charming and decorative as ever, but she turns on all the comic stops at once and overplays consistently.' Undaunted, Gilbert Miller hung her portrait up in the lobby of the Empire next to those of Ina Claire and Helen Hayes, and announced that Gertie too was now 'legit'.

Candle-Light had opened on Broadway at the end of September 1929; a month later, Wall Street crashed and though Gertie had never been much inclined to invest, the collapse of the Stock Exchange drastically affected her friendship with Bert Taylor:

> Bert was up to his ears in financial worries and responsibilities and in the circumstances it seemed impractical for us to marry. At least Bert said it was. I was free to marry him and I wanted to, just to prove that I loved him and not his money... I protested that I was willing to go on working to help things along financially, but that only hurt his pride more deeply. We were at a deadlock.

So she carried on in the theatre, leading a somewhat less lavish private life than in previous Broadway seasons but still revelling in considerable public and private acclaim: 'her performance affected me' wrote Wodehouse later, 'rather as his first perusal of Chapman's Homer had affected Keats...

she had everything'; Burns Mantle noted that she was 'as graceful and accomplished in her first stage comedy as she was witty and charming in her many Charlot revues', and Brooks Atkinson added that she 'has the talent and the presence of the true comedienne.' To those who enquired what on earth the title had to do with a romantic comedy about a Hapsburg heir and a chambermaid (played by Gertie), Wodehouse replied simply that it came from an old Austrian proverb which, roughly translated, stated: 'choose neither women nor linen by candle-light.'

From that somewhat flimsy start they achieved 150 Broadway performances (rather more than a later Cole Porter musical version entitled *You Never Know*), presumably because the extramarital affairs of Viennese princes provided a welcome escape from the grim financial realities of New York in the winter of 1929–30. That Gertie's own spirits remained reasonably buoyant can be gathered from an Equity employment questionnaire she filled in at the time. To the query 'What are your stage ambitions?' her answer was the one word 'Tremendous', and asked if she had ever done any writing she answered 'No, I always cable.' Her parents, she bizarrely noted, had been a celebrated double act known as 'The Moore and Burgess Minstrels' and her hobbies, she added, were 'Backgammon and moving apartments'. *Candle- Light* closed in the Spring of 1930, having made a star of Leslie Howard and a straight actress of Gertrude Lawrence.

Eager to stay in work, and there being no other plays on offer, Gertie then made a thoroughly unwise decision to go back into revue. The show in question was Lew Leslie's *International Revue*, a rare failure from the impresario of *Blackbirds* for which he had decided to counteract America's current introverted mood by importing a large number of foreign stars from Europe and South America. Despite songs by Dorothy Fields and Jimmy McHugh and dance routines by the great Busby Berkeley, not to mention Robert Conche (a Parisian child prodigy who played the violin and the concertina, conducted his own orchestra but soon disappeared forever from the theatrical scene), the *International Revue* was less than triumphant. Anton Dolin had a success with his Apache dance and Gertie sang 'Sunny Side of the Street', 'Exactly Like You' and did a little dancing, but the first night dragged on until a quarter past midnight and even then there were six numbers still unplayed. Lew Leslie had apparently not noticed that a few weeks earlier something called *The Little Show* at the Music Box had revolutionized the whole shape of revue by making it brief and intimate. The unwieldy *International Revue* was still huge and therefore unfashionable.

It did however have one very happy consequence for Gertie. She decided after a few weeks that she would much like to be out of the whole affair, but lacking a good lawyer and unwilling to trouble Bert who still had his own preoccupations, she turned for advice to 'Pat' Dolin who recommended an already celebrated brother-and-sister partnership of New York showbusiness lawyers called David and Fanny Holtzmann. They soon discovered that Gertie's considerable troubles were not merely legal, but also financial. To extricate her from the *International Revue* was no great problem, but while doing so Fanny noticed that Gertie had not only never saved any money for her U.C.S taxes, she had almost never paid any either. Somehow, through all the years of the Charlot Revues and *Oh, Kay!* and the other shows, because she kept criss-crossing the Atlantic, the tax men had not yet caught up with her. When they did, Fanny realized, Gertie's debts would be massive.

But Gertie was never an imaginative lady, and therefore found it hard to grasp a problem that still seemed to lie somewhere in an uncertain future. There was always the hope that when the tax men did finally catch up with her she would be back in London, or that in the current economic uncertainty of the United States, they might not even bother to extract a few hundred thousand dollars from an English actress still not resident there. Gertie was nothing if not optimistic.

Fanny, who was from now on to be her greatest admirer, adviser and manager, did manage to instil a vague sense of impending doom, however, and convinced Gertie there was only one thing for it. She was to get work, stay in work, spend nothing, and hope to God that by the time the tax bills began to come in she'd have saved enough to pay off at least some of them. That seemed to make sense, and when, therefore, André Charlot wrote making her an offer for his *1930 Revue*, Gertie hastily accepted and signed a contract. No sooner had she done so than a script arrived for her in the post. It was a comedy by Noël Coward, and it was called *Private Lives*.

Private Lives happened for Gertie in a roundabout kind of a way; ever since their shared theatrical childhood, and all through their time with Charlot, Noël had promised his beloved friend that one day he would write her a full-scale show, not just another revue number here or there. Indeed when, in the summer of 1928, he had begun working on his first-ever operetta, *Bitter-Sweet*, it had been quite clear in his mind that Gertie was to be its star. But then, as the score developed, it became even more clear to him that it would need a singer with a considerably greater vocal range, and when a year later *Bitter-Sweet* opened in London it was with Peggy Wood in the lead, playing a role later created for Broadway by Evelyn Laye.

All this meant that Noël owed Gertie a show, and that was not a debt she was going to let him forget easily. Indeed when, in the autumn of 1929 while she was playing in *Candle-Light*, Noël had passed through New York on one of his many voyages around the world, Gertie gave him a farewell party and, he recalled later:

> A little gold book from Cartier's which, when opened and placed on the writing-table in my cabin, disclosed a clock, calendar and thermometer

on one side and an extremely pensive photograph of Gertie herself on the other. This rich gift, though I am sure prompted by the least ulterior of motives, certainly served as a delicate reminder that I had promised to write a play for us both, and I gazed daily, often with irritation, at that anxious *retroussé* face while my mind voyaged barrenly through eighteenth-century salons, Second Empire drawing rooms and modern cocktail bars in search of some inspiring echo, some slight thread of plot that might suitably unite us in either comedy, tragedy or sentiment. However, nothing happened. I was aware of a complete emptiness... and I resolved never again to make any promises that implicated my creative ability. They were limiting and tiresome and imposed too great a strain. I would write whatever the spirit moved me to write, regardless of whether the subject matter was suitable to Gertie Lawrence, Mrs Patrick Campbell or Grock; and in the meantime, feeling no particular urge to write anything at all, I closed Gertie's clock with a snap and read a book.

A few weeks later, however, Noël found himself at the Imperial Hotel in Tokyo awaiting the arrival there of his close friend and travelling companion Jeffery Amherst:

> The night before he arrived I went to bed early as I wanted to greet him as brightly as possible at seven in the morning, but the moment I switched out the lights, Gertie appeared in a white Molyneux dress on a terrace in the South of France and refused to go again until four a.m., by which time *Private Lives,* title and all, had constructed itself. In 1923 the play would have been written and typed within a few days of my thinking of it, but by 1929 I had learned the wisdom of not welcoming a new idea too ardently, so I forced it into the back of my mind, trusting to its own integrity to emerge again later on when it had become sufficiently set and matured.

A few weeks later still, by which time Noël was in Shanghai and bed with influenza, the idea re-emerged:

> I lay sweating gloomily in my bedroom in the Cathay Hotel for several days. The ensuing convalescence however was productive, for I utilized it by writing *Private Lives.* The idea by now seemed ripe enough to have a shot at, so I started it propped up in bed with a writing-block and an Eversharp pencil and completed it, roughly, in four days. It came easily, and with the exception of a few of the usual blood and tears moments I enjoyed writing it. I thought it a shrewd and witty comedy, well constructed on the whole, but psychologically unstable; however its entertainment value seemed obvious enough, and its acting opportunities for Gertie and me admirable, so I cabled her immediately in New York telling her to keep herself free for the autumn.

Considering that this was to be the greatest comedy of either of their careers, it would be nice to be able to report that Gertie immediately saw the considerable merits of *Private Lives*. In fact, she saw nothing of the kind and there followed a sustained sequence of telegraphic bickering between Gertie, still in New York, and Noël, whose round-the-world voyage had now got him as far as Singapore:

> She cabled me there, rather casually I thought, saying that she had read *Private Lives* and that there was nothing wrong that couldn't be fixed. I had wired back curtly that the only thing that was going to be fixed was her performance. Now cables were arriving at all hours of the day and night, with a typical disregard of expense, saying that she had foolishly committed herself to Charlot for a new revue – could we open in January instead of September – could I appear in the revue with her, just to fill in – could I wire to Charlot to release her from her contract – that it wasn't a contract at all, merely a moral obligation – that it wasn't a moral obligation at all, but a cabled contract – that her lawyers were working day and night to get her out of it – that she would rather do *Private Lives* than anything in the world – that she couldn't do *Private Lives* at all. In her last telegram she remembered to give me her cable address which, had she done so sooner, would have saved me about forty pounds. I finally lost patience and cabled that I intended to do the play with someone else, and I heard nothing further until I arrived back in England.

By that time, Fanny Holtzmann had not only managed to persuade Charlot to tear up Gertie's revue contract but even more impressively managed to convince Charles Cochran (who was presenting *Private Lives* in London and had, as the producer, last presented Gertie just twenty years earlier as one of 150 children at Olympia in *The Miracle*) that in view of Gertie's impending financial troubles with the American tax people she should be given not only co-starring status in the play but also a cut of the management profits. It was thus not Cochran alone but 'Cochran–Coward–Lawrence' (or CCL as they were known on the posters) who presented *Private Lives*, and Gertie was better off to the tune of several thousand pounds.

Meanwhile, Gertie had retired to the South of France to learn the script, taking Pamela and her devoted friend Helen Downes to stay with her at the Cap d'Ail villa of the designer Edward Molyneux which she had rented, regardless of expense, for the summer. Other visitors were soon on their way down to join her, notably Noël and his new friend, the impresario Jack Wilson. Gertie was informed of this plan by a letter from Noël which read:

> Mr Coward asks me to say that there was talk of you playing a small part in a play of his, on condition that you tour and find your own clothes (same to be of reasonable quality) and understudy Jessie Matthews whom

you have always imitated. Mr Coward will be visiting the South of France in mid-July and he will appear at Cap d'Ail, whether you like it or not, with Mr Jack Wilson on the 20th. If by any chance there is no room at the rather squalid lodgings you have taken, would you be so kind as to engage several suites for Mr Coward and Mr Wilson at the Hotel Mont Fleury which will enable same Mr Wilson and Mr Coward to have every conceivable meal with you and use all your toilets for their own advantage. Several complicated contracts are being sent to you by Mr Coward on the terms you agreed upon, i.e. six pounds ten shillings a week and understudy.

Gertie made room at the luxurious Molyneux villa for Jack and Noël, principally by turning out her now twelve-year-old daughter who never forgave her; but there were other visitors who were allowed to stay on, notably the actor William Powell and the novelist G. B. Stern who thus became the first people ever to see *Private Lives* in rehearsal, as Noël and Gertie pushed back the furniture in the sitting room and set about practising the balcony scene.

They didn't spend all their time rehearsing; once, they heard that George Gershwin was staying at the nearby Hôtel du Cap and they made their way there. Also in residence at the hotel then was a young Simon Harcourt-Smith:

We had come down to Antibes, my mother to recuperate from an illness and I to study for an extremely stiff exam... occasionally 'G' Lawrence would pass my chair, deploying across yards of empty white tables in the hotel's vast dining-room a kind of moonlit charm that drew one's eyes again and again towards her... once she apparently told the manager that I seemed to be working far too hard. But we never spoke until Noël Coward came to lunch with her among the silent tables. I knew him slightly from London, and I could also claim a slight acquaintance with her other guest, no less than the composer George Gershwin... as the two men with G. passed me on the way to her table, Coward greeted me and Gershwin seemed to remember me. Later, at lunch, as my mother complained that the toast was cold, a waiter delivered us a message: would we join Mademoiselle Lawrence and her friends for coffee and brandy? Unfortunately, mother failed entirely to approve of Noël Coward. She had once attended a performance of *The Vortex* and was hardly persuaded that drugs were a suitable subject to be mentioned in a West End play... so despite my pleadings she mounted to her afternoon siesta while I guiltily made my way to my heroine's table. Theatrical gossip of a lively sort played over it: the air was scintillating with allusions which I could hardly catch. Then G. proposed that, as a protest against the *mistral,* an impromptu concert should enliven the afternoon.

Champagne was ordered and we proceeded in leisurely fashion towards the ballroom... George Gershwin slipped the last dust-cover off the piano and sat down before it... her face all animation, husky voice all caresses, G. went into 'Oh! do, do, do what you did, did, did before, baby' and 'The Man I Love' and Someone to Watch Over Me'. Noël sang 'They Can't Take That Away from Me' and 'S'wonderful' and then his own 'Half-Caste Woman' and 'Mad Dogs and Englishmen' while, through the chinks between the shutters, the sunlight slowly reddened... the next day I again flung filial piety and my studies for the moment to the winds and motored G. up to Eze in the hills for lunch... she began to sing 'Parisian Pierrot' and other enchantments I can no longer recall... then I motored her back and it was as if the day before had been stretched far beyond twenty-four hours. Thereafter, until she left for America at the end of the Thirties we remained steadfast friends. She was singularly unaware of her genius, as she was of her defects.

One of those defects was a frequent tendency to overact, especially in comedy, and it was on this above all that Noël worked with her during that Riviera summer. By the time they got back to London at the end of July, most of their scenes together had been pre-rehearsed and (with Noël himself directing and his regular designer Gladys Calthrop doing the sets) they went into full rehearsals with the rest of the cast. The other couple, in Coward's mixed marital doubles, was to be played by his lifelong friend Adrianne Allen (then Mrs Raymond Massey) and a young moustached Laurence Olivier. Their roles, Victor and Sybil, were considered by their creator to be 'little better than ninepins, lightly wooden and only there at all in order to be repeatedly knocked down and stood up again by Elyot and Amanda' who in the play have of course formerly been married to each other, are now on second honeymoons with their new partners, but seriously tempted to get together again.

Noël had approached Olivier because he knew that Victor had to be attractive enough to have become Amanda's second husband, and because he knew that to have a bad part played by a bad actor would be suicidal. On the principle that only a really exciting actor can play a bore without being boring, Noël told Olivier that the play would do him a great deal of good, especially as he was badly in need of a West End hit, having deserted *Journey's End* to go into a recent and disastrous *Beau Geste*. Olivier agreed, and later admitted that much of his comic timing and technique was gained from working this engagement with Noël and Gertie, though it very nearly didn't happen.

With *Private Lives* already well into its second week of rehearsal, the then Lord Chamberlain, Lord Cromer, who still had the power of British stage censor, announced that he was thoroughly unhappy with Act Two in general and the Elyot–Amanda love-scene in particular. Considering that they were now supposed to be divorced and married to new and different partners, this seemed to him altogether too risqué for the public standards of 1930 morality, and his lordship added that unless the act was drastically rewritten he would regretfully be unable to give permission for *Private Lives* to be publicly performed.

Noël repaired instantly to St James's Palace, where he read the play, acting out all the parts in front of Lord Cromer, who was then persuaded that with some dignified direction the Elyot–Amanda love-scene would after all be acceptable without any cuts.

10

THE POTENCY OF CHEAP MUSIC

On 18 August 1930 *Private Lives* had its world première at the King's Theatre in Edinburgh. It was the third time that Noël and Gertie had appeared together on stage, and they were only to work together once more (in *Tonight at Eight-Thirty*); yet theirs was perhaps the definitive light-comedy partnership of the century, and never better expressed than in this one play.

Private Lives almost certainly represents Coward's greatest claim to theatrical immortality. It is in many ways the perfect light comedy, arguably the best to have come out of England since *The Importance of Being Earnest* which preceded it by 35 years; and though at the time of its first production it seemed to many critics that *Private Lives* could only survive for as long as Gertrude Lawrence and the author himself played it, the comedy has in fact been consistently successful ever since, a guaranteed copper-bottomed audience-puller that has temporarily rescued countless local theatre companies from the throes of a bad season. Royalties received, and still being received today, by the Coward estate show that hardly a month passes without somewhere in the world someone deciding to revive *Private Lives*, and it was suitably enough the play which, in a 1963 revival by the Hampstead Theatre Club then transferred to the West End, launched in his own lifetime the 'Noël Coward Renaissance'.

Yet *Private Lives* is a play that stands or falls by the way it is played. On paper, one discovers, there is almost nothing there: brief staccato lines, the occasional aphorism ('women should be struck regularly, like gongs') and duologues which take on a sparkling life of their own, nowhere better than in the second most famous balcony scene of all time:

AMANDA: How was the Taj Mahal?

ELYOT: Unbelievable, a sort of dream.

AMANDA: That was the moonlight, I expect, you must have seen it in the moonlight.

ELYOT: (*Never taking his eyes off her face.*) Yes, moonlight is cruelly deceptive.

AMANDA: And it didn't look like a biscuit box, did it? I've always felt that it might.

ELYOT: Darling, darling, I love you so.

AMANDA: And I do hope you met a sacred elephant. They're lint-white I believe, and very, very sweet.

ELYOT: I've never loved anyone else for an instant.

AMANDA: No, no, you mustn't – Elyot – stop.

ELYOT: You love me too, don't you? There's no doubt about it anywhere, is there?

AMANDA: No, no doubt anywhere.

'Gertie and Noël looked so beautiful together,' wrote Cole Lesley 'standing in the moonlight, that no one who saw them can ever forget; and they played the scene so magically, lightly, tenderly that one was for those fleeting moments brought near to tears by the underlying vulnerability, the evanescence of their love.'

But the dialogue in this comedy of appalling manners is theatrically effective rather than naturalistic; there is virtually no action beyond a fight at the end of Act II and another at the end of Act III; there are no cameo characters to break up the duologues except the maid at the end, and there is really no plot to sustain the actors if their comic talents start to fail them. *Private Lives* is in fact a technical exercise of incredible difficulty for two immensely accomplished light comedians.

After Edinburgh they toured Liverpool, Birmingham, Manchester and finally Southsea where one night the pioneer aviator Amy Johnson was to be found in the audience. Reviews on the tour had been generally excellent, though in this last week *Private Lives* ran into some high moral outrage from one critic who wrote:

> The play, with the exception of a certain amount of smart backchat, consisted of large buckets of stable manure thrown all over the great audience for over two hours... Twenty years ago such a production would have been impossible... of course these four players may in their own private lives be quite moral and respectable. I know nothing about them, and don't want to.

In London, *Private Lives* opened the new Phoenix Theatre in Charing Cross Road with a glittering high-society première on 24 September 1930: Olivier had spent the tour learning not to giggle on-stage, Adrianne Allen remembered 'supreme confidence – we all knew we had a hit' and Noël and Gertie 'enjoyed ourselves tip-top', though the general highspot was reckoned to be their moment at the piano with *Someday I'll Find You* and Elyot's remark about the strange potency of cheap music. 'Don't you just love it' asked Mrs

Patrick Campbell sweeping into the dressing-room afterwards, 'when Noël does his little hummings at the piano?'

Reviews next morning were however mixed, more good than bad but none exactly raves; most critics offered something of the grudging, patronizing, qualified admission of enjoyment with which Allardyce Nicoll was later to dismiss Coward in his book *World Drama*:

> Amusing, no doubt, yet hardly moving farther below the surface than a paper boat in a bath-tub and, like the paper boat, ever in imminent danger of becoming a shapeless, sodden mass.

'Brittle', 'tenuous' and 'thin' were the recurrent adjectives first used to describe *Private Lives* in general and the Noël–Gertie partnership in particular, but there were also references to cocktails, evening dress, repartee and even irreverent allusions to copulation, thereby, noted Noël, causing a gratifying number of respectable people to queue up at the box office.

Private Lives fast became the most popular play in town, especially when it became known that Noël and Gertie had only agreed to play it there for three months before moving on to Broadway. For the two of them, life went on much as it had backstage during that first childhood run of *Hannele*, where in rehearsal Noël took a paternal interest in Gertie's work, in performance they reverted to brother and sister, a couple of loving, squabbling equals who, like Elyot and Amanda, found it difficult to be together and impossible to be apart. There were frequent rows: on one occasion Everley Gregg, playing the small role of the maid, came into Noël's dressing room to find him and Gertie in the middle of a full-scale fist-fight. 'Stop it, stop it,' she cried, trying to tear them apart, 'I love you both,' whereupon Noël and Gertie both rounded on her and threatened to sack her on the spot. But through all of that, Noël's deep devotion to Gertie remained unscathed; a few months later he was to write:

> She has an astounding sense of the complete reality of the moment, and her moments, dictated by the extreme variability of her moods, change so swiftly that it is frequently difficult to discover what (apart from eating, sleeping and acting) is true of her at all. I know her well; better, I believe, than most people. The early years of our friendship set her strongly in my mind. I knew her then to have quick humour, insane generosity and a loving heart, and those things seldom change. I see her now, ages away from her ringlets and black velvet military cap, sometimes a simple, wide-eyed child, sometimes a glamorous *femme du monde,* at some moments a rather boisterous 'good sort', at others a weary, disillusioned woman battered by life but gallant to the last. She appropriated beauty to herself quite early, along with all the tricks and mannerisms that go with it. In adolescence she was barely pretty. Now, without apparent effort, she

gives the impression of sheer loveliness. Her grace in movement is exquisite, and her voice charming. To disentangle Gertie herself from this mutability is baffling, rather like delving for your grandmother's gold locket at the bottom of an overflowing jewel-case.

Her talent is equally kaleidoscopic. On the stage she is potentially capable of anything and everything. She can be gay, sad, witty, tragic, funny and touching. She can play a scene one night with perfect subtlety and restraint, and the next with such obviousness and over-emphasis that your senses reel. She has, in abundance, every theatrical essential but one: critical faculty. She can watch a great actor and be stirred to the depths, her emotional response is immediate and genuine. She can watch a bad actor and be stirred to the depths, the response is equally immediate and equally genuine. But for this tantalising lack of discrimination she could, I believe, be the greatest actress alive in the theatre today.

It was said of Gertie, not only by Noël but by Laurence Olivier, Adrianne Allen and many others who worked with her later, that not only did she never give the same performance two nights running, but there was no way of knowing what she was going to do on the third night either. She was impressionable to a quite remarkable degree; one of her co-stars remembered taking her one non-matinée afternoon to a Maurice Chevalier film, only to have her play the entire evening performance like Maurice Chevalier. But even Noël, her greatest friend and sternest critic, had to admit that when she played Amanda:

> Everything she had been in my mind when I originally conceived the idea in Tokyo came to life on the stage: the quicksilver delivery of lines; the romantic quality, tender and witty, alluring; the swift, brittle rages; even the white Molyneux dress.

True to the agreement they had made to play *Private Lives* on Broadway for Cochran, and with Noël still convinced that three months was the most he could ever play any one role in any one city without a kind of terrible boredom setting in, they closed at the Phoenix at Christmas, having played just 101 performances, much to the rage of those who had failed to get tickets. Noël was told that the day would come when he would bitterly regret his decision, though he never did and never (after Broadway) either experienced or expressed any desire at all to return to the role of Elyot Chase despite being told in print by Sir Cedric Hardwicke that it was unprofessional to close a hit.

Unperturbed, the company set sail for New York (all but pregnant Adrianne Allen, who was replaced as Sybil by Olivier's then wife Jill Esmond) and opened at the Times Square Theatre on Broadway in January 1931. Walter

Winchell reported that the opening night audience 'cheered long and loud when they weren't laughing in a lusty manner' and added that 'Miss Lawrence has never appeared to such advantage, nor has she ever captured an audience in New York as she did last night,' but there was still considerable doubt about the play itself. Brooks Atkinson for the *New York Times* thought that 'though Mr Coward himself appears with competent agility in *Private Lives*, he has nothing to say and sometimes the nothingness of this comedy begins to show through the dialogue.' Burns Mantle for the *Daily News* was however more enthusiastic, and in any case a management decision to play again for only three months guaranteed capacity houses at all performances.

In the most memorable notice of all, it was the *Variety* critic who summarized the plot of *Private Lives*:

> Mr Coward and Miss Lawrence are a couple of cooing meanies... Coward seems kinda grouchy over their scrapping... he goes to the piano and starts to sing.

Nevertheless, the rest of the press reaction was good enough for Metro Goldwyn to put in an immediate and excellent offer for the screen rights. Coward accepted, but as neither he nor Gertie were then (or ever) to he considered genuine film stars, Leslie Howard and Norma Shearer were suggested, though when Howard proved unavailable, the role of Elyot went to Robert Montgomery. For Olivier too, the Broadway run of *Private Lives* led to Hollywood offers; he went straight out to California at the end of the run and started, albeit hesitantly, on a screen career.

One man who happened to see Gertie with Noël during those three Broadway months was her future husband, Richard Aldrich; though they were not to meet for another year or two, he recalled:

> I can think of no two people who have given Broadway a more sparkling and memorable evening than Noël and Gertie in *Private Lives*. Each demanded the best from the other, and always received it; together they seemed to be the very essence of teamwork.

Yet although Noël was happy enough during the run of *Private Lives* in New York, living in a little penthouse on West 58th Street and already hard at work on his epic *Cavalcade*, for Gertie it was a much less happy time. Once through the stage door every evening, things were as usual fine for her, as there was nothing she actually enjoyed more than playing a hit; but in the daytime she had to admit to herself that her life was less than wonderful.

The affair with Bert Taylor had cooled to the point where Bert had in fact got himself another lady, one who didn't expect him at the end of long and increasingly difficult days on Wall Street to wait for dinner until she had

THE POTENCY OF CHEAP MUSIC

played a two-and-a-half hour comedy. Confronted by Gertie, who had heard of Bert's new friend, he admitted her existence and added that if Gertie would give up the theatre he'd still happily marry her, despite the passing of a year in which he had lost most of his own money and what little she had ever given him to invest. The crucial question was not, though, one of money; it was simply whether or not Gertie loved him enough to give up the theatre for him and it was by now all too clear to them both that she did not.

The loss of Bert was however a considerable blow; as Noël told her backstage one night 'You think your heart is broken – it isn't, but your pride is very hurt'; and that pride was at present almost all that Gertie had. As a result, the ending of the affair sent her into a kind of nervous collapse; rather than play *Private Lives* with anyone else (which he never had and never would), Noël sent her to bed and closed the theatre for a fortnight. They then reopened, played the rest of their promised twelve weeks, and handed over their roles to Otto Kruger and Madge Kennedy before sailing smartly back to London.

Gertie was leaving behind her, in New York, Bert Taylor and a mounting pile of debts; though the thousand pounds she had originally invested as her one-third share in the costs of staging *Private Lives* had already been repaid to her fivefold, her bill at Hatty Carnegie's alone was up above the $10,000 line and she was still spending, wrote Fanny Holtzmann, 'like an entire fleet of drunken sailors.' The unhappier she got over Bert and her failure to find any really successful kind of private life, the more she spent. Her generosity now bordered on the insane; once, at a counter in Cartier's, a woman came up to say how much she had enjoyed her performance in *Private Lives*. To the woman's amazement Gertie turned, bought the nearest bracelet in sight and pressed it into her admirer's hand before disappearing with a gracious wave into Fifth Avenue.

On the boat home to England in that summer of 1931, Miss Lawrence had a lot to think about. *Private Lives* had taken up a hugely enjoyable year of her life; it had consolidated her partnership with Coward (they were now and forever to be Noël and Gertie), made her some money, established her as a leading straight-theatre romantic comedienne, and been a lot of fun to do. But now Noël had other projects, ones that did not concern her, and she was again on her own.

Unlike him, she had no real control over her own professional destiny; Gertie couldn't write plays, or direct them. She had, like most jobbing actresses, to look at the offers which came along and try to pick the best of them. But she had no way of planning ahead, or of organizing her professional affairs any more clearly than she was able to extricate her private ones from looming financial chaos. She had, to misquote her own most popular song, no one to watch over her.

Not surprisingly therefore, on that boat home, her thoughts began to turn more and more frequently back to Philip Astley. It had been fully ten years now since he had launched her on London society, and more than three years since the Bert Taylor affair and her increasing devotion to Broadway had signalled an end to their intimacy. On the other hand, they were still deeply fond of each other, and there must have been moments now when Gertie began to wonder whether perhaps marriage might not be a good idea after all.

Fast approaching her 33rd birthday, she was in the uneasy position of being devoted to a branch of the theatre which did not require absolute devotion; had she been a Shakespearian, or any kind of classical actress or dancer, it is possible that the demands of those trades would have taken up so much of her time in rehearsal and performance that she would not have had much left in which to notice any kind of a void. But by its very nature the musical and light comedy theatre of the 1930s left rather more chance for outside activities. Now here she was, for instance, returning to England with absolutely nothing to do but revisit a mother and a daughter with whom she seemed to have even less in common than before, and wait for some sort of a script to drop through the letter-box for the following autumn. It was, she decided, high time to reconstruct a relationship with Astley and ease herself back into a social London life of the kind he and she had been living before the Charlot revues first took her to New York.

But that had been 1923. It was now 1932 and times had changed. For a start, Philip was not at the quayside to meet her. Unperturbed, Gertie moved smartly into the Savoy Hotel and waited for him to call and take her out for dinner, which he duly did. In order to tell her, as gently as possible, that he had just become engaged to Madeleine Carroll.

AMANDA: What's she like?

ELYOT: Fair, very pretty, plays the piano beautifully.

AMANDA: Very comforting.

11

NYMPH ERRANT

Within a matter of months, Gertie had lost the two men on whose arms and in whose beds she had spent most of the 1920s. She was alone again, and she was a lady for whom being alone was about the most terrifying prospect of all. Her greatest friend, ally and partner Noël Coward was a lifelong homosexual who had made it clear that professionally, too, they were to go their separate ways. He would of course write for her again after *Private Lives* (though in fact only once) but there was much else in the theatre that he fully intended to do without her.

Gertie's other early champion, André Charlot, had nothing more to offer Gertie than the chance to revive some of her earlier successes. Wisely she declined. It was, however, to be another two years before anything really worthy of her unique but uneasy-to-cast talent came along, and the fact that in the interim she threw herself into no less than four plays and three films (where recently she had been doing no more than one major show a year) is some indication of just how adrift her career had suddenly gone. It was also an indication of her desperation to stay in work, any kind of work, rather than face up to the collapse of her private life.

The first play she did back in England was a thoroughly curious and fairly disastrous Spanish farce which the Granville-Barkers had rendered into English as *Take Two from One*. As directed by Komisarjevsky (or 'Komanseduceme' as he was irreverently known to the drama students at RADA) this bizarre piece featured Gertie and Peggy Ashcroft at the Theatre Royal Haymarket struggling for the affections of an understandably embarrassed Nicholas Hannen who concluded the play by jumping off the stage into a box, there to disappear from sight. The politest of the reviews called it 'an uneven farce', and the critic James Agate thought the scene where Gertie had to burst into the drawing room 'in the costume of an African savage', having spent several years captured by a tribe there, resembled nothing so much as 'a production number in a Cicely Courtneidge musical'. This was not intended as a compliment, and they were off within six weeks having received from *The Times* a sharp caution to the effect that 'it is time Mr Granville-Barker gets back to his work as a director and gives up interpreting minor matters from Madrid.'

Gertie herself, who treated her customers in a curiously regal way as if she were the archduchess of some middle European state and they her faithful subjects, merely noted that 'the audience did not like me in a role so foreign to the parts I had played.'

Within a month she had hastened over to another play, again at the Theatre Royal Haymarket where the management were keen not to lose her services. With this one, entitled *Can the Leopard?*, she had rather better luck, largely because it was a much better comedy and got her securely back onto home territory – a studio flat in Chelsea. The plot was not admittedly subtle, but it did allow for a certain amount of fun and the wearing of some lavish Norman Hartnell dresses. Gertie played a naturally helpless and untidy young girl-about-town who married a rather stuffy solicitor (Ian Hunter), spent six months trying to become a model housewife and then discovered that her husband had always preferred her untidy anyway, hence the full title quotation about leopards changing their spots. In the wake of *Private Lives*, most fashionable West End marital comedies were supposed to be about four rather than just two people, and so here the quartet was made up by Kay Hammond and Kim Peacock with Kathleen Harrison already starting to do her perennial comic cleaning lady. All in all it was a safe mixture, and it worked: *Can the Leopard?* lasted six months at the Haymarket and Gertie proudly noted that 'in the role I innovated a new fashion – an interesting streak of white hair swept away from the forehead. It caught on immediately and women began flocking to the hairdressers' for a 'Riviera' bleach.'

At the end of the run Gertie herself flocked to the Riviera for her now annual summer holiday on Cap Ferrat. While she was still far from happy, while she had still found no one to replace Philip or Bert, and while her love life consisted at best of the occasional backstage encounter, she had at least had another West End success and was beginning to learn how to live alone again. Her mother was back at the house in Clapham, and her daughter Pamela was now a boarder at Roedean, the most expensive girls' public school in England:

> Mother thought that was socially the right thing to do with me, and so we only ever met in the holidays. She was still a very social animal in the old 'Tatler' sense; she never read much, only ever took me to concerts when she knew somebody who would be there, and though she did occasionally meet up with intellectuals, she never really was anything more than a kind of adornment to their world. Through no fault of her own she had never really been educated, and whereas Noël Coward in later life painstakingly taught himself to think and to understand intellectual concepts, she never did. Her only real care was the theatre, and that on a purely practical, non-intellectual level. If you look at the theatre of her time, outside the Old Vic it really wasn't a very serious place and certainly the scripts that she was getting offered did not require a lot of intellectual analysis. They were jobs, and she did them as well as she could, often better than anyone else could, but they never really gave her the chance or the urge to use her brain, and as a result she seldom did. It was all froth.

We hardly ever got the chance to talk properly together, or to get to know each other, but when she did occasionally begin to unbend and unburden herself to me she would only ever talk about the theatre in terms of the struggle, the terrible need to stay on top, the awful fear of a flop which might mean you were finished. Success and the business of being Gertrude Lawrence were all she ever really thought about; having come up from the bottom, her whole ethos was based on not being poor. Her talent was for making bags of stones into bags of diamonds on stage, and that was a very real talent. In some ways she was a real innocent: 'invincible ignorance', the Catholic Church would call it. Her sophistication was always that of a little girl who dresses up in high heels and her mother's evening gowns: it was skin deep, and that perhaps above all was what made so many men like Philip, Noël, Bert, and later Douglas Fairbanks and Richard Aldrich want to protect her. She needed it, God knows.

For all those reasons, and above all because of an almost total change in the British and American theatre after the war, Gertrude Lawrence left virtually no heiresses: it would be impossible today to find an actress who much resembled her on stage or off, though traces of the Gertrude Lawrence stage presence were, interestingly, soon to be evident in the high-comedy career of her co-star from *Can The Leopard?*, Kay Hammond, who was to be, a decade later, the first actress allowed by Noël to recreate Amanda in *Private Lives* during its first West End revival.

And because there was nobody quite like her, in her own lifetime, Gertie found it often hard to know what she was supposed to be doing next. Her career was decidedly informal, almost to the point of shapelessness, but for all that a number of distinguished talents, by no means all musical, beat a path to her door. That summer of 1932 a script reached her at Cap Ferrat written by the man who, just twenty years later was as director to give Gertie her greatest and last Broadway triumph in *The King and I*. But at this time John van Druten was still purely a playwright, and the script he wanted her to read concerned a woman who, having been retrieved from the brink of suicide, then falls in love with an infinitely distinguished and already married and dying barrister.

Not perhaps the most cheerful of subjects, but *Behold We Live* already had a good deal of distinction attached to it: Gilbert Miller was to present it at the St James's, with a cast which was also to include Sir Gerald du Maurier as the dying barrister and Dame May Whitty as his mother. Gertie, sensing a touch of class, rapidly signed a contract and returned from Cap Ferrat to start rehearsal at the beginning of August.

Behold We Live was to contain, apart from van Druten, another link into her future in that it was to be Sir Gerald's daughter, Daphne du Maurier, who was to write Gertie's one postwar British stage play, *September Tide*. But the play that they were now working on filled them with a certain amount of gloom. Though there is no evidence that he actually knew it at the time, Sir Gerald was by now within eighteen months of his own death; still only on the very verge of his sixties, he had already grown tired of the theatre, perhaps also tired of life. Certainly, in Gertie's view, one of the reasons why Lady du Maurier was seldom seen around the theatre after the first night was that 'she could not bear to watch her husband night after night portraying his own destiny.'

But critics were not of course to know that, and reviews were somewhat mixed; on the one hand, thought Agate, this was a sentimental tale which would have been better done as a Hollywood silent called 'The Salvage of Souls'. On the other hand Ivor Brown wrote of Gertie's 'brave rejection of her sure-fire comedy techniques' and 'her fine grasp that keeps the play from sinking hopelessly into sentimentality.' Above all, many critics noted that she had at last begun to learn some vestiges of self-restraint on stage, and therefore had at last the makings of a good serious actress.

Behold We Live was therefore a worthy, rather than a hugely enjoyable, success, but the best thing about it was the discovery by Gertie and Sir Gerald of how much they had in common. Both at that time were in deep financial trouble, both viewed the theatre as a mechanical money-making function rather than a deep spiritual or intellectual calling, and (though she was little more than half his age) both had become considerably jaded about the way their own lives appeared to be going.

The result was an immediate and loving friendship which soon led them to work together by day as well as by night; during the run of *Behold We Live* Gertie's current lover, Benn Levy, was directing a film for Alfred Hitchcock's production unit at Elstree. It was, considering its Hitchcock–Levy pedigree, an oddly muddled comedy-thriller called *Lord Camber's Ladies,* but in it there were roles for both Gertie (as an actress in danger of being poisoned) and Sir Gerald (as a noble doctor). During the shooting, reported his daughter Daphne, Gerald's dislike of film acting increased tenfold, though no one would have believed it to look at him, with his pockets full of tricks and practical jokes that he let fly amongst the feet of cameramen, electricians and directors in a sort of desperate effort to relieve the tedium. Practical joking during these months developed to a pitch of positive frenzy, until both theatre and studio resembled another Bedlam. The nervy, highly strung Gertie was a boon companion in mischief, and the round-faced Hitchcock a surprising ally down at Elstree. It was a wonder that the picture was ever completed at all, for hardly a moment would pass without some faked telegram arriving, some bogus message being delivered, some supposed telephone bell ringing, until the practical jokers were haggard and worn with their tremendous efforts, and had lived so long in an atmosphere of pretence that they had forgotten what it was like to be natural.

But for Sir Gerald, as for Gertie, these jokes worked as a kind of safety valve which prevented either of them from having to face up to the reality of an unhappy present and an uncertain future. Their work was all they had; because they were in debt, there was no escape from it – even had they wanted one, or known how to take it and what to do once the escape was made. Gertie was now deeply into that tax trap still familiar and much dreaded by actors today. Hoping to find a way of clearing her debts, she threw herself into two other equally undistinguished films in 1932, making them all day while still working in the theatre by night.

The first of these ought to have been hugely distinguished and somehow wasn't; if ever a playwright, apart from Coward, was perfectly suited to Gertie's own brand of high comedy then it was surely the master of the country-house-party satire Frederick Lonsdale. Yet curiously she and he were only ever once to he united, and then for an uninspired film version of his West End hit *Aren't We All?* Harry Lachman shot it in a month (with a cast which also featured Owen Nares, Hugh Wakefield and Marie Lohr) and though it was worth £2,600 to Gertie, it did her film career no more good than *Lord Camber's Ladies*.

Undeterred, she went on to make *No Funny Business*, a United Artists release for which she was reunited with two of her three co-stars from the Broadway *Private Lives,* Laurence Olivier and Jill Esmond. The film was a distinctly hackneyed rewrite of the Coward script, again to do with sudden Riviera meetings in the moonlight and the reawakening of dead marriages, though the plot was kept just far enough away from *Private Lives* to avoid charges of piracy. So too, alas, was the dialogue. 'Miss Lawrence conveys a certain vitality and assurance on screen,' thought the critic of the *Monthly Film Bulletin,* 'but she plays in a manner long outmoded.'

She was, in fact, too theatrical ever to work well in front of a camera and, though she was now the survivor of four films in as many years, not one of them had done her or its backers any real good whatsoever. Back in the theatre, where she belonged, 1933 was to be a vintage year.

As soon as the run of *Behold We Live* drew to its close she went into rehearsal for *This Inconstancy*, a patchy and moralistic comedy by Roland Pertwee and John Hastings Turner. When the plot flagged, as it did quite badly in the second act, Gertie retreated to the piano and there sang a little song specially composed for the occasion by Ivor Novello; for the rest, she contented herself with wearing a series of sparkling Molyneux gowns and trifling with the affections of a husband (Leslie Banks) and two lovers (Hugh Wakefield and Nigel Bruce). 'Ultra Moderns In New Play' headlined the *Daily*

Mail, while Agate thought that 'Miss Lawrence wears with consummate elegance backless dresses in a spineless part, and is as always immensely clever.' Too clever by half, thought another critic, recognizing amid the cocktails and laughter yet another sign of Britain's moral collapse, albeit one for once not written by Mr Noël Coward.

This Inconstancy kept Gertie gainfully employed at Wyndham's through the summer of 1933, but even though she was still filming by day her debts continued to mount up. In something approaching desperation she first took to writing some horrendously twee columns in the *Daily Mirror,* full of (largely ghosted) advice about how to keep a home spick and span and a husband happy, neither of which Gertie had ever had to think much about doing. Then, still in the hope of earning some extra money on the side, she agreed to go into partnership with Lady Diana Cooper and Felicity Tree in founding a Berkeley Square flower shop.

Known to their friends as Fresh Flowers Limited, and to their enemies as Faded Flowers Incorporated, the shop was a perfect microcosm of almost all Gertie's attempts at moneymaking. Though started with the best of all possible motives, quick clear profit, the shop rapidly became a white elephant, costing more to run than it could ever hope to make. Gertie had insisted that the walls were to bear frescoes by Oliver Messel, and that those of her friends who wished to send flowers to other of her friends but found themselves temporarily out of pocket were always to be given extended credit. Moreover Gertie herself naturally considered any flowers in her shop her property, having neatly overlooked the fact that at some point somebody somewhere would actually have to be paid for them.

By the middle of 1933, despite the shop, the *Mirror* column, the films and the plays, Gertrude Lawrence was actually in more debt than she had been a year earlier and there was by now but one hope: Fanny Holtzmann.

Hearing from New York of her English client's financial embarrassment, Miss Holtzmann began to cast around for another big moneymaker. Small films and straight plays were all very well in their way, but Fanny knew even better than Gertie that the big money lay in big shows, preferably long-running musicals. What Fanny needed for Gertie was not just another script but 'a property' and it didn't take her long to discover that Charles Blake Cochran, the impresario of *Private Lives,* actually had one.

He had recently bought the stage rights in a novel written by a young, and then very junior, keeper at the Victoria and Albert Museum by the name of James Layer. Called *Nymph Errant,* it told the simple but enchanting story of an English girl on her way home from school in Switzerland who falls in with a Frenchman and sets out with him on a series of adventures through which she travels wide-eyed, returning home at last totally unaware of what she has just narrowly escaped in the way of sexual and other misadventures.

Cochran originally intended this as a straight play, and had indeed given it to the actor Romney Brent for dramatization. Fanny, however, saw it as a musical comedy and approached Noël Coward with the request that he should write a score for it, and of course for Gertie. Noël replied that, though he was indeed planning to write something soon for his beloved old friend, it would be something totally of his own devising; he was not, he told Miss Holtzmann, a kind of hired hack who could be summoned whenever Miss Lawrence was in need of a vehicle.

Still determined that *Nymph Errant* was to be a musical, and strongly backed by Cochran, Fanny set out in search of an alternative composer. It did not take her long to track down Cole Porter, who read the book in a single evening and was at his piano by early the following morning.

What he had seen in *Nymph Errant,* according to his biographer Charles Schwartz, was: '...the story of an English lass hell-bent on losing her virginity in such offbeat places as a sheik's desert tent, the Parisian follies, a Turkish harem and a nudist camp.' Cole created an extraordinary score for the show that not only kept pace with the heroine's global philanderings but added some wonderfully suggestive overtones of its own. Typical of Cole's breezy suggestiveness was the tune 'Experiment' with its admonitions to 'be curious' and to 'experiment' – presumably in things sexual. Also free-wheeling in approach was Cole's 'Si Vous Aimez Les Poitrines', a number glorifying the size and shape of Parisian women's breasts over other women's, including women in Poona, Bali, Spain and similar romantic Edens of the world. Sung in the show by Iris Ashley, as Madeleine, a well-endowed Parisian cocotte, the tune served as a titillating reminder to mankind that 'when zat feeling comes a-stealing' Madeleine was the one to 'call on'. Another tune that showed Cole at his wicked best was 'The Physician', a humorous anatomical inventory of the heroine's body from the viewpoint of an overzealous medical man who also happens to be one of the schoolgirl's long line of lovers. As recounted by Evangeline, the English schoolgirl played by Gertrude Lawrence, the song deftly enumerated all the parts of her body that the physician adored: her bronchial tubes, her epiglottis, her medulla oblongata, her pancreas and so on. Unfortunately, as the song makes very clear in the last line of the refrain ('but he never said he loved me'), the doctor was too carried away with the individual parts of Evangeline's anatomy to love her for herself.

Cole Porter himself thought that *Nymph Errant* was the best score he ever wrote, although apart from its three hits ('Experiment', 'The Physician' and Elisabeth Welch's great number 'Solomon') it remains among his least known internationally, largely because, at the time, the utter Englishness of the heroine denied the show an afterlife either on Broadway or on film. Indeed so unfamiliar is the show today that the sleeve notes for a recent reissue of some of the songs solemnly announce it to be the musical version of 'Margaret Kennedy's celebrated novel *The Constant Nymph*.'

Though it was clear as soon as Porter began playing his score back in London to Cochran and to Gertie that they were now dealing with a considerably sexier version of James Layer's novel than had originally been contemplated, so delighted were they – and indeed Mr Layer – by Porter's scintillating score that they could hardly wait to get into rehearsal.

Gertie had another cause for celebration that summer of 1932: she had found herself a new lover – Douglas Fairbanks Junior. She had also, she told Bea Lillie, taken a house in Berkeley Square: 'Well, dear,' replied Bea memorably, 'you'll just have to put it back again, won't you?'

Pamela, meanwhile, was still in boarding school; so keen was Gertie to keep establishing her daughter's youth that Woollcott, reminded yet again by Gertie of Pamela's school, was heard to ask, 'And what classes does she teach there?'

12

YOUNG DOUG

I was still in my teens when I first met her, at the time of the first Charlot revue in New York [recalls Fairbanks] and developed a terrible crush on her, but Gertie, Bea and Buchanan were all caught up with much older friends, though they were very kind to me and got kind of used to finding me hanging around the stage door. A few years later, when the revue came out to California, I met them again at a party at my father's house, Pickfair. By this time I was older and had a moustache, and Gertie and I began to seem more or less the same generation. Then, at the very beginning of the 1930s, my father had got his divorce from Mary Pickford and I'd just got mine from Joan Crawford, and so the two of us came to London, at a time when Gertie was living on her own but seeing a lot of Eric Dudley, who used to escort her around town in the same way that Astley always had during the 1920s. Anyway she and I then began seeing a great deal of each other; she was ten or eleven years older than me, but she looked a lot younger, and I guess I must have looked a lot older. Increasingly she began inviting me to her parties and to meet her friends, and I found myself trying to nudge Eric Dudley out of the way so that I could have her to myself.

Dudley was very good-looking, dripped with charm, and both he and his brothers became good friends of mine, which made it all the more difficult to have to fight him for Gertie. She, of course, loved every moment of it; she liked nothing better than having two men competing for her affections the way that Astley and Bert Taylor once had.

I don't think either Gertie or I ever seriously considered marriage, but we had some wonderful times together. She was very temperamental, very jealous, could be exhausting, moody, difficult but also enchanting and alive and very funny. Later we tried to work together and indeed had one big stage success (*Moonlight is Silver*), but it was never easy to keep our professional lives and our private lives separate. In the end I had to go back to the States and we drifted apart, but some of my happiest memories of the 1930s are the months we spent together.

But she could be terrifying. Once we had a great row because I'd been seeing someone else, or anyway she thought I had, and she began throwing furniture at me, so I ran out in the street and jumped on a bus that was passing, and she just ran into the street after me and continued throwing things at the bus with me sitting inside pretending to the other passengers that I didn't know who she was. The bus got into Putney before I dared get off it.

Later, in the Second World War, Fairbanks also met up with Astley – one of the more curious aspects of Gertrude Lawrence's relationships was that many of her lovers tended in later life to befriend each other, presumably to compare notes on survival techniques after the whirlwind of Gertie's tempestuous friendship had passed them by.

Cochran was determined to spare no expense on *Nymph Errant*: he was already paying three creators (Layer for the original novel, Romney Brent for the adaptation and Cole Porter for the score) and he now brought in Doris Zinkeisen to do the sets and costumes, Brent himself to direct and, perhaps most intriguingly, a revolutionary young American choreographer on her first major musical theatre assignment. She was Agnes de Mille, niece of the great Hollywood Czar, and she was soon writing home to mother instalments of a fascinating rehearsal logbook:

> Cole Porter is a small, finely boned and fastidious little man with a round doll head like a marionette's, large staring eyes and a fixed and pleased expression that I rather think has nothing to do with his emotions... he barely speaks but, make no mistake, he is the most powerful person in the theatre not excepting Charles Cochran. His rhymes are fabulous, male, female, middle word which I suppose could be called neuter. 'How do you do this?' I asked marvelling. 'It's easy,' he replied. 'It's just fun. Anyone can. Get a rhyming dictionary.' That's the answer, of course...
>
> Our author, James Layer, is a bookish young man in a bowler, with a muted, slightly eighteenth-century air, the keeper of prints at the Victoria and Albert Museum. It seems he has his raffish moments, this play being one of them. I think it's silly, a mere excuse for good songs and Gertie's dresses...
>
> Romney Brent has ability, and is by all odds the pleasantest person to work with I have yet encountered, as well as the most intelligent. Gertie on the other hand, although warm and charming, has been something rather special to deal with. In fact, I've left every rehearsal cursing with frustration. I finally asked Cochran if she really liked what I was giving her. He says she adores it. It dawned on me then that she actually thinks she is doing exactly what I ask. She never does eight consecutive bars twice the same way. She's more particular about her hats, I can tell you.
>
> Gertie's art is built on instinct and improvisation. She disciplines her performance, I'm told, no more than her rehearsals, changing with whim and temperature and without warning. You expect Gertie downstage; she comes in centre back – even with the curtain up and a paying audience. You expect her to play *grazioso* and gently; she is *allegro vivace* and sharp. You expect her in a dark-green silk; she is in transparent gauze. But she's always fun, on and offstage, always...

Well, perhaps not always. On 16 September, Agnes de Mille was writing home from Manchester:

At dress rehearsal yesterday, Gertie suddenly decided onstage that she hated her first act finale costume although, naturally, she'd been at all the fittings. Suddenly at that moment she couldn't abide it. She pouted and fretted and Cockie, instead of saying it was too late and to get on with her job, patted her on the cheek and said there, there, she'd have a new one on the next night. My heart turned over for Zinkeisen. If anyone had carried on in dress rehearsal about a dance this way! Zinkeisen was already making a pencil sketch of a new red velvet. The specifications were phoned to London and a messenger despatched on the next train with the drawing. Gertie will have it in time for opening. Throughout all this our author, James Layer, sat by admiring. Well, by God, so did I. Before openings, I'm told, Gertie goes to the theatre with three or four outfits of her own for every scene and spends the day choosing. It distracts her from nervous horrors. It also gives the costume designer – who is never consulted – fits.

For James Layer:

> The combination of Cochran and Gertrude Lawrence was irresistible… on the Manchester first night of *Nymph Errant* I took Gertrude Lawrence in a taxi to the Opera House. She sobbed in my arms, crying 'I can't go on! I can't goon!' But, of course, she did go on and in two minutes had the audience at her feet… I suppose I shall never he involved in any capacity in a more 'glamorous' affair. Manchester had suffered an invasion of fur-coats and orchids and white ties. The Fairbanks party had taken a whole row of the stalls for themselves and their friends. The London critics attended in force and, when we got back to the Midland Hotel, the stairs leading up to the dining room were lined five deep with people clapping and cheering Gertrude Lawrence.

For Agnes de Mille, more immediately involved in the show's mechanics than the author of its original book, it seems to have been a slightly less rosy world première:

> The show began and it was, as I'd suspected, piffling. The Cole Porter songs are enchanting. The dances stopped the show, however; that's the God's truth… and Gertie. Ah, Gertie! As Frank Collins, the stage manager said, 'She is like a racehorse. When the curtain goes up, her best foot is always forward. You can count on her as on the Queen. There will be no public error. She delivers. She leads the field. She breaks the tape', and also my heart a little, because it is never by any chance my exact work she is performing. Who cares? She sells tickets. She proceeds as I have told you by improvisation. This may be rough on the play and the other actors but it means that her great nights are incandescent, and on this night she was pure magic. I've never witnessed the like – indeed I haven't. She was, as predicted, nothing like what

she's been in rehearsals; the stage was nevertheless jumping with excitement. Acting shimmered. Gertie moves like a fish through shadows, the creation of her unexpected invention. She is funny, bright, touching, irresistible. When she walks, she streams; when she kicks, she flashes. Her speaking voice is a kind of song, quite unrealistic but lovely, and her pathos cuts under all, direct and sudden. Her eyes fill, her throat grows husky, she trembles with wonder. The audience weeps. She can't sing, but who cares?

The celebrations in Manchester that night involved not only the company of *Nymph Errant*; Fairbanks was there to be with Gertie, as was Noël with his usual acid-sharp advice about cuts needed before London, and so was Sibyl Colefax who seldom missed a party. Such was the American interest in *Nymph Errant* (both Cole Porter and Gertrude Lawrence being regarded there as fundamentally Broadway property) that an entire NBC radio crew travelled to Manchester to broadcast live from there a half-hour coast-to-coast programme about the making of the show. In the interests of drama, Cochran himself agreed to act out a little 'scene' wherein he calmed down a supposedly furious Romney Brent who wished to 'sack' Gertie for arriving late at a rehearsal. He also agreed to interview several of his 'young ladies' who were forming the chorus, and history was therefore made with the first-ever (if somewhat less than totally factual) trans-Atlantic backstage broadcast.

The only person who seemed less than thrilled by the arrival of *Nymph Errant* in Manchester was the father of its author: Arthur J. Layer, a local preacher and chapel steward, gave a lengthy press interview denouncing the show's immorality, though he did admit at the end that he hadn't actually been to see it himself.

There was, however, still a great deal of work to do before *Nymph Errant* was ready to face London audiences a month later: one of the singers got fired for sounding, said Cochran, 'like a Czarina vomiting' and a number that had gone rather too well (while not performed by Gertie herself) was moved to a spot in the show where it would be less of a threat to the star. A decade later, when the same thing happened with a Danny Kaye number in Gertie's *Lady in the Dark*, she had acquired the strength and self-confidence simply to leave the number where it was and rise above it – but not yet. As Agnes de Mille reported a week or so into their Manchester try-out:

> Gertie continues to be unpredictable. The other night she wore two dresses no one had ever seen. Also, she took off all her underpinnings for the Turkish scene, and the actor who was playing opposite her, on being confronted with his star virtually naked, was so surprised he had to leave the stage in order to recover himself. Gertie and young Doug [Fairbanks] thought this very funny.

By early October they were re-rehearsing at the Adelphi in London and, though the box-office queues were unprecedented, or perhaps precisely because they were, a certain insecurity had begun to manifest itself backstage. Agnes de Mille wrote:

> The show is far from first-rate. The loss of morale in the cast has been profound and subtle. Cole Porter has disappeared, as I believe he always does under similar circumstances.

Tempers were now fraying; Cochran was (unusually) beginning to lose his nerve, and much to Miss de Mille's fury he even brought in another choreographer to insert some irrelevant tap routines. Then came the London first night, and Agnes de Mille stopped by Gertie's dressing room to wish her luck:

> She'd been closeted in there since ten in the morning trying on dresses without, by the way, either the permission or the assistance of the designer. Not even her secretary dared speak to her. She was making up in a state of manic euphoria. Beside her were young Doug's flowers, £50-worth. Two men had to lift the basket down from the stage door. The top roses brushed the ceiling... Then she handed me a present. A big box [containing] a milk-white vase from Asprey with a spray of absolutely exquisite pastel-coloured flowers made of feathers. It sounds tacky. It was enchanting – leave it to Gertie.

For James Layer, out front-of-house:

> The foyer of the Adelphi Theatre was full of well-known faces, from Somerset Maugham to Elsa Maxwell, from Lady Lavery to Cecil Beaton. And at the Savoy afterwards the scenes at Manchester were repeated. I suppose it was natural that I should have been made a little dizzy by all this, especially as my share of the royalties was rather more than ten times the amount of my official emoluments. The film rights were purchased by Twentieth Century Fox. I began to toy with the idea of giving up the Museum and living by my pen. It was as well that wiser thoughts prevailed for, in the following year, I paid out in income tax more than my entire earnings from all sources.

Although the first night was a huge social success, the reviews for *Nymph Errant* next morning reflected some of the uncertainty that the cast themselves had begun to feel about the show. Critics generally much preferred Cole Porter's score for *Gay Divorce* (which Fred Astaire was then also playing in London) and accused him here of writing 'minor Noël Coward numbers'. Though ecstatic for Gertie, other notices referred to *Nymph Errant* as 'a sort of pantomime for intellectuals' and the critic of the *Observer* reckoned:

The piece is doomed to failure; in sentiment, on which the English public singly dotes, it is as parched as a pea. And then again there is the deterrent of its unrelenting wit, the one quality of which the English public is uniquely shy. If it is rescued it will be because of 'Solomon', a hot ditty bawled by Elisabeth Welch. This, though I hate it, is undoubtedly the hit of the show.

A combination, however, of the advance bookings and word-of-mouth, which suggested that the show was in fact rather more enjoyable than many critics had indicated, got *Nymph Errant* off to a flying start at the Adelphi. After a week or two Agnes de Mille again dropped by Gertie's dressing room:

It is always a mass of flowers and there is always a bucket of iced champagne in the corner. 'Come in, darling. Come in,' she carols. 'Have some champagne,' her eyes moving beyond me to see if there were possibly a man in attendance. She never looks at me directly. I imagine she looks men in the eyes. But how can I be sure? She has never looked into mine or any woman's I've noticed. She fixes on men wholly, and although sweet and pleasant to women, is in the end oblivious to them. She is a coquette *par excellence,* and unfailingly successful. Many women, however, adore her. In her house in London every night at midnight is spread, I am told, a rich supper pheasant, caviare, crêpes, roast beef and of course champagne. She gathers up whomever she wishes and takes them home. The staff are always ready. She lives on the scale of a duchess. She collects jewels as people collect gramophone records, and after every admirer's visit there is a fine new piece. The white ties and black tails flash in and out of her dressing room like blackbirds, and there have been near encounters and narrow misses. Gertie bubbles through it all, vastly amused, and the new pins and bracelets keep on appearing and being replaced. There was the tale of how on the opening night in a short-lived comedy drama, she found to her astonishment that all the stones in her stage jewelry had been replaced by real ones. There are rumours of Young Doug saying at breakfast to Gertie the other morning, 'Look out the window, Gertie,' and there, tied up in the Thames, was her new yacht right before her new house in Cheyne Row. None of this is to imply that she is anything less than a great big stunning star and deserving of all. Lawrence has bewitching, quicksilver grace, wit, prettiness, chic, and outrageous fun. Her energy is legendary. Her chic and fun have set the style in whatever city or place she graces.

Nymph Errant ran on at the Adelphi through the winter of 1933, achieving a neither spectacular nor shameful total of a hundred and fifty-four performances in a run of just under five months. But it was during this run of *Nymph Errant,* which should have been one of the happiest of Gertie's career for she had seldom before and was seldom again to receive quite the same measure of personal (unconnected with Coward) acclaim in her own native city, that the difference between the way she was living and the way she could afford to live finally caught up with her.

For a long time now she had had a very high standard of living; though she had never lacked wealthy escorts (not only the Earl of Dudley but Ivor Guest, later Viscount Wimbourne, and the Marquis de Casa Maury were among those tactfully referred to at the time as her 'close friends') she had always taken a certain pride, rooted in her own childhood financial insecurity, in paying her own way. This arrangement meant that although she had no qualms at all about accepting, indeed collecting, rich gifts, it was usually she who paid her own very considerable household costs. She may have been (in Agnes de Mille's thoughtful analysis) a coquette, but she was seldom, if ever, a kept woman. She would cheerfully take diamonds, but cash would have been an insult and it was the cash which had long since run out.

For a while, she lived easily and happily on extended credit from everyone; she was after all a very big star, playing in a huge West End theatre in a show which was a popular if not critical success; shopkeepers and traders of the time were by and large an obsequious lot, eager not to lose customers especially if they happened to be famous and in a position to recommend their favourite retailers to others at their own exalted level of society. Miss Lawrence was known to have wealthy friends inside and outside the theatre; true, her bills were seldom actually being paid but that time would surely come, and in the meantime it was always a pleasure to serve her, especially as she made a point of telling all journalists precisely who dressed her and in what.

That whole arrangement, which had lasted throughout the latter half of the 1920s and now well into the 1930s, fell totally apart one winter morning at the beginning of 1934 when the Inland Revenue let it be known that they were after Miss Lawrence for the payment of five years' back taxes on money earned on both sides of the Atlantic. There was at this stage no talk of bankruptcy, but occasional gossip-column references to Gertie's 'financial embarrassment' had the effect of alerting her many creditors to the fact that, if she was having trouble paying the Revenue, then she might also be having trouble finding the money for them. It was not long before some of them decided on some action of their own.

13

TONIGHT AT EIGHT-THIRTY

'**M**y mother never really understood the kind of financial chaos her affairs were in', recalled Pamela, 'largely because nobody in England ever dared to explain it all to her.' Whenever her secretary or someone did find the courage to raise the subject Gertie would fly into terrible rages and so, to quiet her down and make sure she got to the theatre on time, they would simply have to let the matter drop. In the end it took an American, Fanny Holtzmann, to sort the whole thing out and by then it was very nearly too late.

For the time being, however, life went on more or less as usual; true, the creditors were getting a little more restive, but there was still a sizeable salary coming in every week from *Nymph Errant* and the Inland Revenue had as yet done no more than request meetings with Gertie, most of which she managed to forget to attend. Aware that her only real hope of solvency now as always was to stay in constant work, the moment *Nymph Errant* reached the end of its faintly disappointing run in the spring of 1934, she decided to work for the first time with her beloved Young Doug in a play called *The Winding Journey* by Philip Leader, which opened in Manchester towards the end of May and somehow never managed to wind its way into London. As Fairbanks said:

> Neither Gee, nor I, nor Binkie Beaumont, who was presenting it for H. M. Tennent, thought it was really good enough to risk bringing in to the West End, so a great friend of Noël's and Gertie's, the novelist Clemence Dane, was brought in to try and rescue it, but she said she'd rather start again and write us an altogether different play and that duly became *Moonlight Is Silver*.

But first there was the summer and Gertie, in recognition of her increasing financial problems, decided she would not be renting the usual villa in the South of France. Instead, she rented one on Majorca. Fairbanks remembered:

> I didn't have any money then either, but I managed to scrape the fare together and I decided to surprise her, so I took the night boat over, got a taxi to Formentor, changed, shaved at the hotel and asked if there was an English lady renting a little cottage there. The manager pointed to the largest villa on the horizon, so I climbed the hill, rang the bell and waited. Gertie had said, back in London, that she was going there to be alone, to rest up after the winter and to think about her future. But when she

saw me on the doorstep she went ashen, whispered 'Eric Dudley's here – get out,' and closed the door. Disconsolate, I made my way back to London. Years and years went by, and long after the war I was sitting in White's one day reading the papers and Eric Dudley came in, so we began to reminisce about the past in general and specifically about that summer in Majorca, and I told him the whole story of my arrival there and then he too went ashen. He hadn't ever been to Majorca with Gertie. The question is, then, who the hell was she in that villa with? Now she's dead, and we shall never find out.

Back in London, Gertie and Doug began in the late summer to rehearse *Moonlight is Silver,* which Clemence Dane herself was directing with a strong supporting cast including Cecil Parker, Barry Jones, Alexis France, Helen Hayes and Martita Hunt. Given that kind of support and considerable public interest in the offstage affair of the two stars, the play could hardly fail, though a number of critics echoed Ivor Brown's feeling that '*Moonlight Is Silver* is one of those plays which would stop soon after they began if the characters showed a grain of common sense.' It concerned a mining engineer (Fairbanks) who, returning home, is so convinced that his wife (Gertie) has been unfaithful to him that she ultimately decides to let him think she has. In the end, of course, her innocence is proved and all ends happily, but, without the benefit of a strong director, Gertie was apparently up to all her old overacting tricks again. According to *The Times,* 'Miss Lawrence may be a perpetual delight but in a play like this where the one need is for sincerity, she does tend to indulge her mannerisms at the expense of emotional power.'

Miss Dane had, however, borrowed a trick or two from her old friend Noël Coward; when the action was in danger of slowing to near-standstill, Gertie would make her way over to the piano and croon a little number composed by the author and Richard Addinsell:

> Moonlight is silver,
> Sunlight is gold,
> We shall remember
> When we grow old…

The potency of cheap music was however on this occasion not quite enough; though the play was by no means another *Private Lives* it would probably have lasted a little longer than four months had Gertie not developed an abcess in one ear and had to leave the show. This news, by the time it had crossed the Atlantic, had somehow become considerably expanded: DEATH THREATENS GERTRUDE LAWRENCE headlined the *Chicago Herald* for 20 December 1934, and Gertie then had to spend much of her convalescent time writing to friends in New York that reports of her impending demise had been greatly exaggerated.

By the beginning of 1935 she was entirely recovered; Doug had been constantly by her bedside. 'Among his many gifts to her,' reported one gossip column, 'have been diamond and platinum jewellery, a magnificent black sports car and, of course, the yacht which she has duly christened *Grateful*', and now the two of them were planning to work together again, this time in a film version of *La Bohème* to be called simply *Mimi*. It was, reported the film critic of *The Times*, yet another of Gertie's celluloid disasters:

> On the stage, the chief charm of Miss Gertrude Lawrence is her extreme sophistication, her gift of making an amusing line sound wittier than it is, and her ability to take control of any situation. There is no reason why these talents should not have been reproduced on the screen, but in this film good care is taken to see that they are not... Miss Lawrence may be an extremely good actress but she has nothing at all to do with Mimi, who for one thing has consumption – and that is the last complaint from which any character taken by Miss Lawrence should suffer... the film is all very nice in its own uninspired way but the question which hung in the air before the lights went out is still there when they come on again – what has Miss Lawrence to do with it all?

But by early in 1935 Gertie had a great deal more to worry about than a few bad film reviews. Among the huge pile of unpaid bills which had been accumulating these past five years on Gertie's various London and New York desks were two from local laundries, known as the Mayfair Laundry and Cheyne Laundry. Together they totalled just under £50, and the only reason they had never been paid was that Gertie (whose weekly flower bill came to rather more than that) had simply never bothered. The owners of these two laundries, Mr William Cleghorn of Acton and Mrs Katherine MacLean of Church Street, Chelsea, now found themselves in the uneasy position of the child who in the Andersen fairy tale is the first one to remark that the King has no new clothes on. Being small local dry-cleaners, they had apparently not heard of the system whereby big stars of the period were allowed virtually unlimited credit with no questions asked. It seemed to them, after waiting a year or so for their money and still not receiving it, that the reason was probably because Miss Lawrence did not actually have £50, in which case she should surely be declared bankrupt. It was as simple as that, and they duly took out a writ. By 26 February, the whole of Gertie's complex financial affairs was in the hands of the Official Receiver. That morning the *Daily Mirror* reported:

> Liabilities of £24,729 were disclosed at the first meeting held at London Bankruptcy Buildings of the creditors of Gertrude Howley, the actress professionally known as Gertrude Lawrence, residing at Cumberland Place, Regent's Park. Mr S. W. Hood, Official Receiver, dealt with ninety-nine proofs of debt, amounting to £6,802. The chairman reported that

her assets were valued at £1,879. Further liabilities included a claim of £14,000 by the Inland Revenue in respect of the debtors earnings while in America, and, apart from that claim, there were liabilities amounting to about £10,000... the Chairman added that the debtor attributed her insolvency to having lived beyond her means and to the unexpected demand for Income Tax in respect of her American earnings, although she had already paid the full amounts demanded in America.

In fact she hadn't, and there was to be a subsequent bankruptcy hearing when she returned to the U.S.; nor, if gossip-column reports of 'fabulous' jewellery had any truth at all, does it seem likely that Gertie's total worldly possessions only added up to £1,800. On the other hand, she had not been too assuming and meticulous in having her personal possessions valued, it does seem likely that there wasn't much else. She had always lived in rented accommodation, had put the only insurance policy she ever bought in her daughter Pamela's name, and it is entirely possible that the yachts and cars invariably connected with her name in print had in fact been long-term loans from wealthy admirers rather than outright gifts. Jewels aside, then, she was at this juncture quite conceivably worth less than £2,000 and had no difficulty at all in seeing herself as a sudden Cinderella:

> When I came out of the court I had nothing, literally, but the clothes I stood in. Nothing else. My cars, my apartment, my jewels, even most of my clothes were immediately seized... Dorothy, my faithful maid, Mack, my dog, and I stood on the pavement outside the house... we had literally not a roof to crawl under. No money and no credit.

But she was not left there to starve quietly with the dog and the maid on the pavement; her agent and manager at that time was Bill O'Bryen, who happened to be in partnership with Bill Linnit (later of the Linnit & Dunfee theatrical management) and it was Linnit who was duly persuaded to move in with O'Bryen, thereby vacating his flat in Albany for the use of Gertie plus maid and dog. She may have been poor, but she was no longer homeless.

Though she did not much care for the humiliation of the *Daily Mirror* 'Bankrupt Actress' headlines, as all her many other creditors now became considerably more importunate, in one sense the arrival of the Official Receiver had been almost a relief to Gertie. She had always lived in the belief that money was not something she should ever have to think about, and now here was the entire machinery of the British legal system proving her right. Her affairs were for the courts to worry about, and Gertie took the ever-optimistic view that at least her insolvency was at last in professional care, leaving her free to think about her career, which she had always found of considerably more interest than her debts.

That spring she went into an all-star Galsworthian stage epic at His Majesty's; called *Hervey House*, it was billed as the work of 'C. R. Avery' from behind which pen-name there soon emerged the distinguished American actress Jane Cowl. What Miss Cowl had written was a kind of latter-day *Forsyte Saga*, and the management gave it to a young director by the name of Tyrone Guthrie, who rapidly found himself having to tackle several bulls and at least one sacred cow. As Guthrie wrote later:

Hervey House was a fictitious ducal mansion in London; the story was romantic, set in the Edwardian era. There was the duke, very handsome; the duchess, equally handsome and very pure and good; the duke's mistress, very handsome and, to make up for not being very pure, very charming; the duke's secretary; 'character' aunts and uncles; a devoted lady's maid; a good old butler and dear God knows how many footmen, tweenies, grooms, gamekeepers and pantry boys. The scene changed at least fifteen times, from attic to basement of the great house. It had no particular resemblance to real life, but it was written with great verve and conveyed a rather charming admiration for the good old days and the good old English upper orders in a way which no English writer could have managed except tongue in cheek. We decided it would be an appropriate offering for King George V's Jubilee, done on a grand scale with a whopping star cast and lavish production. Nicholas Hannen was engaged to play the duke, with Fay Compton as his duchess and Gertrude Lawrence in the comparatively small but grateful role of the mistress. The cast was also to include Ben Webster, Margaret Rutherford, Alan Webb and Sebastian Shaw, but it was felt that certain alterations were necessary and I was despatched to America to discuss them with the author... I explained that His Majesty's Theatre was very large and that the management intended a lavish and spectacular production. Jane Cowl replied that a large theatre would kill her play, which was intimate. I queried the economic possibility of presenting in a small theatre a play with such a huge cast. She said they could double up, and with a pencil made an efficient plan for this on the tablecloth. I countered with the large number of sets. More plans were drawn, showing how it could all be staged with three good bits of furniture and some plywood screens. The tablecloth began to look like the plan of a maze... in the end I convinced her that it was the alterations or else no production, and the play was then a failure for just the very reason that Jane had foretold. It *was* a small intimate piece, which in my production was blown up to a size in which its charm was lost. The actors did well. The sets by Molly MacArthur were handsome but so complicated that, on the opening night of the try-out in Manchester, one of the actors got lost and flew about in a frenzy through room after room, pre-set on a turntable. The actors on stage, making up lines and pretending to look for their lost colleague in the garden, were startled to see him crawl through the fireplace.

But when Guthrie's production finally reached London the critics were respectful, especially towards Gertie's final scene as an old lady in a white wig 'showing just how gracefully she will still be delighting us in her sixties', a prophecy that was not alas to come true.

The theatre-going public however, not yet ready apparently for Edwardian nostalgia of this *Upstairs, Downstairs* kind, stayed away in their hundreds from *Hervey House*, which closed in the early summer after a run of barely six weeks.

Gertie, eager to escape the nervous demands of her creditors and the rather cramped confines of Bill Linnit's Albany flat, went down to Goldenhurst in Kent to stay for a few days with Noël at his country house.

There he was at last able to show her the basic lay-out and most of the scripts for a new and elaborate vehicle that he had constructed for their respective talents in partnership: a series of ten (nine survived) one-act plays ranging in mood from slapstick comedy through musical romance to high tragedy, in all of which they would both appear, playing them first in London and then in New York as alternating triple bills under the omnibus title *Tonight at Eight-Thirty*.

The success of *Private Lives*, followed by Noël's determination to do something to help his old friend out of her money troubles, had made him think long and hard about another way to bring himself and Gertrude Lawrence together again on stage in parts that would allow them to display their varied acting and singing talents to the best possible advantage. *Private Lives* had, in his view and that of many of the people surrounding him, proved that the combination of 'Noël and Gertie' conjured up a box-office magic which could be invoked again, given the right vehicle. But he needed to write something more than just another light comedy; he needed to write something that would be varied enough to let them both work in their highly individual ways, and also exciting enough to overcome the boredom that he found in nightly repetition of the same role. Given all these requirements, it soon occurred to him that three plays would be better than one and that, by the same token, nine would be better than three.

In the first quarter of this century, however, with a few distinguished exceptions to he found among the work of Bernard Shaw and J. M. Barrie, the one-act play had fallen on hard times; in the provinces some were still being presented, as under-cast and badly produced curtain-raisers, but by and large the *genre* had disappeared as the result of widespread managerial belief that the public would not come to see double or triple bills because they felt that they would somehow be getting less rather than more value for their ticket money. Yet for Noël, the one-act play 'having a great advantage over a long one (in that it can sustain a mood without technical creaking or overpadding) deserves a better fate, and if by careful writing, acting and producing I can do a little towards re-instating it in its rightful pride, then I shall have achieved one of my more sentimental ambitions.'

By the end of August, Noël had finished all of the plays and decided that, after rehearsing first with Gertie at Goldenhurst, where she also played him a mean game of croquet, they would then assemble a company in London under his friend John Wilson's management and open at the Opera House in Manchester in mid-October. Then, after a nine-week provincial tour and a brief Christmas holiday, they would open in London at the Phoenix (scene of their triumphant *Private Lives* six years earlier) in the January of 1936.

During the various provincial, London and Broadway runs of *Tonight at Eight-Thirty* the sequence and arrangement of the plays was altered frequently in a kind of permanent repertoire, and even the title went through such pragmatic local variations as *Tonight at Eight*, *Tonight at Seven-Thirty* and, for matinées, *Today at Two-Thirty*.

The triple bill that launched the whole endeavour in Manchester consisted of *We Were Dancing* followed by *The Astonished Heart* and then *Red Peppers*. Of these, the first was really no more than a curtain-raiser, an acid little comedy about Gertie deciding in the cold light of dawn that she would not after all be eloping from her marriage to run off with a marvellous lover of the night before; the second was a psychological drama (later filmed by Coward with Margaret Leighton in Gertie's role) about a suicidal relationship; and the third was the one which, though the least ambitious, was to become in many ways the most popular and successful of all the play's in the cycle.

In *Red Peppers* Coward managed, with satire tinged by a certain sentimental nostalgia, to recapture the precise flavour of tatty music-hall acts struggling to survive on bad touring dates. Not only the back-stage bickering of Lily and George Pepper but also their appalling musical numbers ('Has Anybody Seen Our Ship?' and 'Men About Town') suggested that Coward had a very sharp eye for the decline of the old 'Halls', and with a faint feeling of guilty delight Gertie realized that she was here going to be allowed to mock precisely the kind of seedy touring life she had been living with Walter Williams back in 1921:

LILY: I'm sick of you and the whole act. It's lousy anyway.

GEORGE: The act was good enough for my Mum and Dad, and it's good enough for you.

LILY: Times have changed a bit since your Mum and Dad's day, you know. There's electric light now and telephones and a little invention called Moving Pictures. Nobody wants to see the 'Red Peppers' for three bob when they can see Garbo for ninepence!

GEORGE: That's just where you're wrong, see! We're flesh and blood, we are – the public would rather see flesh and blood any day than a cheesy photograph. Put Garbo on on a Saturday night in Devonport, and see what would happen to her!

LILY: Yes, look what happened to us!

GEORGE: That wasn't Devonport, that was Southsea.

LILY: Well, wherever it was, the Fleet was in.

GEORGE: If you think the act's so lousy it's a pity you don't rewrite some of it.

LILY: Ever tried going into St Paul's and offering to rewrite the Bible?

14

GROSS EXTRAVAGANCE

While Gertie continued to work with Noel first on the rehearsals and then the tour of *Tonight at Eight-Thirty*, her creditors had a series of private meetings in order to establish what could be salvaged from the wreck of her accounts. A list of her assets published in the summer revealed: jewellery worth £300, a bracelet costing £500, a mink coat valued at £30, furniture and fittings worth £500 and 'a certain amount of pawned jewellery which has still not been redeemed', though whether that list represented Gertie's total worldly assets or merely those she was prepared to have on public discussion remained a moot point. At all events she was now a declared bankrupt: Gertrude Lawrence announced the *Daily Mail* in a sob piece:

> Once a chorus girl, once a musical comedy actress, now a firmly established star is appearing in the Theatre of Tragedy – London's bankruptcy courts. She ascribes her failure to having lived beyond her means; to heavy domestic Expenses; to ill health (sic) and to a demand for Income Tax on her U.S. earnings.

Smaller print revealed that Gertie now had no less than £16,000 worth of jewellery in pawn, and that her pre-tax earnings for the years 1932-35 had totalled £19,000. Her problem, she said, was that though her average annual income was now £6,700, yet her annual expenses including payments to daughter and parents were just over £10,000. 'Somebody', said Gertie in one of her more memorable utterances of this period, 'would have to *do* something about it all.'

As usual it was left to Noël to get the whole thing into a somewhat more cool and clear perspective; during rehearsals for *Tonight at Eight-Thirty* he was asked by the two Bills (Gertie's then managers Linnit and O'Bryen) if he and his own friend and manager Jack Wilson would join them in a united attempt (after one of her more costly shopping sprees) to explain to Gertie the facts of a bankrupt's life. They all agreed to meet for supper one night.

> Gertie [predicted Noël] will be in one of her three moods. Either she'll be very angry and break all the furniture, or she'll he very tearful and make it all wringing wet, or she'll just sit there with her hands on her lap and say that she doesn't understand any of it. I only hope to God she pretends not to understand.

In the event, she simply failed to show up at all.

Halfway through the first week of *Tonight at Eight-Thirty* in Manchester, Coward brought in the second of his three triple bills; this started with *Hands Across The Sea*, a light comedy about Gertie as a London socialite faced with the sudden and total confusion of the arrival in her front hall of two colonial guests and a Maharajah who might possibly have religious objections to the comedian Douglas Byng. It was designed primarily as a vehicle for Gertie, and years later Coward found he still could not think of the play

> Without remembering the infinite variety of her inflections, her absurd, scatterbrained conversations on the telephone, her frantic desire to be hospitable and charming, and her expression of blank dismay when she suddenly realised that her visitors were not who she thought they were at all. It was a superb performance in the finest traditions of high comedy, already now over and done with forever, but as far as I am concerned never to be forgotten.

Coward always denied that the characters portrayed by Gertie and himself were based on Lady Edwina and Lord Louis Mountbatten, both of whom were close friends and not easily fooled by the denials. 'Noël gave us a couple of tickets for the first night,' Lord Louis said forty years later, 'which I always thought was the very least he could have done considering that he got a whole play out of us.' It did not, however, hurt the friendship, and a few years later Noël was to pay Lord Louis an altogether more dignified compliment by portraying him as the noble Captain D in his classic film of the war at sea, *In Which We Serve*.

The second play in this cycle, *Fumed Oak*, was set in an altogether different social milieu, and had Noël as the down-trodden, brow-beaten suburban husband Henry Gow who, in a worm-will-turn final scene, finds the courage to walk out on Gertie as his altogether awful wife. Then the last of the three plays in this second *Tonight at Eight-Thirty* sequence was a return to elegance, a romantic musical fantasy called *Shadow Play* in which Noël and Gertie, impeccably dressed, danced in the moonlight to the echoes of *Private Lives*:

SIMON: Well, here we are.

VICKY: My name's Victoria.

SIMON: Victoria what?

VICKY: Victoria Gayforth.

SIMON: What a silly name.

VICKY: I adore it.

SIMON: That's because you're sentimental.

VICKY: Fiercely sentimental – over-romantic, too.

SIMON: Dearest darling.

VICKY: The wedding went off beautifully, didn't it?

SIMON: Brief, to the point, and not unduly musical.

VICKY: Didn't mother look nice?

SIMON: Not particularly.

VICKY: Oh, Simon!

SIMON: It was her hat, I think – it looked as though it were in a hurry and couldn't stay very long.

VICKY: Was that man who slapped you on the back your uncle?

SIMON: Yes, dear – that was my uncle.

VICKY: I'm so sorry.

SIMON: He ran away to sea, you know, when he was very young and then, unfortunately, he ran back again.

Overpowering charm was exuded through a rather transparent account of a marriage being retrieved from the brink of collapse, but *Shadow Play* (though by no means the most interesting of the plays) retains a certain technical fascination for Coward's use on the stage of such highly cinematic techniques as flashbacks and disconnected scenes played very quickly in pools of light to make up the theatrical equivalent of a montage.

These then were the first six plays of *Tonight at Eight-Thirty*, and alternating them, Noël and Gertie toured the British provinces throughout the autumn of 1935. Meanwhile, from London in November came better news of Gertie's financial affairs. The *New York Times*, which had taken a keen interest in the case, reported on 8 November under the headline 'ACTRESS FREED FROM BANKRUPTCY' that:

Stage and screen star Gertrude Lawrence was today freed from bankruptcy, subject to an undertaking to pay £50 per week out of her earnings until all her debts were cleared. In the course of a public hearing, she admitted that at one period she had received about five times as much in gifts as she had earned on the stage. Chided by a frowning Official Receiver for 'gross extravagance', the actress said that part of her financial woes were due to expenditures in entertaining the friends of an unnamed former fiancé and in spending money on a trousseau which was never used. Miss Lawrence's attorney said she admitted 'gross extravagance' and that though she had nothing left now but her earning power, she was determined to pay off all her liabilities. Mr Registrar Mellor noted that

Miss Lawrence was a distinguished actress, and added that extravagance was to some extent a question of degree. One did not, he concluded, expect people in the dramatic profession to be as careful in their expenditure as those in other classes of life.

And so, at £50 a week, Gertie slowly began paying off her debts; she was not, though, best pleased when her now seventeen-year-old daughter Pamela turned up in the chorus of Cochran's *Follow The Sun* and announced to the press:

I have done this to help Mummy. I hate the life she leads, and I want to get her out of it. What she needs is a long vacation somewhere sunny, with no money troubles. Deep down in my heart, I don't believe Mummy really likes stage life all that much.

Like it or not, and most other evidence suggests that she did, Gertie was now committed to the London and New York runs of *Tonight at Eight-Thirty*. Typically, she had also decided that the £50 a week which had to be repaid to her creditors was not going to involve her cutting back any further on her living standards. She would merely have to earn it on the side, by filming during the day and doing cabaret stints after the shows at night.

The *Tonight at Eight-Thirty* tour had proved extremely profitable (taking just over £26,000 in nine weeks) and towards its end Noël had slipped in a seventh play, *Family Album*, an enchanting little mock-Victorian musical comedy about a missing will, in place of *We Were Dancing*, with which he had never been altogether happy. At the beginning of January 1936, therefore, the first two sets of *Tonight at Eight-Thirty* plays opened in consecutive weeks at London's Phoenix Theatre to a rapturous reception from first-night play-goers among whom were the then Prince of Wales and Mrs Simpson.

Reviews varied from the disappointed to the besotted, but the general feeling was that here was something for everyone; true, Agate reckoned that the score so far was 'for the first trio of plays, one dud, two wows; for the second, one wow, one semi-dud and one dud', but at least no one could now accuse Noël or Gertie of a lack of versatility. The plays offered them countless opportunities for virtuoso musical and dramatic solos and duets which they clutched with both hands, and the whole venture seemed dedicated to the proposition that there was now really nothing in the theatre that this partnership couldn't handle. 'I wonder', mused one playgoer after sitting through all six plays at consecutive matinée and evening performances in one day, 'what they are like on the high wire.'

But early in the London run of *Tonight at Eight-Thirty* (which Noël had warned would again only be for three months pre-Broadway) the death of King George V was announced; he had come to the throne only a few months before Noël and Gertie had first met, and his reign had spanned their entire professional careers. All theatres were of course closed on the night of his death, and the atmosphere of deep mourning in which they reopened made the jokes about bereavement in *Family Album* seem in execrably bad taste; it was therefore hauled out of the repertoire and replaced by *We Were Dancing*.

Gertie meanwhile, determined to make the extra money required for her bankruptcy settlement, had signed with Alexander Korda, the only Czar of the British motion picture industry, to play the somewhat frenetic role of the housekeeper to Charles Laughton's *Rembrandt*. Daily she would commute to the studios, taking, she noted proudly, 'the five-thirty a.m. workmen's train to Denham, filming all day and then returning to the Phoenix to do three plays every evening.' No sacrifice was apparently too great if the money still owing was to be repaid in full (which it ultimately was), though Sir Alexander's nephew, Michael Korda, reports that life on the set was less than easy-going:

> Charles took a vivid dislike to the presence of Gertrude Lawrence... since she enjoyed exchanging dirty stories and theatrical gossip with Alex. It seemed to Laughton that Gertie Lawrence was taking up too much of Alex's time and attention and that Alex was snubbing Laughton by paying court to her. Her voice, he complained, got on his nerves, she talked out loud and laughed in an irritating way while he was preparing his scenes. Finally Laughton had Vincent [Korda] place a pair of soundproof screens around him whenever she was anywhere near the set, and he would retreat there to sulk whenever he heard her voice.

Gertie doubtless objected to the fanatical seriousness with which Laughton approached his work; Noël, though equally dedicated, was a lot more 'fun' to have around. Nevertheless, when a few months later the reviews appeared for *Rembrandt*, Gertie emerged from them with considerably more distinction than ever before in her screen career.

To play three shows a night and make a film by day was however a strain even on her robust health and energy, and shortly after shooting was completed on *Rembrandt* she duly collapsed with laryngitis. Noël insisted (here as six years ago in *Private Lives*) that he could not possibly play without her, and the Phoenix Theatre was duly closed until she recovered her voice. Never in his entire career did Noël ever play a role he had written for Gertie with any other actress, even for a single night. She, however, once played *Tonight at Eight-Thirty* without him: her co-star, in a revival several years after the war, was to be Noël's great and good friend Graham Payn and both were to work then under the Master's own direction.

Despite the laryngitis, Gertie was now in reasonably cheerful shape: the money was pouring in from both *Rembrandt* and *Tonight at Eight-Thirty* (from which she was getting not just a salary but also a royalty since her friend Robert Montgomery had invested in it on her behalf) and she began to think that at last she could see, if not a way out of the woods, then at any rate a decent-sized clearing.

When the Phoenix reopened, Noël brought in the remaining two plays of his original scheme so that, with the reinstated *Family Album,* they could now offer customers three complete triple bills. These additions to *Tonight at Eight-Thirty* were a little high-society burglary sketch written in the Lonsdale vein called *Ways and Means* and, infinitely more intriguing, a railway-station romance for himself and Gertie called *Still Life,* which ten years later he was to expand into the screenplay for David Lean's classic film starring Celia Johnson and Trevor Howard, *Brief Encounter.*

With the repertoire at last complete, *Tonight at Eight-Thirty* ran on at the Phoenix until the end of the third week in June 1936, to achieve a total of just over 150 sold-out London performances. Ivor Brown, summing up for the *Observer,* noted that Coward, 'the man who used to write very slight long plays, has now composed some very full brief ones' and the legendary actor-manager Sir Seymour Hicks, in the audience at the very last performance, was so impressed by Noël's achievement that he insisted on presenting him with one of his own most treasured possessions, a sword which had once belonged to Edmund Kean. Noël kept it, proudly, for thirty years and then handed it on to Sir Laurence Olivier on his formation of Britain's National Theatre Company.

For Noël, the stage partnership with Gertie had again been an absolutely magical if intermittently tempestuous affair; their acting together was still part of a greater private relationship in which the audience were being allowed almost vicariously to participate for an hour or two each night, and though there was never real competition between them there were occasional rows caused usually by Noël's determination not to let Gertie drift off from the top of her form or resort to any of her old tricks of overacting. During February he had cabled to Jack Wilson in New York:

EVERYTHING LOVELY STOP CRACKING ROW WITH GERTIE OVER HANDS ACROSS THE SEA LASTING SEVEN MINUTES STOP HER PERFORMANCE EXQUISITE EVER SINCE.

In March, by which time it had been agreed that Wilson would also present the plays on Broadway the following autumn, another cable from Noël, this one in mock-fury, ran:

VERY SORRY FIND MY ENGAGEMENTS WILL NOT PERMIT

ME APPEAR UNDER YOUR BANNER IN AMERICA UNLESS I
GET A FURTHER 58 PERCENT OF THE GROSS FOR ARDUOUS
TASK RESTRAINING MISS LAWRENCE FROM BEING GROCK
BEATRICE LILLIE THEDA BARA MARY PICKFORD AND BERT
LAHR ALL AT ONCE.

Gertie knew however, that she was among friends and was determined
not to waste a moment of their summer break between closing in London
and opening on Broadway. This year there would be no villa in the South of
France or even Majorca; instead, she immediately signed on for a cabaret
season at the Café Olé, Paris, and agreed to make another film for Korda at
Denham. This, though a much less expensive and ambitious affair than
Rembrandt, was to give her one of the most rewarding of her screen roles.
Called *Men Are Not Gods* and directed by Walter Reisch, who had been
Korda's assistant back in the Vienna of the early 1920s, the film told an
intriguing tragi-comic tale of an actor (Sebastian Shaw) who, while playing
Othello on stage to the Desdemona of his real-life actress wife (Gertie),
decides to strangle her so that be may be free to marry Miriam Hopkins.
Rex Harrison also turned up as a reporter, and the film achieved an
interesting sub-Pirandello confusion of stage reality and actual reality. Best
of all, it cast Gertie as an actress, gave her the chance to have a creditable
stab at Desdemona (her only ever Shakespeare) and allowed her to be what
she always anyway was on screen which *was* theatrical. Only this time the
critics, taking due note of the plot, praised rather than blamed her for it. If
there was a moral here it was perhaps that she should have played more
actresses on screen and maybe on stage, too.

But Gertrude Lawrence was only ever to make one more film, and that in
Hollywood fourteen years later; for now it was back to the theatre, back to
Tonight at Eight-Thirty and back to Broadway, where to her horror she found
precisely the same sort of bankruptcy demands awaiting her as those she had
only recently escaped in London. Again there was a rash of unfavourable
press headlines of the BANKRUPT ACTRESS variety, but at least on this
side of the Atlantic she now had the constant support and advice of her
lawyer Fanny Holtzmann who rapidly negotiated for her the same kind of
deal that she had been given in London – a couple of years to pay off the
debts at around $150 a week to be drawn straight out of her salary. This
however presupposed that she was to stay in more or less constant work, and
she already knew that Noël had therefore agreed to play *Tonight at Eight-Thirty*
for twice his usual three-month season. This was just as well, considering that
shortly before she left England Gertie had bought herself a country house
and small farm in Buckinghamshire, which had the unlikely and

uncharacteristic name of 'Mopes'. It fell, as usual, to her long-suffering agent Bill O'Bryen to try and explain to her that although a lot of money was now coming in, a great deal more still had to go out in repayment of debts before she could be considered free to indulge in such extravagance. By way of a reply, Gertie sent him a cable from New York:

REFERENCE MOPES KINDLY ASCERTAIN COST OF INSTALLING SWIMMING POOL.

With the kind of logic that had always hallmarked Gertie's conduct of her private life and affairs, having for the first time ever just bought herself a house in England she was only once to visit her native country again for more than a matter of weeks, and then only because a play happened to keep her there for a short time.

Apart from that and the occasional English holiday, from the Broadway opening of *Tonight at Eight-Thirty* in November 1936 through to her New York death a little less than sixteen years later, America was to be her spiritual, professional and private home. True, she may neither have known nor have planned that at this time, any more than she ever really knew or planned anything more than about a week in advance unless others organized it all for her; but she was now and forever more to be a Broadway baby.

15

BROADWAY BABY

The end of *Tonight at Eight-Thirty* in London meant not only the end of the 'Noël and Gertie' partnership in England but also the end of her Fairbanks affair. Press reports were now linking his name with Dietrich's, but there was more to it than that, as Fairbanks recalled later:

> In the end, I guess we just decided amicably enough to go our separate ways. There had always been other men in her life, just as there had been other women in mine, but I shall always be grateful for the time that we spent together. She was a very funny woman, you know, and that is still kind of rare; but she was also a great star and that to her was a full-time job. Sometimes we used to escape for a weekend, taking the boat and maybe Pamela and the dog and going off up the Thames for a day or two, and I was always very keen to stay unrecognized, but Gertie after a few hours would begin waving to people on the bank, not people she actually knew but people she wanted to know her. She really loved being recognized, noticed; I think she needed it. She was never one of those actresses who disappear out the stage door after a show in an old coat and a headscarf; her exits from the theatre were as carefully choreographed and arranged as any of her stage exits. She was always 'on', maybe because that was all she knew or understood. She didn't like being alone, almost never was; I don't think she perhaps wanted to find out too much about herself, and she certainly wasn't a lady who needed time to think. I don't remember her ever thinking much. But she could be wonderfully waspish: years after we broke up I'd married Mary Lee and we were both given house seats by Gertie for *The King and I*, so we went backstage afterwards and Gertie put on this terribly regal, condescending performance, patting Mary Lee's cheek and saying, 'Oh you dear little thing, I'm so glad Douglas married you,' and then solemnly taking out of her jewel case some pin that I'd given her and handing it to my wife. I don't think she much cared for her old flames getting married, even if she didn't plan to marry them herself.

Tonight at Eight-Thirty opened on Broadway at the National Theatre in November 1936; in those days, before either American or British Actors' Equity had placed any restrictions on the transatlantic movement of casts, Jack Wilson's management managed to import the entire London company and they were therefore able to open the nine plays on three consecutive nights. After the second, wrote Brooks Atkinson for the *New York Times*:

Noël Coward and Gertrude Lawrence, being tired of the plays they presented on Tuesday, put on three more at the National last evening expecting to keep interested in them until tomorrow when the third bill is scheduled to go on… No student of the drama will ever grind out his doctor's thesis on Mr Coward's contribution to thought on the basis of the current one-act panels, nor will anyone but Mr Coward and Miss Lawrence ever give them much vibrancy on stage, for they are personal vehicles… but although Mr Coward has written his miniatures with skill and acts them admirably, it is Miss Lawrence's triumph and further proof that one who seemed not long ago to be merely an amusing hoyden has now become a brilliant actress.

'Expert razzle dazzle' added the *Post,* and Burns Mantle noted:

Coward and Lawrence fans were so happy to have their favourites back that there was a welcoming demonstration at the evening's close. Mere outsiders looked on and marveled a bit… nothing very serious happens in these plays and nothing dull tarnishes any part of them.

This New York première was preceded by a Boston and Washington try-out, and it was in Washington that Noël had decided, as a joke, to send Gertie a good-luck telegram signed Fiorello La Guardia, then Mayor of New York. Accordingly he dictated it over the phone, ending with the signature:

OPERATOR: But are you really Mayor La Guardia?

NOËL: No.

OPERATOR: Then you can't sign it Mayor La Guardia. What is your real name?

NOËL: Noël Coward.

OPERATOR: Are you really Noël Coward?

NOËL: Yes.

OPERATOR: Then in that case you may sign it Mayor La Guardia.

Their New York opening was eventful, and not only because of the crowds who turned out to welcome them back to Broadway; Lucius Beebe, then a reporter with the *Herald Tribune,* agreed, as a publicity stunt for a Fifth Avenue jewellers, to wear in his lapel a diamond gardenia worth fifteen thousand pre-war dollars. During the first interval it was stolen, not in fact for publicity purposes, by a kleptomaniac English lady of noble birth who'd only returned it to the store after considerable police persuasion.

Soon after *Tonight at Eight-Thirty* opened at the National, news from London about the abdication of King Edward VIII caused Noël and Gertie to issue on behalf of their company a brief and dignified statement of unswerving loyalty to the crown and its new inhabitant, but privately they were both more than a little disturbed and depressed: 'I refuse to give that woman any publicity', Gertie had earlier told reporters. As Prince of Wales, Edward VIII had been a good friend to Gertie, and in private life he had stood for a section of English high society to which she and Noël eagerly attached themselves as soon as they were able to escape their own more humble beginnings. The King's abrupt departure from the throne for the woman he loved seemed to them both unforgivably unprofessional and, worse still, it appeared to fragment a social order whose members had until now found no reason to suppose that it and they would not be secure for some years to come.

It would be an exaggeration to suggest that Gertie's decision from now on to live and work in America was consciously prompted by the events of December 1936; unconsciously, however, she may well have been made aware that the old pre-war England, the England where she had struggled to the top of the social and theatrical heap, was fast coming to its close. As far as America was concerned, she had been born, not in a London suburb, but in a Charlot revue, and she was beginning to think that maybe she liked it better that way.

Tonight at Eight-Thirty ran on through the winter to capacity audiences, but then, in March 1937, the strain of playing nine separate roles in as many plays within a repertoire that often entailed acting no less than six of them consecutively on matinée days began to take its toll of Noël just as, a year previously in London, it had of Gertie. At first he only missed a couple of nights but then, three days after he returned to the cast, he broke down again directly after a performance and this time his New York doctor refused to let him go back to the theatre for at least a week.

On 5 March, therefore, Gertie was able to send a postcard from Atlantic City to her daughter, back in England and now known as Pamela Gordon since she had taken the first half of her father's Gordon-Howley surname, and was intent on some sort of a stage career:

> Darling PG: Noël was suddenly stricken with laryngitis on Saturday last, so we've closed the plays for a whole week and your old Mum packed a grip, picked up the dog and with Dorothy [her maid] running behind made for Pennsylvania Station and the witching waves as fast as her 38-year-old legs would carry her. The dog? Oh yes, he's new, a present from Schyler Parsons, who now breeds them – he's a black miniature schnauzer, the dog I mean not Schyler, and great company. So here we are with our noses full of brine and my heart and eyes filled with the longing to see the white cliffs of Southampton again.

After a few more weeks of the run, she and Noël were both determined to be back in England in time for the 12 May Coronation of King George VI in honour of which occasion Gertie had all of her jewellery dipped in gold: 'I shall always be glad,' she wrote later, 'I saw London again during that Coronation summer. It was wonderful – a last burst of splendour before the storm burst.'

She had no intention of staying there long though. As the run of *Tonight at Eight-Thirty* drew to its close, the ever-present Fanny Holtzmann made it clear to her that though the bankruptcy problems were receding fast, they were as yet by no means cleared and she would have to keep working as constantly as possible for at least another year. It was, therefore, no good waiting around on the off-chance that Noël might have another good idea; something had to be lined up for the autumn, and since there were now many more demands for her services coming from Broadway than the West End, the feeling was that she should consider doing a new show there for the 1937 -38 season. In fact, the one she chose was so successful that it carried her through on Broadway and on a long subsequent coast-to-coast tour until the very beginning of 1939.

The play was *Susan and God*, and it was the work of a pioneering feminist American playwright called Rachel Crothers whose scripts only began to emerge from the undeserved neglect in which they had languished for more than four decades. Born in 1878, Miss Crothers had her first one-act play produced in 1902; but though she was to live until 1958, *Susan and God* was in fact to be the last of her twenty-three full-length dramas. It told the story of lovable, feather-brained Susan Trexel who returns from a European vacation full of the news that she has been converted to a fashionable and wonderful new religion – the religion of love. Subsequent events, involving an alcoholic husband and a repressed daughter, suggest however that what Susan needs is not a new religion but a new understanding of those closest to her. 'God is here – inside us' is the play's final message, and it was topical enough to give Gertie the greatest success she ever had in a straight play.

Meanwhile the film of *Rembrandt* had opened in America, where critics were inclined to pay much more attention to Gertie's part in it: 'As the shrewish housekeeper who becomes Rembrandt's mistress and later second wife,' wrote the *New York American*, 'the former song-and-dance girl Gertie Lawrence shows that she has developed into practically perfection as an actress among actresses', and when, a few weeks later, *Susan and God* opened at the Plymouth on Broadway, Brooks Atkinson added:

> Entertaining, diverting, beaming Miss Lawrence keeps the drama either bubbling or boiling. She bursts into the play like a breath of fresh air...

spirited, witty, dynamic acting that is superlatively keen and alive – if ever there was a virtuoso performance, this is it.

With that kind of attention and adulation being paid her, Gertie did not need much encouragement to stay firmly in America; though Noël had thought of *Susan and God* that 'only the title is right', he was being proved wrong at the box-office, where the play was working well on a whole series of different levels. For those who wanted the old Gertie, here she still was, dressed in a series of stunning fabrics, coping lightheartedly with the problems of a tricky family. For those who wanted something more serious, here was a dramatic sobbing-breakdown ending; for those who wanted something more topical, here (as the *New Yorker* was the first to realize) was a thoughtful, if satirical, attack on the greater lunacies of the Oxford Movement and its discovery of 'the new religion'. Here, in fact, was something for everyone, as Gertie carefully explained to her audiences in a programme note:

> People who see me in the role of Susan Trexel in Rachel Crothers' grand play may be inclined to think that, because the world is so filled with Susans, I might be like her in real life. While I believe wholeheartedly in many of this flighty character's beliefs, I hope that I may never stand out in life as the self-centred person she outwardly represents across the footlights... but I can say without reservation that my role as the woman who has 'found God in a new way' is one of my favourite tasks of all time on the stage. This is no trivial theme that Miss Crothers has spread across the three acts of her work, and if I didn't believe in the final redemption of Susan I couldn't make you believe in her, in spite of yourself. I do believe in *Susan and God* and I want you to also. Because there is a little bit of Susan in all of us.

In more modern terms, *Susan and God* is an attack on encounter groups and, as such, needed all of Gertie's flamboyant stardom to get past the distaste of those fashionable New York theatre-goers who were already deep into the pre-war equivalents of such gatherings. But, in fact, the play itself was – at least by the time Gertie had finished with it – considerably more about Susan than about God and, as John Mason Brown noted:

> All the skill which Miss Lawrence scattered so profusely through the various playlets of *Tonight at Eight-Thirty*, she now consolidates to give the most complete and scintillating performance of her career. Only rarely does she broaden her values in the manner of musical comedy; for the most part her acting of the silly, selfish, insincere and colossally selfishly glittering worldling is as brilliant as it is acid. It is a pleasure to hear her stretch out certain words as if they were taffy; to follow her ever-expressive gestures and graceful body; to respond to the full breeziness of her impersonation and to watch her as from time to time she wrinkles her

nose as if she were sipping from an unseen glass of very bubbly champagne. It is even more pleasing to note how she has grown as a comedienne and to recognize the integrity of her performance.

With praise like that ringing in her ears, Gertie played *Susan and God* happily enough through to the spring of 1938 on Broadway and then, for John Golden's management, embarked on a tour of no less than twenty-seven cities, twenty-four of which duly gave her their keys. Ultimately she played *Susan and God* on radio, in a pioneering NBC television excerpt in August 1938, in a wartime New York revival at City Centre and, for one performance only, at the underground Broadway Temple on Broadway and 174th Street to which she had been invited by Dr Christian Reisner whose policy it then was to have distinguished stage stars perform scenes from their current successes at the end of his equally dramatic sermons.

Reviews on the road were almost equally ecstatic:

Times there are [wrote the critic of the *San Francisco News*] when you think you are watching Ina Claire; at others, you are certain she's Lynn Fontanne, and sometimes you even start to think she's Billie Burke. But, as the show gets under way and Susan becomes more and more familiar, you realize that you are seeing only Gertie Lawrence, brilliant, nervous Gertie, one of the most delightful comediennes of our time.

By the time she got to Chicago in November of that year, she had become an American resident and the flags were still being put out. As the Chicago *Tribune* critic wrote:

Even in these lean years, the Gods do still smile upon the Chicago stage every now and again. The prospect of Miss Lawrence's return here after a lapse of fourteen years had created a suspense in the breasts of Chicago theatre-goers that was nothing short of tantalizing. When she played here before in *Charlot's Revue* she was a breeze ingenue, brought up in the hard school of children's pantomimes and vaudeville tours throughout England's least refreshing centres of culture, and at that time only recently acquainted with wit and culture on their higher levels. Now she has returned to us a world celebrity – and justly so. There is no use trying to avoid being carried along by her inexhaustible vitality, by the high excitement of her enthusiasm and freshness, still completely unspoiled after months and months in the same role. For Gertrude Lawrence is one of those rare actresses in whom the unexpected always seems desirable after it has happened, and the wayward always seems inevitable.

But now that her professional life was back on course with a vengeance, her private life still left a good deal to be desired. Since the ending of the Fairbanks affair there had been no regular man in her life and she was beginning to admit to herself an increasing feeling of loneliness. Noël was working back in England and, though she had made several American friends, they were for the most part new friends, unable to share with her memories of an English past which was no less important to her now that it was over. Fanny Holtzmann alone began to recognize something of what was going on behind the now rather strident vivacity of Gertie's public image. That summer, while she was having a brief holiday in Bermuda, news had come through that back in England her daughter might be about to become engaged to an Indian army officer. Almost nothing Pamela ever did much pleased her mother, but when she wrote indignantly of this to Fanny, the reply was more to do with her own life than Pamela's:

> Oh dear, I do wish the right man would turn up for you and fill your own life. You have reached the top rung of the ladder professionally – now give the private life of Gertrude Lawrence a chance. Your life has been no bed of roses, and while you are still young and beautiful and the most envied woman in the world, I hope that the new season may hold more than professional glory for you.

But somebody less besotted with her than Fanny might have taken a cooler estimate: Gertrude Lawrence that summer celebrated her fortieth birthday, and precious few men, especially of the dashing and glamorous type liked by Gertie, were either free, willing or able to invest themselves in marriage to a tempestuous theatrical superstar who had already frequently admitted that the stage was always going to be the most important thing in her life.

16

TO THE CAPE

When the tour of *Susan and God* finally ground to a halt early in the spring of 1939, Gertie could still see no pressing reason to return to London or her new Buckinghamshire farmhouse. The Charlot management had by now totally collapsed and, though there were occasional expressions of interest from the Cochran office, no specific vehicle for her seemed even on the horizon; Noël meanwhile was working on a revue for Bea Lillie and, though there was no question of a rift in their relationship, they were now on opposite sides of the Atlantic. Both Noël and Gertie remained, as always, utterly confident that they would be working again together soon, but precisely because of that confidence there was no sense of urgency. Six years had, after all, separated *Private Lives* from *Tonight at Eight-Thirty* and there was no way of knowing even then that 1939 was to mark the end of an era.

The one person, apart from Gertie herself, to take a passionate and constant interest in her career was Fanny Holtzmann, and that in itself constituted a good reason for staying in or around New York.

> Fanny's star client [wrote her biographer Edward Berkman] in every sense was Gertrude Lawrence. Lawyer and client were an extraordinary pair, linked by vitality, humour and a kind of mutual envy. To Fanny, as to half the males of the English-speaking world, Gertrude Lawrence was the epitome of alluring sophistication... she was the Fanny that Fanny herself never thought she could be... poised and self-assured. Gertrude in turn was awed by Fanny's law degree, her negotiating finesse and her prestige... to Fanny it was obvious that Gertrude needed total control... she could not be permitted small purchases any more than an alcoholic could be permitted a small drink.

And all that Gertie now had was Fanny; the relationship with her daughter was getting progressively worse, for reasons rooted deeply in Pamela's childhood:

> She had never really been around long enough to be my mother, but suddenly when I got to be about twenty she began taking a lot more interest in me, as if she suddenly thought of me as a younger sister and found that relationship easier to deal with. She didn't care for me trying to become an actress; she wanted me to settle down, to make a 'good marriage', to have lots of children, as if somehow in that way I could make up for all the things she had never managed to do with her life. But it was already too late for us to get along. She desperately wanted to be proud

of me, to be able to boast about me to her friends, but she never really filled me with confidence. Once she came backstage to see me after a show I was doing on tour and told me that my performance reminded her of Nellie Wallace. I think she wanted to put me off the stage as fast as possible, and in some ways she succeeded. For years I blamed her for my failure as a person, though on reflection I now don't think it was actually entirely her fault; I think I inherited also a kind of hopelessness from my father. But Mummy and I both desperately wanted to get to know each other, to get to like each other, yet we never managed it. She wanted the best for me, wanted me to be a kind of golden girl, and I just wasn't cut out for that.

Despite the fact that Fanny Holtzmann was now having most of Gertie's earnings paid straight into her office, then giving her client a weekly allowance in the hope of keeping her finances at long last on a reasonably even keel, Gertie was still (thanks to chequebooks and the miracle of charge accounts) managing to live and to spend in some style. Like royalty, she now seldom had to carry money herself; once, faced with a seventeen-dollar purchase to be made at Woolworths, she told the amazed girl behind the cosmetics counter to charge it. 'There are no charge accounts at Woolworths', replied the girl; 'But then how,' demanded Gertie in genuine astonishment, 'have you all managed to stay here in business so long?'

Gertrude Lawrence was, in the practised eye of the showbusiness columnist Radie Harris, 'the only stage star I'd ever met who managed always to live like a movie star – butler and all.'

Pamela meanwhile, during an Atlantic crossing on the *Queen Mary*, had met a young American doctor by the name of Bill Cahan:

She and I became good friends, first in the summer of 1938, when I was on vacation from medical school and touring England, and then again in New York a year later. The Munich crisis persuaded Gertie that Pamela would be safer living with her in New York, and after a while it became clear that we were seeing a great deal of each other, so I was summoned by Gertie to a meeting where she could look me over as a prospective son-in-law. In fact we didn't marry until 1941, by which time Gertie herself was also married, and, although we managed to be friendly, she wasn't best pleased at having her daughter marry a guy then only earning fifteen dollars a month as an intern. Pamela had also been seeing a lot of a Canadian army officer and I think Gertie would have been a lot happier with him as a son-in-law. Her ambitions for her daughter did not include marriage to a penniless medical student.

Sadly, neither the marriage nor Gertie survived long enough to see Dr Cahan become eminent as one of America's most distinguished cancer specialists.

Even before Gertie finished the long tour of *Susan and God*, she knew precisely what she was going to do next: another long tour. The play this time was *Skylark*, a new comedy by Samson Raphaelson who was the first to acknowledge in print his debt to his star:

> It is a very odd experience, after having five plays on Broadway and having every one of them presented almost precisely as they were first turned in to the producer's office, to become the author of a show which is freely acknowledged to have been rewritten three full times... *Skylark* had already achieved narrative existence as a serial in the *Saturday Evening Post* and Knopf liked it well enough to print in book form... but as soon as I began to work on the stage version (as both author and director) with Gertrude Lawrence, I realized how much more resourceful and witty and vital the central character could be, and had to be, if she was to play it... Miss Lawrence is a light-giving switchboard, and no one can know the extent of her patience and the fullness of her contribution as an actress to the remaking of *Skylark*.

Work on the play started early in 1939 during the closing weeks on the road of *Susan and God*, and they continued working on it right through that summer, playing stock dates all over the country until they were confident enough that they had at last got it right enough for Broadway. *Skylark* was in fact a fairly inconsequential little comedy about the neglected wife of a money-mad advertising man. Donald Cook and Glenn Anders were the two men in her life, a young Vivian Vance was the other woman and though the play was, as John Mason Brown tactfully put it, 'not the kind of drama which need fear winning the Pulitzer Prize', Gertie with her usual unerring eye and instinct for a star vehicle had found another winner here.

> Watching Miss Lawrence [added Brown] is always entertaining. Joy spills from her eyes; her smile is beguiling. She moves with uncanny grace, is charming to look at, dresses smartly and has a voice of velvet which she can wrinkle as amusingly for laughter's sake as she does her upturned nose. Even when she is led into overplaying, when she reverts suddenly to her musical comedy past, and is misguided by the generous abandon of her acting into treating a comedy scene as if it were a black-out sketch, she does not lose her fascination. Hers is no ordinary personality, neither is hers a skill commonly encountered. Her performance may get out of hand at moments, but such uncomfortable moments when they do occur prove no more than air pockets encountered during an otherwise delightful flight.

But even Gertie knew that *Skylark* had to be stronger before she could risk it on Broadway, and in the company's search for a series of summer homes where they could work on it they eventually landed up on Cape Cod at the Cape Playhouse in Dennis, Massachusetts, then being run by a young American called Richard Aldrich:

> It was our policy at the Playhouse to bring there the greatest stars available, on the theory that the summer people would willingly pay Broadway prices for the best that Broadway had to offer... what the Golden [management] office requested for Miss Lawrence's two weeks' stay at the Cape was a cottage by the lake, sufficiently near the Playhouse for convenience but distant enough for complete privacy. Besides generous accommodations for herself and for guests she might care to invite, the star would need rooms for a personal maid and a secretary, garage space for her town car and grounds for Mac, her West Highland terrier. I was instructed to place an order with a florist to keep the vases in Miss Lawrence's cottage filled with fresh flowers, preferably lilies, her favourites. The Playhouse commissary should be at pains to see that Miss Lawrence's refrigerator was well stocked with a list of delicacies that ranged from avocados, caviare and sweetbreads through melons, quail, pâté de foie gras and rainbow trout. Nothing in my previous experience with stars had prepared me for anything like this. Jane Cowl had exhibited no such delusions of grandeur. The previous season Miss Ethel Barrymore had arrived by bus – and in the middle of the night, unexpectedly, before we could prepare an appropriately gala welcome for the First Lady of the American theatre... what, I thought darkly, did Gertrude Lawrence think a summer theatre was? And who did she think she was? I could tell her in less than ten words: a spoiled, pampered actress with a prima donna complex.

It was ultimately explained to an indignant Mr Aldrich, largely by Gertie's now ever-faithful gossip columnist Radie Harris, that most of these requirements were in fact the Golden office's idea of what a star might need rather than Miss Lawrence's own personal requirements. The night she arrived there in person, it was pouring with rain:

> The train drew to a stop [wrote Aldrich later] and people began tumbling out of it, hurrying for shelter from the storm. A white-coated porter swung off the step of one of the cars and stood at attention. I watched a trim young coloured woman descend, carrying a jewel case in one hand and what was patently a make-up case in the other, followed by another woman carrying a supercilious white terrier. Porters began handing down piece after piece of handsome luggage until they grew into a sizeable hillock on the platform. We advanced to the car steps regardless of the pelting rain. Then, with a timing I mentally applauded, a slim, golden-haired figure appeared at the top of the car steps.

This first encounter on his home territory (they had met once before, backstage in London some years earlier) was not, however, the greatest of successes for the couple who were to remain husband and wife from a year later until Gertie's death in 1952. She found him 'passably polite but not overimpressed with me', and he found something uneasy and irritating in her constant cheerfulness. Later that night, at a surprise party given to welcome Gertie to the Cape by the author of *Skylark*, Aldrich found himself 'an awkward anachronism on the edge of the swirl of which Gertrude was the centre. Once or twice I felt her glance on me. It was puzzled, and a trifle pitying.'

As they rehearsed and played *Skylark* on the Cape that summer of 1939, Gertie found herself increasingly drawn to the rather 'Boston Brahmin' figure of Aldrich; feeling himself no part of her Broadway world, he tried at first to stay out of her way until bullied by Radie Harris (who knew something of Gertie's considerable loneliness at this point in her life) into taking her out one night after the show:

> Gertie had had glamorous lovers in the past, but now she had reached that stage of her life when she needed, as she plaintively sang, 'Someone to Watch over Me'. She felt that she had found him in this solid New England rock. Like all stars of her magnitude, Gertie scared men off. They would see her on stage and think, 'Who am I to invite this magical creature out unless I can take her to supper at El Morocco or the Stork Club?' So she would sit alone in her dressing room while the young kids in her company would rush off to their dates.

By the end of the *Skylark* season on the Cape, it was clear to Gertie and Richard and even to a few members of the company – that they might have something going for them. Both had, however, been married unsuccessfully once already, and neither was about to rush into another partnership without some careful thought. Aldrich stayed on the Cape to manage the rest of his theatre's summer-stock season there, and Gertie returned to New York to open *Skylark* that autumn at the Morosco.

Her home country, one she had not seen since the end of the Coronation summer two years earlier, was now at war with Germany; but Pamela was safely with her in New York, both her parents had died peacefully in the previous year, and there were (whatever she would tell the press about her agony at being out of England in its hour of need) precious few links tying her back to Britain. Her life was now a Broadway life, and she spelt it out that autumn in mind-bending detail to a reporter from the New York journal *American*:

> My day starts at 8 a.m. This usually shocks people when they hear it. The popular impression is that every actress sleeps until noon. So why do I get up so early? Well, I've loads to do. I have to exercise to keep in good physical condition, and then a quarter of an hour for massage of feet and ankles to keep these useful appendages slim and unweary.

Then, breakfast in bed. But no ham or eggs or marmalade or pancakes. Just fruit and coffee. Next, the morning mail… fan letters, letters about plays, business matters and lastly of course social correspondence. I have a secretary to help me, but even so dictating an answer to every single letter takes oftentimes until noon. Of course, personal letters I answer by hand. Then, while my secretary is typing, I relax before lunch by arranging flowers. They are my passion, and I love to have all my rooms simply filled with them, and order big boxes of them fresh every day. My favourite colour is white. When these are all beautifully arranged in bowls and vases, it's usually lunch time. If there is half an hour to spare, my secretary and I play a game of chess. This is not only a splendid game but teaches you to concentrate. Lunch, which follows this busy morning is a simple meal of vegetables and salad. Afterwards I sew for a while. I enjoy making old-fashioned samplers, but usually there is not a very long time for this quiet occupation before my producer's representatives call. They visit me every day to discuss the problems that naturally arise in every production. After they leave me there are usually some new scripts to be read. After this I take Mackie my Highland terrier for a walk, thus giving both of us the necessary daily exercise. If I have shopping to do or visits to make, this is the time I do it – but always when I'm playing I make it a rule to be home in time for two hours, rest before going to the theatre, relaxing before the evening's work and making up for too brief sleep at night. I don't like to eat before I go to the theatre. After the performance I am usually very hungry, and I have a big meal usually with friends for if I eat alone I seldom eat enough. It's well after midnight before I am home again and ready to go to bed. And this is what people call a glamorous and romantic life. There may be glamour and romance about certain phases of it, but let nobody imagine that it isn't mostly hard and tireless work. I travel too much to have a real home, and I always say that a new play takes a year off one's life.

If, up there on the Cape, Aldrich was reading all this, it is not perhaps altogether surprising that it took him until the following spring to propose marriage. Marriage to Gertie, he had already discovered, would also mean marriage to Mackie the dog, Dorothy, the English maid and companion, Corinne Turner, the nurse who often looked after her health and diet on tour, Carrie, her dressing-room maid and Hazel, who was Carrie's assistant. Then, of course, there was still Fanny Holtzmann, plus Jack Potter, who was Gertie's touring manager, not to mention Pamela, whom Gertie bullied Aldrich into taking along with him on a long Mexican journey that autumn. Nevertheless their friendship flourished through that winter while Gertie was playing on Broadway in *Skylark*; Aldrich had now taken over sole management and ownership of the Cape Playhouse, and Gertie had promised that in the brief holiday between the end of the Broadway run of *Skylark* in

April and the start of a four-month nationwide tour she would open his 1940 season with a week of *Private Lives* for which her Elyot was the celebrated English actor Richard Haydn. She told Aldrich during that week that she would also marry him, preferably on her forty-second birthday, American Independence Day, 4 July 1940.

It cannot be said that many of Gertie's friends behaved well over her marriage to Aldrich; though undoubtedly a man of the theatre, indeed one of the very few to own and manage one that was virtually his own private property, this was still a summer-stock theatre on Cape Cod, and Cape Cod was still a long way away from Broadway, let alone the West End. Either not knowing or not caring about the desperate loneliness that had begun to overtake Gertie as she moved into her forties, most of her oldest friends reacted in utter bewilderment to what they saw as the rather boring and infinitely stolid image of her prospective husband. Gertie herself had few doubts:

> It was as though he combined in one person the different things I had found and admired in Philip Astley and in Bert Taylor. He was Boston and Harvard, and had been a banker, but above all he loved the theatre. He was the first man in my life who understood what my career in the theatre meant to me – the first man who really understood me.

Noël, on the other hand, took the view that she had married him under the mistaken assumption that he was a member of the wealthy Winthrop Aldrich clan, and Constance Collier merely added, 'Poor man – he thinks he's marrying Miss Lawrence and will wake up to find he has married Myth Lawrence.'

It rained the night of the wedding – just as it had on the night of Gertie's first arrival on the Cape a year earlier – and they were married in Aldrich's own cottage there with only her maid and couple of his friends as witnesses. Fanny Holtzmann was not present, but had ensured before the ceremony that all Gertie's legal and financial affairs were to remain in her own, rather than Aldrich's, control. From Noël there came a telegram:

> DEAR MRS A HOORAY HOORAY
> AT LAST YOU ARE DEFLOWERED;
> ON THIS AS EVERY OTHER DAY
> I LOVE YOU. NOËL COWARD.

A week later, back in New York just before setting off on the rest of her *Skylark* tour, Gertie happened to run into Otto Preminger who had been directing up on the Cape and knew Aldrich. As Preminger recalls:

> He was an attractive but very conservative and serious man, while Gertie was very outspoken and bubbling over with a delightful sense of

humour… She said laughingly, 'I bet you didn't expect me to marry that man.' I was taken aback and protested. I told her I thought he was an admirable choice and hoped they would be very happy. 'Happy or not,' she shrugged, 'it doesn't matter. I needed roots and he is a very firm root.'

17

THE PRINCESS OF PURE DELIGHT

It wasn't only Gertie's friends who were dubious about her marriage; Richard Aldrich's mother, a conservative and puritan old lady who was already having trouble enough getting used to the idea of her son as a divorcé and, perhaps worse still, the manager of a theatre, when asked for an opinion about the new marriage replied memorably, 'We will not mention it to anyone, and naturally none of the people we know will mention it to us.' It says a good deal for Gertie's singleness of purpose that, having decided to make the marriage work, she also managed eventually to win over the entire Aldrich clan including even Richard's sons by his previous marriage, one of whom was to write in later years perhaps the most sensitive and loving of all press tributes to her.

There was now considerable debate as to where precisely Gertie's future should lie; true, she was committed to a new American husband and the end of the *Skylark* tour which might have seemed straightforward enough. But this was the middle of 1940, a time when all English patriots were being called home and when those who had decided to stay away, especially in Hollywood, were being attacked in the British press for having 'Gone with the wind up.' Gertie, sensitive still to public reaction in her own native land, though surely aware that she was unlikely to be fighter pilot material, decided first that her duty was to go to the aid of her country in no matter how vague or unspecified a capacity.

It took, therefore, a combination of her new husband and the British Ambassador in Washington to point out to her that while there was virtually nothing she could do in London that was not already being done there by somebody at least as suitable for the task, there was perhaps a certain amount that she could do for her country by remaining in America. As Gertie was still a British subject and citizen, though now also able to take out American papers because of her status as 'Mrs A.', she could usefully fund-raise for the British war effort in every town the *Skylark* tour took her to, and that was precisely what she then proceeded to do.

She also began sending parcels to friends and distant relatives back home. Though the 'Bundles For Britain' campaign had not yet started, Gertie had always been a compulsive parcel-poster and a lady with a deep understanding of what constituted useful and acceptable gifts. Soon after her marriage she discovered that Clay Smith, her first great patron and the man who had discovered her on tour and got her into the chorus of her very first London revue, was now penniless and blind and living in an old folks home in Illinois. She at once despatched him, a large number of silk shirts from Sulka, and when Richard painstakingly pointed out that woollen shirts would probably be more useful, Gertie explained that they were not talking about usefulness. They were talking about the past, and about luxury, and about something that would impress Mr Smith's acquaintances in Illinois; usefulness was, even in 1940, not everything.

After a twelve-day honeymoon, Gertie departed for a five-month tour of *Skylark* that would take her out to California and the Midwest while Aldrich remained on the Cape to run his theatre; this was not, as he later noted, either the best or the easiest way to start a marriage, particularly as they were both in highly theatrical environments where jealousies spread easily. Gertie, for example, was not best pleased to discover that one of his summer stars up on the Cape was to be Tallulah Bankhead, while Richard found himself faintly uneasy about press reports of what a wonderful time Gertie was having in San Francisco, where the press club gave her the honorary title of 'Scoop', one with which she was frequently to sign letters from then on, and even published an entire special edition of a local paper in her honour.

Though the *Skylark* tour still showed no sign of being grounded, they had now begun to do one-night stands in small cities ('nine states in nine days' was Gertie's proud boast in September) and between train calls she was also helping to organize the evacuation of sixty children from the English Actors' Orphanage (of which both she and Noel were on the management committee) to Canada. Aldrich, Fanny Holtzmann and various other members of the entourage were also roped in to help, and eventually the children landed safely in Montreal and were then bussed to various American homes, thanks to another friend of Gertie's who ran a Chicago transport company and had also answered the call when it came from her. Few ever had the courage to refuse it.

The strain of the one-night stands, and of the Orphanage manoeuvre, left Gertie in a state of physical and mental exhaustion which, though new to her now was to recur with ever-increasing frequency in the twelve years that she had left to live.

Still feeling guilty about being out of England, especially as the war news from there was now getting worse and worse, Gertie continued back in New York on her frantic round of 'war work': fund raising at every possible opportunity, speaking at charity lunches to rich American women who still, it being fully a year before Pearl Harbour, failed to see what the British troubles had to do with them, and generally trying to make herself as useful as possible, even if that did just mean giving endless newspaper interviews about the need for solidarity and hands across the sea. It was a minor public relations job at best, and Gertie knew it, but that at least was better than doing nothing at all.

She still had with her the complete staff including her maid Dorothy, who on first arrival in New York had been asked what she would most like to visit and had replied, 'Strip teas'. What, enquired Gertie in some displeasure, did her maid already know of Minsky's? Nothing, it transpired; Dorothy had just heard the phrase and thought it might be nice to get a cup of a tea and a scone while watching some nudity.

By now the Orphanage children had been safely settled into the Gould Foundation just outside New York where, somewhat to Gertie's dismay, they were treated throughout the war with such care and devotion in conditions of such hitherto undreamt of luxury that, when the war ended, a number of them showed an understandable reluctance to return to England.

Gertie had, meanwhile, had more than enough of *Skylark* which she had after all been doing on and off but mainly on since March 1939, and there was something very much more exciting in the offing, though to grasp it she had to get embroiled in a nasty Equity row with the Golden management, who seemed to be expecting her to tour for them forever. She had, in fact, toured for the best part of a year, before and after the Broadway run, and an indication of her recent war work comes from an interview she gave the *Kansas* City *Times* in September 1940.

> I think [she told their reporter] that Great Britain will be invaded, perhaps with horrific loss of life: but mark my words the Germans will never win. Their greatest mistake was in bombing Buckingham Palace. The British will never stand for that. So far the Allied Relief Fund that I've organised on Cape Cod has sent 2,000 knitted garments, a ton of powdered milk and fifteen hundred dollars for a mobile canteen to Britain. We're starting now to raise another hundred thousand dollars but whatever we British do on this side of the Atlantic can never be enough. I keep thinking of Bea Lillie and the others who are over there giving performances for the soldiers right now.

But Gertie now had one very good theatrical reason for staying right where she was. For several months past an old friend of hers and Noël's, known to Gertie as 'Mossyface' and to the world at large as Moss Hart, had been paying regular visits to a psychoanalyst, partly as the result of a broken engagement to Edith Atwater but mainly as the result of an increasingly desperate feeling that though with George S. Kaufman he was one half of the most successful playwriting team on Broadway (*Once in a Lifetime, You Can't Take It with You* and most recently *The Man who Came to Dinner*), by himself he was nothing. The psychoanalyst not surprisingly recommended some work away from Kaufman, and the first fruit of that spectacular recommendation was a musical about psychoanalysis which Hart wrote, with music by Kurt Weill and lyrics by Ira Gershwin, and called *Lady in the Dark*. His own account of the genesis of this production was published in the Sunday drama section of the *New York Times* a week before the show finally opened on Broadway in January 1941, and so unbeatable an account is it of both Gertie and the *Lady* that it is quoted here in its entirety:

It seems like yesterday, but I'm afraid it was a good fifteen or sixteen years ago that I stood shivering outside the stage door of the old Forty-eighth Street Theatre, waiting for Katharine Cornell to come out. I had pawned my overcoat that night, for a first glimpse of Katharine Cornell and *Candida*, and, though the wind that whistled down the alley was a cutting one, I was set upon making a memorable evening complete by a starry-eyed look at the star herself. Finally, when it seemed that I must perish with the cold, the stage door opened, and, silhouetted against that magic and wonderful background of light that only stage doors glimpsed down an alley on a winter's night possess, stood Candida herself.

Though she has since denied any recollection of it, I could have sworn Katharine Cornell smiled directly at me, and if she didn't whisper, 'You must write a play for me some day' as she brushed by, you have only my word against hers, and the word of a shivering, smitten, and stage-struck young man of eighteen is the one to take, I assure you, or the theatre of the future hasn't a chance. At any rate, that is what I blissfully chose to believe I had heard as I rumbled home on the subway that night, and that, fantastically enough, was the real beginning of *Lady in the Dark*.

For some two years ago, while we were trying out *The Man who Came to Dinner* in Boston, I once again stood in an alley waiting for Katharine Cornell to come out of a stage door and, though now it was a warm autumn evening and the play was *No Time for Comedy*, when the stage door opened finally there stood Candida again. Then it was I decided I must keep my word to that young fellow of eighteen and an hour or so later as we sat and listened to Benny Fields sing 'Melancholy Baby' as only Benny Fields can, I said, 'Kit,' (see how wonderful the theatre is), 'I'm going to write a play for you right away. I'll catch you in Philadelphia – end of March – and read you the first act.'

But by the end of March, with the first act completed, it was apparent to both Miss Cornell and myself that *Lady in the Dark* was not the play for her. Originally conceived as a straight play with recurrent musical themes, it had grown musically to such Frankenstein proportions it was now a little out of her province. We both decided that of a Saturday night in Philadelphia.

Then on a Sunday night I went to a rehearsal of a British war relief party for which George Kaufman and I were to do an act, and Gertrude Lawrence, among others, was there to rehearse her bit.

It was a rather old fashioned boy-and-girl number that she was doing, but as I watched her sing and dance I knew that here, irrevocably, was the

Lady of *Lady in the Dark*. After the rehearsal finished I asked Gertie to come and have a snack with me at the back room of the Plaza, and as we drank our beer I asked her point-blank if she wanted to hear my new play. She was charming and, from even the little I told her, it seemed nothing could be more exciting than the prospect of playing Liza Elliott. She was, as a matter of fact, searching wildly about for a play for the new season and would give me an answer immediately. It was all too wonderful and just Fate, that was all, just Fate. When could she hear it? Tomorrow afternoon? Fine! We arranged a meeting then and there. Had I but known that my life with Gertie was just beginning, it would have been much simpler to have taken a slight overdose of sleeping pills that night and either miss the appointment next afternoon or never to have awakened. But I didn't know it, and the next afternoon, all unaware, I read Gertie the first act in her apartment.

Her apartment is a delightful spot, and Gertie herself, over the teacups afterward, was thoroughly enchanting. She had liked the play. I could tell that. And she literally was the part as she walked about the room talking about it. It was more than exciting, she kept repeating. It was an adventure in the theatre and something she had always hoped for as an actress. Yes, of course she had liked the play and the part – she was mad about it. But her astrologer, reading her horoscope only the week before, had said, 'Do nothing until April seventh,' and since he had also more or less told her that a new play would fall into her lap almost to the minute I had appeared, it would be flying in the face of Providence to do anything but wait until then. Besides, she wanted very much to hear the completed script, and since I worked very fast, why didn't I go down to my farm and finish the play? April 7 was still two weeks away. I could surely finish by that time and she could then say yes to me and her astrologer with a clear heart.

I battled vainly for a half hour or so and then gave in. Cursing Gertie's astrologer all the way down to Pennsylvania, I holed myself in at the farm and worked steadily until the sixth of April. That morning there was a call from Gertie. Was the play finished? Just. And I was coming in that very night to read it to her. 'Wonderful, darling,' said Gertie, 'it's all working out beautifully, because I've just had a cable from Noël and he arrives tomorrow morning. Isn't that wonderful?' It was, I agreed, but what did Noël have to do with it? 'But don't you see, darling,' cooed that lovely voice, 'it all works out! My astrologer said to do nothing until 7 April and I never do anything without Noël's advice and here he is arriving on the very day! You must read the play to Noël and if he says 'yes', I'll do it. It's all working out beautifully. Bless you, darling!'

I groaned as the receiver clicked. Noël Coward was coming over on a war mission for Britain, and I rightly knew that the last thing in the world he desired was to have a play read to him. Certainly the last thing I wanted to do was read it, but I had already taken some measure of my

Gertie and I suspected that was what I was going to have to do. I also realized with that clearheadedness for which I am not noted that Gertrude Lawrence was by no means doing the play as of this nasty moment, and the next morning, bright and early, I called Noël. Noël, as always, was unpredictable, infuriating, and a tower of strength. He made no secret of the fiendish delight he took of the spot I had manoeuvered myself into, but he agreed, busy as he was, to hear the play the next afternoon. It was a nervous lunch we had at my house the next day, and as we went upstairs to begin the reading you could have bought all of Freud and psychoanalysis from me at a very nominal sum.

I began badly and knew it, but as I finally dared look up after the first scene Noël just said, 'Fine,' very quietly and I did pretty well with the rest of it. His comment, at the end, was short but sweet to my ears. 'Gertie ought to pay you to play it,' was what he said, and, the matinée of *Skylark* being just about over, off we both went to tell Gertie the glad news. Gertie's reception of it was typical. 'Bless you, darlings,' she said, and though no mention of an Equity contract was even whispered, I was happy enough to accompany Noël to see the Lints and let them be the first to know.

Only a slight cloud dimmed an otherwise bright horizon, and that little cloud was placed there by Mr Coward himself. 'Uncle Moss,' he said as I left him at his hotel, 'now your troubles are really beginning.' 'But Gertie said yes, didn't she?' I insisted. 'That's just the point, my boy,' he replied, 'Gertie said yes!' and he dashed through the doors before I could grab him.

That was early April. Late in July I was spending a brief two days at Woollcott's island trying to catch my breath, when Noël Coward arrived. He had seen Paris fall, been to bombed London and back since our last meeting, but it was not of the war he spoke as he stepped out of the launch and we shook hands. 'Gertie signed the contract yet?' he asked quickly. 'No,' I answered miserably, and the amount of emotion I apparently managed to get into that one word sent him roaring with pleasure up the path and into what I can only describe as a tribal war dance. But I am getting ahead of my story. Oh, far ahead.

I waited a polite two days for Gertie to read and digest the finished script and then I called her. 'Darling, I love it,' she said, 'and now we must read it to Fanny Holtzmann.' 'Who's that?' I asked with a sense of impending disaster, 'and why must we read it to her?' 'Fanny is my lawyer and business manager. I never do anything without her, darling! We'll be at your house tomorrow for lunch at two. Bless you, darling!'

The next day Fanny Holtzmann came into my life. I say 'came into my life' because in the following weeks and months all of the life that I had lived before – my boyhood, my first loves, everything I had ever done, any place I had ever been, I could only dimly recall. I could only remember that at two o'clock I must see Fanny Holtzmann and be sure to have enough sleeping pills by my bedside that night.

It is a sore temptation to set down here a life-size portrait of Fanny Holtzmann but for one thing Fanny is a little larger than life, and for that reason quite unbelievable, and for another, I shall probably do a play about Fanny some day and I do not like to waste ammunition. Suffice it to say that Fanny is a small, delicate, mouse-like creature given to wearing floppy hats in the spring and creating a first impression of wistful helplessness. Helpless, indeed! Fanny is about as helpless as the Bethlehem Steel Company and as delicate as Jack the Ripper. At any rate, I read the play again this time with Kurt Weill and Ira Gershwin playing and singing the score, and Fanny liked it. 'We'll have it all settled by the end of the week,' said Fanny blithely, as she and Gertie left and as Ira, Kurt, and myself happily congratulated each other.

The next day negotiations began with Fanny Holtzmann. I say 'began', but that is not really the proper term – 'carried on' is what they were, amid Fanny's various other activities, such as bringing over boatloads of child refugees, running the war for England, and making constant calls to the British Embassy. I would leave after a two-hour session, limp and bedraggled, only to be called to the telephone fifteen minutes later, no matter where I was, for at least a forty-five minute conversation. Fanny is a telephone girl and how the British Embassy ever stood up under it I still have no idea. And then, a few days after that, the terms of the contract were finally settled. Gertie was to receive for her services in acting in *Lady in the Dark* my farm, the Music Box Theatre, Sam Harris's house in Palm Beach, half of Metro–Goldwyn–Mayer, a couple of race horses, and five thousand dollars a week. The contract was finally drawn. Gertie, Fanny assured me, would sign it tomorrow. But, the next morning, after the first good night's sleep I had had in a number of weeks, I was awakened early, and it was Fanny herself on the telephone. By some strange coincidence, Gertie had gone off to Dennis to play a week of *Private Lives* in summer stock, and there would be some slight delay. For once, I talked a little longer than Fanny did, and insisted somewhat rudely that I had had enough of Fanny and Gertie and that unless Fanny went up there and brought back a signed contract the following Monday the whole thing was off.

How the British Embassy would get along without her during the three days she was away, Fanny did not seem to know, but, finally, she agreed to do it, and with a gaiety born of complete despair I went down to the country, having first taken the precaution of dispatching Louis Schurr to Hollywood to sound out Irene Dunne and find out if she was available for a play. Monday came and also a call from Miss Holtzmann. Had she brought the contract back with her? No, she had not, nor would she give me any explanation until we could meet privately. I agreed to come into town and meet her that afternoon, but before I left, a telegram arrived from Gertie which explained something of the delay. She had been married the night before to Richard Aldrich, and I suppose it was utterly beyond her to sign two contracts at once. Bitterly, I wired Richard

Aldrich whom I had never met, 'Congratulations and are you sure Gertie said yes?' I decided that, come what may, I would not go up to Dennis and read the play to Richard Aldrich, and while I waited for Gertie to get over the shock of having said 'yes' to something, word came from Hollywood that Miss Dunne was definitely interested and would give me an answer by the next afternoon. That news gave me courage.

I got Gertie on the telephone. As always, I was completely disarmed by that warm, delightful voice and overcome almost at once by a sense of guilt that I was pushing this charming creature into making some hateful decision. But I had lived through three months of this deadly charm and now I managed to shake it off. I told Gertie about Irene Dunne and that she must either make up her mind now, over the phone, or this was the end of it. There was a little silence at the other end of the wire and then, in a voice of complete surprise, Gertie said, 'But, darling, I said yes months ago, didn't I? Whatever are you troubling your little head about? I am coming into town on Monday – let's have lunch at Voisin's and I will bring the contract with me all beautifully signed. Bless you, darling.' Well, I did not quite believe it, but there was nothing else I could do, so I wired Louis Schurr to cancel all negotiations in Hollywood and appeared as bright and cheerful as I could for lunch at Voisin's.

Gertie made her entrance in a little while like a breath of salt Cape Cod air. She was brown and healthy and brimming over with great good spirits, and though I kept eying her handbag hungrily, I had not the gumption to say 'Give me that contract' until we had had a few cocktails. Then I did. And almost jumped out of my seat when Gertie said, 'Darling, the most awful thing has happened. I left it in Cape Cod and Fanny is drawing another one this very minute. We will have it for you the day after tomorrow.' 'But you are leaving for the tour of *Skylark* day after tomorrow,' I said. 'Are you sure to have it?' 'Of course I am, darling,' said Gertie. 'It's all worked out beautifully, hasn't it?' And she was off to Elizabeth Arden's, where I would have given anything to have been the masseur and pummeled the hell out of her. Day after tomorrow finally came, and with it that inevitable call from Fanny Holtzmann. Yes, the contract was all signed just as she had told me it would be if only I had a little patience, and she would meet me at the Music Box Theatre at two o'clock and deliver it herself as a gesture of good will. I was there promptly, and so was Fanny, but after one glance at the contract my heart sank. Gertie had signed it all right, but had not initialed any of the additional clauses, so that the contract was completely useless. This was at two o'clock and at three o'clock Gertie was leaving for Los Angeles. I knew that unless that contract was properly signed before she got on that train the jig was up. Where was she, I demanded to know. She was at the final rehearsal of *Skylark*, Fanny explained. And I could not possibly go over there and have her sign it because that kind of thing upset her. I hollered back that I had been pretty upset too, but Fanny remained adamant. Finally it was agreed that Jack Potter, Gertie's personal manager, would somehow sneak into the rehearsal and grab Gertie as she came out, have her sign the contract properly, and bring it to me at Essex House, where I had an appointment to work with Gershwin and Weill. This was the end of July, mind you, and Gertie had said yes in March.

All three of us, Weill, Gershwin and myself, paced about the room nervously waiting for the telephone to ring. Finally it did. It was Fanny. Gertie had signed the contract all right, but it appears we had rushed her into this so fast that she had forgotten one important clause which must be inserted now – the play must open at the Music Box or the whole thing was off. 'Fine,' I screamed into the receiver, 'the whole thing is off. I will be here for fifteen minutes longer, and if that contract is not here by then just tear it up.' Ira Gershwin, that sweet, simple soul, thought my behaviour had been a little rash, but by this time I would not have cared if Zasu Pitts had played *Lady in the Dark*. And, as a matter of fact, in fifteen minutes our troubles were over for the contract arrived, all properly signed – signed beautifully, as Gertie herself had phrased it.

Not quite over. I must confess that I approached the first rehearsal of *Lady in the Dark* with some misgivings. The play, a difficult one, had to be put on the stage and be ready for an opening in Boston in only three weeks' time. It was the first play I was to direct myself, and, all in all, it was rather a frightening task. Though I had no sense of panic about it, I felt that if Gertie conducted her professional life in the same haphazard and scatter-brained way in which she conducted her business life there would be real trouble ahead. I privately decided that the first time Gertie came late to rehearsals and the first sign I noticed of any dawdling and shilly-shallying I would go right to the mat with her and fight it out, for, when rehearsals begin, the actress is trapped quite as much as the producer and author and at least you fight on even terms.

My fears were groundless. From the first moment of rehearsal Gertie was the very antithesis of her contract-signing self. A brilliant and intelligent actress I knew her to be, but what I did not know was that she was also a perfect angel once past a stage door. Sensitive and kind and completely conscientious, I would have to drive her out of the theatre at night, and there was one element of a working relationship with Gertie that I have never experienced in working with any other actress. That element was fun – rehearsals were unalloyed fun. That is the only way I can explain how we ever did so difficult a job as *Lady in the Dark* in so short a time. In three weeks Gertie made, by her shining good nature and her own special magic, what would have been an otherwise torturous task fun to do. And those four months, while Gertie made up her mind, were completely blotted out by the joy of those rehearsals and the final opening in New York.

All in all, only the pleasant things now remain of my life with Gertie, but next year I am writing a little play – without four revolving stages. In fact the play has no scenery at all. It is to be done on a bare stage with no actors. Just lights. And if she ever says yes again – Gertrude Lawrence.

18

LADY IN THE DARK

Hart's efforts were not in vain: *Lady in the Dark* proved to he among the greatest of both his and Gertie's successes and is now beginning to he recognized (along with *Pal Joey*) as one of the two great pre-*Oklahoma!* pioneers of the modern Broadway musical. Given that it brought together, for this once only, the many and varied talents of Moss Hart, Ira Gershwin, Kurt Weill and Gertrude Lawrence (not to mention Victor Mature in his first starring role and a show-stopping appearance by a young unknown called Danny Kaye) it is perhaps not altogether surprising that the show has become something of a legend to those who saw it.

Gertie played Liza Elliott, a successful magazine editor whose problem is that she 'can't make up her mind', in the words of one of the show's best-known songs (others included 'My Ship', 'Princess of Pure Delight' and Kaye's 'Tchaikovsky'). Liza's indecision spans her own magazine covers and her own life, and in order to help her (the show was once going to be called *I Am Listening*) the psychoanalyst has her describe her many and various dreams, which then form the basis for four major sequences in the show – the glamour dream, the circus dream, the childhood dream and the wedding dream. Weill himself called these Broadway innovations 'little one-act operas which continue the story in musical fantasies while the realistic story stops.'

Gertie was only ever to do one more musical, *The King and I,* and that a decade later; for now, the importance of *Lady in the Dark* lay in the way it stretched her talents for singing, dancing and acting to their limits. This was a hugely ambitious show, and one that for Richard Watts of the *Herald Tribune* established her as 'the greatest feminine performer in the American theatre'. It also made a star of Danny Kaye; at the suggestion of Max Gordon, Hart had been to see Danny in cabaret at La Martinique and wrote for him the role of a silly circus photographer who was to jump from a wooden horse and sing the Gershwin-Weill 'Tchaikovsky', which contained in twelve lines the unpronounceable names of fifty real-life Russian composers from Caesarciu through Stchertbatcheff to Kryjanowsky. On the first night in Boston, remembered Kaye:

> Applause came bounding over the footlights. I was still bowing and smiling and bowing when the awful realization hit me that the great Gertrude Lawrence was also on stage, waiting to sing a number called 'Jenny'. And I knew that, when a star is waiting, the worst crime in showbusiness is to delay her entrance. I bowed all right – but I wanted to bow right out.

I was well aware that greater men than little ham me had been fired for hogging the show. The audience may have liked me, but I was close to being a great flop with the management.

Watching from out-front that opening night in Boston were a select band of the show's creators, plus Pamela and her prospective husband Dr Cahan, plus the director Otto Preminger:

> Moss had invited me to attend the Boston opening. We stood together in the back of the theatre. Gertrude Lawrence, the star of the show, was sitting on a swing when Danny Kaye entered. Kaye was, until then, a night-club performer. This was his stage debut. He had to sing a song especially written for him, and he did it brilliantly. The audience applauded and cheered until he repeated the song, and then stood and cheered until he did it again. Gertrude Lawrence sat on the swing the whole time waiting for him to finish and to follow with her song 'Jenny' which, during rehearsals, had been considered the hit of the play. Moss whispered to me, 'We'll have to move Gertie's song. It is not fair to have her follow Kaye.' But Gertie had made her own plan while watching the long noisy ovation. She had rehearsed her number singing it on the swing with full voice. But now she decided that would not give much contrast to Kaye. So she waited through all his encores and the noisy applause until the audience was quiet. Then she got off the swing, walked slowly to the footlights, and whispered her song. After the bedlam that had preceded her, it was stunningly effective. The audience applauded and cheered her with even greater enthusiasm than Danny Kaye. Thanks to Gertie's showmanship it did not prove necessary to move the number.

Because she had managed to live up to his success, Gertie and Danny Kaye remained on reasonably good terms, though it was not an altogether easy relationship as Kaye recalled:

> One night, while I was singing 'Tchaikovsky', the audience's attention seemed to wander for the first time. Glancing over my shoulder, I saw Miss Lawrence nonchalantly waving a red scarf. It was a good-natured theatre 'incident' and in turn I plotted my equally good-natured revenge. While she was singing, she was startled by an unexpected laugh because I, sitting astride my wooden beast, was doing a little mugging in the background. The lovely Miss Lawrence turned around and raised an arched eyebrow at me. I received the subtle reprimand with a slight bow, and after that we called it quits.

Success overcomes many problems; John Mason Brown thought *Lady in the Dark* 'little short of miraculous', and in the *New York Times* of 24 January 1941 Brooks Atkinson wrote:

All things considered, the American musical stage may take a bow this morning... Moss Hart's musical play uses the resources of the theatre triumphantly and tells a compassionate story magnificently... the music and the splendours of the production rise spontaneously out of the heart of the drama, evoking rather than embellishing the main theme... as for Gertrude Lawrence, she's a goddess; that's all.

Lady in the Dark rapidly attracted other fans: Eleanor Roosevelt declared it 'the best show of this or many another season' and Orson Welles told Gertie in a telegram after the première:

YOU ARE EVERYTHING THE THEATRE LIVES BY.

It was also to give Gertie her longest-ever run: she finally gave it up three years later, having played three entire Broadway seasons (the last at 'popular prices') and toured it through every major city in the continental United States. Had it not been wartime she would also doubtless have brought it to London, where the show did not have a major professional production until the National Theatre staging of 1998.

Kitty Carlisle, who later married Moss Hart and was herself to star in a post-war revival of *Lady in the Dark*, had declined to be Gertie's standby for the original production but remembers tales of her stripping off all nail polish and cutting holes in her underwear in an effort to overcome the heat of a New York theatre. She also recalls her husband having to tell Gertie to cease mugging during Victor Mature's big scene, and instead to sit perfectly still on stage during it without moving a muscle:

Gertie agreed, and Moss went along next night to watch the improvement. Gertie kept her promise. She didn't move a muscle. The only trouble was, just before Mr Mature started on his scene she had lit a match. So there she now sat, motionless as promised, while the flame slowly started to burn down the match towards her fingers. Guess what the audience watched that night? So then the message went around backstage that Gertie was not to be allowed any extra props whatsoever, until one night she went to the stage manager who was Moss's brother Bernie and said that a friend of hers had sent in a bunch of violets, and as the friend was going to be out front that night could she please have the flowers in a vase on her desk during the show? Bernie thought about it, decided there was nothing that even Gertie could do to distract anyone with a bunch of violets, so they duly appeared on her desk and during Mature's big scene she very slowly and very deliberately ate every single one. Another night she took to doing dog barks all through Danny's number.

So *Lady in the Dark* was not plain sailing even on Broadway, as a somewhat acid report in *Variety* (published six months after the show's original opening) indicates:

> Miss Lawrence first developed bronchitis in April, rented a suite in a hospital and spent all the time she wasn't on stage or organising bundles for Britain taking great care of herself. Still, numerous performances had to be cancelled. Her part is one of the longest and most wearing the theatre has ever had, and in addition grippe arrived early and came to stay. Then Miss Lawrence decided she had to vacation from 14 June to 1 September. A number of the cast including all three male leads were then lost: Victor Mature to Hollywood, Bert Lytell in search of a better role and MacDonald Carey also took a film. Their boss was serious enough, but it was Danny Kaye's defection that caused the most Hart-burn... as soon as he became temporarily at liberty because of Miss Lawrence's vacation he was offered five times his present salary to join a Vinton Freedley show. What else is a young fellow with a wife to do? The result is that when the show returns this fall to New York it will having nothing but Miss Lawrence, part of the investment still to pay off, and all of its profits still to be made.

In the end they were, thanks to Gertie's determination to carry on until necessary, even if that was to be 1943.

In the meantime she spent part of that first holiday from *Lady in the Dark* playing for her husband at the Cape Playhouse in one of her earlier London successes, *Behold We Live*. The old Gerald du Maurier role was now being played by Philip Merivale, then newly married to Gladys Cooper, who had a curious amount in common with Gertie, ten years her junior, though the two actresses seldom actually met. Both had been co-stars of du Maurier's, both were lifelong friends of Noël Coward, both had comedies written by him for them, and both were professionally noted for a kind of on-stage *insouciance* as beloved by audiences as it was loathed by other actors. True, Gladys could not sing, but then there were those who claimed that Gertie could not sing much either. Both were possessed of an attitude to work which seemed a great deal more casual than, in fact, it was; both were above all and forever determined not to be caught taking themselves or their chosen professions too seriously, and it is more than likely that had Noël written as often for Gladys as he did for Gertie then her career might have taken a somewhat different turn.

At the Cape that summer Gertie and Richard Aldrich began to get themselves acclimatized to the idea of being a married couple; since their wedding a year earlier they had spent a great deal more time apart than together, and in fact the war and Gertie's career combined to separate them for much of their married life.

Despite her earlier illness, however, Gertie's energies showed no sign of flagging; she joined the Cape Cod Canners' Association, naming the new Aldrich house there The Berries in honour of her devotion to the local cranberries. She also financed and inaugurated the Gertrude Lawrence Mobile Lending Library and Gift Shop, which was in fact an old ambulance with the insides torn out and replaced by bookshelves. This, complete with its own driver, then toured Cape Cod for the benefit of the thousand or so coast guards stationed at lonely outposts along its shorelines.

She also found time that summer to play host to a couple of the evacuee boys from the Actors' Orphanage, and to organize her daughter's wedding to Dr Bill Cahan:

> Pamela and I were married quietly on the Cape, and she then went to work as a secretary for the British-American Ambulance Corps while I was still on fifteen dollars a month; but Gertrude by this time seemed reconciled to having me for a son-in-law. She'd invite me to very glamorous American Theatre Wing parties, and made me feel like I was a member of her family, albeit maybe a rather distant one.

That autumn Gertie went back into *Lady in the Dark* on Broadway and was still playing that there on 7 December 1941. Dr Cahan remembers:

> I was with Pamela at my parents' house that Sunday when the phone rang at lunch-time and it was Gertrude saying, 'Have you heard the radio? Turn it on', and of course it was the news of the Japanese attack on Pearl Harbor. I got into the Air Force as a physician, Richard got into the Navy and our war had started.

Gertie threw herself rapidly and eagerly into the new role of Navy wife; now that America and her husband were both in the war she felt a good deal easier about not having returned to England earlier, and took to organizing a Happiness Ship which was to be sent over to England that Christmas packed with gifts for victims of the Blitz. Meanwhile another minor row had broken out over *Lady in the Dark*, this one concerning a singer called Hildegarde who had managed to rush out recordings of the show's hit songs ahead of Gertie herself; in reprisal, though it was hardly their fault, Gertie refused to sign a limited edition of the score which was to be sold off by the composers for profit. Ira Gershwin, ever ready with the right lyric for the right occasion:

> Gertie made her mind up in '41
> That because of Hildegarde she'd been undone.
> She got even by the autographing she forebore;
> So – no limited edition of the vocal score.

Ira's feelings about Gertie remained reasonably charitable; he had plunged himself into *Lady in the Dark* initially to assuage his grief over the death of his brother George (with whom he had of course written Gertie's *Oh, Kay!* fourteen years earlier) and she assured him that George was 'watching over' their new success, though their friendship took a subsequent beating when she, playing the same show night after night, began to tire of some of the lyrics in *Lady in the Dark* and demanded new ones. Ira, rightly and understandably, refused the request.

Hollywood, meanwhile, had heard of *Lady in the Dark* (though Gertie was not to play it in California until 1943) and had sent an urgent request that Gertie agree to be screen-tested:

> On no account agree [came the advice from Fanny Holtzmann] I urge, plead, pray, beg, implore you *never* to submit to a test here or anywhere. Tests are what the word connotes – for others; you are you *Gertrude Lawrence,* first lady of the Drama – a Goddess! To submit to a test means that you go into competition in a Hollywood projection room or the drawing-room of any fat-bellied producer after he has been well fed at dinner. These uninformed producers then compare you with some Mary Glutz who has no acting ability but whose sweater appeal stands out because she is seventeen years of age.

Paramount, unperturbed and undeterred, went ahead with Ginger Rogers, though as they neglected to include in the film at least one song ('My Ship') which explains a great deal of the plot, audiences left the cinema somewhat bemused.

In June 1942 *Lady in the Dark* closed its second Broadway run and, in the holiday before starting a massive winter tour, Gertie returned to the Cape, to play Julia in her beloved Noël's *Fallen Angels*, a part she was sadly never to play on home territory or anywhere that the Master might have been able to see it. The rest of that summer she spent decorating The Berries, inaugurating the Gertrude Lawrence branch of the American Theatre Wing which was to entertain soldiers stationed however temporarily on the Cape, and driving for the Red Cross.

Then it was time to set off on the tour, a journey that was not undertaken lightly. Richard Aldrich remembers:

> Gertrude's departures for a tour always followed an established ritual, in which each member of the court had an assigned role. With Jack Potter as chief dragoman, the party assembled at the house. Hazel was custodian of the make-up box. Dorothy had the overnight bag and picnic basket. Turner attended to Mackie and his luggage. The other fifty odd pieces, including a case filled with the blue silk sheets and special fine blankets for Gertrude's berth aboard the train, were the chauffeur's affair.

Gertie was thus still living in considerable style, wartime or no wartime; her financial affairs had at last sorted themselves out, not because she was spending less but simply because she was earning more. For *Lady in the Dark*, Fanny had managed to negotiate her an unheard-of $3,500 a week and that applied to the tour as well. Travelling coast to coast for the author she now described as 'Boss Moss' Hart, she began to feel like a member of the Barnum and Bailey outfit:

> One nighters, split weeks, constant dashes for railway stations, making sure all the children in the show are still with us, trying to get increasingly rare cabs to the theatre, eating at drugstores, worrying about my voice.

'Always alike, you singers,' the House Manager at Pittsburgh had said to Gertie in perhaps the greatest of the many tributes she now received as a matter of course, 'You, Flagstad, Lily Pons, Grace Moore, always worrying about your voices.'

The myth that Gertie was a frail and delicate creature took some bashing on this ten-month grand tour, during which she only ever missed two performances. In the opinion of one critic, asked about rumours of her failing health, 'Vitamins should take Gertrude Lawrence.'

19

MRS A.

When the tour ended Gertie went back to Broadway to play a third and final season there of *Lady in the Dark*; that she was now again up to her old overacting tricks is clear from a number of reviews noting that the musical appeared to have 'considerably broadened in emphasis' during its long tour. But by now nobody much cared; the show had a few more dollars still to make, and would then be quietly laid to rest while Gertie went back to her new home on the Cape for the summer, there to fight off press rumours that her marriage was already in trouble and to consider the best way of getting back to England to entertain the troops.

Being an American Navy wife was all very well in its way, but Gertie was still aware that her old friends from the revues, Noël, Bea and Buchanan, were a great deal more involved in the war effort than she was and this troubled her considerably. Throughout all her years in America, perhaps indeed because of them, she had retained a fierce, if vague, patriotism for Britain.

That autumn she went to work regularly in New York for the Red Cross and the Stage Door Canteen, but she declined any offers from Broadway in the hope that there would be a call from ENSA, an abbreviation colloquially understood to stand for 'Every Night Something Awful', which was in fact the Entertainment National Service Association. When the call failed to come, largely one suspects because ENSA already had plenty of entertainers on home territory without going to the additional trouble of shipping one over from America, she took to doing a weekly radio show for Revlon instead.

This was by all accounts an eccentric affair: radio was then very big business indeed and the idea here was that, in the interests of Revlon, Gertie would host a 26-week series (at ten thousand dollars per show, for what was then known as the 'Blue Network'. This 'Revlon Revue' featured Gertie doing highlights from her stage successes, from *Lady in the Dark* all the way back to *Skylark*; it also featured her in conversation with such guests as Uncle Alec Woollcott and Moss Hart, and introducing guest stars in scenes from their current stage or screen hits. Morton Gottlieb, then a young Broadway publicist, was also somewhat involved since his firm was representing the show's producer Charles Martin. Later Morton was to work up at the Cape Playhouse:

> From the first moment I met Gertie in September 1943 I never saw anything negative in her; she may not have been the best mother in the world, and there were indeed those who didn't find her easy to get along with, but to

473

me she was never less than marvellous. Charlie Martin had already done the Lux Radio Theatre and he was brought in to launch her in radio, and very early on she recognised in me somebody who knew something about how to get her in print, and there was nothing she ever loved better than publicity. The more stunts I thought up for her, the more she delighted in doing them; it was a marvellous relationship, and it went on for years both in New York radio and later up at the Cape. She was a publicist's dream, nothing was too much trouble as long as it was going to get her name into print. She had a kind of addiction to newsprint.

The radio series started with massive publicity as a half-hour show that was going to be a formless, sophisticated 'evening in Gertie's dressing-room.' Robert Benchley just happened to be there, and Ray Milland, and Dorothy Kidgallen typing out her column, and Moss Hart just dropped by, so then they went into a four-minute condensation of *Lady in the Dark* using every single song but not quite finishing any of them. It was a wonderful exotic *pot pourri* and then Benchley began doing his own little sequences; during the second show they even did *Private Lives* in five minutes. The reviews were marvellous, New York critics liked it, but the trouble was that nobody else did, so they rapidly had to shift the format towards doing half-hour condensations of movies, much more like the old Lux shows had been. Sometimes the shows were based on original scripts, one even went on to become a movie, and then she'd still find time to talk to guests like Orson Welles and James Cagney and Joe Cotten and Walter Pidgeon and Paul Muni, all of whom would also play scenes from their current movies with her. Ironically, while Ginger Rogers was out in Hollywood trying to become Gertrude Lawrence in New York Gertie was turning all Ginger's old movie musicals into radio shows.

But in less sophisticated climes, however, the Gertrude Lawrence Show was still proving something of a failure; sadly, reading her reviews forty years later, it is clear that she was just ahead of her time. Critics blamed her for leading 'too casually' into the commercial breaks and for conducting conversations with actors that were 'altogether too informal'. Had she lived on into the television era, Gertie might well have hosted a good chat show in the Dinah Shore tradition. As it was, she contented herself with persuading Bernard Shaw to let her do a half-hour version of *Pygmalion* (in itself no mean achievement), though her old friend Noël proved less co-operative about her new career on the radio. Asked by an ambitious producer if he would prepare for Gertie a script based on the life of Bernhardt, he wired back:

TERRIBLY SORRY UNABLE WRITE LIFE OF SARAH BERNHARDT FOR GERTRUDE LAWRENCE AS BUSY WRITING LIFE OF ELEANORA DUSE FOR BEATRICE LILLIE.

Nor was he about to let Gertie do his new comedy *Blithe Spirit* as a radio show, though she was still desperately keen to work with him again. On 12 January 1944 she wrote to him from New York:

> I have not been home in almost seven years and am longing to get back for some War Service... after that why don't we do a play together either here or there? Oh Angel, do let's; it has been so long since *Tonight at Eight-Thirty*. We could finance it again ourselves, and be back once again hand in hand for the curtain calls. You know what might be fun for a change? A really smart mystery drama, very chic and funny. You've never tried one of those, have you? Everybody loves a good mystery and you could write us a corker. Darling please do it; it could start at the home of a very rich woman (me) who lends her dining room out to First Aid classes and the victim would then turn out to be a real corpse or something like that. Ever so exciting and I really am much better on stage nowadays and jolly calm. Do let's.

The idea of a Coward–Lawrence mystery thriller, presumably on the lines of *The Thin Man* film series, was intriguing but did not entertain or engage Noël, and no more was ever heard of it.

Virtually Gertie's entire family were now involved in the war; Richard was serving on a destroyer called the *Maddox* (which Gertie rapidly adopted, crew and all) and her daughter Pamela was with Moss Hart's *Winged Victory* company, of which the resident physician was her husband, Bill Cahan. For Gertie, this made it all the more imperative that she too should get into full battledress and entertain the troops, preferably somewhere in Europe.

At last the call came from ENSA. Waiting in New York only long enough to inaugurate Fiorello La Guardia's new City Centre with a two-week revival of *Susan and God* for which the cast now included a young Doris Day, Gertie started to organize her concert tour for allied troops in Europe. Her diary for 5 May 1944 read:

> Three suitcases have been bought and all proved too heavy to keep my air weight down to the fifty-five pounds allowed. I have packed and repacked a dozen times... new songs have been written, orchestra parts made, dance routines rehearsed, taxes paid, visas and exit and re-entry permits all procured.

At last she got herself a clipper on 16 May and a few hours later was reunited with Richard, now serving in Southampton with the U.S. Navy amphibious forces. Gertie arrived on the same flight as Ernest Hemingway, and was caught by one amazed photographer descending the steps of the plane clutching the great author by one arm and holding two dozen eggs in the other, the latter a gift for her beloved English secretary Evie Williams.

She moved smartly into the Savoy – the war had not changed many of her old habits – and from there set about organizing the Gertrude Lawrence Unit which was soon to set off on tour through England, France and Belgium. D-Day, 6 June 1944, found her still playing the south coast of England but within a month she was at the head of one of the very first ENSA units to play in France after the Normandy landings, an achievement which got her onto the cover of *Life* magazine a few weeks later. Conditions there were not good, but they were at least no worse than she had found them a few days earlier in London. From her diary:

> Sunday night. Am in bed at the Savoy, 10.00 p.m. Alert just gone. Wonder if it's Hitler's dirty-flying bugs again? The window in my bedroom is broken from the blast concussion. But part of Cherbourg is ours tonight; so who cares? 1.00 a.m.: Three of the bloody things have just fallen outside. You hear the beastly droning; then it stops; then it explodes. The whole hotel shudders and my curtains blow into the room from the blast. 1.30 a.m.: one more has just blazed over and dropped with a terrific bang near by. The Strand seems to be the popular target for tonight. Next door a couple are making love. Here comes another! And now it's raining hard to make things harder for the A.R.P. rescue workers. That couple must be fatalists. Wouldn't Hitler be furious at their complete unconcern? There's another. That makes six around here up to now. And our Combined Air Forces are supposed to have been hammering at the robot bases every day. Seven. More rain. Quiet next door now. Eight. What a night. Haven't heard a shot from our guns, but I don't see how they can spot them. The projectiles seem just to come over like fireworks on the fifth of November. Nine. Now it's two-fifteen. Not much lull. The Krauts must be having a gleeful evening across the Channel. This kind of warfare costs them no pilots. I wonder if Hitler has it all arranged so that he can sit at home and push a button that fires the wretched things? Ten and eleven. Two at once that time. Now they are coming in pairs. It's no use trying to sleep in a tin hat and it looks pretty silly, especially when one is alone, so I shall just have to sit up and record this my first real experience of being blindly blitzed by robots. It really is a strange and utterly helpless feeling – not one sound of a plane of ours overhead, or any attempt at gunfire; just these oncoming, droning, phantom missiles loaded with destruction. My room is on a small courtyard, so I can see nothing, but the explosions have been very violent. Much damage must be being done. Being Sunday, and this a business section, there may not be too many casualties but the property loss will be great… I was just going to write 'all over for tonight' but here comes Charlie again, making it a round dozen since one o'clock. How many more? I suppose this is a reprisal for Cherbourg.

Seventeen bombs fell around the Savoy that night, and not surprisingly Gertie suddenly found herself thinking back twenty-six years to the night of another air raid over London, the night when she had rushed out of the Vaudeville stage door after a performance of *Tabs* and realized that she was about to give birth. But with Pamela now safely in California filming *Winged Victory* Gertie completed her ENSA tour (in a company which by now included Margaret Rutherford and her old Charlot understudy, Jessie Matthews) and then collapsed; an attack of dysentery in Normandy, together with the shock to her already taut nervous system of front-line battle conditions, had proved too much for her.

She had however done her duty by ENSA. The drama critic Felix Barker, aware that she was in already poor health, noted in his diary:

8 September. Etretat, Normandy. Gertrude Lawrence and her company are going to play in the Casino again, as in this weather it is hardly feasible to perform in a field. We've put in all our own lighting and curtaining to cover the bizarre interior set for our show and theirs, and the ENSA company, which played here yesterday, in the dimmest gloom, were very pleased... G. Lawrence, back from America after her tour, was in tremendous form. What can one say of her show and performance? That it was great and she tremendous? Well, the supporting company was average and she *won* a triumph out of what looked like defeat. Either from experience of troop shows, or from an idea of her own, she made the initial mistake of playing down to her audience. Almost, one could see her saying to herself, 'I have to deal with a bunch of unsophisticated, braw Highlanders. I must fire every gun I've got', and so, during her first number, we were treated to a full salvo of every trick she knew. But the braw Highlanders, who'd been under fire before, were not impressed. In fact, they thought it rather grotesque. For a ghastly five minutes one of the greatest artists of our stage looked like getting a grouse straight from the moors. But she was too clever for that. A Cockney number, a couple of wise-cracks at the expense of officers and padres, a lovely number from *Lady in the Dark*, and she was back. By the time she was smashing over 'All's Well, M'm'selle', the whole audience was with her and the show ended in one of those red-white-and-blue, First World War, Tipperary-type finales...

Once her show had gone down well she was delightful, and was very sweet afterwards when I told her how sorry I was that I hadn't put up grey curtains instead of blue, which clashed with her dress – insisted that she hadn't *noticed*! But of course she must have done, and was just being gracious.

In our show at that time there was a skit I had written – of all things – about a temperamental ENSA star touring in Normandy entertaining the troops. Gertie had somehow heard of this and said she was determined to see it. She and the company gave up their dinner to see the whole show. Elliot ('Bunny') Playfair was in his best form as Madame Rusticana screaming down the phone at Basil Dean, furious that some other performer is also going to France. I changed the tag of the monologue from her imperious demand, 'Who is Gracie Fields?' to 'Who is Gertrude Lawrence?' and she was delighted.

I was relieved because the whole thing was very near home and I was frightened that Gertie would see the sketch as an extremely impertinent slap in the face. I tried to take out some of the offence when I went out to compère the introduction, but I needn't have bothered. She was marvellously complimentary.

By the autumn she was safely back on Cape Cod, already writing an account of her ENSA touring for the autobiography which was soon to be published as *A Star Danced.* She also found the time to tour briefly for Gilbert Miller in a curiously disastrous war play called *Errand For Bernice* which opened in Buffalo that November and closed on the road without ever reaching hailing distance of Broadway.

But with the war still not yet over, and her autobiography now completed, she decided the time had come to sign up again; not this time for ENSA but for its American forces-entertainment equivalent the USO, which promptly sent her out to Hawaii and from there on to Guam at the start of a long tour of Pacific naval bases with a concert performance of songs from *Lady in the Dark* and *Nymph Errant* and *Oh, Kay!* On her way home from this, passing again through Honolulu, she was persuaded by Major Maurice Evans that the troops might also like something a little more nourishing in the way of entertainment. Evans and she therefore put together a production of Noël's *Blithe Spirit* for which Gertie of course played the ghostly Elvira.

Noël had always seen Elvira as an extension of Amanda in *Private Lives,* and had Gertie not been playing *Lady in the Dark* on Broadway when his comedy first opened she would doubtless have been offered it. As it was, he was less than delighted to find her turning up in a Hawaiian production without his express approval:

Perhaps I should explain about *Blythe Spirit* [replied Gertie by airmail, cheerfully mis-spelling its title]. I had just come back from a gruelling island tour, tired and disheartened; I knew the men now wanted plays instead of just songs. They'd already had Boris K. in *Arsenic* and Moss Hart in *Man Who Came To Dinner,* and they were yelling for *Private Lives* but the USO wouldn't pass it for troop consumption. *Skylark* wasn't good enough and *Susan and God* would never have got past the Chaplains on account of its title and topic; I could hardly do a potted version of *The Lady,* and *Tonight at Eight-Thirty* needed too many sets and versatile players. But the men badly wanted a play with me, and Milly Natwick agreed to fly out and repeat her Madame Arcati so John Hoyt and I went ahead and staged it. We did it jolly well, too; hope you don't mind. Love Gert.

If Noël did mind still, it was now anyway too late as Gertie was back on Cape Cod celebrating the imminent end of the war and publication of her book *A Star Danced* which was, she announced proudly, 'all my own work', though some thought they could discern traces of the pen of Fanny Holtzmann. She travelled the length and breadth of the United States selling it, thereby pioneering the 'author tour' that was to become a feature of post-war publishing but remained at this time an almost unknown adventure.

Back on the Cape, however, the Aldriches were in considerable trouble; many longer-lasting and more securely-rooted marriages had been endangered by the war, and theirs was now on the verge of a total break-up. Aldrich himself, back from the Navy, found that he had no real career to return to; true, there was the possibility of restarting his management of the Cape Playhouse for the summer of 1946, but that remained a part-time affair.

His ambition to become a full-time theatre manager in New York looked unrealistic, and in the meantime on finding to his horror that after a distinguished war he was now nothing more than 'the uniformed husband of the successful star and author Gertrude Lawrence, I did not like it.'

Gertie, having always had, like her Amanda in *Private Lives*, 'the emotional stability of a shuttlecock', was finding certain attractions in other men; nothing very serious or long-lasting, just reflections of a need to remind her husband that 'married or not I'll see whom I like, when I like and where I like. I don't need anyone to manage my life for me. I did it pretty successfully for some years before I ever heard of Richard Stoddard Aldrich.' They had now been married for five years and been together for less than one.

Aldrich took to quoting Browning's *My Last Duchess* ('She had a heart too soon made glad, too easily impressed… Oh sir, she smiled no doubt whene'er I passed her; But who passed without much the same smile?') and Gertie, never at her best in literary contests, took to long silences. Eventually, at the insistence of the inevitable Fanny and various neighbours up at the Cape, they decided to give themselves a year to see if their marriage could be saved before reaching any decision about a divorce. At any time in her past, it is hard to believe that Gertie would have waited that many weeks, let alone months, before heading to a lawyer. But she was now forty-seven, older if not necessarily wiser, and long before their year was up the marriage had been patched together again.

Meanwhile, Fanny was busy getting on with Gertie's stage career; it had been more than four years since the opening of her last success, *Lady in the Dark*, and with the ending of the war Fanny took the view that there was not a moment to be lost. If her star client was to move untarnished into the post-war era, then it was no use her hanging around in the hopes of another big musical or harking back to the now long-dead days of revue. She would have to remind both her public and potential casting directors of her talents as a straight actress too, since that was inevitably where the most theatre work still lay. As Noël had unaccountably never got around to writing the comedy thriller Gertie had asked him for, and now seemed highly preoccupied with retrieving his own career from a sudden post-war slump, Fanny turned to that other well-known playwright George Bernard Shaw.

Even he proved no match for Fanny. The two had first met in the early 1930s during one of Fanny's periodic English visits; from that time on, notes Edward Berkman, 'playwright and lawyer enjoyed a lively friendship' and it was through Fanny that Gertie had managed to get permission to do an abridged *Pygmalion* on her half-hour radio series. That was just the beginning; now Fanny had a still more ambitious idea. She had seen the Leslie Howard–Wendy Hiller film of *Pygmalion*, indeed had made Gertie go with her to a special New York screening before the première. Gertie hadn't much cared for the 'old chestnut' but Fanny was already off on the idea of a musical: 'If an audience will listen to you in *Lady in the Dark*,' she told Gertie, 'singing about psycho-analysis, then surely they won't mind you dancing with a grammarian. This can be the biggest musical of all time.' *My Fair Lady* was of course thirteen years later to prove Fanny had been absolutely right; sadly, however, Gertie never lived to see that, and Fanny had no part of it because at this time Shaw would not contemplate a musical. Fanny persisted, and asked if Gertie could do *Pygmalion* straight; she was, wrote Fanny to Shaw, 'no longer the musical comedy actress of the old days but an accomplished dramatic star.'

Shaw evidently had his doubts. 'I know,' he wrote back to Fanny, 'all about Miss Lawrence in her professional aspect. *Pygmalion* is worn to rags, and filmed.' Finally, however, crumbling under a barrage of letters from Fanny, he gave his consent to a 1945 Broadway production of *Pygmalion* to star Gertie. In the interests of helping save the marriage, Fanny also took the view that Aldrich should be involved in the production, and so it was staged under the aegis of a pioneering, non-profit theatre group he had joined called Theatre Incorporated. The rest of the casting was done somewhat informally, as Raymond Massey relates:

> Dick Aldrich came to my place on 80th Street and told me about the planned play *Pygmalion*... 'We'd like you to direct, or Higgins. What would you rather do? Shaw would rather have you direct'... Nevertheless, without hesitation, I said to Dick: 'I'd rather play Higgins.' He told me, 'You'll be co-starred with Gertie Lawrence. Have you any suggestions about a director?' 'Cedric Hardwicke is the ideal director of any of Shaw's plays,' I said. 'Shall we see if he's free?' I called the Château Marmont in Hollywood and got Cedric at once. 'Cedric? It's Ray here, Ray Massey. Are you busy? Good.' [He says he's in the middle of re-reading a Trollope but is open to offers.] 'There's a production of *Pygmalion* here in New York with Gertie Lawrence and me. Would you like to direct?' [He says yes, of course, he'll direct and George Melville Cooper is there with him and would like to play Doolittle.]

So that was more or less that. They tried out in New Haven and progressed from there to Broadway where they opened at the Ethel Barrymore in December 1945 and lasted 179 performances, thereby breaking the house record for a non-musical. Directing Gertie, Hardwicke found that:

> She has a touch of the divine spark, but it is totally undisciplined. She has an incandescent quality and almost always overacts: when she enters, the stage becomes visibly brighter. Gertrude and her audiences have always had a passionate love affair.

By now though, that affair was beginning to show slight signs of cooling; a number of critics were less than happy about her Eliza, including a young Ronald Bryden, who found it:

> Genteel and slightly lachrymose, where she should have been like a spitfire; but all I can really remember is the tea-party at Mrs Higgins's, where Eliza displays her new vowel sounds exquisitely gowned, her back like an arrow; she moved around the central ottoman like a dancer. It was a pleasure to watch her sit, get up again, stretch her arm out for tea. But there was nothing in the performance to write home about, nothing you could really write down at all. That may have been the mystery about her. The actors that critics write about best are those whose effects bear analysis; who offer a vividly thought-out impersonation, a lucid, communicable approach to a whole role. The notation for Gertie's kind of acting does not yet exist. In her cerebral sense, she was scarcely an actress at all. She moved like a dancer, and probably thought like one, with her body. When it was amused, she was witty; when it was functioning with perfect control and economy, she was beautiful; but all it left on the retina of memory was a line, fading like the trail of a fire-work on the air.

American critics also had reservations about this production: 'New *Pygmalion* Lacks Old Punch' headlined one critic while another merely added 'Shaw Survived'; still, John Chapman for the *Daily News* thought Gertie 'reborn' and George Freedley for the *Morning Telegraph* found her 'lovely – if a little hard to hear.' Undeterred, they played on at the Ethel Barrymore until the middle of June and then (with Dennis King replacing Ray Massey who had a film to make) planned to spend the winter of 1946 and most of 1947 on a lengthy *Pygmalion* tour which took them as far as Mexico City. Gertie, though now getting increasingly physically exhausted, was resigned to these back-breaking tours on which she had always made the bulk of her American money. Others, in the old cliché, may have been *tours de force*; Gertie was forced to tour, and remained throughout her American years the Queen of the Road.

20

QUEEN OF THE ROAD

Back in New York, Fanny was still determined that Gertie should do the musical of *Pygmalion*; she continued to deluge Shaw with requests, eventually suggesting that the obvious man to adapt it for her would be Noël Coward. This finally produced a furious response from Shaw:

> My dear Fanny: Stop cabling crazy nonsense. What you need is a month's holiday. Noël could not possibly interfere in my business. My decision about *Pygmalion* is final: let me hear no more about it.

Fanny conceded; if her client couldn't do a musical version of *Pygmalion* could she at least do an hour-long NEC television version of his *Great Catherine*? Shaw agreed wearily, and a year later Gertie did just that, with Micheál MacLiammóir co-starring.

Meanwhile she returned to the Cape before starting her *Pygmalion* tour, and for their reopening season at the Playhouse there that summer of 1946 the publicity manager was Morton Gottlieb:

> Within six weeks I managed to get two entire layouts in *Life* magazine, one on Gregory Peck, who'd gone up to work there, and one on Gertie rehearsing with the young apprentices. By the following year *Life* had an edict that no Cape Playhouse publicity was to be allowed into the magazine and I took that to be a kind of personal challenge, so I devised a feature on summer activities, and we had the company from the Playhouse fight a water-pistol battle with the people of Dennis, only the pistols were filled with local cranberry juice. Anyway, over one side of the pitch I had a big sign saying 'Cape Playhouse' and over the other side I had a big sign saying 'Dennis', and when that picture appeared in *Life* with Gertie as the umpire there couldn't be much doubt about where she was working.

Richard had that New England delight in making money at the theatre, but he used to find all the publicity and Gertie's everlasting exuberance a little embarrassing, even though he could see how much good it was doing his Playhouse. The Cape did, though, give her a kind of security, and that perhaps she'd never found before.

Between 1946 and 1950 Gertie was to do one play every summer on the Cape; in 1946 it was *The Man in Possession*, though she also gave them a week of her Eliza Doolittle to celebrate the reopening. Eliza was meant to be her sole contribution to the season but, as Arthur Sircom (who directed nine of the ten plays that Gertie was to do at the Cape between 1939 and 1950) recalled, things didn't work out quite that way:

> We offered *The Man in Possession* to several good actresses, all of whom refused it on the grounds that the real star role there was the man's; Gertie agreed in the end to step in, and we started rehearsals keeping quiet about the fact she was in the cast but announcing that a Finnish-English actress called Alexandra Dagmar would appear in the play in her American debut… people were used to seeing Gertie backstage around the theatre so that didn't cause any suspicion, and we refused all interviews for 'Miss Dagmar' on the grounds that she was too busy learning her lines. The Boston critics, curious about this unknown actress, all came to the opening night and in the second act Gertie finally made her entrance. She glided on to the stage down a flight of stairs, brandishing in her hands a perfume atomizer. For a moment there was a stunned silence, then a gasp from everyone in the audience, then someone let out a whoop which caused a roar of laughter, and this started an ovation which lasted for minutes… Gertrude took this in her stride at first, but, as it didn't let up, she started to feel foolish. Rather than just stand there with egg on her face she flourished the atomizer about, resorting to every trick she could think of… she sprayed her hair, her shoes and a lot of the rest of her; then she sprayed the cushions on the sofa and the actress on stage with her; finally she aimed it at the audience and gave them a few whiffs – then she gave such a sparkling and captivating performance that she had everyone starry-eyed.

By her marriage to Aldrich and her residence on the Cape each summer, Gertie had given a kind of star-studded respectability to the straw-hat circuit of summer theatres around there. In return, the Cape Playhouse gave her the chance to lark around, play her incessant theatrical practical jokes, and generally recapture some of the fun she'd first had as an understudy for Charlot thirty years earlier. It was, as she once said, 'so much more jolly than stuffy old Broadway' and she even inaugurated a policy whereby big stars could play the Cape in shows with their own daughters, a policy of which both Helen Hayes and Gladys Cooper promptly took advantage.

Pamela's marriage to Dr Cahan was collapsing as fast as many other wartime marriages; Gertie's relationship with her son-in-law had turned somewhat sour, though intriguingly he was to be the last person to see her alive. At this time, however, Gertie was not altogether surprised to hear from Pamela that she and her husband were separating:

> To which news she responded by telling me that I was being very foolish since I was neither beautiful, nor talented, nor leaving him to go off with someone else! All of which was brutally true. I told her that I was thinking of going home to England as there wasn't anything to tie me to the States.

She was terribly pleased, and envious... not only about that, but she seemed, at that moment anyway, to envy my escape from matrimony.

I did not return to England until a few days before *The King and I* opened in New Haven. The night before I left I spent with her in her apartment on West 54th Street.

I think that night we spent together was the nearest we ever got to being really intimate friends, and it is not just with hindsight that I recall how terribly unwell she seemed to me at that time, which of course I put down to the strain of rehearsals. She must have been ill and in pain very much longer than anyone will ever know. She was that sort of person. Her commitment to the theatre and her responsibility to the public, *her* public, was *everything*.

But there was now to be no turning back; America was Gertie's home, her life and her career and though she would occasionally still murmur about a desire to see England, reports filtering back to her from there had already indicated that England immediately after the war was no longer her England, no longer the England where she and Noël and Charlot and Cochran had ruled the West End. There was no real home for her to go to there. Home was now a house called The Berries on Cape Cod and typically Gertie then made the best of it, the best starting at that time with a massive paint and redecoration job.

Pygmalion was toured through the United States for the rest of 1946, and then in early 1947 Gertie took it on into Canada; there, finally, the show closed and, in May she was unemployed, and suddenly very frightened. It was too late to start anything new that season on Broadway, too early to go to the Cape; Aldrich by now had developed a flourishing theatrical management on Broadway, but was carefully avoiding any professional contact with his wife. Even Fanny had nothing to offer. The best that anyone could suggest was that Gertie should take a holiday, which she then did, paying only her second visit to London since the summer of the Coronation, nine years and a world war ago.

She did not care for what she saw; London in May 1947 was still a fairly bleak place. Noël was doing a revival of his *Present Laughter* with Moira Lister, other friends seemed to have all died or disappeared or settled into a married life which left precious little room for nostalgic meetings with pre-war West End stars. Girls she had known in the chorus at the Vaudeville, Gertie noted acidly, were now Duchesses while she was still 'coping on the good old Cape'. Worst of all, nobody made her an offer of work. Nor could she understand how if England had just won the war everybody there still seemed so badly off; in Paris (which she also visited) there was at least a thriving non-rationed black market where anything could be had at a price. Gertie never understood why London couldn't be run like that.

Soon enough she made her way back to America and the summer season on the Cape, having first left instructions with Noël and Binkie Beaumont, now the head of the H. M. Tennent theatrical organization, that any possible scripts were to be sent to her for the following autumn. A number of possibilities were in fact discussed, including new plays by John van Druten and Emlyn Williams, neither of which seemed to be absolutely right for her return to the British stage after an absence of an entire decade. Rattigan had also written her a play but that had been pre-empted by the Lunts and turned into *Love in Idleness* (in London) and *0 Mistress Mine* (in New York).

On Broadway there did not seem to be much for Gertie either; keen perhaps to do another musical, she thought long and hard about what eventually became the Nanette Fabray role in *Love Life* by Kurt Weill and Alan Jay Lerner, who had just had a huge Broadway success with *Brigadoon*. Gertie's eventual verdict was that 'the Virgin Mary herself couldn't hold that show together' and instead, after a brief season on the Cape doing *The Lady Marie* she decided to take to the road in a revival of *Tonight at Eight-Thirty*.

Noël himself was less than enthusiastic about this project, but pressured by Gertie and Fanny Holtzmann on the one side and Jack Wilson on the other, and knowing that another of his most constant friends Graham Payn was to play his old roles in six of the original plays, Coward finally agreed that they should go ahead. Rehearsals were however deeply uneasy, leading up to a final split in the Coward–Wilson relationship and to Noël himself taking over the production and indeed standing in for Payn when the latter went down with flu in San Francisco:

> I flew down to the theatre, started rehearsing at 1.20 and was on at 2.30, proud of the fact that I didn't dry up once. Performance not bad; company and audience thrilled, but it was all rather exhausting.

It was also the last time that Noël was ever to appear on a stage with Gertie. The tour eventually reached New York where *Tonight at Eight-Thirty* played a brief and not terribly successful season at the National Theatre in February 1948; the general critical feeling was that the plays themselves had 'lost their jauntiness', become 'hopelessly dated' and misplaced their verve since the first production on Broadway twelve years earlier: 'It is not that they have mellowed with age like wine,' wrote Louis Kronenberger, 'but that they have puckered and wrinkled like cocoa.' For Graham Payn, in his first starring roles on Broadway, the memories of Gertie are of:

> ...Her immense kindness and patience and skill. Her career wasn't going terribly well at this time, and I think perhaps she knew there was a kind of desperation in going back to milk an old pre-war success like this one. Fanny Holtzmann got the whole thing going because there wasn't anything else on offer for Gertie at the tine, but Gertie treated the whole thing very

conscientiously and all through the long tour we used to go down to the theatre every night a couple of hours early and rehearse some of the numbers. Yet she was a strange lady, you know; somebody once went to stay with her at her house on Cape Cod, right by the sea, and complained of feeling tired and Gertie in all seriousness said, 'Oh yes, it's the altitude.'

She was still in good health then, though she used to get very exhausted after the show, and she was marvellously good with me, felt she had to look after me a bit because she, after all, had done the shows before and I hadn't. Also I was maybe a little young for her, though I think she tried not to notice that; she never compared me to Noël, never complained that I wasn't playing the plays quite the way that he had. In fact, we didn't do at all badly on the road, but once we got into New York those notices were killers and we were off within the month. 'This theatre is far too empty,' she said to me in the interval one night, 'I think I shall insist that the management remove three or four rows of stalls.' It was a curious experience, but I wouldn't have missed working with her for all the world.

But she was tiring now, in retrospect perhaps tiring faster than a woman of fifty ought to have been, especially one who had never had a serious illness. She vowed that the tour of *Tonight at Eight-Thirty* would be her last, that from now on she would only play seasons on Broadway or in London or at the Cape. Somebody else could take over as 'Queen of the Road'.

That summer, her contribution to the Cape Playhouse season was Rattigan's *O Mistress Mine*, in which she played the Lynn Fontanne role, as she noted smugly in a letter to her old English secretary Evie Williams, 'just as well as Miss Fontanne did it on Broadway and with a great many more laughs!' But by now she had even better news for Evie: in the post, unexpected and unheralded to the Cape, had come a script. It was a new play, a drama about a self-centred young artist who marries a young girl and then falls deeply in love with her mother – this, of course, was the role for Gertie. The author of the play was the novelist Daphne du Maurier, known already to both Aldriches because Gertie had worked with her father, Sir Gerald, and Richard had often been a guest at the du Maurier home in Cornwall when he was stationed there during the war.

Daphne's original plan had been for Gertie to take the play to Broadway that autumn of 1948, but Aldrich took the view that it was altogether too English for that market. Gertie, however, was determined not to lose the role, the best she had been offered in a long time and, though she agreed that the play might just not work out in America, she knew very well that she could make a success of it in London. Plans were therefore made with the H. M. Tennent management and in October Gertie sailed for Southampton on board the *Mauritania,* not best pleased to have discovered that in her absence her husband was to stage a play on Broadway starring none other than her old rival for the affections of Philip Astley, Madeleine Carroll.

Gertie was thus all the more determined that her return to London should be a triumphal and triumphant one. She needed a success in a new play at this point in her career, since for the best part of the last decade she had been doing nothing but revivals; she also wanted very much to re-establish herself in her home city, and to prove to English audiences that she had become a dramatic actress of considerable quality.

To some extent, *September Tide* eventually fulfilled all those requirements, though Gertie's first arrival back in London was a disillusioning experience. Her brief holiday there the year before had still not acclimatized her to all the changes that had overtaken the city and the people of London, both of which Gertie still thought of in terms of the 1930s. As Graham Payn said:

> I think she found the whole thing very disillusioning; nobody hung around the stage door waiting to see her any more, and a lot of her old friends had disappeared, and somehow the whole stardom thing had already changed, and she seemed already to belong to a different era, a theatre that had now vanished from the post-war world. It had, after all been twelve years since she'd last played in London and a lot had happened in the meantime.

Her letters home to Aldrich were at first less than buoyant: Fanny, still nervous about the constantly precarious state of Gertie's finances, had sent her over with no more than two hundred dollars, all of which vanished at once, either paying for the cables she sent to all and sundry from the *Mauritania* announcing her imminent arrival, or else in paying duty on the various presents she was bringing with her to old English friends and ex-servants from her pre-war life.

Though there were ritual articles of welcome in the press and a few photographs, London signally failed to hang out the flags for Gertie and she minded that very much indeed. It was not that anybody much cared (though Gertie of course leapt to the conclusion that they might) about her having spent almost the whole of the war in America, or married an American – if it had been that simple, the truth might have been easier to face – but the truth was quite simply that London had lost interest in her. She was back to do a play, fine; if she had a success, fine. There would of course be critics out in force to cover the first night. But that, in the old days, had only been a small part of Gertie's press coverage. What she missed now was all the old interest in what she was wearing, who she was seeing after rehearsal, where she was going in the evenings. In fact she wasn't going anywhere much, because there was no longer (in terms of nightclubs) anywhere much to go. But in some vague way it annoyed and worried her that nobody any longer much cared about the private life of Gertrude Lawrence. London had ceased to be star-struck by her, and she could never really quite come to terms with that realisation.

But one of the great delights of *September Tide* was to be the friendship it formed between author and star. Daphne du Maurier recalled it thus:

Cinders, I called her, but why? Cinderella. Surely Gertrude was the last person in the world to make anyone want to call her by that name? Yet I did. Cinders... someone of importance had given a party to which she hadn't been invited. I mocked her. 'Poor old Cinders.' It was her name from then on. She retaliated by calling me Dumb Dum. I had been searching my shelves for a copy of the play. I can remember only that it was about a charming, unspoilt widow (Stella) of early middle age who discovers that she and the husband of the daughter she adores fall in love. Not a line of the play comes back to me now. I cannot remember how Cinders looked, what she wore, far less what she said. I close my eyes and it is not my play I see but *Private Lives* with Gertrude and Noël standing beside each other and she is singing 'Someday I'll Find You' That surely was 1930, eighteen years before she appeared in *September Tide*. A few years later she played the lead with my father Gerald in *Behold We Live*, and still I had not met her. I was either in France or in Cornwall and I never saw the play. Then comes the gap of years. I marry, I have three children, I write books, two other plays and then – heaven knows why – *September Tide*. It must have been Binkie Beaumont of H. M. Tennent, who knew she wanted to come to London and offered her the part of Stella. I went and met Gertrude, not Cinders yet, at the station. She was wearing a fur coat. I remembered that Gerald, my father, always gave his leading ladies presents and took them to lunch at the Savoy. I must do the same. I asked Gertrude to lunch at a small table at the Savoy Grill, where we could talk uninterrupted about the play. She took one look at the table, 'But nobody will see me here.' We hastily moved to a table where everyone could see her as they walked into the Grill. She was so right. Then I do recollect presents of champagne, a fur rug either for her flat or her car, I've no idea, but I had an account at Fortnum's, so to some extent I was doing a Gerald.

There was a try-out of the play at Oxford. I remember nothing about it except that Kenneth Tynan, then still an undergraduate, was there. I did not go to the first night in London. First nights of a play written by myself were naturally taboo.

She had taken a flat in London somewhere, and I remember going to see her there one afternoon; she put the kettle on for tea and then shook her finger at it. 'Now don't you go and boil over.' I stared. 'Do you always talk to your kettle?' I asked. 'Always,' she said, 'and it never boils over.'

21

TURN OF THE TIDE

'As I walk through the streets of London this winter of 1948 I see that we are no longer a nation of shopkeepers,' wrote Gertie in an appallingly patronizing 'homecoming' piece for an American magazine, 'but a nation of really hard workers. Teenagers are doing wonderful things which surprise their elders. Britain is on the mend!' Privately, however, she was considerably less enthusiastic about being back in London; they were having to rehearse *September Tide* in the bombed-out remains of the Queen's Theatre, every other stage being fully occupied at the time, and a nasty contractual row had broken out with her old friend and agent Bill O'Bryen, who had looked after her at the time of the first bankruptcy hearings in London but had later been ousted from a share in her affairs by the Holtzmann takeover.

From New York, the news was that Aldrich had had a success with Madeleine Carroll on Broadway ('Your star owed me a good turn' was Gertie's acid comment) and before the West End opening of *September Tide* there was a long provincial tour through Blackpool, Leeds, Liverpool and Manchester in a winter of thick fogs and fuel cuts, neither of which did much for the box-office. Still, business was generally good and playing opposite her, in his first major West End role, was a thirty-year-old Michael Gough:

> In rehearsal she was marvellous, very helpful, very generous, used to bring in bottles of champagne, but she was like a creature from a pre-war world that had evaporated. She was now very lonely. Her husband was in America, and all her old friends from before the war seemed to have disappeared into the woodwork, as if they didn't want to be reminded of a life she had shared with them.
>
> She was full of little tricks on the stage; she used to put scent on the hem of her dress and then on her first entrance do a turn so that the dress would swing out and a marvellous smell would fill the auditorium. Other times, when her hair was a bit greasy, she used to put cotton-wool soaked in cleaning fluid on a comb and then streak it through her head so that her hair literally shone. But in other ways she was a very traditional, rather old-fashioned actress even for that time. If we had a break in rehearsal, she'd always talk about the play or others she'd been in; her whole life was the theatre. She didn't seem to have any other interests or topics of conversation. The world for her was the theatre; anything which happened outside it was simply irrelevant. That made for a rather narrow view, but she had a fascinating intensity; one night

I remember going into her dressing-room and just listening while she and Noël reminisced about their pasts. It was like being a guest in the most wonderful theatrical boarding house in the world.

She didn't really understand why everybody wasn't more interested in her return; she felt she'd been a hero in the war, going over to Normandy and all that, and she expected a hero's welcome which somehow just never happened. Those of her friends who were still around and free to take her out in the evenings found her very highly-strung and terribly demanding. She had a very 1930s idea of how the star should behave in the theatre, and more importantly of how people should behave towards her. I was having an affair with Anne Leon at the time, who was playing Gertie's daughter and whom I later married, and some nights Gertie would summon me to the dressing-room to take her out for dinner and then be furious to discover that I'd made a plan to go out with Anne. It wasn't that she was in love with me or anything like that, merely that as her leading man I was expected to be available, a sort of consort.

She was very bitchy about me and Anne, because I think she was lonely and felt that life was already passing her by; also she never seemed terribly well. Looking back, I think perhaps that final illness had already started.

As a company I think we disappointed her; she loved the play, enjoyed doing it every night, but was furious about Anne and me and somehow couldn't understand how life had changed backstage. Before the war, you see, a company really was a company – they lived together, in and out of the theatre. Or at least the stars lived in one world and the supporting players in another, but they were still within the same family unit, like parents and children. But now, in 1948, that just wasn't true any more; we all had our own private lives away from the theatre and away from her and she could never really come to terms with that.

Also working on this production, as a young assistant stage manager, was the agent Rosalind Chatto:

Gertie was a mixture of very nasty and very nice, and looking back I think perhaps we should have realized that she wasn't really very well by then. She used to get very cross because nobody waited outside the stage door for her as they had in the old days; also most of us in the company were under thirty and had been children when she'd had all her big London hits before the war, so we didn't really know a great deal about her. Another problem was that the author and the director [Irene Hentschell] were both women and she wasn't used to that. Usually the director and the author were the people who took her out for dinner afterwards; she liked to have gentlemen around and there just weren't any except Michael, who was already falling in love with Anne Leon. Gertie didn't care for that either, so all in all I don't think any of us saw Miss Lawrence at her best.

Dressed in long pale green chiffon, unlikely perhaps for a Cornish village drama but it was what she insisted on wearing, Gertie would play one scene while cooking an omelette, so my task off-stage was to get the omelette ready and then shove it through the fireplace to where she was standing. I only got the job because I could cook, though this was still the time of powdered eggs and rationing so she used to complain a lot until I started putting jam in the middle.

She spent a lot of the time being very, very cross; one day her dresser didn't turn up, so I had to help her with a quick change and I caught her in a zip and, in a voice which reverberated round the theatre she said, 'Fucking bitch', and then a second later the curtain was up and the audience, who must all have heard her, were treated to the full graciousness. For the sake of reality she used to slip into a chic little apron for the cooking, but the rest of the time it was all green chiffon.

The audience always seemed to us immensely old, I suppose because most of them were her pre-war customers, and she used to get very angry with them too if she thought there weren't quite enough of them out front at a matinée. Once, when things were going badly on the tour, she said, 'I haven't come five thousand miles to work with a crowd of fucking amateurs,' which surprised us all a bit, as a second or two later there she was being terribly charming again. She was quite extraordinarily variable, and her moods would change in a matter of seconds. She used to make me tremble with fear, but then it was my first job and I don't think perhaps she knew how frightening her rages could be to people who weren't used to them.

One day I told her I was moving house and she announced we'd have an American 'shower' party, which she said meant everyone had to bring gifts. The company weren't best pleased, as you can imagine, but she also announced that it wouldn't be formal, so there were Anne and I in our little wool dresses and she arrived in the full black satin and said, 'Oh, aren't we dressing?' She actually said that. Her whole backstage life was made up of bizarre pre-war manoeuvres like that, and the terrible thing was that it all seemed somehow very irrelevant to London life in 1948.

For the actress Anne Leon, there are many of the same memories:

Gertie didn't much care for me because I was starting to go out with Michael and she thought that was her privilege as the star. Once she hit me quite hard on the neck with a hairbrush, and I'm afraid we were all rather glad when she finally went back to America. But she could still be absolutely magical on stage, and looking back it was a great experience: once you'd worked with Gertrude Lawrence, you could work with anybody.

September Tide opened in London at the Aldwych Theatre in mid-December to reviews that were rather better for Gertie than for the play:

The return of Miss Lawrence [wrote Eric Keown for *Punch*] is an occasion for rejoicing. We have missed her almost more than we care to say, for her utterly charming self and because at present in the English theatre there is no actress who can catch at our hearts as she can; but *September Tide* is an artificial piece of conventional sentiment which leaves the actress's talents unused.

Others were more enthusiastic about the play, but the general feeling was that it had been a faintly muted return home for the star of *Private Lives*; Gertie had never been a mother before on the London stage, at least not of a daughter old enough to have a husband, and though in real life Pamela was soon to embark on her second marriage, the public was somehow faintly uneasy to be thus reminded of the passing years. If Gertie had grown that much older, she who had stood on that terrace in the South of France and talked to Noël about the impossibility of ageing, then surely they her audiences must also have grown that much older? It was not a reassuring thought.

Nevertheless, business at the Aldwych held up well through the winter and into the spring of 1949; also in that *September Tide* cast was a young actor called Bryan Forbes, who later recalled one particularly hilarious matinée:

I had an arrangement with Michael Gough whereby I partly shared the services of his dresser, an engaging and eccentric character named Herbert. Herbert's principal responsibility came during the second act, when Micky had to dive from the balcony of the house into the harbour to rescue the drifting boat. He dived, of course, into a pile of mattresses strategically placed off-stage and out of sight of the audience. He then had to plunge into a bath of lukewarm water to simulate the real thing for his reappearance. Herbert had to be standing by to assist. During one matinée, when the Aldwych was packed with middle-aged matrons all balancing tea-trays on their knees, one of the cleats securing Michael Relph's weighty set suddenly gave way. Ossie [the stage manager Osmond Wilson] dashed in search of stage-hands to repair the damage before the set caved in. Now, it so happened that this incident took place a few minutes before Micky was due to make his celebrated plunge into the harbour. Herbert was waiting in the wings and before he disappeared, Ossie handed him a support rope and told him to hang on to it until help arrived. Meanwhile, on-stage, Gertie and Micky continued with the scene, unaware of the drama being enacted in the wings. Micky leapt from the balcony and groped his way in semi-darkness to the bath of water. During his absence Gertie went to a cupboard in the supposedly deserted house and took some towels out in readiness for Micky's drenched return. It was a vital plot point and carefully established in the dialogue that she and her son-in-law were isolated and alone – the storm was raging and there was nobody for miles around. Unbeknown to Gertie, Herbert was standing holding the rope on the other side of the cupboard door. It was a hot afternoon and he was curiously dressed in pin-stripe trousers, collarless shirt and white tennis shoes. I should also add that he had a small Hitler moustache. The total effect was startling. Gertie opened the cupboard door as she had done for the last two hundred performances, and revealed Herbert. She was too dumbfounded to close the door again, and for a few seconds she and Herbert stood transfixed like characters in a Disney cartoon. Herbert, being of the old school of theatrical dressers was also a stickler for etiquette. He couldn't help himself. He gave a little bow and said, 'Good afternoon, Miss Lawrence.' Up to this point the audience had been mystified but not unduly alarmed by this sudden plot twist. After all, since they hadn't seen the play before, it was conceivable that Miss du Maurier had intended that her central character be suddenly confronted with Hitler in tennis shoes inside a cupboard. But when Herbert paid his respects to Miss Lawrence, the game was up. Gertie managed to close the door and then started to collapse. She turned away upstage in a futile attempt to conceal her mounting hysteria, of course minus towels... I know many a star who would have reacted in anger to such a situation and had the polite and unfortunate Herbert fired on the spot, but Gertie loved a joke.

On another celebrated occasion the audience at *September Tide* one evening included none other than the Queen Mother, then of course Queen Mary. Rumour had it that she was not Gertie's greatest fan, largely because she suspected, not without justification, that the actress had once had a brief affair with her eldest son, who was now Duke of Windsor. Gertie was thrilled at the idea of a royal visit, and had all the company assembled backstage afterwards. Michael Gough recalled:

> Queen Mary came down the line, shaking all our hands and saying how much she'd enjoyed it. Then she got to the end of the line, where Gertie was standing, and said it had been a lovely evening except that she had found it a little hard to hear the ends of sentences. 'Do you hear,' said Gertie, turning to the rest of us, 'now you all got to speak up.' 'Not all them,' said the Queen Mother to Gertie, 'just you.'

Richard Aldrich had flown over to be with his wife at the first night of *September Tide,* after which there had been a poignant meeting in her dressing-room between him and (now Colonel) Philip Astley. But then Aldrich had to return to New York, leaving Gertie to stay alone in London for the rest of the run. In the interests of (minor) economies she had now moved out of the Savoy and into a flat in Park Street, Mayfair, from where she wrote indignant letters home to Richard about the expense, inconvenience and general difficulty of post-war London life.

She did, however, manage to start up a splendid friendship with Bernard Shaw, who took her in the Royal Box to that year's Palladium pantomime.

She also became a frequent Sunday visitor to his home at Ayot St Lawrence and so devoted did Shaw become that he gave her one of his last plays, *Buoyant Billions*, in the hope that she might play it in America, though sadly she never did. She did though manage to get him to grant her husband the Broadway rights in *Caesar and Cleopatra*, which the Aldrich management were keen to present the following winter, and even drove Lilli Palmer down to Ayot St Lawrence so that Shaw might approve her being cast as Cleopatra to Cedric Hardwicke's Caesar. There were times now when Gertie had become the ideal Mrs Richard Aldrich.

She was beginning to build up some kind of a social life (Danny Kaye was then in London and he, she and the then Oliviers would sometimes make up a four for after-theatre dinner) but the run of *September Tide* was still not an easy time for her. On the one hand she felt she had lost touch with her native land, and sometimes thought of nothing but getting back to Aldrich and the Cape for the summer. On the other hand she regarded that as an admission of some sort of defeat; she was still immensely English, not only by birth but by temperament, and simply to let the play close and go back to an American life would be an admission that things had not worked out, that she was no longer at home where she felt she still had the most right to be at home.

Aldrich lay low, refusing to beg her to return to him and determined that when she did go back to America it would be of her own free will. *September Tide* did not seem to lead to any other British offers, and though Noël was already talking about a play called *Island Fling* (which would eventually surface five years later as *South Sea Bubble* with Vivien Leigh in the role originally intended for Gertie) that was still very far from completion, let alone production.

Towards the summer she did some BBC radio work including 'In Town Tonight' and a special called 'The Gertrude Lawrence Success Story' for which Shaw allowed her to do again her celebrated thirty-minute version of *Pygmalion*. But there was really nothing else happening, and by July 1949 with the *September Tide* business starting to fall off, she decided to pack up and head back to America; her telegram to Aldrich read:

SPIT ON THE BRASS CLEAR THE DECKS GET THAT WOMAN OUT OF THE HOUSE AM LEAVING SHOW IN ONE MONTH AND COMING HOME LOVE MRS A.

Though intended and indeed understood as a joke, 'Get that woman out of the house' now had a faintly uneasy ring to it. In the nine years since their marriage, the roles of Mr and Mrs Richard Aldrich had undergone a curious kind of reversal. She had married an unknown theatrical manager, who then had to go away to war, so for at least the first six years of their married life it was always she who made both the running and the news. But now, since the end of the war, Aldrich had built up a thriving Broadway theatrical management, one which frequently involved him in entertaining glamorous actresses in the course of his duties. The press were not slow to notice this, and neither was Gertie; the point was not necessarily that he was unfaithful to her, nor even that he had frequent opportunities to be; the point was that Gertie could now be seen in public, if not in private, as an ageing actress with a handsome husband often photographed in the company of other women.

It didn't actually matter that both Gertie and Richard and some of their closer friends knew the marriage was still strong, or at any rate as strong as it had ever been; what mattered was the subtle shift in Gertie's image from that of the glamorous, romantic, all-winning superstar to that of a middle-aged actress with potential marital difficulties. It had now been three years since she had opened on Broadway in *Pygmalion*, and in three years Broadway was apt to forget. The easy solution would have been for her to grab at the first script, musical or non-musical, that offered her a chance of Broadway stardom for the 1949-50 season and it is hugely to Gertie's credit that on this occasion she took a considerably more difficult and dangerous option instead.

First she did her ritual week at the Cape Playhouse in *September Tide* and then, rather against the judgement of the two who were closest to her, Richard Aldrich and Fanny Holtzmann, both of whom argued for Broadway, she headed out to Hollywood instead. The offer that had come from there was a curious one: to play the mother of Jane Wyman in the film version of Tennessee Williams's *The Glass Menagerie,* a role for which both Tallulah Bankhead and Bette Davis had unsuccessfully tested already.

Almost everything was against Gertie in this: Laurette Taylor had enjoyed a huge success in the stage original, one that Gertie was unlikely to be able to beat on film. Indeed she had not made a film since *Rembrandt* back in England fifteen years earlier, had never worked in Hollywood, and had never played a major role on screen that required anything more from her than minimal acting and very good looks.

Yet now, precisely because it was such a challenge, she was prepared to plunge into a role that many more classically trained and American actresses would have had second thoughts about. It required her to wear 20 lbs of padding in order to age up for the impoverished old Southern belle struggling to preserve a dream of grandeur for her disillusioned children. It also required her to take second billing to Miss Wyman (with Kirk Douglas and Arthur Kennedy also sharing the posters) and to cope with a deep-south accent. It required her, in short, to travel as far professionally as she had ever travelled away from her usual casting, and there were both friends and critics who thought that her courage here bordered on the reckless.

But then Gertie had never been an exactly fearful lady, and in one sense perhaps she knew she had not too much to lose; if the film worked, it would open up a whole new career for her as a character actress on screen, a route that Gladys Cooper and a number of other one-time West End stars had by now chosen. If the film did not work, Broadway was still there and far enough away not to be affected by her California failure.

In the event it *was* a failure; Tennessee Williams himself thought her casting 'a dismal error' and the film itself the worst he had ever seen of any of his work. Other critics were more respectful, but they too had to admit that a once-great stage role had been turned, as Bosley Crowther put it for the *New York Times*:

> By the screenplay and by Miss Lawrence into a farcically exaggerated shrew with the zeal of a burlesque comedienne to see her diffident daughter wed… Miss Lawrence peeks and listens behind the curtains of the tiny dining-room, giving a perfect imitation of a nervous Mama in domestic comedy. This is not what *The Glass Menagerie* is all about.

British critics generally found Gertie 'over-theatrical' and objected on Tennessee Williams's behalf to a tacked-on 'happy ending' as well as to Kirk Douglas's idea of the gentleman caller. But now, in 1980, there are (still admittedly faint) signs that the film may be due for reappraisal. Doug McClelland, writing in a recent issue of the magazine *Filmograph*: 'Now that we have been exposed in subsequent stage and television productions of Tennessee Williams's semi-autobiographical play to such ludicrous Amanda Wingfields as Shirley Booth, Maureen Stapleton and Katharine Hepburn, Miss Lawrence's multi-faceted characterisation looks very good. So does the movie'; and it had other defenders even at the time, most notably Richard Griffith who wrote for the *Saturday Review* about Gertie that 'not since Garbo has there been anything like the naked eloquence of her face, with its amazing play of thought and emotion.' Not altogether bad for her very first Hollywood effort. Sadly it was also to be her last.

22

HOLLYWOOD MENAGERIE

Gertie had never had much luck on film, and *The Glass Menagerie* was to prove no exception to the rule; she did not much enjoy the shooting, did not much care for the Hollywood life (Hollywood was, after all, where her once great mentor, André Charlot, king of the West End and Broadway pre-war revues, was now being allowed to fade quietly away as an extra in B pictures) and she could not wait to get back East, where, in her view, real actors belonged. Sadly, in her haste to escape after the shooting was completed in January 1950, she missed one of the great film roles of all time. Joseph L. Mankiewicz was at this time just starting to cast his classic *All About Eve*; having fought off Darryl Zanuck's idea that Marlene Dietrich should play the role, which eventually went to Bette Davis, Mankiewicz first signed Claudette Colbert. When, however, she accidentally wrenched her back and had to withdraw, Mankiewicz's second choice fell on Gertie. He recalled later:

> Submitting the actual screenplay to her suddenly became a highly complicated procedure. To this day, I don't quite know whether Gertie ever did read it; I'm quite sure that if she had, she would have crawled back to California to play it. Somehow, a protocol of approach to Miss Lawrence had come into being. All scripts were first submitted to, and approved by, the redoubtable Fanny Holtzmann. Miss Holtzmann read the screenplay and called me at home to say she found it very good. There were only two changes she would insist upon: (1) The drunk scenes would have to be eliminated. It would be preferable, in fact, if Miss Lawrence neither drank, nor smoked at all on the screen. (2) During the party sequence, the pianist was not to play 'Liebestraum'. Instead, he would accompany Miss Lawrence as she sang a torch song about Bill (something I thought Helen Morgan had already done, rather successfully). Since my own lawyer had always admonished me to respond to other lawyers with either 'yes' or 'no' and urged me to 'keep the witty ripostes for when you're shaving', I said nothing but 'no'. And that's how Gertrude Lawrence did not play Margo Channing.

Later Gertie would claim in a press interview that it was nothing to do with Fanny, nor yet (as had been reported elsewhere) a dispute with Mankiewicz over dollars. Instead, insisted Gertie, "I did not wish to play the part of the actress as she was characterized in the original script. As a star of twenty-five years in the legitimate theatre, I felt the part would give an unfair impression to the film public of the character and the private lives of leading ladies in my profession.' And, in particular, of her? Meanwhile Aldrich was claiming that she had given up the film purely and simply to get back to his side, and yet again to 'patch up' a marriage of which the last year had been spent by him in New York and her first in London with *September Tide* and then in California with *Glass Menagerie*. Whatever the real reason, for more probably a combination of all these reasons, Gertie was, alas, never to be Margo Channing.

On a holiday with her husband in Florida early in 1950, Gertie had now apparently decided that her marriage was at last to become the most important thing in her life. Aware perhaps that she was nearly fifty-two and that she no longer had any real English affiliations and that Hollywood was a foreign country where things were done differently, she settled back into an East Coast American life as Mrs Aldrich. She was genuinely happy now at the Cape; her initial over-theatrical embrace of the Aldrich way of life had matured and settled into a real devotion to him and his summer theatre. There after all she was the resident queen, able to play gracious hostess to visiting stars from New York on the annual summer-stock circuit. There everybody knew who she was, and she could choose her roles. There too there was a community, of the kind she had once found and loved around the West End but which now existed nowhere else for her.

She was getting on well with her Aldrich step-children (one of whom was to be sent off later that year to Korea), and the marriage to Aldrich himself had at last settled down to the point where each had learnt to live with the other. He now had acquired the confidence of a successful career, she had begun to lose the insecurity which demanded he give her all of his time and attention. Ten years after her wedding, and with only two years left of her life, Gertie had at last learnt about marriage.

For the next year, she announced, she would be devoting herself to Richard and the Cape Playhouse; she was, however, entirely open to offers for 1951 and Fanny at once started on a search for a suitable new vehicle. Clearly it needed to be on stage rather than on screen, since the advance notices were already starting to come in for *Glass Menagerie*. Ideally, perhaps, it should be a stage reunion with Noël, but he had unaccountably still not finished his *Island Fling* comedy for Gertie and in the meantime had nothing else that might suit her. Fanny was now thinking big, perhaps aware that Gertie's career had begun to slide as she moved however gracefully into her fifties. This time it would be no good settling for another safe Shaw or Coward revival, no good just picking up a light comedy and hoping to run with it. Gertie needed something very big, something very starry, and above all something that she could make first and uniquely her own thing. It had, in other words, to be a première, and preferably a musical première.

The choice was a difficult one; it had been nine years since *Lady in the Dark*, and in that time a lot had happened to the Broadway musical. New producers, new composers, new dance directors had come along and none of them were thinking much about Gertrude Lawrence. Mary Martin and Ethel Merman were the big musical stars of the moment; Gertie was associated with pre-war smaller-scale revues and Coward comedies. She was not, in short, getting anything like first pick of the 1950 musicals.

Undaunted as ever, and at her best when faced by this sort of a challenge, Fanny decided that if musicals were not coming in by post then one would simply have to be created for Gertie and expressly commissioned for her. This fairly revolutionary idea (few actresses had ever actually commissioned a musical) would, assuming it could be made to work, have certain distinct advantages: Gertie would not just be another hired hand, but in at the very wrapping of the package and therefore artistically and financially very much more strongly placed. It would be, whoever wrote it and whoever directed it, her musical.

By the spring of 1950 Fanny had all this worked out; what she still lacked was any idea at all as to what the show might be. Then, as if to prove that miracles did still happen, a book arrived on her desk. It was Margaret Landon's 1944 best-seller *Anna and the King of Siam*, and the William Morris office who represented the author had vague hopes that Gertie might fancy doing it as a play. As a film, of course, it had already been done a couple of years earlier with Irene Dunne playing Anna and Rex Harrison the King.

Fanny read it, gave to Gertie, and the two of them immediately reached the same conclusion: here was not a play, but a musical. The only trouble was that somebody still had to write it as such. Gertie suggested Cole Porter, who seemed less than enthusiastic. Fanny Holtzmann's biographer, Edward Berkman remembers:

> Fanny hurried down Madison Avenue, the names of composer-lyricist teams whirling through her mind. Crossing 63rd Street, she found herself abreast of Dorothy Hammerstein who was hastening in the same direction. Dorothy waved a gloved hand: 'Can't talk now, Fanny. On my way to Sammy's Deli to get a sour pickle for Ockie.' Ockie, but of course. What greater master of mellow sentiment and wry humour than Oscar Hammerstein II? And who could pour out melodies as tender as those of his partner, Richard Rodgers, with whom he had already written *Oklahoma!*, *Carousel* and *South Pacific* ?

Anna and the King of Siam was hastily despatched to Rodgers and Hammerstein for an opinion. Hammerstein was immediately keen to tackle this real-life saga of the British widow who, in the 1860s, went out to Siam to tutor King Mongkut's children and ended up tutoring him too; indeed so keen was he on the whole idea of the foreign governess who eventually wins the children and the heart of a crusty despot that ten years later he wrote the whole thing all over again and called it *The Sound of Music*. Rodgers, however, was considerably less enthusiastic at first:

> We had never before written a musical specifically with one actor or actress in mind, and we were concerned that such an arrangement might not give us the freedom to write what we wanted the way we wanted. What also bothered us was that while we both admired Gertie tremendously, we felt that her vocal range was minimal and that she had never been able to overcome an unfortunate tendency to sing flat.

But Fanny had moved fast and buttoned up the musical rights, which meant that if anybody wanted to set *Anna and the King of Siam* to music then they had to do it for Gertie. It was as simple as that, and Fanny had gambled on it eventually proving irresistible even on those conditions to Rodgers and Hammerstein, which indeed it did. They screened the film a couple of times, and as Rodgers later wrote:

> That did it. It was obvious that the story of an English governess who travels to Siam to become a teacher to the children of a semi-barbaric monarch had the makings of a beautiful musical play. There was the contrast between Eastern and Western cultures; there was the intangibility of the attraction between teacher and king; there was the tragic sub-plot of the doomed love between the king's Burmese wife and the Burmese emissary; there was the warmth of the relationship between Anna and her royal pupils; there was the theme of democratic teachings triumphing over autocratic rule; and lastly, there were the added features of Oriental pomp and atmosphere. Here was a project Oscar and I could really believe in, and we notified Fanny that we were ready to go to work.

The King and I was now under way; the Holtzmann office announced the project as a vehicle for Gertie to open on Broadway early in 1951, which gave Rodgers and Hammerstein time to write and Gertie herself the unknown luxury of a year off with no need to worry about what was going to happen at the end of it. From several vaguely unsatisfactory post-war months in London and Hollywood her career had taken another of its sudden lurches upwards, to the point where she was able to announce that Rodgers and Hammerstein were writing her a musical. Ethel Merman and Mary Martin had never been so lucky.

That summer of 1950 Gertie stayed on the Cape, playing housewife and doing a couple of weeks in what was to prove her last part there, Beatrice in the comedy *Travellers' Joy*, which she did for a week at Dennis and a week over at Falmouth where Aldrich now had a second summer theatre. By now she was the undisputed ruler of the straw-hat circuit and even organized the setting up of the first Music Tent on the Cape at Hyannis. This idea of doing shows under canvas, which had recently been pioneered in Florida, was to become a permanent part of the Massachusetts summer theatre scene but it is doubtful if it would have got off to quite so well-publicized or rapid a start in 1950 had it not become a Gertrude Lawrence promotion. She even made sure, typically enough, that 'her' tent at Hyannis had the smartest powder rooms on the whole of the Cape.

She also spent a good deal of time that year redecorating The Berries, playing weekend hostess to the Aldrich New England clan and the various actors who worked the theatre, knitting mittens for Bernard Shaw in the forlorn hope he would give her the Broadway rights to *Doctor's Dilemma*, and organizing picnics for such special guests as Bea Lillie and Robert Flemyng. She also took part in a cabaret at one of her husband's Harvard College reunions and even learned to cook, so determined was she now to prove to the Aldrich family that their boy had not after all made too disastrous a marriage.

Back in New York that autumn, she made a few personal appearances to help *The Glass Menagerie* on its way, but her time was now increasingly being taken up with costume fittings and pre-rehearsal preparations for *The King and I*. With the start of the Korean War, Aldrich had been called back into Naval Intelligence and sent to Washington, so she was now alone again in New York and available for constant casting and other discussions on the new show.

The first idea for the King had been Rex Harrison, who'd already played the part on film; but (this was six years before *My Fair Lady*) he was unenthusiastic about his chances of survival in a musical and in any case already committed to an Edinburgh Festival and London run of T. S. Eliot's *The Cocktail Party*.

The Holtzmann office also made vague overtures to Noël, who of all people Gertie would most have liked to have played opposite; but he was not about to commit himself to a long run in somebody else's musical (he was also to turn down *My Fair Lady* in later years) and meanwhile Richard Rodgers was suggesting Alfred Drake, his *Oklahoma!* hero, who had just had another big success in *Kiss Me Kate*.

Drake however was only willing to sign for six months, and by now the production had already grown to the point where a run of years rather than months had to be economically envisaged. Aldrich himself had refused to take on the role of producer, sticking to his old belief in not confusing private with professional partnerships, and as a result *The King and I* was to become a Rodgers and Hammerstein presentation. The team they built for it during this autumn of 1950 was one of the greatest and most distinguished that

Broadway had ever seen; though the King was still proving tricky to cast, the combination of Gertie and Rodgers and Hammerstein (and an already tried and tested vehicle which had made money as a book and a film) meant that the project attracted the very cream of Broadway's production talent. Thus a young choreographer called Jerome Robbins was handling the dances, Jo Mielziner was doing the settings and lighting, Irene Sharaff was doing the costumes, Robert Russell Bennett the orchestrations and the director was to be none other than Gertie's old playwright friend from *Behold We Live,* John van Druten, who had recently made a name for himself as a director of his own postwar successes *Bell, Book and Candle* and *I am a Camera.* Originally Hammerstein had hoped that Josh Logan, who had worked with him on *South Pacific,* would handle the production of *The King and I* and co-author the book, but when that offer was declined Hammerstein decided he would handle the book himself and the production then became van Druten's.

But still they had no King and they, therefore, began auditioning, since there was no other star actor to whom they could think of offering it. Richard Rodgers:

> The first candidate who walked out from the wings was a bald, muscular fellow with a bony oriental face. He was dressed casually and carried a guitar. His name, we were told, was Yul Brynner, which meant nothing to us. He scowled in our direction, sat down on the stage and crossed his legs tailor-fashion, then plunked one whacking chord on his guitar and began to howl in a strange language that no one could understand. He looked savage, he sounded savage, and there was no denying that he projected a feeling of controlled ferocity. When he read for us, we again were impressed by his authority and conviction. Oscar and I looked at each other and nodded.

Brynner's entire subsequent career can be charted in terms of his rise through the ranks of this musical: when it first opened on Broadway, Gertrude Lawrence was alone above the title and he well below it. For the film, a decade later, he was above the title, but sharing the billing there with Deborah Kerr; for the Broadway and London Palladium revival two decades later still, he was alone above the title, despite the fact that it remains fundamentally Anna's story and show.

But he was, even in 1950, not quite the unknown that Rodgers had taken him for; a former circus acrobat, Brynner had already worked with Mary Martin in a short-lived Broadway musical called *Lute Song* and was a pioneer New York television director then currently hosting his own CBS musical variety show each week, one he was reluctant to quit for the financially less secure offer of a below-the-title Broadway job. But Mary Martin urged Rodgers and Hammerstein to 'kidnap him if necessary – you'll never find a better King' and eventually Brynner was persuaded to quit his television career and start rehearsing.

The King and I was budgeted at $360,000 making it the most expensive Rodgers and Hammerstein musical to date, but there was no shortage of backers: Twentieth Century Fox, who owned the film, came in for $40,000 and other investors included Josh Logan and Mary Martin from *South Pacific*, the composers' families, Billy Rose and Leland Hayward. Gertie was on 10% of the gross plus 5% of the profits, but neither Brynner nor any of Gertie's successors in the role in either New York or London did better than a straight salary. By the end of 1953, profits were running at over $700,000 and that was well before the release of the film or summer-stock rights. One New York lawyer who had originally put in $37,000 eventually, took home another $44,000, meaning that the show in its first run was to return a profit of something like 117%.

The money wasn't made easily though; rehearsals got off to a bad start when Rodgers, thinking to be helpful, arranged for Gertie to attend a piano run-through of the entire score sung by Doretta Morrow, who had been cast as Tuptim, the king's Burmese wife. Gertie refused thereafter to speak to him for the first few weeks of rehearsal, perhaps because she had taken offence at Rodgers allowing Miss Morrow to sing 'her' songs, but more probably because it had panicked her into a realization of the demands of the score and the limitations of her own voice which were even greater than ever before. She had never tackled a show of the musical complexity of *King and I*, which, though rightly regarded as a classic of its kind, did not give her any of the chances for lyrical jokiness which she had always discovered in Coward and Cole Porter and the Gershwins. This was closer to being an operetta, and it frightened the hell out of her.

As a result she was throughout rehearsal edgy and very difficult indeed; she knew she couldn't be sacked, so deeply had she been built in to the show's construction, but she also began to think quite seriously that she had here taken on more than she could handle. As her director, van Druten found himself inexperienced at musicals, and the control therefore reverted quickly to Rodgers and Hammerstein, both of whom had to admit that for all her very considerable comic graces Gertie was not the kind of tough Mary Martin stage star they had grown accustomed to, but instead a very much more fragile and variable creature, given to moods and tantrums which identified her as a rather ghostly 1935 figure instead of a fully functioning part of the new post-war Broadway machine. She was, in short, trouble.

Her singing voice was shaky and very often flat, but Hammerstein was the first to acknowledge that she had a kind of 'magic light' on stage and Rodgers had been careful to write numbers for her in a limited vocal range ('I Whistle a Happy Tune', 'Hello Young Lovers', 'Shall We Dance?') while giving his more demanding songs ('Something Wonderful', 'We Kiss in a Shadow') to the professionally trained singers, Doretta Morrow and Dorothy Sarnoff.

Even so there were complaints about Gertie's flat singing all through rehearsals, and by the time they opened the pre-Broadway tour in New Haven on 27 February 1951 they were in considerable trouble. Expectations were high, bookings were high, but the show was running for almost four hours thanks to Jerome Robbins's immensely long (though innovative) ballet for the 'Uncle Tom's Cabin' sequence. Moreover Gertie had missed the dress rehearsal on account of laryngitis, and had already been replaced at that performance (as at so many others she was later to be) by her old friend and understudy from the Charlot revues Constance Carpenter, who thus became perhaps the first understudy in history to go on for a star even before the show had actually opened.

Still, they seemed to have a winner, though the *Variety* critic thought this was not nearly such a sure thing as the earlier Rodgers–Hammerstein creations despite the fact that Yul Brynner's performance was 'stand-out thesping' and that 'Miss Lawrence, despite a recent illness that kept her away from rehearsals, slinks, acts, cavorts and in general exhibits exceedingly well her several facets for entertaining.'

The *Philadelphia Bulletin,* however, thought that 'Miss Lawrence's already thin voice is now starting to wear a great deal thinner', and this in the very first try-out week; moreover her loss of voice in the final rehearsals had already started to cause a split in the relationship between Gertie and Fanny on one side of the fence and Rodgers and Hammerstein on the other; Gertie wanted to delay the New Haven opening until she was feeling totally back on form. The producers wouldn't hear of it; despite her immense value to the show, the days were long gone when a single star could hold up an entire production simply by getting ill.

The health of Gertrude Lawrence was to be a constant source of worry and acrimony throughout the run of *The King and I*; but neither she, nor her husband, nor anyone involved with the show was to know that she was already dying of cancer, and her frequent indisposition was thus to have two highly contrasting interpretations. Those who loved her took the view that for a woman of fifty-two to have to carry, as Anna does carry, an entire 3½ hour musical during the course of which she walked four miles around the stage at every performance and wore a total of seven massively heavy costumes each weighing 75 lbs and complete with steel hoops which bruised her legs every time she tried to curtsy to the King, was simply asking too much of an actress brought up in a gentler pre-war tradition of British leading ladies. Those who did not love her, and there were a great many of them too, took the not totally irreconcilable view that she was simply past it and masking her inability to sing and her jealousy of Brynner's success by a series of psychosomatic collapses.

In fact, Brynner's triumph was no problem at all: she had lived through all that with Danny Kaye and *Lady in the Dark* a decade before, and was genuinely delighted to have helped make them both into stars, just so long as they never lost sight of the fact that she had got there first. He was not a worry and nor were the collapses psychosomatic; she was beginning to be very sick indeed, though still blissfully unaware of the cause of her physical and vocal exhaustion. *The King and I*, after all, provided a perfect alibi; it was an extremely exhausting show.

It was also, on the pre-Broadway tour, a show in a constant state of change; from New Haven they had progressed to Boston where reviews were quite alarmingly unenthusiastic at first, and it was Gertie who came up with one at least of the show-saving solutions. Between bouts of laryngitis and ill health, and still plagued by a score set in a key too high for her, Gertie yet retained enough of her old-style star's instinct to realize that one of the show's first-half problems was that after 'I Whistle A Happy Tune', sung as the ship docks, she then didn't have another song for a very long time. She was after all still alone above the title, and audiences didn't expect to wait that long to realize why; what she needed was another song up front. Rodgers agreed, and in New Haven suddenly recalled a song he'd written for the young Naval lieutenant to sing to Liat in *South Pacific*. In the event, he'd then written them 'Younger Than Springtime' and abandoned this earlier effort which was still therefore unheard. It was called 'Getting To Know You', and he gave it to Gertie to sing to her Siamese charges when she first is seen with them.

By the time they'd got to Boston they'd also put in the complete 'Shall We Dance?' sequence which was to become the show's most lingering and evocative memory, and by the time they left there for Broadway, Elliott Norton was able to report, '*The King and I* left here with three new songs already inserted; understood Bing Crosby and others already recording, including Sinatra.' Indeed they were; by now the show had excellent word-of-mouth reports going for it, plus a final number which as Irene Sharaff, the costume designer, noted with justifiable pride 'starred Gertrude Lawrence, Yul Brynner and a pale pink satin ball-gown.' Even the fifteen Siamese children had stopped trying to flush their hats down the toilets, and all was set fair for a massive Broadway success, which was exactly what they got: 'an original and beautiful excursion into the rich splendors of the Far East', thought Brooks Atkinson, while Richard Watts reckoned he'd seen 'a show of a thousand delights with the magic of Gertrude Lawrence and a remarkably believable performance by Yul Brynner.'

True, there were those who argued that *Call Me Madam* and a revival of *Pal Joey*, the other main musicals of that 1951 season, were dramatically more exciting, but when it came to Tony award time *The King and I* swept the board: Gertie, Yul Brynner, Rodgers, Hammerstein, Jo Mielziner and Irene Sharaff all won in their respective categories.

Critics began going back to the show at three or six-monthly intervals, to see how it, and specifically Gertie, were holding up; at first all was well. The rapturous first night, followed by rave reviews and a sense of being the musical queen of Broadway again for the first time in ten years, did wonders for Gertie's spirits. She had signed for two years, which would take her through to the end of 1952, and already she was then making plans to star at Drury Lane in what was to be the Coronation summer of 1953. Then, all being well, there would be the film; she was, therefore, to be Mrs Anna for at least the next four years, and all she had to do was survive them. No need to think about other properties or to worry about her career again: *The King and I* had seen to all of that.

Sadly, her health soon began to give way again; in rehearsal her weight had dropped to 110 lb, she was looking painfully drawn, and by the time the summer came, the heat backstage at the St James' was almost more than she could bear. Ironically, this was happening at a time when (singing apart) she had seldom been closer to the top of her form; as her director John van Druten noted:

> Her comedy in the part was gentler, Victorian, almost evasive, and her touch on the sweeter and more personal notes was stronger and surer... her radiance was there, and her star quality indefinable but intensely vivid... she had a power to move not only the audience, but the very boards of the stage as she stepped on them.

That was on the nights she was playing; this time her contract did not allow for her ritual summer holiday on the Cape, but Constance Carpenter was being kept on constant stand-by and was gradually beginning to take over at certain matinées:

> Gertie had never really had an understudy before, and I think (although she was always very sweet to me) that it unnerved her to see me around, because she knew that it meant the management were worried about her health. So was she: I think she knew that even allowing for the demands of the show she ought not to have been getting as exhausted as she was, but though she frequently went for check-ups nobody at that stage seemed to think there was anything very much wrong with her. At first she was furious to have me standing by, but gradually she got used to it and began sending me flowers and little notes when I took over.

23

EXIT MRS ANNA

In the autumn, as the heat receded, Gertie seemed to get her strength back for a while; indeed apart from playing eight shows a week as Mrs Anna, she also agreed to teach a weekly, Thursday afternoon class in drama at the Columbia School of Dramatic Arts and this, so far from leading to further exhaustion, used paradoxically to give her a kind of energy with which to face the rest of the week on stage. Her fees here were used to found a scholarship in drama at Columbia, and she recruited such old allies as André Charlot and John Golden to provide her students with scripts and further advice. She had seldom been happier: for all the years that she had been told she was 'lightweight', a revue star without the intellectual equipment to make the leap into serious theatre, here at last was a kind of revenge. She was now a 'Professor of Drama' and loving every moment of it.

She also threw herself into organizing the charity appeal in the name of Helen Hayes' daughter, Mary MacArthur, who had died an early and tragic death only a few months after playing a season with her mother at the Cape Playhouse and staying there with Gertie. But by Christmas a combination of exhaustion and a recurrence of a bout of pleurisy had left Gertie so weak that she was herself finally sent into hospital for a full week of tests. The medical report at the end of that week, just nine months before her death, read that she 'had the physique of a woman in her twenties and although somewhat tired, this could be ascribed to her having worked through an excessively hot summer without a vacation.'

So there was nothing much to worry about. *The King and I* played into 1952, while the management started to make plans for moving the show to London in the following year. This was proving difficult, as the child labour laws there currently forbade the use on stage of very small children, except for brief periods, and Gertie let it be known backstage that she was 'totally opposed to the use of midgets' for the Siamese princelings.

February brought bronchitis, another week away from the show, and considerably worsening relations with Rodgers and Hammerstein; Gertie and Aldrich (who on frequent trips to New York from his Washington naval assignment was getting increasingly worried about his wife's health, whatever the doctors might have said) asked the R & H management if they would consider closing the show for Holy Week. This they regretted would be impossible; however, they would release her for six weeks from the end of June and put Celeste Holm in as a summer replacement.

Meanwhile, though, the composer and lyricist of *The King and I* were getting more than a little disturbed and irate at Gertie's worsening performances; a letter from them to her dated 20 May 1952 is marked in their files 'not mailed' but there can be no doubt that it only puts on paper what Gertie already knew they were thinking and saying about her work:

> Eight times a week you are losing the respect of 1,500 people. This is a serious thing to be happening to one of the great women of our theatre, and it would be dishonest and unfriendly of us to stand by any longer without making you aware of the tarnish you are putting on your past triumphs and your future prospects.

Everyone except Gertie, it seemed, wanted Gertie out of that show. Audiences were now growing audibly restive at the standards of her singing, boos had even been heard at one or two performances, and both her friends and her enemies were agreed that for Gertie, and for *The King and I*, the best thing would be a parting of the ways. But Gertie was a stubborn fighter. *The King and I* was hers and she was not about to let go, whatever the cost to her health. Nothing had been finally signed about its London run, and if she let go now she might also be losing the chance of what she most wanted, a Coronation summer in a massive hit at Drury Lane; a royal return home.

So she played on, refusing to listen to even her beloved Noël, who that spring begged her for her own good to leave the show and have a prolonged rest, after which he promised her a less demanding light comedy of his own for the autumn, the one that was to become *South Sea Bubble*. But she was not willing to consider that either, and Noël went to Jamaica faintly worried about her unusual state of exhaustion, but having not the remotest idea that he would never see his darling Gertie again.

The summer came and, as Celeste Holm moved into the star dressing-room (turning the show, said one acid reviewer, into 'Anna Get Your King'), Gertie went back to the Cape for a prolonged and idyllic rest. True, they did find her one morning in an apparent faint, but that was put down to the humidity or possibly an unfavourable reaction to a course of injections she had been receiving for a poison-ivy rash on her arm. By Monday 11 August, the holiday over, she was apparently fit and fine again, and back in the show, only faintly indignant to discover that the neon light announcing her name outside the theatre had fused, making her once again, she said, a 'lady in the dark'.

Through a sweltering August she played eight shows a week until one Saturday, after the matinée, she fainted on her way back to the dressing-room. Constance Carpenter again took over as Mrs Anna, and Gertie went into a New York hospital, where doctors now said she was suffering from hepatitis, a painful, but seldom fatal disease of the liver. Aldrich was called to the bedside, friends all over the world were alerted by Fanny, but again there seemed not to be too much to worry about. Gertie had after all been 'off' a good deal this past year, and perhaps at last, now the trouble had been diagnosed, she might start on a proper recovery. That at least was the thinking until 6 September. Her ex-son-in-law, Dr Bill Cahan, recalls:

Pamela and I had long since been divorced, and I therefore hadn't seen much of Gertie these last few years. I was now working across the street from New York Hospital but, although we had remained reasonably friendly, I didn't want to put in a sudden appearance at her bedside for fear of frightening her. The question of cancer did arise, and I had sent one or two of our experts over to have a look at her, but the general view was that this was definitely hepatitis, though we had decided that on the morning of Saturday 6 September there would be an emergency biopsy to see just what was wrong with her liver. I was then living a bachelor life on 69th Street and at six that morning the phone rang and it was Dick Aldrich saying would I come right over, as Gertrude was in a terrible state. I raced over and there she was in a big private room and she was in coma suddenly; I tried to work out what had happened, and apparently we managed to get her out of shock, because she opened her eyes and gave me a 'What the hell are you doing here?' kind of look, and then she died. The autopsy, which I attended, showed that she had a cancer which had been cryptic, very silent, and had completely taken over her liver. We never did find out where it had come from; some thought the gall bladder, others thought the pancreas. Either way, she died of cancer.

By mid-morning the death of Gertrude Lawrence was known all over New York, and by the end of that September Saturday it was known all over the world. Cole Lesley recalled:

We had gone that afternoon to Folkestone Races, where we had great fun, backed several winners and drank rather a lot of cherry brandy. We also, naturally, had to back a horse called Bitter-Sweet, running in the first race at a course somewhere in the north of England. After the last race I ran to get an evening paper to find out if Bitter-Sweet had won, turned to the back page, and in the Stop Press was stupefied to read in large black letters GERTRUDE LAWRENCE DEAD. Noël's grief was dreadful to see, his face ashen during the drive home, and once at home he broke down completely.

A day or two later, Noël wrote in *The Times*:

We first worked together as child actors in the Playhouse Theatre, Liverpool; since then, whether we have been acting together or not, we have been integrally part of each other's lives... I wish so very deeply that

I could have seen her just once more, acting in a play of mine, for no one I have ever known, however brilliant and however gifted, has contributed quite what she contributed to my work. Her quality was, to me, unique and her magic imperishable.

Other tributes began to pour into the Aldrich home and the Holtzmann office from all round the world; that night, in the old 'show must go on' tradition, Constance Carpenter played for Gertie, as she had so often in recent weeks, but it was decided that on the following Tuesday, the day of the funeral, the theatre would close and, in a unique and so far unrepeated trans-Atlantic tribute, the lights would also be dimmed for two minutes all along Broadway and, that same evening, all along Shaftesbury Avenue and Hollywood Boulevard as well. This tribute was fixed, need one add, by Fanny, who reckoned it was no more than Gertie would have wished. Morton Gottlieb described it thus:

> Like most people I was out of town the weekend Gertie died, but as soon as I heard the news I went straight to the Holtzmann office to see if I could help. All the phones were going, with calls coming in from all over the world, and it was decided that we'd manage the funeral just like a Broadway opening night. We sent out invitations to all the drama critics, we had special tickets reserved for her friends, like house seats, and as I was the only one who could instantly recognize all the Broadway people and all the people from Cape Cod as well I stood out front with the police, telling them who to let in. It was a lovely funeral. Dick Aldrich played 'Getting To Know You' on the organ.

In London Pamela heard the news of her mother's death via a phone call from Fanny, and caught the next plane to New York:

> It was grisly. We had this terrible meeting what can only be called backstage at the church, where there was a great boardroom table and there round it were Rodgers and Hammerstein, who had been so awful about her singing, and I thought this is a real mockery. There had been an autopsy and someone had patched her all up and made her face up a kind of putty colour and put her in the last-act 'Shall We Dance?' dress from the show. It was pure Evelyn Waugh, the whole affair. Grotesque. Then we all trailed up to Massachusetts where she was buried with the Aldrich family, and there were photographers practically standing in the grave. I do wish my mother had died in England and was buried here instead. It's where she belongs.

But America had by now claimed Gertrude Lawrence as its own: five thousand people jammed the pavement outside the Fifth Avenue

Presbyterian Church at 55th Street, while there were another eighteen hundred inside – among them Richard and Pamela, of course, and Fanny and David Holtzmann, and the cast of *The King and I*, and Bea Lillie whom Gertie had understudied thirty-five years earlier. Dietrich was there, and Moss Hart, and an entire roll-call of the Broadway stage. Oscar Hammerstein gave the oration:

> Gertrude had a magic light. It had nothing to do with technique, although her technical equipment was considerable. It had nothing to do with physical grace, although no trained dancer could move more gracefully than she. I think it had something to do with a great, warm love for the world and an eagerness to have the world love her. I think she wanted to do things for people to make them love her. And so she harnessed this burning desire and drove it through many theatres until she learned the shortest and most direct ways to the heart of an audience. Nothing was more important to her than this. She cheerfully dedicated her own life to a series of elaborate and glorious imitations of life – imitations that were just a little better, a little brighter, than life itself. This was her fun. This was her mission. This was why she gave herself to us. God bless her for it.

The tributes continued: on television that Sunday night Ed Sullivan put together a weird memorial programme consisting largely of Gracie Fields, Judith Anderson and Winston Churchill's daughter Sarah, none of whom had ever really known her; NBC came up with a rather better documentary tribute to her career, and on the day of the funeral, flags were lowered at Columbia University, where she had so recently been teaching, and by an army entertainments unit out in Korea. Her permanent memorial is a granite seat in Lakeview Cemetery, Upton, Massachusetts, where her body lies next to that of Richard Aldrich's mother and surrounded by other members of the Aldrich clan.

Her estate, left to her husband and daughter, was valued for probate at 'more than twenty thousand dollars'; quite how much more was never publicly established, though it was known that she had recently made £30,000 out of the filming of *Glass Menagerie* and that shortly before her death she had been getting more than £2,000 a week as her share of *The King and I*.

The Museum of the City of New York soon staged a retrospective exhibition in celebration of her career, and one City hospital named its cancer wing in her honour. Two years after his wife's death, Richard Aldrich published a memoir of their life together and Hollywood promptly announced that it was to be filmed with Greer Garson as 'the greatest love story ever told', a plan that came somewhat unstuck when, during the negotiations, Mr Aldrich married a young model whom he had first met during Gertie's lifetime.

When, in the end, they did make a film of Gertie's life it was the 1968 Julie Andrews musical *Star!* That, mercifully, exists now only on occasional late-night American television screenings in a cut version called rather more poignantly *Those Were the Happy Times*.

Yet Gertie lives on: not only as a shadowy figure in white dancing her way through the Royal Ballet production of *The Grand Tour* but also as that enchanting, heartbreaking voice echoing through the many reissues of her few recordings that are now a part of the stock of every London and New York nostalgia store.

Some years after Gertie's sudden death, Daphne du Maurier, who was rumoured to have had a brief lesbian relationship with her, happened to meet Noël Coward at a party in London; the conversation turned to their mutual and now long-lost friend, and Daphne happened to say that Gertie had once told her how bitterly she regretted never having sung his 'I'll See You Again' in *Bitter-Sweet*. A few minutes later, Noël was at the piano singing that very song; only now, its closing words had been altered:

Though my life may go awry,
And I never said goodbye,
I shall love you till I die...

INDEX